# Multilingual Education for Social Justice

# Multilingual Education for Social Justice
## Globalising the Local

*Edited by*
*Ajit K. Mohanty, Minati Panda,*
*Robert Phillipson, Tove Skutnabb-Kangas*

Orient BlackSwan

*Multilingual Education for Social Justice:* Globalising the Local

ORIENT BLACKSWAN PRIVATE LIMITED

*Registered Office:*
3-6-752 Himayatnagar, Hyderabad 500 029 (A.P.), INDIA
e-mail: centraloffice@orientblackswan.com

*Other Offices:*
Bangalore, Bhopal, Bhubaneshwar, Chennai, Ernakulam, Guwahati, Hyderbad, Jaipur, Kolkata, Lucknow, Mumbai, New Delhi, Patna



First published, 2009

ISBN 978 81 250 3698 2

Typeset in 11/13 pt. Times New Roman

*Typeset by*
System Graphics (India) Pvt. Ltd.
New Delhi

*Printed in India at*
De Unique
New Delhi

*Published by*
Orient Blackswan Private Limited
1/24 Asaf Ali Road
New Delhi 110 002
e-mail: delhi@orientblackswan.com

*For*
*Joshua Fishman*
*and*
*Debi Prasanna Pattanayak*

For permission to use the photographs on the cover, the publishers and editors are grateful to the following:

Graham Freer, Progressio.

Ofelia García, Maia Starcevic kindergarten bilingual class, Jefferson School, New Rochelle, New York.

CILA Program, New Rochelle School District. Done by children from Trinity School.

Teresa L. McCarty, Students at Rough Rock Community School, Navajo Nation, USA, used courtesy of Rough Rock Community School.

Teresa L. McCarty, Students' bilingual writing at Rough Rock Community School, Navajo Nation, USA, used courtesy of Rough Rock Community School.

Teresa L. McCarty, Reading in Navajo in Evelyn Sells' kindergarten class at Rough Rock Community School, Navajo Nation, USA, used courtesy of Rough Rock Community School.

Iina Nurmela, MLE programme Nepal. A class in progress, Dhankuta, Nepal.

Minati Panda, A community library, Gajapati district, Orissa.

# Contents

**Part I: Introduction**

*Editors' Foreword* 3

1. **Ajit K. Mohanty**
Multilingual Education—a bridge too far? 5

**Part II: Multilingual Education: Approaches and Constraints**

2. **Jim Cummins**
Fundamental psychological and sociological principles underlying educational success for linguistic minority students 21

3. **Tove Skutnabb-Kangas**
MLE for global justice: Issues, approaches, opportunities 36

4. **Carol Benson**
Designing effective schooling in multilingual contexts: The strengths and limitations of bilingual 'models' 60

**Part III: Global and Local Tensions and Promises in MLE**

5. **Robert Phillipson**
The tension between linguistic diversity and dominant English 79

6. **Kathleen Heugh**
Literacy and bi/multilingual education in Africa: Recovering collective memory and knowledge 95

7. **Teresa McCarty**
Empowering Indigenous languages—What can be learned from Native American experiences? 114

8. **Ofelia García**
Education, multilingualism and translanguaging in the 21st century 128

9. **David Hough, Ram Bahadur Thapa Magar and Amrit Yonjan-Tamang**
Privileging Indigenous Knowledges: Empowering MLE in Nepal 146

10. **Shelley K. Taylor**
The caste system approach to multilingualism in Canada: Linguistic and cultural minority children in French immersion 162

**PART IV: MLE in Theory and Practice—Diversity in Indigenous Experience**

11. **Susanne Jacobsen Pérez**
The contribution of postcolonial theory to intercultural bilingual education in Peru: An Indigenous teacher training programme 183

12. **Andrea Bear Nicholas**
Reversing language shift through a Native language immersion teacher-training programme in Canada 200

13. **Ulla Aikio-Puoskari**
The ethnic revival, language and education of the Sámi, an Indigenous people, in three Nordic countries (Finland, Norway and Sweden) 216

**PART V: MLE in Theory and Practice—Diversity in South Asian Tribal Experience**

14. **Amrit Yonjan-Tamang, David Hough and Iina Nurmela**
'All Nepalese children have the right to education in their mother tongue'—but how? The Nepal MLE Programme 241

15. **Dhir Jhingran**
Hundreds of home languages in the country and many in most classrooms—coping with diversity in primary education in India 250

16. **Rama Kant Agnihotri**
Multilinguality and a new world order 268

17. **Ajit Mohanty, Mahendra Kumar Mishra, N. Upender Reddy and Gumidyal Ramesh**
Overcoming the language barrier for tribal children: MLE in Andhra Pradesh and Orissa, India 278

**PART VI: Analysing Prospects for MLE to Increase Social Justice**

18. **Minati Panda and Ajit K. Mohanty**
Language matters, so does culture: beyond the rhetoric of culture in multilingual education 295

19. **Tove Skutnabb-Kangas, Robert Phillipson, Minati Panda, Ajit K. Mohanty**
MLE concepts, goals, needs and expense: English for all or achieving justice? 313

*About the authors* 335
*References* 343
*Index* 387

# PART I
# Introduction

# Editors' Foreword

*Multilingual Education for Social Justice: Globalising the Local* deals with how using several languages in education can contribute to greater social justice. It is not just about languages, because it documents that marginalised peoples who undergo culturally and linguistically appropriate education are better equipped both to maintain and develop their cultures and to participate in the wider society. It is not just about education: education plays a decisive role in political and economic access and democratic participation. It is about synthesising analysis and local experience in globally relevant ways. It is not just about the needs of linguistic minorities: speakers of a country's dominant language should also have the right to benefit from multilingualism. Multilingual education is just for all.

The editors of this book understand *Multilingual education (MLE)* as meaning the use of two or more languages (including Sign languages) as media of instruction in subjects other than the languages themselves (Andersson and Boyer 1978) and with (high levels of) multilingualism and, preferably, multiliteracy, as a goal at the end of formal schooling. Bilingual education, with just two teaching languages, is included. The languages need not be used simultaneously (e.g. Kui, Oriya and Hindi from grade 1); the teaching can start through (mainly) one language, with other teaching languages added later, but with the earlier teaching languages being developed further. Multilingual classrooms in the sense of children with many first languages can be part of MLE but only if all the languages are used for teaching and are meant to be developed further. MLE is as relevant for dominant language group children as it is for Indigenous/tribal and minority children, for whom it is a necessity and should be an educational linguistic human right. There is some variation in how the authors of the chapters use the concept of MLE. Early-exit transitional programmes use the children's first languages as teaching languages only for a few years. These languages are often not developed further after the transition to a dominant language. Even if such programmes use two or more languages as languages of instruction in the early phases of schooling, they are weak forms of MLE and do not promote the goal of high levels of multilingualism.

Several contributions to this book relate to MLE in the context of Indigenous and tribal children. The terms Indigenous and tribal are used interchangeably, depending on the context: in India and Nepal, for instance, 'tribal' is the legal English term for

*Adivasi*. We use the terms in accordance with the definitions in the *ILO* (International Labour Organisation) *Convention Concerning Indigenous and Tribal Peoples in Independent Countries* (Convention No. 169, 27 June 1989):

> ... peoples in independent countries who are regarded as indigenous on account of their descent from the populations which inhabited the country, or a geographical region to which the country belongs, at the time of conquest or colonisation or the establishment of present state boundaries and who, irrespective of their legal status, retain some or all of their own social, economic, cultural and political institutions.

Self-identification is included within the ILO definition 'as a fundamental criterion for determining the groups to which the provisions of this Convention apply' (http://www.unhchr.ch/html/menu3/b/62.htm). Self-identification is also the only valid criterion for 'mother tongues' for both Indigenous people who have been deprived of the knowledge of their ancestral language but still identify it as their mother tongue (see Bear Nicholas 2009, McCarty 2009, Aikio-Puoskari 2009, all this volume), and for Deaf minority people most of whom only learn Sign language later because the parents do not know it initially (see Skutnabb-Kangas 2000, 2008c, for mother tongue definitions).

Most of the contributors to this volume have worked and published together on bi- and multilingual education issues for decades. This anthology is not yet another set of conference proceedings. Much of the thinking behind it was developed at an *International Conference on Multilingual Education: Challenges, Perspectives and Opportunities* that was held at the Zakir Husain Centre for Educational Studies, Jawaharlal Nehru University, New Delhi, India in February 2008, with worldwide participation. The partner organisations were UNICEF, Save the Children, the Central Institute of Indian Languages, and the National Council for Educational Research and Training. Papers at the conference that could contribute substantially to taking the theory and practice of multilingual education forward were selected for refinement and inclusion in the book. Copenhagen Business School made it possible for the four editors to meet in Holbæk, Denmark to finalise the manuscript. We are also grateful to Ketaki Bose of Orient Blackswan for fruitful, efficient and friendly collaboration throughout the preparation of the volume.

The book is dedicated to two inspiring pioneer scholars who have worked ceaselessly to promote multilingual education, *Joshua Fishman* and *Debi Prasanna Pattanayak*. For many years to come the wisdom that these two very fine human beings and friends shared with us will continue to inspire multilingual education in the service of humanity. This book builds on their invaluable contribution to creating just multilingual education.

New Delhi and Trønninge Mose, with the blessings of *Saraswati*.

**Ajit K. Mohanty, Minati Panda,**
**Robert Phillipson, Tove Skutnabb-Kangas**

# 1

# Multilingual Education
# A Bridge too Far?

*Ajit K. Mohanty*

I met Barun Digal in early 1980s—a bright young grade 9 boy from a rural Nuagaon high school in what was then called Phulbani (Boudh-Kandhamal), one of the least developed districts in Orissa, India. Those were the early days of my research as a psycholinguist. I had just returned from Canada with a Ph. D. and a background of hard core experimental psycholinguistics. Barun confronted me with his naive but searching question. Why was I doing all this? He said the indigenous tribal[1] peoples in that part of the world were too much researched upon but nothing has changed, nothing will. I had sleepless nights groping in the darkness of Phulbani for an answer, for some answer. A few days later, after long hours of waiting on the roadside for our jeep to return from 'research' in some other schools, Barun stopped us to lead me and my party for a walk into the jungle to join them, as previously agreed upon, in a night-time group picnic feast with a tiny lantern struggling to barely pierce the dense darkness of the forest. There he was showing me the way, leading me on to my life's most unforgettable fireside dinner—aroma and taste of freshly cooked food I could not see while eating—and leading my transformation from a dispassionate *'objective'* researcher to someone with human concerns. Nearly three decades down the road, I am still searching for answers to Barun's questions, but in his silent ways Barun had told me that lighting a tiny little lantern to show the way is better than cursing the darkness.

I have tried without luck to get back to Barun and see how he is doing. I know he is there somewhere doing somewhat better than many in his community. He had made it through to take the high school examination which only about twenty in a hundred from among his peers do. Fifty per cent of the tribal children who join school never reach grade 5 and only 20% survive the years of schooling to take the high school examination which only about 8% actually pass. The 80% are counted in *sarkari* (government) records as 'drop-outs'. Did they 'drop out' of their own accord? Did their parents want them to? The untold truth is that they were *'push-*

*outs'* in an unresponsive system that systematically devalues them—their culture, their languages and their identities. The story of each *'pushed out'* child is both complex and a sad reminder of our own failures, which are many.

A tribal child's first steps into school are steps into an alien world—a world she barely understands because, somewhere as she walks into her first classroom, the ties are snapped. Her resources, languages, means of communication, knowledge of her world and her culture are set aside in a system that proudly calls itself human resource development. On the very first day in the school she loses her resources and is left with nothing to be 'developed'. She has been pushed in, to be submersed (and pushed out later), in a system the language of which she barely understands. It would take her three to five years just to comprehend the teacher and by then it would be too late. This tribal child and all others in her community are not alone. All over the world, the Indigenous peoples, the 'natives', the 'first nation' peoples, the aboriginals, the tribes and all the dominated linguistic and ethnic minorities suffer a similar fate unless they have successfully struggled to assert their linguistic and other human rights.

It is a multilingual world of vanishing languages. Nearly every fortnight somewhere the last speaker of a language is dying. While many languages are dead or dying, a large number of languages are marginalised. The relationship between language and power makes it a world of unequal languages. Languages of the marginalised people are treated with discrimination at all levels in the society, stripped of their instrumental significance. It takes over seven to nine years for an Indian child to internalise that some languages are more prestigious, more useful and powerful than others; tribal children learn that their languages have no use for them (Mohanty, Panda and Mishra 1999). Languages of the disadvantaged entail disadvantages in a society that deprives them of their legitimate place in a multilingual structure. Sadly, it is a structure of a vicious circle—languages are marginalised, impoverished and weakened by gross social, educational, statutory, official, and legal neglect, and the furtherance of this neglect is justified on grounds of the poverty of these languages, their so-called weaknesses and inadequacies. In India, constitutional, statutory and policy provisions for mother tongue medium education are not implemented: the number of languages used in schools—both as languages of instruction and language subjects—has sharply declined over the years, with barely thirty languages being used in primary grades as instructional media now (Mohanty 2008a). In the process, there is an alarming 'push-out' rate and abysmally poor educational performance leading to capability deprivation, loss of identity and poverty. These, in turn, trigger further marginalisation, subtractive language learning, loss of mother tongues and loss of linguistic diversity. It is the same story all over the world.

Who suffers? The linguistic minorities and speakers of the dominated languages which are left out of schools. The tribal people in India do suffer the consequences of this neglect. More than 83 million tribal people, constituting over 8.2% of the population and speaking 159 languages, which are exclusive to them, are among the worst sufferers—only 3 to 4 of their languages have a place in schools and most are in the endangered category. Around 58,343 primary schools (grades 1– 5) in India have over 90% tribal children and 103,609 schools over 50%. All these children are taught in forced submersion programmes in dominant majority-language schools with a clear subtractive effect on their mother tongues.

For these and all other similarly placed children throughout the world, their language spells their destiny. What happens to them in the face of such neglect of their mother tongues in schools?This is how I have described a Kandha (Kond) child in grade 2 of a primary school in a remote village in Raikia Block of Kandhamal (Phulbani) district in Orissa, India:

> The child, who has left behind many other children of her age who never came to school, is present in the class with wide-eyed curiosity trying to figure out what is going on. Despite all the pious programmes, improved curricula, Operation Blackboard and many such efforts, she just does not learn to read and write. She is not alone; there are many other such children from Kond families who also do not learn. They are all in each other's comforting company; days pass by but they do not learn. Examinations they may or may not pass but they are certainly passing time. ... any common person can tell you that she does not learn because she does not understand the teacher, the texts, and the curricula all of which use a language she does not know; it is not the language of her family (Mohanty 2000: 104-105).

Numerous studies continue to show the poor educational achievement of children in submersion education which has a subtractive effect on their mother tongues. In contrast, studies do show better performance of children in their mother tongue medium schools. But, is research evidence enough?

Why then are mother tongues neglected despite persuasive evidence to the contrary?As the voiceless minorities suffer the sinister exclusion of mother tongues, the silent elites enjoy the pre-eminence of dominant languages such as English. In the post-colonial world, *'the killer languages'* including English thrive at the cost of other languages, and in many countries the myth of English medium superiority is propagated to the detriment of the poor and the marginalised. English and other 'killer languages' set in motion a hierarchical pecking order of languages which severely disadvantages the other languages, those of the Indigenous peoples and minorities, in particular. And yet, it does not have to be so. In a true multilingual system, all languages can have their legitimate place: mother tongues, languages of regional, national and wider communication. English and all other world languages can play their role; they can be healer languages and not 'killer languages'. In a politically uncontaminated society that would not permit evil entrepreneurs of identity to rob others of their linguistic capital and cultural rootedness, mother tongues and other languages can complement each other with beauty, the beauty of the *'petals of the Indian lotus'*, as Pattanayak (1988) so elegantly puts it, beauty with diversity.

Every child must grow into this beautiful world of many languages capable of nurturing and liberating, sheltering and expanding, enrooting and emancipating.

But how do we foster such growth? Multilingual education (MLE) shows the way. There is hope, since all over the world major international institutions like UNESCO accept multilingualism as a resource, a growing number of nations pledges to honour and foster every child's home language, Indigenous peoples in different parts of the globe strive to revitalise their languages, and smaller nations like Papua New Guinea lead by their success stories of making mother tongues the language of school instruction. MLE is a new commitment, one to strengthen the foundations of a necessary bridge—a bridge between home and school, between languages and between cultures. A bridge from the home language, the mother tongue, to the regional language and to the national language as well as world languages like English; an empowering bridge that leads to meaningful participation in the wider democratic and global set-up without homogenising the beauty of diversity; a bridge that liberates but does not displace.

Is this a bridge too far? At one level, this bridge is an ideological promise, a first step toward a better world of egalitarian social order, equity, justice and human dignity. At another level, it is a concrete reality founded on solid theoretical groundings for realisation of the very best in every child.While there are many small successes in all parts of the world—Africa, Asia, Europe, North and South Americas—as this book shows, there are too many instances of the denial of linguistic human rights in education as well as all other major social domains, and consequent impoverishment of languages and smaller speech communities.Thus, the bridge is both promising and elusive. We know enough about multilingualism and multilingual education to find this bridge promising. However, it takes much more than our knowledge to make this a reality. The movement from theory to practice in all the different and challenging contexts is a difficult task. But developments in the field of multilingual education and numerous demonstrations of successful practical applications make this goal appear quite close and feasible. This book brings together several positive experiences from all corners of the globe: it brings a message of hope, it shows that this is not a bridge too far.

The metaphor of a bridge is compelling, but, at the same time, it is also quite limiting. A bridge is not just a one way link; it has to work both ways and in many ways. How does one build those bridges between many languages and not just between two languages? How does one deal with the problems of number—the number of children and schools and, more significantly, the number of languages? It may look easy and possible to go from one to two—building a bridge; it is not as simple to go from two to three or four or more. How does one link the many? When does one go from one mother tongue to an 'other tongue' or to many other tongues? The bridge metaphor raises more questions than it answers. There are problems of transition *versus* transfer; there are issues of diversity and uniformity; unity of methods and diversity of practices. One script or many? What comes first? Hindi or English? Nepali or Tharu? Do we artificially homogenise varieties and diversities to be able to build the right bridges or do we allow diversity itself to be the bridge? How do we reconcile community aspirations with proven methods? And, more importantly, how does one bridge the gap between theory and practice? How does one take the principles of bilingual education and move to the practicalities of MLE in complex multilingual contexts without being accused of trying to fit a square peg into the complex contours of an uneven hole?

*****

In this volume we have collectively endeavoured to show that such exercises of adjustment, bridging the gap between theory and practice in respect of MLE, not only can but must be undertaken. We have sought to extend the contours of theories of bilingual education to explore their meaningful applications in complex multilingual societies. The fundamental principles of bilingual and multilingual education have outlived the initial scepticism and are now widely accepted. However, as MLE moves to different and challengingly complex sociolinguistic contexts, there is a need to extend and contextualise the principles beyond the simpler 'bilingual' applications and to locate optimal models for diverse multilingual contexts. This book seeks to meet this need to relate theories and practices. It examines theoretical and global issues in respect of multilingual education and then builds on hard data and specific local practices in various aspects of MLE.

In Part 2 of the book, Jim Cummins, Tove Skutnabb-Kangas and Carol Benson provide state-of-the art analyses and new insights into multilingual education for Indigenous, minority and marginalised communities. Cummins offers a pedagogical framework for minority students' academic development in multilingual contexts. He suggests a tripartite division of academic proficiency, stressing the significance of focusing on reading development and transfer of knowledge and skills across languages in MLE. Cummins and Skutnabb-Kangas, as well as many other contributors to this volume, point to the centrality of societal power relations and identity negotiation for the academic development of minority students. Skutnabb-Kangas takes a critical look at the homogenising impact of globalisation and the loss of linguistic and cultural diversity—which as she shows is also closely related to biodiversity. She points out the need for governments and educational authorities to realise that subtractive education in the dominant language amounts to denial of linguistic human rights in education and is a crime against humanity. She also questions the conventional role of researchers and academic discourse in supporting the unequal power relations in a society and pleads for MLE for global justice. Benson examines early models of bilingual education developed in the West and shows their limitations in multilingual contexts and also in classifying the MLE programmes in different sociolinguistic contexts. She takes a critical look at the common forms of bilingual education programmes—submersion, transitional, maintenance, immersion and dual medium models—examining their use and abuse in different contexts. She shows that as the submersion models that lead to inefficient schooling are being increasingly questioned in many countries, MT-based programmes are favoured. Submersion schools in dominant international languages like English, often inaccurately dubbed as 'immersion' models, are also on the increase, with patronage from urban elites. The articles in Part 2 of the book extend current thinking about bilingual/multilingual education to wider global contexts and show the limitations of an uncritical application of existing models.

The global context and promise of MLE are explored in Part 3 through analyses of some overarching issues, local as well as global. The contributors in this part show that persistent shuttling between local practices and global principles is necessary for improved MLE. Robert Phillipson relates the rhetoric of egalitarian multilingualism to the realities of linguistic hierarchisation and marginalisation, and provides historical and contemporary evidence for how English has transformed from the language of colonisation to neoimperialism. He demonstrates that many language-in-education issues in Europe have similarities with postcolonial dilemmas. He cautions against false arguments for English and merely treating English as a '*lingua franca*' when it actually functions as a *lingua frankensteinia* in many parts of the world. He does not deny the role of English in an egalitarian multilingual framework but pleads for careful analysis of how to counter-balance its adverse and subtractive effects on linguistic diversity, multilingualism and MLE.

In Chapter 6, Kathleen Heugh provides a comparative cross-national analysis of MLE approaches in Africa. She points out that the current discourse on languages-in-education issues in Africa reveals collective amnesia of pre-colonial literacy traditions and practices, including mother tongue medium instruction. Through her analysis of African MLE programmes, Heugh illustrates the danger of uncritically borrowing Western models such as early-exit MLE programmes with rapid transition to English or another dominant ex-colonial language. Her data analysis draws on North American and European research (such as Thomas and Collier 2002) but draws significant conclusions in radically different contexts. The solid empirical results described are in many ways revolutionary, as they show that even in some of the world's economically poorest countries, long-term mother tongue medium education programmes can be and have been realised. They lead to better results in most subjects, including in the ex-colonial English language, than early-exit transitional programmes.

In Chapter 7, Teresa McCarty shares her experience of the education of Native American peoples to show some new directions for MLE of global relevance. She underscores the classroom performance benefits and empowerment effects of Navajo bilingual and immersion programmes. She also shows that even when there seems to be limited intergenerational transmission of an Indigenous language like Navajo, it is still integrally tied to youth identities, and the language is a powerful factor in the success of MLE programmes. She relates this experience to other contexts and draws explicit lessons for global use.

Exploration of the relationship between local and global MLE practices continues in the article by Ofelia García, who draws our attention to fluid boundaries between languages in multilingual societies. She stresses the implications of 'translanguaging'—bilingual or multilingual discourse practices—for conceptualising the nature of bi-/multilingualism, and the potential of such concepts as recursive and dynamic bilingualism and plurilingualism (as advocated in the European Union). She refers to monoglossic and heteroglossic types of bilingual education, and different forms of language arrangement and instructional practices in such programmes. A more explicit exploration of translanguaging could be undertaken when analysing the operation of MLE in varied multilingual societies.

In Chapter 9, David Hough, Ram Bahadur Thapa Magar, and Amrit Yonjan-Tamang outline various bottom-up community-based approaches to an empowering multilingual education in Nepal that seeks to revitalise Indigenous languages and cultures. They provide a blueprint for Critical Indigenous MLE Pedagogy grounded in traditional values and knowledge systems among Indigenous communities—from herbal medicines and healing practices to oral history, numerical and mathematical systems. The chapter describes in theory and in practice, trends that are increasingly developing among Indigenous and tribal peoples globally, and which are also recommended as a result of the United Nations Declaration on the Rights of Indigenous Peoples.

Shelley Taylor, in Chapter 10, explores problems in the education of linguistic and cultural minority children of First Nations and immigrant communities in early French immersion programmes in Ontario, Canada. Their mother tongues are invisibilised, which denies them the opportunity to develop additive bilingualism. Based on her studies, Taylor pleads for developing effective strategies for resourceful use of the multilingual composition of classrooms and overt support for the first language development of linguistic minority children. Only in this way can there be enrichment maintenance bilingual education in Canada.

The various contributions to Part 3 of this volume show how the complex reality of multilingualism in education can be and has been confronted, and how false expectations and uninformed policies can be avoided in light of the existing evidence of both successes and failures. The research summarised here engages with tensions, constraints and challenges that are present globally. It elaborates a convincing case for bringing together experience from Africa, Asia, Europe and the Americas when planning what should go into classrooms. It provides evidence and inspiration that is globally relevant and that can be acted on in locally sensitive ways so as to achieve more effective education for Indigenous and minority communities.

The authors in Part 4 provide in-depth studies of how MLE is being achieved for Indigenous communities from diverse settings—Peru, Canada and the Nordic countries. In Chapter 11, Susanne Perez describes her experience of teacher training for intercultural bilingual education (IBE) in Quechua-Spanish bilingual areas in Peru. She discusses how the IBE programme is designed to maintain the indigenous Quechua language and develop Spanish as a second language. She focuses on the processes and issues in the acquisition of Quechua for academic purposes, using traditional knowledge systems in an intercultural pedagogy that builds on teacher identities, and the school-community relationship, both of which are decisive for successful MLE for Indigenous peoples.

The theme of developing and revitalising Indigenous languages continues in Chapter 12, in which Andrea Bear Nicholas shows how the Native language immersion teacher-training programme at St. Thomas University, Canada has contributed to revitalising native American peoples' languages, particularly those of the Mi'kmaq and Maliseet language communities. She is critical of Canadian language policy, which has anomalies and contradictions that lead to the loss of linguistic diversity. She shows how privileging the dominant official languages (English and French) in Canadian teacher training programmes, as well as the inequitable allocation of resources, adversely affect the survival, development and intergenerational transmission of Native languages. Bear Nicholas discusses several positive outcomes of the university-based native language immersion teacher-training programme, and points to some serious challenges facing the programme.

In the next Chapter, Ulla Aikio-Puoskari describes the processes in the ethnic revival of the indigenous Sámi people in three Nordic countries—Finland, Norway and Sweden. She presents a comparative analysis of state policies and multilingualism in these countries, and outlines the nature of Sámi education and the role of language and culture. She shows how multilingualism as a state policy also suffers from biases against the Indigenous and minority communities, which affects the nature and scope of bilingual or multilingual education. A native Sámi herself, having been through the relearning of Sámi and having pioneered academically, politically and in practice the revitalisation process, her careful but realistic optimism can encourage many Indigenous peoples all over the world.

The three chapters in Part 4 bring together diverse Indigenous perspectives and show that MLE as a movement must go and is going beyond conventional approaches to the education of minority and Indigenous children. There needs to be a focus on the enabling aspects of MLE, on teacher training, materials and pedagogies, on designing the overall system of education in the light of existing state policies and the maintenance of a multilingual social structure. In many cases of numerically small Indigenous peoples the outcomes in the struggle against assimilation, historicide and linguicide are still unsure, despite the strong revitalisation movements.

Part 5 of this volume presents the very rich diversity of South Asian multilingualism in the challenging socio-political and linguistic contexts of Nepal and India, and shows how ongoing innovative MLE projects, involving the most marginalised ethnolinguistic minorities—the Tribal communities—strive to transform the challenges into opportunities. They thereby enrich the theory and practice of MLE with new approaches and insights.

Amrit Yonjan-Tamang, David Hough and Iina Nurmela describe, in Chapter 14, the first year of a pilot project of the Nepal Multilingual Education Programme.

This is a collaborative effort of external consultants employed by the Ministry of Foreign Affairs of Finland, in collaboration with the Ministry of Education and Sports of Nepal and a number of Nepalis with specialist qualifications. It involves six language communities. The Programme aims at setting up a sustainable model of mother tongue based MLE for all non-Nepali speaking primary school children by the year 2015. Community participation and ownership, flexible localised curricula and materials based on the Indigenous knowledge systems and oral traditions, a focus on the most endangered languages and marginalised communities in extreme poverty are some of the innovative aspects of the programme. The Nepal experience takes the theory and practice of MLE to new frontiers and can enrich other contexts.

Dhir Jhingran's article (Chapter 15) discusses the languages-in-education policy in India in the context of its linguistic diversity. He assesses the challenges to primary education in India on account of the complex language situations in the classroom and shows how the exclusion of minority mother tongues has a negative impact on children's learning outcomes. Jhingran also discusses some recent Government and NGO initiatives in India to promote mother tongue based education and MLE.

Such initiatives for several tribal language communities in India are the Government MLE programmes in two provinces, Andhra Pradesh and Orissa, that are discussed by Mohanty, Mishra, Reddy and Ramesh in Chapter 17. Mohanty et al. show that a vicious circle of discrimination and exclusion disadvantages the tribal mother tongues leading to poor educational performance, capability deprivation and poverty among the tribal communities. They argue that the tribal children can overcome the language barrier in the classrooms caused by exclusion of their mother tongues by means of MLE that supports the academic development of mother tongues. They discuss the challenges and issues facing the MLE programmes in Andhra Pradesh and Orissa as they strive to move from the theory of MLE to context-and culture-sensitive programmes of mother tongue based MLE for a large number of tribal languages in the region. The specific MLE initiatives in Nepal and India discussed in Part 5 exemplify the diversity of the reality of the theory and practices of MLE and the need for broad structural issues to be taken into consideration, among them macro and micro economic factors, multiple identities, and fluid linguistic boundaries.

Rama Kant Agnihotri, in Chapter 16, uses the fluidity of linguistic boundaries as a take-off point for his alternative view of multilinguality, which he sees as the default situation in classrooms, both in general and in the particular South Asian context. He argues that multilinguality rather than 'a language' is characteristic of being human. Agnihotri questions the notions of a 'standard' language, the sanctity often attached to the association between a language and its script, and other language stereotypes. He draws out some of the implications for language teaching, all of them having significant implications for MLE pedagogy. In his view, the focus on multilinguality is necessary for empowerment of the underprivileged in fighting for a more just and equitable world order.

Part 6 of the volume reflects on the prospects of MLE for social justice. In Chapter 18, Minati Panda and Ajit Mohanty show both in theory and, even more importantly, in practice, how it is possible to take tribal children, through the medium of their own language, from everyday understanding towards Cognitive Academic Language Proficiency-oriented scientific thinking and analysis. They demonstrate the pedagogic processes through which cultural practices can become a classroom reality and lead to better transfer of learning in the classroom and to community empowerment. In the concluding chapter, the four editors reflect on broad issues and the questions of going beyond the diverse local contexts and experiences to making MLE a global practice. They point to the need for clarification of concepts, categories and labels, and offer a synthesis of major insights, pedagogic principles and policy issues in the field of multilingual education drawn from research and practices in the diverse settings reported in this volume. The concluding chapter also addresses some basic issues, including the role of English, economic factors, and linguistic human rights. It stresses the need for multilingual education to facilitate empowerment and development of Indigenous and marginalised communities without linguistic and cultural assimilation. The prospects of MLE as a strategy for human development, poverty alleviation and social justice are highlighted in the concluding chapter.

*****

In sum, this book shows that mother tongue based Multilingual Education (MLE) has become a global movement seeking to provide quality education for ALL. The contributors have presented examples of successful applications and innovations in MLE and strong demonstrations of empowerment though such applications. The contributors have also critiqued some approaches and practices in multilingual education. In effect, this volume seeks to promote new understanding of the principles and uses of MLE, based on analysis of both hard and soft data from a variety of societies and states across different continents—Africa, North and South America, Asia, and Europe. The book significantly has a unique focus on the most marginalised minorities, the Indigenous peoples, who have suffered the consequences of subtractive education. Innovative theoretical insights and practical lessons from diverse understandings of MLE and approaches to it have been culled from many parts of the world. They have been inspired by the initiatives of different communities, Governments, NGOs, and international collaborators. These are distinctive features of this work that seeks to further the commitment, scope and promises of MLE for increasing inclusive social justice.

With mother tongue medium education seen as a critical input for the development and revitalisation of languages, the number of countries joining the MLE movement has shown a rapid increase. This rising interest in MLE is supported by forceful developments in the theory and practice of multilingual education, a large body of committed MLE practitioners and professionals around the world and, of course, the persuasive influence of several international organisations (such as UNESCO, UNPFII and the UN Human Rights Council's Minority Forum). The year 2008, declared by the United Nations as the International Year of Languages, has further kindled hope and promise for the MLE movement.

MLE is not just another vogue, not a fad of experimentation. It opens up the prospect of a glocalising world and a promise of quality education for minorities, for tribal and Indigenous peoples—and for linguistic majorities, as this volume shows. In several countries (such as India and Nepal), the constitution or other laws and regulations do in fact grant all children the right to use the mother tongue as the main teaching language, although these commitments are not always honoured. In many parts of the world, tribal/Indigenous communities have started working together with politicians, school authorities and teachers, in order to change the situation, and to start teaching children in their own languages. Several such initiatives have also started in other South Asian countries, for instance mother tongue based MLE programmes in the Chittagong Hills in Bangladesh through Save the Children and Zabarang, an indigenous NGO, with some support from the state and other international organisations. Elsewhere in the world, for instance in Latin America and in the Pacific, there are successful examples of a variety of MLE programmes including many led by the communities themselves. This volume has presented some of the success stories of MLE—the extensive mother tongue medium education of the Sámi people, the new initiatives in Nepal and India, and the decentralised programmes of education in Ethiopian languages—and there are many more.

All these efforts in Africa, in Nordic countries, and South Asian countries as well as elsewhere in the world have a lot in common and are enormously exciting and pioneering. At the same time, these programmes are also manifestly as diverse as their contexts and sociolinguistic complexities. With a critical mass of people now supporting mother tongue and MLE initiatives, many countries in the world are poised for some fresh developments. But the extent to which the promises are redeemed depends on how effectively the dual gap—between theory and practices and also between the capacity for planning MLE and implementing it—can be bridged. This book, it is hoped, will help in this process. The current MLE programmes in several parts of the globe will also eventually move beyond the experimental stage to become default models of MLE for ALL. This book attempts to meet this need for critical examination of the ongoing MLE programmes and going beyond the available theoretical frameworks and international experiences to face specific challenges arising out of the extreme diversity and complex sociolinguistic realities of classrooms all over the world. Through this collective effort we hope to promote the development of effective strategies for resourceful use of the multilingual composition of many of our classrooms while dealing with the challenges of language disadvantage in multilingual societies.

The growing MLE initiatives all over the world are guided by the international theoretical framework of bilingual/multilingual education developed from the seminal work of eminent researchers in the field and a large number of international programmes of education for biliteracy and bilingualism/multilingualism under the active support of a growing group of researchers and practitioners of MLE. While the initial success of these international programmes for Indigenous and tribal peoples and linguistic minorities has provided much needed impetus for new initiatives in many other countries, analysis of the ongoing MLE efforts in multilingual countries shows that matters are more complex than had been appreciated, and that earlier theories and experimental evidence should not be applied uncritically. The question of transition from the mother tongue to other languages is complicated by the need to develop multilingual (rather than bilingual) competence through formal education, and this in turn is related to the question of the scheduling of skills development in multiple languages. This issue is further challenged in many countries by the presence of culturally less familiar languages like English. Such issues as the relationship between languages, community aspirations for them, the absence of established writing systems for many languages (and, sometimes, the claims of different orthographic systems) and, even more importantly, the poor quality of the existing systems of education for the minorities represent formidable obstacles. They need to be re-examined in light of the theoretical insights and practical lessons to be learned from the kinds of activity and analysis highlighted in this volume. It has also become necessary to have a system of mutual sharing of resources, insights and knowledge gained from different international experiences. This book seeks to foster global understanding based on the sharing of local MLE initiatives.

MLE is not just about building a bridge or many bridges; it is about developing a mindset to overcome the barriers between 'monolingual stupidity' and 'multilingual promise', barriers between a legislated and contrived unity and a naturally flourishing diversity. It is about building a better world, a world of diversity. It is about our survival. Are the small hopes and fragmented dreams enough to realise the promise of this better world? In the small state of Orissa (India) with a large tribal population, for example, as MLE goes to schools, there is hope for many a good bridge. But it is a small beginning. Only in 195 schools, whereas more than 11,000 schools have at least 90% children who speak a language other than the school language. Only 10 out of even the 22 major tribal languages in the state are covered under the Orissa MLE. How long can we wait for MLE to rise from being *'experimental'* programmes in different parts of the world to a just policy for ALL? In the 1980s, Orissa was India's most linguistically diverse state, with 50 languages, of which 38 were tribal. Within about two decades, 16 of the tribal languages have disappeared. Do we wait for more and more languages to die or be *'murdered'* as Tove Skutnabb-Kangas points out? In Andhra Pradesh, yet another state in India with a large tribal population, MLE shows the way. But is this just a path or a way? Where does one go from here? It is the same kind of reluctant beginning in many other parts of the globe. Are we there? Or, is it still a bridge too far?

We may not find all the answers, but we shall try. We may not have all the bridges that we need for effective MLE for ALL but we will hope to connect, sooner rather than later. We must light some lamps and not curse the darkness. And, as we put our minds together in this book, it is our hope that many a lamp will be lit—like in the Indian *Diwali.* Finally, one may still be groping in the darkness for answers to the questions that Barun Digal put to me regarding the future of his people and all others like them, the tribal and Indigenous minorities all over the world, but one hopes that many small efforts like this book are contesting the darkness, and lead to a collective *Diwali*. I am sure, Barun Digal is watching us.

## Note

1 The Indigenous or aboriginal communities in India are officially called 'tribes' (*ādivāsi*) and are listed as 'scheduled tribes' which are identified on the basis of 'distinct culture and language', 'geographical isolation', 'primitive traits', 'economic backwardness', and 'limited contact with the outgroups' and also, sometimes, on political considerations. The Anthropological Survey of India, in its *People of India* project, has identified 635 tribal communities of which 573 are so far officially notified as Scheduled Tribes. In this book the term 'tribe' (rather than 'Indigenous peoples') is used specifically in the Indian context in its formal/official and neutral sense.

# Part II
# Multilingual Education Approaches and Constraints

# 2

# Fundamental Psycholinguistic and Sociological Principles underlying Educational Success for Linguistic Minority Students

*Jim Cummins*

At its most basic level, the term *bilingual education* refers to the use of two (or more) languages of instruction at some point in a student's school career. The languages are used to teach subject matter content rather than just the language itself. This apparently simple description entails considerable complexity deriving from a multitude of sociopolitical, sociolinguistic, psychological, economic, administrative, and instructional factors (see Skutnabb-Kangas 1981, 2000 for extended discussion of these complexities).

The sociopolitical dimensions of bilingual education derive from the fact that use of a language as a medium of instruction in state-funded school systems confers recognition and status on that language and its speakers. Consequently, bilingual education is not simply a politically-neutral instructional phenomenon but rather is implicated in national and international competition between societal groups for material and symbolic resources.

Bilingual programs are usually minimally controversial when they are implemented to serve the interests of dominant groups in the society. In Canada, for example, little controversy exists in relation either to French immersion programs intended to support anglophone students in learning French, or French language programs intended to help minority francophone students outside of Quebec maintain French. These programs serve the interests of the two official language groups. However, there has been minimal implementation of bilingual programs involving languages other than English and French. Similarly, in Europe, there have been very few bilingual programs set up to serve migrant populations in comparison to those that teach the languages of national minorities whose status has been formally recognized within the society.

Typically, opposition to the implementation of bilingual programs for linguistic minority groups is rationalized in psycholinguistic terms. It is frequently argued that linguistic minority students need to become fluent and literate in the majority or dominant language in order to succeed academically; in order to achieve this goal, maximum exposure to the dominant language is claimed to be necessary. Bilingual education involving instruction partly through children's mother tongue is dismissed as 'illogical' on the grounds that it dilutes children's exposure to the majority language. Often parents of minority group children also support this argument—they view the dominant language as the language of power and advancement in the society and want to ensure that their children master this language.

This line of argument no longer has any credibility among researchers who have examined the empirical data on bilingual education in international contexts (e.g. August and Shanahan 2006, Cummins 2001, Genesee, Lindholm-Leary, Saunders and Christian 2006, Mohanty 1994, Skutnabb-Kangas 2000, Portes and Rumbaut 2001). The research data on bilingual education are summarized in the next section.

### General Outcomes of Bilingual Education Programs

A finding common to all forms of bilingual education is that spending instructional time through two languages entails no long-term adverse effects on students' academic development in the majority language. This pattern emerges among both majority and minority language students, across widely varying sociolinguistic and sociopolitical contexts, and in programs with very different organizational structures. Three additional outcomes of bilingual programs can be highlighted.

1. *Significant positive relationships exist between the development of academic skills in first and second languages.* This is true even for languages that are dissimilar (e.g. Spanish and Basque; English and Chinese; Dutch and Turkish). These cross-lingual relationships provide evidence for a *common underlying proficiency* (or what Genesee, Lindholm-Leary, Saunders and Christian [2006] call a cross-linguistic *reservoir of abilities*) that permits transfer of academic and conceptual knowledge across languages. This transfer of skills, strategies, and knowledge explains why spending instructional time through a minority language entails no adverse consequences for the development of the majority language.
2. *The most successful bilingual programs are those that aim to develop bilingualism and biliteracy.* Short-term transitional programs are less successful in developing both L2 and L1 literacy than programs such as dual language programs that continue to promote both L1 and L2 literacy throughout elementary school.
3. *Bilingual education for minority students is, in many situations, more effective in developing L2 literacy skills than monolingual education in the dominant language but it is not, by itself, a panacea for underachievement.* The National Literacy Panel on Language-Minority Children and Youth (August and Shanahan, 2006), established in the United States by the Bush administration to synthesize

the scientific findings on the education of English language learners, concluded that bilingual instruction exerts a positive effect on minority students' English academic achievement. Similar findings are reported other recent reviews (e.g. Genesee et al. 2006). The findings of the two most comprehensive reviews are outlined in the following quotations:

> [T]here is strong convergent evidence that the educational success of ELLs [English language learners] is positively related to sustained instruction through the student's first language. ... most long-term studies report that the longer the students stayed in the program, the more positive were the outcomes (Lindholm-Leary and Borsato 2006: 201).

> In summary, there is no indication that bilingual instruction impedes academic achievement in either the native language or English, whether for language-minority students, students receiving heritage language instruction, or those enrolled in Spanish immersion programs. Where differences were observed, on average they favored the students in a bilingual program. The meta-analytic results clearly suggest a positive effect for bilingual instruction that is moderate in size. This conclusion held up across the entire collection of studies and within the subset of studies that used random assignment of students to conditions (Francis, Lesaux and August 2006: 397).

In summary, the research on bilingual education demonstrates unequivocally that the amount of instruction in the majority language at school is unrelated to student outcomes. In fact, the trend is towards an *inverse* relationship between the amount of instruction in the majority language and minority student achievement in that language.

The data, however, are also clear that bilingual education, by itself, is not a panacea for minority students' educational difficulties. Underachievement derives from multiple factors and, while provision of L1 instruction *can* address some of these factors (e.g. the devaluation of children's language and culture in the wider society), far more than just medium of instruction is involved in reversing school failure.

Language planning to promote academic development among linguistic minority students requires an understanding of both the psycholinguistic and sociological principles underlying the pattern of findings outlined above. The relevant psycholinguistic principles are discussed in the following section.

## Psycholinguistic principles underlying minority students' academic development

Three psycholinguistic principles that are supported by extensive empirical data from a wide variety of sociolinguistic contexts can be articulated:

1. *The language abilities required for academic success are very different from those operating in everyday conversational contexts.* Sustained development of academic language proficiency across the grade levels requires expansion of vocabulary, grammatical, and discourse knowledge far beyond what is required for social communication.

2. *Among bilingual children, transfer of academic language proficiency occurs across languages when development of literacy in both languages is promoted in the school context.* This interdependence of academic language proficiency explains the virtually universal finding that minority students educated in bilingual programs perform at least as well as comparison groups in monolingual programs in the socially dominant language despite less instructional time in that language.
3. *Development of 'additive bilingualism' where both languages continue to develop during the school years is associated with positive intellectual and metalinguistic consequences.* Bilingual children get more practice in using language and this increased use of language results in greater awareness of linguistic operations as well as increased ability to focus intellectually.

These principles are elaborated in the following sections.

### *Language proficiency and academic development*

In order to understand patterns of academic development among linguistic minority students, we must distinguish between three very different aspects of proficiency in a language: (a) conversational fluency, (b) discrete language skills, and (c) academic language proficiency. The rationale for making these distinctions is that each dimension of proficiency follows very different developmental paths among both minority and majority language students and each responds differently to particular kinds of instructional practices in school.

**Conversational fluency.** This dimension of language proficiency represents the ability to carry on a conversation in familiar face-to-face situations. The vast majority of native speakers of any language have developed conversational fluency when they enter school at age 5. However, this fluency involves the use of high frequency words and relatively simple grammatical construction and reflects only a small fraction of the language skills that students will need for academic success. This is why a major focus of schooling for all students, typically over a period of at least 10 years, is on extending students' initial fluency into the registers required for academic success. In contexts where minority students have extensive contact with the majority language, as is the case in many immigrant situations (e.g., on television), peer-appropriate conversational fluency in the majority language typically develops within a year or two of intensive exposure to the language either in school or in the environment. A much longer period may be required in contexts where exposure to the majority language is available only in the context of schooling.

**Discrete language skills.** These skills involve the learning of rule-governed aspects of language (including phonology, grammar, and spelling) where acquisition of the general case permits generalization to other instances governed by that particular rule. Discrete language skills can be developed in two independent ways: (a) by direct instruction (e.g. systematic explicit phonics instruction), and (b) through immersion in a language- and literacy-rich home or school environment where meanings are elaborated through language and attention is drawn to literate forms of language (e.g. letters on the pages of books). A combination of these two conditions appears to yield the most positive outcomes. Students exposed to a literacy-rich environment in the home generally acquire initial literacy-related skills, such as phonological awareness and letter-sound correspondences, with minimal difficulty in the early grades of schooling.

Students learning through the medium of a second language *can* learn these specific language skills concurrently with their development of basic vocabulary and conversational fluency. However, little direct transference is observed to other aspects of oral language proficiency such as linguistic concepts, vocabulary, sentence memory, and word memory (Geva 2000). Similar findings are reported by Verhoeven (2000) for minority language students in the Dutch context and by Lambert and Tucker (1972) in Canada for English-speaking students in French immersion programs.

**Academic language proficiency.** This dimension of proficiency includes knowledge of the less frequent vocabulary of a language as well as the ability to interpret and produce increasingly complex written language. As students progress through the grades, they encounter far more low frequency words, complex syntax (e.g. in English, the passive voice), and abstract expressions that are virtually never heard in everyday conversation. Students are required to understand linguistically and conceptually demanding texts in the content areas (e.g. literature, social studies, science, mathematics) and to use this language in an accurate and coherent way in their own writing.

Numerous research studies have shown that at least five years (and often considerably longer) is required for linguistic minority students to catch up to grade expectations in the majority language (see Cummins 2001, for a review). Thus the 'catch-up' trajectory is very different than in the case of both conversational fluency and discrete language skills. In addition to the complexity of the academic language they are attempting to acquire, linguistic minority students must catch up to a moving target. Every year, native-speakers are making large gains in their reading and writing abilities and in their knowledge of vocabulary. It has been estimated in the context of the United States that in order to catch up to grade norms within six years, linguistic minority students must make 15 months gain in every 10-month school year. By contrast, the typical native-speaking student is expected to make 10 months gain in a 10-month school year (Collier and Thomas 1999).

It is important to distinguish these three aspects of language proficiency because they exhibit different developmental trajectories and entail different implications for instruction. Because academic language is found primarily in books (including textbooks) and classrooms, it is important to encourage extensive reading as a means of enabling students to gain access to this language (see Krashen 2004, Krashen and Brown 2007). Encouragement of extensive writing, across multiple genres, is also a crucial element in enabling students to gain a sense of control over academic language that is active rather than just passive.

*Linguistic interdependence*

The fact that there is little relationship between amount of instructional time through the majority language and academic achievement in that language strongly suggests that first and second language academic skills are interdependent, i.e. manifestations of a common underlying proficiency. The interdependence principle has been stated formally as follows (Cummins 1981: 29):

> To the extent that instruction in Lx is effective in promoting proficiency in Lx, transfer of this proficiency to Ly will occur provided there is adequate exposure to Ly (either in school or environment) and adequate motivation to learn Ly.

In concrete terms, what this principle means is that in, for example, a Basque-Spanish bilingual program in the Basque Autonomous Community in Spain, Basque instruction that develops Basque reading and writing skills is not just developing Basque skills, it is also developing a deeper conceptual and linguistic proficiency that contributes significantly to the development of literacy in the majority language (Spanish). In other words, although the surface aspects of different languages (e.g. pronunciation, fluency, orthography etc.) are clearly separate, there is an underlying cognitive/academic proficiency that is common across languages. This 'common underlying proficiency' makes possible the transfer of cognitive/academic or literacy-related skills across languages.

There is extensive empirical research that supports the interdependence hypothesis. The most comprehensive review was conducted by Dressler and Kamil as part of the Report of the National Literacy Panel on Language-Minority Children and Youth (August and Shanahan 2006). They conclude (2006: 222):

> In summary, all these studies provide evidence for the cross-language transfer of reading comprehension ability in bilinguals. This relationship holds (a) across typologically different languages ...; (b) for children in elementary, middle, and high school; (c) for learners of English as a foreign language and English as a second language; (d) over time; (e) from both first to second language and second to first language;

The interdependence hypothesis involves much more than just linguistic transfer. Depending on the sociolinguistic situation, five types of transfer are possible (see August and Shanahan 2006, for an extended review of research evidence):

- Transfer of conceptual elements (e.g. understanding the concept of photosynthesis);
- Transfer of metacognitive and metalinguistic strategies (e.g. strategies of visualizing, use of visuals or graphic organizers, mnemonic devices, vocabulary acquisition strategies, etc.);
- Transfer of pragmatic aspects of language use (willingness to take risks in communication through L2, ability to use paralinguistic features such as gestures to aid communication, etc.);

- Transfer of specific linguistic elements (knowledge of the meaning of *photo* in *photosynthesis*);
- Transfer of phonological awareness—the knowledge that words are composed of distinct sounds.

One important pedagogical implication of the interdependence hypothesis is that instruction should explicitly encourage students to transfer knowledge and skills across languages. This endorsement of bilingual instructional strategies challenges the common assumption that monolingual strategies are superior both in the context of bilingual and second language immersion programs as well as in second language teaching generally (Cummins 2007, Phillipson 1992).

### *The benefits of additive bilingualism*

Close to 200 empirical studies carried out during the past 40 or so years have reported a positive association between additive bilingualism and students' linguistic, cognitive, or academic growth. The most consistent findings are that bilinguals show more developed awareness of the structure and functions of language itself (metalinguistic abilities) and that they have advantages in learning additional languages. The term *additive bilingualism* refers to the form of bilingualism that results when students add a second language to their intellectual tool-kit while continuing to develop conceptually and academically in their home language.

The general pattern of findings can be illustrated in the series of research studies carried out by Mohanty between 1978 and 1987 in Orissa, India. Mohanty (1994) studied large numbers of monolingual and bilingual Kond tribal children who had varying degrees of contact with the dominant language of Orissa, namely Oriya. The monolingual children came from areas where the original Kui language of the Konds had given way to Oriya monolingualism. In other areas, a relatively stable form of Kui-Oriya bilingualism existed where Kui is used predominantly in children's homes but contact with Oriya through peers and others in the neighborhood results in most children having a considerable degree of bilingualism by the time they start school, which is conducted through the medium of Oriya. Despite the differences in language use, the Konds are relatively homogenous with respect to Kond identity, socioeconomic, and cultural characteristics. This is illustrated in the fact that the Oriya-monolingual Konds perceive Kui as their mother tongue and both Oriya monolinguals and Kui-Oriya bilinguals call themselves Kui people and their structured social organizations are called *Kui Samaj* (Kui Society).

The context thus provides a unique opportunity to study the impact of bilingualism in relative isolation from the social, political and economic factors which frequently confound comparisons between monolingual and bilingual groups. Mohanty's studies show a clear positive relationship between bilingualism and cognitive performance including measures of metalinguistic ability. He suggests that bilinguals' awareness of language and their cognitive strategies are enhanced as a result of the challenging communicative environment in which their bilingual abilities have developed.

## Sociological principles underlying minority students' academic development

Extensive research has been carried out by sociologists and anthropologists on issues related to ethnicity and educational achievement (e.g., Bankston and Zhou 1995, McCarty 2002, Ogbu 1978, 1992, Portes and Rumbaut 2001, Skutnabb-Kangas 2000). These studies point clearly to the centrality of societal power relations in explaining patterns of minority group achievement. Groups that experience long-term educational underachievement tend to have experienced material and symbolic violence at the hands of the dominant societal group over generations. A direct implication is that in order to reverse this pattern of underachievement, educators, both individually and collectively, must challenge the operation of coercive power relations in the classroom interactions they orchestrate with minority or subordinated group students. Challenging coercive power relations within the societal institution of schooling clearly also represents a direct challenge to the more general operation of coercive power relations in the wider society. This claim is elaborated in the sections that follow.

Ladson-Billings succinctly articulates how coercive power relations affect patterns of classroom engagement among African-American students: 'The problem that African-American students face is the constant devaluation of their culture both in school and in the larger society' (1995: 485). This devaluation of identity in both school and society leads many minority students to adopt what Ogbu (1992) terms an 'oppositional identity'. Ogbu contrasts the situation of what he terms *voluntary* and *involuntary minorities*. In contrast to voluntary minorities who come to the host country seeking better economic opportunities or greater political freedom, involuntary minorities have often been incorporated into the host society against their will (e.g. through conquest, slavery, colonization, etc.). He points out that, in certain contexts, voluntary or immigrant minorities often perform well in school and acculturate easily into the host society. By contrast, involuntary minorities frequently experience long-term school failure as a result both of overt discrimination in access to material resources (jobs, adequate schooling, housing etc.) and the long-term devaluation of their identities in the wider society. According to Ogbu, disengagement from academic effort is a function of a collective oppositional identity that involuntary minorities develop in response to their treatment by the dominant group.

While useful in pointing to broad trends and the operation of societal power relations, Ogbu's analysis requires qualification. A simple dichotomy between voluntary and involuntary minorities fails to take account of the many intermediate situations. For example, the experience of migrant workers and refugees in many countries around the world would appear to fall somewhere in-between Ogbu's voluntary/involuntary distinction. Migrant workers and refugees come willingly to the host country seeking better economic or political conditions but are often denied opportunities for structural incorporation into the host country (e.g. through job discrimination and segregated housing and schooling). The second and subsequent generations then assume many of the characteristics of involuntary minorities, 'relegated to menial positions and denied true assimilation into the mainstream society' (Ogbu 1992: 8). The host society frequently demands linguistic and cultural assimilation on the part of the minority group while simultaneously segregating them from the mainstream structures of the society (Schermerhorn 1970).

Portes and Rumbaut (2001) have also pointed to the negative consequences of what they term *reactive ethnicity,* which they define as 'the product of confrontation with an adverse native mainstream and the rise of defensive identities and solidarities to counter it' (2001: 284). Based on a large-scale longitudinal study of acculturation among more than 5,000 second generation immigrant students, they note that '[y]outhful solidarity based on opposition to the dominant society yields an adversarial stance towards mainstream institutions, including education' (285). Disengagement from academic effort is one consequence of this reactive ethnicity or oppositional identity. Similar patterns are illustrated in an Asian context by the low educational levels traditionally attained by the Burakumin minority group in Japan as a result of multiple forms of structural exclusion from Japanese society (Ogbu 1978; Shimahara 1991, see also Skutnabb-Kangas, Phillipson, Minati and Mohanty 2009, this volume). Shimahara, however, points to the fact that social mobilization by the Burakumin in the 1960s and beyond, combined with a strong Japanese economy, have resulted in significant progress toward social and educational equality.

Portes and Rumbaut (2001: 190) highlight the role of *identity negotiation* in mediating patterns of acculturation and academic achievement. They point out that all children of immigrants are inescapably engaged in a process of making sense of who they are and finding a meaningful place in the society of which they are the newest members. Their study highlighted the consistent positive effects of what they term *selective acculturation* both on student self-esteem and academic achievement. In contrast to full assimilation where students largely abandon their parents' cultural norms and home language, selective acculturation slows down the cultural shift and supports partial retention of the parents' home language and norms. Portes and Rumbaut summarize their findings as follows (2001: 274):

> The findings from our longitudinal study consistently point to the benefits of selective acculturation. This path is closely intertwined with preservation of fluent bilingualism and linked, in turn, with higher self-esteem, higher educational and occupational expectations, and higher academic achievement. ... Children who learn the language and culture of their new country without losing those of the old, have a much better understanding of their place in the world. ... Selective acculturation forges an intergenerational alliance for successful adaptation that is absent among youths who have severed bonds with their past in pursuit of acceptance by their native peers.

The implication of these data and other research (e.g. Bankston and Zhou 1995) pointing to the positive effects of home language literacy and a bicultural orientation on academic achievement is that schools should encourage students to develop their home language skills and feel proud of their cultural heritage. The ways in which teachers negotiate identities with students can exert a significant impact on the extent to which students will engage academically or withdraw from academic effort. The intersection of societal power relations and identity negotiation in determining patterns of academic achievement among minority group students is expressed in Figure 2.1 (adapted from Cummins, 2001).

SOCIETAL POWER RELATIONS
influence
the ways in which educators define their roles (teacher identity)
and
the structures of schooling (curriculum, funding, assessment etc.)
which, in turn, influence
the ways in which educators interact
with linguistically- and culturally-diverse students.

These interactions form
an
INTERPERSONAL SPACE
within which
learning happens
and
identities are negotiated.

These IDENTITY NEGOTIATIONS
either
Reinforce coercive relations of power
or
Promote collaborative relations of power

**Figure 2.1** *Societal power relations and academic achievement*

In summary, effective education for minority or subordinated group students challenges coercive power relations in the broader society by affirming students' identities at school. A central goal of education within this framework is *empowerment,* understood as the *collaborative creation of power* (Cummins 2001). Power is generated in teacher-student interactions such that students (and teachers) feel more affirmed in their linguistic, cultural, and intellectual identities and more confident in their ability to succeed in school. By virtue of the fact that it incorporates students' home language as a medium of instruction, bilingual education goes some way to challenging coercive relations of power and affirming students' identity. However, bilingual programs must also encompass effective literacy instruction in both languages if students are to succeed academically. The essential constituents of effective literacy instruction in multilingual contexts are outlined in the following section.

## LITERACY INSTRUCTION IN MULTILINGUAL CONTEXTS

### A PEDAGOGICAL FRAMEWORK

The framework presented in Figure 2.2. posits a direct relationship between literacy engagement and literacy attainment. It also specifies the core conditions that enable immigrant and minority students to engage with literacy from an early stage of their learning of the second language. As outlined in the sections that follow, bilingual instructional strategies and teaching for cross-language transfer are explicitly built into the framework.

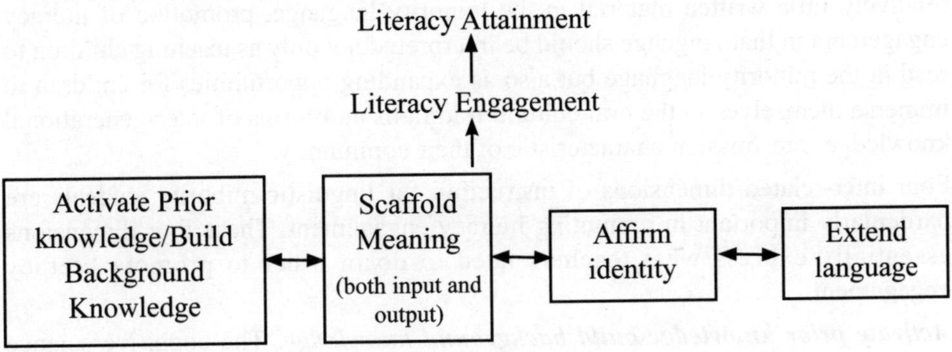


**Figure 2.2.** *A pedagogical framework for promoting academic development in multilingual contexts*

#### *Literacy engagement*

International research has demonstrated that active engagement with literacy is fundamental to student success in school. For example, the Programme for International Student Assessment data on the reading attainment of 15-year olds in almost 30 countries showed that 'the level of a student's reading engagement is a better predictor of literacy performance than his or her socioeconomic background, indicating that cultivating a student's interest in reading can help overcome home disadvantages' (OECD 2004: 8).

Guthrie (2004) has highlighted three major components of literacy engagement:

- Amount and range of reading and writing;

- Use of effective strategies for deep understanding of text;
- Positive affect and identity investment in reading and writing.

Guthrie notes that in all spheres of life (e.g. learning to ride a bicycle, driving a car, cooking etc.), participation is key to the development of proficiency. He notes that 'certainly some initial lessons are valuable for driving a car or typing on a keyboard, but expertise spirals upward mainly with engaged participation' (2004: 8).

It is important to note that school-based literacy is no different in principle from other forms of what Gee (1990) terms *secondary discourses*. Primary discourses are acquired through face-to-face interactions in the home and represent the language of initial socialization. Secondary discourses are acquired in social institutions beyond the family (e.g. school, business, religious, and cultural contexts) and involve acquisition of specialized vocabulary and functions of language appropriate to those settings. Secondary discourses can be oral or written and are equally central to the social life of non-literate and literate cultures. Examples of secondary discourse common in many non-literate cultures are the conventions of story-telling or the language of marriage or burial rituals which are passed down through oral tradition from one generation to the next. In a bilingual education context where there is relatively little written material in the minority language, promotion of literacy engagement in that language should be interpreted not only as teaching children to read in the minority language but also as expanding opportunities for children to immerse themselves in the oral cultural traditions and forms of inter-generational knowledge transmission characteristic of their community.

Four inter-related dimensions of instruction for linguistic minority students are particularly important in promoting literacy engagement. These four dimensions essentially express what teachers need to do in order to promote literacy engagement.

***Activate prior knowledge/build background knowledge.*** The cognitive science research on learning highlights the centrality of students' pre-existing knowledge (Bransford, Brown and Cocking 2000). Snow, Burns and Griffin (1998: 219) express the centrality of background knowledge as follows:

> Every opportunity should be taken to extend and enrich children's background knowledge and understanding in every way possible, for the ultimate significance and memorability of any word or text depends on whether children possess the background knowledge and conceptual sophistication to understand its meaning.

This implies that when students' background knowledge is encoded in their L1, they should be encouraged to use their L1 to activate and extend this knowledge (e.g. by brainstorming in groups). This is true even when instruction is being conducted primarily through L2.

***Scaffold meaning.*** The term scaffolding refers to the provision of temporary supports that enable learners to carry out tasks and perform academically at a higher level than they would be capable of without these supports. Activation of students' prior knowledge and building background knowledge represent one form of scaffolding that operates on students' internal cognitive structures. Other forms of scaffolding focus on modifying the input so that it becomes more comprehensible to students. These include the use of visuals, demonstrations, dramatization, acting out meanings, and explanation of words and linguistic structures. Scaffolding also supports students in using the target language in both written and oral modes. Writing frames, for example, are one way of supporting students in acquiring and using the conventions of different genres of writing (e.g., formal letters, science reports etc.). All scaffolds should be used in a flexible way that adjusts to the progress of individual students. For example, writing frames are a useful temporary support but they should never be implemented in a rigid and formulaic way that is likely to reduce rather than increase genuine literacy engagement.

Students' L1 also represents an important scaffold in certain L2 instructional contexts. Research suggests that encouraging students to use their L1 when necessary to complete a group task can result in higher quality of L2 output than when students are prohibited from L1 use (Swain and Lapkin 2005).

***Affirm identity.*** One of the most frustrating initial experiences for minority students being educated exclusively through the majority language is not being able to express their intelligence, feelings, ideas, and humor to teachers and peers. Under these conditions, it is easy to underestimate what students are capable of and what they aspire to achieve in school and with their lives. By contrast, when students feel that their intelligence, imagination, and multilingual talents are affirmed in the school and classroom context, they invest their identities much more actively in the learning process (see Cummins, Brown and Sayers 2007, for examples). The affirmation of minority students' identity in the context of teacher–student interactions explicitly challenges the devaluation of student and community identity in the wider society.

We have used the term *identity texts* to refer to artifacts created by students that reflect their imagination, intelligence, and linguistic and artistic talents. Students take ownership of these artifacts as a result of having invested their identities in them (see http://www.multiliteracies.ca for examples). Once produced, these texts, which can be written, spoken, visual, musical, or combinations in multimodal form, hold a mirror up to the student in which his or her identity is reflected back in a positive light. These texts frequently become ambassadors of students' identities. When students share identity texts with multiple audiences (peers, teachers, parents, grandparents, sister classes, the media etc.) they typically receive positive feedback and affirmation of self in interaction with these audiences.

This is illustrated in Tomer's comments. Tomer arrived in Canada from Israel in grade 6 not knowing any English but was quickly engaged by his teacher (Lisa Leoni) in writing a dual language book in Hebrew and English. Tomer wrote the book initially in Hebrew and, working with a teacher who spoke Hebrew, translated it into English and published his book on the Internet (http://www.multiliteracies.ca). He expressed his feelings as follows:

> I felt great seeing my book on the Internet because everybody could see it and I don't need to show it to everybody, they can just click on my name in Google and go to the book. I told Tom [Tomer's friend in Israel] to see it and all of my family saw it.

In short, the affirmation of minority student identity within the school explicitly challenges the operation of coercive relations of power in the wider society. The resulting student empowerment, understood as the collaborative creation of power, fuels literacy engagement.

***Extend language.*** As noted above, as students progress through the grades, they are required to read increasingly complex texts in the content areas of the curriculum (science, mathematics, social studies, literature). Students encounter low frequency academic vocabulary and more complex grammatical and discourse patterns predominantly in books. Therefore, students who read extensively in a variety of genres both inside and outside the school have far greater opportunities to acquire academic language than those whose reading is limited. However, it is also essential to focus directly on de-mystifying how academic language works, constantly drawing students' attention to language and how it can be used in powerful ways. Encouraging students to use their L1 as a cognitive tool in acquiring L2 and to compare and contrast their languages contributes to extending students' awareness of language and how it works. Translation in the context of literacy tasks to which students are committed (e.g. writing and publishing dual language books) can also extend students' awareness and knowledge of language in significant ways. This is illustrated in Kanta's reflection on the process of creating a dual language book entitled *The New Country* with two of her friends, Madiha and Sulmana, that told about how difficult it was to leave Pakistan and come to a new country:

> It helped me a lot to be able to write it in two languages and especially for Madiha, who was just beginning to learn English because the structure of the two languages is so different. So if you want to say something in Urdu it might take just three words but in English to say the same thing you'd have to use more words. So for Madiha it helped the differences between the two languages become clear. (from webcast available at http://www.curriculum.org/secretariat/archive.html)

## Conclusion

The debate among researchers and academics about the scientific legitimacy of bilingual education is finished, although there is still much to be discussed and investigated regarding optimal models and practices under different sociopolitical and sociolinguistic conditions. In the context of language planning at both national and local levels, it is possible to distinguish certain core or non-negotiable elements of bilingual programs for linguistic minority students that are essential to educational effectiveness. These include:

- Strong and effective promotion of fluency and literacy in both languages;
- Sustained literacy engagement in both languages, with 'literacy' understood in a broad sense as the oral and written repository of a community's cultural knowledge;
- Empowerment—the collaborative creation of power within the classroom.

Other program components should be decided at the local level because the research suggests that a variety of options can be effective depending on the sociolinguistic and sociopolitical context. These include:

- Language allocation (e.g. 50/50 or 90/10 L1/L2 division in the early grades);
- The appropriate language(s) for initial instruction in reading and writing (L1, L2, both);
- The extent to which the instructional orientation should be to teach for cross-lingual transfer as implied by the interdependence hypothesis (bilingual instructional assumptions) or, alternatively, maintain linguistic separation (monolingual instructional assumptions)

With respect to this last point, as noted above, there are clear instructional advantages associated with teaching for transfer in many bilingual/multilingual contexts. However, in some contexts, these instructional advantages are outweighed in the eyes of community language planners by the importance of normalizing minority language use as a primary and totally legitimate language for social communication and literacy development. Many Māori educators in Aoteroa/New Zealand have strongly expressed this view.

In the context of bilingual education for tribal groups in India, there are many factors that will influence the specific program models that are adopted. Among these are the availability of teachers fluent in tribal, regional, and national languages, the availability of textbooks in different languages, and community beliefs and aspirations for their children's linguistic and academic development. Other chapters in the present volume discuss the complexities of minority language educational initiatives in India. Respectful dialogue among the various stakeholders, academics, and policy-makers will identify the program components and models that are appropriate and feasible in different contexts. However, in discussing these issues, it is important to constantly bear in mind the deep structure of effective bilingual programs that has emerged from the international research. The success of any program will fundamentally depend on (a) the extent to which fluency and literacy in two or more languages is strongly promoted, (b) the extent to which literacy engagement, in both oral and written modes, is promoted across the curriculum, and (c) the extent to which instruction explicitly challenges the operation of coercive relations of power in the wider society through the promotion of minority student empowerment.

# 3

# MLE for Global Justice: Issues, Approaches, Opportunities

*Tove Skutnabb-Kangas*

## Introduction: Corporate Globalisation, Diversities and MLE

In the Communist Manifesto in 1848, Marx and Engels wrote, in a text that stresses many elements of what is now known as globalisation:

> [Bourgeois society] has set up that single unconscionable freedom—Free Trade. In a word, for exploitation, veiled by religious and political illusions, it has substituted naked, shameless, direct, brutal exploitation. [...] The need of a constantly expanding market for its products chases the bourgeoisie over the whole face of the globe. It must nestle everywhere, settle everywhere, establish connections everywhere. [...] In place of the old local and national seclusion and self-sufficiency, we have intercourse in every direction, a universal interdependence of nations. And as in material, so also in intellectual production. The intellectual creations of individual nations become common property. [...] It compels all nations, on pain of extinction, to adopt the bourgeois mode of production; it compels them to introduce what it calls civilisation into their midst, i.e. to become bourgeois themselves. In one word, it creates a world after its own image (reprinted in Mendel 1961, 15, 16, 17).

The class interests that Marx and Engels stressed are now orchestrated through what can be called Corporate Globalisation, which has been extensively described and analysed. 'Globalisation is an attempt to extend corporate monopoly control over the whole globe. Over every national economy. Over every local economy. Over every life' says Michael Parenti.[1] I am asking several questions here. Central issues for the paper are whether and how MLE (Multilingual Education) can support the maintenance of linguistic and cultural diversity (LCD) on earth (and, partially through this also the maintenance of biodiversity), what MLE can do to counter some of the threats to diversities, and to what extent some of the current approaches by researchers are doing this.

I am first asking what Corporate Globalisation is doing to diversities, human and biological. One of the global challenges is whether this globalisation leads to more homogenisation, as this article claims, or more diversification (e.g. through localisation), as some researchers claim. For instance, Mufwene (2008: 227) claims that McDonaldisation does not lead to uniformity because the 'McDonald menu is partly adapted to the local diet'. This reduction to superficial adaptation disregards completely the structural and process-related aspects of this homogenisation (see Hamelink 1994, Ritzer 1996, and Definition Box 6.3 in Skutnabb-Kangas 2000 for discussions on McDonaldisation).[2] Linguistic glocalisation needs to be discussed within a polito-economic framework which relates the hierarchisation of languages to global and local power relations.

'People often think evolution means greater divergence, but now it's going to become a grand homogenisation, a triumph of the average' Jones (2000) claims. Are we facing a grand homogenisation in humans—mixing and leveling of human traits? Ian Sample (2008: 33) states that mass transport leads to 'unprecedented mixing between isolated populations. Genes that have been separated for tens of thousands of years will be reunited in unknown combinations. One consequence will be an evening-out of skin colour, hair colour and other traits, which is expected to happen quickly over the next few centuries.' Grand homogenisation in some parts of the rest of nature, in fauna and flora, is also happening: 'British supermarkets have reduced well over 2,000 varieties of locally grown apple for all practical purposes to two (Bramley and Cox)' (Spurling 2008: 36), and similar figures are true for rice. And more homogenisation is being predicted. 'More and more species which do not belong in Denmark are invading the country and threatening domestic species. The risk is that we get a more homogenised nature with a paucity of species', warns the Research Centre for Forest and Landscape in Denmark (2008). Ecological imperialism (Crosby, 2005) is rampant.

It should be axiomatic that linguistic, cultural and biological homogenisation, biocultural homogenisation, is dangerous for the planet (see also Vandana Shiva's writings, e.g. 1997, 2005). Colin Baker writes (2001: 281).

> In the language of ecology, the strongest ecosystems are those that are the most diverse. That is, diversity is directly related to stability; variety is important for long-term survival. Our success on this planet has been due to an ability to adapt to different kinds of environment over thousands of years (atmospheric as well as cultural). Such ability is born out of diversity. Thus language and cultural diversity maximises chances of human success and adaptability.

Today we are killing biocultural diversity faster than ever before. New species, new languages, new cultures (even if some do evolve) cannot keep up with the pace of present destruction. What needs exploration is how multilingual education (MLE) can address the issues, approaches and opportunities that are connected to contemporary global challenges. Is Glocalisation possible, and what might it mean in education? (see García, Skutnabb-Kangas and Torres-Guzmán (eds) 2006).

## Issues

### *Present situation for languages and the bleak future*

Coming back to the central issue (to what extent, whether and how MLE can support the maintenance of LCD and biodiversity), I start with a short general presentation of the prognosis for the world's languages and the relationships between the diversities. Of the world's almost 7,000 mainly spoken languages[3] (6,912, the *Ethnologue*, 15th edition), at least some 4,500, over half, are tribal/Indigenous (Oviedo and Maffi 2000, Terralingua, www.terralingua.org). There may be only 300 to 600 oral languages left in 2100 as unthreatened languages, transmitted by the parent generation to children (e.g. Krauss 1992, 1995, 1998, Krauss, Maffi and Yamamoto 2004, UNESCO 2003a, b). These would probably include most of those languages that today have more than one million speakers, and a few others. The most vulnerable languages are those with few speakers, especially if the speakers have little power over their economic, social and political conditions, such as logging, mining, oil extraction; availability of jobs without the need to migrate; low social status and few rights (see Skutnabb-Kangas 2000, Chapter 2 for elaboration; see also UNESCO 2003a, 2003b). Lack of a written language may also under some circumstances make languages vulnerable (but see Mühlhäusler 1996). If 90-95% of the world's languages disappear before 2100, most Indigenous languages will go: Almost all languages to disappear would be Indigenous, and most of today's Indigenous/tribal languages would disappear, with the exception of very few that are strong numerically (e.g. Quechua, Aymara, Bodo, Mapuche) and/or have official status (e.g. Māori, some Saami languages).

Thus, if we continue as at present, most of the world's Indigenous languages will be gone by 2100. One serious implication for diversities is as follows. Most of the world's linguistic diversity resides in the small languages of Indigenous peoples. Most of the world's megabiodiversity is in areas under the management or guardianship of Indigenous peoples (e.g. biodiversity hotspots). Terralingua, an international organisation supports the integrated protection, maintenance and restoration of the biocultural diversity of life—the world's biological, cultural, and linguistic diversity—through an innovative programme of research, education, policy-relevant work, and on-the-ground action' (www.terralingua.org, accessed 10 July 2008).

We[4] write on Terralingua's home page (accessed 27 November 2007):

> People who lose their linguistic and cultural identity may lose an essential element in a social process that commonly teaches respect for nature and understanding of the natural environment and its processes. Forcing this cultural and linguistic conversion on indigenous and other traditional peoples not only violates their human rights, but also undermines the health of the world's ecosystems and the goals of nature conservation.

The World Resources Institute, the World Conservation Union, and the United

Nations Environment Programme (1992: 21) also articulate the inter-connectedness of diversities:

> Cultural diversity is closely linked to biodiversity. Humanity's collective knowledge of biodiversity and its use and management rests in cultural diversity; conversely conserving biodiversity often helps strengthen cultural integrity and values.

One reason for maintaining all the world's languages is that linguistic (and cultural) diversity and biodiversity are correlationally and very likely also causally related; historically they have co-evolved, mutually influencing each other. Much of the knowledge about how to maintain biodiversity (especially in 'biodiversity hotspots') is encoded in the small languages of Indigenous and local peoples. Through killing them we kill the prerequisites for maintaining biodiversity (see Harmon 2002, Maffi (ed.) 2001, Skutnabb-Kangas 2000, 2003, Skutnabb-Kangas, Maffi and Harmon 2003, Skutnabb-Kangas and Phillipson 2008a, 2008b, for details).

### *Present situation in Indigenous and minority education: genocide and crime against humanity. Alternatives.*

The goals that any good education must have for Indigenous/tribal and minority (IM) children are 1. high levels of multilingualism; 2. a fair chance of achieving academically at school; 3. strong, positive multilingual and multicultural identity and positive attitudes towards self and others; and 4. a fair chance of awareness and competence building as prerequisites for working for a more equitable world, for oneself and one's own group as well as others, locally and globally. In addition, the same goals that any education, also for linguistic majority/dominant group children has should also be valid for IM children.

When we as educators try to influence educational decision makers, we need to know what the present situation is, and what the consequences of today's education are (does it reach the goals above), and what the alternatives are. In several earlier papers and books, I have stated, just like many others, on the basis of massive research evidence, that the situation today is disastrous but we know in broad terms enough about how to 'do it', even if MLE needs contextualising everywhere. It is also clear from several studies that the costs of proper MLE are even in the short term minor, as compared to costs for subtractive dominant-language-medium education.

Firstly, what we know (e.g. Magga, Nicolaisen, Trask, Dunbar and Skutnabb-Kangas 2005) is that *non-MLE mainly dominant-language medium education for IM children*

- prevents access to education, because of the linguistic, pedagogical and psychological barriers it creates;
- may lead to the extinction of Indigenous languages,
- thus contributing to the disappearance of the world's linguistic diversity;
- often curtails the development of the children's capabilities, perpetuates poverty, and causes serious mental harm.

- It is organised against solid research evidence about how best to reach high levels of bilingualism or multilingualism and how to enable IM children to achieve academically in school.

This subtractive education through the medium of a dominant language can have harmful consequences socially, psychologically, economically and politically. It can (and does, especially for Indigenous/tribal children) cause both serious physical harm, and very serious mental harm: social dislocation, psychological, cognitive, linguistic and educational harm, and, partially through this, also economic, social and political marginalisation (see Dunbar and Skutnabb-Kangas 2008). This education may thus participate in linguistic and cultural genocide, according to two of the five definitions of genocide – II(e) and II(b) - in United Nations 1948 *International Convention on the Punishment and Prevention of the Crime of Genocide* (E793, 1948):

Article 2

In the present Convention, genocide means any of the following acts committed with *intent to destroy*, in whole or in part, a national, ethnical, racial or religious group, as such:

Article II(e): 'forcibly transferring children of the group to another group'; and

Article II(b): 'causing serious bodily *or mental* harm to members of the group'; [emphases added].

Most Indigenous/tribal students (with some exceptions, e.g. Saami, Māori), many national minority and most immigrant minority students in the world are being taught through the medium of dominant languages in *submersion* programmes. Dominant-language-only submersion programmes 'are widely attested as the least effective educationally for minority language students' (May and Hill 2003: 14).[5] Sociologically and educationally submersion models for IM children fit the two UN definitions above (see Magga et al., 2005). Especially subtractive submersion models for IM children but to some extent also many early-exit transitional weak models (see Skutnabb-Kangas and McCarty 2008 for definitions) may fit these two definitions of genocide.[6]

What about MLE? Can *all* forms of MLE (which by definition use more than one language as the teaching language), be endorsed and expected to deliver good results? No. Kathleen Heugh (2009, this volume) states that when children have been taught in their own languages for only a few years, an *early* transition to the international language of wider communication/ILWC across Africa is accompanied by:

- Poor literacy in L1 and L2 (SACMEQ 11 2005, UIE-ADEA study 2006, HSRC studies in South Africa 2007);
- Poor numeracy/mathematics and science (HSRC 2005, 2007);
- High failure and drop-out rates (Obanya 1999, Bamgbose 2000);
- High costs/ wastage of expenditure (Alidou et al 2006).

Weak models of MLE, such as early-exit and, especially, late-exit transitional programmes are more humane for IM children than non-models. But they do not reach the educational goals (see above) of good MLE programmes either (as Kathleen Heugh shows for Africa; see all references to her in the bibliography).

What about the Nepali and Orissa MLE programmes, presented in this volume? So far, they are early-exit. Early- and late-exit transitional programmes are weak models; weak models do not reach the educational goals either.

What should the next step be for Nepali, Orissa etc programmes? Quoting Kathleen Heugh (2009, this volume) again:

> If learners switch from an African MT to FL/L2 medium, they may seem to do well until half way through grade/year 4. After this, progress slows down and the gap between L1 and L2 learner achievement steadily widens. We now know from comprehensive studies in Second Language Acquisition … in Scandinavia, Australia, Russian Federation, India, North America, and, especially in Africa that it takes 6 – 8 years to learn enough L2 to be able to learn through the L2.

Only strong MLE models (for both IM and dominant group children) reach the educational goals:[7]

- Language maintenance (language shelter) programmes for minorities;
- Two-way programmes and the European Union Schools model for minorities AND majorities;
- Immersion programmes for majorities;
- Indigenous revitalising immersion programmes (for IM children who no longer speak the (grand)parents language).

All strong models (for both IM and linguistic majority children) use mainly a minority language as the main teaching language during the first many years. The longer it is used, the better the results in terms of high levels of bi- or multilingualism and school achievement.[8]

This is in no way new knowledge either. There are many indications that Indigenous peoples themselves (e.g. Handsome Lake, Seneca from the USA, in the mid-1700s, see Thomas 2001) knew the devastating results of submersion programmes. So did churches and educational authorities. There are many examples from the Nordic countries (see descriptions and references in, e.g. Skutnabb-Kangas and Phillipson 1989). The USA Board of Indian Commissioners wrote in 1880:

> …first teaching the children to read and write in their own language enables them to master English with more ease when they take up that study…a child beginning a four years' course with the study of Dakota would be further advanced in English at the end of the term than one who had not been instructed in Dakota. … it is true that by beginning in the Indian tongue and then putting the students into English studies our missionaries say that after three or four years their English is better than it would have been if they had begun entirely with English (quoted from Francis and Reyhner 2002: 45-46, 77, 98).

A government resolution was formulated in India in 1904 when Curzon was the Viceroy. It expressed serious dissatisfaction with the organisation of education in India. The extract below shows its present-day relevance, and perhaps suggests that postcolonial education and most minority education has failed to learn from earlier experience.

> It is equally important that when the teaching of English has begun, it should not be prematurely employed as the medium of instruction in other subjects. Much of the practice, too prevalent in Indian schools, of committing to memory ill-understood phrases and extracts from text-books or notes, may be traced to the scholars' having received instruction through the medium of English before their knowledge of the language was sufficient for them to understand what they were taught. As a general rule the child should not be allowed to learn English as a language [i.e. as a subject] until he has made some progress in the primary stages of instruction and has received a thorough grounding in his mother-tongue. … The line of division between the use of the vernacular and of English as a medium of instruction should, broadly speaking, be drawn at a minimum age of 13.[9] (Curzon, cited in Evans 2002: 277-278).

It is very clear that MLE is an opportunity, because good MLE, adapted to local conditions, can really lead to the educational goals listed above. This volume includes many positive, constructive descriptions and analyses of MLE, and how to get there, from many corners of the world. Many opportunities have been lost already—but some promising developments are taking place in many parts of the world, including India, Nepal, Peru, Bolivia, Bangladesh, Ethiopia, Norway, Finland, etc. Still, in today's situation there are many declarations and promises and far too little action. Part of the conclusion in Dunbar and Skutnabb-Kangas 2008, an Expert paper for the United Nations Permanent Forum on Indigenous Issues, PFII[10] is as follows:

> That States persist in such [subtractive] policies, given such knowledge, has been described as a form of linguistic and/or cultural genocide. In Dunbar and Skutnabb-Kangas 2008, we considered the possibility that such policies, implemented in the full knowledge of their devastating effects on those who suffer them, constitute international crimes, including genocide, within the meaning of the United Nations' 1948 Convention on the Prevention and Punishment of the Crime of Genocide (the 'Genocide Convention'), or a crime against humanity. The various forms of subtractive education to which indigenous children have been and continue to be subject result in very serious and often permanent harmful mental and physical consequences. It is now at odds with and in clear violation of a range of human rights standards, and in our view amount to ongoing violations of fundamental rights. It is at odds with contemporary standards of minority protection. In our view, the concept of 'crime against humanity' is less restrictive [than genocide], and can also be applied to these forms of education. In our view, the destructive consequences of subtractive education, not only for indigenous languages and cultures but also in terms of the lives of indigenous people/s, are now clear. The concept of 'crimes against humanity' provides a good basis for an evolution that will ultimately lead to the stigmatisation through law of subtractive educational practices and policies.

In the 2008 Expert paper we 'recommend that the UN Permanent Forum on Indigenous Issues considers what action it might take on this basis'. If we want to learn from research and experience, mainly MT-medium education of Indigenous and minority children should last minimally 8 years. Everything else is irrational and costly compromises. MLE should be extended to all children, including dominant group children, who could have a substantial amount of their education through the medium of an Indigenous or minority language. MLE has to be contextualised, yes, but there is nothing wrong in learning from experience elsewhere. I suspect that the 'West' has more to learn from other parts of the world than vice versa, even if there are some positive signs in the West too:[11]

> The OSCE High Commissioner on National Minorities, Knut Vollebaek, urged OSCE participating States … to ensure protection of the language rights of national minorities as a necessary precondition for peace and stability. 'Linguistic rights are the quintessence of minority rights. The prevention of inter-ethnic conflicts goes hand in hand with the establishment of an adequate system of protection for linguistic rights,' the High Commissioner said. Addressing the challenges of linguistic management in the OSCE area, High Commissioner Vollebaek said efforts to promote one language at the expense of another were particularly harmful. "Such thinking is harmful not just to minorities but also to majorities. When a majority demands mindless obedience and submission from a minority, this is usually regarded as subjugation and increases the chances of that majority not being respected," the High Commissioner said.

Now we can reformulate the issue that we are addressing: Education, especially (mother-tongue-based) MLE, can support the maintenance and intergenerational transfer of Indigenous/tribal and minority languages. Have some approaches by researchers towards the maintenance and transfer of the IM languages (and MLE) been more helpful than others? Are some approaches a threat towards such maintenance?

## Approaches

### *Linguistic and cultural diversity support continuum*

One can place various approaches such as those of parents, educators, researchers, politicians, etc. to the relative maintenance (or otherwise) of Indigenous and minority languages on a continuum where the various approaches result in more, or less, LCD. Few people would argue in *Realpolitik* terms for an approach leading to a situation where the world has one language only and all others have (been) disappeared. For some people this might be an ideal, but people who would in earnest work for killing all other languages would be considered extremists. But is it extremist to work for the maintenance of all or most of the world's languages when we know that diversity (also linguistic diversity) is positive, and homogenisation is negative? In my view, no. But some demagogues seem to think otherwise (see Figure 3.1).

| **More diversity** | | **Less diversity** |
|---|---|---|
| Maximal linguistic diversity; all today's | X X X | Minimal linguistic diversity; only one |
| languages are maintained and developed further | | language maintained & developed further |

**Figure 3.1.** *A demagogical diversity continuum constructs support for linguistic diversity as extremism*

For each point on the continuum, one can assess the relative benefits and costs of the position of supporting/not supporting diversity in terms of both quantifiable factors and qualitative, non-tangible factors[12] (cf. UNESCO's 'Intangible Heritage'). Instead of placing an approach striving towards the maintenance and further development of all today's many languages as one end of the continuum and thus seeing it as extreme (in the same way as striving towards ONE language only IS extreme), maintenance of diversity should be seen as something normal and healthy, as a guarantee for survival. We can ask what a Diversity Continuum might look like which normalises both diversity itself and work towards maintaining diversity (also through MLE). The extreme on the diversity side might be inventing as many new languages as possible, or something similar. It could be useful to place the education systems in various countries on the continuum in Figure 3.2.

| **More diversity** | | **Less diversity** |
|---|---|---|
| Create actively | Maximal linguistic diversity; all today's | Minimal linguistic diversity; only one |
| many new languages and –lects | languages are maintained and developed further | language is maintained and developed further |

**Figure 3.2.** *Continuum normalising linguistic diversity?*

Next I discuss some (obviously over-generalised) prototypes of approaches towards LCD that are closer to the less-diversity end of the continuum. I am here summing up a range of positions from current scholarly literature and presenting three approaches, characterising them with a few statements that are typical of their representatives:[13]

A. Post-(post-) modern 'non-nominalising' myth-makers: 'languages/mother tongues/ do not exist, or they are outsider creations.'

B. Neo-liberal and neo-conservative 'non-essentialising' and rational choice theory myth-makers: 'There is little relationship between language, ethnicity and culture.' 'Mother tongues are not important.' 'Minorities do not want to maintain their languages.'

C. Archivists and other do-gooders: documenting languages but not really supporting their maintenance through active political struggle.

*Approach A: Post-(post-)modern 'non-nominalising' myth-makers.* Languages/ mother tongues do not exist, they are outsider creations (e.g. by missionaries). Some researchers are today questioning the existence of the concepts of mother tongue(s) and language(s). A few examples:

> We start with the premise that languages—and the metalanguages used to describe them—are inventions...First, languages were, in the most literal sense, invented, particularly as part of the Christian/ colonial project. Second, in a parallel process, a linguistic metalanguage...was also invented. Thus, alongside the invention of languages, an ideology of languages as separate and enumerable categories was also created, an ideology founded on a nominal view of language…An extreme extension of this nominal view of language enumerability arises when languages are treated as institutions, a view reinforced by the existence of grammars and dictionaries… (Makoni and Pennycook 2005: 138; see also their 2006).

Jan Blommaert is more contemptuous in his denouncement of language names: Language names such as English, French Swahili or Chinese belong in his view to the realm of folk ideologies of language and popularised or institutionalised discourses anchored therein; only every now and then are they salient as objects of sociolinguistic inquiry. (Blommaert 2005: 390).

Mother tongues as concepts and claiming them is seen as 'outmoded' (Canagarajah 2005: 443), 'irrelevant', 'quaint' or 'antedeluvian' (May 2005: 321) and worse. By negating or ridiculing mother tongues as a concept these researchers may support the invisibilisation of IM mother tongues in precisely those areas where the transfer of IM languages to the next generations is decided, e.g. schools. At the same time, these non-nominalising myth-maker researchers often pose as (leftist and/or post-post-modern) advocates for Indigenous peoples and/or minorities. Many who represent these views are also presenting arguments from approach B below.

*Approach B: Neo-liberal and/or neo-conservative*[14] *'non-essentialising' and rational choice theory myth-makers*

A second approach is represented by researchers claiming that languages have little to do with ethnicity and identity, and therefore there is no need to maintain all the languages. The cultures and identities can be maintained without languages if this is deemed useful. There ARE examples of this—e.g. Konds in India (Mohanty 1995), Irish in Ireland and the USA, Jewishness—but it is rare.

The fact that many people have more than one mother tongue is also seen as proof for the thesis of no link between language and identity. Hybrid people can have no roots, ethnically or linguistically, it is claimed. Linguistic, cultural, or territorial place-related material or intellectual/emotional rootedness is seen as essentialism. Any talk about 'Mother Earth' (and especially by researchers) is seen as suspicious, embarrassing, spiritual neo-religious rubbish, not worth taking seriously.

**Figure 3.3** *Mother Earth*

There is no or at the most a contingent relationship between language, ethnicity, and identity—claiming otherwise is labelled 'essentialism'. According to Stephen May, there is

> ...widespread consensus in social and political theory, and increasingly in sociolinguistics and critical applied linguistics, that language is at most a contingent factor of one's identity. In other words, language does not define us, and *may not be an important feature, or indeed even a necessary one, in the construction of our identities, whether at the individual or collective levels* (May 2005: 327, referring to John Edwards, Carol Eastman, Florian Coulmas, Abdelâli Bentahila and Eirlys Davies; emphasis added).

The consequence of such a view is obvious—if language use were merely a surface feature of ethnic identity, adopting another language would only affect the language *use* aspect of our ethnic identity, not the identity itself: '... there is no need to worry about preserving ethnic identity, so long as the only change being made is in what language we use,' writes Carol Eastman (1984: 275). Thus the loss of a particular language is not the 'end of the world' for a particular ethnic identity—the latter simply adapts to the new language.

The existence of multiple linguistic identities, the fact that many are multilingual from birth, and the existence of hybridity all show according to these researchers that there is no link between language and identity.

Another type of 'proof' of the absence of a link between language and identity presented by the myth-makers builds on rational-choice theory: people weigh different alternative strategies and choose the one that maximises their benefits and profit. If the link between identity and language were strong, the benefits of maintaining a mother tongue would weigh more than the benefits of shifting to a dominant language. The 'exponentially increasing phenomenon of language shift' can only be explained by 'the absence of a link between identity and particular languages', Stephen May writes (2005: 328-329).

Many of these myth-making researchers are also claiming that mother tongues are not important for the minority communities. They are questioning the importance of languages/mother tongues for the identities of those Indigenous peoples and minorities who themselves claim that these are important. The claim is that IM parents do not want to maintain the languages. In fact, the myth-makers claim, IM parents see it as in their children's best interest to forget their languages and learn the power language at the cost of their own, for better education, good jobs and better life chances. These two goals (maintain the MT, learn the power language) are presented by the myth-makers as mutually exclusive, (i.e. high levels of bi- and multilingualism are impossible or at least impractical to achieve; parents have to choose). IF some IM parents still claim that they want to maintain their languages, the myth-makers claim that IM parents are being forced or fooled by sentimental linguists or by their own elites to believe that the languages should be maintained. IF mother tongues are seen as important by the speakers, this impression has been forced on the communities by outsider (socio)linguists (e.g. Laitin and Reich 2003, Patten and Kymlicka 2003). De Swaan claims, for instance (2004: 575) that South Africa's 'recently introduced legislation [was] inspired by the language rights movement, egged on by foreign linguistic sentimentalists.'

Through using both false either/or argumentation and misrepresentation, these researchers often question the importance (and feasibility, also economically) of the maintenance of Indigenous and minority languages.

*Some counter-arguments to myth-maker claims*

Some counter-arguments to the two related types of myth-maker arguments above are presented next. Rama Agnihotri (2009, this volume) explains brilliantly how it is not only possible but necessary to reject many linguists' concept of 'a language' as a bounded, static, normative entity (something that some of the myth-makers also do), at the same time as people can still have 'languages' and 'mother tongues' (denied by the myth-makers). David Hough first (2005) quotes a linguist's claim 'Many minority communities no longer care for their heritage languages and linguists often find it difficult to accept this fact'[15] and then states:

> [it is NOT] 'minority communities' who want to get rid of their languages. It is the linguists—at least the mainstream elitist ones—who are falsely claiming this on behalf of minority communities. At the same time these same linguists are avoiding responsibility for language shift (they claim it is the community's fault). Then they themselves get the lion's share of research funding without receiving the support of the community (because supposedly the community is not interested) to do research which is largely NOT NEEDED and won't help anybody except the individual linguists themselves in climbing their respective career ladders.

Joshua Fishman (2006: 320) sums up his view of the postmodern views represented by the myth-makers:

> More than most other authoritative specialists, the authorities of the educational system are deeply implicated in planned language shift... Education [is] a very useful and highly irreversible language shift mechanism... The usual postmodern critique ... misses the boat completely.

Languages are often core values (Smolicz 1979) for individual and collective ethnocultural identities. Identities are OF COURSE variable and changing, constructed and re-constructed; endangered parts of identities are often focused, treated as central. Elite dominant-language speakers whose own languages may never have been threatened, may have great difficulty in grasping this. Those rejecting linguistic rootedness as a Grand Narrative of Herderian Romanticising Essentialism, may, instead of rejecting all grand narratives, as they claim, be in the process of constructing a new Grand Narrative of Rootless Hybridity. This is presented as a necessary and positive ideal, not only for these elites themselves, many of whom in fact seem to be fighting their own alienation, but also for Indigenous peoples, minorities, and other local people.

Massive evidence shows that many, maybe most, Indigenous peoples and minorities do NOT agree with the myth-makers—they do want to maintain their languages. This often comes as a surprise to administrators and researchers who have said the opposite (see, e.g. the Nepali and Indian projects reported in this volume by Hough, Magar Thapa, Nurmela, and Yonjan-Tamang for Nepal, and Mohanty, Mishra, Panda, Reddy, and Gumidyala for India: see also Mohanty and Panda 2007, Awasthi 2004). For those IMs who *seem* to agree, it is mostly a question of enforced or manufactured consent (see also Skutnabb-Kangas, Phillipson, Panda and Mohanty 2009, this volume). Learning the dominant language has been presented to them as necessarily happening at the cost of their own language, subtractively. Long-term consequences of this (unnecessary) 'choice' have not been clear or known for them. And they have had no choice: additive learning situations (such as MLE) do still not exist for most IMs.

Most Indigenous peoples, who have pronounced on their languages, share the attitudes from Canada, described by Mary Joy Elijah (2002) in her literature review. They see their language as a 'cultural core value' (Smolicz 1979). One example that Mary Joy Elijah quotes is from Resolution No. 9/90, Protection of First Nations' Languages, Special Chiefs Assembly, Ottawa, Ontario – December 11, 1990, Georges Erasmus National Chief.

SUBJECT: Protection of First Nations' Languages

- WHEREAS language is a direct gift from the Creator; and
- WHEREAS First Nations languages are the cornerstone of who we are as a people; and
- WHEREAS our culture cannot survive without our languages; and
- WHEREAS the right to use and educate our children in our aboriginal languages is an inherent aboriginal and treaty right.

> THEREFORE BE IT RESOLVED THAT, as aboriginal people of this country, First Nations languages must be protected and promoted as a fundamental element of aboriginal heritage and must be fully entrenched in the Constitution of Canada; and
>
> FURTHER BE IT RESOLVED THAT the federal government has a moral and legal obligation, through (pre-Confederation) treaties and through legislation, to provide adequate resources that will enable First Nations languages to exercise this right.

Words of the Maliseet Honour Code, written by Imelda Perley, Maliseet from Manitoba, express similar sentiments (quoted in Kirkness 2002: 23):

> Grandmothers and Grandfathers
> Thank you for our language
> that you have saved for us.
> It is now our turn to save it
> for the ones who are not yet born.
> May that be the truth.

Manu Metekingi, from Whanganui iwi, Aotearoa/New Zealand,[16] states beautifully the connection between language, culture and Mother Earth:

> As long as we have the language,
> we have the culture.
> As long as we have the culture,
> we can hold on to the land.

Jeannette Armstrong from British Colombia, Canada, analyses the same connection further:

> The Okanagan word for "our place on the land" and "our language" is the same. We think of our language as the language of the land. This means that the land has taught us our language.[17] The way we survived is to speak the language that the land offered us as its teachings. To know all the plants, animals, seasons, and geography is to construct language for them.
>
> We also refer to the land and our bodies with the same root syllable. This means that the flesh that is our body is pieces of the land that came to us through the things that this land is.[18] The soil, the water, the air, and all the other life forms contributed parts to be our flesh. We are our land/place. Not to know and to celebrate this is to be without language and without land. It is to be dis-placed ... I know what it feels like to be an endangered species on my land, to see the land dying with us. It is my body that is being torn, deforested, and poisoned by 'development'. Every fish, plant, insect, bird, and animal that disappears is part of me dying. I know all their names, and I touch them with my spirit (Armstrong 1996: 465-466, 470).

Mahendra Kumar Mishra[19] writes about the indivisible unity of language, culture, ethnicity, land, and philosophy:

> … Indian constitution promotes education of tribals in MT [the Mother Tongue] and no tribal people know this. Now the awareness is gradually rising among the tribals.

> They fight for the land and now for language, since land and language and ethnicity has one name. 'Saora' is an ethnic group; they are found in Saoraland and they speak Saora language. Land-and-language is signifier of [Saora] tribal identity. I attach a paper on tribal worldview in which language plays a major role in signifying the land, the ethnicity and the philosophy of life as they see it.

The Saura example cannot be generalised to all tribals in India; land issues have often been a road to more awareness of the nexus land – culture – language—ethnicity (see Panda 2009, Skutnabb-Kangas et al 2009, both this volume). Identity negotiation is always a complex process (Saikia and Mohanty 2004).

These are just examples, a 'butterfly collection' as Peter Mühlhäusler calls this kind of soft data. But I think they, coming from all over the world,[20] are still representative. In terms of how people experience those features of their life that may be important aspects of their identities, obviously the very fact that some of them (like languages) have been learned in early childhood, gives them a special character that is not the same for features acquired later. Accepting this is NOT essentialising; it is just accepting that small children experience the world in a different way from cognitively more mature adults. Linguists who claim otherwise know too little about (child) psychology and psychiatry. We should listen to those who are aware of these connections, like Gloria Anzaldúa, in 'How to Tame a Wild Tongue':

'If you want to really hurt me, talk badly about my language. Ethnic identity is twin skin to linguistic identity. I am my language.'

If we really mean it when we call for respect for people's self-identification, the claims by Indigenous peoples and others about the connection between language and identity should be respected; people's own self- identification should be more important than outside researchers' exo-categorisations of people.

Indigenous peoples' and minorities' voices have been more or less completely absent in academic discourses (or, if they have been quoted, they have often been ridiculed, not respected). They have had no right themselves to decide whether they have a named mother tongue or mother tongues and whether this is important for them, and something they want to maintain. This has been 'decided' for them by researchers, administrators, politicians. There has been and is a definite lack of respect for Indigenous and minority voices.

Who stands to benefit from this? If we want to be charitable, the elite dominant language speakers' lack of awareness is partially responsible for the belittling claims made about IM mother tongues. But the participation in the enforced language shift and linguistic genocide that many of the myth-maker elites directly or indirectly advocate cannot be explained by lack of information or awareness only. Representatives of both myth-making approaches discussed above are, I claim, involved in paternalistic power relationships. Their research often mainly benefits their own careers and neo-conservative and/or neo-liberal forces. It may be either irrelevant for or even harm and prevent the realisation of those legitimate LCD goals that Indigenous peoples and minorities have set for themselves, including maintenance of their languages supported by MLE programmes.

### *Approach C: 'Archivists' working with 'dead' and 'dying' languages*

A third approach is represented, for instance, by some (NOT all!) people from SIL, The Summer Institute of Linguistics, and related institutions with Christian missionary goals ('do-gooders', Menk 2000). These 'archivists' as I call them (Skutnabb-Kangas 2000: 237-238) are busy documenting 'dying' languages. Many are not participating in their maintenance through active political struggle, and often the analyses of why languages are dying are devoid of economic and political analyses (e.g. the first versions—not the final one—of what later became UNESCO 2003 a and b; see also Aikio-Puoskari and Skutnabb-Kangas 2007 for a critique).

Building on Christina Bratt Paulston (1994) and others, one could use the following definitions. When a language is *dead*,[21] what is needed is *revival*. When it is *dying*, what is needed is *reversal*, and when it is *neglected*, *revitalisation* is needed. Using these definitions, a Google search 2 January 2007 gave the following figures. There were 249,000 hits on 'language revitalisation' (needed when a language is 'neglected'), 1,110,000 hits on 'language reversal' (a language is 'dying'), and 1,320,000 hits on 'language revival' (a language is 'dead').

There were thus a total of 2.679,000 hits. Most of the entries (49,3%) were about 'dead' (=extinct) languages. The next largest number (41,4%) was on 'dying' ('moribund' = very seriously endangered) languages. The smallest number (9,3%) was about 'neglected' languages, i.e. those that are still used but are endangered, languages that could be maintained if supported, through funds, MLE, research, etc.

This little exercise about definitions and the frequency of the use of the concepts leads to some questions. Is most of the work (research and practical) done on 'dead' and/or 'dying' languages? Is this also true for international organisations such as UNESCO, or UNICEF, etc.? Do funds follow the same principles? More funds for work with 'dead' and/or 'dying' languages? Less for those still in daily use, i.e. languages that would benefit most from funds? Are researchers more interested in describing and 'archiving' languages just before they 'die' or when they are already 'dead', rather than working, also politically, for conditions that enable languages to be maintained and developed by the speakers/signers themselves (sometimes with support from outsiders too)? And, importantly, do the two exclude each other? Even if some Archivists claim that they are doing both, the results often show that they are not. What about Linguistic Human Rights (LHRs) and funds, especially in education, and using MLE, for the 'living' and 'healthy' but numerically small (and thus endangered) languages and especially Indigenous languages and their speakers? Are their LHRs and funds sufficient today? NO.

The quote below describes one action vis-à-vis anthropologists (called 'ideological vultures' by Deloria, 1988). Could that label apply to others too? Should (some of us) (socio) linguists also be 'escorted out'? And the missionaries?

> A couple of years ago Roger Jourdain, chairman of the Red Lake Chippewa tribe of Minnesota, casually had the anthropologists escorted from his reservation. This was the tip of the iceberg breaking through into visibility. If only more Indians had the insight of Jourdain. Why should we continue to be the private zoos for anthropologists? Why should tribes have to compete with scholars for funds when the scholarly productions are so useless and irrelevant to real life? (Deloria, 1988: 95).

Summing up, in addition to the three approaches described here there have been many more approaches which often lead to education that objectively results in less linguistic and cultural diversity. The resulting educational approaches have some educational consequences in common. Either they result in teaching IM children subtractively, through the medium of a dominant language, not their own languages (the first two approaches). Or even if some archivists, such as many missionaries, are involved in supporting educational activities in addition to describing languages, these are either early-exit transitional or, at best, late-exit transitional programmes. In addition to some early primary school materials, most reading matter produced by most missionaries is religious. Still, it must be emphasized that much of the archiving is a useful and necessary activity, often a precondition for more advanced educational work, but only under certain conditions. It should be combined with more pro-active political educational work. It should be done within a framework of structural economic, political and social analysis of the situation of the speakers. And there should be analysis and awareness of the relative roles of literacy and oracy, respectively, for the group and for education (see, e.g. Mühlhäusler 1996 on the last point).

Subtractive education through the medium of a dominant language causes/contributes to language shift. It has negative effects on

- the Indigenous and minority (IM) *languages* themselves
- IM parents' and children's *attitudes*
- the *use* of IM languages.

We are here describing a global phenomenon. Subtractive assimilation is still mostly required from Indigenous peoples for enjoyment of full human rights. In India the term 'backward tribes' is still in official use—they are 'backward' until they are subtractively assimilated. Assimilation through linguistic genocide is in many cases still required from Indigenous peoples and minorities in order for them to achieve human rights and structural/economic and political incorporation (see Schermerhorn 1970 and Cummins 2009, Skutnabb-Kangas et al 2009, both this volume).[22]

## Opportunities

*Governments need to acknowledge that they are committing crimes against humanity with subtractive education*

What can be done now? What might be possible positive approaches? What are the opportunities? I will touch upon two issues only in the rest of the paper. It seems to me that these are important when looking for opportunities for change:

1. Governments need to know that what they are doing now in the education of most Indigenous and minority children is a crime against humanity. This might make them more willing to opt for MLE. Of course there are dozens of other reasons for them to do so, economic, political, etc, and some of them are 'carrots', i.e. benefits for the government and the entire society.
2. We ourselves need to know what our own roles are as researchers/educators, and decide what to do about it. Are we supporting Linguistic Human Rights in education and MLE—or are we participating in crimes against humanity (see Magga et al 2005, Dunbar and Skutnabb-Kangas, 2008).

I start with the governments and educational authorities. Since the most important PEDAGOGICAL reason for both languages disappearing and for 'illiteracy' is the wrong medium of teaching for IMs (meaning mainly a dominant language, in a subtractive assimilationist programme, instead of mainly their own languages), we have to ask: Can LHRs and MLE change this? Is resistance against linguistic genocide and crimes against humanity in education possible through LHRs and MLE?

LHRs in education (which among other things lead to MLE for IM children) are ONE necessary (but not sufficient) prerequisite in the struggle to prevent linguistic genocide. In fact, LHRs are a necessary prerequisite for both demanding and enjoying most of the other human rights (see Skutnabb-Kangas and Phillipson 1994). But there are today very few educational LHRs in international legally binding instruments (see Skutnabb-Kangas 2000, 2008a, 2008b). What we have now of LHRs in education can be characterised as too little, and too late. We can and should spread knowledge about those constitutions, regional and international binding and non-binding instruments that do exist and that do have some LHRs.

We can, and should, through analysis, litigation, argumentation, and, probably most importantly, through political work, try to entice and/or force states and educational authorities to gain more knowledge about the role of LHRs in IM education, *and to act accordingly*. Understanding and analysing the connections discussed above between language, culture, ethnicity, identity, land and water, philosophy of life, presupposes language—one's own language, as well as other languages. Without analysis and understanding, planning strategies and action may be futile or take a direction leading to assimilation.

The vogue denying the connections and belittling the role of HRs and especially LHRs is destructive, and it seems to be spreading from academic discourse also to be used as an argument by some politicians.[23] When states refuse to grant Indigenous peoples and (both 'national' and immigrated) minorities an unconditional right to the most decisive LHR in education, the right to be educated in one's own language in a non-fee[24] state school, they need to know that they are seriously harming both the children concerned and themselves—and our planet. The states have opportunities —will they use them?

*Opportunities for MLE researchers? Our roles?*

The basic approaches already chosen and to be chosen depend crucially on power relations between actors in the field. To see the opportunities, we have to analyse these power relations, and our own role in possibly supporting unequal power relations, and through them, choice of destructive or, at best, compromised educational models, intentionally or unintentionally. Tom Bartlett (2005) has categorised various approaches by researchers, administrators, politicians etc to Indigenous peoples in terms of goals to be reached. One can use his basic categories to analyse the approaches that lead to more or less linguistic diversity, in this case through support to either strong MLE models, or subtractive mainly dominant-language medium educational models (Table 3.1, based on Bartlett 2005).

**Table 3.1** Different approaches by researchers to Indigenous peoples and minorities (who, e.g. want to maintain their languages and cultures)

| Approach | Has the IP or MIN **chosen** the goals? | Is the IP or MIN itself **realising** the goal? |
|---|---|---|
| Paternalism | NO | NO |
| Advocacy | YES | NO |
| Co-optation | NO | YES |
| Transformative empowerment | YES | YES |

Goal = e.g. maintenance of the mother tongue and bilingualism, or language shift.

The first (A) and second (B) type of myth-makers discussed earlier in this article seem to be close to the paternalistic approach, even if the second type sometimes present themselves as advocates (and so do representatives of our approach C). Those IMs who work towards their own assimilation but without having had any real choice, and without enough information of either the possibility of choice or of the long-term consequences of their 'choice', may represent the co-opted approach.

If we want to develop MLE so that we are not giving inappropriate advice that continues to guarantee IM students' failure at group level, loss of global diversity, and continuation of crimes against humanity, some of the questions that we have to seriously answer (and act accordingly) could be as follows:

1. Do Indigenous peoples (IPs) and minorities (MINs) have the right themselves to decide whether they have a named mother tongue or mother tongues, or

is this decided by researchers—here mainly linguists or sociolinguists—(or government representatives, e.g. school or census authorities, who may build on what researchers have written or advised/ advocated)? Are IP and MIN voices heard and respected, or are they silenced, marginalised, ridiculed, stigmatised, etc.

2. Do IPs and MINs have the right themselves to decide whether their mother tongues are an important part of their identities, or is this decided by researchers (linguists or sociolinguists)? Are IP and MIN voices heard and respected, by researchers and government representatives, or are they silenced, marginalised, ridiculed, stigmatised, etc.?
3. Do IPs and MINs get adequate, research-based information about the long-term consequences of their choices, including information about the fact that this is not an either/or question, and that it is perfectly possible to maintain and develop one's own language(s) and learn dominant languages well, i.e. to become high-level multilingual? Do researchers contribute to the creation and distribution of this information, or are they contributing to harmful myth-making?
4. Who stand to benefit from the academic discourses, from the work that researchers/educators are doing and from the processes we are involved in? Who are the losers?

A couple of examples. The *United Nations Declaration on the Rights of Indigenous Peoples*, after 25 years of work, was adopted on 13 September 2007 in the General Assembly, with 144 states voting for it, with 11 abstaining, 33 absent, and 4 against (www.docip.org is an excellent information source). How many sociolinguistic and educational researchers from the only four countries voting against it, namely Australia, Canada, New Zealand and the USA, were lobbying their governments to try to change their minds? Or to try to prevent them making the last minute changes in the Declaration which drastically watered down Indigenous peoples' right to self-determination? Not many. How many have signed protests when Turkey forbids the use of Kurdish in official contexts (see Skutnabb-Kangas and Fernandes 2008)—when, for instance, Kurdish children from a choir, singing an old Kurdish song at the World Music Festival festival (in San Francisco, USA, in October 2007) were taken to court and faced five years of imprisonment for 'terrorist propaganda'?[25] I have not seen any researcher names from our area on the many protests.

### *Finale: intellectuals…*

My role here is NOT to be 'nice'. To explain why, I quote Edward Said on the role of intellectuals:

> The intellectual is...someone whose place it is publicly to raise embarrassing questions... to be someone who cannot be easily co-opted by governments or corporations...Least of all should an intellectual be there to make his/her audience feel good: the whole point is to be embarrassing, contrary, even unpleasant' (Said 1994: 9-10).

I am sometimes accused, often by those who do not want to analyse their own place on the diversity continuum, of politicizing educational language issues. Otto Rene Castillo, the Guatemalan poet and revolutionary, gives an answer that resonates with me—I have quoted the first sentence of it for several decades. Here you get the whole poem.[26]

### Apolitical intellectuals

One day
the apolitical
intellectuals
of my country
will be
interrogated
by the simplest
of our people.
They will be asked
what they did
when their nation
died out
slowly,
like a sweet fire
small and alone.

No one will ask them
about their dress
their long siestas
after lunch,
no one will want to know
about their sterile combats
with the idea
of the nothing
no one will care about
their higher financial learning.
They won't be questioned
on Greek mythology,
or regarding their self-disgust
when someone within them
begins to die
the coward's death.
about their absurd
justifications,
born in the shadow
of the total life.
On that day
the simple men will come.
Those who had no place
in the books and poems
of the apolitical intellectuals,
but daily delivered
their bread and milk,
their tortillas and eggs,
those who drove their cars,
who cared for their dogs and gardens
and worked for them.

And they'll ask
"What did you do when the poor
suffered, when tenderness
and life
burned out of them?"
Apolitical intellectuals
of my sweet country,
you will not be able to answer.
A vulture of silence
will eat your gut.
Your own misery
will pick at your soul.
And you will be mute in your shame.

## Notes

1 From a 'must watch/listen' video/audio at www.informationclearinghouse.info/article11635.htm, accessed on 15 January 2008.

2 For Hamelink, McDonaldisation involves 'aggressive round-the-clock marketing, the controlled information flows that do not confront people with the long-term effects of an ecologically detrimental lifestyle, the competitive advantage against local cultural providers, the obstruction of local initiative, all converge into a reduction of local cultural space' (1994: 112). In Ritzer's definition, the 'basic dimensions of McDonaldisation' are 'efficiency, calculabity (or quantification), predictability, increased control through substitution of nonhuman for human technology, and the seemingly inevitable by-product of rational systems [rational in the Weberian sense]—the irrationality of rationality' (1996: 33).

3 For various ways of seeing the concept of 'language', see, e.g. Skutnabb-Kangas 2000, 6-16, Skutnabb-Kangas and McCarty 2008, García, 2009b, Makoni and Pennycook 2006, Blommaert 2008, Mufwene 2008.

4 I was Terralingua's Vice-President from its start (1996) until 2004; thus 'we'.

5 This is a study commissioned by the Māori Section of the Aotearoa/New Zealand Ministry of Education, http://www.minedu.govt.nz/.

6 See Dunbar and Skutnabb-Kangas 2008 for a legal and sociological discussion of the 'intention' required in Article 2.

7 See Baker 2006, Baker and Prys Jones 1998, Skutnabb-Kangas 2000, Skutnabb-Kangas and McCarty 2008, for definitions of these; see also Benson 2009, this volume, for the need to contextualise and go beyond the models.

8 See, e.g. Ramirez, Yuen and Ramey, Thomas 1991, and Thomas and Collier 2002, the largest-ever study of various educational alternatives, with over 210,000 children—in this case Spanish-speaking children in the USA; for summaries of the research, see, e.g. Collier 1989, and Cummins 2009, this volume, and references in it.

9 Compare this with Cummins and Skutnabb-Kangas and Toukomaa in the 1970s, with Ramirez et al., Thomas and Collier, Cazden and Snow, etc in the 1990s, and with the present USA laws in several states forbidding bilingual education.

10 For PFII, see www.un.org/esa/socdev/unpfii/.

11 From Eurolang News, 25 June 2008, written by Davyth Hicks, http://www.eurolang.net/index.php?option=com_content&task=view&id=3076&Itemid=1&lang=en, accessed 3 July 2008.

12 I have listed and discuss the costs and benefits both in my 2000 book, Chapter 4 ('Linguistic Diversity – Curse or Blessing? To Be Maintained or Not? Why?') and several later articles. François Grin has, among others, presented both theoretical and empirical economic arguments showing clearly that the benefits are greater than the costs (e.g. 2008). See his home page, http://www.geneve.ch/sred/collaborateurs/pagesperso/d-h/grinfrancois/francoisgrin_eng.html.

13 I try to some extent avoid listing people here, because this is more about approaches than approachers. Some of the named ones are by no means the 'worst' representatives

of the approaches. For instance, Stephen May has written thousands of pages supporting (under certain conditions) rather than questioning diversity.

14 The argumentation of such researchers fits into a neoliberal paradigm (see Petrovic 2005 for definitions) even if many of the researchers concerned might detest this label.

15 David Hough had been asked by Tjeerd de Graaf to read and comment on an article (Language Endangerment, Documentation, Preservation and Maintenance) that de Graaf and Matthias Brenzinger wrote for a UNESCO encyclopedia of life support systems. The quotes come from these comments.

16 Manu Metekingi, a Māori man from the Whanganui iwi (tribe), said this in a film shown at the Whanganui Iwi Exhibition, at Te Papa Tongarewa Museum of New Zealand, Wellington, 29 November 2003 - May 2006. The Exhibition told about 'our heartland, the Whanganui River, and our place within it'. The Whanganui iwi write: 'The well-being of our river is intertwined with its people's well-being' (from the brochure describing the exhibition, with the theme: 'Ko au te awa, ko te awa ko au. I am the river, the river is me.' Thanks to the staff at Te Papa for identifying the person for me—neither the quote nor his name is in the brochure, only in the film.

17 The relationship between language and land is seen as sacred. Most non-indigenous people need a lot of guidance to even start understanding the primacy of land in it. One example from Australia. None of the Aboriginal people participating in the reclaiming of the Awabakal language were descendants of the Awabakal (the last speakers died before 1900) but came from other areas and peoples. Still, they speak about 'our language' and 'our identity' in connection with Awabakal. In Rob Amery's words (1998: 94—this is from the manuscript that became Amery 2000) 'the revival of Awabakal seems to be based primarily on the association of the language with the land, the language of the place in which a group of Aboriginal people of diverse origins now live.'

18 This can also be understood completely literally: all our food that builds our body comes from the earth.

19 From an email chat 4 January 2007 with Dr Mahendra Kumar Mishra, co-ordinator of a large MLE project in Orissa, India.

20 There are literally hundreds more in my 2000 book.

21 I resent this terminology, and have criticised it, e.g. in Skutnabb-Kangas 2000, subsections 1.2 and 1.3, but I use it here because of borrowing other researchers' definitions.

22 For details, see my almost 300-page Bibliography on multilingualism, bilingual and indigenous/minority education, linguistic human rights, language and power, the spread of English, etc. on my homepage www.Tove_Skutnabb_Kangas.org.

23 There are, for instance, examples of this in Norway—psychologist Sunil Loona and professor Michael Seltzer, personal information.

24 Even primary education is fee-based in more than 100 countries—see http://www.katarinatomasevski.com/. See also Katarina Tomasevski's http://www.brettonwoodsproject.org/art.shtml?x=542516 on why the World Bank should be debarred from education, and, for some of Katarina's, other brilliant books, http://www.tomasevski.net/books.htm.

25 The Diyarbakir Children's Choir attended the World Music Festival in San Francisco 3-7 October 2007, and sang a march in Kurdish: 'Ey Raqip'. The Diyarbakir Public

Prosecutor's office opened a case against three members of the choir, aged 16, 16 and 17, arguing that the song has been adopted as an official march by the PKK. The indictment, dated 3 April 2008, seeked the imprisonment of three children under the age of 18 for up to five years each. The younger children faced a trial in children's court. The children's lawyer, Baran Pamuk, noted that the song was written by the Iranian-Kurdish poet, Dildar, 68 years ago. Pamuk says: 'That song was accepted as the national anthem of the Mahabad Kurdish Republic, which was proclaimed in 1946 and lasted for one year, and it is now used as an official anthem by the Northern Iraq Kurdish Federal Government. However, it is not possible to accept that a poem written 68 years ago is the propaganda tool of an organisation. The founders of the organisation in question were not even born yet at the time the poem was written. There is no mention of that organisation in the song.' The children were acquitted in June 2008, after massive protests from all over the world. (Source http://www.antenna-tr.org).

26 The poem can be downloaded from http://www.geocities.com/marxist_lb/otto_rene_castillo.htm.

# 4

# Designing Effective Schooling in Multilingual Contexts: Going beyond Bilingual Models

*Carol Benson*

## Some limitations of bilingual models

In the field of bilingual education, a well recognised set of models—including submersion, immersion, transitional (early- and late-exit), two-way or dual medium, and developmental maintenance—have allowed both researchers and practitioners to classify and discuss educational programmes according to the degree to which they develop each language, and to what end. These models, an outgrowth of an earlier highly detailed classification of 90 different bilingual schooling patterns by Mackey (1970), were solidified in the literature by Skutnabb-Kangas (1984), who made critical points not only about the pedagogical processes involved but also about the ideological assumptions underlying them. From that point on, we could distinguish between transitional use of the mother tongue (to assimilate or transition to a dominant language) and true development and maintenance of both/all languages (to foster bi- or multilingualism). Another important distinction was made by Baker (e.g. 2006) between weak programmes, which take a subtractive view of bilingualism and are based on the erroneous idea that the L1 should be removed from the equation so that the L2 can be learned, and strong programmes, which take an additive view more consistent with educational research findings, i.e. that the most effective language learning builds on L1 development.

This set of models has clearly been valuable as a practical and strategic tool, particularly in drawing attention to the hidden curriculum or underlying values inherent in choosing which languages are to be used in school and how. Classification of bilingual programmes has also allowed us to describe expected outcomes, combining research-based language learning principles with socio-psychological factors. We can demonstrate, for example, that monolingual dominant language policies and practices do not necessarily result in effective dominant language learning, nor do all so-called bilingual policies and practices promote bilingualism among learners.

Yet despite the usefulness of the models, problems have arisen in their application in policy and practice internationally. The first problem is some are not models at all, and some are not bilingual at all; for example, submersion is the *lack* of an approach that recognises learners' own languages in the classroom, and immersion is often *monolingual* in a language that learners do not speak at home. Another problem is that any one model encompasses a wide range of approaches, practices and ideologies, making it difficult to generalise about how languages are being used or about the outcomes; for example, when determining the parameters for their large-scale longitudinal studies, Thomas and Collier (2002) were forced to define a range of approaches that could be included under each 'model', having realised that they could not rely on what schools happened to call their own programmes. Related to this is the problem that models developed to accomplish certain aims in one sociolinguistic context cannot necessarily be expected to accomplish the same aims in a different context. Finally, models address inputs and outputs but rarely the processes involved, and because they are oversimplifications they 'do not explain the successes or failures or the relative effectiveness of different types of bilingual education' (Baker 2006: 215).

An examination of educational language policy across countries and contexts reveals that such problems have led to misapplication of models, misinterpretation of their potential to achieve desired goals, and even misnaming of programmes for political ends. From a practical standpoint, there are still some nagging questions about the hidden messages inherent in the models adopted, as well as about how to operationalise models on a daily basis in the classroom.

I believe that these problems have arisen internationally because there has been too much of a focus on models and not enough attention paid to the language and learning principles underlying them. The purpose of this paper is therefore to explore the limitations of classifying bi- or multilingual programmes according to bilingual models, using examples from multilingual Southern contexts. (I have adopted the geographically imprecise terms of North and South for ease in distinguishing between high-income and low-income countries in this analysis.) I will review the research-based thinking about languages and learning and discuss some of the challenges of applying them in real-life situations. Finally, I will propose a more comprehensive approach to designing effective educational programmes.

## Northern models and Southern realities

While most of the models represent policy and practice in minority contexts in North America and Europe, during the past twenty to thirty years, some of them—overwhelmingly the weakest ones—have been discussed and applied extensively in the context of low-income Southern countries (see e.g. Dutcher 1994, 2004, Heugh 2006, Hornberger 1991, Skutnabb-Kangas 2000). This section describes the basic models that are most often discussed, including the form they may take in multilingual contexts.

Figure 4.1 lists the most common models that will be discussed according to whether they are weak/strong and subtractive/additive, including their basic features such as which language(s) are used and the results that can be expected. Please note that while these models are intended for 'bilinguals', young learners have not necessarily been exposed to the dominant language prior to schooling, though they may be bi- or multilingual in local languages.

**Table 4.1.** Common bilingual models

| Type of programme | Type of learner | Medium of instruction | Educational aim (societal aim) | Most likely outcome (societal outcome) |
|---|---|---|---|---|
| MONOLINGUAL (subtractive) | | | | |
| Submersion | Non-dominant lang./culture | Dominant lang. | High L2 competence (Assimilation to dominant lang./culture) | Limited bilingualism, limited literacy (Marginalisation |
| WEAK (subtractive) | | | | |
| Transitional | Non-dominant lang./culture | From non-dominant to dominant lang. | High L2 competence (Assimilation to dominant lang./culture) | Limited bilingualism, L1 literacy sustained or not sustained (Possible integration |
| STRONG (additive) | | | | |
| Maintenance | Non-dominant lang./culture | Bilingual, initial focus on L1 | Bilingualism/ biliteracy (Pluralism, enrichment) | Bilingualism/ biliteracy (Pluralism if change in dominant attitudes) |
| Immersion | Dominant lang. and culture | Monolingual; or bilingual with initial focus on L2 | High L1 & L2 competence (Pluralism, enrichment) | Bilingualism/ biliteracy or limited bilingualism (Pluralism if change in dominant attitudes) |
| Two-way/ dual medium | Mixed dominant and non-dominant | Bilingual | High L1 & L2 competence Pluralism, enrichment | Bilingualism/ biliteracy (Pluralism/enrichment for both groups) |

### *Submersion*

As mentioned above, submersion is not a model of bilingual instruction at all, but exists because of either unintentional (*laissez-faire*) or intentional (*assimilationist*) policies, where speakers of non-dominant languages have no choice but to attend schools in languages they do not understand. If the policy is intentional, its only justification is the myth of 'maximum exposure', i.e. as much exposure as possible to the dominant language at the expense of the mother tongue. This myth has been thoroughly debunked (Cummins 1999, 2000) but still persists in many parts of the world. Submersion, also known as 'sink or swim' (Skutnabb-Kangas 1984), is a cruel form of schooling in both Northern and Southern contexts that forces children to try to make sense of a foreign medium of instruction while devaluing their languages, cultures, identities and overall self-esteem. In the North, it has been imposed on speakers of regional and minority languages as well as immigrant groups, resulting in disproportionately low educational results for learners from these groups.

Submersion in the South has been imposed on numerical majorities as well as minorities, even in places where no learners speak the school language and teachers themselves find it difficult. In African and Latin American contexts, it has its origins in colonial schooling for local elite, which was then expanded to mass education without consideration for people's learning needs. Throughout Asia, dominant languages have been given roles similar to colonial languages, which is why *castellanización* throughout Latin America—literally the 'Spanishising' of indigenous peoples (see e.g. Albó and Anaya 2003)—has a parallel in places like Vietnam, where Khmer, J'rai and other ethnic minority groups are 'Vietnamised' through exposure to Vietnamese language and culture, beginning as early as possible through pre-school education and boarding schools (Kosonen 2004, 2005).

### *Transition*

Transitional schooling is generally characterised as a weak form of bilingual education because the L1 is used only or mainly as a bridge to the L2 and is not necessarily seen as an end in itself. In reality, transitional models range from short-term oral use of the L1 at the preschool and/or early primary levels to developing L1 literacy skills over a number of years before *transitioning*, or changing the language of instruction from the L1 to the L2. The justification for this is Cummins' (1981) concept of *common underlying proficiency*, whereby the knowledge of language, literacy and concepts learned in the L1 can be accessed and used in the second language once oral L2 skills are developed, with no re-learning required; this is known as the process of *transfer* (see also Bialystock 2001).

To capture the difference between less or more L1 development before transitioning to the L2, a distinction has been made between *early-exit* and *late-exit* transitional models. Late-exit programmes, which use the L1 throughout most or all of primary school, have been found to achieve comparatively better results than early-exit ones in large-scale longitudinal research (Thomas and Collier 2002). This is because transfer from L1 to L2 is most successful when a good foundation of language and literacy is developed in the mother tongue. Even if the focus is on learning the L2 and the L1 is eventually phased out, late-exit transitional models give learners comparatively more of the L1 support needed to do well in school, as well as more affective benefits such as higher self-esteem.

Among Southern countries that have some form of bilingual schooling, the early-exit transitional model is unfortunately the most common (Heugh 2006). These programmes attempt to transition from the L1 to the L2 after only two or three years, a period which is insufficient to develop the literacy, communication and academic language skills necessary to promote effective transfer from the L1 and learning through the L2. Based on her exhaustive review of African experiences, Heugh (2006) is highly critical both of early-exit models and of any specialist who promotes them internationally, even as interim measures. I am also suspicious of early-exit models because they often represent minimal educational and/or political concessions to non-dominant groups, and because difficulty in demonstrating significant results (especially in terms of desired L2 proficiency) may convince educators and parents to push for greater exposure to the L2 instead of recognising the importance of the mother tongue (Benson 2004a).

*Maintenance*

This model, also known as developmental maintenance, encompasses a range of programmes that differ in the amount of time and effort put into each language; however, all of them share the goal of bilingualism (highly competent understanding and speaking of both/all languages) and biliteracy (highly competent reading and writing of both/all languages). Regarding development of the mother tongue, some programmes front-load it, i.e. begin with mother tongue literacy and learning and oral L2 learning to promote L1 to L2 transfer, while others back-load it to support cognitively challenging, abstract learning in the content areas at upper levels of schooling. What they have in common is that the non-dominant language is developed and remains a significant component of the curriculum, ideally for as long as learners are in school but minimally through to the end of primary schooling.

There is strong research-based support for maintenance and development programmes, including the principles discussed below which are related to home language development (minimum 12 years required), second language learning (minimum 5 to 7 years required), building mother tongue competence as a solid foundation for second language learning, and continued development of the mother tongue throughout the schooling process (see e.g. Cummins 2000). It should be noted that all of these principles are commonly followed throughout the world in designing education for speakers of dominant languages. Even the South has cases, for example schooling for speakers of English and Afrikaans in South Africa (Heugh 2003).

There are not many instances of maintenance programmes in the South for speakers of non-dominant languages, however. Bolivia and South Africa both have official policies that call for maintenance and development of non-dominant languages, study of non-dominant languages by members of dominant groups, and intercultural education for all; unfortunately, there are large gaps between policy and practice. In the case of South Africa, the policy is not equitably applied to African languages. In the case of Bolivia, lack of trained teachers for upper primary and secondary has greatly limited L1 development, meaning that schooling by default takes more of an early-exit transitional approach (King and Benson 2004). Ethiopia provides a better example, with an education policy supporting mother tongue as medium of instruction for the full 8 years of primary schooling (with national language Amharic and official language English taught as subjects). Although implementation is incomplete, this model is practised for the majority of non-dominant language speakers in three decentralised regions, which have performed better than other regions in all subjects on national assessments at grades 4 and 8 (Heugh, Benson, Bogale and Gebre Yohannes 2007).

### *Immersion*

Immersion is also considered a strong bilingual model in the typology, but it is not easily applicable to Southern contexts. The best known immersion programme was developed in Canada in the 1960s, where the two languages involved, English and French, are both relatively prestigious and where formally educated parents who opt to put their children into the programme can assist them to become bilingual and biliterate. Immersion programmes use second language teaching methods to teach children beginning literacy and content instruction in the L2, but the L1 is not ignored; in fact, most immersion programmes include L1 literacy instruction, and even those that do not can count on the family promoting L1 literacy and oral development at home (Genesee 1987). This model has also been applied to language revitalization programmes for regional minority groups in Europe (see Baker 2006). Learners in immersion programmes attain high-level receptive skills in the L2 within a few years, but the productive skills of reading and writing require more development (Swain and Johnson 1997).

Immersion programmes have distinctive features that make them difficult to apply in other contexts, whether North or South, because: (1) the bilingual teachers are highly competent speakers of the learners' L2, (2) they have access to research-based methods and materials, and (3) the L1 is used both for literacy and for later content instruction (Tucker 1986 in Hornberger 2003). Swain and Johnson feel there are 'unwarranted extensions of the term' immersion by programmes that lack the necessary overt support for the L1 (1997: 6). Thus attempting to apply an immersion model in a minority Northern context or any Southern context would most likely result in a weaker model more closely resembling submersion. Indeed, this has happened, e.g. with 'structured immersion' in the US, where learners have been taught through 'sheltered' L2 only (Lambert 1984).

### *Two-way (dual medium)*

The final strong form of bilingual education to be discussed here is two-way bilingual education, also known as dual medium, which like immersion is not easily applicable to most Southern contexts. Classrooms using the two-way model combine equal proportions of children who are native speakers of two different languages. Whether the languages are dominant or non-dominant, participants have made a choice to learn each other's languages. Teachers are proficient in both languages, and plan teaching so that all students develop in the L1 while learning (and learning through) the L2. In some contexts this takes the form of a 50:50 balance between the two languages in teaching and learning; in other contexts there may be greater (90:10) stress on the non-dominant language. The latter context represents a combination of maintenance for learners from the non-dominant group and immersion for learners from the dominant group (Skutnabb-Kangas 2000).

The interaction between learners from two linguistic backgrounds contributes to the high performance results documented for dual-medium programmes in US comparative studies (Lindholm-Leary 2001, Thomas and Collier 2002). Yet two-way models in the North are rare, due mainly to the challenge of finding enough learners from the dominant group who want to learn a non-dominant language. In the South, where socioeconomic gaps between groups are even more pronounced, and where only a small, elite group speaks the dominant language, a model like this is not likely to attract learners in the appropriate proportions. One possible context would be in semi-urban areas where speakers of both dominant and non-dominant languages interact in markets, social services and the informal sector, in which case both groups might feel there would be a benefit to learning each other's language. There have been attempts to teach elite children non-dominant languages, for example in Bolivia and South Africa due to the above-mentioned intercultural policies, but the predominant view still seems to be that bilingual intercultural education is for non-dominant groups to learn the dominant language and culture (Albó and Anaya 2003, Chatry-Komarek 2005).

## Challenges in applying these models

As demonstrated above, the models in Figure 4.1 have different connotations and consequences in the South than in the North due to contextual differences and more extreme socioeconomic gaps between dominant and non-dominant ethnolinguistic groups. This section, adapted from Benson (2008), describes recent trends in Southern bilingual education policies and practices to demonstrate how models are being used—and abused.

### *Submersion in a dominant language: Less common for the rural poor, more popular for the elite*

Submersion schooling has never had explicit support from international organisations, rights-based groups or educational language specialists, but until recently educational development efforts have tended to follow national language-in-education policies without interfering. Now there is growing recognition that submersion makes schools highly inefficient and exclusionary, and that if Education for All is to become a reality, it is essential to use languages that learners speak well. Evidence of this trend comes from a range of initiatives: the adoption of large-scale pro-mother tongue education policies in countries like South Africa and Ethiopia; the widening (to additional mother tongues) and occasional deepening (to more than a couple of years of mother tongue use) in countries like Malawi that already had some experience in bilingual education; the introduction of national languages in countries like Cambodia, Mozambique and Thailand based on experimentation and experience in non-formal education; and even the planned re-introduction of national languages in Ghana and Guinea-Conakry. Papua New Guinea has distinguished itself recently by managing to bring 350 to 400 languages into lower primary education (Kosonen 2005).

Meanwhile, Southern elite are investing significant personal resources in sending their own children to private schools that submerge learners in a European language, very often English. Underlying this practice is the unfounded assumption that the dominant language is best learned if it is the (sole) medium of instruction. In this context the term used is immersion, but the actual pedagogical practices are closer to those of submersion because the mother tongue gets little or no attention. The increasing demand for private schooling through 'international' languages has caused private immersion schools to sprout up in cities all over the world, creating a see-saw effect: while more and more children of non-elite parents are entering such schools, the quality of teaching and learning is becoming more and more questionable (see Rubagumya 2003 on this effect in Tanzania, and Mohanty 2006 regarding India). While elite families can afford higher quality schools and have more resources to promote their children's learning through a European language, lower-income families aspiring to the same thing are making great sacrifices to put their children in low-quality 'immersion' schooling, possibly missing opportunities for a much higher quality mother tongue-based education.

### *Aspiring to unrealistically high competence in a second/foreign language*

Even if a model that includes the mother tongue is adopted, virtually all stakeholders from policymakers to parents aspire to the ideal that learners should acquire native-like competence in the dominant language. It would seem that after generations of imposing these languages on speakers of other languages, educators would recognise two things: one, that native-like competence is unlikely, even for the cleverest of multilingual learners; and two, that only or mainly the elite benefit, due to their inherited cultural and linguistic capital and enhanced opportunities (Bourdieu 1991). Alexander (2000) has called this unrealistic aspiration 'English unassailable but unattainable' in the South African context.

Native-like competence in a European or urban standard is not only unlikely, it is virtually impossible according to current language acquisition and learning theory. For learners to gain high-level competence in a second or foreign language, they require input from highly competent speakers of that language along with regular and sustained practice through communicative interaction in different domains, usually in an environment where that language is used regularly, in addition to study of grammatical, phonetic and other linguistic features (Baker 2006, Cummins 1999, 2000). In the South this goal is completely unrealistic for all but the few who have a native speaker at home or who can be sent to places where the language is widely spoken. It is similarly unreachable in the North—for Swedes learning English in Sweden, for example. Neither the 'native-like' nor the 'standard language' aspect of the goal is reasonable to expect in a non-native environment. This does not mean that learners in multilingual contexts can not gain reasonable levels of competence in a second or foreign language, but they require an enabling learning environment that includes building a solid foundation in the mother tongue.

### *Backwash effects of testing and the requirements of further education*

When there are inconsistencies between different levels of an education system, a negative backwash effect is created, because learners are likely to reject what they are asked to do in the early years if they see that will have no benefit for what they are asked to do in the future. This analogy comes from backwash (or washback) in testing, which refers to the extent to which a test asks learners to perform what they have been taught to perform (see e.g. Hughes 2003). Heugh made this analogy in Ethiopia, where our four-member research team was commissioned to determine how the different semi-autonomous regions of the country were implementing mother tongue-based schooling (Heugh et al 2007, 2009 this volume). As mentioned above, the sound national policy calls for mother tongue medium for the full eight years of primary schooling, which could be considered a *maintenance and development* model, and learners from the three regions most consistent with the policy have achieved the best results on national examinations. Yet despite the sound policy and strong evidence of its success, other regions have not adopted the eight-year model, there is public pressure to use English as medium of instruction earlier and earlier, and private English-medium schools proliferate. Why? The answer lies in what comes after primary in the Ethiopian education system, i.e. English-medium secondary schooling, and in large-scale efforts by the Ministry of Education and English-speaking donors to promote English throughout the system. There is no such effort to support mother tongue education, nor is there any mention of an educational role for Amharic, a widely spoken national language (Heugh et al 2007). In this case, inconsistencies in the system have caused an effective mother tongue model to be challenged instead of expanded.

## Contexts and Clarifications of Language and Learning Principles

In light of the challenges of applying bilingual models in different contexts, I propose a shift in focus to a set of widely agreed principles of language learning and cognitive development and how they may be applicable. These principles, based mainly on research in high-income countries, are likely to be relevant in the South because they deal with human linguistic development, though we clearly need to consider where multilingual contexts may be different. If some of these understandings can be put across to policymakers, they are more likely to be able to design their own models based not only on what is desirable but also on what is possible in their contexts. Similarly, if these understandings can be put across to practitioners, they will be better equipped to design their own materials and methods, and to make adaptations if they see that certain strategies are not working with their particular students.

It will not always be possible to design educational programmes in multilingual contexts that are immediately in line with these principles due to constraints like teacher availability, materials development and financial resources, and some adaptations must be made for multilingual learners. However, if these principles are kept in mind, measures taken in the short term can be directed toward building up conditions that enable the planning and implementation of more theoretically sound (and thus feasible) programmes that are more likely to support effective learning.

### *The importance of mother tongue development*

Children are still developing competence in the mother tongue at adolescence, including more complex, adult-like grammatical structures and many other features of communicative competence; there are various estimates of how long this process goes on, but a modest estimate based on research reviewed by Dutcher (1994) is that it continues at least to age 12. For effective development to occur, children require input and interaction with more knowledgeable speakers of the mother tongue, as well as exposure to a range of new information and experiences like what schools can offer. Reading, writing and cognitive development contribute significantly to this process (Cummins 2000). Thus if children begin school at age 6 or 7, it will be optimal for them to gain initial literacy in the L1, study it as a language, and learn through the L1 until at least grade 5 or 6.

In multilingual contexts, especially those that rely almost exclusively on oral rather than written communication, the relationship of age to 'adult-level language' has not been researched to my knowledge. It would also be interesting to see research in the South on multilingual oral competencies among young children and how these could be better utilised and developed in school. There is evidence that in the absence of children's actual mother tongues, a 'close' second language can function well because of its linguistic or social proximity to the home language. This second language might be a *lingua franca* like a creole (see e.g. Benson 2003 on the Kiriol experiment in Guinea-Bissau; Siegel 1997 on creoles in education), a national language like Kiswahili in Tanzania or Amharic in Ethiopia, or a related non-dominant language like some state languages in Nigeria (Bamgbose 2000) and India (Mohanty 2006).

Regarding beginning literacy in a non-dominant language, there are at least two reasons to examine appropriate methodologies for Southern contexts. One reason is that teachers who learned through foreign languages have a tendency to use repetition and rote memorisation when children should be decoding on their own and reading for meaning (Benson 2004b). Another reason is that oft-used phonemic literacy teaching methods may be inappropriate for the linguistic features of the mother tongues being taught, as Trudell and Schroeder (2007) have recently suggested in the case of Bantu languages.

*The need for L2 development if it is to be used for content instruction*

A modest estimate is that children require 5 to 7 years of school-based second language learning before they can learn academic subjects exclusively through the L2 (Hakuta, Butler and Witt 2000). This is due to the decontextualised and abstract nature of academic language, which represents a serious challenge to students from grade 3 on (Cummins 2000, 2009 this volume). Basic communicative skills in the L2 are useful, but they are not enough to support high-level thinking and learning skills. Use of the L2 as a medium of instruction can contribute to second language learning if teachers use techniques to make the input comprehensible (Krashen 1985, 2002, Krashen and Brown 2005).

This principle is based on research in Northern contexts where the L2 is widely spoken by highly competent speakers inside and outside of the school. In another context, Spolsky and Shohamy (1999) reported that 7 to 9 years were needed for immigrants in Israel. It can not be expected in Southern contexts that the L2 will be an effective medium of instruction, at least not exclusively, within a 5- to 7-year time period. The critical point around grade 3 between learning to read and reading to learn is especially problematic in low-income countries (Heugh 2006, 2009 this volume), as evidenced by markedly high dropout rates, and can not be separated from language issues. In addition, it may be unrealistic to expect that L2 teaching can be communicatively based; it may be more effective to teach the L2 'for specific purposes', i.e. to prepare students to comprehend content materials, while instruction should continue through the L1 or bilingually.

*Building competence in the L1 facilitates learning of additional languages*

Though it may appear counterintuitive, the bilingual programmes that result in the best student performance in L1, L2 and subject areas by the end of primary school, are those that continue to invest in L1 thinking and learning. The quality of teaching and learning in both languages is much more important than early and/or maximum exposure to the L2 (Cummins 1999, 2000, Heugh 2006, Thomas and Collier 2002). Systems that rush learners to 'transition' to all-L2 learning are depriving them of a strong, L1-based foundation of prior learning, experiences and competencies. Students should therefore have the opportunity to learn through the mother tongue for as long as possible, and the mother tongue should remain part of the curriculum (at least as a subject of study) throughout their school careers. Even if a system requires knowledge to be demonstrated in the L2 at certain points through national examinations, both/all languages should be assessed, and bilingual content examinations will allow learners to demonstrate their full capabilities.

There is some evidence from Southern contexts that long-term mother tongue use generates the best results in L2 and the content areas. This evidence comes from the six-year Yoruba primary project in Nigeria (Akinnaso 1993), whose positive results were unfortunately never generalised in the country (Bamgbose 2000); from former Bantu Education in South Africa, which despite its apartheid roots generated better school achievement results than present-day English submersion (Heugh 2003); and from countries like Eritrea (Walter 2008) and Ethiopia (Heugh et al 2007) that are using their languages for primary schooling.

*Transfer is a process that can be facilitated*

The reason that L1 development facilitates learning of and in additional languages is that there is transfer of linguistic features, concepts and meanings. Introduction of an additional language into the curriculum does not necessitate the re-learning of concepts already learned through the L1. Hakuta (1986) among others has provided clear evidence that basic literacy and numeracy concepts need to be learned only once in life. As Tucker says, we still need to learn more about the contexts and strategies that facilitate transfer, but 'the fact that such transfer occurs should not be a topic for debate' (2003: 467). While transfer can happen from L2 to L1 (and indeed this is often a condition in training of new bilingual teachers whose prior education was exclusively in a second language), it is clearly most efficient to begin with cognitive skills and strategies in the more familiar language (Krashen 2002). Transfer between languages can be facilitated through explicit instruction of features that are not common to the two, such as phonemes, graphemes, and grammatical structures (see e.g. Baker 2006).

Transfer is a feature of human learning that has equal import in Southern contexts. An innovative evaluation method used by Hovens (2002) in Niger demonstrated the power of transfer in either direction by testing students in bilingual and French submersion classes in both languages, despite the fact that submersion students had never been taught L1 literacy. He was able to establish that the highest scores were attained by bilingual students tested in the L1, then by bilingual students tested in the L2, followed by submersion students tested in the L1, and in last place submersion students tested in the L2. Submersion students were therefore able to apply their L2 literacy to knowledge of the home language enough to facilitate understanding of the tests, while still out-performed by those who studied in their L1.

There are two other aspects of transfer in Southern contexts that are worthy of mention here. One is the potentially beneficial but yet untapped level of metalinguistic awareness that multilingual children in the South may be bringing to their schooling experience. An example of this is what Alexander (2007) calls a 'fifth dimension' of multilingualism: the capacity to interpret/translate between languages with facility. Another is the ability to transfer literacy competence between languages that use different writing systems. Kenner's recent work (2004) indicates that children may experience simultaneous biliteracy, which means that transfer is less linear than envisioned, and that Cummins' (1981) concept of interdependence holds true for bi- and multilingual literacies (see also Bialystock 2001).

To conclude this section, Tucker makes the following point regarding such principles: 'If the goal is to help the student ultimately develop the highest possible degree of content mastery and second-language proficiency, time spent instructing the child in a familiar language is a wise investment' (2003: 466). It should be noted that there are many other excellent arguments to use a familiar language, including affective benefits, rights-based and biodiversity reasoning (Skutnabb-Kangas 2000) which I have not included in this discussion, but which are equally relevant.

## Designing effective schooling based on realistic strategies

To summarise the argument, I believe that rather than discussing models we should be promoting understanding on the part of all stakeholders of the principles of language acquisition and learning. This would help people to evaluate the existing conditions, define relevant goals, and determine the most realistic means to reach these goals. The procedure might include the following steps:

- Raising awareness of principles of language acquisition and learning
- Determining a set of educational and linguistic goals
- Looking at the available human, material and financial resources realistically
- Determining what interventions are required in the short, medium and long term to reach the goals
- Designing programmes that address the goals in an ongoing way
- Implementing a cyclical process of planning, piloting, reflection, evaluation and analysis

Planning can begin once stakeholders have understood the language and learning principles discussed above. The first step would be to realistically assess the situation(s) for which an educational language programme will be designed. While this can be done at the national level in a generalised way, there may be difficulty if different regions present exceptions to the rule, and every effort should be made to survey the different regions or language groups that will be involved.

Figure 4.2 is an illustration of how critical language-related competencies on the part of learners, educators and family members can be included in planning discussions. This chart has been completed with fictional information that is likely to be true in many parts of the Oromiya Region in Ethiopia. Once actual language competence has been assessed, the current situation can be compared with educational aims.

This will reveal what kind of language teaching and/or learning is being expected of whom. Finally, reference to the principles (as well as other research-based information) can provide information about how long it might take realistically to reach those aims, and what inputs would be necessary.

**Table 4.2.** Illustration of language competence for planning

| | **Language A** L1 = Afaan Oromo | | **Language B** L2 = Amharic | | **Language C** L3 = English | |
|---|---|---|---|---|---|---|
| | **List/Spk** | **Read/Wr** | **List/Spk** | **Read/Wr** | **List/Spk** | **Read/Wr** |
| **Learners** Incoming | High | --- | Low | --- | --- | --- |
| **Families and communities** | High | --- | Low | --- | --- | --- |
| **Teachers** | High | Moderate | High to moderate | Moderate | Low | Low |
| **School directors** | High | Moderate | High | High to moderate | Moderate | Low |
| **Trainers and curriculum developers** | (*Varied*) | (*Varied*) | High | High to moderate | Moderate | Moderate |
| **Aim** | **High** | **High** | **High** | **High** | **High** | **High** |

As the chart shows, children enter school with high oral skills in Language A (their mother tongue, Afaan Oromo) and some possible oral skills in Language B (the national *lingua franca*, Amharic), but no exposure to Language C (the official language, English). Let us assume that the goal of the school system is for them to reach high levels of competence in all three languages.

In this case, learners are exposed completely or mostly to **Language A** outside the school, since members of their families and community are A speakers, so this is their strongest language and the one that should be used to build a strong literacy and learning foundation in primary that continues throughout secondary schooling. A is currently used for literacy and learning for the entire 8 years of primary schooling in the Oromiya Region. Since learners are expected to reach high levels of literacy in A, teachers and school directors may need to improve on their moderate literacy levels; fortunately, since their oral skills are high, a short course and/or practice with a local intellectual will probably suffice. Depending on their prior experience and training, they might also benefit from inservice workshops on L1 methodology. Only some trainers and curriculum developers can serve as resources for A, and they may also require methodology training.

As for **Language B**, learner exposure outside the school is limited, since it is spoken by some members of the community (usually youth or adults) in some domains. This outside exposure may increase as learners grow older, but it is likely that that their main input in B will be through the school. B is currently taught as a subject beginning at grade 3 or grade 5, and is a required subject throughout secondary schooling, but until recently the same curriculum has been used for native speakers and learners of B. Based on the fact that B is an important *lingua franca* and national language of Ethiopia, our research team recommended strengthening its study and use as an L2 (Heugh et al 2007). This would suggest giving B more of a role in the primary (and secondary) school curricula, i.e. strengthening teaching and learning of B as a second/foreign language beginning in lower primary and using some bilingual methods in upper primary so that both A and B can be used in secondary schooling. Since learners will rely almost exclusively on their teachers for their B input, teachers will need ongoing training and practice in B literacy, building on their moderate to high speaking competence. In this case A and B have different writing systems, so teachers may need reminders and/or clarification of B writing conventions. Further, teachers will require strong inservice training in second/foreign language teaching methodology as well as access to appropriate B as L2 curriculum and materials. School directors, trainers and curriculum developers can be good language resource people but may need to upgrade their L2 methodology background.

Regarding **Language C**, neither learners nor their families are exposed to input outside the school, and even teachers' and school directors' exposure and competence is highly limited. C is currently taught as a subject beginning at grade 1, and it becomes the exclusive medium of instruction of secondary schooling beginning at grade 9. All primary teachers are meant to attend an inservice programme to upgrade their language skills as well as to learn second/foreign language methodology, and radio broadcasts provide classroom support during C lessons. However, due to lack of use of this language and/or insufficient training, primary teachers' competence in C is too low for them to teach effectively at this time, nor can their school directors give them the support they require. Based on current conditions in primary schooling and the fact that secondary education in C is not comprehensible to the majority of learners in Ethiopia, our research team recommended taking C out of the primary curriculum until teachers can gain the appropriate competence, and we seriously questioned its usefulness as a medium of instruction at the secondary level (Heugh et al 2007). Since trainers themselves have only moderate competence in C, it is currently unrealistic to expect primary school learners to reach high levels of spoken and written C. There is little choice but to adjust the aims of schooling to more realistic levels, at least until appropriate training and language assessment mechanisms can be put into place. Meanwhile, strong mother tongue-based learning and more reliance on Language B as L2 should give learners in Oromiya Region the best opportunity to gain a quality education.

This example from one region in Ethiopia illustrates how educational planning in a multilingual context can benefit from a realistic approach to language and learning. More subtly, it shows how Ethiopian policy has apparently relied on a kind of trilingual model that begins with the L1 in primary school, adds the L2 and L3 as subjects and 'transitions' to the L3 at the secondary level. As a model it might seem somewhat logical and even progressive because of its use of the L1 for the full 8 years of primary schooling. However, a more careful examination of learners' existing language skills and the available human resources reveals that the aims of the system are currently unattainable. Coupled with an understanding of language and learning principles, this analysis provides insights into how to design a system that builds on existing resources in a pedagogically effective way.

## DIRECTIONS FOR THE FUTURE

This paper has discussed how a set of bilingual models from the North has impacted on policy and practice in the multilingual South. I have claimed that application of these models has limited potential for informing effective decision-making concerning mother tongue-based schooling, and I have proposed an alternative approach to bi- or multilingual programme design that focuses on language and learning principles to determine how to reach educational goals given existing resources.

The Oromiya Region illustration above highlights the importance of investing in teachers and building on their strengths, a point that has been made strongly by Chatry-Komarek (2003) and Komarek (2003) and supported by cost-benefit analysts (as reviewed in Heugh 2006). As I have noted elsewhere (Benson 2004b), teachers from the same communities as their students have a repertoire of useful skills along with their languages—metalinguistic awareness, cultural insights, local credibility, good communication with parents/caregivers—but they usually require L1 literacy and vocabulary development along with bilingual methodologies. Furthermore, their competence in additional languages needs to be developed and fairly assessed. As the Ethiopian case demonstrates, it is pointless to have a foreign language in the curriculum if neither teachers nor students have had the opportunity to develop the necessary language skills.

How can teachers develop the necessary skills? Recent work with a colleague in Angola reminded me that it is difficult to initiate mother tongue-based educational programmes if the professional work force consists of teachers, teacher trainers, curriculum developers and linguists who have little or no background in using local languages. Where university linguists in Angola have historically worked in European languages, efforts are now being made to include national languages in descriptive and applied linguistics faculties. In Southern contexts like Angola, there is an urgent need for applied researchers with a commitment to improving the quality of educational services available to members of non-dominant linguistic communities. They could benefit greatly from links with the nonformal education sector, as community-based literacy and alternative education programmes tend to have much more experience in using local languages (see Malone 2005 in Asian contexts).

Finally, as mentioned earlier, there are a number of areas where research in multilingual Southern contexts could contribute a great deal to the field of bilingual education. Some research topics mentioned were: the relationship between learners' multilingual oral competence and literacy; language-appropriate strategies for teaching L1 literacy; time and quality of L2 input needed to facilitate transfer; and effective methodology for teaching an L2 used only/mainly for future learning, not for communication. Such research would provide invaluable inputs into the proposed reality-based process of designing mother tongue-based programmes in multilingual contexts.

# Part III
# Global and Local Tensions and Promises in MLE

# 5

# The Tension between Linguistic Diversity and Dominant English

*Robert Phillipson*

The paper explores how we think of English, through looking at the causes, past and present, of its expansion, and the implications for other languages. It also reports on a number of educational developments that are of global relevance, including what looks like becoming a 'three language formula' for schoolchildren in Europe. Influential pan-European bodies, the Council of Europe and the European Union, advocate the learning of the mother tongue and two other languages, with English invariably one of them. In higher education in some parts of Europe the latest goal is to require academics to have 'parallel competence' in English and a national language. This is shorthand for all university faculty developing the same level of competence in writing (publications) and speaking (lecturing, supervising) in English as in Danish, Swedish, etc. The paper stresses the need for conceptual clarification: reference to English as a '*lingua franca*', as 'global' or 'international', is special pleading, the beguiling rhetoric that promotes the *project* of establishing English worldwide. The *product* is branded and marketed through a variety of overt and covert *processes*. The advance of English in any given context, and whether it constitutes a threat to other languages, needs to be analysed in terms of the triad of project, product and process.

Gandhi and Nehru, key architects of independent India, warned against an excessive concentration on English. Even if much has changed in patterns of communication, trade, politics, and technology in the meantime, their warnings strike me as being of global relevance now. We live in the age of universal corporate-driven Pax Americana —meaning Bellum Americanum for any state or movement that defies US demands, corporate America's war on the majority of the world's citizens. Bush's 'you are either with us or with the terrorists' is unalloyed state terrorist discourse that friends and 'enemies' are supposed to accept as gospel. By contrast the discourses marketing and entrenching English are more discreet. However, they often serve the cause of

American empire, not least when insidiously legitimating educational policies that see English as a panacea. Such discourse too often goes unchallenged, leading to the co-opting of minds. The function is 'manufacturing consent' to a world order that is inequitable, unsustainable, and in conflict with international human rights law. As educationalists, we have an obligation to promote more just alternatives.

These were the warnings over a fifty-year period of Mahatma Gandhi (cited in Naik 2004: 255) and Jawaharlal Nehru (cited in Gopal 1980: 507, 525):

> To give millions a knowledge of English is to enslave us. The foundation that Macaulay laid of education has enslaved us (Gandhi 1908).
>
> Of all the superstitions that affect India, none is so great as that a knowledge of English is necessary for imbibing ideas of liberty, and developing accuracy of thought. English is a language of international commerce, it is the language of diplomacy, and it contains many a rich literary treasure, it gives us an introduction to western culture. For a few of us therefore, a knowledge of English is necessary…today English has usurped the dearest place in our hearts and dethroned our mother-tongues. It is an unnatural place due to our unequal relations with Englishmen… To get rid of the infatuation for English is one of the essentials of Swaraj (Gandhi 1921).
>
> Some people imagine that English is likely to become the lingua franca of India. That seems to me a fantastic conception, except in respect of a handful of upper-class intelligentsia. It has no relation to the problem of mass education and culture… even the most rabid of our nationalists hardly realize how much they are cribbed and confined by the British outlook in relation to India (Nehru 1936).
>
> I am convinced that real progress in India can only be made through our own languages and not through a foreign language. I am anxious to prevent a new caste system being perpetuated in India—an English-knowing caste separated from the mass of our public. That will be most unfortunate. ... I cannot conceive of English being the principal medium of education in India in the future. That medium has to be Hindi or some other regional language. Only then can we remain in touch with our masses and help in uniform growth (Nehru 1956).

Nehru also rightly noted that while language is a unifying factor of society, it can also promote disunity (in Constituent Assembly Debates 1946-50: 1411, quoted in Agnihotri 2007a: 194). Failure to heed these warnings in independent India has led to inequitable societal policies: 'In today's India, English is the language of power, used as an indication of greater control over outcomes of social activities… Over the post-Independence years, English has become the single most important predictor of socio-economic mobility… With the globalized economy, English education widens the discrepancy between the social classes' (Mohanty 2006: 268–9).

The effects of this are ironically described by an Indian who has personally experienced the intense discrimination that results in the vast majority of Indians being 'disenfranchised not merely politically, but also economically, academically, culturally and intellectually':[2]

> It wasn't until he was 18 that Kanchhedia Chamaar realized that God spoke and understood English and nothing else. Because unfamiliarity with the *lingua divina* was a matter of intense shame at Delhi School of Economics in the 1970s, he started learning English on the sly, and continues to be consumed by the process to this day. Over a period of three years after his master's degree, no fewer than one hundred and eight Indian firms found him unfit for gainful employment. While doing his PhD in the 1980s, he found that at Universities in the US, even those not fluent in English were treated as human beings, a dignity that not everybody seemed willing to accord him in Delhi. He has been hiding in the US ever since (Chamaar 2007).

It is awareness of agonies such as Chamaar's and the co-articulation of privilege with use of English worldwide that triggers the widespread wish for English-medium education. The issue of medium of instruction in the subcontinent has been documented and vigorously debated over the past two centuries. There is a wealth of scholarly literature, primarily by local experts, on multilingualism past and present, and of the multiple roles that English now plays in India, Pakistan, and Sri Lanka. This does not need recapitulation here (on Africa, see Heugh 2009, this volume). What I shall attempt to do is to explore how linguistic diversity is being threatened by expansionist, subtractive English globally and locally, and consider ways of resisting it and ensuring a more just linguistic order.

Reference to a 'divine' language is a reminder that Christian missionaries have played a crucial role in global Europeanisation, starting with the Americas. The first charter of the East India Company, granted by the English queen, Elizabeth I, dates from 1600. When the charter was renewed in 1698 (the year in which the Society for Promoting Christian Knowledge was founded), it included a 'missionary clause' requiring 'the company to maintain ministers of religion on their business premises and take a chaplain in every ship of 500 tons or more' (Parasher 1991: 29). In 1838 the 'Board of Foreign Missions of the USA', then consisting of thirteen 'colonies', propounded 'a belief in the manifest destiny of Anglo-Saxon culture to spread around the world' (Spring 1996: 145). Such activity continues to this day, as can be seen on the website of a missionary body, the United Society for the Propagation of the Gospel,[2] which seeks to Christianise China covertly in the guise of providing English teaching:

> Amity [Foundation] has a team of people witnessing at a grassroots level that Christianity is not anti-Chinese or solely western. As missionaries are still banned from China, it represents one of the most effective ways to support Christians in China through the sending of teachers of English from overseas.

Such activity raises profound ethical and professional questions for associations of English teachers such as TESOL, the US-based Teachers of English to Speakers of Other Languages. The issue is hotly debated at annual conventions. The topic is explored in depth in an anthology that presents the case for and against evangelists who are simultaneously English teachers (Wong and Canagarajah, eds, 2009).

There are similarities between the missionary goal of spreading Christianity worldwide and the secular gospel of 'global' English. The Wycliffe Bible Translators, the partner organisation of the Summer Institute of Linguistics, which produces the Ethnologue list, declares that its goal is to make 'the Bible accessible to all people in the language they understand best. To make this vision reality, Wycliffe also focuses on literacy development, community development and church partnerships'.[3] The project of Christianisation can thus be promoted through processes that overtly appear to be a matter of general education. The missionary goal is covertly masked as culture-free education, whether a minority language or English is used. The imperial promotion of English and Christianity are symptoms of the USA global dominance project.

## Manifest destiny and US world dominance

The neoliberal project that was hatched by the likes of Cheney, Wolfowitz, and Rumsfeld in the late twentieth century (www.newamericancentury.org), was assessed in *Harper's Magazine* 305 in 2002 (by D. Armstrong, cited in Harvey 2005: 80):

> The plan is for the United States to rule the world. The overt theme is unilateralism, but it is ultimately a story of domination. It calls for the United States to maintain its military superiority and prevent new rivals from rising up to challenge it on the world stage. It calls for dominion over friends and enemies alike. It says not that the United States must be more powerful, or most powerful, but that it must be absolutely powerful.

This US mission has been in place for two centuries. President Harry Truman stated in 1947: 'The whole world should adopt the American system. The American system can survive in America only if it becomes a world system' (cited in Pieterse 2004: 131).

The dominion over friends has been worked through in the European Round Table of Industrialists, the Transatlantic Business Dialogue, and the Transatlantic Economic Partnership (Monbiot 2000) as well as in the main international fora (NATO, UN, IMF, World Bank, WTO etc). The UK has spearheaded the adoption of this model in Europe, with its key role in global finance and its energetic military engagements as visible symptoms of commitment to US strategic interests.

Language policy has been central to the process of world domination (Phillipson 1992, 2008a, 2008b). An article frankly entitled 'In praise of cultural imperialism?' in the establishment journal *Foreign policy* (Rothkopf 1997: 45) proclaims:

> It is in the economic and political interest of the United States to ensure that if the world is moving toward a common language, it be English; that if the world is moving toward common telecommunications, safety, and quality standards, they be American; and that if common values are being developed, they be values with which Americans are comfortable. These are not idle aspirations. English is linking the world… Americans should not deny the fact that of all the nations in the history of the world, theirs is the most just, the most tolerant, the most willing to constantly reassess and improve itself, and the best model for the future.

As is well known, the language is used on both sides of the Atlantic. Prime Minister Winston Churchill declared in the House of Commons on 24 August 1941: '… the British Empire and the United States who, fortunately for the progress of mankind, happen to speak the same language and very largely think the same thoughts …' (Morton 1943: 152). These thoughts were not shared by Gandhi (whom Churchill referred to as a 'half-naked *fakir*')[4], even if they were expressed in English. It is, of course, a truism that any language can be used for good or evil purposes, a reality that often muddies discussion of language issues since interlocutors may be talking at cross purposes.

## European integration and language policy

English played no role in the institutions of the European Union (EU) before Great Britain, Ireland, and Denmark joined in 1973. Since that time, English has progressively been established as the dominant language. This consolidation has taken place simultaneously with a rapid process of economic, political, military and cultural integration in Europe. The EU started life as an economic union of six member states in 1958, and gradually expanded to twenty-seven in 2007. In principle the dominant language of each member state has equal status with all other EU official and working languages, currently 23.[5] The world's largest translation and interpretation services facilitate multilingual communication in the key institutions, the European Parliament, the Commission, and the Council of Ministers (Phillipson 2003). Exploring EU language issues is complicated because there is a great deal of diversity and fluidity in language policy in Europe. This relates to

- an unresolved tension between linguistic nationalism (based on the monolingual ideologies of the 'nation' state), EU institutional multilingualism, and English becoming dominant in the EU system;
- competing agendas at the European, state (national), and regional or local levels;
- much EU rhetoric endorsing language rights and linguistic diversity, but very uneven implementation at both the supranational level (e.g. on EU websites, or the availability of EU documents in all languages for meetings) and in the 27 member states;
- increasing grassroots (immigrant and national minority) and elite bi- and multilingualism, but low levels of foreign language proficiency in many EU countries;
- a largely uncritical adoption in member states of Englishisation, English as the *lingua economica* or *lingua Americana.*

In theory each member state has exclusive responsibility for matters of culture, education, and language, but the EU has had a 'supportive' role in these fields since 1992, and in reality there are many overriding forces. Languages are no respecters of borders when integral to the unfree market forces of the international economy, media and popular culture. Over and above the 23 EU official languages, roughly 300 languages are in use in EU member states, often with few rights.[6] Many NGOs work for the rights of minority groups. The Council of Europe[7] has a Language Policy Division that works to strengthen policy formation—it can be asked to survey language policy issues in a country—and foreign language learning. It also oversees the operation of the Framework Convention on National Minorities,[8] and of the European Charter for Regional or Minority Languages.[9]

A core problem for European integration is the major uncertainty at both government and grassroots level in each EU member state about what 'Europe' is (Skutnabb-Kangas 2000: 181-194), what the EU is for (Phillipson 2003), and where the European 'project' is taking its citizens. This is clear from the referenda that went against accepting the draft EU Constitutional Treaty in France and the Netherlands in 2005, and the reluctance of the governments of many states to hold a referendum on its successor 'reform treaty', the Lisbon Treaty. Ireland was constitutionally obliged to hold a referendum: Irish voters rejected the Treaty in June 2008, triggering a major crisis for the EU, and confirming the gap between elites and citizens. This is popularly known as the EU's 'democratic deficit'. There is also uncertainty and disagreement about the criteria that should determine whether applicant states such as Turkey qualify for membership (Phillipson 2003: 29-35).

Many of the visionary politicians who devised the formation of institutions and structures that would serve to bring European wars to an end through creating a single market were impelled by a wish to create the United States of Europe (Winand 1991). The EU is not exclusively a European project, since it would never have come into existence if it had not also been US policy. There are annual EU-US summit meetings that coordinate policy. Recent meetings have endorsed a Transatlantic Economic Integration Plan, as well as the co-articulation of foreign policy globally. In effect this means that the EU accepts corporate America's global agenda, as loyal but junior partners.

English linguistic hegemony has been progressively asserted in the EU system, which can be seen in the figures for choice of language in the initial drafting of EU texts (laws, directives, policy statements) over the past forty years—see Table 5.1. These reveal a dramatic decline in the use of German and French, and a progressive and accelerating increase in the use of English as the default in-house language. This clearly strengthens the interests of the English-speaking member states, and of the countries in northern Europe where proficiency in English tends to be high.[10]

**Table 5.1.** Language choice in drafting EU texts 1970-2006.

| | French | German | Other | English |
|---|---|---|---|---|
| 1970 | 60% | 40% | 0% | 0% |
| 1996 | 38% | 5% | 12% | 46% |
| 2004 | 26% | 3% | 9% | 62% |
| 2006 | 14% | 3% | 11% | 72% |

The EU's democratic deficit goes hand in glove with a set of linguistic deficits. One can argue that there is now *European linguistic apartheid* of three types (Phillipson 2007):

- the exclusion of most minority mother tongues from schools, public services and recognition;
- the *de facto* hierarchy of languages in the EU system, in internal and external communication;
- inequality between native speakers, particularly of English, and other Europeans, in international communication and especially in EU institutions.

## English expansion and the discourse of a *lingua franca*

The consolidation of the dominant position of English in the EU and in European education systems is integral to the way English is expanding in the commercial, political and military worlds and in 'international' organisations. Proficiency in English is increasingly expected of Germans and Greeks, the Portuguese and the Polish. Is it reasonable and correct then to refer to English simply as a *lingua franca*, as is often done when using English is considered 'normal' and 'natural', especially by advocates who are oblivious of the consequences of hegemonic and linguicist practices?[11] I have explored elsewhere the origins of the term *lingua franca*, its varying senses and uses, and the implications of misusing it in an age of US-dominated empire (Phillipson 2008b), but here follow a few key points.

Reference to English as a *lingua franca* generally seems to imply that the language is a neutral instrument for 'international' communication between speakers who do not share a mother tongue. Any purported neutrality needs to be weighed against the fact that the language serves key societal purposes in many domains. English might be more accurately described as

- a *lingua economica* (in business and advertising, the language of corporate neoliberalism),
- a *lingua emotiva* (the imaginary of Hollywood, popular music, advertising, consumerism and hedonism),
- a *lingua academica* (in research publications, at international conferences, and as a medium for content learning in higher education),
- a *lingua cultura* (rooted in the literary texts of English-speaking nations that foreign language learning traditionally aims at in many countries, and integrates with language learning as one element of general education).
- the *lingua bellica* of wars between states (aggression by the US and its loyal acolytes in Afghanistan and Iraq, building on the presence of over 700 US bases worldwide).

In many postcolonial contexts, including India, English is a key language of *elite formation*. Consolidating this process suited the elites that were in power when political independence was gained (including Nehru: it is significant that in the 1956 quote above, he refers to Hindi and India's regional languages but not to the totality of India's languages), reinforced and actively promoted by massive 'aid' from Britain and the US, and later by the World Bank. The worldwide presence of English as a *lingua americana* is due to the massive economic, cultural and military impact of the USA.

Labelling English as a *lingua franca,* if this is understood as a culturally neutral medium that puts everyone on an equal footing, is therefore simply false. It is an *invidious* term if the language in question is a first language for some people but for others a foreign language. It is *misleading* if the language is supposed to be disconnected from culture and very specific purposes. It is an *inaccurate* term for a language that is taught as a subject in general education. Ironically, there is a historical continuity in the way the term originated (from Arabic and Persian) as a designation for the hybrid language of European crusaders who were out to recapture Jerusalem and eliminate Islam from Asia Minor, while now English is viscerally connected to the crusade of global corporatisation, marketed as freedom and democracy (Poole 2007). Human rights have been dropped from this rhetoric, as they are manifestly no longer on the agenda, except when criticising 'enemies'.

The role of the British, especially Tony Blair, in this global scenario, is captured by the eminent playwright David Hare:

> it is now impossible to imagine any American foreign policy, however irrational, however dangerous, however illegal, with which our present Prime Minister would not declare himself publicly delighted and thrilled… They know we have voluntarily surrendered our wish for an independent voice in foreign affairs. Worse, we have surrendered it to a country which is actively seeking to undermine international organisations and international law. Lacking the gun, we are to be only the mouth. The deal is this: America provides the firepower. We provide the bullshit (Hare 2005: 207, 208).

Such discourse is integral to empires old and new. During fruitless negotiations for Indian independence in London in 1931, Gandhiji wrote 'Perhaps, there is no nation on earth equal to the British in the capacity for self-deception'.[12] US hubris follows the same pattern.

The elimination of linguistic diversity has been an explicit goal of states attempting to impose monolingualism within their borders: linguicist policies favour the *lingua frankensteinia*[13] in the sense of a language that terrifies and exterminates others, leading to linguicide (Skutnabb-Kangas and Phillipson 1996). This was the case in the internal colonisation of the British Isles and in most Europeanised parts of the world. Skutnabb-Kangas (2000) avoids seemingly innocuous terms like 'language death' and 'language spread', concepts that obscure agency, by referring to *killer languages*, *language murder*, and *linguistic genocide*, basing the latter term on definitions in international human rights law and the historical evidence of government policies. Swales (1996), after a lifetime of work on scientific English, is so concerned about other languages of scholarship being on the way to extinction that he labels English a *lingua tyrannosaura*. The widespread concern in political and academic circles in Northern European countries with *domain loss* signifies a perception that segments of the national language are at risk from the English monster, hence the concern that Danish, Finnish, Norwegian, and Swedish should remain fully operational in all domains. Here the risk is often expressed that an English-using class (in Nehru's terms a caste) is emerging, one which is cut off from the mass of the population, as a result of the 'self-colonisation' of elites who are enamoured with English.

The EU Commission has for nearly a decade been attempting to counteract infatuation with English and an excessive concentration on learning the language at the expense of other foreign languages in European schools. Its ambitious *Framework Strategy for Multilingualism* (2005) recommends that member states undertake the following:

- the learning in education of mother tongue[14] plus two,
- the formulation of national plans to give coherence and direction to actions to promote multilingualism, significantly including the teaching of migrant languages,
- improved teacher training for foreign language learning,
- early language learning,
- Content and Language Integrated Learning (CLIL), i.e. the merging of a foreign language with another school subject,
- more study of multilingualism in higher education,
- introduction of a European Indicator of Language Competence, a Europe-wide language testing scheme,
- greater use in language learning of Information Society technologies,
- the harnessing of languages to 'the multilingual economy'.

What the local impact of any EU initiatives will be is impossible to predict, since it is entirely up to member states to follow or to ignore what 'Brussels' decides. Language policy issues do not figure prominently on the agendas of the meetings of EU Ministers of Education, but governments are expected to report back to the Commission regularly on implementation. The Council of Europe (a completely different body with far more member states) has developed a range of language policy activities and instruments. In recent years a number of significant European schemes have been devised, covering various approaches to foreign language learning, language testing, and the advocacy of national language policy formulation to cover all languages in a country, along with the creation of a 'language-friendly' public sphere.[15]

There are also many symptoms of crisis in language policy in Europe. Market forces are strengthening English in the Bologna process, a scheme to create a single Europe-wide higher education and research area. In the policy statements of the forty-six countries involved, no attempt is made to ensure that international collaboration and student mobility schemes should aim at students becoming bilingual (Phillipson 2006). On the contrary, 'internationalisation' seems to mean Europe-wide 'English-medium higher education', especially at the MA or graduate level. Similar pressures are building up behind English in the internal management of multilingualism in EU institutions. Translators and interpreters for demographically 'small' languages like Danish and Swedish, as well as the newly arrived Baltic and central European languages, are convinced that their languages are being treated as second-class. There is manifestly a conflict between the rhetoric of supporting all languages and the realities of linguistic hierarchies and marginalisation.

While the use of English in higher education in continental Europe is extensive at the postgraduate level in a few countries, it is minimal or non-existent elsewhere at present. In the natural sciences and business studies, and increasingly in other fields, many course books and much scholarly literature is in English. When students have course work in both the mother tongue (say, Dutch or Finnish) and in English, such studies fall within the definition of bilingual education as instruction being in the medium of two languages. It is also common in universities in the Scandinavian countries for course books to be in English and the local Scandinavian language as the medium of instruction. What the position will be in 10 or 20 years' time is impossible to predict, but the Swedish and Danish governments are considering legislation to ensure that the national language is not eliminated from higher education.

What Europe is currently experiencing is influenced by many factors, external/global and internal/local. The same is true of former colonies. A survey of histories of decolonisation—written from a British perspective—stresses that many narratives and interpretations have emerged, because so many variables are involved, factors in the ex-imperial power and in each periphery context, pivotal global changes, including the delicate balance in Anglo-American relations, and the way massive US economic and military activity facilitated the prolongation of British power into the postcolonial age (Darwin 1999: 552, 556):

> The history of decolonization requires the careful fusion of three 'sub-historiographies': the domestic politics of 'decline'; the tectonic shifts of relative power, wealth, and legitimacy at the international level; and the colonial (or semi-colonial) politics of locality, province and nation. As so many respectful histories of official policy reveal, archives all too easily turn their readers into captives, and the self-serving official minute is insidiously transformed into historical narrative. …the advance of decolonization as an academic subject of the widest relevance and importance—what other recent historical experience unites so much of the world's population?—depends upon maintaining the delicate balance between our knowledge of metropolitan, international and colonial processes, and on our sensitivity to the historical experience of ex-subjects as well as ex-rulers.

Postcolonial states have been significantly influenced by the role that English has played during decolonisation. English has serviced the Commonwealth that brings ex-colonial elites together, and impacts significantly on decisions about medium of instruction in education (Phillipson 1992). It is therefore plausible to claim that market forces and the many pressures, overt and covert, that are currently serving to strengthen the position of English worldwide, in postcolonial and post-communist countries and even in western Europe, may be propelling English forward as the language of empire in ways that threaten well-established European languages. Hence the urgent need for active language policy formulation and implementation in each country.

Here Europeans can learn from African experience, where developments in education in recent years have seldom served the majority of the continent's people well, in large measure because an excessive focus on European languages, English in particular, contributes to and determines educational failure (Heugh 2009, this volume). A Tanzanian scholar, Rubagumya (2004) rebuts the position of Brutt-Griffler, whose *World English: A Study of its Development* (2002, reviewed in Phillipson 2004) has been warmly embraced by those who regard the expansion of English worldwide as unproblematical. Rubagumya fundamentally disagrees with Brutt-Griffler's claim that English was 'not unilaterally *imposed on* passive subjects, but *wrested from* an unwilling imperial authority as part of the struggle by them against colonialism' (Brutt-Griffler 2002: 31, italics in the original). He insists that

- European languages were *imposed* on Africa in the colonial period. African people as communities did not *choose* to learn those languages…
- Individual Africans do not necessarily *choose* to learn these languages (French, English, Portuguese). Since the language of instruction in almost all African countries is the language of the former colonial power, going to school does not leave any choice.
- Individuals who do not go to school, and therefore do not learn European languages, do not choose not to go to school. They do not have access to schooling (Rubagumya 2004: 134).

> Rubagumya adds (136-139) that in the global village there are 'a few chiefs—very powerful economically and militarily—and a lot of powerless villagers. …The market has indeed replaced imperial armies, but one wonders whether the effect is any different. …It is therefore not the case that more English will lead to African global integration; the reverse is more likely. …Giving false hopes that everybody can have access to "World English" is unethical'.

English should be learned, but only additively.

It is important not to under-estimate the powerful forces behind English. Its power adjusts to new contexts, whether postcolonial, post-communist or western European. Its expansion is all the more insidious when 'experts' declare that the language now 'belongs' to all its users and has become detached from its Anglo-American roots and serves all equally well. This is a fraudulent claim that is as untrue in York as New York or New Delhi. I agree with Wierzbicka's analysis (2006: 14) that 'In the present-day world it is Anglo English that remains the touchstone and guarantor of English-based global communication.' And her warning of 'The tendency to mistake Anglo English for the human norm'. Probal Dasgupta (1993: 203, 215–216) makes a similar point:

> English is not a space. It is a piece of real estate. Its owners—whose biological identities keep changing, as in the case of any real estate, —enforce normative spelling, punctuation, grammar, and phonological and lexical limits (within which accents and dictions may vary) throughout the domains of English discourse. Indian use of English will forever remain a tolerated, degenerate variant of the norm in the eyes of the owners. Hence the striving by Indians to attain near-native command, to count as individuals who may be co-opted into the metropolitan Herrenvolk.
>
> ...The forces that keep this fact in place have not been and are not being contested. You and I may coin a new expression for our private games in the language: but our coinage will not be part of the language unless the Anglo-American mint canonizes our doings in standard reference works.

## Project, Process and Product

Any more detailed analysis of the current role of English in Europe and in many other contexts would benefit by seeing the language in terms of *the project*, as *process,* and as *product.* Nobody is questioning whether English ought to be optimally learned or not. There is no dispute about the fact that proficiency in English is massively useful in the modern world, and that English serves multiple purposes, some constructive, some benign, and some evil. But while English opens doors for some, it closes them for others. More in-depth research is needed into how English functions globally and locally, for which the following pointers may be useful. They relate to the interlocking of project, process and product, and the way these three mutually reinforce each other.

The *lingua franca/frankensteinia* ***project*** can be seen as entailing the following:

- the imagining of a community, in the same way as polities are imagined (Anderson 1983), an English-using community without territorial or national boundaries;
- the invention of traditions (in the sense of Hobsbawm and Ranger 1983), customs, activities and discourses that connect people through a merging of the language with multiple agendas at many levels, the local, the national, the regional, the universal and global;
- ultimately the project reflects metaphysical choices (Schumacher 1977) and philosophical principles (Kant 2004) that underpin the type of community we wish to live in, a topic that Gandhi devoted his life to—the beliefs, values, and ethical principles that guide us, in a world that is currently dominated by neoliberalism, unsustainable consumerism, violence, and linguistic neoimperialism (Phillipson 2008a);

- our choices can either serve to maintain diversity, biological, cultural and linguistic (http://www.terralingua.org) or to eliminate it, and current trends are alarming;
- all of which lead to visions of and for English, and if these do not define *lingua franca* in such a way as to ensure equality and symmetry in intercultural communication, but are essentially one-sided promotion of English, the project tends to be more that of a *lingua frankensteinia.*

The *lingua franca/frankensteinia* ***process*** can be seen as entailing

- building communities of practice, of language use and language learning
- that people identify with at various levels
- which can be personal, interpersonal, intercultural, and sub-cultural
- in contexts of use, discourses, and domains
- which conform to norms of linguistic behaviour that are institutionally reinforced, legitimated and rationalised
- in societies that hierarchise by means of race, class, gender, and language
- leading to English being perceived as prestigious, 'normal', and normative, hence the feeling of native speakers that the language is universally relevant and usable, and the need that others experience to learn and use the language, in some cases additively, whereas in others the process is subtractive.

The *lingua franca/frankensteinia* ***product***

- interlocks with economic/material systems, structures, institutions, and US empire
- is supported ideologically in cultural (re-)production and consumption, and
- in political, economic, military, media, academic and educational discourses
- through narratives of the 'story' of English, the 'spread' of the language, that rationalise the 'death' of other languages and legitimate linguicide
- through metaphors of English as 'international', global, God-given, rich, its use being 'natural' in the modern world
- with the prestige code that of elites in the dominant English-speaking countries, and embedded in the lexis and syntax of the language.

Heuristic ways of clarifying whether the advance of English represents *lingua franca* rather than *lingua frankensteinia* trends would entail asking a series of questions, and relating each of them to English as project, process and product:

- Is the expansion and/or learning of English in any given context additive or subtractive?
- Is linguistic capital dispossession of national languages taking place?
- Is there a strengthening or a weakening of a balanced local language ecology?
- Where are our political and corporate leaders taking us in language policy?

- How can specialists in English Studies, education, and sociolinguistics contribute to clarifying the many roles of English in the contemporary world?
- How can academics contribute to public awareness and political change?
- If dominant norms are global, is English serving local needs or merely subordinating its users to the American empire project?

These questions could be explored in relation to many of the country studies presented in this volume, for instance those dealing with African education, and in the analysis of Tanzania by Rubagumya, where English clearly functions as a *lingua frankensteinia*. The same phenomena may be present in many Asian contexts too. Education through the medium of English serves the *project* of elite formation, excluding the mass of the population. This is a project that local political and corporate elites, in coordination with external commercial and political forces, are committed to. The local needs that the project serves are those of the urban elites, who are complicit with the forces of the global economy, which means in effect subordination to the US empire project. The *processes* involved entail the subtractive learning of English, distancing learners from their ancestral languages and cultures, push-out from school of most children, and a weakening of the local language ecology when there is a harsh pecking order of languages (in Tanzania, a triglossic situation, with English at the peak, Swahili below it, and other languages marginalised). Dispossession of national languages takes place when resources are not allocated to validate, update and use them in the modern economy and political domain and throughout education. The *product* is Anglo-American English in its core, even if there are major modifications of vocabulary, grammar, and in particular of pronunciation to adapt to local needs and levels of intelligibility or formality.

In many Asian contexts it is highly probable that English is being learned subtractively, despite the warnings of many scholars from India and Pakistan. The project of increasing the learning and use of English represents a threat to other cultural values unless education is organised so as to build on the languages and cultures that children bring with them to school, after which other languages can be acquired additively. This is how education has traditionally been organised in European countries, with a primary focus on developing competence in the national language and thereafter the effective teaching of additional—foreign—languages. Bilingual or multilingual education is not widespread except in Luxembourg. Many continental Europeans (the Swedes, Dutch and others) have developed high levels of competence in English, French, German and other foreign languages without any suggestion that the language should be introduced as a medium of instruction. The current concern with an excessive use of English at university level is therefore a very recent one which has usefully served to highlight why explicit language policy formation for multilingualism, for meeting national as well as international needs, is essential. In the European case, it ought to prove possible to resist English as a *lingua frankensteinia* and ensure that the language is learned additively. There is also now much wider recognition of the case for maintaining minority languages and building on them in education, and that bilingual education of this sort in no way represents a threat to dominant languages. It leads to greater social justice. This is precisely what multilingual education in an Asian or African context ought to be able to achieve.

Empirical studies that explore the many tensions, at micro and macro levels, between linguistic diversity and dominant English are needed, in tandem with a refinement of the theoretical framework for understanding these changes in the global and local language ecology. The massive forces behind English and the US empire project promote inequality and destruction. The more we can contribute to counter balancing them the better.

## Notes

1 Footnote to 'A resolutely uncivilised colonial bumps into postcolonialism', *Studies in Language and Capitalism*, 2/1, 145-154, May 2007. The article was initially published in an in-flight British Airways magazine, in response to the airline's misuse of Hindi. The name Chamaar means 'shoe maker' in Hindi, a Dalit designation (information from Giridar Rao).

2 www.uspg.org.uk, accessed on13th March 2008.

3 http://www.wycliffe.org/, accessed on 13th March 2008.

4 Quoted in Parekh 2001: 21, who reports (citing Louis Fischer) that Gandhi thanked Churchill for the 'compliment', and wrote that 'he would love to be a naked fakir but was not one as yet.'

5 The exceptions are states with more than one official language, Belgium, Finland and Ireland.

6 According to the Federal Union of European Nationalities (http://www.fuen.org) 'FACTS: In the 45 states belonging to Europe live 337 ethnic and national minorities with almost 105 million members. This corresponds to about 14 % of the total population. The number of peoples in Europe amounts to 87 of which 33 peoples belong to a kin-state'. See also www.eurolang.nete.

7 http://www.coe.int/T/DG4/Linguistic/Default_en.asp.

8 http://conventions.coe.int/Treaty/Commun/QueVoulezVousasp?NT=157&CM=1&DF=2/17/2007&CL=ENG.

9 http://conventions.coe.int/Treaty/Commun/ListeTraites.asp?CM=1&CL=ENG&NT=&NU=148. For details, for instance of recent ratifications, see http://conventions.coe.int/Treaty/EN/v3News.asp.

10 It is, however, doubtful whether Dutch or Swedish interests are served optimally when representatives of these countries use English in high-level negotiations. This issue, often pointed out by interpreters, can be addressed by analysing how the interpretation system operates, how it is managed and funded, and criteria of efficiency and equity in communication.

11 Linguicism is defined as 'ideologies, structures and practices which are used to legitimate, effectuate, regulate and reproduce an unequal division of power and resources (both material and immaterial) between groups which are defined on the basis of lan-

guage' (Skutnabb-Kangas 1988: 13). Most education systems worldwide reflect linguicism (Skutnabb-Kangas 2000).

12 Gopalkrishna Gandhi, 2008: 320.

13 *Frankenstein* is the title of a novel (1818) by Mary Shelley whose eponymous character constructed and gave life to a human monster. The term therefore refers to a 'terrible creation; a thing that becomes terrifying to its creator' (*New Shorter Oxford English Dictionary*, 1993). It is often wrongly used as the name of the monster itself rather than its creator.

14 Whether this refers to minority mother tongues or the dominant national language is left unclear.

15 Report on the implementation of the Action Plan 2004-2006 'Promoting language learning and linguistic diversity' http://ec.europa.eu/education/policies/lang/policy/report_en.html

Recommendations of the High Level Group on Multilingualism set up by the EC http://ec.europa.eu/education/policies/lang/news/index_en.html.

European Language Indicator (plans for an EU-wide survey of language competence) http://ec.europa.eu/education/policies/lang/key/legislation_en.html.

Though there is increasing evidence of the Commission drawing on advice from independent experts, it is doubtful whether the career eurocrats who at any point of time might be attached to a language policy unit are professionally qualified for liaising with national authorities or educationalists and making an impact. They might just as well be dealing with fish quotas, energy, or air pollution, and may well be doing so in their next posting.

# 6

# Literacy and Bi/Multilingual Education in Africa: Recovering Collective Memory and Expertise

*Kathleen Heugh*

## Introduction

Current language education debates, practices and research in Africa need to be viewed through a historical lens. Language policy and education in most sub-Saharan African countries have evolved through several historically bounded phases: pre-colonial, colonial, early independence and developments since UNESCO's 1990 Education for All Conference in Jomtien (cf. Alidou 2004). The partition of Africa by and amongst various European powers, and accelerated after the Berlin Conference of 1884-5, resulted in a division of sociolinguistic communities, often exacerbated by a renaming of 'cross-border' languages. Historical revisionism became a necessary instrument of the geopolitical partition and the creation of new identities after 1885 and it continued as an integral component of political and economic control by the colonial and post-colonial state structures as well as neo-colonial agencies concerned with global influence from the second half of the twentieth century onwards (see other post-colonial critiques, e.g. Bourdieu 1991, Canagarajah 1999, May 2001, McCarty 2005, Mohanty 1994, 2006, Phillipson 1992, 2008c, Rassool 1999, 2007, Skutnabb-Kangas 2000, 2004, 2007, Stroud 2003, 2007).

In the domain of language education policy, revisionism in Africa is manifest at four levels. First, there is an apparent loss of memory regarding the use of African languages in written form and as the primary mediums of education in pre-colonial times. There is little recollection of the linguistic and literary continuum from the Egyptians' hieroglyphics to numerous scripts used amongst linguistic communities in East and West Africa. That modern day Amharic and Tigrinya have emerged from the Ancient Ethiopic, Giiz (Ge'ez) is barely known beyond Ethiopia and Eritrea. It is seldom acknowledged that the spread of Islam since the seventh century AD gave rise to the use of Arabic script, Ajami, in the transcription of many West African languages (Abdulaziz 2003, Alidou 2004). The late twentieth century discovery in Timbuktu of a large store of educational documents from the university mosques of the twelfth to the sixteenth centuries provides extensive evidence of literacy and formal education across a wide range of fields in several languages. Despite existing practices and evidence from the past, most education officials and advisors in African countries claim, amongst other things, that African languages are: too plentiful, without written traditions, and do not convey mathematical or scientific concepts.[1]

Second, although the colonial period introduced one or more of English, French, German, Spanish and Portuguese in formal education in the first half of the twentieth century, the practice of mother tongue medium (MTM) continued in the early years of education in territories under British control. Furthermore, there are several other post-independence examples of MTM or use of an African language as the medium of instruction in Ethiopia, Somalia, Madagascar, Guinea Conakry, Tanzania, Malawi, Namibia, and South Africa. Yet, these experiences and collective expertise are ignored in most high-level government and development agency debates on education on the continent. It is as if they have been expunged from the consciousness of contemporary education documents to the point that even in some universities students are taught that African languages cannot represent mathematical thought.[2] The implication is that African languages are too primitive to convey high level cognitive processing. Few recognise the irony that this argument is itself unscientific and contrary to the evidence.

Third, while communities in Africa are usually bi/multilingual, education systems drive towards an ill-fitting monolingual educational straightjacket. While political, educational and economic agents are impelled towards the apparently simple and efficient concept of a single *lingua franca*, usually the former colonial language in most countries, this is in conflict with communicative practices. De facto communication amongst communities is negotiated through '…a multilayered and partially connected language chain that offers a choice of varieties and registers in the speaker's immediate environment…' (Fardon and Furniss 1994: 4). While this multilayered chain may include what is regarded as a *lingua franca* elsewhere, it is not confined to a single linguistic entity. Dynamic multilingualism, rather than a static monolingual variety, is the African *lingua franca* (following Fardon and Furniss 1994). The incompatibility of colonial/neo-colonial linguistic determinism within the African context is at the heart of policy mismatches on the continent. Educational policies based on the assumption that contemporary education can only be delivered monolingually in a former colonial language have been attempted for 120 years, unsuccessfully.

Fourth, a relatively recent form of revisionism has emerged through policy documents, programme design and materials production in a number of 'anglophone' countries. In particular the Association for the Development of Education (ADEA)-UNESCO Institute for Education (UIE) Report (Alidou, Boly, Brock-Utne, Diallo, Heugh and

Wolff 2006) uncovered evidence of serious misuse of the discourse, terminology and theory about the role of the mother tongue medium (MTM) in education and additive bilingual education, notably associated with the work of Jim Cummins, Tove Skutnabb-Kangas and others (e.g. Cummins 1984, Skutnabb-Kangas and Cummins (eds) 1988). In essence, this involves the labelling of very limited MTM (one to three years) plus an early transition to English medium (usually by the second or third year of school) as additive bilingual education. Mislabelling or terminological slippage, deliberate or not, has the potential to ruin the educational progress of students across the continent. Three categories of stakeholders are involved in this process: government departments of education, programme providers, and well-meaning but confused educational academics and consultants.

European languages have generally come to be used for high-level purposes in each African country south of the Sahara. English has even come to occupy a significant position in at least two African countries which were never under British colonial rule, i.e. Namibia and Ethiopia. French, Spanish and Portuguese were used throughout the education system of territories which fell under the rule of southern European countries. Mother tongue medium (MTM) education,[3] however, was used for primary education to the mid-twentieth century in most countries under British colonial rule, and this was replaced by English-only (Zambia) or early transition from MTM to English medium after independence in several countries. Tanzania, South Africa, and Namibia for different political reasons retained and extended the use of the African languages to the end of primary school. Malawi retained one local language as medium for four years. Political changes since the early 1990s, however, have resulted in a similarly diminished use of African languages coupled with an accelerated transition to English medium in Namibia and South Africa. The history of Ethiopia was somewhat unique in that formal education in the twentieth century has moved from English medium only, to Amharic medium followed by transition to English medium, to the current policy which provides for various MTM options, although this has been interpreted differently from one region to the next.

By and large, there has been a convergence towards an early transition from MTM education to a second language (L2) education system across most sub-Saharan African countries, even though this is not compatible with contemporary education research. The research illustrates the interdependence of first and second language acquisition, cognitive development and academic achievement (e.g. Cummins 1984, Skutnabb-Kangas and Cummins (eds) 1988, Thomas and Collier 2002). Early transition from the MT to the educational second language in African settings does not facilitate the requisite competence in the second language. High-level linguistic competence is necessary for meaningful access to the curriculum and without this the student is unable to engage with educational materials and discourse. Education in the former colonial (second) language therefore, does not offer equity with MTM education and it cannot deliver quality education. The comprehensive ADEA-UIE stock-taking evaluation of mother tongue and bilingual programmes across sub-

Saharan Africa found no evidence that second language only or early transition to the second language programmes produce successful academic achievement for students (Alidou et al 2006).

Language education policy developments, as these articulate with memory loss and revisionism in the 'anglophone' countries of the region, particularly South Africa and Ethiopia, are examined here. The collective and collaborative (cf. Bourdieu 1991) amnesia in regard to the earlier and even contemporary use of African languages in education and the suspension of disbelief regarding past and present language and literacy practices across most of the continent are widespread. Elsewhere, the Canadian indigenous Maliseet researcher, Andrea Bear Nicholas, following the notions of 'linguicide' and 'linguistic genocide' (Skutnabb-Kangas 2000), calls this process 'historicide' (Bear Nicholas 2003). The purpose here, therefore, is to restore some historical, theoretical and pedagogical accuracy, to explain some of the contemporary manifestations of misapplied policy decision, and to illuminate practices which demonstrate the efficacy of MTM within dynamic multilingual environments.

## (Pre) colonial practices

It is necessary to recollect that richly textured oral traditions have been significant conduits for history, literature and knowledge systems to be preserved, expanded and transmitted from one generation to the next for thousands of years in Africa. Oral traditions were not, however, the only vehicles for language and education development. The Ancient Egyptians' use of hieroglyphics influenced many writing systems in countries further south. The Gicandi script of the Kikuyu in Kenya, the Nsibidi pictograms of the Efik in Nigeria, the Mende script of Sierra Leone and the Loma script of Liberia, as well as Dogon, Bambara and Bambum (Cameroon) scripts show similarities to Egyptian hieroglyphics (Battestini 1997, Ki-Zerbo 2003: 31). Modern Ethiopian languages, such as Amharic and Tigrinya have emerged from the Ancient Ethiopic, Giiz (Ge'ez), a South Semitic language in which the Holy Book, *Kebra nagast,* is written (Bloor and Tamarat 1996).

Discussions of language practices in Africa usually neglect the historical use of local languages in education. The rediscovery of the Malian Timbuktu manuscripts has drawn recent attention to extensive and sophisticated pre-colonial literary use of African languages and *Ajami* scripts for fields of study including religion, philosophy, music, astronomy, history, law, medicine, mathematics and commerce, in several West African languages at university mosques from the twelfth century onwards (e.g. Timbuktu Education Foundation 2002).

African languages received later attention from various nineteenth century missionary groups that travelled through Southern Africa and believed that their evangelical work would be advanced through the transcription of local languages, translation of the bible, the introduction of mother tongue literacy and primary education. Schools established by missionaries for a small percentage of children in

British colonies used MTM or African language medium for four to six years (e.g. Gorman 1974). This practice suited the British colonial administration's general policy favouring segregation; thus education was left largely to the missionaries. Education in the French, Portuguese and Spanish colonies, however, did not include the use of African languages. From the early twentieth century, various education commissions recommended the maintenance and use of local or domestic languages alongside the addition of an international language (e.g. Gorman 1974). Missionary education in 'anglophone' countries was compatible with these recommendations, particularly those of the influential *Report on the Use of Vernacular Languages in Education* (UNESCO 1953).

The linguistic credentials of the missionaries and the consequences of their activities have, however, been criticised. Missionary groups favoured different orthographic conventions and their expertise in linguistics was uneven. They often mistakenly identified close varieties of one language as separate languages and this, coupled with different orthographic systems, contributed to what Msimang (cited in Cluver 1996) has termed a 'linguistic balkanization' of Africa; or a 'misinvention' of African languages (Makoni 2003). The net result has been to inflate, artificially, the number of languages and establish different orthographies for the same or related language/s (e.g. for Sesotho as written in Lesotho vs. Sesotho as written in South Africa). Several arguments, including the apparent costs of such 'multiplicity' and, more recently, the 'artificiality' of languages, are advanced by post-colonial governments as part of a bank of reasons why African languages cannot be used in education. Schmied (1991), Obanya (1999) Bamgbose (2000) and Ouane (2003), nevertheless, offer detailed rebuttals to these arguments.

There are positive aspects of early missionary transcriptions and production of texts in African languages. Together, with the rediscovery of the Timbuktu manuscripts, they demonstrate the feasibility of materials production in and education through African languages. Language committees established in the late 1920s in South Africa built on earlier missionary work. The limitations of earlier divergent processes were recognised, and linguists sought to resolve orthographic differences and re-route developments along a convergent path (Cluver 1996).

## Post-colonial preoccupation with international languages

Post-colonial developments in the second half of the twentieth century in most African countries were accompanied by the identification of official languages for use in the political, economic and educational domains. In most instances, the international languages rather than local languages came to be selected for high-status functions in the former colonies.

The focus below is on countries which have chosen English to perform high-level functions. Tanzania, Malawi and Zambia gained independence in 1964, Botswana and Lesotho in 1966, and Swaziland in 1968. Under Julius Nyerere, Tanzania opted for a single African language, Kiswahili, as the official language and medium of instruction throughout primary school. Although Kiswahili was not a dominant MT of any particular group it had been advanced under both German and British rule as a language of trade and *lingua franca*. In Malawi, President Banda's home language was declared an official language alongside English and renamed Chichewa (although it continues to be known as Nyanja in Zambia and Mozambique) after independence in 1964. Chichewa was used until recently as the medium of instruction for the first four years of school with a switch to English medium thereafter. Zambia opted for English-only education after independence, ostensibly to avoid inter-ethnic rivalry (Tripathi 1990). The educational development and use of particularly Kiswahili (see Blommaert 1997, Brock-Utne 2005, Rubagumya 1994) and, to a lesser extent, Chichewa (Williams 2001) illustrate that African languages can and do offer viable educational opportunities.

The history of language education in Ethiopia took a slightly different path. Ethiopia remained free of colonial conquest, except for the short-lived Italian occupation between 1935 and 1941. Despite the literary traditions arising from Ge'ez, and there having been no history of British conquest, early twentieth century formal education in Addis Ababa was delivered through English. The Italians attempted to introduce MTM education but this did not take effect and the few existing schools proceeded with English-medium education upon the departure of Italy, largely owing to a sense of gratitude towards the British who helped to oust the Italian occupation (Bogale and Gebre Yohannes 2007). A policy change between 1955 and 1958, pre-empting later Tanzanian and Malawian decisions, identified one domestic language, Amharic, as the medium of instruction for primary education and this policy was implemented in the early 1960s (Bogale and Gebre Yohannes 2007).

Unfortunately, however, the advancement of only one African language in Tanzania, Malawi, Ethiopia and Botswana has resulted in the perceived marginalisation of other linguistic communities (e.g. Nyati-Ramahobo 2000). This is particularly the case for the fragile San communities of Botswana which have effectively been 'invisibilized' (Skutnabb-Kangas 2000) by the political dominance of Setswana. On the other hand, Zambia's English-only policy, adopted to avoid such ethnolinguistic inequities, has had other consequences. It has arrested further development of and production of texts in African languages. Those which had been developed earlier fell into disuse and went out of print. The English-only policy has resulted in neither high levels of English language proficiency nor educational success. It has also not arrested socio-political discontent, since those who are proficient in English and access higher education are resented as part of a political elite, impervious to the needs of those on the fringes of society (Tripathi 1990).

In each of these cases, the 'multiplicity' of African languages after independence and/or during the second half of the twentieth century was seen as a threat to national unity in the post-colonial years (Obanya 1999, Bamgbose 2000), and language policy reflected a tendency to marginalise most language communities and select either a single international or domestic language. Missionary development of languages other than Kiswahili, Chichewa/Nyanja, and Setswana, lost momentum or ceased altogether. Inevitably, this meant declining literacy activities and a gradual loss of literary resources in many languages.

Similar post-colonial developments were delayed by political events and sizable European settler communities in South Africa, Zimbabwe, Namibia and Mozambique (Schmied 1991). South Africa occupied 'German' South West Africa (now Namibia) during World War 1 and retained control until independence in 1990. Language policy and practices changed in both countries with a new government in 1948. Policy was marked by a two-pronged approach: official Afrikaans – English bilingualism (with special consideration for German in Namibia) and development and use of African languages to reinforce separatism. Earlier British colonial ideology of separate development, infused with European fascism of the 1930s, was refined into 'grand apartheid'. Convergent approaches to linguistic development amongst African languages were replaced by deliberate divergence. Apartheid logic included separate ethnolinguistic education systems. This meant eight years of MTM education for African children, followed by a transition to an equal number of subjects in Afrikaans and English in secondary school. The use of MTM education under such circumstances tainted its educational legitimacy amongst African language communities in South Africa.

With the exception of apartheid's expanded use of African languages, and the development of Kiswahili, Chichewa, Amharic and (for a short period) Somali in education in other East and Southern African countries, and several languages of Guinea Conakry in West Africa, the range of MTM options in education shrank across most of the region during the first decades of independence. Initial MTM education in the 'anglophone' countries was replaced either by a single African language followed by transition to English, or English-only. Political events were soon to alter the trajectory in South Africa and Namibia as well. Resistance to the compulsory use of Afrikaans medium for half of the subjects in secondary school for African students culminated in a student revolt in Soweto in 1976. Government was forced to make Afrikaans medium optional and MTM education was reduced from eight to four years of primary. All the while, MT speakers of Afrikaans and English continued to enjoy MTM education plus the other of these languages as a subject, to the end of secondary. At no point were Afrikaans or English speakers compelled to learn an African language.

At the time, heated political debates deflected attention from the de facto achievements of MTM education in South Africa. The secondary school leaving pass rate for African students rose to 83.7% by 1976. The English language (as subject) pass rate improved to over 78%. Within a few years of the reduction of MTM education to four years and earlier transition to English, the school leaving pass rates declined to 44% by 1992, with a parallel decline in English language proficiency (Heugh 2002). Macdonald (1990) was to show that students could not become sufficiently proficient in English by the end of the fourth year to facilitate a successful transition to English medium in grade 5.

Although African parents hoped that extended and earlier access to English in school would deliver higher-level proficiency in English and education success, the educational gap between speakers of African languages and speakers of Afrikaans and English, who have MTM education throughout, has widened. The knock-on effect of this is that those leaving school and going into the teaching profession are now less well-equipped for teaching and there is a downward spiral of teaching competence across the entire system (see discussion in following section below). The gap in educational achievement of African children vis-à-vis children of European descent is more noticeable in South Africa than in other countries because of the size of the 'settler' community and the analytical scrutiny which followed apartheid.

The implications of a significant longitudinal study, the Six Year Primary Project in Nigeria in the 1970s, in a politically more neutral environment were debated at length across the continent. This project demonstrated the educational and linguistic efficacy of extended use (six years) of MTM in conjunction with expert teaching of English as a subject (e.g. Bamgbose 2000). Other investigations into the use of African languages in education continued and were reported on through various education channels. In 1986 the Organisation of African Unity committed itself to the Language Plan of Action for Africa (Mateene 1999) which included the extended and expanded use of African languages in education. Subsequent and similar declarations regularly support this line of argument. Even though these debates were not tainted by the association of apartheid ideology with MTM education, none of the declarations or statements of intent have materialised in practice. Post-colonial debates in Africa (e.g. Alexander 1999, Bamgbose 2000) and beyond (e.g. Bourdieu 1991, Canagarajah 1999, May 2001, McCarty 2005, Mohanty 1994, Phillipson 1992, Rassool 2007, Skutnabb-Kangas 2000, Stroud 2003) demonstrate the resilience of ideological conditioning which reproduces earlier inequitable government practices. International aid agencies have also been reluctant to support the development and use of African languages in education (e.g. Schmied 1991). Alidou (2004) points out that since 1990 most African states have committed themselves to greater use of African languages, yet most continue to implement early transition from MTM to the former colonial or international language medium (L2) models. In essence, the continued privileging of the international and sometimes one of many other African languages reproduces inequality and educational failure for those who receive education in an unfamiliar language. In other words, the emphasis towards a single African language, for example: Amharic in Ethiopia, Kiswahili in Tanzania, Chichewa in Malawi and Setswana in Botswana, may result in linguistic, educational and other inequalities for speakers of other languages.

Ironically, by accident rather than design, apartheid education offered optimal opportunity for first and second language development alongside cognitive and academic development from 1955–1976. Despite the intention of separate and unequal education, an unintended consequence was greater educational success than other education policy in the region. The feasibility of using several African languages to the end of primary school was demonstrated. Seven South African and several Namibian languages were elaborated for educational use and textbooks were translated from Afrikaans and English into these languages for the duration of primary school. Most significantly, this was accomplished with minimal costs: the expenditure per capita on African education was a fraction of that for other population groups at the time (Heugh 2002).

The common thread across Southern and Eastern Africa is that education has been expected to deliver access to high level competence in an international language, which is English in most of the countries of the region. This has been and continues to be presented as feasible in a predominantly second or even foreign language education system. Evidence of the academic success of students who experienced extended MTM along with systematic teaching of English as a subject in what we now know as additive bilingual programmes, in Nigeria and South Africa, have been ignored. As mentioned earlier, a parallel or symbiotic phenomenon is that as English or other international languages gain prestige in African countries, recollections of African literary traditions fade and their very existence and use for mathematics and science and other educational domains comes to be denied on influential platforms (see endnote discussions).

## LATE TWENTIETH AND EARLY TWENTY-FIRST CENTURY DEVELOPMENTS ETHIOPIA AND SOUTH AFRICA

During the 1990s political changes across the region, especially in South Africa and Ethiopia, brought renewed attention towards education and language policy.

### *Ethiopia*

In Ethiopia, speakers of languages other than Amharic felt aggrieved at the use of only one Ethiopian language in primary education and political changes brought about new education policy in 1994. This has extended the use of other Ethiopian languages on a regional basis. The policy specifies eight years of MTM, plus Amharic as a subject for those students who do not have this language as a MT, plus English as a subject to the end of year 8, and a transition to English medium in year 9 (Ministry of Education 1994). Although there is some residual resentment about the earlier dominance of Amharic, it continues to have a utilitarian and functional use as a *lingua franca*. A feature of multilingual communities in Africa is that they are able, simultaneously, to hold apparently contradictory attitudes towards the same language. English, on the other hand, has little practical use outside of government departments in Addis Ababa, and functions as a little known, but most desirable foreign language of aspiration.

Despite the eight year MTM national policy, decentralisation of authority to the regions has made it possible for inconsistent implementation. Some regions implement eight years, some six years and others four years of MTM, followed by transition to English medium. In two of the regions where there are many minority communities, Amharic medium, rather than the MTM is used. What is instructive about the Ethiopian situation is that because of the variation of time during which MTM is applied, and because the systemic assessments are regularly undertaken, important data for language education internationally is available for scrutiny.

The system offers current data on the academic achievement of students in an additive bi/multilingual education system (at least eight years of MTM plus an additional language as a subject and very late transition to this language in the ninth year). It also offers comparative data on academic achievement of learners who have fewer years of MTM, i.e. learners who have late transition to English and those who have an earlier transition to English medium.

**Table 6.1.** Year 2000 Grade 8 achievement scores across regions

| Regional State | Medium of Instruction | English score | Math score | Biology score | Chemistry score |
|---|---|---|---|---|---|
| **Tigray** | **Tigrinya** | **39%** | **45%** | **56%** | **47%** |
| **Oromiya** | **Oromifa** | **39%** | **40%** | **56%** | **45%** |
| **Amhara** | **Amharic** | **34%** | **44%** | **61%** | **45%** |
| Harar | English | 45% | 40% | 48% | 43% |
| Addis Ababa | English | 46% | 39% | 44% | 40% |
| Benishangul Gumuz | English | 40% | 36% | 43% | 41% |
| Dire Dawa | English | 39% | 37% | 41% | 39% |
| SNNPR | English | 37% | 36% | 43% | 36% |
| Afar | English | 34% | 36% | 39% | 36% |
| Gambella | English | 36% | 27% | 37% | 33% |

(Data prepared by Gebre Yohannes for Heugh, Benson, Bogale and Gebre Yohannes 2007: 79).

**Table 6.2.** Year 2004 Grade 8 achievement scores across regions

| Regional State | Medium of Instruction | English | Math | | Chemistry | Physics | Composite |
|---|---|---|---|---|---|---|---|
| **Oromiya** | **Oromifa** | **41.6** | **42.8** | **48.3** | **43.6** | **39.3** | **43.2** |
| **Amhara** | **Amharic** | **39.1** | **41.4** | **48.3** | **44.6** | **41.8** | **43.0** |
| **Tigray** | **Tigrinya** | **39.1** | **44.4** | **49.1** | **43.0** | **39.5** | **43.0** |
| **Somali** | **Somali** | **42.4** | **42.6** | **36.3** | **37.8** | **34.5** | **38.6** |
| Harar | English | 46.8 | 43.4 | 39.4 | 42.5 | 35.1 | 41.5 |
| Dire Dawa | English | 42.4 | 41.0 | 37.7 | 38.2 | 33.5 | 38.6 |
| SNNPR | English | 41.0 | 39.7 | 36.8 | 37.5 | 31.3 | 37.4 |
| Addis Ababa | English | 42.3 | 40.5 | 33.7 | 35.9 | 31.1 | 36.7 |
| Afar | English | 39.6 | 36.6 | 32.0 | 33.8 | 30.7 | 34.6 |
| Benishangul Gumuz | English | 37.0 | 33.3 | 31.2 | 34.5 | 28.4 | 33.7 |

(Data prepared by Gebre Yohannes for Heugh, Benson, Bogale and Gebre Yohannes 2007: 79).

In Tables 6.1 and 6.2, the students in the regions with eight years of MTM (Oromiya, Amhara, Tigray and Somali) have higher levels of achievement across the curriculum than those students with six or four years of MTM. Their English language achievement does not appear to lag behind other regions, except the more wealthy and urban city states of Addis Ababa and Harar where students with six years of MTM do show a consistently higher level of English language achievement. This is to be expected for socio-economic reasons and also because urban students have some access to English beyond school. In summary, the data show that the longer students have MTM, the better their overall academic achievement. This data confirms the last three decades of international research on bilingual education (e.g. Skutnabb-Kangas and Toukomaa 1976, Cummins 1984, Thomas and Collier 2002).

Although English is seldom used and has limited foreign language functions in Ethiopia, the school system follows a transition to English medium by secondary school. It is important to note that in other 'anglophone' countries, English has a long history of use and it functions as a second language in urban if not rural contexts. In Ethiopia, however, English does not function as a second language and teachers have an even more limited proficiency in the language than in other countries that experienced British colonial rule. Its use in education as a medium of instruction creates an impossible situation for students and teachers alike.

Concurrent with the MTM policy, increased attention has been directed towards improving English language proficiency in secondary school because it is believed that this would better prepare the few who will proceed to university. This has had a strong negative washback effect across the school system whereby pressure is exerted towards an earlier switch from MTM to English medium, and this in turn exerts pressure on teacher education to ensure that teachers have the proficiency to teach through the medium of English earlier. The government response since 2005 has been to allocate more than 40% of the teacher education budget to a system-wide cascade model of providing English language improvement programmes for all teachers in the system. This is provided in 200 hours of which 120 is contact time in an intensive school holiday period with 80 hours of distance education. This skewing of resources towards English reduces resources for teacher education in other educational fields, levels and languages. There is no evidence that the investment in this expenditure shows a positive return (Heugh, Benson, Bogale and Gebre Yohannes 2007). It is simply not possible to increase the English language proficiency of teachers across a system in a 200-hour programme and these resources might be more profitably allocated to other areas of teacher education. Of most concern is that despite the assessment data, the pressure towards English is such that revisionist implementation plans which undermine the eight-year MTM policy have been introduced. Even in a country which did not experience British colonialism, the power and allure of English is such that decisions give more prominence to this language despite research, theory and systemic assessment data (see also Skutnabb-Kangas and Heugh forthcoming).

*South Africa*

In South Africa, apartheid rule gave way to a democracy in 1994. The finalisation of a new South African Constitution (Republic of South Africa 1996) introduced the principles which would guide new language policy developments. Two official languages, Afrikaans and English, were complemented by the addition of a further nine African languages. A new language education policy re-introduced the principle and right of MTM education within the context of 'additive bilingual and multilingual' models of education (Department of Education 1997). Discriminatory linguistic practices of the past were to be jettisoned. The language education policy further declared South African Sign Language a twelfth official language for educational purposes. The policy included strong recommendations regarding the promotion of languages for trade and diplomacy purposes. This promised to position South African language education policy as one of the most progressive in international contexts. The profiling of multilingualism in this framework was specifically supported during Nelson Mandela's presidency. After new elections in 1999, implementation of the new language policy ceased. Post-colonial analyses (e.g. Bourdieu 1991) demonstrate the difficulty of changing paradigms. However, the conditions in South Africa appeared for a short period of time to be sufficiently elastic to accommodate change. Elasticity was short-lived and a default to English option, when in doubt, took precedence.

Language education policy was kept separate from, rather than integrated into curriculum transformation, and this provided the loophole for government to avoid its implementation. By 2002 it became clear that the language policy had been overtaken by curriculum revision and of the six aims of the original policy only two had been partly included in the curriculum. The Revised National Curriculum Statements (Department of Education 2002) make a vague reference to the 1997 language education policy, and where additive bilingual education is mentioned, it is explained as if it were the same as early transition to English. The curriculum documentation, therefore, misrepresents the theory and pedagogical principles of additive bilingual education and also the principles of the language education policy. The misrepresentation involves terminological slippage. South African teachers and parents do not understand the new terminology and are confused by the replacement of the term 'second language' which most understood to mean English. The term second language has been replaced by the term 'first additional language'. In South Africa the terms 'first language' and 'mother tongue' are synonymous. Therefore, use of 'first additional language' as medium from grade 4 onwards in the context of 'additive bilingual education' discourse does not appear to be contradictory. Repeated reference to students 'who will learn in their first additional language' is a convenient rhetorical device used in the documentation to normalise the transition to English medium by grade 4.

Early transition from MTM to the second language has thus been cemented into the application of the new curriculum for 75% of learners who speak African languages as MTs, and passed off as if it were consistent with additive bilingual education. It is difficult to accept that this has been an accidental process of revision.[4]

## Revisionism in other contexts

The Ethiopian and South African examples of promising additive bi/multilingual education policy which undergoes systematic revision towards early transition to English have parallels in Mozambique, Zambia and Malawi since the mid-1990s. In each of these countries, concern regarding underachievement in literacy and general education led to proposals for a new language education policy supportive of extended use of African languages and additive bilingual principles. In each case, however, through a process of redrafting and revision of policy, there have been compromises in regard to the period of time afforded to MTM education. Zambian language policy revision has finally accommodated literacy in the mother tongue for grade 1 (extended to grade 2) but the medium of instruction remains English from grade 1 (Muyeeba 2004). In Malawi, the proposed expanded use of MTM in languages other than Chichewa for four years has been whittled down to two years. Mozambique has begun implementation of three years of MTM education. Namibia has similarly opted for three years of MTM. Each example demonstrates early transition to English or Portuguese; not one is attempting an additive bilingual option.

## Assessment, monitoring and evaluation

It is not surprising that attempts to transform education and achieve equitable provision and outcomes for students have had disappointing results in African countries. Systemic assessments of literacy and numeracy in grades 3, 4, and 6, in South Africa since 1998 are alarming and show the discrepancy between those students who do have MTM education throughout and those who do not.

In Figure 6.1, English- and Afrikaans-speaking students who have MTM throughout education (dotted line) outperform those who have switched to their second language, English, by grade 4 (solid line) across all provinces in South Africa, with a national average of 69% for MTM students and 32% for second language students.

Despite a huge financial investment in education since 1994, South Africa has been placed last in the Third (now Trends in) International Mathematics and Science Study (TIMSS) (UNESCO 2000, Reddy 2006). A common thread across these and other studies shows a correlation between students who are studying through their second language, English, and the lowest levels of achievement. South African students studying through their MT, Afrikaans and English, exhibit the highest levels of achievement in this country. These findings are predictable when viewed through the perspectives of psycholinguistics, second language acquisition, and bilingual theory. This is especially the case in relation to the interdependence of language, cognition and academic achievement (e.g. Macdonald 1990, Thomas and Collier 2002, Doughty and Long 2003, Abadzi 2006).

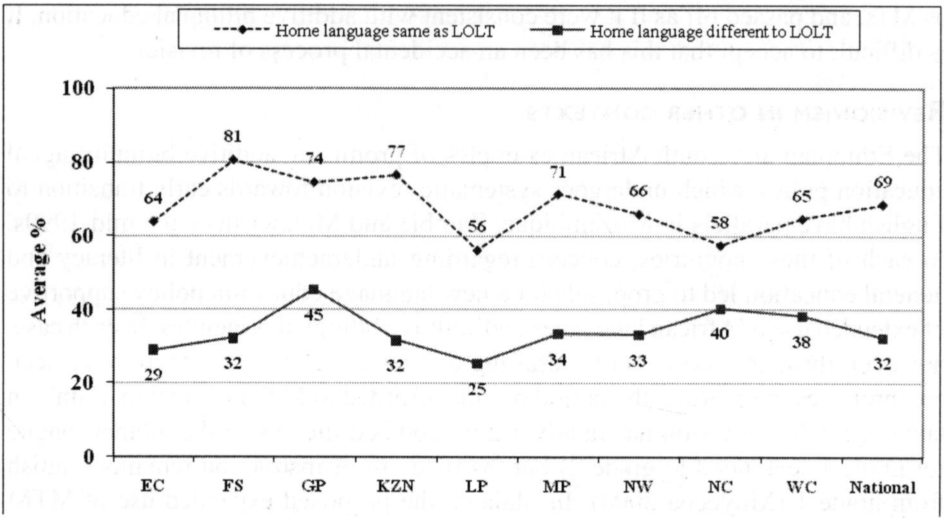


**Figure 6.1**. *Language (LOLT) achievement by home language / mother tongue and province, Grade 6 Systemic Evaluation National Report, South Africa* (Department of Education 2005: 77).

The language model used in South Africa, early-exit from MT and transition to English for African children, is one which is used across most other countries in sub-Saharan Africa, and its design guarantees educational failure. The question is: why since 1990 has there been an accelerated convergence towards this model when there is no evidence that it can offer success? Spolsky (2004) argues that blame cannot be directed at governments only, and that there needs to be an introspective examination of the role of advisors and experts. Post-colonial literature and debates referred to earlier may explain macro-level constraints which impel developments away from democratic principles. Less frequently documented are meso-level issues involving experts and advisors. Some of these are presented below.

Terminological slippage, as shown in the South African example, where an 'early-exit transitional bilingual' model is passed off as 'additive bilingual' education is clearly a government responsibility. However, it is becoming evident that there are other stakeholders involved in similar terminological slippage. In the literature about 'additive bilingual' education, Cummins (e.g. 1984) has consistently used the term 'transfer' to refer to a cognitive process in language acquisition, where knowledge developed in the MT may be transferred to the second language, and this is dependent upon the retention of the MT, not the suspension of MTM education. Unfortunately the terms 'transition' and 'transfer' appear to be similar to those who are not familiar with language education theory and research. Therefore, one might expect that laypersons might confuse the terms and even transpose them. However, there is no excuse for applied linguists who work in the area of language education to misuse them. Documents and second language programmes currently circulated in African countries increasingly contain terminological slippage and rhetorical

devices similar to those in the South African curriculum discussed above. The influence of the English second language (ESL) industry, mainly in Britain, North America and Australia is such that ESL programmes designed in those contexts have been transposed to African contexts in the form of early-exit from MT literacy and transition to ESL programmes, e.g. in materials borrowed from Britain and modified in South Africa by the Molteno Project. These materials, when analysed along with other mother tongue and bilingual programmes in Africa (Alidou et al 2006) revealed serious terminological inaccuracies. Early transition to English medium education was presented as consistent with additive bilingual education.[5] Additive bilingual education requires a minimum of six years of MTM under ideal conditions, and usually eight years under those found in African education systems. The Molteno Project made use of the additive bilingual discourse of the South African language education policy to advance its initial MT (Breakthrough to Literacy / BTL for grade 1) and early transition to English (Bridge to English from grade 2) reading programmes, as if they were consistent with additive bilingual education. These programmes were presented to the ministries and departments of education in numerous 'anglophone' African countries which were impressed with apparent changes in South Africa, including Malawi, Zambia, Uganda and Ghana. Programme material, including that on the project's website, referred to the 'transfer' of reading skills from the MT to English in grade 2 as if this were consistent with the theoretical work of Jim Cummins from the early 1980s. The documentation should have called this 'transition to English'. It is difficult to understand how this could have been accidental, since the Molteno Project is staffed by applied linguists and supported by several senior academics. Immediately after the attention was drawn to the erroneous use of terminology and theory, the Molteno Project dispatched letters to UIE which had commissioned the research, threatening legal action against the agency and the researcher who made this finding. The erroneous use of terminology was nevertheless simultaneously removed from the Molteno's website.
Independently, similarly erroneous terminology has been found in recent advisory documents supplied to the governments of Sierra Leone and Ethiopia. The extent to which the slippage is intentional obfuscation or genuine error is not always clear. An unfortunate consequence of information technology is that theoretically flawed documentation is circulated on the internet along with more academically rigorous material and government officials are not well-placed to distinguish between these.

As Schmied (1991) and others point out, there are several donor organisations concerned with L2 programme delivery in African countries. Evaluations for the donors of initial MT literacy and early-exit transitional (L2) programmes, however, are often flawed. Firstly, control groups are selected from a usually dysfunctional mainstream system, thus any intervention will look promising in comparison. (Most evaluations do not control for the well-known Hawthorne effect, where the performance of subjects under observation is expected to demonstrate improvement.)

Secondly, as the research of Thomas and Collier (2002) shows, evaluations of most types of bilingual programmes show similarly positive results during grades 1–3. The differences start emerging during grade 4 and are increasingly obvious from grade 5 onwards. This is the point at which the cognitive and linguistic demands of the curriculum increase sharply. It is also where it becomes clear that students from early-exit programmes who have not developed sufficiently strong foundations in literacy and numeracy experience a slowing down of their academic progress. Evaluations of programmes seldom reflect longitudinal effects of the transition to L2, so claims of success prior to an analysis of grade 5 data are premature and should neither inform policy nor its implementation (Heugh 2006). A former senior World Bank official who has had significant influence over development aid for education in African countries, mostly in the form of early transition to the former colonial language, vigorously attempted to prevent the presentation of the ADEA-UIE stocktaking report at the Meeting of Ministers of Education in Africa in Libreville, Gabon in March 2006. He insisted that 'we cannot now tell African Ministers that they have to invest in longer mother tongue education because for years we have been advising them that three years of mother tongue is sufficient' (Adrian Verspoor 2006, personal communication).

In the meantime, several cross-national studies show disturbing signs of poor achievement in literacy, mathematics and science, in the second language, across the region (UNESCO 2000). SACMEQ II (Southern and Eastern Africa Consortium for Monitoring Education Quality) 2000-2002—shows that 44% of learners in 14 countries achieve minimal levels of literacy at grade 6 whereas only 14.6% achieve the desired level of literacy achievement (Mothibeli 2005). These studies suggest that current language models fail most students and that the early transition to second language medium contributes to failure and attrition.

An adequate explanation for the reproduction of a flawed language model, one based on a language unfamiliar to teacher and student alike, includes both macro- and meso-level reasons (e.g. Alidou et al 2006, Benson 2004). The long-term effect of the wrong language model has been opaque or difficult to recognise in most countries where universal primary education has not yet been achieved and through-rate to secondary has been low. In South Africa, however, the evidence has been readily available, but obscured by the political-ideological aversion to apartheid and its education system.

The challenge, however, goes deeper than policy, language teaching or learning programmes and ideological considerations. A detailed study of literacy practices in the primary schools of Limpopo Province in South Africa (Reeves et al 2008) reveals that the current orientation towards the teaching of literacy (particularly reading and writing) which has been included in the country's new outcomes-based curriculum, is inadequate for students who come from vulnerable communities with low levels of literacy. An overly enthusiastic, naïve, adoption of the contemporary discourses of critical and social literacies, along with whole language approach (e.g.

Bloch 2006), has left teachers in rural African settings confounded. The national education system, encouraged by persuasive stakeholders, adopted these approaches without having ensured that they had been rigorously trialled under local conditions. Teachers have been encouraged to discard explicit teaching of reading and writing skills and to adopt vague notions which are not made explicit in any documentation. This has left teachers disempowered and students without the explicit scaffolding they require to develop strong reading and writing in the MT and/or the second language (see also Abadzi 2006, Macdonald 2002).

A further significant difficulty in South Africa is that students in vulnerable settings are seldom allowed to take schoolbooks home, in other words they have minimal or no reading matter out of school. This is because the schoolbook industry has responded to an ill-considered, politically correct, call from government and other educational stakeholders for glossy covered materials. School management teams in poor rural or township schools cannot afford to supply each child with these expensive schoolbooks, and pupils invariably have to share books. When schools have such materials in stock, students are seldom allowed to take them home. They simply cannot afford to replace lost or damaged books. It is only children of the middle-class and professional communities whose parents can afford to purchase books. Those who cannot afford books do not have them, and the socio-economic gap continues to widen.

Another study of literacy and numeracy of students in the Western Cape Province (Heugh, Diedericks, Prinsloo, Herbst and Winnaar 2007) shows that almost 80% of students cannot read or write material required across the curriculum at grade 8. This applies to both the mother tongue and the second language. It also shows that students have been retained and promoted through the system despite the fact that they cannot read or write. What this and other recent systemic assessments show is that achievement in literacy after a decade of the whole language approach, and the social and critical literacies' orientation, is weaker now than during the height of the apartheid years. Whilst whole language and social literacies approaches may suit students in English-dominant societies where there are high levels of community literacy and printed materials are readily available beyond the classroom, these conditions seldom apply in Africa.

Finally, whilst there are many challenges for education in Ethiopia, including inconsistencies of policy across the different regions, inadequate provision for learners from minority languages, and continual pressure to introduce English medium earlier across the system, there are important positive lessons for other countries. Ethiopian policy decentralises many educational decisions to the regions, including the publishing of school textbooks and other materials. Large foreign-owned publishers have not been allowed to take over the schoolbook market in Ethiopia. This limits the impact of foreign literacy and language programmes and is far less costly for the country. Materials are produced on inexpensive paper and students have learning materials which they are allowed to take home and use, unlike the situation in South Africa. South Africa is arguably the wealthiest and Ethiopia is considered the poorest of countries in Africa. Yet, it is Ethiopia which furnishes schoolbooks to most students while South Africa does not. The issue of cost and resources therefore needs far closer interrogation. In South Africa huge resources are spent on learning materials which are mostly in English and they are too expensive to provide to all children. In Ethiopia, on much more modest budgets, most primary school materials are produced in Ethiopian languages and although delivery of materials is patchy in some regions a high proportion of students receive textbooks.

An advantage of the Ethiopian decentralisation of education is that authorities in Oromiya, Tigray, Amhara and Somali regions, and two city-states, Addis Ababa and Harar, can concentrate on producing materials in the major language/s of those regions cost-effectively. However, where there are several minority languages, as in some of the Southern and Western regions, the regional bureaus of education experience financial and logistical difficulties. The use of human language and other electronic technology, however, could reduce the complexities and facilitate a broader coverage of languages over time.

## Conclusion

The research in South Africa and Ethiopia discussed above follows the ADEA-UIE Report (Alidou et al 2006) which points towards the high risks of policy informed by poor research, evaluation and advice in many countries. That study finds that inadequate decisions are made by a range of stakeholders, including policy makers, education consultants, academics and publishers who are therefore co-responsible for educational failure. The discussion in this chapter underscores those findings with subsequent and more detailed data from the Ethiopian (cf. Skutnabb-Kangas and Heugh forthcoming) and South African studies. It also illuminates four simple implications of the recent research for language and literacy education in Africa. The *first* is that collective memory regarding past and current experiences of African languages as educational mediums needs to be preserved in Africa. Amnesia and denial of African literary traditions and scholarly research is a pervasive and negative aspect of the post-colonial condition and allows revisionism to take root. The *second* is that literacy and language learning programmes and materials which originate from or which may be currently fashionable in English-dominant contexts beyond Africa cannot be trans/im-ported successfully to Africa. The *third* is that African research shows that children who enter formal educational contexts in African schools require explicit teaching of literacy in the MT and the L2; and that MTM education is required for at least eight years of schooling, along with second language teaching and learning. The *fourth* is that this can and does happen as found in one of the poorest countries in Africa, which is perhaps the most instructive point of all.

## *Notes*

1 There are several other arguments which are directed against the use of African languages in education and which have received comprehensive rebuttals, for example by Bamgbose (2000) and Ouane (2003).

2 Notably in the work of Douglas Young, University of Cape Town and Stanley Ridge, University of the Western Cape. For example both claimed that African languages are not capable of expressing mathematical or scientific concepts during symposium discussions at the 2002 AILA Conference in Singapore and Ridge emphasised this point to the author after these discussions (Ridge 2002, personal communication). Young reiterated this point at the Southern African Applied Lingustics Association (SAALA) Conference in Polokwane, July 2004.

3 It needs to be emphasised that in the African context, mother tongue education does not necessarily mean that every child has one mother tongue and has received or needs to receive schooling in a single, rarefied language. The term, mother tongue, is understood to include any or all of the linguistic repertoire of the child upon entry to school. Thus, although one's mother may use Fulfulde, one's father may prefer Djula, and one's neighbours speak Wolof, the linguistic repertoire includes all of these and any or all of these can be used successfully as medium/s of instruction at school. The term, mother-tongue education, therefore, should not be misunderstood in any narrow, monolingual sense. It needs to be understood as a far more nuanced and dynamic linguistic continuum of the language/s acquired and used for efficient communication in the community outside of formal education (cf. also Fardon and Furniss 1994). While there are many red-herring debates which include objections to the term mother tongue from gendered or narrow linguistic perspectives, the term is used in this chapter in the widely accepted sense it has across the continent.

4 This is particularly since this author has consistently pointed out the slippages to the Ministers of Education and senior education officials both in private and public discussions in South Africa and during continent-wide education conferences. At the March 2006 Meeting of Ministers of Education in Africa sponsored by ADEA and UIE in Libreville, Gabon, the South African Director General of Education, Duncan Hindle, told the author that although the Ministers of Education in Africa might appear to acknowledge the research, none of them had an interest in the implementation of MTM education (Hindle 2006, personal communication). At the UNESCO Regional Literacy Conference in September 2007 in Bamako, Mali, the South African Minister of Education's special advisor, Martin Mulcahy, argued that since MTM had been used under apartheid's separate and unequal education system, it could not now be used in the education system. He furthermore advised this author to desist from public presentation of the research supporting MTM lest she be accused of supporting apartheid (Mulcahy 2007, personal communication).

5 The Molteno Project's Breakthrough to Literacy (BTL) programme's origins were based on an approach for teaching of English as a first language (Letshabo 2002). This was modified for Southern African conditions and BTL came to be associated with one year of BTL in an African MT followed by Bridge to English from the second grade of school (i.e. an early exit from the MT and transition to English medium).

# 7

# Empowering Indigenous Languages What can be Learned from Native American Experiences?

*Teresa L. McCarty*

Native American education is characterised by a multiplicity of Indigenous languages and cultures. There are 62 classes of Native American languages, each as different as are Sino-Tibetan and Indo-European. Every one of these languages is in a perilous state of decline. The causes of Native American language loss are complex, but are ultimately traceable to Anglo-European colonisation, Christianisation, and physical, cultural, and linguistic genocide. The stakes are high, for unlike immigrant speech communities, Indigenous communities have no external pool of speakers from which to replenish their numbers. Language endangerment is heightened by the fact that these are traditionally oral societies. While grammars and practical writing systems exist, it is the spoken word—powerful but fragile oral tradition—that is the foundation of tribal societies (Sims 2005), and this foundation is in danger of being lost in our lifetimes.

Of 300 languages indigenous to what is now the United States and Canada, 210 are still spoken, but according to the linguist Michael Krauss (1998), 141 of these languages—67%—are spoken only by the grandparent generation and older. 'Our…languages are in the penultimate moment of their existence in this world,' Northern Cheyenne language educator and activist Richard Littlebear warns (1996: xv). Thus, one cannot talk of 'good practices' or 'successful language education programmes' for Native American children without considering how those practices and programmes are 'good for' restoring health and vitality to Indigenous mother tongues.

Understanding these issues requires understanding the unique legal and political status of Native peoples in the US. The term Native American encompasses diverse American Indian tribes, Alaska Natives, and Native Hawaiians who share a status as first peoples. American Indians and Alaska Natives have a legally defined status as tribal sovereigns.[1] Tribal sovereignty—the right to 'self-government, self-determination, and self-education' (Lomawaima and McCarty 2006: 10)—both predates and is recognised in the US constitution. From their first encounters, American Indians and Europeans interacted on a government-to-government basis. The federal–tribal relationship was subsequently codified in treaties, judicial rulings, and federal law. In exchange for land, Native peoples entered into a trust relationship with the federal government in which it recognises a binding responsibility to honour certain guarantees in education, health, and other areas. This legal–political relationship is unlike that of any other US ethnolinguistic group. It has profoundly influenced the present status of Native American languages, and, as discussed later in this chapter, it continues to shape the possibilities for Native American language education today.

With this background, and in the comparative spirit of this volume, this chapter distills four lessons for bi-/multilingual education based on Native American education experiences of which I have been part, either as a direct participant or as a long-time and close observer. To situate this work, I need to say a word or two about my own background. I am a non-Native educator and anthropologist and have worked in the field of Native American/Indigenous education for nearly thirty years. In that time, I have been fortunate to collaborate with many excellent Native American educators who are 'teaching against the grain' (Simon 1992) by bringing children's mother tongues and natal cultures into a historically alien space—school—and by taking schooling into the community. The resulting social–educational transformations have been enormous, but they have not come without cost. I have also witnessed—and fought—the threats to those transformations posed by 'dominant English' (Phillipson 2007a, 2009, this volume) and its users.

What can we learn from these experiences about empowering Indigenous mother tongues? This chapter addresses that question by raising four more:

1. What do Native American experiences teach us about 'good practices' for developing bi-/multilingualism when children's primary language is not the dominant or school language?
2. What lessons does Native American education hold for teaching Indigenous/minority languages as second or 'heritage' languages—that is, when mother tongues are weakened and language revitalisation is a primary goal?
3. What can we learn by listening to the supreme stakeholders in multilingual futures, Indigenous youth? And finally—
4. What do Native American experiences teach about the possibilities for a counter-hegemonic project that relocates Indigenous education from the margins to the centre—an education in which *all* citizens have a stake?

To situate these lessons, I begin with a brief demographic and social–linguistic profile of contemporary Native American communities.

## DEMO-LINGUISTIC PROFILE

Figure 7.1 shows Native American lands in the US today. In viewing this map, one can envision the march of Anglo-European colonisation from east to west. Tribes in the eastern US were hit hard and early by the European invasion. As a consequence, although Native American people reside in every US state and its territories, the majority of Native lands and peoples today are in the western and southwestern US.

At the turn of the twenty-first century, 4.1 million people in the US (1.4% of the population) identified as American Indian and Alaska Native (AI/AN), including 2.5 million who reported only American Indian and Alaska Native heritage (US Census Bureau 2002). An additional 874,000 people identified as Native Hawaiian and 'other Pacific Islander', with 141,000 reporting only Native Hawaiian heritage (US Census Bureau 2001: 1, 8). Approximately one-third of AIs/ANs are children under 18, and more than one-quarter live below the federally established poverty line—a figure double that of the US population as a whole (US Census Bureau 2006: 12). As Table 7.1 shows, the most populous tribe is Cherokee, with 729,533 members, of whom 281,069 report 'Cherokee heritage alone.' Navajo, with a population of more than 298,000, is the second most populous tribe and has the largest land base, with a reservation the size of the country of Ireland (US Census Bureau 2002; see Table 1).

**Table 7.1.** Ten most populous American Indian/Alaska Native groups: 2000

| Tribe/tribal grouping | No. reporting 'American Indian tribal grouping alone or in any combination' | No. reporting 'American Indian tribal grouping alone' |
|---|---|---|
| Cherokee | 729,533 | 281,069 |
| Navajo | 298,197 | 269,202 |
| Latin American Indian | 180,940 | 104,354 |
| Choctaw | 158,774 | 87,349 |
| Sioux (Lakota, Dakota) | 153,360 | 108,272 |
| Chippewa | 149,669 | 105,907 |
| Apache | 96,833 | 57,060 |
| Blackfeet | 85,750 | 27,104 |
| Iroquois | 80,822 | 45,212 |
| Pueblo (includes multiple Pueblos in Arizona and New Mexico) | 74,085 | 59,533 |

*Source:* US Census Bureau 2002: 10

Seventy-two per cent of AIs/ANs 5 years of age or older report speaking only English at home; *Ethnologue* reports a total of 361,978 speakers of NativeAmerican

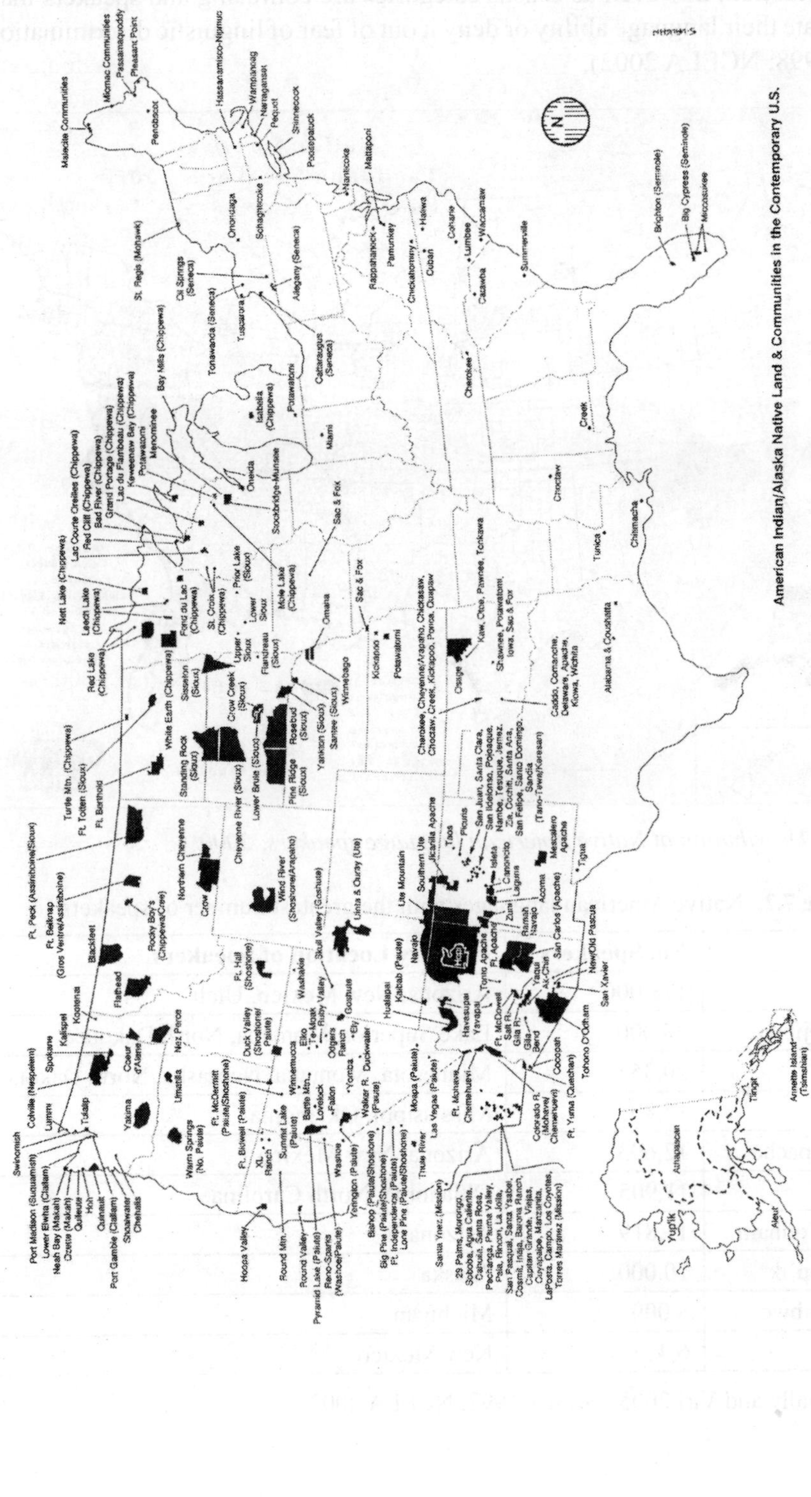


**Figure 7.1** *American Indian reservations and Alaska Native lands*

**Source:** McCarty and Watahomigie 2004: 80

languages (NCELA 2002; US Census Bureau 2006: 7). These numbers should be used with caution, however, as census categories are confusing and speakers may overestimate their language ability or deny it out of fear of linguistic discrimination (Krauss 1998; NCELA 2002).

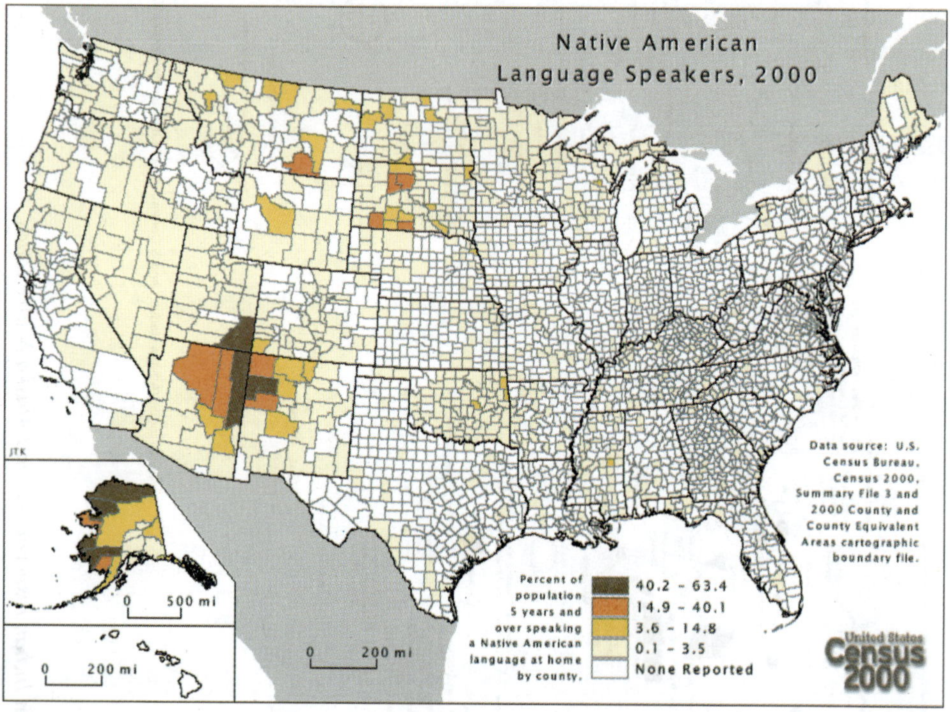


**Figure 7.2** *Distribution of Native American language speakers, 2000*

**Table 7.2.** Native American languages with the greatest number of speakers

| **Language** | **No. Speakers** | **Primary Location of Speakers** |
|---|---|---|
| Navajo | 178,000 | Arizona, New Mexico, Utah |
| Western Ojibwe | 35,000 | Lake Superior, Montana, North Dakota |
| Dakota | 20,355 | Minnesota, Montana, Nebraska, North Dakota |
| Choctaw | 17,890 | Mississippi, Oklahoma |
| Western Apache | 12,693 | Arizona, New Mexico |
| Cherokee | 11,905 | Oklahoma, North Carolina |
| Tohono O'odham | 11,819 | Arizona |
| Central Yup'ik | 10,000 | Alaska |
| Eastern Ojibwe | 8,000 | Michigan |
| Zuni | 6,413 | New Mexico |

*Source:* Benally and Viri 2005; Grimes 1992; NCELA 2002

Figure 7.2 shows the distribution of Native American language speakers in 2000. The largest numbers of speakers reside in Alaska and the Southwest. Navajo, an Athabaskan language related to languages spoken from the circumpolar north to the US border with Mexico, has the most speakers (178,000 in the 2000 census). As Table 7.2 shows, most Native American languages have many fewer speakers and more than a third have just a handful of elderly speakers. Eyak, for example, a language once spoken by people indigenous to what is now southern Alaska, lost its last speaker, Marie Smith Jones, in 2008.

## Lesson 1: 'Good Practices' when the home language is not the school language

With that introduction, I want to now concentrate on Navajo as a way into the first question about 'good practices' when the home language is not the school language. The Navajo Nation straddles three states in the Four Corners region of the US, so-called because it is the only region in the country where the borders of four states touch at a single point (see Figure 7.3). This is a stunningly beautiful landscape of red-rock buttes and monoliths, multihued canyon lands, and pine-studded mesas and forests ringed by four mountains held sacred by Navajos, or Diné (The People).

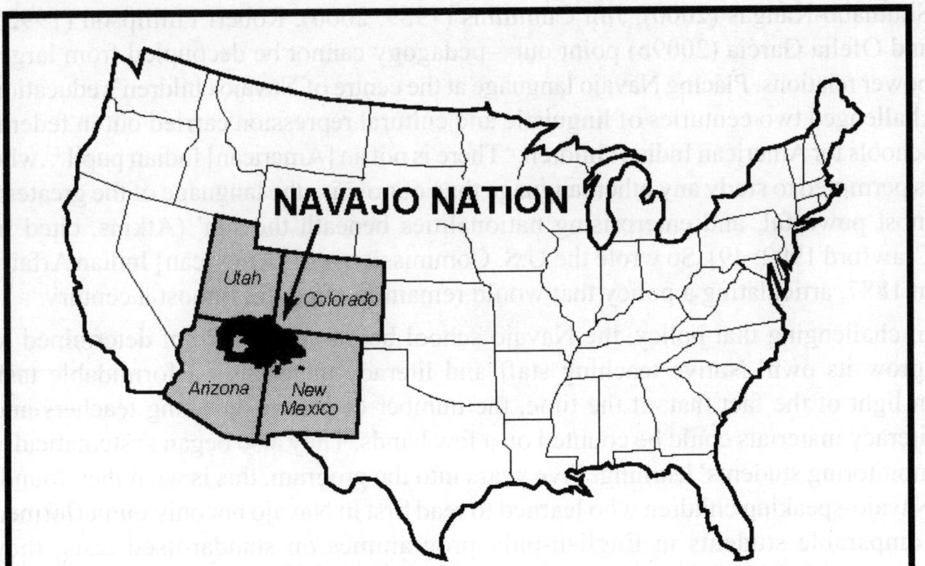


**Figure 7.3** *Four Corners region of the US*

This is the place where, in the late 1960s, a radical experiment in Native American education took root and began to grow. The premise of the experiment was simple: Teach Navajo-speaking children to read and write in their primary language first—an approach that goes unquestioned for children who speak the dominant language.

But at the time, teaching Native American children to read and write in their mother tongue was, quite simply, revolutionary. As one of the cofounders of this movement, the late Agnes Dodge Holm, told me in a 1996 interview: 'People were shocked when we suggested using Navajo in school. Nobody has ever suggested using Navajo in the school to *learn*, so how can you do that? School is to learn English.' (cited in McCarty 2002: 113).

Agnes Holm and her husband, Wayne Holm, were part of the Navajo Reading Study directed by Bernard Spolsky at the University of New Mexico in the 1960s and 1970s. Agnes—who was Diné—and Wayne, who is Anglo—went on to found an internationally acclaimed bilingual, bicultural, biliteracy programme at a small Navajo reservation school in Rock Point, Arizona. Their work, and that of a few other revolutionaries, would forever change the content and process of Native American education. As Wayne Holm told me in the same 1996 interview, never again could educators justify why they 'were not attempting to have community-based education' in Native American schools (cited in McCarty 2002: xvi).

Returning now to Spolsky's and the Holms' question—'Why *not* teach Navajo children to read in their mother tongue first?'—I must add a caveat. They were asking a pedagogical question—yes—but as they and scholars such as Tove Skutnabb-Kangas (2000), Jim Cummins (1989, 2000), Robert Phillipson (1992), and Ofelia García (2009b) point out—pedagogy cannot be decoupled from larger power relations. Placing Navajo language at the centre of Navajo children's education challenged two centuries of linguistic and cultural repression carried out in federal schools for American Indian children. 'There is not an [American] Indian pupil…who is permitted to study any other language than our own…the language of the greatest, most powerful, and enterprising nationalities beneath the sun' (Atkins, cited in Crawford 1992: 49). So wrote the U.S. Commissioner of [American] Indian Affairs in 1887, articulating a policy that would remain in effect for almost a century.

In challenging that policy, the Navajo school board at Rock Point determined to 'grow its own' Native teaching staff and literacy materials—a formidable task in light of the fact that, at the time, the number of Native-speaking teachers and literacy materials could be counted on a few hands. They also began systematically monitoring students' learning. Five years into the program, this is what they found: Navajo-speaking children who learned to read first in Navajo not only outperformed comparable students in English-only programmes on standardised tests, they surpassed their own previous annual growth rates, and they did so by greater margins each year (Holm and Holm 1990, 1995, Rosier and Farella 1976). Because they were being taught in their own language, children were able to 'actively *participate* in their own education from day one' (Holm 2006: 33). As Wayne Holm describes the programme's effects on student achievement: 'They succeeded in school *through* Navajo. More importantly, they came to *expect* to succeed in school, and they did' (2006: 33). Meanwhile, these students had the advantage of becoming literate in two languages (Rosier and Farella 1976: 388).

In a 25-year retrospective on the Rock Point programme, the Holms describe the 'four-fold empowerment' it generated: (1) of Indigenous school leaders, who acquired increasing trust and credibility with parents, staff, and students; (2) of Indigenous teachers, whose pedagogical vision and expertise were validated within and outside their community; (3) of Navajo parents, who for the first time, were invited into their children's schooling instead of being excluded from it; and (4) of Native students, who came to 'value their Navajo-ness and to see themselves as capable of succeeding because of, not despite that Navajo-ness' (Holm and Holm 1990, 1995). In short, Navajo 'claimed its space,' to quote Mäori scholar Linda Tuhiwai Smith (2007), carving out new possibilities for bi-/multilingual education that have been implemented with success in Native American communities throughout the US.

## Lesson 2: 'Good Practices' for teaching Indigenous/tribal languages as Second ('Heritage') languages

As groundbreaking as this early work was, it has not been sufficient to stem the tide of language shift. Figure 7.4 shows students at the Rough Rock (Navajo) Community School where I worked during the early 1980s. All spoke Navajo as their primary language. These students are now adults with children of their own, and for the most part, their children speak English as a primary (and sometimes sole) language.

**Figure 7.4** *Navajo schoolchildren at Rough Rock Community School, 1983 (photograph by Fred Bia, courtesy of Rough Rock Community School)*

How did this situation come about? A leading cause of language shift in Native American communities was an explicit federal policy to eradicate Indigenous languages and remake Native children 'into brown White citizens' (Benally and Viri 2005: 89). Stories abound of children being viciously beaten, ridiculed, and having their mouths 'washed' with soap for speaking the mother tongue in school (see, e.g., McCarty 2002 ch. 4, Watahomigie and McCarty 1996). These experiences left a residue of linguistic ambivalence and, as later sections of this chapter discuss, linguistic shame. Add to this the impact of modern English media and technology, and it is easy to see how children come to view English as the language of power and to feel uncertain about their mother tongue.

Given this situation, what lessons does Native American education hold about 'good practices' for teaching Indigenous/tribal languages as second languages? Space limitations prohibit an extension discussion, but the following example, again from the Navajo context, is illustrative. (For additional examples, see Hinton and Hale 2001, McCarty 2008, McCarty and Zepeda 2006, Reyhner, Cantoni, St. Clair and Parsons Yazzie 1999). The programme began in 1986 as a Navajo-language track in an English mainstream school that has, in recent years, blossomed into a K-8 Navajo-medium school called Tséhootsooí Diné Bi'ólta (The Navajo School at the Meadow Between the Rocks, or TDB). When the original programme began, less than a tenth of five-year-olds at the school were considered 'reasonably competent' Navajo speakers (Holm and Holm 1995). At the same time, they were identified as 'limited English proficient' (LEP) based on their performance on English standardised tests (Arviso and Holm 2001: 204-205, Holm and Holm 1995). In parallel fashion to developments at Rock Point a generation before, local educators, with parents' support, began a voluntary Navajo immersion programme for Navajo second-language learners.

In the lower grades, reading and writing are developed first in Navajo, then English. Math is taught in both languages, with other subjects included as content for speaking or writing (Holm and Holm 1995: 149-150). The programme includes 'situational Navajo' to develop students' oral language abilities while also using Navajo for high-level cognitive tasks. In the lower grades, all communication occurs in Navajo. Thereafter, the amount of English instruction is increased until a 50-50 ratio of Navajo and English is achieved (Johnson and Legatz 2006).

Table 7.3 summarises findings from the programme's first seven years. By the fourth grade, Navajo immersion (NI) students performed as well on local tests of English as comparable students in mainstream English (ME) classes. Immersion students performed better on local assessments of English writing, and were 'way ahead' on standardised tests of mathematics, discriminatory as those tests are (Holm and Holm 1995: 150). On standardised tests of English reading, students were slightly behind, but closing the gap. In short, the students had accomplished what research on second language acquisition from around the world predicts, acquiring *both* Navajo and English and performing as well as or better than their ME peers by the fifth grade (Arviso and Holm 2001: 211-212, Holm and Holm 1995: 150).

**Table 7.3.** Comparison of Navajo immersion (NI) and mainstream English (ME) student performance

| Assessment | NI Students | ME Students |
|---|---|---|
| *Local evaluations of English* | Same as ME students | Same as NI students |
| *Local assessments of English writing* | Better than ME students | Worse than NI students |
| *Standardised tests of mathematics* | Substantially better than ME students | Worse than NI students |
| *Standardised tests of English reading* | Slightly behind but catching up with ME students | Slightly ahead of NI students |
| *Local assessment of Navajo* | Better than ME students | Worse than NI students and worse than their own kindergarten performance |

*Sources:* Arviso and Holm 2001, Holm and Holm 1995

One additional finding is worthy of note. By fourth grade, not only did NI students outperform comparable ME students in Navajo (what we would expect), but ME students actually scored *lower* on those assessments than they had in kindergarten; in effect, they *lost* whatever bilingual proficiency they possessed on entering school (see Table 7.3). There is much debate about what schools can and cannot do to enhance bi-/multilingualism and reverse language shift (Fishman 1991, Krauss 1998, McCarty 1998). These data demonstrate the powerful negative effect of the absence of bilingual/immersion schooling, and, conversely, its positive effects on heritage language maintenance and English acquisition.

This brings us to lesson 2: Heritage-language revitalisation and academic achievement, including proficiency in 'academic' English for high-level tasks, are not mutually incompatible goals. Academically rigorous, sustained, and cumulative heritage-language education over 5 to 7 years is a highly effective counter-pedagogy to English-only schooling, even for students with limited proficiency in the heritage language.

## Lesson 3: We can learn a great deal by listening to youth !

I turn now to the third question: What can we learn about 'good practices' in bi-/multilingual education by listening to the supreme stakeholders—Indigenous youth? My attention to this is driven by a recent five-year study (2001–2006) of Native language shift and retention undertaken with my colleagues, Drs Mary Eunice Romero-Little and Ofelia Zepeda, at seven schools and four tribal communities in the US Southwest. Five Native languages were represented in the study. Study sites included communities in which intergenerational transmission of the Native language still occurs, trilingual communities in which a Native language is spoken along with English and Spanish, and a community in which the Native language is spoken by a handful of elders. The sites represent a continuum of rural-reservation, urban, and urban periphery settings. The total Native American student enrollment at all seven schools is 1,739. Language education programmes at these schools include pull-out Native language and culture classes for a half-hour to an hour a week, stronger forms of bilingual education (partial Native-language immersion), and 'non-forms' (structured English immersion/submersion) (see Skutnabb-Kangas and McCarty 2008 for programme definitions).

As part of the study, we conducted 212 in-depth interviews with adults and youth, administered 600 sociolinguistic questionnaires, spent hundreds of hours observing language use and teaching inside and outside of school, and collected academic achievement data. (For a full discussion of the study's methodology, see McCarty, Romero-Little and Zepeda 2006a, 2006b, Romero-Little, McCarty, Warhol and Zepeda 2007.) Of all these data, what impressed us most was what we learned from the interviews with Native American youth.

It is often assumed that youth are disinterested in their heritage language and culture. What we found instead were remarkably thoughtful, articulate, and bright young people who are deeply concerned about their languages and cultures and who, when asked, have a great deal to say about what should be done. Much of what they say is at odds with conventional wisdom as reported by adults:

- Whereas educators tended to report that students are unlikely to hear the Native language spoken in their homes and communities, youth overwhelmingly reported that they hear the Native language spoken regularly at home, at church, in tribal offices, and at tribal cultural events.

  *What youth are telling us:* These are language-rich, not language-deprived environments. There is more 'languaging' (Shohamy 2006) going on in youth's cultural worlds than is apparent on the surface, and this is a resource for multilingual and multi-literacy development.
- Whereas educators often described youth in deficit terms (e.g. 'semi-lingual'), we observed youth actively processing multiple varieties of one or more Native languages, English, and sometimes Spanish. Minimally, most of these youth possess receptive abilities in their heritage language. Many more than expected are fluent speakers, and some are able to read and write their Native language. Further, youth understand and can articulate how different language varieties work in their community: who speaks what variety, where, and for what purpose, and how language varieties mark speakers' locale, age, and social status.

  *What youth are telling us:* Even if they are not fluent speakers of the Native/heritage language or of academic English, youth are actively processing multiple language varieties for different purposes. These are social-linguistic strengths that may go unrecognised or be treated as deficits in school. There is more 'translanguaging' (García, 2007, 2009b) going on in youth's cultural worlds than adults may credit, and this is a further resource for multilingual and multi-literacy development.

- Whereas adults tended to characterize youth as indifferent toward their heritage language, most youth expressed deep concern about their language and were eager to learn it. These interview excerpts are representative (emphases added):

  For me it's important because it's *my language* and…when I speak the language, I think it makes me more [name of tribe]. (Youth interview 6/1/04)

[The Native language] is *our blood language*…. (Youth interview 6/1/04)

I would like to know *my cultural language*…. (Youth questionnaire response)

[Knowing the Native language] helps me not to lose the *identity of who I am,* of where I come from…. (Youth interview 5/6/04).

I really am speaking *English instead of my culture*. (Youth interview 6/1/04)

*What youth are telling us:* The Native language is integrally tied to identity. Youth are not indifferent toward their heritage language and culture; they know that their language is in trouble, desire to learn it, and recognise the stakes for future generations. This is a powerful motivational resource for multilingual and multi-literacy development.

Youth and adults agreed, however, that within youth peer culture there are pressures that create conflicting feelings of language embarrassment and shame, and that this constrains youth language practices. 'It's being told that [the Native language] is stupid…to speak [American] Indian is the way of the devil,' a 16-year-old declared, adding: 'you…forsake who you are, you give up having to learn [the Native language]…in order to accommodate the mainstream life' (Youth interview, 5/6/04). Linguistic shame leads many youth to 'hide' their Native-language abilities. As one youth explained, linguistic discrimination against 'non-standard' English leads some youth to 'feel dirty' about speaking the mother tongue and to present themselves as non-speakers of, or as indifferent to, their heritage language (Youth interview 5/504).

The latter findings are both complex and troubling, and we have written about them elsewhere at length (McCarty et al. 2006a, 2006b). For present purposes, what is important to point out is that linguistic shame is not a function of language per se, but rather of wider societal discourses that marginalise and demonise Indigenous/minority languages and their speakers, associating them with poverty, traditionalism, and 'backwardness', while privileging standard(ising) English (see also Bonner 2001, Lee 2007). As Navajo scholar Tiffany Lee observes in her study of Navajo youth's language attitudes, and as our data also show, even in the presence of these pressures, Indigenous youth 'inherently…value their heritage language' (Lee 2007: 25). This is an opportunity, Lee adds, for educators to support youth in placing language shift in context by critically assessing the history of colonisation and cultural change, and thereby strategically reposition peer influence to promote Native-language learning and use.

## Lesson 4: Repositioning Indigenous/minority education from the margins to the centre

Previous sections have illuminated 'good practices' for teaching Indigenous languages as first and second (or third) languages, foregrounding the quiet revolutions and the significant, if often untapped, heteroglossic resources in Indigenous communities (García 2007, 2009b). Lessons from these efforts also show that power inequities are not totalising; Native American communities continue to claim an Indigenous space. These efforts are, as Luis Enrique López (2008) observes, the 'unquestionable victories' of Indigenous peoples worldwide for the right of choice: not the manufactured either–or choice that characterizes colonial schooling—*either* the language of wider communication and opportunity and success, *or* the Indigenous/minority language and school and life failure—but Indigenous self-determinant choice about the content and medium of children's education.

As López (2008) also notes, the next revolutionary movement involves transforming the received 'compensatory condition' of Indigenous/minority education; that is, making bi-/multilingual education 'good practice' for *all* learners. At one level this requires ideological clarification in which Indigenous communities engage in their own healing dialogues and action (see Dauenhauer and Dauenhauer's [1998] penetrating discussion of the challenges and opportunities inherent in this process based on their experience in southeast Alaska). At another level, (re)positioning Indigenous/minority education from the margins to the centre entails dialogic engagement and activism among multiple social sectors. This is an equally tough proposition, but there is a great deal to learn from Indigenous examples. I close with one more.

Outside the entrance of the Raukaumanga Kurakaupapa (Māori-medium) School in Huntly, New Zealand is a beautiful wood and metal sculpture representing the school's philosophy. The sculpture depicts a piece of wood piercing steel, which Robyn Hata, the school's former deputy principal, explains represents the school's philosophy of 'crashing through barriers' (personal communication, November 2007). For more than two decades, crashing through social, linguistic, and political barriers is exactly what the Māori language revitalisation movement has done. In similar fashion, Native Hawaiians have established Hawaiian-medium education as a pre-K through postsecondary school option for *all* students in Hawaiian public schools.

Models of 'good practice' such as these are enormously instructive, challenging us to continue to 'crash through barriers' where they exist. As this work moves forward, I am reminded of the vision of the 'seventh generation' in American Indian prophecy—not the next, or the next, or the next, or the *next* generation, but the seventh generation to come. With that vision in mind, a final lesson from Native American education experiences is to involve youth directly in these processes—not only as language learners, but as active and vested language users, planners, and researchers in their own right.

## *Note*

1 Political incorporation into the US has been different for American Indians, Alaska Natives, and Native Hawaiians, and among American Indian tribes themselves. The sovereignty of some tribes is recognised by states but not by the federal government, and many tribes are not recognised by either states or the federal government. Native Hawaiians, whose internationally recognised sovereign kingdom was illegally overthrown by the US military in 1893 and who were not officially incorporated into the US until Hawaiian statehood in 1959, are still fighting for federal recognition of their sovereignty. The experience of Alaska Natives, who include American Indians and Aleut, Inupiat, and Yup'ik peoples, is different still. Nonetheless, all Native Americans share a distinct status as Indigenous peoples that entails tribal sovereignty and a singular legal-political relationship with the US government.

# 8

# Education, Multilingualism and Translanguaging in the 21st Century[1]

*Ofelia García*

## Introduction

Throughout the world bilingual[2] children are the norm. Most of the time children grow up in homes where parents and families have various ways of speaking. Other times, children acquire different language practices as they move from the family context to that of the community. Yet other times, children move with parents to other geographical regions where they acquire additional languages and ways of 'languaging'.[3] Most often, however, children grow up in homes where people 'language' in one way, and go to schools in what is considered another language, or they learn an additional language in school. Regardless of how children come to be bilingual or multilingual, children throughout the world most commonly engage in *bilingual languaging* or what I have termed elsewhere *translanguaging*[4] (García 2009b).

Translanguaging is the act performed by bilinguals of accessing different linguistic features or various modes of what are described as autonomous languages in order to maximize communicative potential. It is an approach to bilingualism that is centered, not on languages as has been often the case, but on the practices of bilinguals that are readily observable in order to make sense of their multilingual worlds. Translanguaging therefore goes beyond what has been termed *code-switching*, although it includes it. For me, the concept extends what Gutiérrez and her colleagues have called 'hybrid language use', that is, a 'systematic, strategic, affiliative, and sense-making process ....' (Gutiérrez, Baquedano-López and Álvarez 2001: 128), that is important for all bilinguals in multilingual contexts.

But the facility to language bilingually is seldom recognized by education systems throughout the world. Children who come to school speaking in ways that differ from the language practices of school are often stigmatized and assigned to remedial education tracks. This is so whether the child comes to school as a monolingual student speaking in ways that are different from those of school, or whether the child engages in bilingual practices that differ from the monolingual ones schools most often impose.

Two questions frame this paper—(1) What assumptions do we have about monolingualism and bilingualism, and how are those reflected in our current understandings of bilingualism and the development of bilingual and multilingual education programs? (2) What kinds of multilingual education programs and what kinds of language practices would have to be nurtured in order to equitably teach language minority students[5] and facilitate their learning?

I will argue here that the educational system's denial of the bilingual potential of children has much to do with the concept of *governmentality* as proposed by Foucault (1991). Foucault focuses on how language practices in schools 'regulate' the ways in which language is used, and establish language hierarchies in which some languages, or some ways of using language, are more valued than others. This has to be interpreted within the framework of *hegemony* developed by Antonio Gramsci (1971)[6] which explains how people acquiesce to invisible cultural power. Erickson (1996: 45) defines *hegemonic practices* as:

> routine actions and unexamined beliefs that are consonant with the cultural system of meaning and ontology within which it makes sense to take certain actions, entirely without malevolent intent, that nonetheless systematically limit the life chances of members of stigmatized groups.

One such hegemonic practice has to do with our understandings and beliefs regarding monolingualism, but also bilingualism. When seen through a Western scholarly lens, monolingualism is routinely accepted as the norm. And bilingualism is accepted only as double monolingualism. As such, it is then monolingual and monoglossic[7] language ideologies, policies, and practices that are imposed by schools. As agents of the state, schools insist on monolingual practices, silencing the ways in which bilingual children 'language,' and thus limiting their educational and life opportunities. Even when bilingual programs are developed, schools often demand the total control of two bounded autonomous language systems instead of honoring and capitalizing on the children's bilingual practices. Bilingual education programs that insist on two separate languages end up denying the complex multilingualism of much of the world.

## Questioning some assumptions about bilingualism

Although the greatest linguistic complexity exists in Sub-Saharan Africa (the belt from the West African coast through the Congo basin and to East Africa) and Southeast Asia (India, peninsular Southeast Asia, and the islands of Indonesia, New Guinea and the Pacific) (Nettle and Romaine 2000), most scholarly work on bilingualism has been developed in North America, and especially in Canada—a region known for low to medium language diversity.[8] (On First Nations languages, see Bear Nicholas 2009, this volume.)

The impetus behind the work on Canadian bilingualism was the Royal Commission on Bilingualism and Biculturalism established in the 1960s in response to the notion of two founding nations (the French and the English). Aiming to establish a balance between English and French, bilingualism in Canada was proposed as the two wheels needed to move within a bilingual federation, ignoring the languages of the First Nations and of the increasing number of immigrants. *The Official Languages Act of 1969* declared Canada to be bilingual in English and French. But in 1977, *Bill 101, the Charter of the French Language*, made French the language of work, business and education in Québec (Ricento and Burnaby 1998).

Working to balance these tensions between the bilingualism of the federation and the increasing insistence on French monolingualism in Québec, Wallace Lambert and his colleagues in McGill University established the first Early Immersion Bilingual Education programs in St. Lambert (Lambert and Tucker 1972). And Lambert (1975) then proposed the two models of bilingualism that have dominated the scholarly literature—*subtractive* bilingualism and *additive* bilingualism.

In subtractive bilingualism, the first language is taken away as the second language is added, resulting in monolingualism in a second language (L1 + L2 – L1 = L2). In contrast, in additive bilingualism, a second language is added without any loss of the first language (L1 + L2 = L1 + L2). Lambert argued that additive bilingualism is socially and cognitively beneficial, whereas subtractive bilingualism results not only in monolingualism, but also in inferior academic achievement (Lambert 1975).

But the subtractive and additive models of bilingualism have proven to be inadequate to describe the linguistic complexity of the twenty-first century. On the one hand, the additive model insists on developing a second full language that could be accessed entirely on its own, that is, it results in double monolingualism. On the other hand, both models start with, or end in, monolingualism, naming one language as clearly the first, and the additional one as the second.

The additive model calques or traces the language practices of a monolingual individual, simply multiplying them by two. If monolingualism is like a unicycle, bilingualism, in this view, is having two fully balanced wheels of a bicycle (Cummins 2000). At any time, these bilingual individuals can be seen to rely on their unicycle, wheeling each of their wheels independently of each other, or at most, always at unison and at the same speed. But in the twenty-first century, we need to recognize that this type of bilingualism will not work in the rough communicative multimodal terrain for which two balanced wheels are no longer adequate. Beyond the bicycle, we need to develop discursive practices that adapt to the ridges and craters of multimodal communication and that include complex ways of languaging. We need to develop wheels that turn, extend and contract, that make up for each other, that are able to turn in different directions—as those of an all-terrain-vehicle. And we certainly need to have more than two wheels.

The subtractive/additive models also consider a first and a second language, based, of course, on monolingualism as the norm. But in the communicative complexity of the twenty-first century, spurred by the movement of people, information, goods and services that are the result of globalization and richer technology, the concept of a first and a second language has also begun to unravel. Instead, communication includes complex discursive practices with different modalities—visual, audio and spatial semiotic systems, besides written-linguistic modes of meaning (Cope and Kalantzis 2000, Kress 2003, New London Group 1996)—and their use in integrated fashion. When bilingualism and languaging bilingually are taken as the normal mode of communication, it is difficult to identify a first or a second language, as bilingualism becomes the heart of the matter.

Much like the banyan tree so common in Southeast Asia, bilingualism, and especially multilingualism, needs to be recognized for its interconnectivity and multiplicity, grounded not only vertically, but also horizontally. It is precisely these associations and linkages that potentialize not only communication, but also that protect the structure, the temple that is the individual speaker.

I have proposed elsewhere (García 2009b) that two other models of bilingualism need to be considered today to include these different realities of the twenty-first century —*recursive* bilingualism and *dynamic* bilingualism. Recursive bilingualism refers to cases when bilingualism is developed after the language practices of a community have been suppressed. In these cases, the development of the community's mother tongue is not a simple addition that starts from a monolingual point, since the ancestral language continues to be used in traditional ceremonies and by many in the community to different degrees. Bilingualism in these cases is recursive because it reaches back to the bits and pieces of ancestral language practices, as they are reconstituted for new functions and as they gain momentum to thrust forward towards the future. This recursive bilingualism does not stem from a monoglossic vision that starts out from monolingualism (as does additive bilingualism), but it originates in already heteroglossic languaging practices, in bilingualism per se. I have annotated this model of bilingualism as in Figure 8.1:

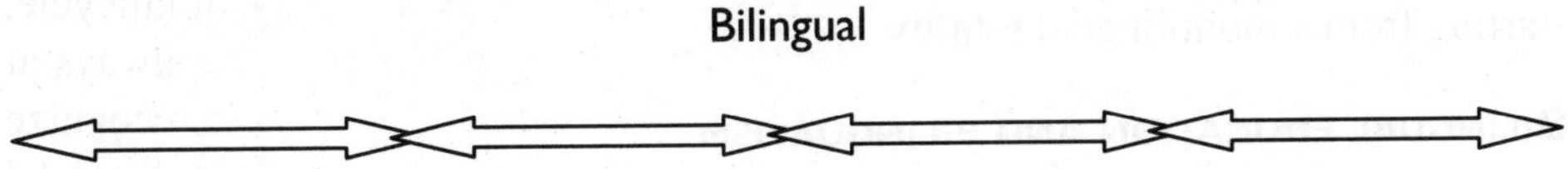


**Figure 8.1** *Recursive bilingualism*

Dynamic bilingualism refers to language practices which are multiple and ever adjusting to the multilingual multimodal terrain of the communicative act. This model has nothing to do with the linear models of the past, responding to language interaction that take place in different planes that include multimodalities and multilingualism. I have rendered this model with the diagram in Figure 8.2:

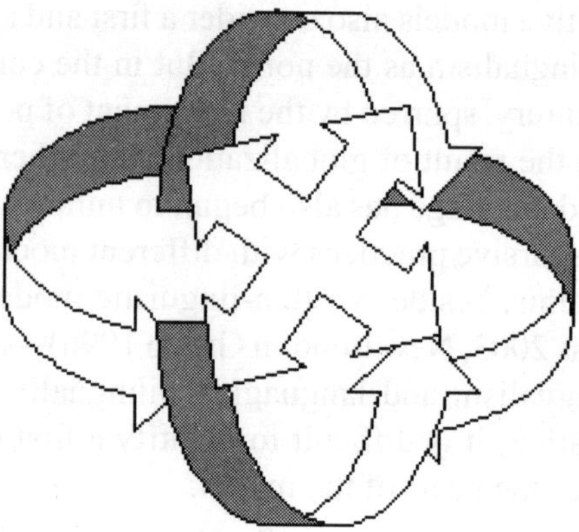

**Figure 8.2** *Dynamic bilingualism*

My concept of dynamic bilingualism has much to do with the way that the Language Policy Division of the Council of Europe[9] defines the concept of plurilingualism as the ability to use several languages to varying degrees and for distinct purposes. The *Common European Framework of Reference for Languages* defines it as the ability 'to use languages for the purposes of communication and to take part in intercultural action, where a person, viewed as a social agent, has proficiency, of varying degrees, in several languages and experience of several cultures' (Council of Europe 2000: 168). Dynamic bilingualism refers then to the varying degrees of abilities and uses of multiple language practices needed for people to cross physical or virtual borders.

The progression from subtractive and additive models of bilingualism to include recursive and dynamic models has to do with ideologies that recognize the value of heteroglossic discourses and multiple voices. Heteroglossic ideologies and practices not only assert the functional interrelationship of languaging bilingually, but in so doing, they break the cycle of power that has held monolingual practices as dominant. Languaging bilingually or translanguaging is then considered the norm, as speakers are seen to occupy different points in the bilingual continua instead of starting from a monolingual totality.

## Bilingual education and bilingualism

The use of two languages in education is not new. Mackey (1978: 2-3) describes how the 16,000 tablets unearthed in Aleppo, Syria in 1977, indicated that bilingual schooling is at least four to five thousand years old. And Glyn Lewis (1977) has shown how in the West, from the second century onward, Greek–Latin bilingual education was the way to educate boys from Roman aristocratic homes who were expected to learn the language of the admired Hellenic civilization. And throughout history, two languages have been used to educate prestigious social and religious groups. However, scholarly attention became focused on bilingual education in the second half of the twentieth century. It was then that the *immersion* bilingual education programs started to be developed in Québec,[10] as a way to make the majority Anglophone children bilingual. Immersion bilingual education programs use the child's second language as the only medium of instruction at the beginning, followed by the equal use of the child's first and second languages.

It is also during the mid-twentieth century that the United States starts to develop bilingual education programs for their language minorities, in particular for U.S. Latinos. Those bilingual education programs were mostly of a *transitional* kind, using the child's first language for subject instruction, along with English as a second language instruction. This approach is used only until the child speaks enough English, when the child is transferred to monolingual English-only medium classrooms. In cases when Latino parents have acquired enough power, they are able to establish *maintenance* bilingual education programs, where both languages are eventually used throughout the child's primary education. But those programs were, and continue to be, rare.

Whereas immersion bilingual education, maintenance bilingual education, and *prestigious* bilingual education correspond to a model of additive bilingualism, transitional bilingual education follows a subtractive bilingual model. This distinction also has repercussions on the language arrangement, that is, the ways in which languages are used in instruction,[11] and the language practices allowed in instruction. Whereas immersion bilingual education, maintenance bilingual education, and prestigious bilingual education try to keep the two languages strictly compartmentalized, the transitional bilingual education type allows code-switching in the classroom. The argument is made that bilingual education programs that follow an additive model of bilingualism have to protect a functional compartmentalization, reflecting a diglossic[12] relationship between the two languages (Fishman 1977). In this view, language separation is good and language education, even if bilingual, needs to have protected monolingual spaces.[13] On the other hand, in transitional bilingual education programs teachers are encouraged to code-switch, thus violating the diglossic compartmentalization between the two languages, and eventually favoring the majority language (Garcia 1993). For years, and with few exceptions (Jacobson 1981; Jacobson and Faltis 1990), the bilingual education profession argued that language separation was always good, and that code-switching, which mirrored the ways in which bilinguals used language in communities, was bad (see, for example, González and Maez, 1980). Table 8.1 displays the relationship between model of bilingualism, type of bilingual education, and instructional bilingual arrangement.

**Table 8.1.** Bilingualism, Bilingual education, and Bilingual arrangement

| Model of Bilingualism | Type of Bilingual Education | Bilingual Arrangement |
|---|---|---|
| Additive Bilingualism<br>L1+L2 = L1+ L2 | Prestigious bilingual education<br>Immersion bilingual education<br>Maintenance bilingual education | Complete language separation |
| Subtractive Bilingualism<br>L1+L2-L1 = L2 | Transitional bilingual education | Code-switching |

## Bilingual Education and Translanguaging

By the end of the twentieth century, the types of bilingual education that had been developed in the west proved to be insufficient for the type of complex bilingualism that globalization brought to the forefront. Besides making more visible than ever the complex multilingualism of Africa and Asia, and of regional minorities everywhere, globalization brought increasing linguistic complexity with the movements of people, information, services, and goods, that accompanied it.

India may serve as an example of the heteroglossia of many Asian and African contexts. Pattanayak (2003: 129) gives this example:

> One of my students, an Oriya boy, married to a Tamil, speaking English at home, lives in Calcutta in Bengali surroundings, where the children are brought up by a Hindustani ayah and a Nepali Gurkha security man.

In India, two languages are simply not enough. Furthermore, there is fuzziness of language boundaries and fluidity in language identity (Khubchandani 1983, 2001). Mohanty (2006) has described the very different multilingual nature of India—widespread bilingualism at the grassroots level; maintenance norms supported by the non-competing roles of languages and their complementarities in the lives of people; the multiplicity of linguistic identities; and bilingualism as a positive force. Increasingly, this linguistic complexity characterizes the rest of the world, as translanguaging becomes the most important communicative tool in an increasingly multilingual world.

Little by little, bilingual education programs have grown and expanded, to include this increasing heterogeneity. Grounded in the possibility of reversing the language shift of groups that had been politically oppressed, and building on the successes of Canadian immersion programs, *revitalization immersion* bilingual education programs have been developed. This type of bilingual education program has been especially useful for Indigenous peoples that have suffered the most language loss. Examples are the Kura Kaupapa Māori and the Kula Kaiapuni Hawai'i programs. These programs clearly respond to a recursive model of bilingualism, respecting an expansive range of bilingual practices.

Ethnolinguistic groups who through considerable agency and effort have resisted efforts to stamp out their languages do not always need immersion revitalization bilingual education programs. Based on the success of prestigious bilingual education programs, they establish *developmental* bilingual education programs for the purposes of expanding their languages. Often they are groups that have been given regional recognition, and thus some limited power. Because they often include children who come from families with different home language practices, there is also an expansive range of bilingual practices in these classrooms.

Even in the US and Europe, the bilingual education programs of the past prove insufficient today. Especially in the United States, what are called *two-way dual language* bilingual education programs have come into being, including children with different linguistic profiles. And in Europe, *Content and Language Integrated Learning (CLIL)* programs, where all children are taught an academic subject through another language, are being promoted as a way to substitute for traditional core foreign language instruction. In reality, both two-way dual language bilingual education programs and CLIL programs remain rare.

But these more complex bilingual education types that respond to a broader range of bilingual practices are quite distinct from the heteroglossia evident in multilingual states such as India and the Philippines. In these more multilingual contexts, bilingual education of the more traditional kind would be insufficient. *Multilingual* education programs are increasingly used to recognize the bilingual and multilingual practices of children, as they develop multiple language practices and spread them throughout an entire population. Often these multiple multilingual programs weave languages in and out of the curriculum, dropping them, expanding them, and using them for one function or the other, depending on particular instructional circumstances.

What is common among all these newer types of bilingual education is precisely the breadth of the linguistic range in the classroom, and the increased tolerance, at the classroom-level, towards multiple languaging practices. In these classrooms, practices of languaging bilingually are often accepted as the norm, as both students and teachers capitalize on this translanguaging. These classrooms have the potential to expand on the multiple discursive practices that the children bring, and consider translanguaging an important educational practice—to construct understandings, to make sense of the world and of the academic material, to mediate with others, to acquire other ways of languaging.

Seen from a bilingual and heteroglossic angle, and not a monolingual and monoglossic one, the term *code-switching* loses meaning, as students and teachers accept and adopt translanguaging practices that enable them to function effectively, and educate and become educated. The traditional concept of diglossia *could* make way, in these classrooms, to a *transglossia* where bilingual practices are neither strictly compartmentalized nor are they random, but sense-making. Transglossia could offer flexible spaces for language practices that are associated with making meaning and improving communication among participants who are different, and yet participate more equally. Translanguaging is then a responsible communicative practice that offers communicative and educational possibilities to all. Nevertheless, it is important to understand that translanguaging is nurtured within instructional spaces that most often respond to separate language arrangements. For example, dual language classrooms separate languages strictly for instruction, although the mixing of children with different linguistic profiles coupled with a progressive child-centered education that builds on collaborative grouping facilitates the translanguaging. The embeddedness of translanguaging within a diglossic language separation arrangement is often precisely what is responsible for the transglossia (García 2006, 2009b)

**Table 8.2** Displays the relationship between model of bilingualism, type of bilingual education and bilingual instructional arrangement.

| Model of Bilingualism | Type of Bilingual Education | Bilingual Arrangement |
|---|---|---|
| Recursive bilingualism 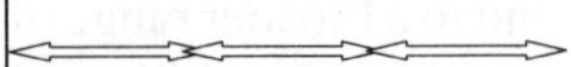 | Immersion revitalization bilingual education | Translanguaging within language separation arrangement |
| Dynamic bilingualism  | Developmental bilingual education<br>Two-way or Dual language bilingual education<br>CLIL bilingual education<br>Multiple multilingual education | Translanguaging within language separation arrangement |

## Multiple multilingual education and translanguaging

This section focuses on the last type of bilingual education considered in the section above—multiple multilingual education—increasingly the type of education that we need to develop for all children. This multilingual education must be much more than simply bilingual education in more than two languages. I call it *multiple multilingual education* because I want to emphasize its multiplicity. I am referring here not only to the use of more than two autonomous separate languages in instruction, but to the intertwining of language practices, to the translanguaging that must be the *modus operandi* of schools that tend to heteroglossic ethnolinguistic groups whose language practices are multiple. These multiple multilingual programs mix and blend types of bilingual education programs as they see fit, and develop standard academic language use in one or more languages. To do so, however, they increasingly build on the children's heteroglossic language practices—a product of lived multilingual experience.

## The potential of multiple multilingual education

One of the problems of establishing bilingual education programs for highly linguistically diverse populations is precisely its reliance on two or more autonomous language systems. But as Mühlhäusler (2000: 38) has said, the 'notion of "a language" makes little sense in most traditional societies where people engage in multiple discursive practices among themselves.' Speaking of the Pacific region, Mühlhäusler (1996:7) says: '[t]he notion of "a language" is one whose applicability to the Pacific region, and in fact most situations outside those found within modern European type nation-states, is extremely limited'. Romaine (1994: 12) concurs with Mühlhäusler when describing the complex language use in Papua New Guinea:

> [T]he very concept of discrete languages is probably a European cultural artifact fostered by procedures such as literacy and standardization. Any attempt to count distinct languages will be an artifact of classificatory procedures rather than a reflection of communicative practices.

As pointed out before, India's multilingualism is complex, and so is that of the Philippines. Understanding that traditional bilingual education programs would be insufficient in these contexts, both India and the Philippines have tried to establish multilingual education policies and programs (For a review of the multilingual education programs in India, see Jhingran 2009, Mohanty et al. 2009, Panda and Mohanty, 2009, all this volume). And yet, although there are thirty-three languages used in education in India, including English, and there are forty-one languages available for study in school (NCERT 1999), education in India, as Mohanty (2006: 279) says, is not really bilingual: '[E]ducation in India is only superficially multilingual, and it remains monolingual at an underlying level. The official three-languages formula is more abused and less used.'

In the Philippines the Indigenous languages were restored as auxiliary teaching languages in the initial grades of schools in 1987. A trilingual system is now used in the early grades, with the vernaculars, Filipino and English supposedly used up to grade three, at which point the use of the auxiliary languages ceases. During this transitional stage a *bimedial system* of instruction is supposed to be used. The instructor gives the gist of the lesson in the language prescribed—Filipino or English—and then explains to students in the local vernacular (Gonzalez 1998).[14] This policy officially moves away from the total separation of languages in instruction, although it does not go far enough in recognizing the translanguaging of the students, as they make sense of their multilingual learning environment.

Because of the resistance to the expansion of truly multiple multilingual programs, multilingual education in India and the Philippines has proven to be insufficient for the equitable education of all children. Despite the multilingual character of some programs in both India and the Philippines, there is little *official* recognition of the fuzziness of the language practices in this population, and of the language hybridity that includes Indigenous languages, regional languages and official languages. Thus, the potential of translanguaging within these multilingual educational context is not explored.

Other states that have faced the multilingualism of their population have developed multiple multilingual education programs. It is the policy in Luxembourg where children start out being schooled in Luxemburgish, with German added for literacy purposes in the first year, French introduced after year 3, and French then becoming the main medium of education in secondary schools (Beardsmore and Lebrun 1991). Despite the fact that these programs succeed better than others in accessing the children's and the community's languages to teach and learn, there is a limitation, at least in curricular design. These programs are conceived of as sequential programs, where one language is introduced after the other, without serious consideration of how to build from the simultaneous dynamic bilingual practices that children already possess—from the translanguaging that takes place in the community. It is then the official recognition of translanguaging that is missing from many of these multiple multilingual education programs, the topic of our next section.

## The Potential of Translanguaging in Education

The main advantage of building on translanguaging to educate all children bilingually has to do with its potential as the building block of all bilingualism. It is impossible to live in bilingual communities and communicate among multilinguals without translanguaging. In fact, it is translanguaging itself that enables us to make sense of the multilingual worlds we live in. It enables us to understand our multilingual linguistic landscape (Shohamy 2006) and to understand the different signs—visual, audio, physical and spatial, written and linguistic—that surround us. One cannot make sense of communication in the twenty-first century without putting together all the different signs and modes that we come into contact with. Signs that have been assigned to one language or the other are just that—and being linguistically competent for the twenty-first century requires that we access them all, mostly simultaneously, but sometimes also sequentially.

Those of us who have worked in the education of linguistic minorities have experienced the detrimental effects, for both teachers and students, of strict language policies that separate minority and majority languages. In the case of minority languages that are being revitalized or that are stigmatized, there is great linguistic insecurity among the teachers who are often reacquiring the language themselves. This linguistic insecurity then may sometimes lead to the use of language that may be 'standard,' but that is impoverished in meaning, in metaphors, in poetry, and that is restricted in form.

Language minority students also feel extreme linguistic uncertainty in the languages they speak at home, often leading to silence in classrooms. This lack of confidence and increased anxiety then may lead to little investment on the part of students in learning and owning the minority language (Norton 2000). In fact, the insistence on language separation for language minority students may accelerate distance from the minoritized language and eventual language shift to the dominant language.

In cases of language revitalization, the minority language is often used in education in ways that have little to do with the language use in the minority community. After years of contact between Quechua and Spanish, for example, Quechua speakers have adopted five vowels, but Quechua educators insist on using only three vowels, a reflection of traditional classical Quechua that has little to do with today's Quechua use in Indigenous communities. Thus the insistence on using only an academic standard may promote more linguistic insecurity and linguistic failure than if the Quechua had been left behind in the community and kept away from school (see Pérez 2009, this volume, Luykx 2000).

If for the sake of people's self-esteem and people's educational and social opportunities, the ways of languaging of minority communities cannot be left behind and must be included in the educational system, then we must accept that building on the community's linguistic and cultural strength includes ways of languaging that are in themselves bilingual to begin with. This translanguaging has little to do with monolingual standards as have been conceived by many linguists and educators (Makoni and Pennycook 2007).

Even when minority languages are not in need of revitalization, and community monolingual spaces exist, there is much value in translanguaging as a pedagogical practice. In classrooms all over the world, language minority children are often taught in a language they do not understand—usually a colonial language that has now increased in importance because of globalization. Educating children in a language they do not understand usually leads to educational failure. If the majority language space does not include the children's languaging, and if the teacher does not maximize communication using the children's language practices, failure in communication and education is sure to occur.

Pedagogical code-switching, which for me is an instance of translanguaging, is becoming vindicated, as education scholars call for their responsible, and not random, use (Van der Walt, Mabule and De Beer 2001). Gajo (2007) and Serra (2007) have shown how its use enhances cognitive skills for non-language subjects like mathematics or history. Merrit, Cleghorn, Abagi and Bunyi (1992) have found that teachers in Kenya use it to focus or regain students' attention and to clarify or reinforce lesson material. Arthur (1996) in the case of Botswana, Bloom (2008) in the case of Chinese bilingual teachers in New York, and Lin (1996) in the case of Hong Kong, have observed that translanguaging is a pedagogical scaffolding technique in bilingual classrooms, making the additional language more comprehensible. As Martin-Jones and Saxena (1996) have established, it is not necessarily code-switching that is bad, but rather how language is used and by whom that shapes the students' perceived value of the two languages in a bilingual classroom. Translanguaging is also a way to develop students' metalinguistic understandings and metacognitive awareness, important for bilingually educated individuals in the twenty-first century (see Bialystok 2001, Mohanty 1994).

Pedagogical practices for all children, but especially for language minority children, must rest on two important principles—social justice and social practice (García 2009b). Neither of these two principles can be observed if the children's home language practices are not included in education.

The *social justice* principle values the strength of bilingual students and communities, and builds on their language practices. It enables the creation of learning contexts which are not threatening to the students' identities but that builds multiplicities of language uses and linguistic identities, while maintaining academic rigor and upholding high expectations. Another important element of this principle has to do with advocating for the linguistic human rights of students (Skutnabb-Kangas 2000) and for assessment that includes the languaging of bilingual students.

The *social practice* principle places learning as a result of collaborative social practices in which students try out ideas and actions (Lave and Wenger 1991), and thus socially construct their learning (Vygotsky 1978). Learning is seen as occurring through doing (Dewey 1897). And translanguaging among students, especially in linguistically heterogeneous collaborative groups, becomes the way in which students try out their ideas and actions and thus, learn and develop literacy practices. In linguistically integrated group work, students *appropriate* the use of language, and although teachers may carefully plan when and how languages are to be used, children themselves use their entire linguistic repertoires flexibly. Often this language use appropriation by students is done *surreptitiously*. For example, many two-way bilingual education classrooms in the United States carefully compartmentalize languages and a have a clear policy of language separation. But when children with different linguistic profiles are involved in group work, children violate the language use norms of the classroom, using languages flexibly to support their understandings and building conceptual and linguistic knowledge. Language flexibility is built in, as the children appropriate both the content and the language, both oracy and literacy (García 2006).

In classrooms, children also use translanguaging to mediate understandings, to co-construct meaning, and to include others. And it is perhaps this translanguaging, more than any other language arrangement that is responsible for children's bilingual acquisition and for their learning. Examples from United States bilingual education classrooms with which I am deeply familiar follow.

## Translanguaging in US bilingual classrooms

In a fifth grade two-way dual language education class, the teacher often lectures in Spanish, but students take notes in English. Sometimes students read in one language and write in another. And students always refer to material in one language or the other in order to compose their own oral or written texts. The difference between translanguaging as language practices and in the way used by Cen Williams to refer to a pedagogical approach is that here translanguaging occurs naturally, as students appropriate the language use in the classrooms.

In this same fifth grade class, Social Studies is taught in Spanish. Although the New York State Social Studies test is offered in both English and Spanish, all students, except for one of the students in this class who has recently arrived from a Spanish-speaking country, choose to answer the exam questions in English.[15] Thus, for the extensive review that takes place for a month, there is much translanguaging. The readings that have been done during the entire class time, and the accompanying notes drafted by the students, are written in Spanish. During the review sessions, the discussion is mostly in English, since the teacher follows English language tests. But the students look up their notes written in Spanish, and consult their Spanish language textbooks, as they translanguage orally to get to the meaning. All these understandings are then rendered into academic English, for the students understand that the assessment only values answers in a monolingual standard.

In a fourth grade bilingual class, a recently arrived Spanish-speaking girl writes a sophisticated Spanish essay in September. But during the ESL class, she can only copy simple English language sentences which she illustrates in child-like ways —'I see a teacher', 'I see a student,' 'I see a clock'. But when the teacher gives her the option to write in any language she wants, the student immediately tries to incorporate new English words and phrases into her Spanish essays. Translanguaging as she writes her essays serves as the springboard that allows her, five months later, to write an essay entirely in fluent English.

The two kindergarteners in the example that follows are in a side-by-side dual language program. They are having snack in an integrated period which happens to meet in the English classroom. A Spanish-speaking boy, Adolfo, whose bilingualism is at the very beginning stages, is snacking besides Gabriela, a Spanish-speaking girl whose bilingualism is more advanced, although still emerging.

| | |
|---|---|
| Adolfo: | [Looking out the window and talking to himself] |
| | *Está lloviendo mucho*. 'It is raining a lot.' |
| | Look [telling the others]. It's washing. There's washing *afuera* 'outside.' |
| Gabriela: | *Está lloviendo?* [She asks him] |
| | [Turning to me] He says raining. He speaks Spanish, only Spanish |
| | [Turning to boy] Adolfo, raining. |
| Adolfo: | Raining. (10/19/2007) |

Although Adolfo had no word for 'raining,' and used 'washing' to communicate, the translanguaging that occurred allowed a meaningful interaction between Adolfo, Gabriela, and myself, and enabled Adolfo to acquire the lexical item that he needed without any intervention from the teacher. Thus, translanguaging in the classroom enables language acquisition without having to wait for the teacher to assume a direct teaching role.

On another day, in the same kindergarten class, I observe the following interaction between a bilingual Latino boy (Marco) with another Latino boy who has very limited English (Angel) during the unstructured 'work choice' in the English language classroom. The pair has chosen to draw, something in which Angel excels. The fully bilingual boy, Marco, therefore, becomes Angel's 'helper'. Marco would have preferred to speak in English. However, because of Angel's dominance both in Spanish and in drawing, Spanish is the language of choice. And yet, it is translanguaging that helps them co-construct the meaning in this activity and to share each other's skills—Angel his drawing ability, but also his knowledge of Spanish by offering the word 'cola'; Marco his English ability to translate the teacher's request for writing the name, and his bilingual ability to use one and the other language, but also his more advanced writing ability, by showing Angel how to write his name.

| | |
|---|---|
| Marco: | *¿Quieres deste así?*<br>'Do you want this this way?' |
| Angel: | OK |
| Marco: | *Cortando algo.... Pa pegar... Ahí.*<br>'Cutting something... To glue... There!'<br>And now we're going to put a line.<br>*Quieres así éste, pero ¿mucho?*<br>'Do you want this one this way, but, a lot? |
| Teacher: | Angel, are you writing your name? |
| Marco: | *Tu nombre. Así Angel*....[Writes Angel's name across the paper] *Mira.*<br>'Your name. This way Angel...., look....' |
| Angel: | Ohhhhh |
| Marco: | *Quieres más?*<br>[Asks me, How do you say in Spanish [pointing to the bottle of glue? Before I can answer, Angel replies] |
| Angel: | Cola |
| Marco: | Angel, mira. Now we got to just color. (9/23/2007) |

That translanguaging is important for children to develop bilingualism is especially evident when one listens closely to children talking to themselves, a practice that is prevalent among kindergarteners. The translanguaging practices that are constructed always bring the other language to the forefront, even when that language is not being activated by the instruction. In the next example, the teacher, has taken the ESL children outside and is showing them the trees and teaching them how to compare them. Adriana is constructing language through translanguaging:

Teacher: This tree is bigger. That tree is smaller.

Adriana: [Tries out under her breath]. This tree is *grander*. (9/23/2007)

In this two-way bilingual kindergarten, children with different linguistic profiles often work, learn and play together. Playtime becomes a translanguaging negotiation event and the only way in which activities can continue across the different languages. In the example that follows, there is an interaction between Alice who is English-speaking, Bruno who is Spanish-speaking, and Carolina who is bilingual:

Alice: Are you done? [As she tries to take over the block area from Bruno and Carolina who have been speaking in Spanish]

Bruno: Yes, I done. [As he starts to walk away]

Carolina: [To Alice] Do you want to play with us? [They start playing, translanguaging] (10/17/2007)

Translanguaging, a practice that teachers in their quest for accepting only the standard academic language often shun, is an important practice, pedagogically to teach, but also cognitively to learn.

The examples above have made clear that bilingual and multilingual education must go beyond just using multiple languages in instruction. Bilingual and multilingual education must be multiple itself, drawing also on students' and teachers' translanguaging practices as they write, read, and speak.

## Conclusion

Multiple multilingual education must not only teach (and teach well) two or three standard academic languages. But multiple MLE must also build on the translanguaging practices of the classroom actors—both students and teachers. In so doing, children will develop the linguistic security and identity investment that they need to learn and be successful. The task for multilingual education in the twenty-first century will not only be to add more languages, but to recognize the multiple language practices that heterogeneous populations increasingly bring and which integrated schooling, more than any other context, has the potential to liberate.

Our discussions of multilingual education have often been clouded by conceptualizations derived from ways of thinking about bilingual education from a Western monoglossic point of view. But if multilingualism in most of the world today is characterized by its widespread nature, along with the fuzziness of language boundaries and fluidity and multiplicity in language practices and language identities, then multilingual education must develop ways of supporting not only multiple languages and literacies, but also interrelated functional complementarity of language practices.

The development of these more heteroglossic multiple multilingual education programs still has a long way to go officially, even in contexts that are highly multilingual and heteroglossic. In other words, the state that controls educational systems rarely supports these practices. Academic discourse continues to be monoglossic, even in multilingual settings. Yet those of us who carefully observe language practices within good classrooms in multilingual programs rarely see instruction that does not rely on the translanguaging of students and teachers, as they make sense of content. The challenge for educators in the twenty-first century will be to acknowledge that monolingual, and even monoglossic bilingual practices, are not sufficient. And that in an increasingly heterogeneous world, where children in school are of all kinds and bring different language practices, the only way to build equitable educational systems is to develop multiple multilingual programs that acknowledge translanguaging as a resource for engaging cognitively and socially, as they also develop standard ways of communicating in dominant languages.

## Notes

1 I want to thank the editors of this volume for their insightful comments on an earlier draft of this paper.

2 I use the term bilingual to encompass what others refer to as multilingual. Bilingual in this paper refers to all language practices that include features beyond those described by linguists and educators as forming a single autonomous language.

3 I use 'languaging' and 'to language' to refer to the way people use language, their discursive practices, and not to the conception of a 'language' as constructed by states, missionaries and linguists. I am using 'to language' as a verb. See Makoni and Pennycook, 2006.

4 I borrow the term 'translanguaging' from Cen Williams who coined it to refer to a specific bilingual pedagogy. To learn more about Williams' work, see Baker (2001).

5 By language minority children I am referring to Indigenous/tribal children (even if in principle they are not minorities), autochthonous ('national' minorities), and (im)migrant minorities.

6 Gramsci was a founding member of the Italian Communist party and was imprisoned by Mussolini's Fascist regime.

7 Monoglossic ideologies treat languages as bounded autonomous systems without regard to the actual language practices of speakers. On the other hand, heteroglossic ideologies respect multiple language practices in interrelationships. I base this use on Bakhtin's (1981) use of *heteroglossic* as multiple voices. For more on this difference, see del Valle (2000).

8 Of course there is a lot of work on bilingualism that has been done in other places and in other languages. Nevertheless, the most popular work stems from a North American tradition.

9 The Council of Europe groups 48 countries at its seat in Strasbourg, France.

10 I am aware that there was much bilingual education in other places beyond North America much earlier.

11 Language arrangement refers to explicit policies mandated by school officials for how teachers ought to use the two languages in classrooms.

12 Diglossia is the relationship between a H(igh) variety of one language or a language for certain prestigious functions, and a L(ow) variety or a language in ordinary functions.

Whereas Ferguson popularized the concept and referred to only varieties of languages, Fishman extended it to include different languages.

13 In discussing English language teaching (ELT), Phillipson (1992: 185) identifies as the first key tenet of the ELT profession the principle that English is best taught monolingually.

14 I am not implying here that there is any serious commitment to the marginalised languages.

15 In practice, the children are allowed to use both language exams side-by-side, although they can only answer questions in one or the other.

# 9

# Privileging Indigenous Knowledges Empowering MLE in Nepal

*David A. Hough, Ram Bahadur Thapa Magar and Amrit Yonjan-Tamang*

What kind of education should be prescribed for the tribal population of our country? By making them run after us, we shall perhaps make them bankrupt, the way we lost ourselves following the English, what is your view on this?

(Chittaranjan Das 2007: 117).

Science is an expression of human creativity, both individual and collective. Since creativity has diverse expressions, I see science as a pluralistic enterprise that refers to different 'ways of knowing'. For me, it is not restricted to modern Western science, but includes the knowledge systems of diverse cultures in different periods of history

(Vandana Shiva 1997: 8)

Indigenous cultures of Nepal have democratic practices in them. Some of these practices are sidelined and others are at the verge of extinction.

(Prabha Devi Kaini 2007:3)

## A Sociohistorical Sketch of the Languages and Ethnic Groups of Nepal

This paper describes the underlying vision and theoretical constructs which inform a bottom-up community-based approach to multilingual education (MLE) in Nepal. The programme, which both empowers and is empowered by indigenous knowledge systems, began in January of 2007, and involves six pilot language communities. It is a joint effort on the part of the Ministry of Foreign Affairs (MoFA) of Finland and the Ministry of Education and Sports (MOES) of Nepal. Although the programme is funded top-down by the governments of Nepal and Finland, it varies from many other educational sector projects in that it takes a bottom-up community-based approach to design and implementation, wherein indigenous knowledge systems, beliefs, values and practices inform both content and methodology. Here, local indigenous and minority communities are empowered to take control of both the content and method of their learning and teaching, and to have voice in framing and further modifying language planning and policy at the national level.

Although the exact number of languages spoken in Nepal is unknown, the 2001 census lists 92, Ethnologue (2005) lists 126 and the Indigenous Linguistic Society of Nepal (ILSON) lists 143 (Yonjan-Tamang 2006). When dialects/different speech communities are added in, the number may come to well over 200. These can be divided into four distinct language families and one isolate: Tibeto-Burman with more than 120 languages (the largest group), Indo-European with at least sixteen (including Nepali, the dominating language), Austro-Asiatic with three, Dravidian with two, and finally the Kusunda language, an isolate of unknown origin. According to 2001 census figures, the total number on non-Nepali speakers in the country stands at 50% of the population of 23 million.

Indigenous and non-Nepali speaking minorities in Nepal have suffered nearly 500 years of discrimination. Beginning in 1559, Drabya Shah dismissed the Magar State in Ghorka. For 240 years from the middle of the eighteenth century, Nepal had an official policy of one language, one culture and one religion (Hindu). During this period, the official slogan was 'One king, one country, one language, one culture.' In addition, during the 104 years of Rana family rule (1846-1951), all indigenous languages and cultures were banned.

This legacy of discrimination has had—and continues to have – a devastating impact on indigenous and minority children when carried over into the school system, and has been well documented (see Awasthi 2004). Here, it will be helpful to consider what happens at the psychological level to people when their mother tongue is ***not*** taught in schools. These are some of the results as abstracted from interviews, discussions, academic papers, published reports and indigenous scholarship worldwide:

1. Lack of appreciation for indigenous culture, values and languages;
2. Feelings of inferiority and humiliation when exposed to the dominating culture;
3. Denial of one's culture and language;
4. Self-hate which can be either externalised or internalised (e.g., domestic violence or suicide);
5. Colonisation of the mind (learning to perceive oneself and the world through Western categories); [1]
6. Retarded cognitive development (based on foreign benchmark educational standards);
7. Increased dropout, repetition and failure rate at the early grades.

Problems caused by the devaluing of one's mother tongue are endemic to indigenous communities worldwide. They are not voluntary but are brought about by the domination of one language over another. Skutnabb-Kangas (1999) writes, '…if people are forced to shift their languages in order to gain economic benefits of the kind which are in fact bare necessities for basic survival, this is a violation of not only their economic human rights but also their linguistic human rights.' As noted above, the results in terms of human psychology range from feelings of inferiority, humiliation and self-hate to outright denial of one's culture and heritage. Here, it could be argued that denying children the right to learn in their mother tongue is a form of linguistic genocide (see Dunbar and Skutnabb-Kangas 2008 UNPFII expert paper for a thorough discussion of this issue).

In 1990 indigenous peoples in Nepal began organising themselves in mass to demand radical change. They called for the creation of a democracy which would protect their languages and cultures. They also began to legally register their own organisations[2] as a step toward the realisation of linguistic and cultural human rights. In 1991, NEFIN (Nepal Federation of Indigenous Nationalities) was founded as an umbrella organisation to assist in the struggle. In 1995, NFDIN (the National Foundation for the Development of Indigenous Languages) was established as a government body to assist in addressing indigenous issues. Both organisations have been extremely active in MLE. They are both on the steering committee of the MLE Programme (see below; see also Yonjan-Tamang, Hough and Nurmela, 2009, this volume), and both actively participate in and monitor the MLE project in the field and at regional and national workshops.

The indigenous people's democratic struggles which started in 1990 and 1991 reached a high point in 2006 with the demand that the monarchy be abolished and that the nation be restructured as a secular republic based on federalism. This would include constitutional rights to use at least some indigenous languages as administrative languages within the federalist system. During this period, the indigenous peoples also demanded proportionate representation in the constituent assembly which was finally elected to office in April 2008.

As an umbrella organisation NEFIN has fought for the rights of indigenous peoples since its inception in 1991. Its policy has been to rely on the strengths, talents and power of indigenous peoples themselves, rather than employing outsiders to mediate for them, or otherwise to 'represent' their interests. All of NEFIN's activities are rights-based rather than welfare-based. It believes that the latter only serves to create or exacerbate colonising dependencies. This also applies to the right of indigenous peoples to use their own languages in schools and to develop their own teaching materials using their own culturally appropriate methods of teaching and learning. This is in keeping with the spirit and intent of the *United Nations Declaration on the Rights of Indigenous Peoples* (see http://www2.ohchrorg/english/issues/indigenous/declaration.htm). Although non-binding, both Nepal and Finland voted in favour of the declaration. Some important provisions of the declaration regarding indigenous knowledge systems in the context of language, culture and education are as follows:

> *Article 13, Paragraph 1*: Indigenous peoples have the right to revitalize, use, develop and transmit for future generations their histories, languages, oral traditions, philosophies, writing systems and literatures, and to designate and retain their own names for communities, places and persons.
>
> *Article 14, Paragraph 1*: Indigenous peoples have the right to establish and control their educational systems and institutions providing education in their own languages, in a manner appropriate to their cultural methods of teaching and learning.

These two paragraphs call for the right of self-determination in indigenous education. Paragraph 13 gives indigenous peoples the right to control the content of their teaching, while Paragraph 14 states that the teaching of this content should be based on methods of teaching and learning which are appropriate to indigenous peoples.

Given the immense size of the indigenous and minority non-Nepali speaking population, it is imperative that the government address these educational needs. In particular, it is absolutely vital for high level administrators and policy makers in Nepal to understand how languages come to be threatened and as a result how people are marginalised. Here, de Varennes (2004) notes that 'A State's decision to adopt an exclusive language as medium of instruction virtually guarantees that children with limited or no proficiency in the chosen language, usually minorities —will endure serious disadvantages and fall behind as they either struggle to keep up or simply withdraw into a world of their own.' Likewise, Mohanty and Panda (2007) report on a similar situation in India:

> These languages are pushed out of major domains of power and development such as official, legal and other formal use, education, trade and commerce. This, in effect creates shift pressures from the dominant contact languages threatening their survival. In face of such threats, the speakers of these languages adopt what has been characterized as 'anti-predatory strategies' (Mohanty 2004, 2006) to ensure survival by a passive withdrawal into domains of lesser power and visibility. In effect language shift does not occur; but there is considerable domain shrinkage with languages barely maintained mostly in the domains of home and in-group communication. (p. 3).

## A BOTTOM-UP APPROACH

A key aspect of the approach used by the MLE programme is that it is bottom-up. The term 'bottom-up' has a variety of meanings and applications, which are summarised below. The first involves the issue of language domination. In Nepal, the major dominating languages are killing the less dominating ones in a top-down manner. English is killing Hindi, which is killing Nepali, which is killing Nepal's major indigenous languages, which in turn are killing local indigenous languages. The question is where to intervene. If programmes are developed for the major indigenous languages only, the result will be to continue the process of killing smaller languages since regional languages will dominate (and eventually kill) local ones. To avoid this continuing linguistic genocide, it is necessary that all indigenous languages (including what some would call dialects) must have equal status and access to mother tongue medium of instruction.

Another important aspect of the bottom-up approach comes from the Education for All (EFA)[3] goal of decentralised education as a tool in empowering local communities to take control of their own learning needs, a goal which is also supported by MOES, the Nepalese Ministry of Education and Sports.

Empowering a community means working with its knowledge base to build MLE programmes. Those with the greatest knowledge of the language and culture within the community rarely have teaching credentials. Often while they may be 'illiterate' in terms of western educational benchmarks, they at the same time possess a treasure of oral knowledge. Shiva (1997), for example, argues that in many areas of science, indigenous knowledge systems are superior to Western scientific models:

> Indigenous knowledge systems are by and large ecological, while the dominant model of scientific knowledge, characterized by reductionism and fragmentation, is not equipped to take the complexity of interrelationships in nature fully into account. This inadequacy becomes most significant in the domain of life sciences, which deal with living organisms. (8)

Further support for this argument comes from numerous indigenous scholars worldwide (see among others, Alfred, 1999; Deloria, 2002, 2003; Deloria and Wildcat, 2001; Fixico, 2003; Hemara, 2000; Mihesuah, 2004; Smith, 1999; Warrior, 2002). Vine Deloria, Jr., leading North American indigenous scholar, for example, argues that the whole process of Western science is based on finding common denominators that can describe large amounts of data in the most general terms, while rejecting anything that refuses easy classification as 'anomalous'. Indigenous knowledge systems, on the other hand, are holistic, experiential and based on a deep historical knowledge of place (Deloria 2001). Tove Skutnabb-Kangas (in personal correspondence 2007) reports at length on the value of traditional knowledge:

> At the Johannesburg World Summit on Sustainable Development (August – September 2002) there seemed to be a breakthrough in the sense that 'orthodox' western scientists now also acknowledge the relationship between traditional indigenous knowledge and science in a way which suggests that science has learned and should learn from traditional knowledge; they should be equal partners.

This knowledge is by no way static either, as Four Directions Council in Canada (1996, in Posey 1999: 4) describes:

> What is 'traditional' about traditional knowledge is not its antiquity, but the way it is acquired and used. In other words, the social process of learning and sharing knowledge, which is unique to each indigenous culture, lies at the very heart of its 'traditionality'. Much of this knowledge is actually quite new, but it has a social meaning, and legal character, entirely unlike the knowledge indigenous people acquire from settlers and industrialized societies.

All of this suggests that Western educational standards and practices—including humanistic and communicative approaches to language teaching and classroom management—may require critical re-examination and radical restructuring if not a process of dialectical friction and creative replacement by indigenous ways of knowing. Deloria (2001) offers the following perspective on this:

> The answers that we will receive, when we ask elders and when we read recorded accounts of beliefs and practices, will often seem strange and many times irreconcilable with our scientific knowledge. But we must not use the scientific method to determine the truth or falsity of our comparison. We must learn to place the difference within the tribal context and there reconcile conflicting points of view. As Indians we know some things because we have the cumulative testimony of our people. We *think* we know other things because we are taught in school that they are true. The proper transition in Indian education should be the *creative tension* [emphasis added] that occurs when we compare and reconcile these two perspectives. (86)

Re-phrased, it suggests that there may be a vast untapped resource in the local communities that can be utilised in an MLE context—both in terms of content of mother tongue medium of instruction, and in terms of methodology. Many qualified teachers in village schools lack fluency in the local language and knowledge about the culture. Currently all teacher training is conducted in Nepali and teachers are not encouraged to use local languages as a medium of instruction (ProDoc 2006: 12). This kind of universal teacher training and education programmes not only fail to recognise local knowledge that is lost, they also fail to recognise the valuable human resources in the community. The International Council for Science (ICSU 2002) reports:

> Universal education programs provide important tools for human development, but they may also compromise the transmission of indigenous language and knowledge. Inadvertently, they may contribute to the erosion of cultural diversity, a loss of social cohesion and the alienation and disorientation of youth. ... In short, when indigenous children are taught in science class that the natural world is ordered as scientists believe it functions, then the validity and authority of their parents' and grandparents' knowledge is denied. While their parents may possess an extensive and sophisticated understanding of the local environment, classroom instruction implicitly informs that science is the ultimate authority for interpreting 'reality' and by extension local indigenous knowledge is second rate and obsolete. Actions are urgently needed to enhance the intergenerational transmission of local and indigenous knowledge.

There is, however, a way to turn all of this around. The objective situation in most schools attended by speakers of indigenous and minority languages in Nepal is that the majority of teachers do not speak the local language, while the students do not speak Nepali—and therefore do not understand their teachers. This has been presented as a problem to be solved, and can be represented by the two circles (one for the students and the other for the teachers). By adding a third intersecting circle, representing the community, the problem is easily solved. For example, most communities have local speakers of the language who possess SCLs (school leaving certificates). Many also possess primary school teacher certification. These individuals, along with local indigenous knowledge (or IK) holders[4] can be brought together to create MLE learning materials and strategies appropriate to their needs. In many schools, this may take the form of multigrade, intergenerational programmes where these three groups interact to teach each other.

Thus, an expert on herbal medicines, a master carver or storyteller might be called on to share their knowledge in the local language with students and teachers (see Hough 2003, 2005). These stories can serve as a vehicle for MLE instruction where teachers not fluent in the language can learn at the same time that they are facilitating. Later, students and teachers, including those fluent in the language, can work together to transcribe these stories. Students may also take these materials home to share with family and friends. They may even take on the role of teacher and impart literacy skills based on these stories and written materials to their elders. Exactly how students, teachers, parents and community members work together is up to each community. In some cases it may involve children drawing pictures and collecting stories from elders with parents and teachers helping to transcribe and edit written material. In communities with strong oral traditions, ways of designing oral teaching materials may be emphasised. In others, picture dictionaries, wall posters, wall magazines, wall pamphlets, calendars, and books of oral histories, songs or rhymes may be produced. In still others, the emphasis may be on local resources rather than printed materials.

A third meaning of bottom-up involves documentation. Communities also need to be enabled to make video documentaries of their own progress. These can be used in teacher training, in multicultural and multilingual awareness raising activities, in advocacy projects, and as part of a dialectical process of community empowerment. The entire process of empowerment begins when communities are given the opportunity to develop their own MLE learning materials, pedagogically sound intergenerational teacher training and resource practices, and awareness raising programs. Through the process of engaging in these activities, the community also becomes aware of truly how deep its collective knowledge and talent really is. The 2006 Project Document, for example, notes the following about the pedagogical awareness of a community described as 'backward':

> …the project preparation team met with communities that presented strong demands for children being instructed with their mother tongue as a medium of instruction. A community generally described as backward and having no understanding of the value of education presented pedagogically valid and sound arguments for their demands. (12)

Such activities should also lead to what can be termed a critical indigenous pedagogy—a pedagogy which is grounded in indigenous epistemologies, metaphysics and values, but at the same time, allows for dialectical tension with transformative Western knowledge systems, as acknowledged, among others by the sociohistorical psychology of Vygotsky and the liberation pedagogy of Paulo Freire (1985).

In a personal conversation with Dr Mere Kepa, indigenous Māori and Post Doctoral Fellow at the University of Auckland, at her home in 2005, one of the authors of this article (David Hough) asked whether or not Western critical pedagogy might historically turn out to be nothing more than the latest version of 'great-white-fatherism'. She replied that there was always that danger, but that so long as it was grounded in the aspirations and empowerment of the oppressed, it also possessed seeds of liberation. Out of this conversation came the realisation for the need to raise to a level of critical consciousness the dialectical interplay between developing traditionalism (see Alfred 1999) and Western critical pedagogy. A key aspect of both, however, is that they seek to be transformative—to critically understand the world and be active agents in making it better.

## Toward a Critical Indigenous Pedagogy

The history of universal compulsory education dates back to the advent of the industrial revolution. It was a mechanism whereby malleable and (with the concurrent development of the nation state) patriotic national workforces could be trained. A key component of this training was the introduction of individualised and competitive techniques for instruction, diagnosis and testing. A second key component of this system was the imposition of Western linear (i.e. cause and effect) notions of empirical science. Both these components run counter to traditional values and epistemologies, which are (a) largely based on generosity and sharing, collectivism and cooperation, and (b) understand the world in a dialectic relational way rather than as a set of isolated cause-and-effect variables. There is a wide body of literature that critically analyses the legacy of universal compulsory education in the sociohistorical context of globalisation and which further documents the value of indigenous ways of knowing. It is therefore imperative that government agencies, donor countries and organisations, as well as others in positions of power, both understand the merits of traditional values and epistemologies, and critically re-examine the basic, often implicit, assumptions of mainstream (market-based) educational models. As Henry Giroux argues (in Freire 1985), it is necessary for educators to understand how school culture has 'functioned not only to confirm and privilege students from the dominant classes but also through exclusion and insult to discredit the histories, experiences, and dreams of subordinate groups.' (xv). Therefore, we must not simply say, 'Education for all is the answer.' We must also ask 'What kind of education?'

What follows is an overview of some of the ways in which the Nepalese MLE programme has attempted to encourage local development of critical indigenous pedagogies. It is based primarily on a workshop held in Rasuwa with teachers and community members from two Tamang-speaking schools in the area. Participants began by developing lists of generic themes which they thought could be used in developing culturally appropriate learning and teaching materials and methodologies. The themes chosen were: (1) herbal medicines and healing practices, (2) traditional and modern knowledge and skills, (3) history, numerical systems, weights and measures, (4) religion, belief systems and practices, and (5) life rituals, feasts, festivals, songs and poems.

Where appropriate, reference is also made to similar workshops conducted among indigenous communities in other parts of the country. Both NEFIN and NFDIN as well as other local IPO's actively participated in these workshops.

*Herbal medicines and traditional healing practices*

Tamang herbal medicines and healing practices are not part of the primary school curriculum, although certain aspects of Western hygiene are. This lack of inclusion (or replacement) serves to devalue indigenous knowledge and privilege Western health education—a fact which is reflected in the many health education materials that INGOs, NGOs and donor countries produce for use in the schools, both as supplementary and non-formal education sector materials. Nevertheless, Tamangs consistently report that they have long experience and knowledge about the effectiveness of indigenous treatments, and that in actual practice, their preference is to use self-medicated local treatments first, seek local healers second, and only go to a clinic or hospital as a last resort.

Participants listed the Tamang names of numerous plants, roots, leaves, vines, etc. which they wanted included in the school curriculum. They added brief descriptions of their uses as well as random notes about the locations and seasons where they can be found, who prepares them and how, and which types of plants and/or knowledge is endangered.

From the materials collection and development side, discussion focused on how students and teachers could gather stories from IK holders which were rich both in detail about medical knowledge and practices as well as personal information about the lives of the IK holders themselves. To this, drawings, samples, songs and other cultural information intended for different age groups could be added. For example, interesting and relevant stories about indigenous healthcare for younger children could be supplemented with problem posing questions for older students about why such practices are dying and what can be done about it.

This led to some initial tentative ideas about the transformative aspect of what a critical indigenous pedagogy might seek to offer. Themes of possible interest regarding indigenous healthcare issues might include: (1) how indigenous healthcare practices are holistic and have scientific value; (2) how Western stereotypes about poverty and disease in Third World countries often serve to devalue indigenous knowledge and practices, and (3) in a contribution by Kepa at a later workshop, how indigenous knowledge must be protected from theft by international pharmaceutical companies claiming intellectual property rights[5] (See also Shiva 1997, 2005 for elaboration).

Such materials would not have to be printed in book form but could be handwritten and bound by students and teachers using only local resources. They could then be made part of a school or community library for use both inside and outside of the classroom.

Interest was also raised regarding how such indigenous knowledge was traditionally passed on,[6] and how these methods could be either brought into the classroom, or the classroom brought outside to the community. For example, experiential and intergenerational learning were considered culturally appropriate ways of teaching and learning.

### *Traditional and modern knowledge and skills*

This category covered a wide range of indigenous knowledge and skills, all of which are devalued and under threat from outside, dominating forces of globalisation and mainstream education. The participants themselves were aware of this and felt the need to better understand the processes of change within a transformative educational context by critically contrasting the traditional and modern. Also, as with herbal medicines and traditional practices, curriculum materials can be designed for use with different age groups,[7] and can be shared intergenerationally with members of the community. The following is a brief summary of the points raised.

Traditionally Tamang practices relating to agriculture and food are threatened by the introduction of pesticides as well as from increased imports of processed foods, including junk food. This shifts people away from subsistence economy which is seen as ecological, and exacerbates economic dependency (including the need for income from outside remittances from family members who are forced to leave the villages).

Historically, the Tamang have relied on local materials for producing pots, baskets, bags and containers for transport and storage. These containers were both functional and artistic (reflecting the indigenous individuality of the makers), were ecologically friendly (both durable and disposable containers being biodegradable), and were inseparable from indigenous relations of production and distribution (collective relations of love, generosity and sharing). Today, these containers are being replaced by those made from plastics and other materials which are non-biodegradable. They do not reflect the dialectical unity of indigenous art and function, and generally not being biodegradable thus pose an ecological threat (plastic bags and throw-away containers now pollute the landscape), and they destroy indigenous relations of production and distribution (replacing them with an individualised and segmented consumer mentality).

A similar situation exists with weaving and the production of indigenous clothing. The love and care associated with sewing or weaving well-made, personalised clothing still exists, but is today being overtaken by the purchase of mass-produced ready-made clothing imported from factories in India and China, and increasingly the sweatshops of Kathmandu and other Nepali cities. All of these changes also impact on the economic power of indigenous women who are forced into roles of dependency. Children also become victims and rarely does the current education system help.

All of these and many other questions need to be carefully considered and integrated into a critical indigenous pedagogy that must ultimately replace the mainstream compulsory education models which dominate today.

*History, numerical systems, weights and measures*

For the Tamang of Rasuwa, both their history and numerical systems are cultural treasures which are endangered, albeit in different ways. At the start of the workshop, participants expressed an overwhelming desire for advice and suggestions on how to stabilise words and cultural artefacts which are dying, and how to revive and use the Tamang counting system, both in the classroom and in the wider community.

As participants began to transcribe an oral history of their peoples, they noted that there were many old, even archaic, terms and structures (including the use of high language), which some felt might prove difficult for young students to understand, and which should therefore be simplified. In subsequent discussions, however, it was noted that this was much of the same language that people feared was dying and needed to be stabilised. Discussion then turned to ways in which this language could best be incorporated into the curriculum, and how oral histories could indeed be an untapped resource in helping to reverse language shift.

The rich context of the oral histories argued against lexical and syntactic simplification. Here, two accounts were given as to how young students could actually benefit from exposure to this type of language. The first involves the way societies with oral traditions generally pass on their history. The second involves problems encountered in mainstream American education when such language is simplified (and consequently decontextualised).

Societies with oral traditions record their histories in ways which are as good if not superior to those with literary ones. In fact, their knowledge and use of a vast array of mnemonic devices makes them the world's most expert memorisers. One such device is the use of children—particularly between the age of four and puberty—to be the keepers of valued information, such as tribal history. Children at this age have tremendous capacity for rote learning. Rote memory can be further enhanced if the information to be stored is recorded as a song, poem or chant. By way of example, the combination of rhyme and rhythm (i.e. the rhythmic pattern) actually limits the possible number of words in the language that can logically fit within a given phrase. This can be demonstrated by the fact that cloze exercises (often used in foreign language teaching) based on songs or poems are easier than ones based on textual material. Other 'tricks of the trade' include repetition (a cyclic rhetorical style), dance/body movement and the contextualisation of the information to be stored in the form of a story. The use of beaded or knotted strings, dolls, and other contextualising objects which can be seen, felt, heard, inhaled or even tasted further enhance memory. The area of the brain which controls the sense of smell, in fact, is physiologically connected to the area which controls memory.

Stories, including oral histories, which are memorised using the above techniques, are so strong that children easily remember complex words and grammatical structures (including archaic ones) even if they do not understand the actual meaning of all of the words themselves. Two examples from English children's songs and rhymes are 'Ring Around the Rosie' and 'Little Miss Muffett.' Even though the deep meanings of these stories may not be fully understood by young children, there is nevertheless enough context to allow for both overall comprehension and gradual acculturation. Deeper cultural understanding begins at puberty with the development of greater cognitive skills and is enhanced throughout life with experience.

In contrast to this rich oral tradition of indigenous education, modern Western educational doctrine argues that learning materials must be graded, simplified and reduced to easily learnable/identifiable chunks for diagnostic purposes. The result is often boring, decontextualised textbooks, readers, supplementary materials and lesson plans, which serve to dumb out large numbers of students, most particularly those from indigenous, minority and other marginalised groups. A study done in the United States in the 1960s, for example, revealed that since the 1890s children's readers had regularly been simplified and decontextualised to the point that by the 1950s children were having major difficulties learning how to read. This resulted in the revolution of Dr Seuss books which attempted to make reading richly contextual and fun again.

The second issue of language endangerment raised by the Rasuwa Tamang community involved their numeral system, which is highly endangered. Although still known by many older members of the community, it is no longer used in daily intercourse, and is no longer being passed down. Instead, Nepali, Hindi and English terminology along with Western metric (and to a lesser extent the British Imperial) systems dominate.

Reasons for this particular form of endangerment must also be addressed in a manner which allows for transformative consciousness raising and empowerment. Here, we return to the fact that dominating languages kill weaker ones. As weights and measures are standardised from the West, indigenous systems are often lost. Worldwide standardisation of weights and measures occurred shortly before the industrial revolution and the beginning of compulsory education. Two major systems competed for dominance: The British Imperial system and the French metric system. As these systems were adopted in schools worldwide, other systems began to die. Many have been lost or only remain in folklore, songs and poems.

Assistance both in reversing language shift in this area, and in further developing curricula, may come from work in the field of ethnomathematics. Ethnomathematics is an attempt to look at the mathematical ideas which are embedded in indigenous cultures worldwide. These ideas and the way they are expressed vary from one culture to another. The concepts or ideas can include art, navigation, religion, record keeping, games and kin relationships (Ascher 1998). Mnemonic devices taken from indigenous oral traditions also have application for the teaching of mathematics, and can thus be employed in the revival of the numeral system.

### *Religion, belief systems and practices*

Participants felt strongly that stories which reflect the morals and values of the Rasuwa Tamang community should be included in the local curriculum. Here, community members collected Buddhist parables which teach about human relations, helping others, and harmony with the environment. Shamanistic practices, which traditionally played a significant role in Rasuwa Tamang culture, appear highly endangered and may need further investigation. Also, there are various democratic community institutions which were used for resource distribution and conflict resolution that appear endangered and need further study. All of these appear to be grounded in a holistic worldview and may be of help in elaborating culturally appropriate classroom methodologies.

In order to accomplish this, communities may wish to explore how their underlying values, epistemologies and learning methods might be utilised in the classroom. The following is a general list of values, which has been compiled from anecdotal information and testimonials given by indigenous peoples in the Pacific, Far East Russia, and North America, as well as Nepal. Similar lists have been published in books and journals of indigenous scholarship. The list may be used as a tool as communities develop culturally appropriate learning content and teaching methodologies:

1. Generosity/sharing;
2. Caring for each other;
3. Collectivism (as opposed to individualism);
4. Cooperation (as opposed to competition);
5. Relatedness to one another;
6. Relatedness to nature/spirituality;
7. Individuality (respect for difference/tolerance);
8. Matrilineal bonds (gender equity);
9. Respect for elders/wisdom;
10. Intergenerational learning;
11. Patience;
12. The use of time and space as a function of the above.

When lists such as the above are compiled by the community, they may be contrasted with the experiences children have had in school based on foreign benchmark educational standards (for example: individualised instruction, competitive testing, separation of students by age, etc.).

*Life rituals, feasts, festivals, songs and poems*

This final category also had numerous potential applications for mother tongue medium of instruction as well as the elaboration of indigenous teaching methods. Participants told stories about hospitality and welcoming people into their homes and taking leave. They described how they look after each other in rituals from birth and marriage through death. They told stories about division of labour and responsibilities for sharing, about local democratic practices and how they make rules for the group, and about committees designed to resolve disputes. And finally, they talked about how many of these practices are breaking down.

Stories such as these have great transformative and liberatory potential. In *A Tortured People: The Politics of Colonization,* Howard Adams (1995), a Canadian Métis, writes that in order to achieve true liberation, it is necessary to develop counter-consciousness:

> Without an indigenous consciousness, Indians, Métis, and Inuit peoples' only claim to Aboriginality is race and heritage. This is not enough to achieve true liberation. To accomplish self-determination, we need more than racial pride. We must have Aboriginal nationalism, an understanding of the state's capitalist ideology and its oppression, and, ultimately, counter-consciousness. (45)

One way to develop such a consciousness is though story. Lee Francis, Laguna Pueblo, argues that young American Indians need to reclaim their identity by learning 'the stories of the People'. They need to learn, remember, and tell the ancient origin and migration stories, the stories that focus on Native values, attitudes and beliefs' as well as new stories which 'incorporate the wisdom of the People' (2003: 79).

## Making new histories—where we go from here

History is not simply a thing about the past. It is also about the future and making new futures, new histories. In order to make truly liberating histories, however, we need many tools. The values listed above, the use of story, and the empowerment of indigenous communities to control both the content and methodology of teaching are some. The Black American civil rights leader Malcolm X once said that to be liberated, it is not enough to know what is happening on your block or in your ghetto, or even what is happening in your city or your country. You must also know what is happening in the world. On a similar note, Linda Tuhiwai Smith, a Māori indigenous scholar and Pro Vice-Chancellor Māori University of Waikato, tells us that the key issue is what indigenous peoples can teach each other:

> What is more important than what alternatives indigenous peoples offer the world is what alternatives indigenous peoples offer each other. The strategies that work for one community may well work for another. (2001: 105)

In looking to indigenous peoples around the world for directions and ideas about paths to a critical indigenous pedagogy, we turn to the writings of Taiaiake Alfred, a Kahnawa:ke Mohawk scholar and Director of the Indigenous Governance Program at the University of Victoria, Canada. He writes:

> Within a traditional framework, we must acknowledge the fact that cultures change, and that any particular notion of what constitutes 'tradition' will be contested. Nevertheless, we can identify certain common beliefs, values, and principles that form the persistent core of a community's culture. It is this traditional framework that we must use as the basis on which to build a better society. I am advocating a self-conscious traditionalism, an intellectual, social, and political movement that will reinvigorate those values, principles, and other cultural elements that are best suited to the larger contemporary political and economic reality. Not only has the indigenous voice been excluded from the larger social and political discourse, but even within our own communities it has been supplanted by other voices. The notion of traditionalism I am promoting demands cultural give-and-take with non-indigenous people—respect for what both sides have to contribute and share. It also demands self-respect and the confidence to build on what we know to be good and right for our own people. As a movement to gain respect for indigenous people, this form of traditionalism is not predicated on racially constructed conflict. It is a matter not of red versus white, but of right versus wrong, considered within the broad framework of values we all share: freedom, justice, and peace. (1999: xviii)

Applied to the MLE program, this suggests a pedagogy grounded in indigenous values which can transcend the negative contradictions of globalisation and development, a pedagogy that sees indigenous peoples as experts in wide-ranging fields from biological, cultural and linguistic diversity (and related areas of ecology, land and forestry management), to democratic governance, participatory dispute management, the arts, literature, the humanities and law.

Finally, if this story is incomplete, it is because it is still very much of a work in progress. There are many detractors but hopefully we will not fall down. It is our great collective responsibility.

> The tribal community has its own sustainable strength in promoting their economic life and social order. They have their natural habitat with an integrated worldview, which enriches their mind with nature and culture. (Mahendra Kumar Mishra 2006).
>
> I think the poor and the people who can't read and write have a sense that without structural changes nothing is worth really getting excited about. They know much more clearly than intellectuals do that reforms don't reform. They don't change anything… Now if you could come to them with a radical idea… where they see something significant, they'd become citizens of the world. (Myles Horton 1990).
>
> The essentials of the… school that I have started have touched so deep that many conflicts would of course arise. The elites would at first scorn at us, scold and then there would be much anger but still they cannot make us fall. Slowly everybody would come to our side. And then you never think about yourself alone. No, you have to harden your skin and make progress! (Kristen Kold[8], in Das 2008).

## Notes

1 See Duran and Duran (1995) for an excellent elaboration of both self-hate and colonisation of the mind.

2 Indigenous Peoples Organizations, or IPOs, could be legally constituted under Nepali law. However, indigenous peoples had been intimidated for so long that very few were legally registered. During this period many IPOs registered as legal entities. In addition many new organizations were formed.

3 Education for All (EFA) is a worldwide UNESCO supported program to create universal primary education by the year 2015. It is part of the United Nations Millennium Goals. The MLE Program in Nepal supports EFA.

4 The terms TEK, or traditional ecological knowledge, and IK, or indigenous knowledge, are used synonymously. Among indigenous and minority groups in Nepal, the terms IK and IK holder are preferred.

5 Dr Kepa noted that if indigenous knowledge systems and practices are included in the curriculum they must be protected through intellectual property rights. Otherwise they become part of the public domain and could be patented or copyrighted by outsiders.

6 Note was also made of the fact that certain knowledge is secret and cannot be compromised.

7 Here we use Vygotsky's concept of zones of proximal development.

8 Kristen Kold was a pioneer of the Danish High School movement in the middle of the nineteenth century.

# 10

# The Caste System Approach to Multilingualism in Canada: Linguistic and Cultural Minority Children in French Immersion

*Shelley K. Taylor*

## Introduction

A recent report describes Canada's largest city, Toronto, as 'pushing past New York and London as the world's most diverse city' (Spicer 2008). To support this claim about Toronto's diversity, the report notes that half of the residents of the city were born outside of Canada, and over 300 languages are spoken in the city (Spicer 2008). This has huge ramifications for the education system as English is now spoken as a second language (L2) by more than 70% of all school-aged children in Toronto. Similar figures have been reported for English language learners (ELLs) in Montréal and Vancouver, Canada's other largest urban centres (Allen 2007, Dagenais, Armand, Walsh and Maraillet 2007, Lamarre and Dagenais 2004). An earlier census taken by Statistics Canada (2001) showed that 20% to 40% of the residents of these large Canadian cities spoke non-official languages at home (i.e., neither English nor French).

These extreme levels of diversity are not characteristic of smaller urban centres. A recent report by Statistics Canada (2008) suggests that approximately 34% of all Canadians aged twenty or older live in Toronto, Montreal or Vancouver. That means 66% of all Canadians do not live there. In comparison, 75% of all immigrants admitted to Canada after 1996 do live in those three cities. The report further notes that the post-1996 immigrant settlement pattern differs from the pattern for immigrants admitted to Canada before 1986 as they did not congregate in major cities to the same extent. Therefore, the current degree of linguistic and cultural diversity in these three cities is unprecedented. One might expect creative programs to be implemented in light of the changing face of Toronto schools, including innovative educational language programs such as multilingual education (MLE); however, that is not the case. MLE is not flourishing in Ontario, Toronto's home province, where the majority of immigrants settle; rather, MLE is illegal in Ontario.

Instruction is only allowed in English and French (Canada's official languages) in the Ontario public school system. That is, while courses teaching international languages are offered, only the official languages can be the medium of instruction for courses such as math, social studies, physical education, etc. Attempts to place mother-tongue based instruction of minority languages on the educational map during the instructional day have been thwarted since the 1980s (Cummins and Danesi 1990). This limitation is not widely known throughout Ontario, but recently garnered the spotlight: much to the shock and embarrassment of an Ontario school board. In a medium-sized town in Southern Ontario, a public school board tried to implement Arabic-medium instruction for children whose mother-tongue was Arabic at the kindergarten level (Valpy 2007). This attempt was met with a public outcry and the board being chastised by the Ontario Ministry of Education, creating a public relations fiasco for the board (Wolfson 2007). While Ontario (and Canada in general) are known for cutting-edge L2 teaching strategies and innovative approaches to incorporating culturally and linguistically sensitive pedagogy (Cummins 2007, Duff 2007, Lotherington 2007), the implementation of these strategies and approaches is limited to mainstream classroom settings. The only form of bilingual education allowed by the Ontario Ministry of Education is French immersion, which features French- (and later English-) medium instruction.

This paper reports on the findings of recent studies that I have conducted in French immersion classrooms in average sized cities to investigate the degree of linguistic and cultural diversity in Ontario schools outside 'the world's most diverse city' (Spicer 2008); that is, in cities with less intensive immigrant settlement. I examine the educational experiences of multilingual immigrant and First Nations students whose varying degrees of trilingualism develop without the support of *bona fide* MLE programs. I examine the sorts of circumstances that constrain these students' access to French immersion programs, how their presence challenges the theoretical underpinnings of the program as a vehicle for the development of additive bilingualism, what would be required to remedy the situation (Swain and Lapkin 2005), and reasons why those remedies are not forthcoming. This paper also examines attrition issues that arise among the multilingual students admitted to the program (Taylor 2006, Taylor and Yu in preparation). The results suggest that the dearth of linguistic and cultural minority children in some urban French immersion settings may be attributed to a 'caste'-like approach to multilingualism linked to outdated but potent attitudes about language development, bi-/multilingualism, and (deficit-based) views of minority populations.

The paper argues that attitudes and views such as these must be identified and addressed at the societal level. Furthermore, minority groups' awareness of the need for mother-tongue based multilingual language education must be raised. Only then can individual and group action incite, fuel and galvanize grassroots level calls for MLE. Whether the impetus comes from majority or minority groups, minority language children will benefit from the implementation of MLE in Ontario schools. This paper is testament to advances in the MLE movement in India and Nepal. It is also testament to García, Skutnabb-Kangas and Torres-Guzmán's (2006) book *Imagining Multilingual Schools* and UNESCO Bangkok's (2007) publication *Promoting literacy in multilingual settings*, which document how MLE has been imagined and implemented elsewhere.

The sections that follow contextualize my work, and then outline theoretical and ethical considerations in my advocating for the presence of cultural and linguistic minority students in French immersion. Following this, I highlight the findings of related research, then present and discuss the results of my recent investigations involving cultural and linguistic minority students in French immersion. I conclude with lessons learned and lessons to learn.

## Ontario's caste-like approach to the development of child multilingualism

Since there are no MLE programs in Ontario other than French immersion programs, I distinguish these from 'multilingual classrooms' in the sense of classrooms in which the enrolled students speak a wide range of mother tongues (L1s). They are not children who receive L1-based instruction alongside instruction in the dominant language of their country of residence, and another language as a 'foreign' language. Cummins (2007) defines 'multilingual classrooms' as 'mainstream' or 'English-as-a-second-language (ESL) classrooms' that 'focus on English as the target language for students who are learning English as an additional language', and French immersion classrooms in which French and English are used for instructional purposes (222). Minority language children whose L1 is a non-official language in Ontario (i.e. minority languages other than French) may receive L1 support after regular school hours in heritage language schools or may learn their L1 as a subject (not as a medium of instruction) during the regular school day in high school; however, they have more chance of receiving instruction in a less widely spoken minority language in a heritage language setting than at high school. In other words, while a Chinese-speaking student may take a course in an 'international' (read: non-official, foreign, or modern) language in high school, outside of the Toronto area they are likely to be limited to Spanish or German language courses. Until now, First Nations[1] students have been almost as likely to have the option to study their L1 as they were to study Latin (i.e. a language rarely taught in Ontario). As a case in point, in 2007–2008, future teachers only had the option of gaining teaching certification in Spanish and German in two Faculties of Education across Ontario; in 2008–2009, they only have the option of gaining teaching certification in Spanish, and only in one Faculty of Education in Ontario. Many more supports are in place to gain certification in teaching French as a second language (FSL). Subsequently, more programme options are in place for students to learn FSL. That said, not all students have equal access to those options.

Table 10.1 provides a breakdown of the most widely spoken (non-French and non-aboriginal) minority languages in Canada. When reviewing this table, the reader should bear in mind that Spanish is the most widely taught *international* language in Ontario high schools today.

**Table 10.1.** Ranking of (non-official / non-Aboriginal) minority languages according to the Canadian census figures of 2001

| Rank | Language | Number of Speakers |
|---|---|---|
| 1 | Chinese | 872,000 |
| 2 | Italian | 681,000 |
| 3 | German | 636,000 |
| 4 | Spanish | 611,000 |
| 5 | Punjabi | 339,000 |
| 6 | Arabic | 290,000 |
| 7 | Portuguese | 265,000 |
| 8 | Polish | 250,000 |
| 9 | Tagalog | 245,000 |
| 10 | Hindi | 227,000 |

(Adapted from Edwards 2004: 10)

A close examination of Table 10.1 shows that there are fewer Spanish speakers in Canada than there are speakers of Chinese, Italian and German. Therefore, the figures do not support the practice of offering Spanish as the main international language course across the province. The figures also highlight the paltry support that multilingual children receive to learn minority L1s as subjects during the regular school day. Some people may view prioritizing the teaching of Spanish as making economic sense since Canada, the US and Mexico are all 'Free Trade' partners (i.e. Canada and the US already have English, therefore it would be beneficial for Canadians to know Spanish to do business with Mexico). However, more is at stake than trade agreements. Research supports L1-based instruction (e.g. Cummins 2001, Skutnabb-Kangas 2000, Mohanty 2006, Traoré 2001a) and Table 10.1 indicates that Spanish is just one of many minority languages (4th in terms of its prevalence) that merit being taught at school.

French immersion is offered all across Canada while bilingual education programs are, as noted, illegal in Ontario, but offered in other provincial public school systems (Cummins 2007, Cummins and Danesi 1990). Canadian bilingual education programs feature instruction in English and First Nations languages (such as Cree), or instruction in English and an immigrant language (such as Ukrainian). Some of the 50 or more remaining First Nations languages in Canada are offered as subjects, even in Ontario public schools. Furthermore, some First Nations communities in Ontario have established language immersion programs to maintain or revive their languages. Many First Nations communities established these programs because they were rapidly losing the remaining L1-speakers of their ancestral languages (Richards and Burnaby 2008). *Kanerahtahere* Michelle A. Davis (2008) describes the linguistic and cultural immersion programme her community founded in the local *Kawenni:io/Gaweni:yo* School. Schools such as hers operate outside the provincial school system in Ontario. They are independent schools located on Band land, and Band Councils run the school boards that oversee them.

Until now, the Ontario government has not seemed willing to support immigrant or Aboriginal students' L1 or ancestral language, and has not seemed to understand the importance of these languages to the learning process. For example, the Ontario Ministry of Education (2003) allocated $17 million in 2003 to support English- and French-speaking L2 learners (in the English and French school systems, respectively), but did not allocate any funds for non-official L1 support. In 2007, Ontario invested 23 million dollars in new programs for Aboriginal students. The stated goals of this Aboriginal student funding were to close the education gap between Aboriginal and non-Aboriginal students, and meet Aboriginal students' needs. While linguistic revitalization was not included among the strategies identified as likely to encourage and sustain Aboriginal student success, part of the funds was ear-marked for developing more Aboriginal cultural and linguistic programs (Ontario Ministry of Education 2007a, 2007b). Generally though, non-official languages do not rank very high on the list of the Ontario government's priorities.

This trend lays the background for why mechanisms are not in place to develop linguistic and cultural minority children's L1s and ancestral languages in French immersion programs across Ontario. In Ajit Mohanty and Minati Panda's (2007) terms, program structures can veil the multilingual composition of students. The net effect of invisibilising French immersion participants' minority L1s is to disadvantage them because they do not benefit from the same opportunity to develop additive bilingualism as do their majority language peers. In the MLE project proposal that Mohanty and Panda (2007) presented to the *van Leer Foundation*, they related inequalities in Indian society 'where social divisions, based on caste, class, culture, language, religion etc., are pervasive' to unequal access to educational opportunities (1). My analysis of the Ontario situation in the remainder of this paper will show how the exclusion and non-accommodation of minority L1s that Mohanty and Panda describe in the Indian context also pertains to educational practices in Ontario.

Mohanty and Panda (2007) explain how 'multiple layers of discrimination' feed into and maintain links between caste-like social divisions and educational opportunities (2). I argue that *multiple layers of discrimination* exist in Ontario for two reasons. First, (c)overt limits are placed on non-official language minority and Aboriginal children's access to enrolment in French immersion programs, thus disadvantaging them. Second, the presence of those child multilinguals who make it into the program is veiled, thus doubly disadvantaging them. My purpose in presenting the findings of my investigations into these topics in the Ontario French immersion context is as follows. I wish to contribute to the development of effective strategies for resourceful use of the multilingual composition of today's classrooms, while dealing with the challenges of language disadvantages in a multilingual society.

## Theoretical and ethical considerations

### *The ostrich approach to contemporary EFI: Ignoring growing pains*

Three decades ago, researchers Bruck (1978) and Genesee (1976) asked whether early French immersion (EFI), the primary form of bilingual education in Canada, was suitable for all learners, including speakers of a non-official L1. In the decades that followed, the Canadian immersion model spread worldwide (Gaffney 1999), leading researchers in different national contexts continue to pose the same question but, as Genesee (2006) laments, with no response. The 'suitability for all' issue has never been resolved despite its importance and the public interest it has garnered.

In larger Canadian urban centres, the population of minority language children in EFI continues to grow. Their presence in the program adds an unexpected twist to its theoretical underpinnings—a twist that holds major implications for program design. Their presence is currently unaccounted for in program design. This oversight challenges the premise of French immersion as a successful vehicle for the development of 'additive' bilingualism (i.e., a program in which children learn an L2 at no cost to their L1). English-speaking children develop literacy in both languages, making EFI an 'enrichment maintenance' program for them (Skutnabb-Kangas 2007, McCarty and Skutnabb-Kangas 2007). Comparable structures are not in place for linguistic minority children in the program to maintain their L1 or develop L1 literacy in the program. In that sense, EFI places them in a double bind. To coin Wong Fillmore's (1991) expression, it places them in a position of having to learn a second and third language (French and English) even though that may mean losing their first language (through lack of educational support for its development).

Since the aim of the program is neither to maintain their L1 nor develop their L1 literacy, EFI is now missing two of the 'core' features of immersion programming identified by Swain and Johnson (1997). One core feature that is missing from EFI for linguistic minority children is overt support for their L1 development. The second core feature missing for them is the possibility to develop additive bilingualism. Without these components, Canadian EFI can no longer be called an enrichment maintenance bilingual education program for all.

Recognizing the poor fit between the old design and the country's new linguistic realities, Swain and Lapkin (2005) reworked some core features. They stress that Canadian immersion programs still aim for additive bilingualism, but note the need to recognize the presence of multiple L1s and to build overt support for all L1s into the program. Genesee and Gándara (1999) call for principles of MLE to be applied in French immersion classrooms. For this to happen, structural changes are needed.

A major change that would go a long way towards restoring the core features of EFI would be to legalize instruction via the medium of non-official languages in Ontario. Thus far, there have been few calls for change of this nature, and even they have gone unheeded. This evokes the image of an ostrich with its head in the sand, oblivious to the multilingual composition of today's classrooms and research supporting the viability of L1-based MLE.

I investigated the theoretical viability of minority language children enrolling in EFI back in the early 1990s in a longitudinal study involving a Cantonese-speaking child (Taylor 1992). In that study, I questioned the 'common sense' attitude that minority language students are 'obviously' better served by learning English before French by reviewing Weber and Tardif's (1990) description of children's initiation to French in an EFI classroom at the kindergarten level. I viewed EFI kindergartens as highly supportive environments for learning French as an L2 or additional language because:

- EFI kindergarten teachers are cognizant of the fact that the children in their classrooms do not speak the language of instruction yet;
- They incorporate a great deal of meaning-making scaffolding techniques into their instruction (i.e., paralanguage such as gestures, body movement, intonation and expression), and
- They also incorporate concrete materials, pictures, symbols and rituals into their instruction.

The advantages of that sort of teacher awareness of language learner needs, and those forms of instruction for linguistic minority kindergarten children (versus in a 'mainstream' English classroom) include:

- Starting on a linguistic basis equal to majority language-speaking peers who are also non-speakers of the language of instruction (French);
- Acquiring basic interpersonal communication skills (BICS) in French with the aid of teacher scaffolding (Cummins 2001);
- Not experiencing roadblocks to cognitive development due to lexical gaps since they and their majority language peers are both rank beginners in the language of instruction;
- Developing BICS in English in kindergarten and the primary grades (ages 4-8) since English is the *lingua franca* of social interactions among children in the classroom until their French develops sufficiently (around age 6.5 or 7), and remains the *lingua franca* of the playground throughout their elementary school years;
- Not being required to use English for academic purposes until the junior grades (ages 9-12) at which point they have a much more solid grasp of the language (Cummins 2001).

That is, they have three years to develop interpersonal communicative skills in English before being required to use it for academic purposes.

To sum up, Taylor (1992) argued that minority language children in EFI were better served than their minority language counterparts in *mainstream* classrooms. In the mainstream setting, their peers were unlikely to receive the same degree of teacher understanding or teacher scaffolding in the language of instruction (English). They would thus be at a linguistic disadvantage in comparison to peers for whom the language of instruction was their L1. This suggests that EFI is a viable (if not superior) option for the schooling of minority language children. It would be an even better option if its design were revamped to regain its designation as an enrichment maintenance bilingual program for all. This is also recommended on ethical grounds.

### Ethical questions

ELLs and Aboriginal children are commonly classified in the 'at-risk' category. To deny *at-risk* children access to EFI is to drastically reduce their chances of becoming functionally bilingual in Canada's two official languages. Limiting them in that way is highly problematic as functional bilingualism satisfies national goals in the Canadian context, and leads to higher paid jobs. Genesee (2006) questions whether it is ethical to dissuade some parents from enrolling their children in EFI or outright bar certain children from enrolling in the program because they are deemed at-risk. He bases his question on the findings of an exhaustive literature review he conducted on the suitability of EFI for all children. Genesee (2006) found that there is 'insufficient evidence to support decisions to exclude at-risk students from immersion on an a priori basis' (21). He concluded his review by stating that more evidence is needed before parents and schools can make informed choices about whether to enrol these children in the program.

For now, atheoretical decision-making is the rule of the day. Skutnabb-Kangas (2000) explains popular myths underlying people's understanding of language development and views on monolingualism, bilingualism and multilingualism. King and Mackey (2007) emphasize the power of these myths, which frequently carry more sway than research findings in policy-making. Myths can also dictate which children get profiled as 'good' or 'bad' candidates for EFI. Monolingual Canadians who construct English-medium instruction as the norm (hence, legitimate) and bilingual education as exceptional (hence, 'harder' and illegitimate), and bilingual Canadians who buy into monolingual ideologies, do not endorse EFI for cultural and linguistic minority children. These views are then transmitted in messages to cultural minority parents such as First Nations parents, and parents with home languages other than English. The messages can range from covertly dissuading parents from enrolling their children in the program to overtly informing them their children do not qualify for enrolment (Genesee 2006, Taylor 2006). The intent and outcomes of these messages raise the issue of whether EFI should it be publicly funded if it is not suitable for all? To make EFI work for all learners means that educational leaders must take their heads out of the sand, and develop the will and the way to make the program work. This not only has implications for L1-based MLE, but also for EFI teacher preparation and student services such as ESL.

## Related research

Two earlier studies led me to conduct research into the educational experiences of multilingual immigrant and First Nations students in EFI. The first was a longitudinal, ethnographic case study conducted in Toronto, which involved the previously mentioned Cantonese-speaking child, 'Victor'. I followed his academic, social and linguistic adaptation to the program for three years: from junior kindergarten through to grade 1. The second took place in a small town bordering on two Maritime provinces on the east coast of Canada. A substantial number of First Nations students were involved in the EFI program in that school. *Victor*'s case showed that, as Wong Fillmore (1991) and King and Mackey's (2007) work suggests, minority language children in North America are becoming English-dominant well before residing there for three generations. In Victor's case, he learned English since it was the *lingua franca* of the immersion program. His mother reported that he was English dominant by the end of grade 1. In fact, he was becoming so resistant to speaking Cantonese that he was shifting his whole family's home language to English (Taylor 1992). Prior to enrolment in the program, Victor was cared for by his grandmother who only spoke Cantonese. Therefore, though he was a third generation immigrant, he entered school monolingual in Cantonese, but was not barred entry to the program because he was 'ESL'. When asked why she and her husband chose EFI for Victor and his sister before him, she said: 'Canada is bilingual. (French) is part of our heritage' (Taylor 1992: 745). In fact, Victor inherited a trilingual heritage, but was losing part of himself (his Cantonese heritage). He was not experiencing additive bilingualism in the EFI program. Neither was it an enrichment bilingual program for him.

The second study involved Mi'kmaq children whose home community had experienced language shift in their parents' generation. Their grandparents had been through physically, emotionally and psychologically scarring residential schools where speaking Mi'kmaq became strongly associated with suffering (Knockwood 1992, Milloy 1999). Therefore, they consciously decided to not transmit the language to their children: the parents of the children in my study.

Interview reports suggested that the Mi'kmaq children initially gained entrance to the EFI program 'through the back door': What began with the occasional, isolated child enrolling in the program had escalated to a third of the kindergarten and grade 1 cohorts being Mi'kmaq by the time of my study (Taylor 2000). Findings of my ongoing, ethnographic observation suggested that these First Nations children exhibited an average range of academic ability, ranging from low average to above average, such as one would expect from a variety of learners. They acquired oracy and literacy in French, their L2, and L1 literacy in English on par with their dominant group peers. They also studied Mi'kmaq as a subject during the regular school day, in a provincial elementary school—an option which few First Nations or immigrant children enjoy in Ontario. Unfortunately, while they studied their ancestral language, their dominant group peers received Social Studies instruction. That led some First Nations parents to withdraw their children from Mi'kmaq rather than miss out on Social Studies instruction throughout their elementary school years (Taylor 2000).

Neither Victor nor his immigrant peers nor the Mi'kmaq children were dissuaded from enrolling in EFI and all fared well academically, socially and linguistically in the program. Their relative success led me to wonder how immigrant and First Nations children fare outside Toronto, Montréal and Vancouver—in cities with populations of 100,000 – 400,000. Population figures recently released by Statistics Canada (2008) show that while slightly more than 1 in 5 Canadians live in a small town or rural area with a population under 15,000, the corresponding proportion of immigrants is less than 1 in 40. The same report shows that the most striking difference between where immigrants settle in Canada involves their country of origin: 'Immigrants [who settle] in small areas come mostly from Europe and the United States, while immigrants [who settle in] large urban centres come mostly from Asia. Nevertheless, more than 1 in 4 immigrants in the smallest areas come from Asia and the proportions of immigrants from Africa in very large urban areas and small urban areas are similar' (Statistics Canada 2008). My intent was to examine the assumption that the cultural/linguistic minority student enrolment in EFI phenomenon would be isolated to Ontario's major urban centre, Toronto. I investigated multilingual and First Nations students' access to EFI in two smaller cities, and push-out or attrition issues that arose amongst those minority children enrolled in the program.

## Three investigations

### *Settings, participants and research measures*

I conducted the first study in the highly populated southern part of Ontario, and two studies (in the same city) in the under-populated north. Brief sketches of the two settings and studies conducted in both are provided next.

### *Southern Ontario*

The town had a population of 300,000. The school that housed the EFI program was a French immersion centre. For purposes of this paper, I refer to this school as Southern School A. It is located in a lower socio-economic status (SES) part of the city, but draws on students from diverse SES backgrounds. That is because it has a large encatchment area and home-school bus services are provided free of charge.

As Southern School A was an immersion 'centre', all of its 600 students were enrolled in EFI. I administered a web-based survey to students in grades 4 through 8. One-third of all grades 4-8 students completed the survey midway through the academic year. I also conducted participant-observation in one grade 6 classroom, focussing my attention on classroom practices, teacher attributes and the educational experiences of four students. Two were linguistic majority children whose L1 was English, and two were linguistic minority students whose L1 was Arabic. The latter students attended pull-out ESL classes. I also conducted participant observation in their EFI and ESL classrooms, and interviewed the four children, their parents, their EFI teacher, and the ESL teacher.

### *Northern Ontario*

The town had a population of 100,000. I conducted my first northern study in two 'dual track' schools, which housed EFI and English-medium programs. For this paper, I refer to the larger school with 750 students as Northern School A. It was located in an average/above average SES part of the city, and had an average sized encatchment area. The northern school board also provides free, city-wide, home-school bus services.[2] Thus, the potential for students from a wide variety of SES backgrounds to attend the program was in place.

The second school, Northern School B, was also a dual track school with 450 students. Roughly half of them were enrolled in the EFI program, with the other half in the English-medium program. Free bussing was also provided to the EFI program in this school. The school is in a low average/average SES area, and had a larger encatchment area than its sister school. There is a low income housing area which was in the adjacent encatchment area. Many First Nations members lived in the housing complex—many of whom had recently moved off small, isolated northern reserves and settled in the city. Students in that housing area had the option of attending their local English-medium school or being bussed out of their encatchment area to attend the EFI program at Northern School B.

I administered the same web-based survey to grades 4–8 students in these two northern schools as I had in the southern school, but very late in the school year. Only 1/10$^{th}$ of the 300 possible EFI students agreed to participate in the study. The low number of participants precluded my focussing on minority language students who spoke the same L1. I conducted participant-observation in several grades 4–8 classrooms in both schools, but less intensively than I had done in the one grade 6 classroom in the south. I again focussed on classroom practices, teacher attributes and the educational experiences of minority language students, but was unable to observe them in pull-out ESL classes as none were offered. I was informed that there was only one ESL classroom in the school board, and it was not housed in either of the schools in my study. Furthermore, the principal of Northern School A informed me that if children required ESL services, they would not be allowed to enrol in EFI.

Only two 'minority language' children from different classrooms participated in the study at Northern School A and no First Nations children participated in the study. No children self-identified as minority language-speakers at Northern School B. Therefore, I only interviewed majority language children there. I also interviewed majority language children at Northern School A, and one EFI teacher in each school.

During the course of my classroom observations at Northern School B, I became aware of a noticeable number of First Nations children in EFI. The administrator in charge of the school at the time informed me that 10%–15% of all EFI students at the school had First Nations backgrounds. With this in mind, I planned a follow-up study in the same northern setting, but only in that school. I later completed a follow-up study targeting First Nations students (i.e., cultural minorities) participating in the program, but found that far less than 10%–15% of the program participants had a First Nations background.

Two First Nations students were enrolled in the same grade 6 EFI classroom at the school. They consented to participate in the study and complete the online survey. I conducted participant-observation in their classroom over a one-week period, and interviewed them and their EFI homeroom teacher. I also conducted telephone interviews with their parents. I informally observed two other First Nations students at the school in a Kindergarten EFI classroom. As they were too young to complete the online questionnaire, I did not formally include them in the study. I also had impromptu discussions with other EFI and English-medium program teachers at the school.

## Results

The quantitative measure, the online survey, included 29 items. It elicited data on the students' overall (socio-psychological and academic) well-being. Items included 'rate your school performance', and 'rate your social life'. The goals of the survey were to elicit data on the students' language practices, feelings and attitudes. Specifically, it yielded descriptive data on:

- the breadth of their language usage and proficiency,
- their emotional attachment to their L1, L2s and, possibly, L3s,
- their sense of pride/stigma associated with speaking English, French and, for some, a minority language, and
- the ethno-linguistic vitality of their non-official languages.

### *Southern setting*

Figure 10.1 shows the percentage of respondents who described themselves as bi-, trilingual or multilingual.

**Table 10.1** Percentage of respondents who described themselves as bi-, tri-, or multilingual

Bilingual = Two languages spoken; Trilingual = Three languages spoken; Multilingual = Four or more languages

Please describe yourself. Are you bilingual, trilingual, or multilingual?

| Selection | # | Count |
|---|---|---|
| Bilingual | 30 | 58.8% |
| Trilingual | 18 | 35.3% |
| Multilingual | 3 | 5.9% |

The results indicated that 44.2% of the respondents considered themselves tri- or multilingual. This figure was noteworthy because only 4% of all school-aged children in the board receive ESL instruction. The city in which this study was conducted is not a major magnet for immigrants. The high representation of linguistic minority students at Southern School A was not typical of other EFI schools in the city. One teacher suggested that immigrants in the area had negative views of neighbourhood schools that drew on lower SES populations. She further suggested that parents enrolled their children in the EFI school for one of two reasons. The first was to avoid sending them to a local school in which children from predominantly lower income families enrolled. The second was because they viewed EFI as publicly funded private schooling.

The three main minority languages spoken by respondents were Spanish, Polish and Arabic, and this reflects the main minority languages spoken in the city and in the surrounding rural areas where many Spanish-speaking Mexican Mennonites reside. Other survey results for the minority language children included:

- As a language in which to convey their emotions, 2/3 of those surveyed preferred English, ¼ preferred their L1, and only 1 preferred French,
- 5/6 of those surveyed preferred to communicate with their friends in English, and 1/6 were equally comfortable communicating with their friends in English or French; none of them chose a minority L1,
- 2/3 of them wanted to stay in French immersion in high school,
- They identified math, physical education, music and art as their strongest school subjects, science as their weakest subject, and nobody thought they would fail a grade,
- 94% responded that they would continue college or university studies after high school, and only 1 respondent said s/he would do 'something else', and
- the majority said they felt comfortable to very comfortable with their school social lives, and nobody said they were unhappy.

These results were on par with their English-speaking peers' responses with one exception: one Arabic-speaking student profiled in my study. He expressed feeling weaker academically than many others, did not like French, wanted to switch to the English stream, and reported feeling less satisfied with his social life than the majority of English-speaking or minority language respondents. The other Arabic-speaking student did not enjoy French any more than the first, but reported feeling better socially and academically adapted in the program, with the exception of his written French work.

These boys were English-dominant and the main language of their home was English with some Arabic, but their EFI teacher viewed them as Arabic-dominant, ESL students. That surprised their mothers, given the boys' proficiency in English and limited proficiency in Arabic. Both mothers stated they did not understand why their sons were receiving ESL pull-out. Their EFI teacher attributed their weakness in written French to being 'Arabic dominant' and 'ESL'. And their ESL teacher was undecided as to whether they had some form of learning difficulty or were spoiled and lazy. Their EFI teacher succeeded in convincing the boys' parents to transfer them to the English stream in grade 7, a decision that their ESL teacher disagreed with, as she thought a change of language of instruction would not be a 'magic bullet', especially as 50% of instruction in EFI is already in English from grades 5-8.

### *Northern setting*

To call the two children who self-identified as linguistic minority children 'trilingual' at Northern School A would be a stretch. They had virtually no passive understanding of their heritage languages. Both children had one parent for whom English was the L1 and one parent whose L1 was a minority language (Finnish or Italian). Since their parents' common language was English, Finnish and Italian were not spoken in the home. The children's only exposure to their heritage languages was through their grandparents. Therefore, there had been a home-language shift in two generations due to intermarriage.

No First Nations students participated in my first northern study: neither in School A nor in School B, and no linguistic minority children participated in the study in School B. As noted, the two 'minority language children' who participated in my study from School A were actually bilinguals. Their survey data did not differ to any noteworthy extent from that of the other English-dominant 'bilingual' children who participated in Phase 1 of my northern study in either School A or B.

For my return trip up north in Phase 2, I targeted School B as I had noticed First Nations students in EFI while observing in different EFI classrooms. That had led me to wonder what role their length of residence in the city played in their enrolling in EFI. I also wondered whether the families of the First Nations students in EFI had resided in the city for some time or were recent arrivals from northern reserves. I hypothesized that recent arrivals' ancestral language would be intact, and that students whose families had resided in the city for some time would be English-dominant. I further hypothesized that monolingual myths might block First Nations students whose L1 was an ancestral language from enrolling in the program, but not block English-dominant First Nations students from enrolling.

The school records showed that, of the total school population of 450 students, 58 were First Nations students (or 12.8% of the total school population). They also showed that roughly half of the total student population was in the EFI track. Only four First Nations students were enrolled in EFI at School B—a far cry from the 10%–15% suggested in Phase 1. Indeed, there were only seven First Nations children enrolled in EFI in the entire northern school board. Those four students accounted for 1.7% of all students enrolled in EFI at that school. That figure also stands in stark contrast to the percentage of First Nations students enrolled in the school overall (12.8%), and shows that the vast majority of First Nations students were in the English-medium track of the school. A 1.7% enrolment figure of First Nations students in EFI stands in even starker contrast to the enrolment figure (33%) for linguistic minority students in EFI in Southern School A. This finding suggests that one group of cultural minority students (i.e. First Nations students) is noticeably less present in EFI than linguistic minorities. It must also be noted that there are major discrepancies in the number of linguistic minorities present in EFI (virtually nil) in northern Ontario as compared to in southern Ontario (33%).

Of the four First Nations children in EFI at Northern School B, two were in my target grade range. Both were girls, and both were in the same grade 6 classroom. Therefore, I conducted participant observation in their classroom. Since they were English-dominant, they would not have attended ESL pull-out classes even if the board provided them to EFI students. The girls' only contact with their ancestral language, Ojibwe, was through their grandparents. Their survey results showed individual differences, suggesting one preferred French and English language arts more than the other. Their teacher confirmed this, but stressed both were solid 'B' students (i.e., quite average). Not surprisingly, their cultural minority status in no way predetermined their success in the program.

Statistics Canada (2007) identifies Finnish, Italian and Ojibwe as the main non-official languages spoken in that northern city. The results of my study support those statistics: While the two students who self-identified as linguistic minorities were not fluent in Finnish or Italian, they were the descendents of Finnish and Italian immigrants. Furthermore, the school board web site cites the Aboriginal community as the fastest growing segment of the city's population (XX Public Schools[3] 2007). Therefore, if their enrolment figures remain low in EFI, the program will miss out on an important segment of the student population pool and potential enrolees. I did not discover any differences between the two 'quasi' minority language children's responses or in any of my observational or interview data regarding them when I conducted my first study in the northern setting. In the second phase of my northern study when the focus was on the two First Nations children in grade 6 at Terry Fox public school, the results were the same: They too was faring well in EFI. What differed was perceptions of my focus.

In Phase 1, all concerned found my interest in multilingual students in EFI interesting, but nothing out of the ordinary, with the exception of the Northern School A's principal who rejected the premise of ESL students enrolling in the program. In Phase 2, when the focus of my investigation shifted to the presence of First Nations children in EFI, the board, principal of Northern School B, and EFI classroom teacher were very interested in the premise of my study and extremely supportive of the equity issues involved. The English-medium teachers at Northern School B were, on the other hand, aghast at the suggestion of First Nations children being schooled in French. As one vehemently stated: 'They come to school with no language. They have no language. Why put them in French?' (personal communication, 13 December 2007). The opinion overtly (if not boldly) expressed by this teacher in a public forum suggests that she would limit First Nations students' access to EFI, and would not be averse in principle to pushing-out ones currently in the program.

As noted, the purpose of my two-phase study in the different settings was to investigate cultural and linguistic minorities' access to EFI and push-out from the program. Table 10.2 summarizes my findings related to these layers of possible discrimination.

**Table 10.2** Layers of discrimination

| | **NEGATIVE (×) AND POSITIVE(✓) STRUCTURAL FEATURES** | |
|---|---|---|
| **LOCATION, SCHOOL AND PHASE** | **ACCESS TO THE EFI PROGRAM** | **PROGRAM PUSH-OUT** |
| Southern School A (Phase 1) | *Few linguistic minority students in the city*<br>*First Nations students concentrated in other EFI encatchment areas*<br>√ ESL students have access to EFI<br>√ Linguistic minority participation in program positively disproportionate for overall school enrolment | X LD push-out AND<br>X Subtle ESL push-out for two students profiled |
| Northern School A (Phase 1) | *Few linguistic minority students in the city*<br>*Many First Nations students in the city*<br>X ESL students do not have access to EFI<br>√ Cultural minority students (First Nations students) have access to EFI<br>X No First Nations present | N/A |

| | | |
|---|---|---|
| Northern School B (Phase 1) | – *Few linguistic minority students in the city*<br>– *Many First Nations students in the city*<br>X ESL students do not have access to EFI<br>√ Cultural minority students (First Nations students) have access to EFI<br>√ Several First Nations in EFI (but not participating in study) | N/A |
| Northern School B (Phase 2) | √ First Nations students have access to EFI<br>√ A few First Nations in EFI and a couple participating in the study<br>X First Nations participation in program <u>negatively disproportionate</u> for overall school enrolment<br>X Cultural minorities: some teachers overtly express monolingual ideology, deficit perspectives towards First Nations students and support barring access | X Cultural minorities: potential for push-out due to monolingual ideology/deficit perspectives towards First Nations students held by some teachers<br>√ No push-out for the First Nations students profiled |

To summarize the findings presented in Table 10.2, linguistic minorities have access to EFI in Southern School A, but the two linguistic minority students that I profiled experienced subtle push-out effects. That is, their homeroom teacher attributed supposed learning difficulties to their 'ESL' background, and covertly suggested withdrawing the children from the program to their parents. There was an overt policy in effect in the two northern schools to not accept ESL (linguistic minority) children into the program. Therefore, access to the program was a major issue. Program push-out due to students' ESL status was a non-issue as such children were not allowed into the program. While no similar policy exists to dissuade First Nations (cultural minority) parents from enrolling their children in the program, some teachers frankly expressed exclusionary ideas. The two students whom I observed did not experience any push-out attempts by their EFI homeroom teacher who stressed that they were average students faring well in the program.

It is worth noting, however, that their teacher had no idea that the two students were cultural minorities before I conducted my study. That confirmed my hypothesis that First Nations students in EFI would be from English-dominant families who had lived in the city for a long time. The students were also the products of intermarriage between First Nations and European background parents, and were blonde. This raises the issue of how First Nations children who were L1-speakers of an ancestral language and did not 'blend in' with Canadians of European descent would fare in EFI (if they gained access to the program)?

## Discussion and conclusion: lessons learned and lessons to learn

It is interesting that one of the reasons that immigrant parents in Phase 1 of the study in the southern setting appeared to choose EFI had 'white flight' qualities. That is, they chose an EFI school to avoid enrolling their children in an English-medium, local school in a lower SES neighbourhood where students deemed 'undesirable' would be their children's peers. The same sort of flight to EFI did not occur in Northern School B even though most of the students at the English-medium school adjacent to the EFI school lived in a public housing complex with a bad reputation for crime. Many of those students were First Nations students. Would they have had access to the EFI school if they had tried to 'flee' there? Would the reception they received have differed if their children's ancestral language was still intact and they had recently migrated south? Do factors such as these explain the dearth of cultural minority children in some urban French immersion settings? Can the English-medium teachers' outrage at the mere mention of EFI possibly being a better option for First Nations children be attributed to a caste-like approach to multilingualism? To what extent do outdated (yet potent) attitudes about language development, bi-/multilingualism, and minority populations result in (c)overtly denying some children access to the program? The mere fact that the results of these studies lend themselves to such questions is cause for concern. They suggest the presence of caste-like attitudes, which are also cause for concern. Such attitudes create a climate in which discrimination against minority children can occur by institutionalizing structures of unequal access to educational opportunities. Caste-like attitudes can also compromise the ethical nature of the EFI program.

In summary, a principal flatly rejected the idea of permitting 'ESL' children to enrol in EFI, and some teachers expressed outrage at the thought of First Nations children enrolling in EFI. These comments reflect deep-rooted attitudes about the viability of EFI for 'at-risk' students. Genesee (2006) cautions that there is 'insufficient evidence to support decisions to exclude *at-risk* students from immersion on an *a priori* basis' (21), yet my findings suggest that this is being done. Genesee (2006) classifies such behaviour as unethical because it excludes a segment of Canadian society from French immersion: 'the most effective educational means for promoting bilingual competence given...global realities' (5). Research evidence—not preconceived, deficit-based notions about language development in general, and linguistic and cultural minority students in particular—is needed before parents and schools can make informed choices about which (if any) children should not enrol in French immersion. In conclusion,

- linguistic and cultural diversity does exist in EFI outside of Canada's major urban centres,
- in both the southern and northern studies reported on in this paper, the linguistic diversity found in the EFI programs reflected the linguistic diversity of the cities in which the studies took place,

- cultural and linguistic minority students have varying degrees of *de facto* access to EFI in different settings, but (deficit-based) preconceived notions can constrain their actual access to the program,
- access (denied) to EFI matters as it has major implications for social justice and the future of the program as a vehicle for the development of official bilingualism,
- there are sufficient numbers of linguistic minority students in EFI to warrant reconsidering program design so that all students can benefit from an enrichment model of bilingual education,
- greater awareness is needed of the importance of linguistic and cultural minority students gaining access to EFI and those enrolled not being pushed-out, and
- grassroots efforts are urgently needed to put MLE on the educational map in Ontario and institutionalize equitable access to learning opportunities for minority students.

To sum up the issues, outdated (yet potent) deficit views and caste-like positioning of linguistic and cultural minority students must be addressed. Only then will immersion and other forms of bilingual education programs be implemented in the public school system and MLE gain a toehold on the educational landscape of Ontario. Linguistic and cultural minority children may not have been the intended program participants in EFI, but they are there. The lessons that parents, teachers, administrators and policy-makers must take away from the results of these studies are as follows. They must take the necessary steps to allow more children with diverse backgrounds into the program; they must alter program design and structures so all children can benefit equally; they must eradicate caste-like attitudes so that diverse children can stay in the program. Only then will EFI be equitable for all.

## Notes

1 The global term used to describe Canada's indigenous people is Aboriginal. The term 'aboriginal' encompassed indigenous people of First Nations, Métis, or Inuit backgrounds. For purposes of this paper, I will primarily refer to First Nations people (e.g. Mi'kmaqs, Ojibwe, etc.).

2 Bussing is not provided for students to attend English-medium schools out of their encatchment area; students must attend their local English school.

3 I refer to this city as 'XX' here and in the References to protect it and my participants' anonymity.

# Part IV
# MLE in theory and Practice—Diversity in Indigenous Experience

# 11

# The Contribution of Postcolonial Theory to Intercultural Bilingual Education in Peru: An Indigenous Teacher Training Programme

*Susanne Jacobsen Pérez*

## Introduction[1]

In many South and Latin American countries, for instance Peru, Bolivia, Ecuador, Guatemala, the debate on bi- and multilingual education has been nourished for decades on the experience of multi- and intercultural educational programmes. A common point of reference has been what is generally termed 'Intercultural Bilingual Education' (IBE). In 2000 this educational model was in use in seventeen Latin American countries (López and Küper 2000: 4). Throughout the continent, IBE and bilingual education are mainly for the indigenous population.

The development of bilingual education and the changes the model has undergone seem to have been influenced by postcolonial nation-building processes and the ways that state and nation are perceived by various social agents. Defining the nation determined simultaneously how indigenous peoples should be in order to fit into the nation: 'Latin America's option for the indigenous peoples has, from the beginning of the Republican era of the nineteenth century until very recently (and perhaps even still) been one of cultural and linguistic homogenisation' (López and Küper 2000: 26).

Peru can serve as an example of how bilingual and intercultural bilingual education have been developed within the framework of a predominantly homogenising state policy towards the indigenous peoples. Various social and educational agents have influenced the development of bilingual education models, which now reflect competing discourses about nation and state—a monocultural homogeneous nation-state versus a multicultural heterogeneous nation-state. The meaning of bilingual education and the way it is practised by state agents, teachers and trainers depends greatly on the way they perceive indigenous peoples' role in society.

The Peruvian experience clearly shows that the development of bilingual education and IBE is an ongoing process of negotiation between the various agents. It also shows that the way groups are defined and define themselves can strongly influence whether bilingual education can be implemented in a region. Bilingual education has developed in two regions in Peru: the rain forest regions, generally referred to as Amazonia, and the highland Andean region.

Indigenous rain forest movements have played a key role in influencing the existing bilingual education state policy not only for indigenous education but also in introducing the concept of interculturality to the entire education system. By contrast IBE has been applied by the state in Andean regions where most of the population is bilingual but do not define themselves as indigenous peoples.

This is the case with the region described in this article. Cusco is an Andean region where the indigenous language Quechua dominates, but most of the Quechua-speaking population do not define themselves in terms of ethnicity, but rather as peasants, i.e. in terms of production.

For many years bilingual teacher training focused on the need for bilingual education in order to achieve better academic results for children whose mother tongue was Quechua. However, results were relatively poor, and neither teachers nor parents were convinced of the utility of bilingual education. But in recent years several teacher training projects have started to focus on the inherent coloniality of formal education. I will refer mainly to an in-service teacher training programme for teachers from bilingual, rural areas around Cusco, Peru.[2] The programme underwent significant changes in training content, methods and activities after starting to emphasise the concept of interculturality, which resulted in an appropriation of the IBE model by teachers and local villagers.

## History of Intercultural Bilingual Education in Peru

### Policies and Practices

Peru has always been a multilingual and multiethnic country. Today the country has 42 living indigenous languages, Spanish, and several immigrant languages. The biggest indigenous language, Quechua, is spoken by more than 3 million, which is almost 17% of the population. It can be found in all Peruvian regions, but is dominant in the highlands. Forty indigenous languages are spoken by 0.7% of the Peruvian population, mainly in the rain forest lowlands. Because of the power and status of Spanish and 'hispanification' processes, many of these languages are in danger of extinction (Trapnell and Neira 2006: 258-262). Formal education has played a central role in the promotion of a Spanish-only policy:

> [I]n Latin America, school generally came to the rural zones hand-in-hand with Spanish. This fact stood out, and still does, in the conceptions that indigenous people have about this institution, and about the roles and functions that the various languages occupy in it. For many people, their language still does not belong in the school, nor can it be used in it. It is believed that Spanish alone is the language of reading and writing, and many parents still believe that learning to write means learning Spanish,

the language required to operate more fully and exercise their citizenship rights. (López and Küper 2000: 28–29).

Even if there were instances of indigenous languages being used initially in schooling, since the end of the eighteenth century indigenous education has been dominated by the use of Spanish as the medium of instruction (ibid.: 26). This did not change after the country′s independence in 1821, as it was now governed by a small Creole elite which considered itself the direct heirs of European superiority and therefore continued to promote Spanish as the national language (Manrique Galvez 2003: 6).

In the 1930s and 40s, however, due to a strong national indigenist current, it was officially recognised that two of the indigenous languages, Quechua and Aymara, should be used as mediums of instruction (MoI) during the initial years of primary school. Teaching through the mother tongue was considered necessary in order to assimilate the indigenous peoples into the nation (López and Küper 2000: 26–27).

Concurrently the protestant North American Summer Institute of Linguistics (SIL) started offering its services to Latin American countries, i.e. linguistic studies of indigenous languages, teacher training, and materials for primary schools in indigenous communities. In 1952, SIL became the first government-authorised institution to train indigenous teachers in bilingual education in Peru (Trapnell and Neira 2006: 255, López and Küper 2000: 28). The aim of the teacher training was to 'create a type of school that gives the pupils the essential elements of an initial culture, trains them for productive work, teaches them basic norms of civilised life, the concept of nationality and hygienic-sanitary practices.' (Supreme Decree 909, 1952, quoted in Lùdescher 1998). The indigenous languages were definitely only to be used transitionally during the first two years, until children were able to use Spanish (Trapnell 1985: 125).

After some years it became clear that SIL was not only training young indigenous people as bilingual teachers, but also to become evangelist priests (Lüdescher 1998: 241). Indigenous organisations and anthropologists were severely critical of SIL's approach in the 1970s: its work was based on two false assumptions, that indigenous culture and tradition were backward and inappropriate for modern life, and that every culture has good and bad parts. Thus SIL established a logic whereby traditional life is the same as idleness and the cause of poverty whereas progress is achieved by hard work and a civilised life. By not revealing to indigenous teachers the real causes of their poverty, SIL was reproducing and contributing to the dominant discourse that legitimates the exploitation and domination of the indigenous peoples as cheap labour. Since indigenous culture was perceived negatively, it was not reflected in the curriculum either. Thus indigenous cosmology was completely ignored in SIL's approach (Trapnell 1985: 125–128).

Several alternative teacher training programmes arose as a result of the critique. One of the most important is 'Programma de Formación de Maestros Bilingües de la Amazonía Peruana' (FORMABIAP) which was the kind of education that the indigenous movements wanted. FORMABIAP is qualitatively different from what most Peruvian teacher education institutions offered, and has greatly influenced the politics of indigenous peoples' education. Since 1998 FORMABIAP has functioned as an NGO through a contract between the indigenous organisation 'Asociación Interétnica de Desarrollo de la Selva Peruana' (AIDESEP[3]) and the state teacher education institution 'Loreto'. It is based on the Amazonian indigenous organisations' claim for culturally relevant education. Together with the first students and indigenous adults an alternative curriculum for the Amazon region was elaborated, and approved by the Ministry of Education (MoE). The curriculum was both clear in language strategy and based on indigenous cosmology. The students spend half of their time in the institution and half in their communities or a school belonging to their language group, where they have to investigate aspects of their culture and apply IBE strategies.

Through the foundation of FORMABIAP in the Amazon region and similar projects in the Andean region in the 1970s and 80s, interculturality became a fundamental concept in bilingual education. It was felt to be necessary to introduce the concept explicitly in order to distance these programmes from assimilationist approaches to bilingual education.

The first national policy on bilingual education, in 1972, was supportive of this trend (Trapnell and Neira 2006: 267). The policy had resulted from expert meetings in the 1960s and reflected both linguistic and cultural considerations. It explicitly stated that bilingual education should be offered to children with an indigenous mother tongue or were incipient bilinguals in an indigenous language and Spanish. It recognised the use of bilingual education at pre-school level and the need for methodological variation depending on the pupil's degree of bilingualism. However, it only decreed the use of indigenous languages as MoI until the fourth grade of primary education.

Not much has happened in bilingual education policy since the 1970s. According to the 2003 Education Law, Art. 20, IBE should be '...offered in the entire education system' to children from indigenous minorities, '...guaranteeing acquisition [of curricular content] through the medium of the pupil's mother tongue and of Spanish as a second language, as well as the acquisition of foreign languages afterwards.' Even if the law states that bilingual education should be offered at all educational levels, in reality it is still only offered in primary education, and in some cases kindergarten (Trapnell and Neira 2006: 267).

The concept of interculturality was not mentioned explicitly in 1972, but the policy was embedded in an overall educational reform policy which aimed at overcoming the indigenous population's poverty and addressing social and economic realities (ibid.). Since 1989 interculturality has been explicitly incorporated in Peruvian bilingual education policies, and since 1991 it has been applied to the entire primary education cycle (ibid.: 268). When the concept was incorporated, it referred mainly to the inclusion of indigenous knowledge in the curriculum during initial schooling and thereafter gradually bringing in content from other cultural traditions. From 1991 interculturality and the acknowledgement of cultural diversity were to permeate all education (ibid).

This becomes even clearer in the Education Law of 2003. Here, interculturality as a principle is described as follows:

> Interculturality…sees the country's cultural, ethnic and linguistic diversity as richness and regards the recognition of and respect for difference, as well as knowledge about and an attitude of appreciation of others as the basis for living together in harmony and for interaction between the world's different cultures. (General Education Law 2003, Art. 8).

In addition an 'intercultural approach' is perceived as a necessary tool to reach 'universal coverage, quality and equity in education' (2003, Art. 10).

The use of the term interculturality in the education policies of the 1990s has been criticised by several authors because it does not spell out reform. It is rather part of multiculturalism, which retains the idea of cultures as separate entities based on difference. The philosophy of difference leads to compensatory policies and policies of positive discrimination for certain groups. By doing this, it maintains the power relations that are in force between these groups (Tubino 2003, Walsh 2003).

Recently several authors have therefore used the concept of interculturality to make a break with the coloniality of social and economic relationships (Tubino 2003, Fuller 2003).

> It is necessary to differentiate between interculturality as a de facto situation and interculturality as a normative principle. The first expresses the concrete fact that in a majority of nation-states different cultures co-exist, which may live together harmoniously or, as in the case of a huge part of Latin America, may reject and discriminate each other. The second refers to an ethical-political proposal which seeks to improve the concept of citizenship with the aim of adding the recognition of the cultural rights of the people, cultures and ethnic groups that coexist within the frontiers of a nation-state to the already established rights of liberty and equity in the eyes of the law. (Fuller 2003: 10).

The civil war period between 1980 and 2000 may have made even clearer the need for radical changes in Peruvian society. It is estimated that almost 70,000 Peruvians were killed and that the main regions affected by the civil war were '…regions which were marginalised as to political and economic power and leaving the indigenous rural population as the victims *per excellence.*' (Comisiòn de la Verdad y Reconciliación 2003).

The new discourse of interculturality, which proposes institutional changes in all sectors, has also penetrated educational practice in some regions and some projects. Even if it is not part of a coherent state policy, its potential can be analysed by looking at some of the concrete changes that have occurred in a teacher training programme when it integrated postcolonial criticism of education and state policies into its strategies.

Even if bilingual education has now officially existed in Peru since 1952, its actual extent is reckoned to be no more than approximately 10% of needs (Trapnell and Neira 2006: 267). This means that 90% of indigenous pupils still receive education that does not involve their language or culture. In addition, formal IBE teacher education is still very restricted in the country. The MoE has developed teacher training plans for bilingual education, but in fact the principal developers and implementers of minority mother-tongue based education have been NGOs, universities and research centres which have financed experimental projects (ibid.: 269). The MoE's lukewarm treatment of IBE was manifest when the department in charge of IBE was merged with the department of rural education.

IBE policies and practices are thus still very weak, as they are not supported by a coherent state policy. Most of the achievements that have been reached are due to indigenous organisations' struggle for their cultural and linguistic rights and the insistence of anthropologists, linguists and national and international NGOs working with education.

## Teacher training

Between 2003 and 2007, I worked in a Peruvian in-service teacher training programme for indigenous bilingual teachers (hereafter 'the programme'). It is one part of a local education NGO that has worked in and around Cusco since 1981. It was established in 1998, training teachers who worked in semi-urban schools with a high percentage of Quechua-speaking pupils. Since 2002 the programme has trained teachers in rural schools, and I will only refer to that part of the experience.

The aim of the programme is to qualify teachers working in rural, bilingual areas with methods from intercultural and bilingual education. The main activity of the programme is teacher training, along with producing some school and training materials. Each year the programme investigates a particular aspect of IBE.

The programme is a small-scale one, as only fifty teachers in service attend at a time over a three-year period, but the programme is interesting in itself, because it has moved from a culturally assimilationist bilingual education model towards a culturally revitalising and re-affirmative model.

### *The teachers and schools*

The programme trains teachers working in rural schools in bilingual areas. In order to assure sustainability, several criteria are applied when choosing participants for the programme. One of the criteria was to work with 'school networks'. Peruvian schools in rural areas are organised into school networks: teachers from schools which are relatively close to each other decide on a joint education policy for their schools, including joint training needs and activities, and apply for funding for development projects. Administratively, every network has to present yearly reports to the local MoE office, with details of school year plans, teacher training needs, etc.

For the last two project periods, the programme has decided to work with teacher networks instead of volunteer teachers, as this had several advantages. Working with volunteer teachers assured teacher motivation, as they had chosen to attend the course, but often other teachers at the same school or the principal were against the teacher's ideas and methods. By contrast, working with networks means working with all the teachers at a school and at all levels from kindergarten to secondary school. It is thus easier to commit all teachers to an educational proposal. It also means that one is working within a relatively small area. This makes school visits, coordination and cooperation with the local communities and the local MoE offices much easier. Finally, working with networks enables the teachers to discuss and integrate a joint education and language policy in their schools, as this is part of the network aims.

*Characteristics of the schools*

The programme works with kindergarten, primary and secondary school teachers. The kindergarten level in Peru covers children from 3 to 6 years. It is not obligatory, but more and more children at this age are sent by their families to kindergarten. In villages where kindergartens cannot be established, normally due to the fact that there are not enough children in the village, alternative informal kindergarten education is offered to the children. While the teachers employed in a kindergarten need to be professionals, those who work in the informal kindergartens are generally people from the village who have finished secondary school and who may have received some kind of training.

Primary education is offered from grades 1–6 in Peru. Most of the schools that the programme works with have between one and three teachers, covering all six grades or in the case of some small villages, only grades 1–4. Only the bigger villages and the district capital schools have enough teachers to cover all grades, and only in the case of the district capital schools is there a school principal with no teaching duties.

Even if 90% of all rural schools, or 75% of all public primary schools in Peru, are characterised by having less than a teacher for every grade (Cordero, Contreras, Ames, Dippo, Durán, Alsop, Fynbo, Sánchez, Gonzales and García 2005: 832), mainstream teacher training does not cover methods or classroom organisation that take into consideration this reality.

Secondary education is offered from grades 7 – 11. In rural areas, secondary schools are generally in the district capital. A few can be found in bigger villages, but often only offering the first grades of secondary education. Distance to the secondary school has been identified as one of the crucial factors for parents' decisions on whether to let their children continue in school or not. Secondary schools are often so far away from the villages that children cannot get there and back on the same day. Thus sending the children to secondary school often implies extra costs for accommodation, food and transport.

### *Characteristics of the teachers*

Apart from the village kindergarten teachers, all teachers have been trained. Even if they work with bilingual children, almost none of them have been formally trained in bilingual education when they start in the programme. But most of them are fluent bilinguals in Quechua and Spanish, and many have lived in rural areas during their childhood and youth. This fact has been crucial when the programme applied strategies of linguistic and cultural revitalisation.

There seemed to be an interesting difference in the level of linguistic and cultural sensitivity between trained teachers and villagers who taught in the alternative kindergarten programmes. Thus village teachers often responded much better to the intercultural approach. This difference has also been observed by Trapnell (2005), who interviewed indigenous village kindergarten teachers about the utility of supposedly contextualised teaching guidelines elaborated by a kindergarten expert. The village women working in the informal kindergartens showed systematically how the guidelines did not correspond to indigenous teaching strategies, led to misunderstandings, and bored children.

All teachers, with few exceptions, live in Cusco, which is the biggest city in the area. Therefore many of the teachers have to stay at their schools during the week, or even a month at a time, as the villages they work in are far from Cusco. The teachers' living conditions in the schools are often poor and their access to conventional educational materials such as books, maps, and photocopies is restricted. On the other hand, the teacher training experience shows that teachers spending so much time in the villages can be turned to advantage.

### *Bilingual education model*

The bilingual education model recommended by the programme follows the ministerial recommendations and models used by other teacher training programmes in the region. Basically the indigenous language, Quechua, is maintained as the language of instruction until grade 6 of primary education, though more and more time is dedicated to teaching Spanish as a second language and using it as MoI.

The programme also recommends the use of Quechua as MoI in secondary school. Nevertheless, it is very difficult to convince teachers of the necessity of using the children's mother tongue as MoI. Even at the grade 4 of primary school, teachers do not approve of using Quechua as MoI, and often they end up teaching less than recommended through the language.

Table 1 shows the language education recommendations given to the schools that participate in the programme.

**Table 11.1.** Bilingual education model recommended by the IBE teacher training programme

| Year | Language subjects: Quechua, Spanish and English | Language of teaching and learning |
|---|---|---|
| Kindergarten | Spanish is taught as a second language every day for 20 minutes (only oral Spanish). | Quechua |
| Grades 1 and 2, primary education | Quechua as a language is taught within the subject 'Integral Communication'.<br>Spanish is taught as a second language every day for 30 minutes to one hour (only oral Spanish) | Children acquire literacy skills through the medium of Qechua. All other curriculum content is also taught through the medium of Quechua. |
| Grades 3 and 4, primary education | Quechua as a language is taught within the subject 'Integral Communication'.<br>Spanish is taught as a second language two entire days a week (oral and written Spanish) | All new curricular content is taught through the medium of Quechua.<br>Well-known curricular content can be integrated in the Spanish as a second language lessons. |
| Grades 5 and 6, primary education | Quechua as a language is taught within the subject 'Integral Communication'.<br>Spanish is taught as a second language two and a half days a week (oral and written Spanish) | New curricular content should preferably be taught through the medium of Quechua, but may be integrated into the Spanish as a second language lessons. |
| Secondary education | No recommendations by the programme. Quechua is generally not taught as a subject, except for one school where it is taught for two hours a week (replacing English lessons).<br>Spanish is taught as a subject (though without L2 methodology). | Spanish is used as the medium of teaching and learning.<br>The programme recommends that secondary teachers at least use Quechua as an oral medium of instruction when explaining complex academic concepts. |

### *Spanish as a second language*

The MoE has elaborate detailed guidelines for Spanish as a second language, which many teachers use actively, and which are used in teacher training also. The guidelines are based on a communicative approach. They stipulate the communicative aims, words and phrases to learn, and the underlying grammatical aspects of communicative situations to be practised. They contain detailed instructions for activities and should therefore make it relatively easy for teachers of Spanish as a second language.

As well as the communicative approach, the programme has added a rights-based approach to Spanish as a second language lessons. Spanish is a colonial language and much of the real-life communication in this language is neither amicable nor on a basis of equality. It is often a tool for discrimination. Pupils should therefore also have the opportunity to prepare themselves to confront and respond to discriminatory attitudes.

This is how two schools have organised in Spanish as a second language teaching.

1. At a single-teacher school with four grades, the teacher had trouble in making the children switch to Spanish on the 'Spanish days'. Especially the smallest pupils were very shy and often did not participate actively. As he had only one classroom, the teacher decided to transform his own office into the Spanish language classroom. Together with the pupils he creates scenery and objects from real-life communication. Situations like 'shopping at the local store' or 'going by bus to Cusco' become real. The result has been that even first grade pupils are now participating actively, as they recognise situations and activate their passive vocabulary.
2. At a three-teacher school with six grades, teachers found it problematic that children within the same grade managed Spanish at very different levels. Therefore they decided to group children not according to grades, but according to their proficiency in Spanish. Within a few months it was clear that children achieved much more Spanish when placed at the right level.

## Quechua as a Medium of Teaching and Learning, and as a Subject

Teachers are not generally reluctant to switch from Spanish to Quechua as the medium of teaching and learning, as most of them are fluent Quechua speakers. However they identify several problems that the programme is trying to address.

### *Written Quechua and Quechua grammar*

Most of the teachers speak Quechua, but due to their own monolingual training in Spanish, they have never acquired the official orthography and syntax rules. As many of the teachers are responsible for introducing pupils to literacy, they are worried about transferring wrong spelling and syntax.

Their insecurities are moreover complicated because of an ongoing public dispute between two groups of experts, referred to as the three-vowel and five-vowel groups, about the Quechua alphabet and spelling. The three-vowel group includes the MoE, which with a group of linguists, Quechua experts and Quechua speakers has ratified a unified Quechua alphabet and spelling rules for all Peruvian Quechua dialects. The five-vowel group is represented by the 'Academia Mayor de la Lengua Quechua' which basically defends dialectal variation that is visible in different spellings.

While the programme follows the MoE position, many of the teachers are members of the Academia and therefore defend the other position. Even so, discussions during training sessions may have helped other teachers to become aware of certain characteristics of Quechua language.

### *Translating academic content from Spanish to Quechua and creating academic text in Quechua*

The MoE has elaborated national textbooks and workbooks for the four curricular areas and all grades which are distributed in all schools. But these materials are written in Spanish. Even if the MoE has started producing books in some indigenous languages, these are often criticised by teachers due to a massive use of neologisms or unfamiliar sentence structures. While some teachers simply rule out using the materials, others use parts of them.

Basically all programmes in IBE are simultaneously involved in the production of educational materials both in the indigenous languages and for teaching Spanish as a second language. In the Cusco region, NGOs exchange their materials in order to make them accessible in as many schools as possible. The IBE network also decided to catalogue the existing materials so that teachers and other interested persons can know what is available for IBE.

Even if the volume of teaching materials for IBE has increased, it neither covers all areas of the curriculum nor all levels of education. Especially in relation to abstract concepts, very little has been done. A lot of academic terminology has not been elaborated in Quechua, so that words like 'cell', 'atom' or 'atmosphere' need to be invented. Mathematical terminology has been created, but not enough social and natural science terminology. Especially in secondary school this is a growing problem.

As long as no agreed terminology exists, the programme generally recommends that teachers borrow the term from Spanish, but explain the concept in Quechua. As it is not the word 'cell' which causes problems for the pupils, but the concept, the programme advises teachers to explain in their own words in Quechua what is meant, and feel free to give examples and to elaborate on the concept in a meaningful way. Teachers are applying this strategy both orally and in writing. This may be one of the ways to get more acceptance of the indigenous languages as medium of teaching and learning.

## Questioning the neutrality of academic knowledge

A rather different question is whether academic language should become part of the indigenous languages *at all*. This leads to considering the importance of postcolonial theory and analysis when discussing the purpose of bilingual and intercultural education. This should not be reduced to a 'technical' question of finding the best indigenous word for 'cell' or 'atmosphere', but requires discussion of the ideological implications when it is assumed that the introduction of what counts as academic knowledge, reasoning and 'truths' is good.

Indigenous peoples, anthropologists and others have questioned this truth, but their efforts were branded as 'ethno-academic', for instance ethno-mathematics, ethno-biology, ethno-medicine, and ethno-astronomy. But why is some knowledge classified as 'ethnic' in contrast to 'pure' knowledge, as in 'pure mathematics'?

> Nowadays, 'ethno-' is used in a quite liberal way…, in order to indicate that the investigation of a particular field of study (as biology or astronomy), is made from the perspective of and based on the knowledge of a 'traditional' non-occidental society. (Urton 2003: 21).

By classifying non-occidental knowledge as 'traditional' or 'local wisdom', it is fixed in time and space. At the same time, words like 'abstract', 'neutral', 'pure science' or 'universal knowledge' hide the fact that all knowledge is produced *by somebody, at a certain time in history and at a certain place in history*. By defining academic knowledge as time- and spaceless, Western scientists are trying to hide their own philosophical foundations (Urton 2003: 21).

> '[T]he 'history' of knowledge is marked geo-historically, geo-politically and geo-culturally; it has a value, colour and a place "of origin" ' (Walsh 2004: 2). Thus when indigenous epistemologies, philosophies and ways of 'doing science' are questioned and reduced to 'local wisdom', or 'ethno-sciences' by occidental scientists, they are actually reproducing colonial and neocolonial power relations. It is a colonisation of knowledge. Access to occidental academic knowledge is presented as access to the 'modern world' and 'development', which ultimately reproduces the bonds of colonialism.

In order to make a break with the colonisation of knowledge, Walsh proposes the construction of an 'epistemic interculturality':

> …the construction of new epistemological frames that incorporate and negotiate occidental and non-occidental knowledges, indigenous but also black (and their theoretical and lived bases, from the past but also from the present), always maintaining as fundamental the necessity of confronting coloniality of power to which these knowledges have been submitted. (Walsh 2004: 4)

In her article three steps are proposed, which have been used by the programme in teacher training sessions as a tool for reflection:

- To recognise that knowledge has a value, colour, gender and place of origin and hence, the place from which you think, *is* important.
- To recover, re-value and apply ancestral knowledges, but also to question the temporality and locality attributed to them and that tries to reduce them to 'ancestral wisdom' rather than 'knowledge'.
- Knowledges should not simply be related to each other as blocks or clearly identified and closed entities, but rather as critical contributions to new processes of intellectual intervention. (Amawtay Wasi in Walsh 2004:6).

## Content based on indigenous cosmology

One of the ways that the programme has worked with epistemic interculturality as proposed by Walsh is by strengthening the status of Andean indigenous knowledge (and of the bearers of this knowledge) by bringing it into the school curriculum and giving it the same status as 'universalised' Western knowledge or knowledge based on Peruvian dominant discourses.

In principle this can be done relatively easily, as diversifying the national curriculum is allowed. Teachers, schools, or regions can recreate the national curriculum taking into consideration local circumstances and the local context both in content and methodology. In practice though, the task of diversifying the national curriculum needed to be discussed in many teacher training sessions. Teachers had to train analytical skills, recover their own knowledge about Quechua cosmology, modify their view of the local population that they generally looked down on and did not identify with, and they also needed to learn to apply the new strategies in practice.

Between 2003 and 2006, training sessions about this theme had the following topics: Geopolitics of knowledge; why should we know Andean cosmology?; what does 'quality of life' mean to indigenous peoples?; Andean cosmology is part of our pupils' way of thinking; teachers are also 'knowers' of Andean cosmology; how to recover indigenous concepts; mathematical thinking in Andean cosmology; introducing literacy in a culturally appropriate way; curricular diversification and planning the school year and classes through the community calendar.

Apart from teacher training sessions, in 2005 teachers were invited to participate in a special project; they were asked to plan and implement a school project under the following conditions: the project should use the communal calendar and be based on a local (mainly agricultural) activity; the pupils should be participants in the local activities, and members of the community should be integrated in the project as knowledge persons and teachers.

Every participant teacher was given a camera in order to document the process and central activities. Afterwards they asked the community to comment on and explain what could be seen in the photos. The projects were published in 2006 (Asociacîon Pukllasunchis 2006). They gave other teachers in the region ideas for how they could plan sessions and projects based on the community calendars. Some of the projects were filmed throughout the year to produce videos as educational material for schools. Finally the knowledge gathered through the teachers' projects has also been produced as interactive CD-ROM materials for teachers, pupils and other interested persons. In 2006/7 a group of volunteer teachers received intensive training during their vacations about the relationship between biodiversity, indigenous cosmologies and the school as an institution. Amongst other things, they were taught by community members about agro-diversity and the communal calendar.

When teachers open up for indigenous ways of thinking in school they often do not stop with the content, but start to redefine other aspects of school, like for instance methodology, educational materials, school traditions, language use, even clothing used in schools.

## Redefining the relationship between school and community

When entering the programme, teachers generally identified with their profession, their schools and the national curriculum, including very specific ideas about 'development', 'quality of life', 'progress', etc. The majority did not—as could be expected—identify themselves as belonging to an ethnic group or identify with the communities they worked in, even if many of them had grown up in similar conditions and contexts.

Therefore the aim of the programme was triple: to restore many teachers' identity, as they had abandoned Quechua and rural identity due to discrimination throughout their life and the absence of alternatives to Western thinking about 'the good life'; to re-establish the relationship between school and community, making school part of the community and redefining the school's role in it and in society in general; to actively involve teachers in community life and to create space for communities to influence the kind of school they want; and to open up for communities to participate on equal terms in other public spaces.

Training sessions that treated themes related to the role of school in society and for indigenous peoples were, for instance: the goal of schooling in society; the colonial history of languages of instruction in schools in indigenous villages; teachers' perceptions of the community and pupils; *iskay yachay* ('both knowledges'); cultural and linguistic discrimination in school; discrimination in the classroom.

Apart from training sessions, a pilot project was initiated in a secondary school where teachers and villagers together redefined the goals of school and, as a result of this, school curriculum, structure and subjects taught. The main change has been that villagers and teachers stop considering higher education as their sole source of inspiration, and instead identify local developments and employment routes that would not mean 'just to continue in poverty as our parents' but are based on the region's potential.

Other initiatives to strengthen the communities' voice and participation, especially in education, are radio programmes and videos elaborated by teachers and villagers, and an annual conference where education is discussed.

In 2006, teachers and villagers together made half-hour radio programmes in which they presented the community, development opportunities or problems in the community. The programmes were bilingual in Quechua and Spanish and broadcast in the local region. This was followed up in 2007 by a process whereby villagers had the opportunity to produce videos that were to be broadcast on local television.

In order to make education as a theme more visible in the local region, in 2006 the programme decided to arrange a two-day conference in a provincial capital. To assure sustainability, the conference was organised together with local authorities and with a minimum of NGO input, since the idea was to produce a conference model that could be used year after year with or without the presence of the NGO. The purpose of the conference was to make visible the opinion of the local indigenous population about the role of school and education; to discuss the role of school in society in general and especially in relation to indigenous peoples; to strengthen the ongoing decentralisation process and to give teachers an experience of being just as competent as external education experts.

The title of the conference was 'Gathering two knowledges. Challenges and possibilities in IBE'. The title referred to Western and Andean knowledge systems and the way they can be brought together. The first day focused on rights and citizenship and the second day on the role of school in society.

Before the conference, workshops were held in all districts in the province to collect demands and wishes for a better education system from the local population. Every district was invited to send representatives to the conference.

Teachers from all districts were also invited to present papers about their experience under the different headings of the conference. It was important for the programme to ensure that teachers presenting papers would have the same status as national or international 'experts' on the theme.

The conference was not held in the regional capital, Cusco, but in a provincial capital. This was in order to show that decentralisation can be a reality if dominant social and political actors are willing to follow the principle. To strengthen the status of Quechua, the conference was held as far as possible in Quechua, including papers given by the teachers.

To embed the conference in local traditions, a local shaman[4] conducted an opening ceremony, meals were prepared by local women, and the night programme was a typical dance session of the kind used on special occasions when different communities or districts gather. More than 300 teachers and villagers participated in the conference. The conference was repeated in 2007, which suggests success and sustainability.

## The Potential of Decentralisation

The strategies presented above would only have been anecdotal, if they had not been followed up by political action. The education sector is part of a national decentralisation strategy which has opened up for very interesting participatory processes and the possibility of influencing regional education policies in the direction of IBE.

All regions in Peru are asked to elaborate a 'Regional Educational Project' (REP). In Cusco, I had the opportunity to observe and partly participate in the construction of the REP. At the end of 2005, several of the IBE NGOs had participated in regular meetings where the REP was constructed. In spite of their presence, the working document neither reflected the region's linguistic and cultural diversity, nor the role of IBE. Possibly the education NGOs that work with IBE were busy with other work and did not always sent people from the IBE teacher training programmes.

To establish IBE as a strategic issue in the REP, IBE NGOs formed a network with the purpose of 'affirming and developing intercultural bilingual education in Cusco'.[5] Network representatives have since been sent to the REP formulation meetings, to concentrate only on the IBE aspects. As a network the IBE NGOs obtained sufficient status for them to be able to revise the document, make more visible the linguistic and cultural diversity in the region, and ensure appropriate pedagogy through, for instance, IBE.

The network also became involved in regional policy-making in other sectors than education. Thus through participatory involvement it made sure that there was public discussion of bilingualism and interculturality by all political parties in the election debates in 2006.[6] It also ensured that a congress where a regional development agenda was to be formulated offered a workshop on interculturality, and that there was simultaneous interpretation between Quechua and Spanish during the entire congress.[7]

## Perspectives

In many multilingual postcolonial societies, bi- and multilingual education have been introduced in order to improve the education of groups whose mother tongues are not the colonial language. The choice of a bilingual education model often not only depends on theories of language pedagogy but also on the way the population to be educated is perceived by those who make the policies.

When introducing the concept of interculturality into the discussion on bilingual education, several questions have to be asked: is bilingual education just a tool in an acculturation process or is it a tool that can lead to a multicultural state and intercultural citizenship? If so, which other aspects of society need to be reformed in order to make this happen? It is apparent that the concept of interculturality is not only a methodology in education, but rather can potentially reopen discussion of the colonial conditions that remain in place in many postcolonial societies.

Thus bilingual education does not in itself guarantee a break with colonial social structures. On the contrary, Peruvian history shows that bilingual education from the 1950s until today has mainly served to assimilate the indigenous population to the dominant political, economic and social order. The introduction of the concept of interculturality by indigenous organisations in the 1970s was crucial, and has resulted in a permanent focus on the cultural hidden curriculum in teaching methods, educational materials and curricular content and on the ways in which formal schooling reproduces colonial power relations. However, it is very recent that that the claims of interculturality as a generalised ethical-political project have been formulated all over Latin America.

IBE agents can play an important role in showing how to construct an intercultural society. In the case of Peru, decentralisation processes have opened up fresh opportunities for local networks within civil society to influence regional political agendas, not only within the education sector but more broadly.

Peruvian history shows that political advocacy is an important tool for all IBE agents so as to ensure long-lasting regional solutions or to influence state education policies. The existing state IBE policy can thus be understood as a product of, on the one hand, the elite's desire to integrate the Indians into a national project and, on the other, civil society's and indigenous organisations' struggle for education which they have influenced.

## *Notes*

1 Citations from Spanish sources are in the author's translation.
2 Proyecto 'Escuelas rurales cercanas a la ciudad', Asociación Pukllasunchis.
3 AIDESEP constists of a conglomerate of almost all Amazon indigenous organisations and is therefore important politically.
4 A shaman has several functions. S/he often knows to cure and to carry out rituals necessary for assuring harmony between nature, gods and human beings.
5 Comité para la afirmación y el desarrollo de la EIB – Cusco.
6 In 2006 there were presidential, parliamentary and regional and local elections.
7 This had never happened before at a congress.

# 12

# Reversing Language Shift through a Native Language Immersion Teacher-Training Programme in Canada

*Andrea Bear Nicholas*

## THE CANADIAN CONTEXT

The first ever native language immersion teacher-training programme in Canada was established in Fredericton, New Brunswick in 2001. It grew out of a number of events and opportunities, but mostly out of the tragic reality that the First Nations languages in the Maritime Region of eastern Canada, like most Indigenous languages in Canada and around the Western world, were critically endangered and not expected to survive the present century (Canada 1990). Before relating the details of this project it will be useful to begin with some general information on the Indigenous language situation in Canada.

Canada is part of the block of 'First World' countries that Tove Skutnabb-Kangas (2000: 549-550) describes as 'directly or indirectly responsible for most of the linguistic and cultural genocide in the world', insofar as these countries have generally demanded that other countries respect minority rights while denying 'the same rights to minorities in their own countries'. The hypocrisy and double standard involved is evident in the fact that Canada constantly promotes itself as a champion of human rights, but has ratified little more than half of the Universal Human Rights Instruments. Indeed it stood in 2001 with such 'un-notable' countries as Azerbaijan, Barbados, Belgium, Bolivia, Switzerland and Uganda in having ratified only 31 of the 52 international human rights instruments (Skutnabb-Kangas 2000: 594, 556). In 2007 Canada demonstrated its double standard, yet again, having been one of only four of the countries in the world that voted against the Declaration on the Rights of Indigenous Peoples in the General Assembly of the United Nations (143 voted for it and 11 abstained). Indeed, it appears that Canada not only voted against the Declaration, but also lobbied hard to prevent its passage. Sadly, this means that the linguistic and other rights of Indigenous Peoples in Canada will continue to be denied even the legal support of what is merely an aspirational human rights instrument.

Before colonisation there were about 63 languages in Canada belonging to 11 different language families, the largest being Algonquian. Of the 63 languages at least 6 are considered to be in a critical state with fewer than 50 speakers, while only 3, Cree with 80,000 speakers, Ojibway with 23,000, and Inuktitut, with 29,000, are considered to be healthy enough to survive the present century (Norris 2002). All the others, mostly with fewer than 1000 speakers, are expected to disappear from the face of the earth unless drastically new strategies are implemented to reverse the trends. Like climate change, the factors in this phenomenon are multiple and complex, and like climate change, the consequences are multiplying exponentially (Krauss 1992: 4-10, Fettes 1998, Nettle and Romaine 2000).

In Canada there is some correlation to be made between size of population and linguistic survival. In other words, those having the largest populations, such as the three Aboriginal languages mentioned above, have generally the best prognosis, while those having the smallest numbers, such as Han, Munsee or Western Abenaki, are experiencing some of the sharpest declines. But even size is not always an indicator since the Mohawks, who speak an Iroquoian language, have a population of at least 40,000, yet only a small number of Mohawks, 425 according to the 2001 census, are fluent speakers (Norris 2002).[1] Other factors, such as isolation or proximity to urban centres, also tend to correlate with the degree of language survival. For example, the majority of First Nations having relatively healthy languages (Cree, Ojibway, and Inuit) are located in northern regions of Canada, farthest from the heavily populated urban centres in the south. At the same time, there have been other factors at play that do not seem to fit any expected pattern. For example, some of the languages, such as Mi'kmaq, or Maliseet,[2] the language of my people, the Wblastbkwewiyik, have experienced heavy contact with Europeans for four centuries and yet are still spoken today, with Mi'kmaq having over 7000 speakers and Maliseet well under 1000.[3] Meanwhile, other languages, such as Han, Tagish, and Tahltan that have been in contact with Europeans barely a century are now nearly extinct (Task Force on Aboriginal Languages and Cultures 2005: 34-36).

One way of measuring the state of Indigenous languages is to count the number of speakers and to track that number over time. According to one study by the Department of Indian Affairs only one in four Aboriginal people (24%) spoke an Aboriginal language in 2001, and that number had declined from 29% in 1996 (Norris 2002: 19).[4] In New Brunswick a noticeable decline in child speakers began about four decades ago, which was about the same period of time that the Federal government began imposing the integration (actually 'forced assimilation') of First Nations children into public schools (Bear Nicholas 1996). Though generally lamented, there was a feeling that this declining trend in child speakers was the way of the world, even a mark of progress which no reasonable person would oppose. The more highly educated families, including my own and my husband's, came to passively believe the stigma attached to their language by the dominant society—that it probably served no useful purpose, and that any effort spent on teaching it to children would probably confuse or seriously hinder the learning of English. My father who was raised with the language in a more traditional hunting and trapping lifestyle off-reserve on the American side of our territory, was eventually forced to attend school by the time he was eight or nine. He later became a teacher in public schools in the 1930s, and did not maintain the language or teach it to us.

During the same period the language on-reserve was doing significantly better, in spite of the punitive laws requiring parents to send their children to strictly English-only schools, or risk being jailed. For most this meant day-schools on-reserve, but for some it meant residential schools hundreds of miles away where children were subjected to extreme abuses for speaking their language (Knockwood 1992, Milloy 1999). Yet, what happened to my family off-reserve is now happening several generations later on-reserve. The older generations in my husband's family still speak the language fluently, but none of the younger generations could be considered fluent. All generations now are quite well educated, including in their numbers a judge, a former chief, (recently decreased) and many who are university-educated. Indeed, some even became educators who taught only in the English language, in spite of fluency in their mother tongue.

How did this come to be? Again, it has been the cumulative effect of assimilative laws, intense indoctrination, and subtractive language learning, primarily in school, that has produced this state of affairs as part of the larger colonial reality of English as a 'killer' language (Pakir 1991). That we as First Nations people have come in varying degrees and various ways to cooperate in this worldwide project of linguistic genocide (Dunbar and Skutnabb-Kangas 2008) is one of the most difficult situations to address, but it is not unique to my people.

It was only after World War II that Canada began to question its program of residential schooling for First Nations children, not for their harsh assimilationist goals, but rather for the supposed slow rate of assimilation that they had accomplished. Segregation was now seen to be the problem, and integration into public schools, the solution. From 1947 to 1961, as residential schools began to close, the numbers of First Nations children enrolled in public schools rose dramatically from 137 to 10, 822, and by 1969, 60% of all First Nations children were attending public schools (Milloy 1999: 201, 208). It was this policy of forced assimilation, noted above, that constituted a second form of assault on First Nations languages with drastic results, particularly in areas such as New Brunswick where relatively small numbers of children had attended residential school.

By the 1960s the project of assimilation by integration in public schools had become an open policy, especially after the results of a government-funded study advocating assimilation were released (Hawthorne 1966). It was not, however, until three years later when the government extended this policy of integration to include the political integration of First Nations into the mainstream (Canada 1969), that First Nations began to resist (Cardinal 1970). In response to the educational aspects of the new assimilative policies, the National Indian Brotherhood (1972) issued a position paper titled 'Indian Control of Indian Education' (ICIE). Though intended as a rejection of assimilation through education, this paper set in motion a massive programme that, ironically, served to accelerate the assimilation process. This program funded universities across the country to train First Nations people to become teachers in their own schools. On the surface it seemed a valid and much needed project, but in reality it trained fully fluent Native people for forty years to teach only in English (or French in Quebec). In effect, it served to indoctrinate whole cohorts of teachers-to-be into monolingualism, since most went home and then taught children in their own communities almost exclusively in the medium of English.

By teaching only in English these teachers provided no support or opportunity for children to maintain or become proficient in their mother tongue. Indeed, it is quite likely that the modelling provided by First Nations teachers who taught only in English may have actually been more effective as a tool of linguistic genocide than non-First Nations teachers teaching only in English. This is not to demean the intentions of such teachers, but only to demonstrate the effectiveness of the hegemonic indoctrination process, and the degree to which we, ourselves, have become unwitting partners in the destruction of our languages, if only by silently accepting these processes (Herman and Chomsky 1988).

For twenty years no one dared to criticise these teacher-training programmes in Canada until the middle 1990s when one First Nation educator publicly noted that the state of Indigenous languages in his province had actually plummeted in the same period after First Nations teachers had begun to teach in their own communities (King 1995: 8). It now appears that the damage done was possibly more serious than what the residential schools had accomplished by themselves in all the previous years. Of course, residential schools were still a factor in the decline of First Nations languages to the extent that many of the teachers trained under ICIE had been 'educated' in residential schools, and to the extent that community opinion about the priority of English-only had been engendered by the colonial education process for decades. And there were other new factors as well, in the sudden decline, factors such as the proliferation of television and the increased mobility of reserve-based people. Nevertheless, the indictment implied by this educator's comments concerning the role of teacher-training programmes in the process of linguistic genocide, still stands.

We now know, thanks to the exhaustive work of Tove Skutnabb-Kangas (2000: 318-365), precisely how dominant language medium of instruction actually accomplishes linguistic genocide in education. The problem is that not enough people know this. In fact, most of us, including too many of our education leaders, still labour under the indoctrination of past decades that holds bilingualism to be useless and our languages to have no utility in the modern world. As a result, First Nations parents and communities still overwhelmingly choose English (or French in Quebec) as the medium of instruction for their children believing that it represents their best interests. It is this self-colonisation that stands as one of our greatest challenges.

Even where Indigenous parents would prefer Mother tongue medium (MTM) education for their children there are all kinds of other barriers, most importantly the serious lack of financial resources to make the development of such an education possible. Canada, in fact, is seriously, and even criminally, lacking in the will both to promote and to fund such programmes, in spite of the growing and overwhelming evidence of the benefits of bilingualism and MTM education. First Nations' schools, in general, receive at least one-quarter to one-third less funding than public schools in Canada.

This lack of resources may be largely attributed to the fact that, unlike some Nordic countries (Aikio-Puoskari 2005), Canada has no positive linguistic rights for Indigenous Peoples (Skutnabb-Kangas, 2000: 511-514), hence no laws providing for the maintenance and financial support of their languages in education. The only positive minority linguistic rights recognised in Canada are the rights of the French minority. In that case, over $260 million is allocated annually to the maintenance of French schools, with nearly $10 million alone going to one province[5] that has fewer than 2000 French people. Meanwhile, less than $4 million is allocated annually to nearly a million Aboriginal people representing more than 60 languages in Canada (Norris 2002). Under a new agreement worked out several years ago that amount would have increased to $17 million annually for a period of ten years, but even that was clawed-back by a relatively new national government in 2007. Had positive and protective language legislation been in place there is a good chance that this claw-back might not have been possible. There is, also, a very good chance that were Canada to be taken to court on the matter, it would lose (Leitch 2005). Considering the great destruction done deliberately to First Nations' languages since colonisation (and only recently admitted in the raging debate over residential school compensation) there should be much more funding apportioned to First Nations to maintain and/or regenerate their languages. And to ensure this support over time First Nations leaders need to push hard for legislation in all jurisdictions to protect their languages.

Another barrier to the survival of First Nations languages in Canada is that created by a separation of funding for First Nations languages and funding for First Nations schools at the national level (Bear Nicholas 2007). Heritage Canada, the federal department responsible for matters relating to the culture and language of all cultural groups in Canada, is responsible for disbursing the funds for First Nations' language programmes, while Indian Affairs Canada, the federal department responsible for all Aboriginal Peoples in Canada, including the Inuit, is responsible for funding First Nations and Inuit schools. This separation strictly disallows funding from the language source (Heritage Canada) to be used in schools for Indigenous children, a problem conspicuously not addressed in the most recent study on strategies for Indigenous languages in Canada, which was funded by Heritage Canada (Task Force on Aboriginal Languages and Cultures 2005). In large part, this policy appears to reflect the old linguicidal ideology which held that schools had a particular duty to eradicate Indigenous languages by teaching in the medium of the dominant language, while communities were to be the only locus for Indigenous languages to be used, at least until the schools could accomplish their linguicidal goals.

For most of my adult life I had focused on raising our three children while involving myself in various struggles facing First Nations in Canada. One was the struggle of Native women to address the inequalities in the Indian Act (Jameison 1978). Another was the struggle to research and bring to light the history of my people for use in the schools. As one who had grown up without Maliseet as a first language, I did not feel well enough placed to speak on behalf of the language, but I was growing increasingly concerned that children, even in homes where both parents were fluent speakers, were not learning to speak the language. As a result we had raised our children almost entirely in English, even though my husband was a fluent Maliseet speaker.

In 1989 I had a life-changing experience in the opportunity to attend a talk by Dorothy Lazore, the founder of the Mohawk Immersion Programme at Kahnawake near Montreal, Quebec (Grenoble and. Whaley 2006: 86-94). In this programme begun in 1981, Mohawk children who spoke only English were instructed by bilingual teachers in the medium of their mother tongue, thus fitting the description of an immersion programme for Indigenous Peoples and Minorities, as defined by Skutnabb-Kangas and McCarty (2008). The results of this programme were astounding. We plied Dorothy with questions mostly aimed at proving that her community must have had all the preconditions necessary for such a programme, while ours did not! One by one she countered our questions with answers that proved her community had dealt with the same kinds of barriers, and even many more than we faced in our community. Her community may have been large, but the percentage of fluent speakers had been much lower than even ours. Hers had had barely a dozen speakers out of a population of 7000 at the outset of their project in 1981, and her community lived closer to a very large city (Montreal) while we were relatively isolated in a rural area. We assumed that the divisions between religious factions in our community might be a serious barrier, but the Mohawks had faced many more such divisions, even within religious factions. What was most remarkable was that they had been successful in creating a generation of young people who could speak Mohawk relatively fluently! Secondly, they had been successful in creating an entirely different attitude of love and respect in the school, to the point that the school had experienced virtually no vandalism, and the children literally cried when it came time to graduate, at the end of grade 8. And thirdly, the children in the immersion programme seemed not only to love school, but also to do as well or better, academically, than their peers educated entirely in English. It was an enormous revelation that not only might a language on the brink of extinction be saved, but that children in such a programme might actually do better in school!

For the first time ever, I had hope, but I still felt a sense of powerlessness and lack of moral authority to say or do much.

## Genesis of a University-Based Immersion Teacher-Training Programme

Late in 1992, I was appointed to the Endowed Chair in Native and Aboriginal Cultures of Atlantic Canada at St. Thomas University, a small university in Fredericton, New Brunswick, which had had both a full Native Studies degree programme and the endowed Chair since the 1980s. While I was hired primarily for my work in Maliseet history, it slowly occurred to me that unless something could be done to address the rapidly declining state of our languages in the Maritimes, both Maliseet and Mi'kmaq, that our histories would ultimately be threatened, too.

At the time, the Mi'kmaq population was about 20,000 with about 7,000 speakers in 32 communities spread over five provinces and the American State of Maine. While the Mi'kmaq language was expected to remain strong for at least forty more years, there were many small Mi'kmaq communities where no one but a few elderly people spoke the language. As for Maliseet, the total population was about 5,000 in eight communities in New Brunswick, Quebec and Maine, with only about one-fifth of that population able to speak the language. Indeed, two communities in French areas had no speakers at all, while another three communities with fewer than 200 people had only a small number of elderly speakers each. Only in the three largest Maliseet communities (with populations ranging from 500 to 1,200) was the language still regularly spoken, but even in those communities it was spoken primarily by people over 40 or 50. This language has been judged to range variously from critically endangered (Canada 1990), to viable (Norris 2002), but it is now estimated to have only about ten more years of viability before it is gone, if present trends continue. As for the 2500 Passamaquoddies in the American State Maine, who speak virtually the same language as Maliseets, approximately the same situation pertains with only about one out of five people able to speak the language.

As for written work in Mi'kmaq and Maliseet, both languages were first alphabetised only in the mid- to late nineteenth century, and then primarily by missionaries who produced materials mainly for liturgical purposes (Rand 1888). Around 1900 an amateur linguist began to collect and write oral traditions in Passamaquoddy, the sister language to Maliseet that is located mostly just over the border from New Brunswick in the American state of Maine (Prince 1921). But it was not until the mid-twentieth century that interest on the part of linguists began to produce more standardised orthographies in both Mi'kmaq and Maliseet (Battiste 1987, Teeter 1967). Some of these materials found their way into classroom materials, particularly for the Mi'kmaq (Battiste 1987) and the Passamaquoddy (Leavitt 1979) who now have a sizeable body of literature, though primarily for young people. Since the orthographies developed for the Maliseets tended to end up only in museums and archives, Maliseet language teachers tended to develop and use their own unique systems of writing. As a result, there is now an array of writing systems used within each linguistic group today, which has, sadly, tended to inhibit cooperation between communities in language revitalisation efforts.

At a 1993 symposium sponsored by St Thomas University on the matter of what universities, particularly Native Studies programmes, should be doing for First Nations, it was very clear that language survival was the number one concern in the minds of the Mi'kmaq and Maliseets in attendance. Remarkably, the participants even concluded that immersion would be the best solution to address the situation in our communities, even though immersion was not as well-recognised then, as it is today, as one of the most effective methods of language revitalisation (Grenoble and Whaley 2006: 51). It was also concluded that the universities must help in the process of developing immersion programmes by providing whatever training that they could.

Since St Thomas University had not been as involved in teacher-training for First Nations as the University of New Brunswick had been, we approached UNB to see if they would consider developing an immersion teacher-training programme. They declined for reasons unknown, and so we at St Thomas embarked on a challenging journey. We began in 1995 by offering a two-day workshop on immersion in two communities in the Fredericton area, to which over one-hundred Mi'kmaq and Maliseet educators converged from across the province. That autumn, the Director of the Headstart programme in the Mi'kmaq community of Big Cove (now Elsiboktok) began its first ever immersion programme for three-year-olds, and we at St Thomas began preparing our first course, an introductory course in Native Language Immersion education.

The same year a small study was conducted on the state of the Maliseet language in the three communities in the Fredericton area. This is the study which found that the language had declined most drastically in the previous thirty-year period, approximately the same period that Maliseet children had been integrated into public schools (Bear Nicholas 1996). Other troubling facts were also found: that there were virtually no speakers under thirty years of age in any of the participating communities, and that there was a negative correlation between level of fluency and level of education, which findings pointed to integrated (monolingual, English-medium) schools as the single most important factor in the drastic decline of the language. It also found that among Maliseet students of high school age, a core language programme in Maliseet had been provided for almost all of their school years, yet, since none of these students were able to carry a conversation in Maliseet, it was evident that these core programmes had had no effect at all in maintaining or producing child speakers.

While this research provided new impetus for us to continue developing immersion teacher-training courses, its results did not seem to shake any of the involved Maliseet communities into new strategies for language maintenance. Two of the communities had their own school and one did not. Of the two that already had a school, one was planning for a new and larger one to be built at the time. Though it had used the need for language maintenance as one justification for the new school, a confidential report about a study by a non-native educational consultant strongly urged community decision-makers not to include immersion in the school, arguing that they were 'not ready for it'. The result was that immersion was not implemented, and it still has not been implemented to this day.

The possible reasons for this resistance to immersion are varied. One may certainly have been the unwillingness of the Department of Indian Affairs to provide extra funding for the development and implementation of an immersion programme, or for the cost of an extra teacher per grade in order to provide both a Maliseet stream and an English stream. In other words, schools may have been free to offer such programmes, but only as long as there was no extra demand on the government for funding. Another reason for resistance may have been the need for considerable extra space for an immersion stream. Yet another likely reason was that decision makers were still bound to varying degrees by the old ideologies, and still not convinced of the value or feasibility of immersion. Most existing teachers were either not Maliseet or not fluent in Maliseet, which likely posed difficult political or legal issues, if not personnel issues. Quite possibly too, the communities may have been shocked into despair by the findings of the study, and/or overwhelmed by the enormity of the work required to establish immersion (Grenoble and Whaley 2006: 160-204). For whatever reason, excitement and interest in immersion as a practical strategy began to wane in the three communities that had been part of our study, and participation from those communities in immersion teacher-training courses also began to wane[f].

While interest definitely declined in the three Fredericton-area communities, at least two other Maliseet communities and several Mi'kmaq communities remained committed to continuing the training. Over the next several years we worked with Dorothy Lazore to develop and offer a series of courses, thirteen in all: two foundational courses, five methods courses, three linguistics courses in either Mi'kmaq or Maliseet, and two courses to be taught entirely in either Mi'kmaq or Maliseet, one in history and another in literature and writing. The introduction of these last two courses marked the first time that any courses had been offered entirely in an Indigenous language by any university in the Maritimes.

Luckily the university has been very supportive and open to this programme. In one area it already had a needed component, a mature student policy which allowed students without the requisite high school diploma to register in two university courses. If they could pass these courses they would be eligible to enroll as full-time students. This allowed some of our most fluent speakers, who for the most part had not completed high school, to be trained as immersion teachers.

The university has also been quite willing to bend in several other areas to permit the programme to be offered. First, it has allowed us to offer the courses in a different format from the standard pattern of once, twice or three times a week over a whole semester. Nearly all of our courses are offered as extension courses in the participating communities as either three-week intensive summer session courses, or as intensive weekend courses, thirteen hours per weekend, with three weekends per course. These arrangements were necessary for several reasons. In the first place, most of our students held full-time jobs in areas quite distant from the university, and our principal instructor for the introductory and methods courses, Dorothy Lazore, maintained a full-time teaching position in various Mohawk communities, over a thousand miles away. Considering that she needed to be flown in to New Brunswick to teach the courses, they needed to be offered in as concentrated a manner as possible for cost effectiveness.

As for price, the university graciously agreed to offer any course in the programme for the basic cost of the instructor with no extra tuition fees to be charged, as long as the participating community could cover all additional costs, such as instructors' travel and accommodations. This arrangement has allowed the university to offer courses with fewer than the required minimum of fifteen students per course, and has provided certainty that courses would not be cancelled at the last minute if we did not have the minimum number of students. The arrangement has also allowed communities to field as many students as possible at no extra cost, which, in many cases, means a lower per capita cost to a community. With the added benefit of having two or three communities share the cost of offering one course at a time, the cost per community has been significantly lowered, as well.

Finally, in light of the reality that the most fluent speakers have generally not been educated to the Masters degree level, the university has given credit for life work in language education or immersion, and allowed us to hire instructors with less than the usual requirement of a Masters degree. Had this not been the case we might never have been able to find qualified instructors. In the year 2000 we obtained internal university approval for the programme as a certificate programme in Native Language Immersion Teaching, and in 2001 we received certification from the regional post-secondary accrediting agency, the Maritime Provinces Higher Education Commission. The only problem was that our graduates would only be able to teach in a preschool programme and not in the primary grades unless they already had a Bachelors of Education, but it was a start.

## Impact of the Native Language Immersion Teacher Training Programme

In 2003 we graduated our first cohort of twenty-four immersion teachers including fourteen from Cape Breton, Nova Scotia, mostly from the large Mi'kmaq community of Eskasoni, where an immersion programme was begun by their teachers while they were taking our training. Out of ten other students graduating in that first group, one launched a pre-school immersion programme at the Mi'kmaq community of Elsiboktok, New Brunswick, and another established one in the Mi'kmaq community of Eel Ground, New Brunswick. Other graduates from Elsiboktok went on to assist either in the pre-school programme or in the development and improvement of their core language programmes.

Only four out of the first group of twenty-four graduates were Maliseets, and they were all from my community at Tobique, about 200 kilometres north of Fredericton. In this community the Maliseet language was in a better state than it was in the Fredericton area. At the time, about one in three people in this community was a fluent speaker. This relatively good state of the language by comparison to the other communities, was due in part to the fact that it was the largest Maliseet community (population about 1200), and in part to its distance from any large urban area. Still this community had had no fluent child speakers for a decade or more, and most speakers were over forty-five years of age, the result of the combination of factors discussed above. While none of the people who graduated from the immersion teacher training programme in this community are currently teaching there, they have exerted considerable influence in the direction of immersion, to the point where there is now an immersion programme for four and five-year-old pre-schoolers.

In spite of a decreasing proportion of speakers in this community (in 2007 about one in four), it now has the best set of circumstances to develop a Maliseet immersion programme into the primary grades. Indeed, there is a great onus on this community to move into immersion quickly, not only because of its own declining number of speakers, but also because it is realistically the only Maliseet community with enough teachers and immersion teachers-in-training who are sufficiently fluent to implement and sustain an immersion programme. As such it has the best chance of creating child speakers once again.

Other communities that have now begun immersion teacher training include two Mi'kmaq communities in Quebec. Both are tri-lingual with French, English, and Mi'kmaq, and both have had some experience with immersion programming in Mi'kmaq. One currently has a Mi'kmaq immersion programme for four-year olds, and the other had a short-lived Mi'kmaq immersion programme in the primary grades about three decades ago. In both communities a noticeable and disturbing decline in the number of child speakers has awakened them to the need for immersion in the schools, though evidence of support for the idea varies. In one, there is still more support for English or French immersion, but in the other, a recent study has shown parental support for Mi'kmaq immersion to be above 90% (Jerome 2007). For both of these communities the presence of teachers trained in immersion methods will be critical both to advocate for immersion and to implement immersion programmes as soon as the communities are ready.

Results for which our immersion teacher-training programme can take some small credit can be seen in a recently published study of ten exemplary First Nations schools across Canada by the Society for the Advancement of Excellence in Education. One of the communities studied was Eskasoni (Wade 2007: 144–148), a community for which we had provided the full round of immersion teacher training courses on site.

As the largest Mi'kmaq community in the Maritimes (population 3200), it began developing a kindergarten to grade 4 immersion programme in 2003, and it has already produced some dramatic results. In addition to a significant increase in the level of Mi'kmaq language proficiency and a heightened pride in being Mi'kmaq, the programme has produced a marked improvement in overall academic achievement among the immersion students, as compared to non-immersion students. As the study points out, these results are remarkably consistent with the results from other studies of immersion (see Lindholm and Aclan 1991, Benson 2004). The results also go a long way to validate immersion teacher-training at the university level.

While major credit for the Eskasoni Immersion programme must be given to the determined team of educators in that community, other factors have contributed to making it a reality. Indeed, the groundwork was laid for immersion with the establishment of the Eskasoni School Board more than two decades ago, and with the establishment of the Mi'kmaw Kina'matnewey (MK), an organisation of ten Mi'kmaq school boards in 1999, which quite literally took over jurisdiction and responsibility from the provincial and federal governments for the education of Mi'kmaq children in the ten communities involved. A decision-making body, MK allocates funding from the government, and provides needed research and support services for the communities it represents. And, as is now evident, the result has been both a substantial improvement in the educational outcomes for Mi'kmaq children, and a renewed hope for the future of the language (Fulford 2007: 125-150).

## Challenges to Immersion Teacher Education and Possible Solutions

The immersion teacher-training programme which we have developed is, to our knowledge, the only such university-based programme in North America. In our opinion, every university that can, should find ways to provide similar training. To date most university-based language programmes have focused only on teaching Indigenous languages (See Wesche 2000: 187-208, Johns and Mazurkewich 2001: 355-366), rather than on teaching in the medium of such languages. As a result, our programme has begun to attract increased interest outside of our region, particularly in northern Canada. Most are interested in our methods courses. Some are also urging us to consider developing our programme into a full Bachelor of Education programme in immersion teaching (more on this below). Clearly, these requests have forced us to address existing challenges, as well as the new challenges raised by these expressions of interest in our programme from outside our region.

In the remaining pages portion of this paper we list challenges and possible solutions in no particular order of priority. One is the lack of solid support for immersion from the Department of Indian Affairs, the body responsible for the education of First Nations children, even though immersion has now demonstrated enormous academic promise for First Nations. Indeed, the Department appears oblivious to the excellent research results now available on immersion (see Grenoble and

Whaley 2006, Thomas and Collier 2002, McCarty 2008). This inexplicable lack of support has been evident in all stages. For example, neither our programme, nor the community schools in the region have received either encouragement or financial support from the Department of Indian Affairs for immersion programming. This seems especially odd considering how much criticism the department has received for the poor overall academic performance of Aboriginal students in education. While this resistance may stem simply from uninformed or negative attitudes towards bilingualism and Indigenous languages, it also indicates that the old assimilationist policies of the government still exist (Neu and Therrien 2003).

Clearly, one solution to such governmental resistance has been the action taken by one group of Mi'kmaq communities in Nova Scotia to establish the Mi'kmaw Kina'matnewey and to make educational decisions for themselves. Another would be increasing research into the relationship between immersion and academic performance, as in the recent study of the Eskasoni school. There has to be some point at which it will be impossible for the Department of Indian Affairs to ignore such research. Still another important solution to this problem would be language legislation, as discussed earlier in this paper. Ideally, such legislation should also mandate funding at the very least equivalent to that provided to Official Language Programmes for French, and it could help solve the serious shortages in teacher training and curriculum development which now serve as deterrents to immersion programme development.

Another simple, but necessary solution that could be offered by both research and funding agencies would be unequivocal policies privileging MTM programmes for priority in funding, especially at the pre-school level, since funding for that level is not always provided by the government. Unless such programmes are privileged in this way, First Nations will continue to see the establishment of English-only education programmes for their children, and a continuing linguicidal assault on their languages, which will, in turn, perpetuate a demand for English-only teacher-training, rather than immersion teacher training.

Another huge problem facing immersion programming lies in community disinterest, or even opposition, to the need for immersion and immersion teacher training. One source of the opposition is clearly the massive indoctrination to which all First Nations have been subjected. Another arises from fear on the part of non-First Nations teachers or non-fluent teachers who expect that immersion will put them out of work. Still another source of opposition certainly derives from the lack of resources from the Department of Indian Affairs for teacher training, staffing, and curriculum development for immersion. Finally, the numbing effect of sudden and drastic language shift may operate so as to make the project of revitalisation seem insurmountable to people who experience it (Lindholm 1990: 91-105).

For post-secondary institutions to assist Indigenous Peoples in the work of maintaining and revitalising their languages, it will require far more than just offering courses or even whole certificate programmes in immersion teaching, though that would be essential. It will require these institutions to assist communities in multiple ways to address the specific barriers to MTM education that centuries of colonial education systems have created. It will require ongoing research and dissemination of research on bilingualism, immersion education, and linguistic rights. It will require attention to making this research accessible to more than scholarly circles, as in the development of readable and attractive materials promoting bilingualism, immersion, and linguistic rights (See Edwards and Newcombe 2006: 137–149, Skutnabb-Kangas 2000: 479–566).

An increasingly serious challenge facing immersion teacher training in many First Nations lies in the very problem our programme was designed to address—the rapidly aging and declining numbers of fluent speakers in particular language groups. A decade ago the inception of a programme to create child speakers of Maliseet might have begun to produce potential teachers by now, or at least before the current group of fluent teachers becomes too old to teach. But now that window of opportunity is nearly past, since, contrary to the supposed findings in the 2001 census (Norris 2002: 21), there are virtually no known fluent second-language speakers of Maliseet, and any child speakers created today may barely be educated and trained to teach before our present crop of fluent teachers reaches retirement age. This situation has required us at the university level to begin developing new courses to promote accelerated methods of teaching Indigenous languages, if only to raise fluency levels as rapidly as possible, especially among teachers and potential teachers lacking sufficient fluency to teach in immersion.[7]

Another serious challenge facing mother tongue medium education is the fragmentation of funding. Ironically, it is the multiple sources of funding for languages together with a strict separation of funding for education and funding for Indigenous language (described above), which is leading to a detrimental fragmentation of energies and solutions. And this situation will most certainly linger in the absence of effective language planning and development, both nationally and within each linguistic group. For example, one programme from Heritage Canada to promote native languages is dispersed solely through First Nations and Inuit political leadership, rather than through language-wide planning committees which would have the best view of the overall needs of a language and how best the funding can be pooled to produce the most benefits. Of course, funding from Heritage Canada is not available for schools at all, which ensures that its funding cannot even be used for in-school immersion programmes. Clearly planning within language groups is desperately needed to establish priorities in each language as a whole, and to dedicate resources to projects most beneficial to the survival of the language as a whole (See Hinton 2001: 51–59). Indeed, the simple per capita or per-community dispersal of funds to the leadership may be politically expedient, but of questionable benefit to Indigenous languages as a whole, and it could even exacerbate existing language disparities between communities.

Yet another serious challenge facing our immersion teacher-training programme is the fact that graduates of the programme are allowed to teach only in pre-school and not in the primary grades, unless they already have a Bachelor of Education. Fluent speakers who wish to teach in an immersion programme in the primary grades must, therefore, spend the equivalent of one year in our programme and another year in a B.Ed. programme. This creates an extra burden for fluent speakers to become immersion teachers. It could also lead to the unlearning of methods and skills taught in an immersion teacher training programme. Without a doubt, there is a critical need for B.Ed. programmes to be developed in immersion teacher training for fluent speakers of First Nations languages.

A last serious challenge now facing community immersion programmes is the desperate need for curriculum materials. Were it not the case that immersion teachers generally need both to teach and to develop curriculum, there would likely be many more fluent speakers eager to seek immersion teacher training and more communities eager to implement immersion programmes. Ideally, communities and/or language groups should have teams of curriculum developers to develop curriculum in their languages in order to relieve immersion teachers of that burden. But to meet this need much more funding is desperately needed. To begin addressing this need, national native political or educational organisations could coordinate the development of sharing of a set of curriculum materials in various languages with English versions that could be readily translated to other Indigenous languages. Though less preferable than for each language to develop its own unique materials first, this strategy could at least help smaller communities and language groups without sufficient resources for curriculum development to start their own immersion programmes.

In closing, a little reflection is offered here on what can be learned from this experience since there are likely millions of people in the world facing struggles for linguistic survival similar to those of the Maliseet and Mi'kmaq people in Atlantic Canada. **First,** there needs to be a commitment to the principle of education in the medium of the mother tongue, at least on the part of a few individuals willing and able to work for it. **Secondly**, a handful of parents and potential teachers fluent in the language would need to be convinced of its necessity. To accomplish this, existing immersion programmes for minority languages could be visited, or immersion activists or educators could be invited to speak. **Thirdly**, literature could be developed to promote the Indigenous language and mother tongue education among parents and teachers. **Finally**, once there is community support for such education, both political and institutional support needs to be sought. Universities, especially, need to understand the colonial roles they have played in linguistic genocide, both in the past and in the present. And they need to understand the role that they can play in turning this story around to assist Indigenous communities to maintain or revitalise their languages. In some parts of the world this is already happening in places like Hawaii and Norway. In other parts of the world it will require people educated in these matters both within and outside of Indigenous communities to effect the necessary changes. Ideally, at least some of these activists can gain positions within post-secondary institutions where they may be better positioned to help those institutions begin working with Indigenous peoples to develop programmes that will assist in the struggle for MTM education and linguistic survival. Precisely what this work could entail will depend on local needs and priorities, but at some point or another it should include training of Indigenous speakers to teach in their own mother tongue. There can be no substitute for such training if mother tongue medium education is to be achieved, and if Indigenous languages are to survive.

## *Notes*

1 Norris (2002: 13) reports only 425 speakers of Mohawk, while the Task Force on Aboriginal Languages and Cultures (2005) reports at least 7000 speakers of Mohawk!

2 Maliseet is virtually the same language as the Passamaquoddy language located mostly in the American state of Maine, and partly in New Brunswick. While the language is often referred to as Maliseet/Passamaquoddy, this paper will use the term 'Maliseet' and focus on its speakers in Canada.

3 According to Norris (2002)], there were over 800 speakers of Maliseet in 2001 representing an increase of nearly 200 new speakers over 1996, a figure which appears hugely inflated, while the Task Force on Aboriginal Languages and Cultures (2005: 36) reports fewer than 200 speakers of Maliseet in 1996. The truth is probably somewhere in the middle.

4 The same study also found that out of the number of people who could speak their language in 2001 approximately 20% had learned it as a second language.

5 For Official Languages funding see http://www.cmec.ca/protocols/OLEP2009.en.pdf.

6 One hopeful new development in 2008 has been a request by at least one education director in the Fredericton area for talks to begin on the possibility of establishing an immersion programme in Fredericton for pre-schoolers from all three Fredericton area Maliseet communities.

7 The most recent courses in our programme designed to address this problem include 'Language Arts in Immersion', and 'Accelerated Methods in Adult Immersion'.

# 13

# The Ethnic Revival, Language and Education of the Sámi, an Indigenous People, in three Nordic Countries (Finland, Norway and Sweden)

*Ulla Aikio-Puoskari*

## Introduction

The Sámi are an indigenous people who live in the territories of four states: Norway, Sweden, Finland and Russia. There are some 70–100,000 ethnic Sámi in these states, about 40–60,000 in Norway, about 15–20,000 in Sweden, about 9,000 in Finland and approximately 2,000 in Russia (www.sametinget.se, www.samediggi.fi, www.samediggi.no, accessed on 9.7.2008). The core areas of the Sámi are situated in the northern parts of these countries (see Map 13.1). The Sámi have their own language(s) and distinct culture(s) that differ from the cultures of the neighbouring populations.[1] Five out of the ten original Sámi languages are currently used as languages of instruction and taught as school subjects in three Nordic states. One of the languages, Kildin Sámi, is taught in Russia to a limited extent.

From the mid-nineteenth to the mid-twentieth century, the Sámi were subjected to a conscious and, at times, very harsh assimilation policy. For centuries, many people have predicted that Sámi culture, which they have characterised as primitive, and the Sámi languages, which they have considered unfit for civilised people, will disappear. Despite such predictions, the Sámi languages and culture still survive but in conditions that are very different from what prevailed as recently as the mid-twentieth century. The present situation is characterised by an intensive struggle between a language and cultural shift on the one hand, and revitalisation and cultural survival on the other. The school and the teaching of and through the native languages are of great significance for the outcome of this competition.

Over the past 50–60 years, Sámi society and culture have gone through a drastic change, which many researchers have compared to a revolution (e.g. Eidheim 1997: 29). The change has had a profound effect on all spheres of life: on mentalities,

**Map 13.1.** Explanations for the coloured areas in three countries

**Norga/ NORWAY. The Administrative Area of Sámi Language:** Municipalities of Kárášjohka/ Karasjok, Guovdageaidnu/Kautokeino, Unjárga/Nesseby, Porsáŋgu/Porsanger, Deatnu/Tana, Gáivuotna/Kåfjord, Divttasvuotna/Tysfjord and Snoasa/Snåsa. **The Special Sámi Schools in Norway** are located in Snoasa/Snåsa, Árborde/Hattfjelldal, Romssa Málatvuopmi/Målselv in Tromsø.

**Ruotta/ SWEDEN. The Administrative Area of Sámi Language:** Municipalities of Giron/Kiruna, Váhčir/Gällivare, Johkamohkki/Jokkmokk and Árjjatluovvi/Arjeplog. **The Special Sámi Schools in Sweden** are located in Gárasavvon/Karesuando, Láttevárri/Lannavaara (will be closed in 2008), Giron/Kiruna, Johkamohkki/Jokkmokk, Váhčir/Gällivare and Deartná/Tärnaby.

**Suopma/ FINLAND. The Home Area of Sámi / The Area of Cultural Self-determination of Sámi:** Municipalities of Ohcejohka/Utsjoki, Anár/Aanaar/Inari, Eanodat/Enontekiö and the northern part (the reindeer herding area called Sámi bálggus/Lapin paliskunta) of Soađegilli/Sodankylä material and social conditions. It has also accelerated the change that has been going on in the languages. Above all, it has resulted in the emancipation of the Sámi community and the creation of emancipatory politics in Anthony Giddens's sense of the term (Giddens 1991: 210-211, Lindgren 1999, 2005: 48, Huss and Lindgren 2005). Today the Sámi community consciously promotes its political strategies[2] in order to develop and defend its language, culture and traditional sources of livelihood, and in order to pass them on to new generations by means of education, as well as to create conditions that permit the Sámi culture to survive. Because of the fact that the Sámi live in several states, it is not possible to say there would be one common strategy shared by all the Sámi. There is a lot of cooperation and a growing awareness of Sámi as one people but, for their political strategies to succeed, the Sámi have to understand and act in the political, administrative and cultural systems of four different kinds of society. Recent developments in cooperation between the Sámi Parliaments and the governments of three Nordic countries suggest something quite new in Nordic cooperation and in the field of human rights. A proposal for adopting a Nordic Sámi Convention was released in 2005 and the states are now preparing to sign it. The main purpose of the new Convention will be to harmonise national legislation and Sámi rights (Åhren, Scheinin and Henriksen 2007).

Education—all its levels from compulsory schooling to higher secondary and vocational education and colleges and universities—is central to how the Sámi language, history, cultural knowledge and skills can be passed down to new generations. Education is important for whether children and young people are provided with the chance of growing up and living their lives as Sámi, as citizens who know their own culture, have good skills in their own language and have a strong identity and a sound self-esteem. At present, everyone needs to know, in addition to the main language of one's native country, at least one foreign language, mostly meaning English, which is becoming more and more prevalent in the Nordic countries. Every Sámi young person who goes to school today is more or less a world citizen, using the Internet for global communication and exposure to cultural influence of every kind. On the other hand, every Sámi is nowadays also aware of the other indigenous peoples of the world and of the fact that their own languages and cultures are threatened. The Sámi have been deeply involved in the international ethno-political movement of the world's indigenous peoples since its start. Torill Nyseth and Paul Pedersen (2005: 76) describe the change as follows: 'The enlargement of awareness, which sees Sámi as an Indigenous people, implies a change from local and specific ethnic group identification to the general concept of indigenousness, where the Sámi become a part of the international movement of Indigenous peoples.' The first president of the United Nations Permanent Forum on Indigenous Issues was a Sámi, Ole Henrik Magga.

The world was a great deal smaller in the days when my grandmother Elsa-Marja Aikio (1891–1979) grew up. In the early 1900s, one's identity was interlaced with one's first language and the Sámi way of life that one happened to be part of. My grandmother was born in a Sámi tent, or *goahti*, in the woods; she was born to a nomadic Sámi family that spoke the local variety of the North Sámi language. Of the ten original Sámi languages, North Sámi is the most widely spoken one. Today it is used in schools, the mass media, literature and cross-border cooperation between the Sámi to a greater extent than any other Sámi language. When my grandmother was a child, the Nordic countries did not yet exist as the states we know of today. However, the establishment of the first school system that was to provide compulsory education was under way in the final decades of the nineteenth century. In the schools of my grandmother´s generation, the Sámi language was non-existent. Only the youngest of her grandchildren were provided with some training in their native language. The teaching of the Sámi language did not begin in any of the three Nordic countries in which I was educated—Norway, Sweden and Finland—until a new 9-grade system of compulsory schooling was created in the 1960s and 1970s.

This article examines Sámi education historically with a focus on educational policy. Initially and for a long time, Sámi education was considered only a linguistic issue. Over the past 10–15 years we have reached a new phase in promoting Sámi education: we do not focus only on the language, but also on the content of instruction and on the position of native culture in education. I need to stress that these are concerns of recent origin. At present the most important issues are the right to self-determination in education and the potential of reviving the language and culture with the help of the school.

## Northern multilingualism and the roots of Sámi education

In the north, in the traditional Sámi areas, the borders of Norway, Sweden and Finland cut through the linguistic and cultural communities. In all three countries, three different Sámi languages are spoken: in Norway and Sweden, North Lule and South Sámi; and, in Finland, North Inari and Skolt Sámi. The northern parts of these countries are a real mosaic of languages and cultures. In the northern parts of Norway and Sweden, there are also minorities that speak, in addition to the Sámi language, different varieties of the Finnish language. In Sweden, this Finno-Ugric language spoken is *meänkieli* [= our language], which is officially recognised as a regional minority language. In Norway, it is the *Kven* language, which has been defined as a historical minority language. In addition to the northern minorities, these countries also have other traditional minorities. The Swedish-speaking population of Finland (some 5.8% of the whole population) probably has greater recognition than any other linguistic minority in the world (McRae 1997). Finland is officially a bilingual country, with Swedish as one of its two national languages. In addition, there are other linguistic minorities of long standing in these countries, for example Sign language, the Roma, the Russian-speaking population (in Finland), and a range of new immigrant minorities, whose native languages are to some extent also taught in school as subjects. Thus, the three countries are, due to history and recent immigration, multilingual and multicultural.

The Sámi, who are the indigenous people of these states, represent the oldest languages and cultures of these countries, long pre-dating the present-day states.[3] The first Sámi author Johan Turi (1854–1936) wrote in his world-famous novel of 1910:

> Nobody claims that the Lapps have come here from somewhere else. The Lapps have been an ancient inhabitant right across Lapland, and when the Lapps lived here by the coast in ancient times, there were no other inhabitants here and so the Lapps were free to do so. And the Lapps have also lived all over the place on the Swedish side in ancient times. There were no farmers anywhere at that time; the Lapps were unaware of the existence of any people other than themselves.[4] (Turi 1910; English translation www.eng.samer.se, accessed on July 9, 2008).

Thus one might think that the Sámi languages would have been, and would still be, an integral part of the systems of compulsory schooling of these states. However, this is not the case. Furthermore, the development has been a most paradoxical one in Sweden, which was the first state to begin the formal education of the Sámi (as early as the eighteenth century). In Sweden, there are still a few small Sámi schools (*sámeskuvla* in Sámi/ *sameskola* in Swedish) that began to provide education before the first general system of compulsory schooling (*folkskola*) was launched. These schools, which were called 'nomad schools' (*nomadskola* in Swedish) until the 1970s, were originally special schools intended for the children of reindeer-herding Sámi families. Paradoxically, they did not even teach the Sámi language as a subject, although one of their objectives in the early twentieth century was to make sure that the children would not become alienated from their own culture. The Swedish policy of the nomad school period can be seen as *protective segregationist*, segregating the reindeer-herding Sámi from the rest of the Sámi population and from ethnic Swedes. According to this policy, the reindeer-herding Sámi were 'the real Sámi' whose culture was to be protected, whereas the other Sámi, a majority of the Sámi population, were to be assimilated into the Swedish population (e.g. Svonni 1997). This division is still highly visible in Sweden: it can be seen in the language situation and the education of the Sámi, in the prevalent stereotypes of the Sámi, and even in Sámi politics. In comparison with the other two states, the state that began to formally educate its indigenous people long before its neighbouring states now lags behind in its Sámi education, if we consider this education from the point of view of today's assessment criteria for Sámi education.

Norwegianisation, a harsh and overtly assimilationist official policy that was launched in Norway in the mid-nineteenth century, was implemented specifically through educational and economic policies (Eriksen and Niemi 1981; NOU [Norwegian Committee Reports] 1985: 14,15, Lehtola 2002: 44–48, Minde 2005a). This assimilation policy lasted for about a hundred years. For decades, it was forbidden to use the Sámi language and to *yoik*—to sing in the traditional Sámi way—in the school; being a Sámi was a marked stigma. In Finland, the policy of assimilating the Sámi was not as overt, nor as harsh as in Norway. Nevertheless, it was based on a similar way of thinking. The objective of 'civilizing the primitive Sámi' through assimilation became visible later in many conflicts, when the Sámi demanded that Sámi children be taught their own language in compulsory schooling (e.g., Itkonen 1970).

The first systems of compulsory schooling were created in the late nineteenth century during the period when the three Nordic countries that I discuss here evolved into present day nation-states. In line with the ideals of the time, the school system was based on the idea of a united, monolingual nation. Such a system had only room for the main languages of the countries and for schools that were, in terms of their content, similar throughout the country, from south to north. From the point of view of the Sámi, this phase in history was a distressing period that led to a rapid language and cultural shift. Paradoxically—again from the point of view of the indigenous people—the first steps towards a new direction were not taken until the 1960s and 1970s, when immigration to the Nordic countries increased. As a result, and especially in Sweden and Finland, the system of compulsory schooling began to provide some opportunities for teaching the native language of the Sámi at schools—on an equal footing with the 'other minority languages'. Thus, immigrants helped advocacy for and the launch of the teaching of the Sámi languages, the indigenous languages of the Nordic countries.

Norway, which had attempted to root out the Sámi language and Sáminess in the most forceful way in the Nordic countries also experienced the most drastic change in the other direction. This was caused by a conflict that took place at the turn of the 1970s and 1980s in connection with the building of a power station on the River Alta (Paine 1992, Magga 1990, Lehtola 2002: 76–77, Lindgren 1999, Huss 1999: 76–77, Minde 2005b). In one sense the Sámi lost the conflict, as the river was dammed, but through active protest they achieved many things. Officially, the policy of Norwegianisation had been abolished as early as the 1950s, but an active Sámi policy only evolved after the Alta clash between the state and the Sámi. The new policy focused on promoting the rights of the Sámi to their native language and Sámi education. This change in Norway triggered the ethnic movement of the Sámi that had already begun to grow stronger in the 1950s (Magga 1990, Lehtola 2002: 70–77, Lindgren 1999, Seurujärvi-Kari 2005). This development is still continuing, and the cross-border cooperation of the Sámi—their stepping forward as a united nation—has developed many new political, cultural and administrative forms. The most important ones of these are the Sámi University College (*Sámi allaskuvla*) and the Sámi Research Institute (*Sámi instituhtta*), which was founded in the early 1970s and is now affiliated to the Sámi University College (founded in 1989). To promote cooperation between the elected Sámi Parliaments, a Sámi Parliamentary Council was established at the beginning of the 2000s. The Russian Sámi also participate in all these institutions. In addition the Sámi have a cooperative body, the Sámi Council *(Sámiráđđi)*, which was established for non-governmental Sámi organisations as early as the 1950s.

## The Sámi language and culture in education

The dominant historical tendencies are not abolished within one generation but go on for long after they have officially been forsaken. The Sámi community still carries the burden of the active assimilation policy on its shoulders. As a result of this, the present generation of Sámi pupils is heterogeneous in terms of its linguistic background and identity. Only a limited number of children and young people, perhaps one in four or one in three, now speak Sámi as their first language. Many parents wish that the school could give the children back the language that they have lost. The children and young people who speak Sámi as their first language are usually bilingual, some even trilingual: in addition to their native language, they speak the main language of the country as their second mother tongue. Other young people can speak some Sámi, and the rest do not know the language at all. Some of the young people have become assimilated both in terms of language and culture. On the other hand, some young people who have lost their language still identify themselves strongly with the Sámi community and its culture, trying to reclaim and learn the language. Unfortunately there are neither research results nor statistics available on the linguistic situation of Sámi children and youth on these aspects.

Other consequences of the assimilation policy include the negative attitudes that still affect the improvement of the status of the Sámi language and Sámi education, and, likewise, the ignorance, and the stereotypes of the Sámi population that still prevail. However, the language is still the most important element of the identity for the Sámi —in addition to self-identification and the feeling of belonging to a Sámi family. But it is also possible to see a change in attitudes, especially in attitudes of Sámi youngsters. According to a new report, prepared by the Children's ombudsperson in Finland, the Sámi youngsters of today say 'it's cool to be a Sámi' (Rasmus 2008). That is something our parents and grandparents would never have said, because of their experience of shame and discrimination on the basis of their ethnic and linguistic background. We also need to remember that the issue of language never deals with 'just' language: it is also about the culture and the cultural changes that the language sustains and lives in. Therefore we need to ask whether the compulsory schooling of the Nordic welfare states today takes into consideration the language, culture and identity of the children and youth of the indigenous peoples of these states. Is compulsory schooling a counter-force to the language shift that was about to break the cultural backbone of the earlier generations, or does it promote the shift?

According to present regulations, the Sámi language *can be* the language of instruction, or a subject called 'the mother tongue/ first language', or 'a foreign/ second language' in the schools of Norway, Sweden and Finland. However, there are great differences between the three countries. Sámi education in these countries can be compared to an unsolvable jigsaw puzzle, the pieces of which differ from each other in terms of their size (= resources and accessibility), forms (= forms of education) and colours (= the guidelines for education policy) (Aikio-Puoskari 2005, 2006 and 2007). As regards the status of Sámi education in the schools of these countries, there is one common feature: the rights and possibilities of a Sámi pupil to learn his/her own language are guaranteed especially in 'the core Sámi areas' (see map 13.1). In Sweden, these core areas can be defined as the special Sámi schools, in Norway the Administrative Area in which the Sámi Language Act is to be implemented (*sámegiela hálddašanguovlu* in Sámi) (The Sámi Act, L 1987: 56; the amendment concerning the Sámi language in Chapter 3, in law 1990: 78, § 3, Sect.1.), and, in Finland, the Sámi Area as prescribed by the Act on the Sámi Parliament (*sámiid ruovttuguovlu* in Sámi) (The Law on the Sámi Parliament, SSK 1995/974, § 4.). In the latter areas, the Sámi also have rights that concern their own language in other spheres of public life. Outside these areas, teaching in Sámi and the teaching of the Sámi language are restricted in many ways. It is estimated that as many as 50% of the Sámi people live outside the core Sámi areas.

*Sweden*

In Sweden, Sámi education has been organised in three different ways: (1) the six small special Sámi schools in the North, (2) home language/ mother tongue instruction, and (3) integrated Sámi education in other-than-Sámi schools. The special Sámi schools are situated in the traditional areas of the reindeer-herding Sámi. They have a long history and are today open to all Sámi children. According to the Education Act (SFS 1985: 1100, SFS 2008: 317, Chapter 1, §1 and Chapter 8, § 3), Sámi children can get their compulsory education in separate Sámi schools that are part of the public school system. The Sámi schools are run by the state and administered by the Sámi School Board (*Sámeskuvlastivra* in Sámi, www.sameskolstyrelsen.se), which is appointed by the Sámi Parliament of Sweden. The education provided in the Sámi schools corresponds to the education provided in grades 1–6 of Swedish primary schools, but Sámi children must have Sámi content (SFS 1985: 1100, Chapter 8, § 1). The Sámi schools have both the Sámi language(s) and Swedish as their languages of instruction (The Statute on Sámi schools, SFS 1995: 205, Chapter 3, § 2) and, according to the curriculum (The 1994 curriculum for compulsory schooling, pre-school education and free-time activities, Lpo 94, SKOLFS 1994: 1) the schools are to ensure that every pupil who has gone to the Sámi school is familiar with the cultural heritage of the Sámi and can speak, read and write the Sámi language. Sámi is used as the language of instruction only in the Sámi schools, in which teaching provided through Sámi was strengthened in the 1990s. The Sámi School Board is also responsible for integrated Sámi education (see below) and the pre-school education of the 6-year-old children that is provided in connection with the Sámi schools. In addition, there are now kindergartens that are connected to the Sámi schools and function in the Sámi language(s); they also arrange after-school activities. At present, the special Sámi schools of Sweden are like small distillations of Sámi culture; they are effective cultural centres that have a great impact on the neighbourhood. They are very much Sámi in their appearance and in them, Sámi culture is drawn on in the teaching to a great extent. The Sámi schools could be of great significance for the future of the Sámi, if they were extended to more than currently just 5–10 % of Sámi children in Sweden.

Outside the Sámi schools, the Sámi language(s) is/are taught according to the school regulations that deal with mother tongue instruction, until 1976 called 'home languages' (*hemspråk* in Swedish). Home language or heritage language instruction was launched in 1976. The subject is now called the mother tongue (*modersmål* in Swedish), and the teaching usually consists of 1–3 weekly lessons. (The Statute on Compulsory Schooling, SFS 1994: 1194 and 2008: 97, Chapter 2, § 9–14). To have the right to learn one's mother tongue in school, the pupil must have, according to the statute (SFS 1994: 1194 and 2008: 97, Chapter 2, § 9), basic skills in the language. This has provided a reason for some schools to refuse to arrange teaching in South Sámi (e.g. Rådmansö, Gräddö School in Norrtälje 2003). The regulations on Sámi pupils' right to be taught Sámi as a mother tongue provide no right for those Sámi pupils who have already lost their native language to study the language at school. According to the statute the municipality is also obliged to arrange teaching in the mother tongue of the pupil only if there is a suitable teacher available (Chapter 2, § 13). Lack of teachers is certainly one of the main reasons why this form of Sámi education only reaches about 200 pupils yearly.

The third type of Sámi education, called Integrated Sámi education, means teaching about Sámi culture as an integral part of the ordinary subjects of compulsory schooling. A municipality can provide this education for Sámi pupils in its comprehensive schools if it makes an agreement about it with the Sámi School Board. Integrated Sámi education means for many pupils continuing the education of the Sámi schools in grades 7–9. Most integrated education is still given in Swedish, and not all the pupils who have asked for it have been able to get it, because the Sámi School Board does not have sufficient funding to organise it for all pupils wanting it (personal communication with the staff of Sámi School Board, 2007).

All three of these types of Sámi education in Sweden taken together reach a total of some 10%–20 % of the Sámi pupils of compulsory school age. The regulations about Sámi education have remained approximately the same from the 1970s until today and there have not been any major changes in the total number of pupils getting Sámi education since the 1970s. The proportion of instruction through the medium of Sámi has risen since the 1990s. Part of it can be defined as revitalisation immersion education (Skutnabb-Kangas and McCarty 2008) because there are also Swedish-speaking Sámi pupils getting instruction through the Sámi language. The statistics from the school years 2002–2004 illustrate the situation (Figures 13.1–3):

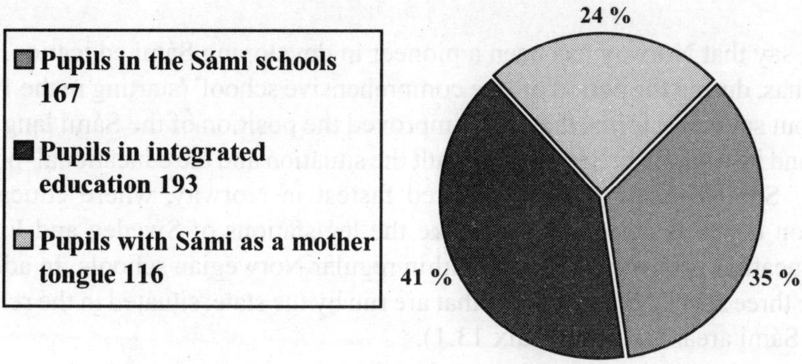


**Figure 13.1.** *Pupils studying the Sámi language and culture in Swedish comprehensive schools in 2002–2003, altogether 476:*

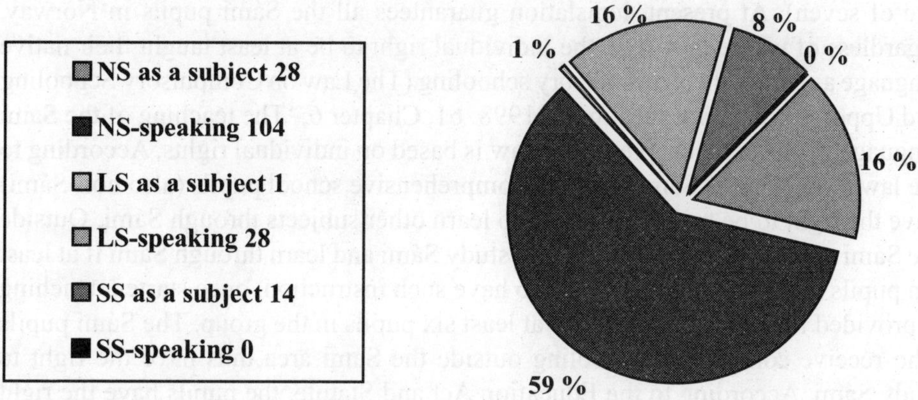


**Figure 13.2.** *The pupils of the Sámi schools in Sweden by language in 2003–2004, altogether 175. Pupils taught in Sámi: 132 = 75%.*

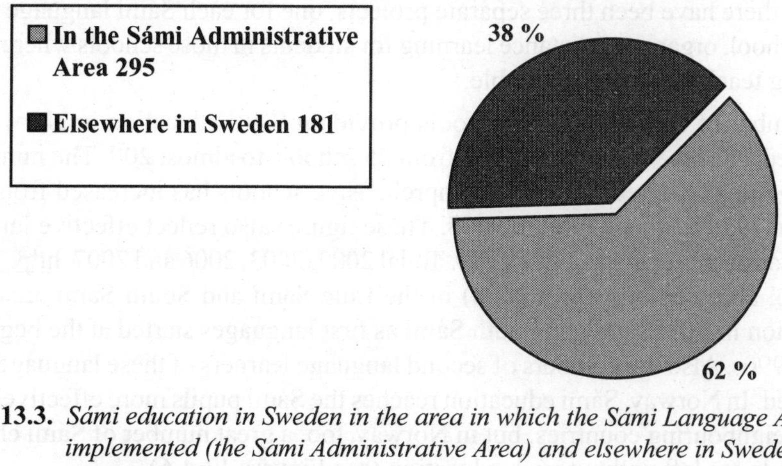


**Figure 13.3.** *Sámi education in Sweden in the area in which the Sámi Language Act is implemented (the Sámi Administrative Area) and elsewhere in Sweden in 2002–2003:*

*Norway*

One can say that Norway has been a pioneer in developing Sámi education, as the country has, during the period of 'the comprehensive school' (starting in the 1960s), carried out several reforms that have improved the position of the Sámi languages, culture and instruction in Sámi. As a result the situation and the educational–political status of Sámi education has improved fastest in Norway, where educational legislation contains clear rights—unlike the legislations of Sweden and Finland. Sámi education is mostly provided within regular Norwegian schools. In addition, there are three special Sámi schools that are run by the state, situated in the reindeer-herding Sámi areas (see Appendix 13.1).

The latest school law reform in 1998 meant that a system of ten-year comprehensive schools was established, and school started at the age of six years (Sweden and Finland have nine-years of comprehensive school and children start school at the age of seven). At present, legislation guarantees all the Sámi pupils in Norway, regardless of where they live, the individual right to be at least taught their native language as part of their compulsory schooling (The Law on Compulsory Schooling and Upper Secondary Education, L 1998: 61, Chapter 6, 'The teaching of the Sámi language'). The sixth chapter of the law is based on individual rights. According to the law (§ 6-2) in the Sámi area[5], all comprehensive school pupils (also non-Sámi) have the right to be taught Sámi and to learn other subjects through Sámi. Outside the Sámi area, pupils have the right to study Sámi and learn through Sámi if at least ten pupils in the municipality want to have such instruction; once started, teaching is provided for as long as there are at least six pupils in the group. The Sámi pupils who receive compulsory schooling outside the Sámi area thus have the right to study Sámi. According to the Education Act and Statute, the pupils have the right to alternative teaching methods if their school does not have a teacher who could teach them. This means that the internet and distance education, for example, have a legal basis in the educational legislation. Since the beginning of the twenty-first century there have been three separate projects, one for each Sámi language taught in the school, organising distance learning for students in those schools where Sámi-speaking teachers are not available.

The number of comprehensive schools providing Sámi education in Norway has increased since the end of the 1970s from 25 schools to almost 200. The number of pupils getting Sámi education in comprehensive schools has increased from 1175 pupils in 1979 to about 3000 in 2008. These figures also reflect effective language revitalisation projects (see Huss 1999, Todal 2002, 2003, 2006 and 2007, http://www.arran.no, accessed on 9 July 2008) in the Lule Sámi and South Sámi areas. The instruction in Lule Sámi and South Sámi as first languages started at the beginning of the 1990s. Also the numbers of second language learners of these languages have increased. In Norway, Sámi education reaches the Sámi pupils more effectively than in the neighbouring countries, but in Norway, too, a great number of Sámi children and pupils are left without such education (see Figures 13.4-6).

**Instruction in Sámi for 963 pupils = 35% (+30 pupils studying Sámi as the subject 'First language' > altogether 993).**

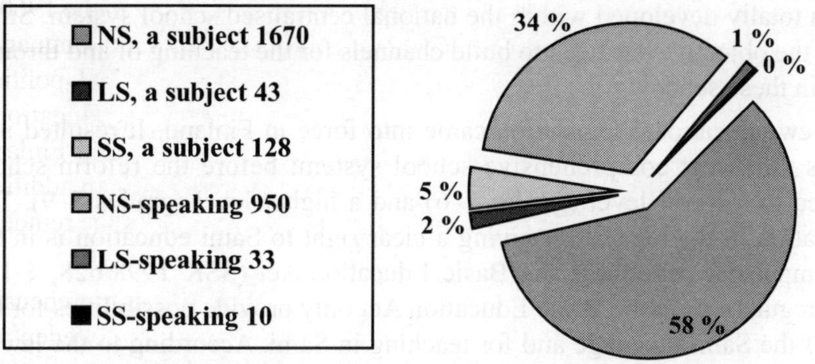


**Figure 13.4.** *Pupils studying Sámi in Norwegian comprehensive schools by language in 2003–04.*

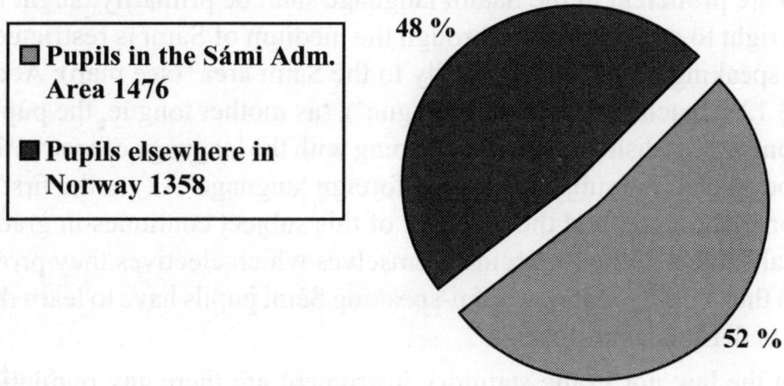


**Figure 13.5.** *Sámi education in Norway: Sámi in the area in which the Sámi Language Act is implemented (Sámi Administrative Area) and elsewhere in the country in 2003–04.*

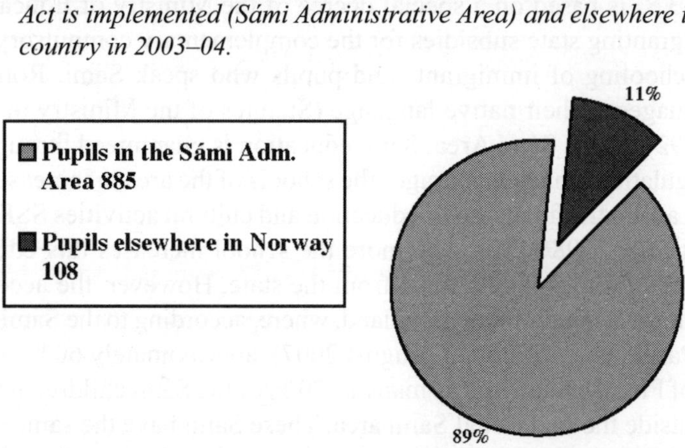


**Figure 13.6.** *Pupils studying in Sámi in the Sámi Administrative Area and elsewhere in the country in 2003–04.*

*Finland*

In Finland, Sámi education is provided in regular Finnish schools, which means it has been totally developed within the national centralised school system. Since the 1970s, the objective has been to build channels for the teaching of and through Sámi within these schools.

In 1998, new educational legislation came into force in Finland. It resulted in a continuous nine-year comprehensive school system; before the reform school was divided to a lower level (grades 1–6) and a higher level (grades 7–9). The only regulation in the legislation giving a clear right to Sámi education is in the law on compulsory schooling, the Basic Education Act (SSK 1998/628, § 10). The other regulations in the Basic Education Act only provide possibilities for the teaching of the Sámi language and for teaching in Sámi. According to the law (§ 10, 'The language of instruction') 'the language of instruction and the language used in extracurricular teaching shall be either Finnish or Swedish. The language of instruction may also be Saami, Roma or Sign language...Pupils living in the Sámi Area who are proficient in the Saami language shall be primarily taught in Saami.' Thus, the right to get instruction through the medium of Sámi is restricted firstly to the Sámi-speaking pupils and secondly to the Sámi area[6] (see map). According to the law (§ 12, 'Teaching the mother tongue'), 'as mother tongue, the pupil shall be taught Finnish, Swedish or Saami, in keeping with the language of instruction.' Sámi can also be an elective subject ('second foreign language' A2) in the first grades of compulsory schooling, and the teaching of this subject continues in grades 7–9 as an optional subject. Schools decide themselves which electives they provide. This regulation thus implies that non Sámi-speaking Sámi pupils have to learn their native language under the label 'foreign'.

Neither in the law nor in the statutory instrument are there any regulations about teaching outside the Sámi area. This teaching (realised to a very small extent, see Figure 13.8) is based on a special decree of the Ministry of Education on the grounds for granting state subsidies for the complementary compulsory and upper secondary schooling of immigrants and pupils who speak Sámi, Roma or other foreign languages as their native language (Statutes of the Ministry of Education, SSK 2007/392). In the Sámi Area, Sámi education is guaranteed through a special financing regulation which encourages the schools of the area to increase their Sámi education (Law on the financing of education and cultural activities SSK 1998/635, Amendment SSK 1998/1186). The more the school increases this education, the higher are the subsidies it gets for it from the state. However, the accessibility of Sámi education is a big problem in Finland, where, according to the Sámi Parliament (The Sámi Parliament of Finland, August 2007), approximately 60 % of the whole population of Finnish Sámi and as many as 70 % of the Sámi children under the age of 10 live outside the traditional Sámi area. These Sámi have the same opportunity to be taught their own language as immigrants. At most they can have 2.5 hours of teaching per week, and there are always great difficulties in arranging this instruction.

The situation is similar to the situation in Sweden, where schools other than the Sámi schools base their teaching in the Sámi language on the same regulation as the one that also allows the new minorities, that is, the immigrant groups, to be taught their own languages. Thus, the educational policies of Finland and Sweden treat the indigenous people who live outside their traditional territories as if they were immigrants!

The number of pupils getting Sámi education in comprehensive schools rose from about 350 pupils in 1979 to about 550 pupils in following ten years. As a consequence of the increasing immigration from the Sámi area to towns and cities further south, the number of pupils in Sámi education has decreased, to about 430 in comprehensive schools in 2008 (see Figures 13.7–9). The latest reforms in educational legislation (1998) strengthened instruction through the medium of Sámi in the Sámi area. Thus the development in Sámi education in Finland has taken place within the instruction itself (i.e. using Sámi as a medium instead of studying it as a subject only has increased), not in the numbers of pupils. For most pupils who now get instruction through the Sámi language, Sámi-medium instruction usually covers close to 100% of their school subjects. The language revitalisation activities, run by the active Sámi associations and the Sámi Parliament, are mainly special projects funded by the EU and the Finnish Cultural Foundation, thus they are limited in relation to length and resources. The most effective one has been the Inari Sámi-speaking language nest for children under school age, started in 1997, following the model developed in Aotearoa (see Huss 1999, Pasanen 2005, Olthuis 2003, 2008). As a consequence of the language nest, Inari Sámi-medium school instruction was started in 2000. The revitalisation of Inari Sámi will continue with a teacher-training project funded by the Finnish Academy in 2008 (Olthuis, personal communication).

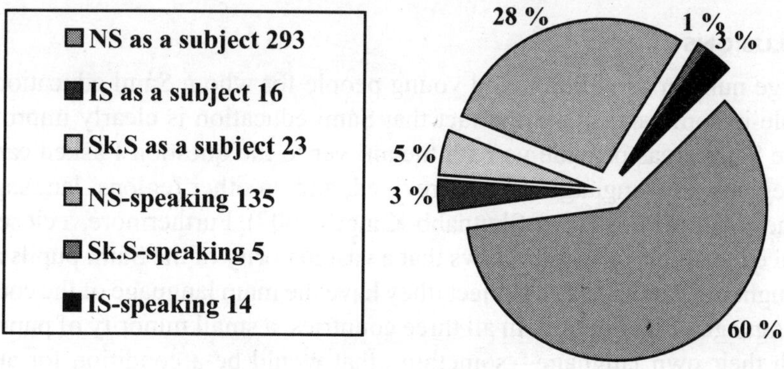


**Figure 13.7.** *Pupils studying Sámi and learning through Sámi by language in Finnish comprehensive schools in 2003-2004, altogether 486. Pupils taught in Sámi: 154 = 31,7%.*

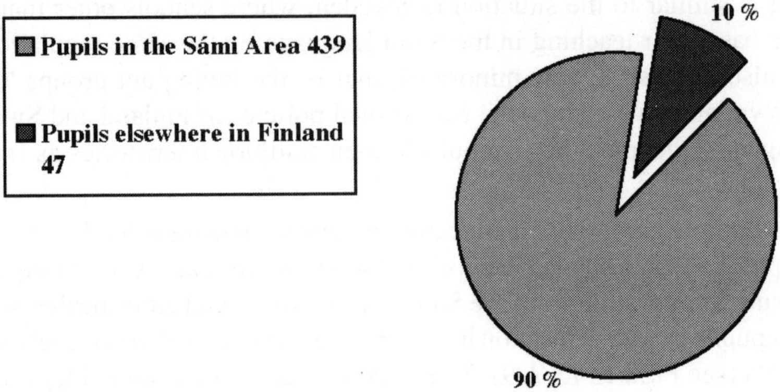


**Figure 13.8.** *Sámi education in Finland in the Sámi Area and elsewhere in Finland in 2003-2004.*

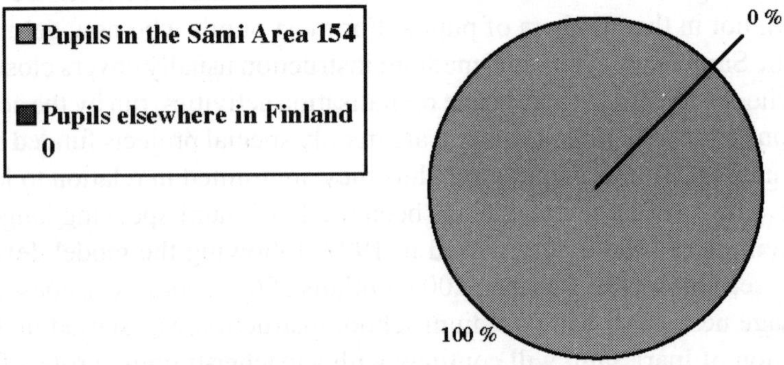


**Figure 13.9.** *Pupils studying in Sámi in the Sámi Area and elsewhere in Finland in 2003-2004.*

## Conclusions

The large number of children and young people for whom Sámi education is not available in some areas, and the fact that Sámi education is clearly improving in the core Sámi areas provide us with the answer to the question I asked earlier: in some regions, the language is being revived, and, in other regions, language shift continues (Aikio-Puoskari & Skutnabb-Kangas 2007). Furthermore, a closer study of Sámi education as a whole shows that a vast majority of the Sámi pupils are still only taught the language as a subject: they have the main language of the country as their language of instruction. In all three countries, a small minority of pupils learn through their own language—something that would be a condition for attaining a high level of bi- and multilingualism. Multilingualism and multiculturalism are prominent themes in the education policies of the Nordic countries. In reality, Sweden and Finland in particular only seem to be tolerating the languages that the majority does not know, and implementing the principle of non-discrimination, meaning granting negative rights only. The goal of bilingualism which is part of the curricula of Norway, Sweden and Finland, applies only to indigenous peoples and minorities; there is no reciprocity even in the traditional Sámi areas so that the linguistic majority would learn an indigenous or minority language. The only exception is the Swedish language in Finland that is to be taught to every pupil in the country. In their educational policy, the Sámi themselves consider bilingualism and multilingualism as a valuable capital which should now be maintained. Nevertheless, bilingualism is threatened as long as one of the two mother tongues of a bilingual person is endangered.

The objective of making the school thoroughly Sámi—of making Sámi culture an integral part of the content and methods of education—has advanced furthest in Norway, as the country has passed two equal versions of the curriculum for compulsory schooling: the national (Norwegian) and the Sámi curriculum (the first one in 1997, O97S, The Sámi Curriculum for the Ten-Year Comprehensive School; the latest in 2006, *Máhttolokten—Sámi oahppoplánabuvttus, Læreplanverket—Kunnskappsløftet Samisk*). The national curriculum of 1997 (L97) also defined, for all subjects (except mathematics) and for all grades, the aspects of Sámi culture that were to be taken into consideration everywhere in Norway. These 'Sámi pillars' became then, for the first time, an obligatory part of the national curriculum, and they should fulfill the objective that the Government of Norway defined for education in the first part of Reform L97; according to this principle, Sámi culture is a part of the national heritage which all the children in Norway should be familiar with. Fundamental aspects of Sámi culture are therefore part of the teaching that is provided in the common curriculum of compulsory schooling (Parliamentary Notice (*St. melding*) No. 52 (1992-93): 16). The new national curriculum also includes the contents of Sámi culture (*Oversikt over samisk innhold i Kunnskapsløftet, Læreplaner for gjennomgående fag i grunnskolen og videregående opplæring,* 2006, http://www.skolenettet.no, accessed on 9 January 2007). As a new goal the Norwegian pupils all over the country now have to learn the alphabet of a Sámi language.

The Sámi curriculum especially emphasises traditional Sámi skills and the strengthening of the pupils' sense of being part of the local nature, culture, traditions, livelihoods and ways of life. In connection with the evaluation of the Sámi curriculum, Sara (2003, 121–138) shows how difficult it is to realise these objectives: he considers it necessary to provide the schools and teachers with a real chance to enhance their professional knowledge in the sphere of traditional skills and to put time and effort into this. Lauhamaa also shows in her study (2008) how difficult it will be to transfer indigenous knowledge into the school. The school culture that is shaped by Western schooling history is often slow and even reluctant to change established practices. 'For instance, the use of local people and nature and flexible scheduling were included in teaching to a limited degree, although these are fundamental measures in the education of Native peoples, such as among the New Zealand Māori and the native Americans,' she states. In the present situation, the objectives concerning the teaching of traditional skills can be used as a landmark leading to a new school culture, which will, in the future, force the school to adopt new ways of thinking and working.

What can be learned of the linguistic history and today's educational situation of one of the smallest indigenous peoples in the world, a people living in the richest welfare states of the world? Is there anything similar to the linguistic and educational situation of the indigenous peoples and minorities in India or Nepal and elsewhere? Scandinavian countries and Finland are linguistically very homogeneous if we compare them with Asian countries such as India, a country with more than one thousand mother tongues. Still I can see many kinds of similarities. In other words, because we are all human beings and we share the same worry about the right to maintain our native identity, the right to be accepted such as we are. We will need recognition and acceptance in the official school systems. The special needs, rooted in assimilation policies and its consequences, seen in the heterogeneous linguistic and cultural background of our children and youngsters today, need to be accepted in the official curricula. That means that we need different kinds of teaching programmes: language nests for children under school-age, revitalisation immersion programmes for those who have lost their native language, protective language shelter programmes for mother tongues, revitalisation programmes for adults. And, finally, the basis for all this, we need teacher training that is closely connected to the native cultures and languages of the pupils. A large and challenging task will be to formalise and transfer the native/ indigenous knowledge into the school curriculum. All these changes are under way in several parts of the world among indigenous peoples and minority groups. We already have a lot of knowledge and understanding from people/s, from researchers and from theories developed even on the other side on the globe. We are building further on these efforts.

## Notes

1 The Sámi community consists of a group of regional Sámi cultures. The groups differ in terms of their traditional sources of livelihood, popular culture, folklore and languages, though the languages are closely related.

2 See the websites of the Sámi Parliaments of Finland, Norway and Sweden www.samediggi.fi, www.samediggi.no, www.sametinget.se and the website of the Saami Council, a rainbow organisation for Sámi NGOs www.saamicouncil.net.

3 Norway became independent (after Danish and Swedish rule) in 1905, when Sweden's current borders were fixed. Finland became independent (after Swedish and Russian rule) in 1917.

4 Turi used the ethnonym 'Sápmi' of his people, but the translation quoted has replaced it with 'Lapp'. 'Lapp' has today been replaced with the Sámi language ethnonyms ´Sápmi´ (for the country and also for the people) and ´Sápmelaš´ (about the people only), rendered Sámi or Saami in English. The ethnonym ´Lapp´ is now considered a (derogatory) name given to Sámi by outsiders.

5 'Sámi area' in Norway refers to the administrative area where the Sámi Language Act is to be implemented (see map). Sámi Language Act refers to Chapter 3 concerning the Sámi language in the Sámi Act (Sámeláhka/ Sameloven, L1087:56). The amendment was made in 1990 (L1990: 78).

[6] 'Sámi area' in Finland refers to the cultural self-determination area of Sámi in Finland. It was specified for the first time at the beginning of 1970s. The latest regulation on the Sámi area is included in the Law on the Sámi Parliament, SSK 974/1995, §4.

**Appendix 13.1.** *The conditions of Sámi education in Nordic compulsory schooling during the 2003-2004 school year*[1].

| | ***SWEDEN*** | ***FINLAND*** | ***NORWAY*** |
|---|---|---|---|
| **SCHOOL SYSTEM VS. SÁMI EDUCATION** | - **6 special Sámi schools** which have the same status as the education provided in grades 1–6 in compulsory schooling (in comprehensive schools) (Láttevárri/ Lannavaara, Giron/Kiruna, Váhčir/Gällivare, Deardná/Tärnaby, Johkamohkki/ Jokkmokk, Gárasavvon/ Karesuando)<br>- **Integrated Sámi Education** in the municipal schools with which the Sámi School Board has made an agreement about the matter<br>- the teaching of the native language **(mother tongue)** in public schools | - all Sámi education is provided by **ordinary public schools** (comprehensive schools)<br>- in schools that provide teaching in Sámi, the Sámi- and Finnish-speaking classes work side by side | - **2 state-owned special Sámi schools** in the South Sámi area (Snoasa/Snåsa and Árborde/Hattfjelldal)<br>- **1 special Sámi school** owned by the municipality in the North Sámi areas (in Málatvuopmi/ Målselv in the province of Troms); its activities are financed by the State<br>- otherwise, teaching in Sámi and the teaching of the Sámi language take place in the ordinary municipal schools, in which the Sámi- and Norwegian-speaking classes work side by side |
| **THE SÁMI LANGUAGES TAUGHT IN THE SCHOOLS** | North Sámi<br>Lule Sámi<br>South Sámi | North Sámi<br>Inari Sámi<br>Skolt Sámi | North Sámi<br>Lule Sámi<br>South Sámi |

| | | | |
|---|---|---|---|
| **SÁMI AS THE LANGUAGE OF INSTRUCTION (=teaching in Sámi)** | - in the Sámi schools (grades 0–6) at least 5 weekly lessons/ grade<br>- Lule Sámi as the language of instruction in 2 Sámi schools in 2003-04<br>- South Sámi **was not** used as the language of instruction in 2003-04<br>- in the Sámi schools (grades 0–6) of Gárasavvon, Giron and Váhčir, about 50% of the teaching is provided in North Sámi<br>- part of the integrated Sámi education (grades 7–9; in Gárasavvon, Giron and Johkamohkki) in North Sámi<br>- Sámi is not the language of instruction outside the Sámi schools and integrated Sámi education | - is realised best in the schools of the Sámi Area, in grades 1–6, in North Sámi; teaching usually covers almost 100% of the pupil's lessons<br>- is limited to the Sámi Area (in Vuohčču, a few weekly hours of language immersion)<br>- teaching in Inari Sámi is increasing; Skolt Sámi is also being used as the language of instruction<br>- teaching in North Sámi is about to begin in grades 7–9; at present, it decreases radically at the beginning of grade 7 | - mainly in the area in which the Sámi Language Act is implemented and to some extent in other areas (e.g. Málatvuopmi Sámi School, in the city of Romsa/Tromsø, in Loabat/Lavangen and in Oslo)<br>- in grades 1–7, teaching in North Sámi usually covers about 100% of the pupil's lessons<br>- teaching in Lule Sámi is increasing; little and scattered instruction in South Sámi<br>- all instruction in Sámi decreases clearly at the beginning of grade 8 |
| **TOTAL NUMBER OF PUPILS IN COMPULSORY SCHOOLING/ teaching in Sámi, the teaching of the Sámi language + teaching in the Sámi language and culture** | **476** | **486** | **2834** |

| **Teaching in North Sámi and the teaching of North Sámi**, total number of pupils | The figures for the different languages and those on the language of instruction for Sweden apply only to the Sámi schools and are from the 2003-2004 school year[2]:<br>**132** | **428**<br>(=88% of all the Sámi pupils of the country) | **2620**<br>(=92,4% of all the Sámi pupils of the country) |
|---|---|---|---|
| **Teaching in Lule Sámi and the teaching of Lule Sámi**, total number of pupils | **29** | | **76**<br>(=2,7% of all the Sámi pupils of the country) |
| **Teaching in South Sámi and the teaching of South Sámi**, total number of pupils | **14** | | **138**<br>(=4,9% of all the Sámi pupils of the country) |
| **Teaching in Inari Sámi and the teaching of Inari Sámi**, total number of pupils | | 30<br>(= 6,2% of all the Sámi pupils of the country) | |
| **Teaching in Skolt Sámi and the teaching of Skolt Sámi**, total number of pupils | | 28<br>(= 5,8% of all the Sámi pupils of the country) | |
| **TEACHING IN SÁMI**<br>- total number of pupils<br>- percentage of all who participate in some form of Sámi education in the country | **132**<br>? | **154**<br>31,7% | **963**<br>34% |

| | | | |
|---|---|---|---|
| **Teaching in Sámi by language:**<br>- in North Sámi | 104 | **135** | 950 |
| - in Lule Sámi | 28 | | 33 |
| - in South Sámi | 0 | | 10 |
| - in Inari Sámi | | 14 | |
| - in Skolt Sámi | | 5 | |
| **PUPILS STUDYING SÁMI AND LEARNING THROUGH SÁMI IN COMPREHENSIVE SCHOOLS IN THE SÁMI ADMINISTRATIVE AREAS**<br>- total number | **295** (2002-03) | **439** | **1476** |
| - % of all the pupils studying Sámi in the country | 62% | 90,3% | 52,1% |
| - Sámi-medium instr. | ? | **154** (=35% of the pupils who study Sámi in the Sámi Area) | **885** (=60% of the pupils who study Sámi in the Sámi Adm. Area) |
| - study the language (and culture) as a subject | ? | **285** (=65% of the pupils in the Sámi Area) | **591** (=40% of the pupils who study Sámi in the Sámi Adm. Area) |
| **PUPILS OUTSIDE THE SÁMI ADMINISTRATIVE AREAS**<br>- total number | **181** (2002-03) | **47** | **1358** |
| - % of all the pupils studying Sámi in the country | 38% | 9,7% | 47,9% |
| - instruction in Sámi | - | - | **108** |
| - study the language (and culture) as a subject | **181** | **47** | **1250** |

## *Notes*

[1] Aikio-Puoskari 2004, Chapters 3-5. The sources of information: for Norway, the Educational Office of the province of Finnmark and the Department of Education in the Sámi Parliament; for Sweden: the Sámi School Board and the national statistics office

*Statistiska Centralbyrån*, SCB; for Finland: the municipalities and schools of the Sámi Area, the Education Office of the Sámi Parliament and the State Provincial Office of Lapland. For Sweden, the data are from two school years (2002/03 and 2003/04).

2 It is impossible to calculate the percentage, because the other data on the number of pupils in Sweden are from the 2002-03 school year. It is not possible to calculate how many pupils study each of the Sámi languages outside the Sámi schools (2002–03), because the information provided by the SCB, *Statistiska Centralbyrån* is unclear.

# PART V
# MLE in Theory and Practice—Diversity in South Asian Tribal Experience

# 14

# 'All Nepalese children have the right to education in their mother tongue'—but how? The Nepal MLE Programme

*Amrit Yonjan-Tamang,*
*David A. Hough, Iina Nurmela*

## Some background and assumptions

This paper describes the first year of project work and implementation of the Nepal Multilingual Education Programmeme. A joint effort on the part of the Ministry of Foreign Affairs (MoFA) of Finland and the Ministry of Education and Sports (MOES) of Nepal, the programme began in January of 2007 and involves six pilot language communities. It aims at setting up a sustainable model by July of 2009 whereby all non-Nepali[1] speaking primary school students in the nation will be able to study in their mother tongue by the year 2015. A detailed account of the theoretical underpinnings of the programme's approach appears in 'Privileging Indigenous Knowledge: Empowering MLE in Nepal' (Hough, Thapa Magar and Yonjan-Tamang 2009, this volume).

All Nepalese children have the right to education in their mother tongue. Both national legislation and education policy documents support this right. Nepal's 1990 constitution states that the medium of instruction in Nepal shall be Nepali but allows for education at the primary level to be given in the mother tongue. The interim constitution of Nepal (January 2007) further elaborates the equal rights of every citizen by giving each community the right to choose education in its mother tongue.

Non-Nepali speaking students have been found to be a disadvantaged group in the Nepalese school system, where the medium of instruction is Nepali. The enrolment and participation of non-Nepali speaking students in primary education is low. Their achievement at school is lower than that of Nepali-speaking students. The dropout rates are highest among non-Nepali speaking groups (see Awasthi 2004).

In order to transform this situation and facilitate mother-tongue medium of instruction at primary school for all, MOES submitted a project proposal in December 2004 entitled *'Bilingual Education Programmeme for All non-Nepali Speaking Students of Primary Schools of Nepal'*. In May 2006, MOES in collaboration with MoFA completed a final joint Project Document for Finnish Technical Assistance (ProDoc 2006), to advise on implementation. The project began in January of 2007 and in August was formally renamed the Multilingual Education Programme. The programme comes under the umbrella of the Nepal Education For All (EFA) 2004-2009 Programme, and is being coordinated by an MLE technical assistance team funded by MoFA.

An important aspect of the programme comes from the EFA goal of decentralised education as a tool in empowering local communities to take control of their own learning needs, a goal which is also supported by MOES. This involves the MLE technical assistance team working closely with six non-Nepali (or mixed Nepali and non-Nepali) speaking communities, where students, parents, teachers, and members of the community at large—including those with valuable local knowledge (hereafter referred to as indigenous knowledge, or IK holders)—are empowered to develop their own learning materials and teaching methodologies, and then to pass this accumulated knowledge and experience on to others in neighbouring communities. This can be achieved by using a cascade model whereby representatives from pilot schools, after having received training and gone through the process of developing local MLE capacity themselves, will then go on to train others. These newly trained communities will, in turn, train other communities. This approach is supported by MOES and MoFA in the joint Project Document (2006: 20), which stresses the importance of local participation and ownership:

> The bilingual education project is not a mechanism which transfers directives from national to local level; it has to be based on the needs and aspirations of linguistic minorities. It is of utmost importance to create a sense of ownership among all local stakeholders, and to directly involve them in the preparation phase in planning and implementing concrete activities that will be carried out.

The project document further cites UNESCO (2003) and OSCE (1992) reports, which call for curricula to be localised and flexible enough to integrate local content in both teaching and testing (ProDoc 2006: 10). This allows local communities to take ownership of the project, both in terms of actual results as well as in terms of the processes used to achieve them.

Close coordination at the district and central levels, and with the Curriculum Development Centre (CDC) and the Department of Education is also vital. Here, CDC specialists at the national level may suggest ways in which locally produced lessons, drawings, stories, etc. may be integrated into the core syllabus for content courses. Teacher training may be informed in a similar way with local, regional and national workshops that include IK holders, teachers and administrators.

Another key component of the programme is engendering appreciation and respect for the tremendous value of Nepal's rich linguistic and cultural diversity. Indigenous and minority peoples face discrimination in all areas of Nepali society from education to employment and beyond. In the education sector, the 2006 project document notes that 'the school system has failed to recognize, accept and appreciate NNS [non-Nepali speaking] children's culture and linguistic competencies and values' (2006: 10). It also reports on national research findings (Awasti 2004) which show that these students are treated unresponsively by school administrators, teachers and staff, causing them to feel disgraced, discriminated against and devalued to the lowest level of the social hierarchy. This often results in parents and teachers trying to change or cover up their linguistic identity (2004: 10). In order to turn these discriminatory attitudes and practices around, the 2006 project document calls for an action research team to be established, which will produce video documentaries that can be used in awareness training programmes at the local, regional and national levels.

## STARTING OUT

A working group was set up in March 2007 to make recommendations on criteria for the speech communities to be targeted. There are over 143 languages spoken in Nepal (Yonjan-Tamang 2006). The working group was mandated to select speech communities in up to six districts for pilot testing. The following criteria were established for selecting speech communities and schools:

### *Selection of Language or Speech Communities*

1. That there be a balance of communities from Nepal's three regions: mountain (Himal), hill (Pahadi) and lowland (Terai);
2. That Nepal's four main language groups (Tibeto-Burman, Indo-Aryan, Austro-Asiatic and Dravidian) be represented and that no more than one speech community/dialect from each language within the four groups be included (e.g. only one speech community from Magar, Rai, Tharu, Tamang etc.);
3. That most pilots be from relatively small speech communities and not represent a dominant dialect;
4. That at least one language be highly endangered;
5. That the communities represent a mix of long literary, developing literacy and oral traditions, with priority given to communities with developing literacy and oral traditions;
6. That priority be given to areas for which materials have not been produced.

### *Selection of Schools*

1. That the community wants and requests the project;
2. That the school(s) in the speech community have a very low level of academic achievement;

3. That there be a high level of marginalisation and poverty in the community;
4. That pilots include schools with both monolingual and multilingual student populations;
5. That at least some of the pilots include schools where not all teachers speak the local language;
6. That at least some of the pilots include schools where materials and support for multilevel classes is needed;
7. That additional factors be considered as deemed necessary by specific conditions.

Based on the above, a tentative list of six speech communities was selected. They are as follows: Rasuwa Tamang (Mountain Region), Palpa Barahmagarant Magar (Hill Region), Dhankuta Athapahare Rai (Hill Region), Kanchanpur Tharu (Terai Region), Sunsari Uraw (Jhangar)/Maithili (Terai Region), and Jhapa Santhali (Terai Region).

Once these districts and speech communities were chosen, it was necessary to select specific schools/school communities. This process involved discussions among district and central educational administrators, District Education Office (DEO) representatives and educational administrators, and local indigenous peoples organisations (IPOs). Following these consultations, and in order to ensure that the process would become bottom up, local IPOs were empowered make the final recommendation as to which school communities best met the pilot project criteria.

After final recommendations had been made, visits to the specific schools were arranged so that the team could explain the programme and determine if the school community wanted to take part in the project. Community members described their feelings about current educational practices and what types of changes they wanted. Through this process, the community committed itself to being actively involved in the project. They also agreed to train five other schools as part of the cascading process, intended to expand the MLE programmeto all 28,000 schools in Nepal by the year 2015. In attendance were: the head teacher, teachers, students, parents, PTA members, school management committee members, IK holders, members of the community, representatives of the DEO, representatives of national and regional IPOs, education officials from the centre including the Department of Education (DOE), CDC, MLE technical advisors and the action research team.

After members of the school community expressed interest in becoming part of the project, they were recruited to take part in the activities. On the first visit, it was decided that students, teachers and community members would work together to develop some kind of materials which could be produced quickly and returned to the school on the second visit. The MLE team felt that it was vital that local communities see some tangible results from the project as soon as possible. In looking at similar programmes in other parts of the world, one major problem has been that materials take so long to develop that the local community loses interest or trust. Added to this is the fact that the budget for a particular project often runs out before the final product is complete, making it unsustainable.

Each community decided what they wanted to do for their first project. The Rasuwa community asked for a picture dictionary which the children could produce. Other communities asked for readers based on local stories and customs. Here, it was decided that IK holders would tell traditional stories to groups of children, and that the children would write abbreviated versions of the stories and draw pictures about them. Materials would first be used to produce wall posters for the school and additional A4 sized copies for each of the students. These materials would be printed and distributed on the second visit. The readers and picture dictionaries would be produced later (hopefully in time for the start of the April 2008 school year). Decisions as to what language or languages to use was also in the hands of the community. In addition to the language or languages of the local speech community, most schools opted to have materials in Nepali and English.

In communities which asked for readers, IK holders were selected to tell stories in their local language. This included a brief training session in order to familiarise community members and school staff with the process of materials collection. The following steps were explained in the training session: (a) students divide into groups of five or six, (b) community members tell a short story, (c) students are given paper and pencils, (d) students write their names and class on the back of the paper, (e) students write the story, (f) students are given drawing paper and crayons, (g) students write their names and class on the back of the paper, (h) students draw the picture. It was important that the stories be told in the mother tongue. In many cases, this was the first time that students had the opportunity to learn about their own culture in their own language at school. Also, where necessary, students had help in writing and drawing from the other students, teachers, IK holders or community members who were present.

In the case of the Rasuwa picture dictionary project, IK holders were also used to find culturally appropriate words and themes. In all cases, choice of orthography was also based on community wishes. Generally, the Devanagari script was used. Later, work was proofread, and translated into the language(s) specified by the community. Group photographs were taken of all students to be included later. Audiotapes were also made of the complete versions of the stories so that they could be transcribed and used in the readers. Finally, the MLE action research team, made up of indigenous young people, documented the process for later use in teacher training sessions as well as for advocacy purposes.

## The Second Visit

This section is based on the MLE technical assistance team's second trip to the Tamang-speaking community of Rasuwa. This was the third in the team's series of second-round visits and involved a two-day workshop in addition to school visits.

The visit began at the schools by returning materials, either complete or in basic printed form for final proofreading, to the schools and students. All schools received classroom posters and students were given A4 copies to take home. Parents and other community members attended and shared the posters with the children, often pointing out pictures that particular children had drawn. As it had been several months since the last visit, the team reviewed the original purpose and asked for feedback. Lively conversations ensued with questions (about teacher quotas and timelines), hopes for the future (about passing their language and culture on to their children, giving them pride), fears (about continued language shift), anger (about how their demands for mother-tongue education had been ignored by the authorities for so many years, and how the culture and language was always being devalued), and expressions of empowerment (about how they could make the programme work for themselves). These conversations were videotaped by the action research team for future use in teacher training and awareness building documentaries.

The two-day workshop followed, and was attended by the head teacher from each school, teachers, parents, PTA members, school management committee members, IPO representatives, IK holders, interested members of the community at large, DEO representatives, and educational officials from the national centre including the DOE, CDC, MLE advisors and the action research team. Although only 30–35 participants were expected, more than 45 attended. All took an active role throughout the workshop.

The MLE team opened the meeting by outlining basic purposes and objectives of the workshop: (1) to listen to the expectations of the participants, (2) to collectively assess their own teacher and community needs, (3) to collectively explore their own knowledge systems, ways of knowing and appropriate teaching methodologies, (4) to plan together how to continue the process of curriculum development, (5) to explain cascading, and (6) to give maximum time to allow education administrators and officials to hear the voices of the community.

Participants then expressed their expectations from the workshop. These were written down on large sheets of paper and hung from the walls of the workshop. This allowed everyone to reflect during the workshop and make modifications as necessary (e.g. by noting which expectations were being addressed and which either needed to be or were no longer important). It also allowed for further reflection and discussion at the end of the workshop. In all, participants listed fourteen things which they wanted to learn about. These are grouped here into three general categories: (a) how to maintain the Tamang language and culture, (b) what approaches can be used in teaching and encouraging the use of Tamang, and (c) specific plans and ideas for implementation and sustainability of the programme.

Concerns about maintenance of the Tamang language and culture played significantly in the list of expectations and included the desire for general suggestions on how to maintain and enrich Tamang as well as more specific questions relating to how to stabilise words and cultural artifacts which are dying, and how to revive and use the Tamang counting system (both in the classroom and outside). Questions were also asked about how to teach Tamang to children who have lost their language, how to teach/encourage parents to use Tamang in the home with their children, how to teach both Tamang and Nepali in the classroom, and which of four existing orthographies to use (there are several scripts including Devanagari, Tibetan, a modified Tibetan and a Roman script). Questions were also raised about which grades could have Tamang language teaching, and how to teach Tamang from the beginning. Finally, issues of implementation and sustainability included questions about how to implement the programme within two-and-one-half years, how to make it sustainable, the desire that the programme be extended to the non-formal education sector (particularly for adults who wished to return to school), and the feeling that ultimately, for the programme to be truly sustainable, it must extend to higher education as well.

Following discussion of expectations, participants were divided into two groups of (a) teachers and administrators, and (b) members of the community, and asked what types of resources and assistance they felt they would need in order to implement the programme from their side. Teachers and administrators listed the following: (1) Tamang language teachers, (2) training for all teachers, (3) materials development, (4) Tamang language materials, including ones which teach math and measurements in Tamang, (5) assistance from linguists and other experts in carrying out the project, (6) funding for Tamang language teachers (if no quota is established), and (7) the training of a current teacher to teach Tamang (if no quota is established and there is no extra funding available). Community members listed the following needs: (1) financial support, (2) Tamang language stories and books (including literature and cultural history), (3) teaching in Tamang about the use of herbal medicines, belief systems and shamanic practices, (4) materials which link traditional and modern practices, (5) the linking of moral knowledge and practical skills (both traditional and modern), and (6) language and culture experts to help in the process of MLE development. These lists were also written on large sheets of paper and posted on the walls.

After completing the needs analysis, workshop members broke into small groups to discuss the indigenous knowledges that were important to them, and which they wanted to pass on to their children. Here, the posted wall sheets of expectations and needs were helpful to participants in the process of categorisation. After some animated discussion as to how to categorise their interests, group leaders presented the assembled body with the following lists:

1. Herbal medicines and traditional healing practices;
2. Traditional and modern knowledge and skills;
3. History, numerical systems, weights and measures;
4. Religion, belief systems and practices;
5. Life rituals, feasts, festivals, songs and poems.

The groups then spent the rest of the afternoon, and worked into the night and the next morning to expand on their lists, collect relevant stories, and pose questions and concerns about approaches to implementation, based in part on their earlier posted lists of workshop expectations and assessed needs. They then shared their work with the assembled group, again using large sheets of paper hung on the walls. Each group chose one or two representatives to present their findings. A detailed analysis of these findings is presented in Priviledging Indigenous Knowledges: Empowering MLE in Nepal (Hough et al., 2009).

## Following from here

It is assumed the government will implement a policy of recruiting teachers who speak the local language of the community, and that preference will be given to female teachers. Additionally, the project calls for models to be developed in schools where teachers do not speak the students' mother tongue. It further calls for empowering the communities themselves to produce learner and locally generated materials based on appropriate cultural content. Local community participation and leadership in this process is vital and requires the full cooperation of all government agencies.

The 2006 ProDoc (18) notes that 'Transfer of government officials is still frequent. In both districts the project preparation team visited, the District Education Officers had been working only a month. Trained key staff of the project may be transferred, which would result in the loss of input for the capacity building of the concerned institutions.' Based on discussions with the Finnish Embassy, the Technical Assistance team will attempt to incorporate capacity building seminars to be given by key government transformative agents who attend conferences and study tours. It is hoped that this will enhance the sustainability of capacity building activities.

There were serious problems in collecting baseline data during the preparation phase of the project. Disaggregated data based on local linguistic communities is currently unavailable. NEFIN (Nepal Federation of Indigenous Nationalities) has nationwide statistics based on ethnic group, and has conducted some qualitative research on specific speech communities (See: JEP, 2005; NEFIN, 2004). There is also district level data (not disaggregated by speech community) available from various national sources (See, for example, CBS 2004). This lack of accurate baseline data has been recognized as a problem by NPC[2]. As a result, they have requested the World Bank and DFID (the Department for International Development, UK) to devise a new social inclusion index. Even here, however, data from small communities will be clustered. Lynn Bennett, the World Bank project leader, has suggested in a personal conversation that the MLE team needs to collect its own anecdotal data in cascading communities.

Finally, rapid implementation and cascading of the programme is imperative if it is to be sustainable. Indigenous and minority peoples in Nepal have been demanding mother tongue medium of education for many years. Without immediate and positive action which empowers local communities 'to establish and control their educational systems and institutions providing education in their own languages, in a manner appropriate to their cultural methods of teaching and learning' the threat of further political instability is exacerbated. (Art. 14.1 of the *UN Declaration on the Rights of Indigenous Peoples*, 2007 A/61/L.67). Nevertheless, while transition to MLE nationwide needs to begin immediately and be modeled on a bottom-up, community-based approach such as the one outlined in this paper, this transition must also be carried out in close cooperation and with a developing appreciation for linguistic and cultural diversity on the part of all government agencies and education sector donor organisations. Only if sustainable models are established now and cascading begins within the next two years, can the EFA goal of MLE nationwide by 2015 be achieved.

## Notes

[1] This paper uses the terms 'non-Nepali' and 'indigenous' interchangeably. Both terms, however, are problematic. The term 'non-Nepali', while inclusive of minority linguistic groups who were not the original inhabitants of the land, nevertheless deprives all non-Nepalis of combined ethnic and national identity (e.g. as Nepali-Magars, Nepali-Tamang etc), and further privileges the dominating group as singularly Nepali (all others being non-Nepali). Some have suggested using the term 'Nepali Khas' for the dominating group and further delineating non-Nepali groups as Adhivasi, Janajati, Mahedesi etc. Others have suggested a more inclusive interpretation of the term 'indigenous' to mean all non-Nepali groups (similar to the approach taken by the United Nations Permanent Forum on Indigenous Issues). This issue is still in process of resolution.

[2] This is a global problem and has been a PFII recommendation for years.

# 15

# Hundreds of Home Languages in the Country and many in most Classrooms: Coping with Diversity in Primary Education in India

*Dhir Jhingran*

Language is not merely a means of communication. Language, thinking and learning are inextricably linked. When children are forced to study through a language they cannot fully understand in the early primary grades, they face a serious learning disadvantage that can stunt their cognitive development and adversely affect their self-esteem and self-confidence for life. This is especially severe in deprived socio-economic situations where there is little exposure to the school language, outside the school. This gets further exacerbated when the children's culture, along with their language, is completely excluded from the classrooms.

The education system in India has not been able to respond to the complex cultural and linguistic diversity in the country. Language-in-education policies have attempted to provide some standardised solutions which have not proved very effective. This paper attempts to cover some ground on the following issues: (a) what is the nature of the challenge at the primary school stage on account of the diverse language situations in the country (b) what is the impact on children's learning outcomes (c) what have been the policy and programmatic formulations on the language-in-education agenda and (d) what are some challenges that need to be addressed on a priority basis.

## Language diversity in India

Like many other countries in this part of the world, India is pluri-lingual and pluri-ethnic. The language situations in India are like a mosaic with a bewildering variety of speech patterns that get woven together in an 'organic pluralism'.[1] It is usually difficult to attach language labels to the varied speech patterns that differ from place to place. There is little agreement on which languages be called 'languages' and which ones be categorised as 'dialects' and why. A significant proportion of the population is multilingual—even if their repertoire of the other languages is limited; different languages are used in different domains of life; there are many 'contact' languages that are used in inter-group communication, which are often hybrids of other languages; there are constant language shifts that are taking place; in most parts of the country, language assimilation is taking place resulting in increased homogenisation, especially in many tribal areas; there are several diglossic patterns among many communities, for example, parents using the regional language when speaking with their children, while using their ancestral language with their elders.[2] Thus, like several other countries in South Asia, language use patterns are complex and difficult to capture and any attempt at documenting speech patterns is a complex exercise.

The national decadal Census attempts to enumerate speakers of different 'mother tongues' (MT).[3] The 2001 Census has identified 1652 mother tongues. These mother tongues are then 'rationalised' into recognised languages. In the 2001 Census, these 1652 mother tongues were grouped into 122 languages. This is an artificial exercise and mother tongues (or languages) grouped under one language could be very different from each other. For example, the mother tongues of Sadri, Lambadi and Chattisgarhi are grouped under the language—Hindi. Speakers of these languages would have low mutual intelligibility and also would not find it easy to understand the standard dialect of Hindi. Similarly, the classification between Scheduled and Non-Scheduled languages has been guided by several non-linguistic considerations.[4] Four languages have been added to the list of Scheduled languages in 2003, taking the total of such languages to 22. Bodo, Dogri and Santali were earlier included in the list of Non-Scheduled languages and Maithili was a mother tongue grouped under Hindi.

The 2001 Census recorded that 57 languages had more than one million speakers, including 27 'mother tongues' listed under Hindi. Hindi, with all its mother tongues formed the largest language group with 422 million speakers.[5] Two hundred and thirty-four Mother tongues were reported as having more than 10,000 speakers. These include mother tongues listed under Scheduled and Non-Scheduled languages. It is estimated that more than one-third of India's districts are linguistically heterogeneous, i.e. more than 20% of the population speaks languages that are not the dominant language of the district. There is a high level of linguistic diversity, even within a block, an administrative unit with 100–200 villages and a similar number of primary schools (see Table 15.1).

Thus, language situations are really complex, with a variety of languages being spoken even within a small geographical area along with link or contact languages. The Census does not provide information on young children's language proficiencies. To be able to understand the language situations in schools, especially primary schools, it is important to conduct sociolinguistic surveys that document language proficiencies and attitudes of young children, especially 5–6 year old children who are ready to join school. There have been very few sociolinguistic surveys that have focused on young children. We often tend to generalise that most children in India, like adults are multilingual. While this may be true for children who are slightly older, for very young children this is usually not true, especially those living in remote parts of the country.

**Table 15.1.** Language context in a block

| |
|---|
| The situation in the Kharsian block in Raigarh district of Chattisgarh state in Central India, exemplifies the complexities of language situations in India. In this multiethnic and multilingual block, tribal groups speak Nagesia, Oraon, Gondi, Kond and Kharia languages. But some of the tribal groups have adopted Sadani as their home language in the eastern part of the block. Chattisgarhi is used as the link language between different tribal groups. However, in many areas of the block parents and children communicate with each other in Sadani/Chattisgarhi even at home. The tribal mother tongue is still used with elders in the family in most households. In some areas, children have to learn four or five languages by the time they complete primary school. For example, a child in a Mundari-speaking household in Raigarh district in Chattisgarh would speak Mundari with his parents, Chattisgarhi with his friends and neighbours and learn Hindi at school as the language used for instruction and try to pick up English from grade 3 onwards. |

## Varied Language Situations in Classrooms

The language situations in classrooms where students face a learning disadvantage on account of the language used at school are very varied. Some important variables that would help define/describe these contexts are:

a. First Language(s) of children (L1):[6] In primary schools in remote areas, classrooms could be monolingual, i.e. almost all children speak the same local language. However, the most common situation is that there are students with at least two-three first language backgrounds in the same classroom.
b. Official Medium of Instruction (MoI): The standard language used in the textbooks and also prescribed for transacting the curriculum.
c. Language used for Instruction: This is the language(s) actually used by the teacher for transaction of the curriculum. This could be of the following types:
   i. A strict standard language (MoI) environment, where children are not allowed to speak their first language(s)
   ii. While instruction is mainly in MoI, children's L1 is used to explain certain concepts and difficult words or while giving complicated instructions
   iii. The teacher freely and extensively uses the children's L1 in teaching process. Often the teacher uses the link language commonly used in the area.

However, very young children, say in grade 1, may not be familiar with this language.

d. Language background of the teacher: Her proficiency in the children's first language(s) and the MoI.

The teachers' attitudes towards students who do not speak the standard school language also influence the learning situation.

There is really a spectrum of complex language and school situations in India. In a geographic area where students in a school/classroom belong to diverse first language backgrounds, there is sometimes a link language that is used for communication in the area. But what needs to be understood is the level of understanding of the link language that young children have at the stage of entry into school.

Another important factor that determines the degree of disadvantage faced by children in understanding the school's standard language is the literacy situation at home and the neighbourhood and the extent of exposure to the standard language through print and visual media. The aspiration level of the families and their desire to help children do well at school in the regional language go a long way in influencing the children. The most adverse situation for young children who do not understand the school language is when the teacher does not know or use their language in the classroom and looks down upon their language and culture. Monolingual classroom situations, where all children in a class have a similar first language background, are not common and obtain only in the more remote tribal areas. Mixed first language situations are the most common.

The school system, however, does not make any allowance for these situations and the curriculum and teaching process is based on the assumption that the classrooms are monolingual and all children understand and speak the standard language used in the textbooks.

## Languages Used as Mediums of Instruction

### Learning Disadvantage

Of the 122 languages recorded in the census, only 26 are used as mediums of instruction at the primary stage. Only 6 of the non-scheduled languages, of the 100 recorded in the 2001 census, (all spoken by tribal groups in North-Eastern India) are used as mediums of instruction. No Non-scheduled language, outside North-Eastern India is used as a medium of instruction.

English is used as the medium of instruction in all government primary schools in three states of India—Jammu and Kashmir (Kashmir Valley), Nagaland and Arunachal Pradesh. A significant proportion of private schools in the cities and small towns of the country use English as the medium of instruction from grade 1 itself. Thus, a large number of children in India begin school studying in an unfamiliar language. A rough assessment indicates that almost 25% of primary school children face moderate to severe problems in the initial months and years of primary school on account of the their home language being different from the school language. The following groups of children face a moderate to severe learning disadvantage on account of their home language being very different from the language of instruction at school:

a. *Children belonging to Scheduled Tribes (ST)* who speak their indigenous language at home, especially those living in remote, tribal dominated areas. In several parts of the country, tribal communities have adopted the dominant local language or the language of the market or neighbourhood as their home language. However, this language is usually still very different from the standard language used at school. Based on school-wise data for 2006–07, it is estimated that 165,869 primary schools had more than 50% children belonging to scheduled tribes (ST), 128,873 primary schools had more than 75% ST children and 103,732 schools had more than 90% ST children.[7] Thus, about 10% of the 1.02 million schools with primary grades had more than 90% ST enrolment. An interesting feature of the enrolment of ST children is that almost 85% of the total ST children enrolled in primary schools are enrolled in schools that have 50% or more ST children. This implies that it is easy to identify primary schools where most children belong to the scheduled tribes, and are, therefore, studying through an unfamiliar second language.

b. *Children who speak a language that is considered a 'dialect' of the regional language*, and have very low comprehension of the standard language used at school. Many of these languages are actually quite different from the regional language and cannot be called dialects. For all practical purposes, the school language is a second language for these children.

c. *Children of migrants* who are living in a state that has a different official language and those residing in inter-state border areas who have a different language as their mother tongue, and do not get the facility of studying in their own language. The problems faced by seasonally migrating families who move along with their children for varying durations in search of work are more complex. Tracking these families is a huge task. Also, since a significant proportion of seasonal migration is across states, it is a challenge to provide schooling facilities in the medium of education in which the children had been studying when they left their homes for a few months.

d. *Children whose first language, though written and well developed, is not used as a medium of instruction at school.* This is of course a very diverse category including speakers of Sindhi, Urdu, Kashmiri, Dogri, Konkan, etc.

The extent and nature of learning difficulties faced by the children who do not speak or understand the language used as MoI depend on several factors—such as level of intelligibility of the language used as the medium of instruction, the socio- economic background of the children including literacy level of family members, exposure outside school to the standard language used at school, motivation to learn the school language, the teaching methodology adopted at school in the early grades and the linguistic competence of the teacher in the first language(s) of the children.

Apart from the issue of an unfamiliar language being used at school, the alienation is compounded by the attitudes of the teachers towards the languages and cultures of the students belonging to particular ethno-linguistic groups. This is especially true in the case of non-tribal teachers working in schools with tribal students.

## This is a 'quality of education' and learning issue

There is no denying the psychological trauma faced by young children when confronted with an alien language in school (see Magga, Nicolaisen, Trask, Dunbar and Skutnabb-Kangas 2005, Dunbar and Skutnabb-Kangas 2008). Also, the textbooks and instruction have no reference whatsoever to their local culture and traditions. But the education system understands the language of 'quality of education' and the learning outcomes of children. So, it is best to highlight the learning dimension of the challenge faced by these children. In this age, where everyone talks of Education for All (EFA) which is clearly understood to include 'learning for all', it is surprising that this serious learning issue has received scant attention. The system does not provide an equal opportunity to these children to learn. They are being deprived of the right to basic education of good quality. The education system ensures that from their first day in school everything that is thrown at children during the teaching process is completely 'unknown' to them. Educationists, who cry hoarse saying that the most inviolable principle of a good curriculum and teaching practice is that 'we need to build on the child's existing knowledge' and move from the 'known to the unknown' do not recognise that in these situations, the child starts with the completely unknown and can only sink deeper into incomprehension with each passing month. The language deficit that is forced upon the child the day she joins school becomes a learning deficit that only becomes bigger each year.

In India, in the past fifteen years, there have been a series of initiatives for improving quality of basic education. These include the Minimum Levels of Learning (MLL); Joyful Learning; Child-centred, activity-based teaching methodology; multi-grade and multi-level teaching; remedial teaching, etc. The buzzword today is 'constructivism'—promoting curriculum and teaching that help children construct knowledge based on their earlier knowledge and experience and the learning experiences organised in the classroom. What no one seems to talk about is—what kind of knowledge can children construct on their own if they do not understand or only partly understand the language being used in the classroom?

All these 'new' pedagogical approaches were conceptualised at some central level and also implemented in a 'top-down' manner. The implicit assumption was that the teaching–learning materials and training programmes developed under these approaches were uniformly applicable and useful throughout a state or region. They did not encourage a reflective approach at the district, block or cluster levels to understand real issues in the classrooms in varied contexts. The dimension of the diversity in children's languages when they first come to school has rarely been considered when these initiatives were launched at regular intervals.

## Impact on Children's Learning

There has been very limited rigorous, large-scale research in the country to understand the impact of the monolingual teaching practices, especially on children who come from a different language background. Typically, standardised assessments of children's learning in reading, language and mathematics conducted by state agencies or NGOs have seldom used the dimension of children's mother tongue to understand the variations in learning outcomes. Usually, these surveys use social group categories like scheduled caste and scheduled tribes to profile the children.[8] The only analysis that can possibly be made is with respect to the learning outcomes of tribal children when compared with those belonging to other social groups, with an assumption that all or most tribal children speak their mother tongue. The analysis shows a mixed situation, where tribal children generally score the lowest among all social groups; but often the differences are not significant. This could be on account of the fact that tribal communities in India do not form a homogenous group with the same level of physical and social isolation and students' performance scores aggregated at the state level for thousands of schools miss out on the picture in specific, marginalised situations. More importantly, it could also reflect the generally low levels of learning of most children in government schools. Also, since school based examinations at the primary school stage usually test only for rote memorisation, and not higher order thinking and language skills, most children manage to somehow get the minimum scores required.

However, a more in-depth analysis at the school level brings out the serious learning difficulties faced by tribal and other children who study in schools through a language that is totally different from their first language. A small study conducted in 2004 (Jhingran 2005) in four states documented the language environment in the classrooms (languages used by teachers and children), language teaching methods, learning problems faced by students and an assessment of basic language skills in eight primary schools with different language contexts.[9] The salient findings for grades 1 and 5 are presented below:

### *Language used by the teacher*

In schools where the children's first language is very different from the language of instruction (as used by the teachers), children in grade 1 (after about six months of the academic session) are not able to comprehend the language spoken by the teacher. Some teachers who know the children's first language also do not use it for classroom transaction because they feel that this would be against the official policy of use of the standard language for instruction and/or they believe that the exclusive use of the standard language would help provide maximum exposure to the standard language which would help the children pick up the language quickly. These teachers speak in long monologues since there is no possibility of response from the children who do not understand what the teacher is saying.

In classrooms where the children's first language is very different from the standard language, some teachers use the first language to communicate with children, give instructions and also explain the content of the textbook. In such classrooms, there is much greater communication between the teacher and the children. The children understand the teachers' instructions and are not completely silent (unlike the situations in the classrooms where the children's first language is not used at all). This situation is, however, not very common in tribal areas because there are fewer tribal teachers and many of them hesitate to use tribal language extensively in the classroom. The use of the local tongue is much more common in situations where the local language is a variant (often called a dialect) of the standard language. Since in such areas, teachers are mostly from the locality of the school and are often not so well versed in the standard language, they tend to use the local language extensively in the classroom.

In almost all mixed language background (multilingual) classrooms that were observed, teachers used the standard dialect (textbook) or the local variant of the language that is the dominant language in that area.

In grade 5, the standard language is used for instruction in almost all schools. The basic assumption is that students have, by this stage, acquired proficiency in the standard language.

### *Language teaching methodology*

In grade 1, it was observed that children copy letters of the alphabet and numerals from the blackboard or the textbook and very little oral work is done. Children are mostly passive and spend most of their time reciting or copying. These activities provide no scope to start understanding the unfamiliar language being taught to them. In multi-grade schools, teachers do not spend much time in grade 1. Thus, children who need the most attention and conversation–communication support in their first few months in school for navigating an unfamiliar language have the least time with the teacher.

In each of the eight schools that were observed, teachers in grade 5 were aware of the very limited second language proficiency of the children, and felt that they had no option but to get the students to copy from the textbook or blackboard and memorise the answers. Almost all the classrooms that were observed followed a similar teaching methodology. The text is read out aloud, either by the teacher or by the students, often followed by chorus repetition by the students. The teacher then offers some explanations and word meanings, which are usually inadequate to make the children understand the content. Later, the answers to some of the questions at the end of the lesson are written on the blackboard by the teacher for the children to copy. The children do not ask many questions or say anything on their own. Overall, the stress is entirely on rote memorisation of the answers.

*Children's language skills*

In schools where the children's first language is very different from the language of instruction (as used by the teachers), children in grade 1 cannot recognise letters of the alphabet, except when arranged in a sequence. They cannot speak even a few words in the standard language. A majority of the children name objects shown to them in their first language easily. However, they cannot articulate simple answers even in their first language and mostly use one or two words to reply to questions. They are, however, clearly more comfortable in their first language.

In some areas, tribal children also speak the local version of the regional language, though they have only a limited vocabulary when they first enter school. In such areas the tribal children do not appear to be at a greater disadvantage than the general (non, ST) children who also face a problem in understanding the standard dialect. Children whose first language is similar to the language used as the medium of instruction could respond to simple questions, recognise alphabets and also read and write simple words in grade 1. In the same class, children whose first language is different, mostly tribal language speaking children, performed poorly on reading and oral comprehension tests.

In several such schools with mixed language background children, the observations in grade 1 clearly indicate that children who speak a language which is of a different stock (linguistically very different from the language of instruction), and have limited exposure to the regional language when they enter school, definitely face a greater disadvantage than other children who may speak a language which, though quite different from the standard language used as MOl, has some similarity with it.

In general, tribal children (whose first language differs substantially from the MoI) can only read with a lot of effort, mostly word by word, even in grade 5. Their oral skills in the second language are poor and they are definitely more comfortable speaking in their mother tongue. Such children cannot frame sentences correctly and have a very limited vocabulary. While they can partially comprehend texts (of grade 2 level), they are unable to formulate answers to simple questions in the standard language. In most schools, the tribal language speaking children could not score a single mark in the reading comprehension test. Teachers generally had low expectations of tribal children in almost all the schools that were observed.

In schools with a multilingual situation, i.e. where there are some children who are native speakers of the standard language or those who speak a similar dialect and some who speak a tribal language, the spoken language abilities of the tribal children in the second language were somewhat better (than in schools where there were no children who spoke the regional language). But their performance in reading and writing tests was not significantly better. Obviously, peer group interaction helps the tribal children in picking up conversational skills in the regional language. In some of these mixed population villages, there is also a greater exposure of the tribal children to the regional language in its local form.

Generally, children whose first language is a dialect of the main regional language (whose standard form is the medium of instruction) pick up the school language quickly, especially in areas that have high literacy levels. In two schools, due to extensive use of the local dialect, the children did not acquire any proficiency in the standard language even in grade 5 and continued to use words and expressions from the local dialect.

Overall, students in grade 5 could not express their thoughts freely and coherently even in their mother tongue. Academic and higher order language skills in the first language do not develop since the language is not used at all in school.

Generally, the ability to comprehend a simple unknown text and answer questions based on an understanding of the text was very unsatisfactory. Almost no child could correctly answer questions that did not have a direct answer in the text. The skill to write in their own words had not been cultivated in the students. The ability to write creatively on an open-ended topic was almost non-existent.

## Language-in-Education policies...and practice

Article 350 A of the Indian Constitution states that every state and local authority shall endeavour to provide adequate facilities for instruction in the mother tongue at the primary stage of education for all children belonging to linguistic minority groups. This is reiterated in the Programme of Action (POA), 1992, that is based on the National Policy on Education, 1986. The National Charter for Children, 2005 also states that primary education should be provided in the mother tongue of the child. Even before that, the Provincial Education Ministers' Conference in 1949 and the Conference of Chief Ministers in 1961 had resolved that 'whenever there are at least 40 students in a school or 10 in a classroom speaking a particular mother tongue that is different from the regional or state language, teaching would have to be done in the mother tongue of these children by appointing at least one teacher.' However, this decision has not been implemented in practice.

The issue of education in the mother tongue at the primary stage has not become a right and has remained only as something that is desirable. It is completely up to the state governments to decide the languages to be used as mediums of instruction or as subjects at the primary stage.

We have noted earlier that twenty-six languages are used as mediums of instruction at the primary school stage in India. This is a much larger number than most other countries in Asia. There are several reasons why many languages have come to be used in primary schools in India. Traditionally, much before the British came to India, basic education was imparted in the regional languages in the local educational institutions like *pathshalas* and *maktabs*. Languages like Sanskrit, Prakrit and Arabic were used for higher education at different points in time. The Constitution authorised each state to choose its own official language(s). The reorganisation of states on a linguistic basis in the late 1950s and early 1960s helped to create and reinforce strong linguistic identities and strengthened the regional languages. The federal nature of the Indian polity ensured that primary education largely remained the responsibility of the states and they could take decisions on the languages to be used in education.

In addition to their own state official languages, most states have schools with other mediums of instruction too. Twenty-three of the twenty-eight states have more than three mediums of instruction; while 12 have five or more mediums of instruction. However, school facilities in the mother tongue for children residing in inter-state border areas and for migrant families residing in another state/region tend to be very inadequate. The number of primary schools offering education in the language of the migrants or border area residents is not enough; there are very few, if any, schools at the upper primary and secondary stages of education; such schools are often neglected and do not have adequate number of teachers who can teach in the children's language and textbooks are often not delivered in time for the school session. These are languages that are fully developed and already being used as mediums of instruction in other parts of the state or other states. The other issue is that the work being carried out in a state for improving the quality of education including curriculum and textbook revision, training of teachers and on-site academic support to teachers does not get done in these languages (which are not the state/regional languages). Thus, these schools do not benefit from all the quality improvement initiatives being implemented in a state. The state level apex academic institutions responsible for curriculum revision and teacher training usually do not have any staff with these language backgrounds. One language that has consistently faced neglect in several states is Urdu. There is an acute shortage of Urdu medium schools in several parts of the country. The number of such schools is steadily declining, mainly because new Urdu medium teachers have not been recruited for some time. Training of Urdu teachers and revision of the curriculum for Urdu medium is delayed or neglected in several states.

Overall, we seem to have done well in promoting our regional languages and their use in education. However, our record in the use of other, less powerful languages has been dismal. Only six non-scheduled languages are used as mediums of instruction and only in North-Eastern India.

To address the various demands of regional identity, retaining Hindi as a national link language and to provide a place for English as the language of progress and power, the Three Language Formula was evolved in 1961 and developed in to the following policy in 1968:

a. The First language to be studied must be the mother tongue or the regional language.

b. The Second language:
   - in Hindi-speaking states, the second language will be some other modern Indian Language or English
   - in non-Hindi-speaking states, the second language will be Hindi or English.

c. The Third language
   - In Hindi-speaking states, the third language will be English or a modern Indian Language not studied as the second language, and
   - In non-Hindi-speaking states, the third language will be English or a modern Indian language not studied as the second language.

The intention of the Formula was to ensure that every student in India learns at least three languages in school by the secondary stage of education. However, the Three Language Formula, never really a national policy, but only a consensus strategy, has not been implemented in most states in the right spirit. In Hindi speaking states, Sanskrit is being taught instead of another regional (preferably South Indian) language as the third language. In South Indian states, Hindi is not being taught and only the regional language and English are included. Private schools do not follow the Formula and a large proportion use English as the first language. Also, the medium of instruction is usually the regional language and not the mother tongue of the children. The regional language is a second language for most children in the early primary grades and the Three Language Formula does not require that children must receive primary education in their mother tongues. Therefore, this strategy does not really support initiatives that aim at introducing mother tongue based multilingual education.

The National Curriculum Framework (NCF), 2005, developed by the National Council of Educational Research and Training is strongly supportive of the use of mother tongue at the primary stage and the addition of other languages gradually. It also identifies the importance of multilingualism and promotes the use of children's languages as resources in the classroom. Unfortunately, the NCF is not a policy that is binding on all states and its formulations are only of an advisory nature. Also, the Framework does not go beyond talking of ideal approaches to suggest practical strategies to implement these approaches. Thus, the NCF has failed to become a prime mover for multilingual initiatives.

## The issue of English

There is really no national policy on language-in-education for the government education system. The private school system usually has the freedom to adopt any choice of languages for the primary stage. In the towns and cities in India, there is a surge in the establishment of 'English medium' primary schools. A vast majority of these schools have under-qualified and untrained teachers, but their Unique Selling Point is the English medium. English is seen as the language of power and the vehicle for getting better jobs. Even poor families in urban areas aspire to send their children to these private English medium schools. Here children are taught through English from their first day in school. Often their parents do not speak the English language and there is no English speaking environment anywhere in the neighbourhood. The teachers usually do not have the competence to teach English even as a subject. This makes for poor quality teaching and a huge burden of non-comprehension for these children. The rate at which such schools are mushrooming, now even in the better-off rural areas, is scary. There is a much smaller number of high fee charging elite English medium private schools.

The government school system, which is anyway perceived as of lower quality, is trying to keep pace with this demand for education in English. Almost all states have introduced English as a subject from grade 1 or grade 3. This has been done despite the knowledge that there are no teachers in primary schools who can teach English. It is also common knowledge that in several parts of the country, English could be a fourth language for the children (home language, local link language, school or state language being the first three) and they have very limited exposure to English outside school. Till about ten years ago, English was taught as a subject from the upper primary stage, beginning with grade 5 or 6. The argument provided in favour of this early introduction of English is that this would help children learn English better. The other explanation offered is that the government schools need to meet parental demand and the competition from private schools. When some educationists raised the issue of inappropriateness of teaching English from grade 1, the central government took the stand that this was the prerogative of the state governments and no advice could be sent from the centre. The following extract from a government resolution (Curzon, cited in Evans 2002: 277–278) formulated more than a hundred years ago (1904) in Viceroy Curzon's time seems to have said exactly what is required to be asserted today in government policy and practice.

> As a general rule the child should not be allowed to learn English *as a language* [i.e. as a subject] until he has made some progress in the primary stages of instruction and has received a thorough grounding in his mother-tongue. It is equally important that when the teaching of English has begun, it should not be prematurely employed as the medium of instruction in other subjects.

## Educational Programmes and Language Related Initiatives in Primary Education

There have been some initiatives at the national and state levels to address the problems faced by children who study through an unfamiliar language. Most of these have targeted situations where the school has a monolingual situation (in terms of children's home language) in tribal areas and the medium of instruction is a completely unfamiliar regional language.

a. The National Council of Educational Research and Training, the Central Institute of Indian Languages and the Tribal Research Institutes in several states produced a large number of primers in several tribal languages for the initial primary grades. These primers were based on the 'bilingual transfer model'. Thus, the grade 1 primer was almost entirely in the tribal language and in the following grades the proportion of text in the tribal language was reduced, till the primers in grade 4 were entirely in the state language. Ratios like 90:10; 70:30; 50:50; 20:80 and 0:100 reflecting the proportion of the two languages in the primary grades (1–5) formed the basic building block of the curriculum. However, these initiatives were really half-baked and were guided by a welfarist perspective of 'let us do something for the poor tribal children' rather than a rights perspective on language and culture. These books were mere translations of the state language books and were not based on local culture and knowledge. They were often prepared only for the language subjects which did not address the issue of non-comprehension of the curriculum in other subjects. The approach was confined to the publication of these textbooks or readers. Components of teacher training, regular academic follow-up and evaluation were not included. Many schools where these books were introduced did not have 100% tribal children with the same first language. Many of these schools did not have bilingual teachers. There was little grounding of the approach in theoretical perspectives of second language learning. The teachers did not understand how to transact the text that was in both languages and how to help students in moving to the second language. These pilot experiments did not have the policy backing of the state governments and slowly withered away. Worse, they were declared failures. This queered the pitch for any further effort at introducing more comprehensive bilingual education programmes.
b. As sporadic efforts in a few states as a part of EFA programmes, several states prepared two kinds of materials: (a) Bilingual inventories of words in some tribal languages to help non-tribal teachers understand what children say in the early primary grades and use some of these words to explain the content in the textbooks and (b) Some teaching-learning materials using words familiar to children for use in the first few months of grade 1—like word cards, alphabet cards and charts. Some of these materials were used to help 'transition' from the local tribal language to the state language in six months.
c. Under the influence of the 'joyful learning' initiative of UNICEF, some states collected rhymes, riddles and folktales in the children's mother tongues (in a few languages) for use by teachers in grade 1 for 30–60 days as a part of their 'school readiness packages'. However, these remained like add-ons, distinct from the regular teaching learning process and aimed mainly at making children comfortable in the first few weeks of school.

d. Introducing children's home or ancestral languages as language subjects from grade 2 or 3 onwards has happened mainly in North-Eastern states. This has been done mainly for appeasing certain ethnic groups and their sociocultural associations that were demanding some political autonomy. These initiatives did not originate in any understanding of the problems faced by young children in grades 1 and 2 when studying through the state language, which continues to be the medium of instruction.

e. Two states have been running training courses for non-tribal teachers in tribal languages. However, this strategy has met with very limited success. It is not easy for teachers to learn a language that belongs to a totally different language stock. especially, when there is little motivation to do so. Often, non-tribal teachers have negative attitudes towards tribal languages and cultures. In this context, the experiment of 'attitudinal training' of teachers in Orissa (a state in eastern India), to help introspect their beliefs and assumptions about tribal cultures (Mishra 2008) and develop more positive attitudes that can help improve their interaction with tribal children, is worthy of study and emulation.

Most of these efforts suffered from severe limitations. These were half-hearted measures that were not grounded in a sound theoretical understanding of how children learn a second language. Some of them were tokenistic in nature, e.g. the use of bilingual language inventories for teachers or word and alphabet cards for children in the initial months of grade 1. The understanding in all these initiatives was that children need to be initiated into literacy with their home language, but then can be quickly transitioned into the school language. Thus, these were 'very early exit' transitional bilingual programmes. Most of these initiatives were not grounded in state policy and were discontinued once key personnel got shifted away from key EFA programme positions.

Some NGOs have implemented small MLE programmes in learning centres and alternative schools outside the formal school system. *Prashika*, the primary education programme of an NGO called *Eklavya* sought to promote good materials and teaching–learning practices for the teaching of languages in government primary schools.

Presently, two very promising pilots of MT based MLE programmes are being implemented in the states of Andhra Pradesh and Orissa in eight and ten tribal languages respectively in about 400 primary schools. Since these two experiments are detailed elsewhere in this book (see Mohanty et al. 2009, this volume), we will not discuss them here. The distinguishing features of both these experiments are: (a) maintenance of the MT has been planned at least till grade 5, though the MT is not proposed to be used for teaching other subjects after grade 4; (b) the entire process has drawn strength from the motivation of local communities; (c) the curriculum has been developed by incorporating local knowledge and culture and the materials are, therefore, child-centred in the true sense; (d) these are comprehensive approaches that include dimensions of curriculum development, teacher development, additional supplementary materials; and (e) they are state-owned and part of the regular state-run EFA programmes and are, therefore, more likely to be sustained. While, these two MLE experiments hold great promise, there are serious issues to be addressed. There is a need for developing a strong research and evaluation component as part of the programme design. The strategy for bridging to the state language could be strengthened. As the programmes expand, it would be necessary to keep the community initiative and involvement sustained. Regular academic monitoring of schools has to be ensured. The policy support from the government is still not unequivocal and greater advocacy is required to ensure sustained support from the government. The research and development tasks will need to be anchored in existing institutions, rather than being supported through temporary project arrangements.

## Conclusion

Here are some suggestions for policy makers, education planners and administrators that could help in improving the education system's response to the challenge posed by the varied language contexts in India:

1. For remote, tribal areas with primary schools that have 100% tribal children with the same home language background, comprehensive MT based multilingual education programmes on the pattern of the present pilots in two states of India would need to be implemented. These should not be early-exit transitional bilingual education programmes of the subtractive type, but should maintain children's home languages till a late stage (beyond the primary grades). It is crucial to ensure that there is a long term state commitment backed by policy formulations and institutional support for these MLE programmes.
2. With the fluid language patterns, a structured approach with a fixed set of materials and bridging strategies will not work in most parts of the country. The approach of the present MT based MLE programmes would be relevant only in areas with a monolingual home/first language situation. For most other language contexts, a more flexible approach that focuses on use of children's home languages in the early grades and appropriate teaching–learning strategies for acquiring proficiency in the school standard language would be needed. Such an approach would require a high level of teacher competence, motivation and sensitivity to children's needs. Thus, training of teachers in assessing the local situation and working on flexible strategies and materials would be the key elements. Pre-service training and refresher courses for teachers should include a strong component of appropriate language teaching practices in early grades, e.g. time for oral work, communicative use of language, etc. In addition, teacher development strategies must include orientation and dialogue on issues of marginalisation and diversity within classrooms and beliefs and attitudes of teachers about certain sociocultural and ethnic groups that could adversely affect children's development.

3. The challenge of developing appropriate strategies for multilingual classrooms is daunting. While there are some ideas, there has been little research and experimentation in our country on this issue. Some linguists (Agnihotri 2007b) and educationists do talk about the use of children's languages as a resource in the classroom and also as a part of the teaching strategy, but this has remained in the realm of theoretical discussion. We probably need to identify and study experiments that are being tried out in other parts of the world and promote such work in India.
4. State governments need to provide adequate schooling facilities in other mediums of instruction (other than the state's official language(s)). This is a big need in inter-state border areas and where migrants from other states have settled. Also, there needs to be adequate investment of resources in training of teachers, revision of curriculum, academic supervision, etc. for these 'other' language medium schools. A bigger challenge is to address the needs of children who migrate seasonally with their families across states that have different mediums of instruction.
5. Irrespective of what strategies are adopted for various language contexts, some basic pre-requisites that can be called non-negotiables, need to be ensured by the education system for addressing the language disadvantage faced by children who do not fully understand the standard school language when they first join school. Four such basic conditions are:
    - Understanding and mapping school language contexts to help identify appropriate approaches.
    - Promoting use of children's first languages in school by teachers and students, even if these languages are not used for instruction.
    - Bilingual teachers who understand the children's language(s) and the school language.
    - Appropriate early grades teaching strategies, especially language teaching methods that focus on oral work, conversation and meaning and flexible use of language.
6. We must recognise that the teaching of English from the early primary grades is here to stay. The government school system cannot remain insulated from the market forces fuelling the growth of 'English-medium' schools. From a language development perspective, this may be totally inappropriate. But, given the momentum of this change, there is no likelihood of a reversal. So, we need to put our heads together to understand and develop strategies to minimise the harm that can be caused to young children in grade 1 trying futilely to learn several new languages all at once. For example, the teaching of English in grades 1 to 3 could be limited to only oral work—simple words, conversation, rhymes, etc.
7. Pre-school education could offer the best window for promoting children's home languages. At present, the coverage and quality of pre-school education is really

unsatisfactory. But, a good one or two year pre-school programme could be the ideal precursor of an MLE strategy at the primary school stage.

## *Notes*

1 Khubchandani (1983) distinguishes the Indian cultural and linguistic pluralism, which he calls 'organic' from the more 'structured' pluralism as seen in some European countries like Switzerland and Belgium.

2 As reported in the 1991 Census—almost 20% of India's population is bilingual and 8% trilingual. These could be underestimates.

3 The Census in 2001 used the following definition to record the mother tongue exactly as mentioned by the respondents—'Mother tongue is the language spoken in childhood by the person's mother to the person. If the mother died in infancy, the language mainly spoken in the person's home in childhood will be the mother tongue. In the case of infants and deaf mutes, the language usually spoken by the mother should be recorded. In case of doubt, the language mainly spoken in the household may be recorded.'

4 The Indian Constitution in 1950 recognised the multilingual character of the nation. Fourteen languages were listed in the Eighth Schedule of the Constitution initially. They are called Scheduled languages. These were the traditional 'literary' languages. Thereafter more languages got included in the Eighth Schedule since this provides some economic and political benefits. The remaining languages are called Non-Scheduled languages. The 2001 Census recorded 96.56% of the country's population to be speaking one of the Scheduled languages as their mother tongue; the remaining 3.44% is accounted for by one of the Non-Scheduled languages.

5 India's total population in 2008 is estimated as 1.13 billion.

6 Here, the first language of the child is that language in which the child has oral proficiency at age five or six, at the time of joining preschool or primary school. This may not be the commonly understood 'mother tongue' or ancestral language of the family.

7 This database, called the District Information system for Education (DISE) is maintained by the central and state governments under the EFA programme called *Sarva Shiksha Abhiyan*. It is designed to include information for each primary and upper primary school in the country.

8 We analysed the following assessments: (a) Grades 3, 5 and 7 Students' Learning Achievement Surveys carried out by the National Council of Research and Training in 2002, 2005 and 2006, (b) Learning Assessment Study for Quality Education- Measuring Learning Achievement in 13 States, a Study on behalf of UNICEF conducted by Educational Initiatives (P) Ltd. and (c) Annual Status of Education Report (ASER) 2008, a large, country-wide survey carried out annually by Pratham, an NGO.

9 The study was conducted in government primary schools in the states of Assam, Gujarat, Madhya Pradesh and Orissa.

# 16

# Multilinguality and a New World Order*

*Rama Kant Agnihotri*

## Introduction

Given that large-scale linguistic genocide and attendant loss of cultural, educational and socio-economic space and human dignity (Skutnabb-Kangas 2000, Crystal 2000, Nettle and Romaine 2000, Tollefson and Tsui 2004, Dunbar and Skutnabb-Kangas 2008 among others) and that English imperialism and attendant economic and cultural exploitation (Ram 1983, Viswanathan 1989, Suleri 1992, Phillipson 1992, Niranjana 1993, Trivedi 1993, Pennycook 1994, Agnihotri and Khanna 1997 among others) are stark realities, we need to work towards a more just world order that is marked by equity and democracy. We need to formulate an alternative view of 'language' and 'multilinguality' in both theory and practice as well as at least begin to conceptualise a new world order. So far as the interface between language/ multilinguality and the new social order is concerned, there is hope primarily for three reasons: English can survive more constructively in the implementation of 'multilinguality' as proposed in this paper and there is no reason to believe that what could happen to Greek, Sanskrit, Latin, Persian etc will not happen to English; secondly, technology which was hitherto almost exclusively exploited by English is increasingly accessible to other languages. And finally it does seem possible to examine multilinguality as a site that would not only help fight highly dangerous sociolinguistic stereotypes but will also promote divergent thinking, higher levels of linguistic and scholastic achievement, cognitive flexibility and most of all social tolerance (Cummins and Swain 1986, Mohanty 1994 among others). In societies such as India (Pandit 1969, 1972, 1988, Pattanayak 1973, 1981, Khubchandani 1983, 1988) multilingualism facilitates rather than obstructs mutual communication and survival and different groups create new meanings out of day-to-day interactions, maintaining a multiplicity of dynamic identities simultaneously. I do believe all communities are like that, of course, to different degrees. We also know that there are socio-political and linguistic processes at work which construct excluded underprivileged groups of various kinds including women, untouchables, lepers and deaf, for example. It is not being claimed that a focus on multilinguality will alone make our society democratic and participatory; it is a path that may provide several alternative leads. Unless we dream of a different world order, we will not even try to get there.

## Our debt to linguistics and sociolinguistics

For a long time now both formal linguists and sociolinguists have worked under the spell of the concept of 'a language'. It has been assumed that for doing 'science of language', there is no option and one would readily and gratefully acknowledge that this approach has yielded a large number of insights about the nature, structure, acquisition and change of language and about the relationship of language and mind. Enquiry on these lines where 'a language' is examined as an abstract idealised artefact or where an attempt is made to structure and accommodate inherent linguistic variability that in practice cuts across language boundaries into 'a language' must continue. It is such extremely carefully conducted enquiry into language by Chomsky and others that has given us the confidence to at least formulate a reasonable hypothesis to Plato's Problem in terms of Universal Grammar and the poverty of stimulus. The Language Faculty that constitutes the basis of extremely complex and rich linguistic systems is common to all. The research into the social aspects of language has shown how language varies systematically in terms of time and space and in terms of person, place and topic. That most linguistic enquiry shares a common paradigm may be seen in, for example, Agnihotri 2002b and 2002c.

In the same breath, we also need to recognise that this conceptual machinery and its implementation, not always unwittingly, have also caused incalculable damage to human societies, in particular towards widening the gulf between the elite and the underprivileged. The way the global economy is structured and local and state educational institutions function, grammars of underprivileged indigenous languages remain covered in dust on the shelves of some library (after of course the ceremonial release, see Illich 1981). What does get into the public domain as the 'pure standard' that needs to be acquired by anyone who aspires for higher education or social mobility gets enshrined in the grammars of languages of the privileged; these of course are based on 'intuitions' about what the linguist would regard as 'grammatical'. I don't think any educational system across the world is free from the bondage of this near 'absolute standard'.

However, some work done in both formal linguistics and sociolinguistics in the past few decades, I think has clearly shown that more meaningful insights into the nature and structure of language and its use with attendant sociological, political and pedagogical considerations can only be obtained if we discard the concept of 'a language' and accept multilinguality as the default human situation (Le Page 1968, Crawhall 1992, Agnihotri 1995, Singh 2001, Agnihotri 2007a, b among others). I think what is constitutive of being human is multilinguality and not 'a language'. What defines us is fluidity rather than stagnation; probably the concept of a verbal repertoire is more useful. Languages do not have any boundaries; they are porous and flow into each other, continuously changing themselves; there is no doubt that this is facilitated by the blueprint of a Universal Grammar. There is no way of demarcating either in terms of space, time or community where one language really ends and the other begins. Even in terms of the most distant languages you can conceptualise and empirically verify areas of overlap of all kinds. If we really wish to understand the structure and politics of language and infer useful social and pedagogical implications, we need to keep linguistic flux and fluidity at the centre of our discussions. We in a sense need to revise and re-examine our meta-language about language. Let's not commit the same kind of mistakes that the people who propagated the cause of monolingualism committed. Multilinguality and multilingual communities and classrooms are the default situations. We need to examine language behaviour in its social context and understand the social, political and pedagogical implications of such an enterprise. To quote Sarangi (2001: 56):

> The core question to ask is: how can sociolinguistic analyses of talk relate to social theory—even theories which invoke language in some explicit sense? A weaker claim here is that close analyses of text can sharpen social theorists' assumptions and claims about social reality. A somewhat stronger position would be to see if our understanding of social action is helped by such an application.

In my Foundation Day Lectures at the Central Institute of Indian Languages (CIIL), Mysore, India (Agnihotri 2002c), I had strongly argued that linguists, including sociolinguists, have long enjoyed the luxury of ivory tower isolationism and that the time to participate in social action is here. Since language powerfully mediates all social, political and pedagogical discourse, this social responsibility is all the more pressing. In spite of the fairly robust nature of Chomsky's innate Language Faculty hypothesis and Piaget's stages of cognitive growth, it is Vygotsky's idea of proximal development that seems more relevant to us. Despite our shared Universal Language Faculty, our minds are crafted in the society we live in, with language providing the most important scaffolding for our thoughts, to the extent of often completely structuring them. In fact, for several modern social theorists including Foucault, Bourdieu and Habermas, language is social action.

## Sociolinguistic stereotypes

One major hurdle on the path of promoting multilinguality and equity is the set of stereotypes shared almost without exception across policy makers, academia, parents, educationists, teacher trainers and teachers. We need to carefully identify and examine these stereotypes and then redress them; we also at the same time need to outline innovative pedagogical interventions at the levels of curriculum, syllabi, teacher training, teaching materials and classroom transaction. I suggest that unless we locate both of them in multilinguality, we may not succeed in any significant way in bringing about a new world order. We must focus on the concrete steps that mediate between the dream and the reality (for some modest beginnings see Agnihotri 1995, 1997, 1998, 2000, 2001, 2005, 2007a and 2007b; Crawhall 1992; National Language Project 1994; Edwards 1998; Edwards and Walker 1995; NCERT (National Council of Educational Research and Training) 2006 among others). During the preparation of the NCERT's Position Paper on the Teaching of Indian Languages, it was the struggle against these stereotypes that was always centre-stage. It has indeed also been the case whenever we have been engaged in conducting workshops involving language anywhere in the world. Even though the Position Paper is an integral part of the NCERT's National Curriculum Framework 2005, the opinions even within the NCERT are divided and it is likely to take the planners and the teaching community a long time before a scientific and socially sensitive view on the nature and structure of language becomes widely accepted.

### Language and dialect

That a language is only a dialect with an army and a navy seems so obvious to linguists that they do not even entertain the thought that there is a whole world out there engaged in rearing and educating generations of children that looks at 'languages' with a sense of awe and respect and regards all 'dialects' as stigmatised, inferior varieties. The State, academia and a whole range of agencies involved in pedagogy are, often consciously, sometimes perhaps unwittingly, engaged in perpetuating such myths as 'tribal languages are underdeveloped and cannot therefore be used for education' or 'these children mix their languages and are therefore not competent in any language' or 'there is no real option to the use of one standard language in education' etc. I strongly feel that we need to design modules in different print and electronic formats for the policy makers, teacher trainers, teachers and the general public which clearly demonstrate that in the case of language, 'Kings, the Macedonian swineherds and Confucius … walk together.' (cf. Sapir 1921) and that if that's not what is believed, something is wrong with us and NOT with (people who speak these) languages.

Multilinguality constitutes an eminently suitable site for preparing such materials. It is here that we salute the formal linguistics enterprise which empowers us to demonstrate beyond any doubt that ALL languages are equally rule-governed, rich and complex at the levels of sounds (or cheremes, in the case of Sign languages), words, sentences and discourse and that each one of them would have some fingerprints of the Universal Grammar. It is eminently possible to engage with a group of policy makers or teacher trainers (an exercise I have often done) from a variety of different linguistic backgrounds (the default case, as I claim) in a process of formal linguistic analysis through the steps of data collection, classification and categorisation, rule formation and verification to appreciate the rule-governed nature of all languages and their apparently strange but fairly rule-governed mixtures. Such an exercise is empowering in a variety of ways: it gives the target audience enormous confidence and respect for their own languages; it changes their attitudes, even if in a minimal way, towards the languages children bring to the classrooms. The obsession with 'a standard' is so strong that neither the policy makers, nor teacher trainers, nor parents or teachers even think of making capital out of what comes so naturally to humans. And if we can design syllabi and classroom materials that are rooted in multilinguality (small beginnings of such efforts may be seen in National Language Project 1994, Agnihotri 2007b, Agnihotri, Rajan and Khanna 2008, the forthcoming Vidya Bhawan Society ELT Project, among others), we are already on the path of radical pedagogical and social change.

It is not easy to estimate the emotional and psychological damage that is done to a child when we insist that she be taught in a foreign language. We have for a long time treated the languages of the underprivileged child as 'objects of wonder' (Illich 1981). It is not just that she does not understand what is going on; she feels small, insulted and humiliated and more often than not simply drops out (or, rather, is being pushed out, to borrow from Ajit Mohanty) of the school system. As Tollefson and Tsui (2004: 17) have argued, the use of a foreign language as medium of education 'hampers not only academic achievement and cognitive growth, but also their self-perception, self-esteem, emotional security, and their ability to participate meaningfully in the educational process'. As Skutnabb-Kangas (2000) points out, prohibiting the use of the language of the group in daily intercourse or in schools is (as per the definition of the final draft of what became the United Nations Genocide Convention) linguistic genocide. This happens equally effectively when a child is psychologically(and structurally) prohibited from speaking (and wanting to speak) her own language, and is psychologically transferred to another group, made to want to identify with a dominant group instead of, rather than in addition to her own (xxxiii).

For girls from the underprivileged sections of society, this is in addition to their domestic responsibilities and threats of early marriage and sexual harassment that they face in the family network, street and school. We need to talk in terms of 'diffusion and focussing' (Le Page and Tabouret-Keller 1985; Pandit 1972). The earlier we get rid of the concepts of a standard and pure language and the oft-repeated distinction between language and dialect, the better.

## Speech and Script

Consider another stereotype: that a language whose script approximates to its spoken form is inherently superior to the one that apparently does not. Notice that script, though marginal to a variety being recognised as language per se, is very central to formal schooling and is an essential component of learning to read and write. With substantial empirical evidence, three points in connection with this issue need to be put across to every person interested in a better world. It does not take very long to invent a script for a language; you can actually do so very successfully in a single session in a workshop and with some practice all the participants begin to write in the new script the same day. Script is therefore not something that can distinguish a language and a dialect, as most people believe. Secondly, it is with a sense of great joy that participants realise that all the languages available among the audience can be written in one script with minor modifications and one language can easily be written in all the scripts of the world. No sanctity therefore needs to be attached to the almost religiously held faith about the association between a language and its script. Notice that even the Constitution of India (Government of India 1950), one of the most linguistically sensitive documents ever written (Austin 1966/ 2000), says (as perhaps a reasonable solution to the complexity of the then historical and political situation) that 'the official language of the Union shall be Hindi in Devanagari script' (Art. 343). Thirdly, with some examples, participants begin to appreciate that, in principle, all scripts must start with some kind of isomorphism between the spoken and the written word and that over a period of time that isomorphism will inevitably break down. Writing systems cannot keep pace with the fast changing world of speech. Multilinguality once again constitutes an eminently creative site for a discussion of this phenomenon which otherwise is extremely difficult to unpack.

## Some additional stereotypes

Nothing weighs heavier on the minds of teachers and parents than the errors children make. It needs to be demonstrated with suitable examples that no system of knowledge including that of language is acquired without going through a fairly well understood progressive path whose milestones are 'errors'. More often than not, errors are indicators of systematic knowledge than ignorance; they in fact only show adult ignorance about children's systems of (phonological, grammatical and other) knowledge at different points of time (see, for example, Agnihotri 1984, 1988).

Explicit teaching of grammatical rules as a route to achieving proficiency in a given language is another stereotype that inflicts attitudes to language and language pedagogy. Imagine the number of person hours that are wasted across the world in teaching grammatical rules about the structure of languages; neither the teachers know these rules in any meaningful way, nor do children make any sense of them. They of course contribute very little to language proficiency. The work of Krashen (1982, 1985) has shown that the role of the formal Monitor in language acquisition and learning, which largely takes place through active interaction with comprehensible, interesting and challenging input, is rather minimal even when used by well-trained teachers. I am now convinced that all grammar classes at all levels MUST be converted to proper linguistics classes. It is eminently possible to create a class-wise curriculum, syllabi and teaching materials that negotiate problems of linguistic analysis with students. We will of course need to train teachers and this can easily be done in pre-service and in-service teacher training programmes, a greater part of which is generally devoted to such mechanical exercises as 'lesson planning' in the worst of behaviourist modes.

## LISTENING TO BACON: A SCIENTIFIC OUTLOOK

In his *Novum Organum* (1620), Francis Bacon (1561-1626) warned us long ago about the 'Idols of Tribe, Cave, Market Place and Theatre' which hamper any scientific understanding of any phenomenon under investigation. Even though he was a hard-core empiricist, his warnings are worth paying attention to by scientists of all paradigms, inductive or deductive. As members of the human tribe, we do tend to take for granted solutions as we would want to see them rather than as they are. For example, one of our major struggles has been to convince Indians and others that according to the Constitution of India, Hindi is our 'Official' and not 'National' language and that it is NOT necessary for every country to have a national language to fit into the equation 'one nation, one religion, one language'. It is indeed unfortunate that in spite of the hard work of the Constituent Assembly, the facts and spirit of the Indian constitution have not been appreciated and implemented. Austin (1966) subtitles his chapter on the issues of Language in the Indian Constitution as 'The Half-hearted Compromise' since it was asked to accommodate a great diversity of claims of Hindi, Sanskrit, English, Urdu, Bengali, Tamil and several other major and minor languages in different domains of State activity. However, he concludes the chapter by saying:

> Yet the language provisions are not just an unhappy compromise; they have a more positive side. They show that the large majority of the Assembly believed that the use of many Indian languages and of English was compatible with national unity and with the evolution of a national spirit. (Austin 1966/ 2000: 307)

Idols of the cave concern individual minds which are prone to all kinds of unexamined belief systems arising for example from a blind admiration for antiquity. Since Sanskrit is an ancient language, a common stereotype is that Sanskrit is the mother of all Indian languages (even all the languages of the world) and that it is beyond any doubt the most perfect language of the world. Many scholars and teachers would perpetuate these stereotypes without any hesitation. Kemal Atatürk's language ideology in Turkey in the 1920s is another case in point: Turkish was proclaimed the mother of all the world's languages (Skutnabb-Kangas and Fernandes 2008). One of the major hurdles for Turks to overcome has been to accept that Kurdish, spoken by over 20% of the population, is a language—it was called Mountain Turkish. Idols of the market place and theatre arise through human interaction and through hidden agendas of various kinds. For example, most people strongly believe that Hindi and Urdu are two different languages and not the same language largely with two scripts (King 1994); so they would say are Serbian and Croatian. It may not be a great exaggeration to say that 'people one night slept with Hindustani and woke up next morning with Hindi in the Devanagri script in India and Urdu in Perso-Arabic script in Pakistan'; that people slept with Serbo-Croatian and woke up with Serbian and Croatian (Agnihotri 2002a). Or vice versa: they slept with Turkish and Kurdish, and woke up with Turkish and Mountain Turkish. Or the mother languages of Hindi, such as Awadhi, Braj, Maithili, Maghai and Bhojpuri would soon be declared the dialects of Hindi.

## GLOBALISATION

Globalisation has only helped to intensify the faith in these stereotypes in addition to making this world increasingly unliveable for the poor and those living on the margins for reasons of gender, caste, religion or language. As I showed in Agnihotri (2007b), increasing investment by major international agencies into the area of literacy/ education has resulted in celebrating English and in marginalising multilinguality. No amount of romanticism about reviving 'locally self-sufficient mini-democracies' is going to check that process. The important thing is to analyse the kind of threats and promises that globalisation brings with it. The greatest threat is the intensification of the forces of exploitation, as the resources of production and means of distribution get increasingly concentrated in the hands of a few. The other threat is the way different manifestations of violence are going to multiply; not just in terms of levelling out indigenous variability but also the violence of the market place, violence to local systems of knowledge, culture and language and the violence of the mass media—all staring in our face as major threats of the future.

However, the most promising aspect is that a focus on multilinguality, even though in a minor way, may empower the underprivileged to fight for a more just and equitable world order. Even though Pennycook (1994) feels that the formation of counter-discursive positions in English may hold out the greatest hope for a possible decolonising of the coloniser's mind, it should be clear that such discourses, if any, are confined to the elite and reinforce rather question the hegemony of English at the cost of multilinguality. As I have suggested above, multilinguality and variability are constitutive of human existence. People need their own food and dress styles and birth, marriage and death ceremonies etc. to assert their distinct identity; they also need their own variety of multilinguality as a linguistic identity marker. The site for subversive discourses is NOT English but multilinguality. One is reminded of Martinet (1962: 105):

> Once the familiar and comfortable idea of the homogeneity of linguistic communities is abandoned, the world appears as an ocean of conflicting attractions, convergence here breeding divergence there, with new centres of attraction developing at all times and threatening to disrupt existing ensembles.

There is every reason to sustain the kind of multilingualism we hear in the voices of young Delhi college students such as the following (also see Agnihotri 2007b) in spite of the fact that they are under severe pressures of globalisation:

> Since Hindi is my mother tongue and I've learnt it at my home, I feel very comfortable to use it while talking to my parents. In school, I learnt English; therefore while relating to friends and siblings, I prefer English. Hindi is also my language with my friends and siblings. Some of my relatives hardly know any other language but Bhojpuri. I like this language as I've been using this since childhood. With my teachers and

strangers, English is quite comfortable being an international language. Also to sound formal I love using English.

Even though in urban areas, English is making increasing inroads into the domains of family and friendship, the local ties are strong enough to demand the use of a multiplicity of languages (Agnihotri 2005); on the other hand, in the rural areas where the grassroots multilingualism may face serious internal and external threats, fairly significant efforts have already been mounted by different institutions and NGOs such as the Central Institute of Indian Languages, Mysore and Eklavya, Bhopal to strengthen the local languages. What one regrets in India is the increasing withdrawal of the State from welfare sectors and its constitutional responsibilities as a result of interventions made by the World Bank, International Monetary Fund, MNCs or other international agencies.

## What can we do?

What I suggest is that we keep 'language defined as multilinguality' at the centre of our discourse about education and society and briefly outline a future course of action for us. I must confess that I address these issues in all humility, fully aware that they are highly complex and there are large areas of knowledge in relevant disciplines of which I am completely ignorant. As Wittgenstein says: whereof one cannot speak, thereof one must be silent. I only propose small possible beginnings.

I suggest that sociolinguistics must assume an active role in contemporary society. Multilinguality can constitute a potential site for eliminating, in a scientific way, the kind of stereotypes discussed above. For example, it does not take long to write languages from different regions and families such as English, Bengali, Tamil, Angami and Hindi (or let us say, languages of the same region, such as Hindi, Bundeli, Gondi, Bagheli and Bagri, a set of such languages will always be easily available in any class or workshop) in say Roman or Devanagri to explain how arbitrary in some sense the relationship between the sounds and symbols of 'a language' is. You can similarly elicit data, say, regarding number or gender systems, or regarding forming 'yes–no' and 'wh-' questions, examine it carefully in groups and then arrive at linguistically significant generalisations to show that ALL languages are systematic and are complex in different departments. You can also show easily how languages flourish in each other's company and regularly borrow from each other without any visas and passports. Multilinguality actually becomes a resource to fight these dangerous stereotypes which come in the way of social tolerance and are often used for political exploitation. It is also a resource for creating extremely challenging teaching–learning materials and not just through translation and genre-conversion but also through using the well-known *mani praval* tradition of 'mixing languages' in which some of the most celebrated literature gets written. It can help build bridges across disciplines through textual analysis; it can help people unfold their own minds and examine them critically to appreciate the kind of social and linguistic biases they nourish. The point I wish to make is that processes of globalisation have brought us to a point where the role of sociolinguistics has become far more critical than at any time in the past. Though the pressures of global political economy have unleashed forces that legitimise homogenisation at all levels, the multilingual human fabric has the vitality and robustness to absorb that shock and maintain its dynamic and fluid equilibrium and help create a more just world order.

* Thanks are due to Dr Amrit L. Khanna who read the paper twice. Most of his suggestions have been incorporated.

# 17

# Overcoming the Language Barrier for Tribal Children: MLE in Andhra Pradesh and Orissa, India

*Ajit K. Mohanty, Mahendra Kumar Mishra,*
*N. Upender Reddy, Ramesh Gumidyala*

Languages are said to make us human; but they also dehumanise when they become instruments of power for some and shame and guilt for others. For some, language is a road to upward mobility and for others it is a barrier to even the marginal life of choice and dignity. For millions of people, whose languages are rendered powerless in a society where only one or few languages are dominant, exclusion of mother tongues from social domains of significance has serious consequences for basic survival and well being. Educational failure of linguistic minorities all over the world is primarily related to the mismatch between the home language and the language of formal instruction. This issue has been severally discussed in the literature on minority education (see, for example, Skutnabb-Kangas 2000, Skutnabb-Kangas and Cummins 1988 and various chapters in this volume). State policies in respect of languages in education often recognise but ignore in practice the problem of exclusion of languages. In the post-colonial world—Africa (Heugh 2009, this volume), India (Jhingran 2009, this volume), Pakistan (Rahman 1998), Nepal (Yonjan-Tamang, Hough and Nurmela 2009, this volume), Sri Lanka (Kandiah 2001) —as in other parts of the more developed world, policy proclamations appear to support the rights of minor and minority language communities for preservation, use and development of their languages and, in many cases, there are explicit statutory provisions for education in mother tongues. But, as several contributions to this volume show, there are contradictions between policy provisions and actual ground level practices. Forced submersion of minority children in dominant or majority language classrooms with subtractive effects on their mother tongues continues to be the most pressing educational issue in multilingual settings. Two reactions to minority languages are often implicit in state educational practices. Diversity is considered a nuisance and multilingualism a socioeconomic burden, privileging the practices of preference for homogenisation and standardisation. Further, minority languages are considered inadequate, impoverished and underdeveloped and, hence, unfit for educational and scientific use. These reactions lead to stigmatisation and invisibilisation of less powerful and marginalised languages, pushing many into the inferior status of dialects. Languages without a script, for example, are often stigmatised as dialects, ignoring the fact that writing systems developed much after the languages and are not essential properties of language. As Agnihotri (2009, this volume) points out, one script can be used to write all languages and any language can be written in many scripts. Hegemonic position of dominant languages, imposition of their norms on the languages of minority and disadvantaged groups and common biases in assessment of verbal skills of bilingual/multilingual children have led to propagation of the myth of linguistic deficit (Mohanty 2000: 106):

> What is often forgotten in the parochial vision of linguicism is that language varieties are simply different symbol systems with their own logical bases and, therefore, the languages of the minority mother tongue speakers, of the poor and the disadvantaged are not deficient; they are only different.

No language is inherently deficient or illogical; the association between some languages and their so called deficiency is social in origin, resulting from unequal treatment of languages. The sociocultural conditions of language use and the inequalities between languages propagate a misconception of some languages as 'substandard' languages which entail inherent disadvantages for their users. The real disadvantage of the languages of the disadvantaged is related to social attitudes and the conditions under which these languages get located lower down the hierarchy of social power. Unfortunately, in most societies, schools represent such social attitudes and become instruments for perpetuation of inequalities among languages. Disadvantages accrue to speakers of some languages not because their languages are substandard or deficient, but, because social biases against these languages and their exclusion from significant social domains, from schools for example, form an essential part of the very definition of disadvantage (Mohanty 2000, 2008b).

Languages are deprived of their legitimate place, marginalised, kept out of the domains of power, privileges and resources and, in the process, impoverished. The consequences of prolonged deprivation lead to further disadvantage to the languages and their speakers in a vicious circle. This chapter shows how this vicious circle of disadvantage and the language barrier in schools for tribal children in India are linked to poor educational performance, capability deprivation and poverty of the tribal communities. MLE programmes in two states of India—Andhra Pradesh and Orissa—are discussed as positive examples of multilingual education for tribal children demonstrating a possible way out of the vicious circle of disadvantage.

## The vicious circle of language disadvantage

Kept out of the major domains of power and resources such as official, legal and formal use, education, trade and commerce, languages become vulnerable to shift pressure from the dominant languages and their survival is threatened. This process is associated with loss of linguistic diversity and death or 'murder' of languages. Some times, however, minority languages under such pressure seem to survive in multilingual societies like India by a passive withdrawal into domains of lesser power and visibility following what has been called 'anti-predatory strategies' (Mohanty 2006). Although rapid language shift does not occur, these languages are marginalised with considerable domain shrinkage; languages are barely maintained in the domains of home and close in-group communication with clear signs of declining intergenerational transmission. As the languages are pushed out of significant domains they become impoverished with limited functions restricting their scope for development. For example, many tribal languages in India are pushed out of a number of public domains of economic significance for the communities. One of the domains which show rapid loss for tribal languages is the weekly village market. During the early 1980s the Kond women of Phulbani, Orissa who brought their household produces for sale in the village markets spoke their Kui language and used traditional notions of weights and measures for all commercial transactions. They had the better of the bargain with customers who were generally non-tribals with limited or no knowledge of Kui. Within over two decades, Kui has been pushed out of the village markets and the Kond women of their bargaining power. Panda (2004, 2007) observed extensive use of Saora language and Saora number system in market transactions in Gajapati district of Orissa. Use of the indigenous language and traditional knowledge systems which empowered the people of the Saora tribe in this important economic domain is also on the decline. As Panda (2004, 2007) shows, languages are cultural tools for encoding and transmission of indigenous knowledge systems such as mathematical and scientific knowledge among the tribes (see also Hough, Magar and Yonjan-Tamang 2009, this volume). Thus, when languages are kept out of some domains of use, the indigenous knowledge systems are endangered and languages weakened. Most of the indigenous languages in the world today are systematically impoverished due to large scale social neglect. Exclusion of languages from education, as we will show in case of tribal language communities in India, has direct negative consequences for educational performance, socioeconomic well being and sense of identity and empowerment of the speakers of minority and indigenous languages, severely restricting the chances of their development and survival. Social and educational neglect strip languages of their vitality and contribute to their weakness which is used to justify further neglect in a vicious circle of language disadvantage (see Figure 17.1).

The so called poverty of minority languages and disadvantages often associated with them are not inherent to the languages. Language disadvantage and inequalities across languages are socially constructed and transmitted (Mohanty, Panda and Mishra 1999) through institutionalised discrimination of some languages in political, economic, social and educational domains reinforcing their stigmatisation as weak languages. Unfortunately, attribution of insufficiency and weakness leads to justification of further social exclusion and, more importantly, educational neglect perpetuating inequality. Exclusion of languages from formal education does contribute to loss of diversity due to what has been characterised as 'linguistic genocide in education' (Skutnabb-Kangas 2000) and, more immediately, to educational failure, capability deprivation and poverty for the indigenous communities. This is particularly evident in case of the tribal peoples in India whose languages are disadvantaged due to layers of discrimination and exclusion in the system of formal education.

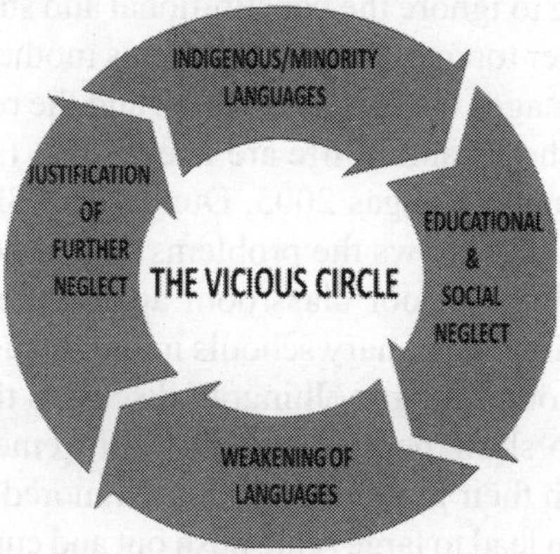


**Figure 17.1.** *The vicious circle of language disadvantage*

## Tribal communities in India: education and the language barrier

With a population of 84.3 million, the Scheduled Tribes[1] (STs) constitute 8.2% of the population of India. The 623 tribal communities speak 218 languages out of which 159 are exclusive to them (Singh 2002). Most of the tribal languages do not have a script[2] and are written in the script of either the dominant regional language or another major language; but some tribal languages, such as Santali,[3] have developed their own writing system. The *Sixth All India Educational Survey* of the National Council of Educational Research and Training (NCERT 1999) shows that, out of 41 languages used in schools[4] (grades 1–10) as languages of teaching or the medium of instruction (MoI) and as school subjects, only 13 are tribal languages, all but one (Nicobaree) from the North-Eastern States which have a much higher concentration of tribal population compared to the rest of India. Further, only three to four of these 13 tribal languages are used regularly as MoI (Jhingran 2005) whereas the others are taught as school subjects or used as MoI in occasional special programmes. Less than 1% of the tribal children have any real opportunity for education in the medium of their mother tongues. Exclusion of tribal languages in school education is problematic since a very large number of classrooms throughout the country have a sizable proportion of tribal children (see Jhingran 2009, this volume).

It is also quite striking that the tribal mother tongues are denied a place in formal school education in practice, despite constitutional and other policy related provisions which mandate education in mother tongues particularly for the linguistic minorities (see Jhingran 2009, this volume, Mohanty 2006, 2008b for more elaborate discussion of languages-in-education policy in India). In view of the poor educational performance among the tribal communities in India, various programmes of special intervention have been floated from time to time. But surprisingly, even if mother tongue education has traditionally been emphasised in India and use of mother tongues is widely viewed as crucial for better educational performance, the actual school practices continue to ignore the constitutional and statutory commitments in respect of minority mother tongues. When children's mother tongues are left out of classrooms, the disadvantages that accrue to them and the resultant damage to their chances of success in schools and in life are irreversible (see Magga, Nicolaisen, Trask, Dunbar and Skutnabb-Kangas 2005, Dunbar and Skutnabb-Kangas 2008). Jhingran (2009, this volume) shows the problems of non-comprehension (also see Mohanty, 2009, this volume), poor classroom achievement and severe learning difficulties of tribal children in primary schools in India taught in a language which is different from their mother tongue. Jhingran discusses the findings of his study in four states in India to show poor classroom achievement of tribal children in primary schools in which their mother tongues are ignored. The problems in tribal children's early education lead to large scale push out and cumulative failure through out all levels of education which, in effect, push the tribal population to the lowest level of educational attainment in India. Some indicators of non-attainment of the tribal population will be briefly discussed drawing comparisons between the two most disadvantaged populations in India, namely, the Scheduled Tribes (ST) and the Scheduled Castes (SC).

### *Literacy, school enrolment, push out rate and educational achievement of the STs*

The crude literacy rate (the percentage of literates in the total population) for STs is 38.41% compared to 54.51% for the total population and 45.20% for SCs. Effective literacy rate (percentage of literates among the population aged 7 years and above) is 47.10% for STs and 54.69% for SCs and 68.81% for the rest of the population. Thus, the ST population shows a literacy gap of 21.71% compared to 14.12% for the SCs. The Gross Enrolment Ratio (GER) or the percentage of children enrolled in schools in the age group of 6 to 11 years (grades 1–5) is 98.67 for STs, 95.61and 95.39, respectively, for SCs and the total population. The enrolment ratio is relatively high in the early grades due to special government programmes to universalise education up to 14 years of age for STs in recent years. However, in the grades 6–8 (11 to 14 years) the GER is 48.19% for STs and 56.28% and 60.99%, respectively, for SCs and the total population. When the grades/age groups are combined to cover grades 1–8 (6 to 14 years), the corresponding GER for the STs, SCs and the total population are 80.50%, 81.06% and 82.51%, respectively. The percentage of students joining grade 1 and then leaving school by grade 5 is 51.57% for STs, 41.47% for SCs and 34.90% for the total population. By grade 10, the push out rates are 80.29%, 71.92% and 62.60%, respectively, for STs, SCs and the total population.

These figures, taken from *Selected Educational Statistics, 2002–2003* (Ministry of Human Resource Development 2004), show that tribal children face major barriers to their enrolment and retention in schools.

An assessment of learning achievement of students at the end of grade 5, by the National Council of Educational Research and Training (NCERT) with a national sample of 88,271 children (Singh, Jain, Gautam, and Kumar 2004), shows that the ST students scored significantly lower than the 'other' students (i.e., excluding SCs and STs) in tests of learning achievement in Mathematics, Environmental Studies, Language, Reading Comprehension, and Grammar and Usage. The tribal students performed somewhat better than their Scheduled Caste counterparts (except in Mathematics), but their performance was significantly below that of the other students. The performance of tribal students in high school examinations is also found to be poorer compared to SCs and the rest of the population. The percentage of ST students who pass the high school examinations in different states in India is about 40 on the average, less than the other groups. With 80 out of 100 children pushed out before high school examination, this means that, of the 20 in 100 who appear the examination, only about 8 pass. Mohanty's (2008b) analysis of the results of state wide common annual high school examinations in Orissa (where STs constitute over 22.13% of the state population) for the period 2003 to 2005 shows that ST students have a higher failure rate and low levels of achievement (percentage of marks in the examination) compared to SC and other students. The results of 2006 and 2007 examinations also show the same trend. Lower levels of school achievement of tribal students effectively reduce their chances of joining institutions of higher education in which ST representation is quite low.

Beginning from primary schools, the proportion of ST students declines with higher levels of education—from 9.67% in primary (grades 1–5) to 5.37% in (grades 9–12) (Mohanty 2008b). The representation of ST students in higher and technical education is even lower. The percentage of ST students in higher and technical education in India during the years 2000–2001 and 2001–2002 varied from 2.97% to 4.64% (Planning Commission 2004), far below their 8.2% share of the national population.

### *The language barrier and education of tribal children*

The language barrier that the tribal children face on their school entry is a major factor in their poor educational performance and consequent socioeconomic deprivation. The language barrier also comes with a content barrier since the daily life experiences and culture of tribal children are hardly present in textbooks and other curricular material in the dominant language schools. As pointed out earlier, school practices in respect of tribal children in India have often been predicated on the assumption that there are weaknesses and disadvantages inherent to tribal languages and that maintenance of these languages is a cognitive and socioeconomic burden. Contrary to these beliefs, our studies among the Konds in Orissa over a period of nearly two decades show that the Kui-Oriya bilingual Konds (who had maintained their indigenous language) performed better than the Oriya monolingual Konds (who had lost their language although they still identified with it, calling themselves Kui people) in a host of tasks assessing their cognitive, intellectual, metalinguistic and metacognitive skills and educational achievement (Mohanty 1994, 2000, 2003a, 2003b; see also Skutnabb-Kangas 1995 for a review of Mohanty 1994). The Kond studies also showed that maintenance of Kui and community level bi/multilingualism promoted social integration in contact situations. Thus maintenance of the indigenous language is a social and psychological resource and not a burden for the language community. Rather, the problem lies in its denial and exclusion.

The exclusion of tribal mother tongues from education limits tribal children's chances of adequate classroom learning and success in academics and, consequently, limits their freedom and ability to influence the direction of their lives. A number of Indian studies show that tribal children (Saikia and Mohanty 2004, Sema 2008) as well as other groups of children (Nayak 2007) perform significantly better in MT medium classrooms compared to their matched counterparts in classrooms in which the MoI is another dominant language. As several contributions to this volume show, educational benefits of the use of mother tongue in regular classroom settings have been clearly demonstrated in a number of studies all over the world. Any barrier to the continued use of children's home language in schools is debilitating and imposition of another dominant language as the MoI has long term adverse effects not only on their mother tongue but also on their capabilities, entitlements and freedom of choice.

## Education, Capability Deprivation and Poverty in the Tribal Population

Amartya Sen conceptualises poverty as 'capability deprivation' and 'unfreedom' (1982, 1985; Dreze and Sen 2002). Capability, according to Dreze and Sen (2002: 35–36), refers to 'the ultimate combinations of functionings from which a person can choose' and freedom to 'the range of options a person has in deciding what kind of life to lead.' Sen relates social discrimination to lack of opportunities and freedom, capability deprivation and poverty. According to Sen, education is a major capability input and illiteracy a lack of freedom restricting economic opportunities. School education directly enhances opportunities through easier access to jobs and income and, equally importantly, it adds to social and cultural freedom and empowers persons for adequate participation in exercise of political rights. Dreze and Sen (2002) speak of the substantial problems of 'voicelessness' of the disadvantaged groups in India, particularly the scheduled tribes, arising out of the large-scale illiteracy and lack of education both of which impede economic development. They attribute non-attendance and school push out to lack of interest (of parents as well as children) and to a host of 'discouragement effects' due to alienating curricula, inactive classrooms, indifferent teachers, and social discrimination in the classroom.

Linguistic and cultural discrimination, arising out of prevalent inequalities, is central to the relationship between illiteracy and educational failure, lack of freedom, capability deprivation and poverty. While education is the enabling factor for economic development, mother tongue is the enabling factor for access to quality education. Mismatch between home and school languages and neglect of mother tongues force the tribal children in India into subtractive language learning in a form of submersion education in the dominant language and leads to poor educational achievement reinforcing inequality and leading to capability deprivation. Educational failure, at least partly due to the systematic exclusion of mother tongues, is clearly reflected in the economic underdevelopment, and general poverty of the tribals in India,[5] which evidently is a complex multidimensional phenomenon.

The system of education in India, which is officially named as human resource development, neglects the most powerful resource that a tribal child comes to school with—her mother tongue—and in the process fails to enable her for a life of choice; rather, it fails to develop the human resources and leads to cumulative disadvantages. Exclusion of mother tongues in education limits access to resources and perpetuates inequality by depriving language communities of linguistic human rights, democratic participation, identity, self-efficacy, and pride. In case of the tribals in India, linguistic discrimination forms the core of their capability deprivation through educational and social neglect which contribute to their poverty in a vicious circle. As has been pointed out, their languages are weakened by marginalisation and exclusion from education and other instrumentally significant domains and then stigmatised as weak and inadequate justifying further exclusion. It is necessary to realise that mother tongue in education is not a problem; it is the solution.

## From mother tongue to multilingual education in India

The system of school and higher education in India has not responded to the prospects and challenges of its multilingual ethos (Mohanty 2008b). Maintenance of mother tongues, multilingualism and linguistic diversity are cognitive, educational and social resources for the tribal people as well as the society at large. As Mohanty (2006: 281) writes:

> (T)he core of Indian multilingualism is in complementary relationship between languages and in the need to bridge the gap between the minor, minority, and tribal languages, and the languages of wider communication, including the regional and state level languages - Hindi and English. Multilingual education holds a central position in planning for a resourceful multilingualism that does not marginalize and deprive the minor, minority, and tribal language groups.

The existing systems of public and private education in India fail to appreciate the role and consequences of mother tongue for quality education (Mohanty 1989, 1994, 2006, 2008a); they do not support the weaker languages nor do they promote high levels of multilingual proficiency. Some Government of India agencies such as the Central Institute of Indian Languages (CIIL) made substantial efforts for development of tribal and other weaker languages. Pattanayak (1981), who was the founder Director of CIIL, pleaded for mother tongue education in India and initiated experimental programmes in several states for introduction of tribal languages in early school education (see Mohanty, 1989). These programmes, however, could not be developed further and they were gradually dropped. The recent National Curriculum Framework (NCF) (NCERT 2005) sets MT-based multilingualism as a goal of school education in India but, in the absence of specific formulations on the methodology of multilingual education (MLE), it remains an unrealised framework for promotion of multilingualism through education and for preservation of the multilingual character and diversity of the society (see Jhingran 2009, this volume for discussion). It is necessary to have a comprehensive languages-in-education policy in India for empowerment of tribal and minority languages and promotion of multilingualism for all (Mohanty 2006). MLE in India needs to be developed as a process of education that starts with development of MT proficiency forming the basis for development of proficiency in all other languages with functional significance for specific groups including the tribal peoples. As several contributions to this volume show, the theoretical foundations of such a process are well developed and supported. Jhingran (2009, this volume) has discussed some of the initiatives to deal with the problems of mismatch between the home language and school language in India through various forms of MLE most of which are weak transitional programmes for soft assimilation. In recent years, more structured experimental programmes of MLE for tribal children in India have started with government initiatives in some of the states with substantial tribal population and are planned in few others. The following section gives a brief description of the programs in two states—Andhra Pradesh and Orissa—which pioneered the current MLE programmes in India.

## MLE for Tribal Children in Andhra Pradesh and Orissa

### Challenges and Opportunities

In the year 2003, the Government of India under its *Sarva Siksha Aviyan* (SSA, Education for All) programme approached states with substantial tribal population to introduce mother tongue based MLE for tribal children. The same year the government of Andhra Pradesh[6] decided to start an experimental pilot project of MLE in eight tribal languages[7] in 1000 schools. Initial preparations involved development of curriculum, textbooks and teaching learning materials and teacher training. The programme started for grade 1 children in the selected schools in 2004. With the first batch of children moving up to grade 5 in 2008, the Andhra Pradesh programme now covers all children from grades 1–5 in the selected schools. Orissa[8] was the second state in India to launch the programme with 10 tribal languages[9] in the year 2006. The Orissa MLE program started with grade 1 children of 195 selected schools in the year 2007. These children have moved to grade 2 in 2008 and the MLE programme in Orissa has added 300 more schools taking the total number of schools under the programme to 495.

### *The structure, nature and evaluation of the MLE programmes*

The MLE programmes in the two states are planned to strengthen children's mother tongue through its use as the language of teaching for few years in the school and then gradually develop competence in the dominant state language, Telugu in Andhra Pradesh and Oriya in Orissa. However, as pointed out earlier, MLE in India must develop high level multilingual competence among children in at least 3 to 4 languages—mother tongue (for tribal and linguistic minority children), state majority language (like Telugu or Oriya), English and Hindi. Thus, the MLE programmes seek to develop competence in English and Hindi besides the mother tongue and the state majority language. The programmes envisage the children in the (experimental) MLE schools to join the mainstream majority language medium schools at the end of the primary grades (grades 1–5). In other words, in grade 6, the MLE children in Andhra Pradesh and Orissa are expected to join schools in which Telugu or Oriya are the languages of teaching (MoI) for all school subjects except for the language subjects. However, the manner in which teaching of languages is scheduled in the MLE programmes of the two states does show some differences. In both state programmes, the tribal mother tongue is the only MoI or the language of teaching for all school subjects[10] for the first three years. L2[11] (Telugu/Oriya) oral skills are sought to be developed from grade 2 onwards with introduction of teaching of L2 reading and writing from grade 3. Oral English (as L3) is also a part of the grade 3 curriculum in Orissa and grade 4 in Andhra Pradesh. The tribal language (MT) as well as Telugu (L2) are used as MoI with 50% time sharing for teaching of all school subjects (except the languages) in grade 4 in Andhra Pradesh MLE programme and bilingual textbooks are used for the school subjects. The grade 4 programme in Orissa MLE is planned to use Oriya (L2) as the sole language of teaching (MoI) for all school subjects and continue with the MT as a language subject. Reading and writing skills in English (L3) constitute a part of the grade 4 curriculum in Orissa MLE. Thus, the Orissa MLE programme plans for a change from the use of MT as MoI to Oriya as MoI from grade 4 with MT and L3 (English) retained as school subjects. The same structure continues into grade 5. In Andhra Pradesh MLE, on the other hand, there is a gradual switch over from MT as MoI to Telugu as MoI. Following equal time sharing in grade 4, MT and Telugu (L2) are used as languages of teaching (MoI) for all school subjects (other than languages) for 25% and 75% of the school time, respectively. Teaching of reading and writing in L3 (English) is introduced in grade 4 in Andhra Pradesh and it continues as a school subject beyond grade 5. The children from the MLE programmes in both the states are expected to become a part of the regular school programme from grade 6 onwards with the state language (Telugu or Oriya) as the language of teaching (MoI). In both states, Hindi is introduced from grade 6 as a fourth language (third language for the majority language children) while English also continues as a language subject; there is no plan to use MT (either as MoI or a school subject) after grade 5. However, the use of tribal MTs in MLE schools has led to growing indications of involvement and appreciation of parents and communities. Further, the MLE programmes have generated some printed texts—curricular as well as extra-curricular—in tribal languages and the children in these programmes are showing better educational attainment. Such positive developments are expected to have ripple effects creating demands for continuation of the tribal MTs in the school programmes beyond grade 5.

The tribal mother tongues are written in the script of the state language—Telugu in Andhra Pradesh and Oriya in Orissa—with some modifications wherever necessary to accommodate to the phonological features of the target language. The MLE programmes make special efforts to incorporate cultural and daily life experiences of children and the indigenous knowledge systems, games, songs and stories from the tribal communities into the curriculum, textbooks, pictures and illustrations, teaching-learning materials and children's learning activities all of which are developed and worked out and vetted in groups which include teachers, community leaders, writers and artists from the target language community along with experts. The national and state curricula are closely followed in listing the grade specific competencies sought to be developed through the MLE programmes. The competencies in different curricular areas such as mathematics and language are integrated with different cultural themes by a theme web approach in which the different themes and competencies are mapped so that a specific set of skills can be developed through several culture specific classroom activities and learning processes. For example, the number skills are sought to be developed through songs, games and other culture specific themes. The sequencing of the text materials, stories, songs, and other teaching learning activities is decided by a village calendar approach which notes seasonal and periodic community activities, festivals, and special events in different months of a year which form a part of the children's cultural experiences around which the curriculum materials are developed. Children are encouraged to participate in the classroom and in different activities. Some activities are also undertaken in the community settings with involvement of community members in children's learning process. The teachers in the MLE programmes are drawn from the target language communities and, in some cases, the eligibility criteria are relaxed to recruit teachers from the community if teachers with the required training and qualifications are not available. Manuals for teachers have been developed in the programme and all MLE teachers are given specific training on MLE. The programmes are monitored by the state MLE Project cells as well as by the community. Language development activities such as development of dictionaries in different tribal languages and special community programmes are also undertaken as a part of the state MLE programmes. The impacts of MLE in Andhra Pradesh and Orissa have been periodically evaluated internally and also by external agencies.

The Andhra Pradesh MLE programme has been evaluated in two major studies as well as through internal feedback from teachers and communities and also by the project monitoring group. One comparative evaluation of classroom achievement of MLE children and those in Telugu medium schools was undertaken in 2005 by the Andhra Pradesh Tribal Cultural Research and Training Institute and another external evaluation study in coordination with SSA in 2007.[12] Both studies show that classroom achievement in the school subjects was significantly better in the MLE programmes for all eight tribal languages compared to the Telugu medium schools. The MT based MLE improved the basic competencies of literacy and numeracy among all children, increased their school attendance and participation and resulted in greater parental satisfaction and community involvement. The Orissa MLE program has been evaluated[13] on the basis of the regular classroom assessment of grade 1 children in the experimental MLE schools as well as in the Oriya medium schools in 2008 at the end of the school year. Feedback from the teachers and community also forms a part of the evaluation. The evaluation shows better classroom achievement of children in the MLE schools in all of the ten tribal languages at the end of grade 1 compared to their Oriya medium counterparts. The MLE schools also reported better attendance and participation of children, greater teacher satisfaction, positive parental feedback and community involvement.

## MLE programmes for tribal children in India: some reflections

The MLE programmes in Andhra Pradesh and Orissa clearly provide a better quality of education than the traditional programmes of submersion education in a second language. However, systematic formative evaluation of the state programmes seems to be necessary to make them more effective in dealing with the language and content barriers that tribal children face in the mainstream schools. Planning of MT based MLE programmes for these children faces a formidable task of developing multilingual competence in at least four languages. While learning of the state majority language as also Hindi is supported by greater degree of exposure to these languages through their presence in several social and public domains such as market place use, intergroup communication and popular media, the same cannot be said for English in rural areas. However, there is a national trend favouring early introduction of English in the school curricula which has effectively pushed Hindi down in the order in which languages are taught in the schools. The problem of variations in the degree of exposure of the tribal children to the state majority language, Hindi and English gets even more complicated in case of classrooms which are much more diverse in terms of their multilingual composition. The current experimental MLE programmes in the two states have minimised this problem of multilingual variation within the classrooms by focusing on homogeneous groups of children from a single tribal language community. Even then, the manner in which use of the different languages in the MLE schools is distributed in the school curriculum varies between the states. The issues in respect of scheduling of languages and the timing of exit from the mother tongues need to be sorted out after careful analysis of the current programmes and their outcomes for development of multilingual competence. In any case, in diverse multilingual contexts (see Agnihotri 2009 and Jhingran 2009, both this volume), the MLE pedagogy faces the difficult challenges of dealing with multilinguality, classroom linguistic diversity and societal preferences for different languages.

The current experimental MLE projects in Andhra Pradesh and Orissa are quite limited in their scope and coverage both in terms of number of tribal languages taken up for MLE and the number of schools in the program. In the absence of a clear policy in these states and in India in respect of MT based MLE for all tribal and linguistic minority children and with limited resources for expansion of the programmes, how and when would MT based MLE become regular programmes of minority education in these states and throughout the country remain doubtful. The programmes in Andhra Pradesh and Orissa have provided a good beginning and a lot of expectation; they have demonstrated the potentials of MLE in enabling and empowering the tribal communities to escape the vicious cycle of language disadvantage in India. One hopes that these initiatives will usher in an MLE movement in India for quality education and a just society.

## Notes

1 See Endnote 1 in Chapter 1 for clarification of this term.

2 Twenty-five scripts are used for writing Indian languages. Eleven major scripts are used to write the main scheduled languages and thirteen minor scripts are used for writing some minor and tribal languages. Besides, the Roman scrip has been adopted by some languages in recent years.

3 The Santals have developed a script of their own – *Ol Chiki* - invented by Guru Gomke (the 'Great Teacher') Pandit Raghunath Murmu. This script has become the rallying point for the identity of Santali tribals. There are other tribal communities where sporadic and uncoordinated efforts are made to evolve language specific writing systems.

4 As Jhingran (2009, this volume) reports, 26 languages are used as media of instruction (MoI) in the primary grades (grades 1–5).

5 See Mohanty (2008b) for a discussion of various indicators of poverty among the tribal people in India which place them at the bottom in comparison even to other disadvantaged groups and the relationship of poverty with exclusion of the tribal mother tongues.

6 There are 35 tribal communities in Andhra Pradesh. These tribal peoples constitute 6.59% of the state population and have a literacy rate of 37.04% whereas the same for the state is 61.11%.

7 The tribal languages covered in the MLE programme in Andhra Pradesh are: Gondi, Koya, Kalami, Kuvi, Savara, Konda, Adivasi Oriya, and Banjara.

8 There are 62 tribal communities in Orissa. These tribal peoples constitute 22.13% of the state population and have a literacy rate of 37.37% whereas the same for the state is 63.61%.

9 The 10 languages in Orissa MLE programme are: Kui, Saora, Santali, Koya, Munda, Kuvi, Oram, Kisan, Bonda, and Juang.

[10] The school subjects include Language and Mathematics from grade 1 onwards. Environmental Studies as a curricular area is included from grade 1 (as a part of the language textbook for grades 1 and 2 and then as separate subject from grade 3 onwards) in Orissa. In Andhra Pradesh, on the other hand, Environmental Studies as a subject is part of the curriculum from grade 3 onwards.

[11] Labelling of languages as L2, L3 and L4 only refer to the order in which they are introduces in the MLE programmes; no other assumption is made about the manner in which they are developed, taught or learned.

[12] Details of the Andhra Pradesh MLE programme and these evaluation studies are available from the last two authors of this chapter and also from the Andhra Pradesh SSA web site (www.ssa.ap.nic.in).

[13] The details are available from the second author of this chapter and also from the Orissa Primary Education Programme Authority (OPEPA) web site (www.opepa.in).

# PART VI
# Analysing Prospects for MLE to Increase Social Justice

# 18

# Language Matters, so does Culture Beyond the Rhetoric of Culture in Multilingual Education

*Minati Panda and Ajit K. Mohanty*

Multilingual education (MLE) is much more than just bringing in languages into the process of education; it is, in fact, deeply rooted in a philosophy of critical pedagogy that seeks to actively empower the learners and their communities. If MLE is to be seen as providing a powerful model for the education of the indigenous/tribal and linguistic minority communities, it needs to replace the authoritarian, rigid, pre-ordained knowledge approach of dominant-culture-centric education by a system of critical educational experiences empowering them to become valued, equal, and responsible members of their own and the larger society outside their community and not feel estranged from it (Panda 2006). At one level, strong MLE practices seek to develop children's home language competence from basic interpersonal communication skills (BICS) to cognitive-academic language proficiency (CALP) in the mother tongue through at least five to eight years of schooling before bringing in gradually second, third and other languages into formal education. And, at a deeper level, such programmes of MLE develop strong multilingual competence, identity and a few vital collective processes that sustain the linguistic and the eco-cultural diversity of the society (see Cummins 2009, this volume, for elaboration of the psycholinguistic principles underlying MLE and the role of empowerment; Skutnabb-Kangas 2009, this volume).

In India, experimental programmes of MLE have started in government schools for tribal children in Andhra Pradesh, Orissa and are about to start in Chhattisgarh and other states with very high tribal population (see Mohanty, Mishra, Reddy and Ramesh 2009, this volume). Seeking to provide quality education for tribal children who are otherwise forced into subtractive type submersion education in the mainstream majority language government schools (see Mohanty 2008a for a discussion), this experimental programme of MLE started in Orissa under the government *Sarva Sikhsa Aviyan* (Education for All) initiative for 10 tribal languages in 195 schools in Orissa. The first batch of MLE children is now in grade 2 in these schools. A special intervention called *MLE Plus* (MLE+)[1] is being simultaneously implemented by the authors in eight of the government MLE schools for the children of Saora and Kond tribal communities speaking Saora and Kui languages respectively, with an objective of strengthening the MLE practices in these schools by establishing a bridge between tribal children's everyday discourse[2] and the scientific/academic discourse of the school.

This chapter provides a description of the MLE+ approach based on our ongoing project *Education in Mother Tongue and Other Tongue.* The MLE+ intervention in this project envisages good MLE practices to be holistic, culturally situated and historically informed of culturally embedded social, mathematical, literacy/oracy and science practices. Taking a Vygotskyan (1978) line, the MLE Plus approach takes off from exhaustive ethnographic survey of the everyday practices and knowledge of the communities with a view to using the cultural practices to evolve a set of classroom as well as community based activities. Various intervention strategies at the school and community level such as motivating parents to send their children to school and close monitoring of the academic history of these children, developing the reading environment both in the community and in the school through a synergistic *'Read Together'* approach are discussed in this chapter with a focus on making classroom learning a culturally shared collaborative activity. We illustrate and discuss some specific classroom interventions based on ethnographic data and developed as activities using a Cultural Historical Activity Theory (CHAT)[3] approach to facilitate critical dialectic exchanges and movements from culture to classroom making the linkages from language to mathematics and to science easy, smooth and culturally meaningful for children (see Panda 2006, 2007 for a discussion). The paper concludes with the assertion that the use of linguistic and cultural diversity as resources in the classroom is central to MLE and, therefore, to any enterprise that concerns the education of children from the dominated and minority communities. Use of these resources in the official/formal space of school is also viewed as necessary to augment the process of cultural maintenance. It may be pointed out that the MLE and MLE+ programmes for the tribal children in Orissa that we discuss here need to be viewed in the context of the nature of societal multilinguality and the current languages-in-education practices in India which are dealt with in this volume (Jhingran 2009, Agnihotri 2009, Mohanty et al. 2009). As has been shown in these chapters, Indian multilingualism is both a resource and a challenge. Given the inequalities across languages, tribal languages suffer gross neglect and exclusion from significant social, political, economic and educational domains leading to serious language disadvantage of tribal children and large scale failure and 'push-out' in dominant language classrooms, where their mother tongues have little space. As discussed in Mohanty et al. (2009, this volume), this has led to some experimental MLE projects in several states.

## MLE INITIATIVES FOR TRIBAL CHILDREN IN INDIA

After several aborted efforts to bring in mother tongue based education for tribal children in several states such as Orissa (Mohanty 2006), some states have now started structured programmes of MLE for tribal children whose mother tongues are different from the state majority language used as language of classroom instruction. There are also some local programmes under the initiatives of several non-government organisations throughout India which claim to be mother tongue based programmes of bilingual/multilingual education. Such programmes are mostly soft assimilation type transitional early exit programmes seeking to ease minority language children's transition to majority language classrooms. However, in the absence of any shared documentation of these programmes, it is difficult to analyse their nature. Large scale government programmes have started in two states—Andhra Pradesh and Orissa—and a few more are being planned. The multilingual education programme in Andhra Pradesh (see Mohanty et al. 2009, this volume) started in 2004 in eight tribal languages. Another state level programme is in place in Orissa. The initial evaluation in Andhra Pradesh and Orissa shows that the MLE programmes are somewhat more successful than the traditional programmes of submersion education. These MLE programmes have a deliberate focus on bringing in elements of children's culture into the classroom and curricular materials. However, the theoretical and methodological groundings of the programme planners have not been explicitly stated so far. Hence, the pedagogical practices needed to help children to gradually move from everyday (empirical) discourse to a theoretical discourse are not clear and the programmes face the risk of being reduced to a set of routines. This is typical of the nature of the current Indian experimental MLE projects in different states, including some planned initiatives in Chhattisgarh, Jharkhand and other states. Some aspects of the Orissa MLE programme will be discussed here before we describe the MLE Plus approach.

## MLE IN ORISSA

As mentioned in Mohanty et al. (2009, this volume), the MLE programme in Orissa started in 2006. The schools selected have nearly 100% children who speak a tribal language. Thus, the classrooms are quite homogeneous[4] with all the tribal children and their teacher speaking a common language. For each of the 10 tribal languages, teachers and language resource persons were selected from among the tribal communities for development of teaching–learning materials (such as picture cards, stories, songs and activities) and the content and design of the text books, following a curricular framework common to all the schools in Orissa. Community culture is being integrated into the curricular materials through what is known as the village calendar and the theme web approach which are used to select the text themes. The calendar year is divided into seasonal village activities from which the content of the textual and teaching–learning materials are derived. Basic skills in different curricular areas such as language, mathematics, and environmental studies are related to different activities and thematic content. For example, a particular theme is related to writing as a broad skill. This is then related to specific skills such as writing a word list and individual workbook writings. The theme web is divided into two tracks or roads, one for accuracy and correctness and the other for meaning and communication. Corresponding to these tracks, the instructional materials for language, such as alphabet charts and alphabet books are grouped under the accuracy and correctness track whereas the storybooks are grouped under the meaning and communication track. The instructional materials developed through a series of workshops were pilot-tested in schools and through community feedback. Besides the materials development, teacher training and attitudinal training of teachers were also undertaken through a series of specific programmes. Singh and Mishra[5] (2008) report some initial success for the MLE programme in Orissa assessed in terms of increased student interest, attendance and community involvement.

## Cultural-philosophical underpinnings of Orissa MLE

As there is no one uniform kind of MLE programme, it is imperative to ask a few questions in order to map out the nature and the form of MLE that is in place in Orissa. How are 'culture' and 'activity' defined and treated within the epistemic system of the Orissa MLE approach? What forms of empowerment models and pedagogic practices are in place? If children's everyday activities are used as critical cultural resources to teach in the classroom, how are the relationships between everyday (empirical) and school (theoretical/academic) concepts viewed? The processes of acquisition of an everyday concept and a mathematical concept are very different as both are part of two very different epistemic practices—home and school (Bernstein 1996; Panda and Cole 2007). Use of many examples of everyday concepts does not necessarily lead to an understanding of a corresponding theoretical concept. It requires use of carefully planned intervention by the teacher where the children are assisted to perceive, for instance, a quantity in relation to another quantity and move gradually from the notion of sharing to the theoretical concept of ratio. In terms of discourse, the child's discourse moves qualitatively from the everyday (empirical) discourse to scientific (theoretical) discourse (see Karpov 2003 for detailed discussion on everyday and scientific concepts). Even though everyday examples and discourses are vital to start with, the use of everyday examples and discourses in the classrooms may not in itself be sufficient to ensure children's access to academic mathematics and science discourse.

In the MLE programmes in Orissa, the mother tongue is the teaching language in grades 1 and 2. The second language is used for oral communication in grade 1 and grade 2 and increasingly as a language of teaching from grade 3 onwards. In grade 5, the second language will be used as the medium of teaching and the place of the MT remains unspecified. From grade 6, the second language is supposed to become the sole medium of instruction. A number of issues remain unclear which the Orissa MLE programme needs to address in the coming years. If the use of the mother tongue stops in grade 6, what happens to children's cultural resources? The current programme envisages the use of books and other teaching–learning materials written in the MT and drawing almost exclusively from their experiential and cultural resources till the point of complete transition to the second language. It is likely that the withdrawal of children's mother tongue from the classroom as early as grade 6, would lead to sudden loss of children's cultural capital since the standard Oriya textbooks for use in the classrooms are common to all the children in Orissa and usually they represent the culture of the dominant Oriya community. In that case, this system of transition with an early exit programme could be a trap, as it cleverly would click to a minimalist agenda of the government and, at the same time, caters to the concerns of the a few optimistic reformists. Unless some of these issues are addressed before the first batch of children reach the point of transition to the second language only, the extent to which the present MLE programme in Orissa succeeds in providing the necessary scaffolding from children's cultural resources will remain in doubt. On a positive note, there are clear signs of growing interest in MT based MLE for tribal children and the MLE programme in Orissa has just decided to continue with the tribal MTs at least till grade 5 and a proposal to have these languages as a school subject thereafter is being seriously examined by the Government of Orissa. Further, the MLE programme in Orissa is now poised to be extended to at least six more tribal languages.

## Packaging! An inevitable trap

Our observations of MLE schools in Orissa show that what has been transcribed in training the MLE teachers is a package, one which is often performed as a routine in actual classroom practices.

The teachers were found to be holding a big book and reading a sentence from the book aloud followed by the children repeating the sentence in chorus. In grade 1 of one Saora area school, the teacher read a sentence aloud four times and then called on a student, who moved her index finger over the words while reading. The student was made to read the sentence four times. The teacher then asked the student to identify one particular alphabetic symbol. In another class, the teacher read the sentence aloud seven times followed by the chorus produced by children. The teacher then asked the children one by one to identify specific alphabetic symbols. The process of reading was almost the same across the schools. These observations reveal continued emphasis on only repetitions and rote memorisation as a strategy. It was obvious that in such pedagogic practices, the rules and the grammar of the package were transferred and not the theory or the principles underlying such an approach. Theme web was a concept, an idea that was used to organise the curricular materials and the teaching–learning programmes. But in practice it was treated as yet another routine in the class, a calendar that has to be followed. Activities that occur in a season were often routinely picked up and discussed in the class without treating them or converting them into a classroom activity in a Vygotskyan sense. It is often ignored in the process that a web of concepts which exist in an interrelated manner needs to be unpacked and discussed in order to facilitate transfer from everyday to scientific discourse.

The current MLE programmes are still an improvement over the earlier programmes which almost completely excluded children's language as well as culture. For a change, the children in MLE classrooms looked happy and confident and they seemed to be relating to the classroom themes transacted in their mother tongue. The children found the materials such as big and small books,[6] activity charts, storybooks and a small book on mathematics familiar. However, the approach was still very much materials- and teacher-centered. Moreover, the way the children's culture was represented in the classrooms seemed to be subscribing to a mentalistic[7] definition of culture (Ratner, 2001). The programmes looked quite structured, as the same model is used everywhere and teaching–learning activities are often performed as a routine using methods which are, at the most, close to the Initiation-Response-Evaluation format (see Mehan, 1979).

The MLE teachers were found to have very little idea of an everyday concept and its relationship to a theoretical/scientific concept. There was little understanding of how cultural artifacts like agricultural practices, art, craft and games mediate learning in the classroom. Our observation showed that a limited understanding of the concept of 'activity' led to limited empowering of teachers; they continued to axiomatically follow the given teacher training modules and manuals exercising little independent control on their own. Everyday knowledge was romanticised without converting it into a strong resource for education in formal schools for children. One therefore fears that among the teachers, a cadre of hardcore believers in the MLE routines of the kinds mentioned above may emerge. This may subsequently limit the prospects of developing dynamic and strong MLE practices.

## MLE Plus: A Culturally Rooted Holistic Approach

MLE Plus programme therefore aimed at strengthening the existing MLE practices in the schoolrooms taking the Cultural Historical Activity Theory (CHAT) approach of Vygotsky (Cole and Engeström 2007). This programme was implemented in four MLE schools each in Phulbani (for Kui speakers) and Gajapati (for Saora speakers) districts of Orissa. This approach envisages good MLE practices to be holistic, culturally situated and historically informed of the culturally embedded social, mathematical, literacy/oracy and science practices. This action research project sought to further the MLE objectives through a different kind of bridging between school and homes of Kui and Saora children. In the MLE Plus programme, the children's own cultural resources such as language, cultural artifacts, institutions and practices are used for teaching them formal concepts and theories. A number of activities were planned to empower not only the children but also the parents so that they participate in children's learning processes. Activities were planned at the level of both school and community for developing effective classroom pedagogy based on children's everyday experiences. These interventions included motivating parents to send their children to school and closely monitoring the academic history of these children, developing the reading environment both in the community and in the school through a synergistic *Read Together* approach, providing authorship to the tribal villagers in these selected villages for the documents/books published on the basis of oral narratives provided by them on the local history, ecology, stories, songs etc. and making these books part of the *Read Together* programme. MLE Plus sought to develop the community's interest in children's schooling by developing community reading and learning resource centres in which the oral tradition (story telling, songs and rhymes in the community) was linked to written texts.[8]

Besides this, the action research through the MLE Plus initiative aimed at adding value to the government MLE programmes by monitoring children's transition to other school languages based on strengthening their mother tongue by increasing the cultural inputs into language as well as mathematics, science and environmental studies curricula through the use of ethnographic analyses. Community awareness and involvement was particularly emphasised since most of the tribal children were the first generation that joined formal schools for learning.

## Ethnographic survey

The MLE Plus approach began with an extensive ethnographic survey of the everyday practices and the knowledge systems in these two tribal communities of Orissa—Kond and Saora. The programme placed a special emphasis on teachers themselves making efforts to use these knowledge systems to strengthen the existing MLE practices in the schools. This was facilitated by regular interaction between the Community MLE Workers (CMW) who undertook this survey and the Government MLE teachers. An exhaustive exercise of concept mapping was done to identify various mathematical and science concepts the Saoras and Konds use in their everyday activities. These concepts are angle, length, force, weight, pull, shapes like square, rectangle, rhombus etc., and units for measurements like weight, length, volume etc. The cultural activities like folk games, weaving, art/craft, agricultural practices and house construction etc. were documented and analysed to show how these concepts, notions and ideas are embedded in these activities. The most noteworthy part of this documentation process was the careful analysis undertaken to examine how Saoras and Konds use these concepts to talk about balance, stability, equilibrium, best fit and gravity etc. The exact linguistic terms used for these concepts were documented. Where, why and how the communities use these concepts and the meanings embedded in their use were analysed. The CMWs collected the pictures of wall painting, *rangoli* and crafts that contain mathematical concepts like pattern, symmetry, progression etc. and interviewed Saora and Kond adults about the knowledge that helped them produce these crafts/arts. Mathematics/Science knowledge and ideas embedded in weaving were documented. Various aspects like what patterns do the clothes have, how do the villagers describe a pattern, and how do young learners learn specific designs, motifs and patterns were documented. Agricultural tool making, irrigation, laying plots for irrigation and sowing, buying and selling agricultural lands were analysed to show what concepts Saoras and Konds have to describe angle, length, force, gravity etc. The deep design structures of houses in these regions were analysed for similar purposes. Video recording and analysis of at least five to six folk games played by children in their communities were carried out for understanding the rules of the game and the kind of mathematics people use to play the games. The indigenous knowledge and classification systems used by Konds and Saoras in respect of trees, plants, and herbs, the soil properties for growth of plants and trees and their medicinal use and animal types, habitats, food and ecology were documented. Contextual use of linguistic terms for everyday discourse in respect of the social institutions, local governance, the line of authority and inter-community relationship and the larger democratic system of political governance and the conceptual relationship of these notions to the villagers' notions of time, history, geographical boundary, rights and duties were documented and analysed. These knowledge systems were then used as some guiding principles in workshops to develop culturally relevant and meaningful pedagogic activities (Panda 2007, Panda and Cole 2007).

## Moving from Everyday to Scientific Discourse

By the time young tribal children come to school, they already possess a vast repertoire of knowledge about their environment, family, relationships, quantities, numbers etc. Their knowledge is built around loosely connected everyday concepts rooted in their everyday practices. For example, our ethnographic data showed how different mathematical concepts and ideas are embedded in various cultural practices like cooking, agriculture, house construction, folk games, buying-and-selling etc. Children do possess basic knowledge of some of these mathematical concepts and ideas. So, one of the major objectives of MLE Plus programme was to link students' everyday knowledge as an epistemic system and the academic mathematics discourse so that the children could easily build the latter on the basis of the former (see Panda, 2008 for details). Vygotsky (1987) described conceptual development as an interaction between spontaneous everyday concepts and the organised systems of concepts referred to as 'scientific' concepts. He proposed that through formal instruction, children are given access to scientific concepts that enable them to reconceptualise their everyday experiences. In this sense, scientific concepts replace children's everyday concepts and they can begin to work within the more formal and generalised conceptual frameworks associated with schooling. But this is possible only if children's own knowledge systems, beliefs and values are used as the basis for development of more formal scientific knowledge. The interaction between scientific and spontaneous concepts can also be described as an interweaving process where scientific concepts grow downward through spontaneous concepts, while spontaneous concepts grow upward through scientific concepts.

In the present programme the children, while playing a folk game, are made to mathematise the situation in hand, talk about the mathematical concepts used in the game and the meanings of those in the given game context. Sometimes they are put in buying-and-selling activity or use a barter system to assess equivalence, determine the value or the price of the object, and handle money using their own Saora or Kond number system. Once they make certain transactions, they are asked some questions that require mathematisation or, at least talking about the transactions using a few mathematical terms. Here, the role of the instructor is crucial. Therefore, when mathematical activities are developed using folk practices, the teachers' roles become crucial. Often the moderation of the discussion is so managed that the children gradually learn to mathematise everyday experiences using the conventional school mathematical discourse and its symbols. Like Davydov's approach (1990), the children's notion of quantity, equality, more, less etc. are used along with numerous modal logic terms from everyday discourses to conceptualise the conventional mathematical symbols of equal (=), addition (+), subtraction(-) etc. Many folk games are manipulated where the notion of equity is evoked by making unequal distribution of objects or misappropriation and the children are asked to do justice to the partners. When the children redistribute the objects, they are asked to describe the process. Here, children often used the terms like 'I took back these many from Rama', 'Gave these many to Shyam', 'I saw to it that both get equal numbers' etc. These descriptive terms are then replaced by the symbols in the next step in which the students are not allowed to use the descriptive terms any more. They were given specific symbols that mean the same. Only after sufficiently dealing with the quantity concepts and school mathematics symbols in the context of folk games, stories, barter games etc. in their own number system, do the children learn to use numbers, symbols and algorithms formally.

In the state MLE programme, the Saora children were taught counting first up to 20 in the Saora number system and then up to 30 in grade 1. The textbooks treated number 10 as the base value and the concept of base value was introduced by showing pictorially a bundle of 10 sticks, and a number like 11 was shown as the bundle along with one loose stick. Subsequently, one loose stick was added each time to show 12 till 19 and twenty is shown as two bundles of 10 sticks each.

If one looks at the Saora number system carefully, one finds the use of two base values: 12 and 20. There are thirteen basic numbers in the Saora number system. These are *ariba*(0), *abay*(1), *bagu*(2), *yagi*(3), *unji*(4), *manlai*(5), *turu*(6), *gulji*(7), *tanji*(8), *tinji*(9), *galji*(10), *galmuai*(11), *migal*(12). The numbers from 13 to 19 are created by adding base numbers to migal (12). So, 13 is m*igalbay [(migal (12) + abay (1)]*. Similarly, fourteen is formed by combining twelve with two i.e m*igalbagu [(migal(12)+bagu (2)]* and so on until nineteen i.e. m*igalgulj [(migal (12) +gulji (7) ]*. They use *kudi* (20) then as a base for counting up to 39 (Panda, 2004). It is obvious that if one is using the Saora number system to teach counting and provide a basic understanding of the relationship between quantities and the numbers, 10 as base value should not be introduced right away. The Saora children should be helped to deconstruct the numbers from 13 to 19 as 12 plus 1, 12 plus 2 etc. Similarly, 20 becomes the base value for generating numbers from 21 to 32. Once the Saora children get the notion of base value, they can be introduced to the Oriya number system. When they deconstruct values higher than 10 and compare those with the Saora number system, they understand the mathematical concept 'base value'. The CMWs attempted to help children look at their own number system and talk about 12 and 20 as base values for creating bigger numbers and then to show that other number systems including the Oriya number system have base values too, though they may be different. It is important to note here that pedagogues and teacher trainers in Orissa (as also in other states with large tribal populations) often complain about lack of ability among the tribal communities to conceptualise 10 as base value and put the blame on their oral traditions and lack of literacy among parents. Our MLE Plus intervention programme shows that this problem could be tackled only when the children's own knowledge and experiences are brought into focus in understanding the scientific concepts rather than being viewed as a deficit and interference and, hence, excluded. The base value issue is only one of many mathematical and science concepts in the schools which are clearly related to the everyday discourse of the tribal children. They can be accessed by the children more effectively through activities based on everyday knowledge; use of their everyday knowledge increases the ontological qualities of mathematical experiences and the discourses.[9]

Saoras do not have a writing system. The numbers are basically words that are spoken. Therefore all the calculations in the Saora system are done orally. Our earlier studies show that Saoras use various regrouping methods for doing basic calculations like addition, subtraction etc. (Panda 2004, 2006). So the Saora children were not introduced to the written symbols for numbers in the beginning of class one. The concept and the use of numbers and the number system were first strengthened orally through careful selection and analysis of everyday activities of children. Different everyday activities were planned to talk about numbers and some of the basic properties of the number system. The notion of odd numbers and even numbers, the concept of basic numbers, numbers growing till infinity, that the numbers can be added and subtracted and arranged in different patterns were discussed in the context of children's everyday activities. The deep design structure of craft objects like hat and umbrella made out of bamboo strips were brought to the classroom and discussed to show how different crafts use different systems of progressions of numbers and that there is a regularity or pattern in most of the crafts. In other words, the children are made to discover the use of the number system and its properties in almost every activity of human life. The conversations are organised in such a manner that the children can discuss the number system in as many ways as possible. Pattern recognition and mathematisation of patterns were specially promoted through these activities as higher mathematics builds on this knowledge system. So, it is not only the use of the mother tongue that accounts for the difference in children's learning, it is also the more careful use of their everyday discourses in the classroom that makes learning possible.

Since this intervention programme is for three years, it is imperative to provide a theoretical distinction between 'replacement' (i.e., the substitution for an 'everyday' understanding of a more sophisticated conventionalised academic understanding) and 'interweaving' (i.e., maintenance of and interaction between the everyday and the scientific concepts) and make our position on these two clear. Integrating everyday and scientific discourses is regarded as essential in developing a deep understanding of specific domains of knowledge. The process of integration, however, may occur in quite different ways such as 'replacement' format and 'interweaving'.[10] 'Replacement' format refers to a process that emphasises substitution of an 'everyday' understanding with a more sophisticated conventionalised academic understanding, whereas 'interweaving' stresses maintenance of and interaction between the everyday and the scientific concepts in the classroom. We have noted that too much focus on 'replacement' may deter students from actively participating in socially constituted practices such as 'conjecturing' and 'justifying'. This may constrain creativity on the part of the students. Similarly, greater focus on 'interweaving' may result in children continuing in everyday discourse longer. This may sometimes reduce student inquiry to a process that lacks mathematical substance and clarity. Therefore both 'replacement' and 'interweaving' could be seen as necessary elements of the discourse practices of a classroom community. In the beginning, interweaving could be the dominant mode of transaction where the everyday spontaneous concepts form the basis of transaction. Once the children get the theoretical concepts, the everyday discourse may be replaced by the conventionalised academic mathematics discourse.

In an intervention study, a folk game called *Apphuchi* was used in grade 7 to teach the Saora children probability (Panda and Cole 2007). Initially, when the game was played by the children on the board (drawn with fingers on the ground) using four tamarind seeds as dice to earn points so that the players can move the counters on the board, the game itself evoked spontaneous concepts like chance, relative value, bias and many modal logic terms like *would, could, should, maybe* etc. Chance, bias and relative value are called spontaneous concepts because these are loosely defined and regarded as everyday concepts by the children. When the children discussed the rules of the game using these terms and subsequently reflected on probability (the teacher tried to moderate the discourse so that the children examine the concept of probability in the context of the game), at one point the teacher realised that actual outcomes of the tosses interfere in children's acceptance of the theoretical probability of equal chances. At this point the teacher decided to dispense with everyday examples and engaged the children in theoretical possibilities. He discussed the concept of actual probability and theoretical probability with the children, drawing on their notion of bias evoked in the context of the folk game

*Apphuchi*. When the children freed themselves from the real life event to appreciate theoretical probability, they were given more abstract questions so that they indulged in more conventionalised mathematical discourse. At this point, 'interweaving' was replaced by the 'replacement' as the dominant mode of pedagogic approach for teaching probability. However, the interweaving method continues in other areas of mathematics and also for students who make a late transition (some spontaneously) to the theoretical concept of probability. Therefore we decided to use 'replacement' and 'interweaving' patterns of discourse as alternatives to the Initiation-Response-Evaluation format[11] (as advanced by Mehan 1979) that pervades classroom talk and as an initial heuristic to process information. A judicious alternative use of 'interweaving' and 'replacement' patterns of discourse in the mathematics class helped the MLE teachers understand how the everyday and scientific concepts could be linked in classroom talk to promote deep understanding among the tribal children. This, no doubt, requires a very different kind of teacher preparation.

## Community MLE workers: The link between culture and school

Though the teaching–learning activities are taken from the community itself and the curriculum is organised in accordance with the seasonal activities of Konds and Saoras in state MLE programmes, there was a limited dialectical exchange between epistemic knowledge and practices in the community and in the classroom processes. This is mainly because the teachers were often not in dialogue with the communities. Further, they do not develop the activities themselves; rather they transact a pre-ordained programme under MLE. As mentioned earlier, the use of cultural materials within the framework of the theme web alone does not make the classroom transactions of the MLE teachers in government schools child-centered and joyful. In the MLE Plus programme, the CMWs provided this missing link. The MLE Plus programme essentially revolves around the issue of linking school to community as efforts are being made to simultaneously empower both and to use one to enrich the other. The growth of one is integrally linked to the growth of the other. Regular meetings of the CMWs with the parents, the development of community libraries run with the help of the *mukhia* (tribal leaders or heads of the village) and the schoolgoing children, documentation and printing of the stories, songs, rhymes and riddles with the speakers' authorship, and inclusion of these books in both school and community libraries are a few of these steps towards this end. In fact, the very act of undertaking the ethnographic survey was a significant first step towards bridging the gap between school and community. In MLE Plus, the ethnographic survey served two purposes; one, to make available a systematic documentation of the relevant cultural knowledge systems and epistemic practices that were subsequently used to evolve a culturally situated pedagogic practice, and two, to train the CMWs to look at everyday activities/practices from the children's learning perspective and to develop these activities into culturally informed pedagogic tools.

The CMWs meet once every month for three days in a workshop where not only MLE issues (materials production, pedagogic issues) are discussed but also relevant teaching–learning materials and activities are developed on the basis of the ethnographic survey data. In this workshop, the State Project Manager, MLE+ Teachers, CMWs, and Language Group Coordinators jointly discuss various pedagogic and materials-related issues and problems and share best practices. Periodic observation of classroom processes by the Project Directors (the authors of this chapter) and the state level project staff such as the State Project Manager and the district level Language group Coordinators helped us identify specific issues and to address them both in the monthly meetings and in the workshops. Every month, one day is devoted to sharing and discussing each others' issues and problems like 'how best can the MLE Plus workers monitor each child's progress', 'how do they support individual children's learning and the transition from one language to another' and 'how do they prepare the community for children's education'.

## **SYNERGISTIC *READ TOGETHER* PROGRAMME**

The synergistic *Read Together* programme is a specially designed programme to facilitate the process of developing a sense of continuity between oral and written practices by collecting folk tales, stories and songs from individual community members and transcribing them into written texts with authorship and photographs. These and other selected reading resource materials go into a community library/resource centre for children, parents, and other adults in the community. In every village where an MLE+ School is located, a community resource centre is opened with the help of villagers under the leadership of village head (*mukhia*) and the members of Village Education Committee. The Kond and Saora community members were first approached by the CMWs to provide a space for opening this library/resource centre. A storage box was provided to store the reading materials. In most villages, a common meeting ground (ground space under a big tree located in the place where villagers meet) was used in the evening hours from 4–5 p.m. to read and discuss the books. The village heads (*mukhia*) have generally agreed to keep the storage box in their houses when not in use. In the first few months, community workers (CMW) go to the village during this hour, collect the box with the help of villagers from the *mukhia's* house and spread the books on a mat in the common meeting ground. In the first phase of this initiative, the CMWs used to read the story books, or asked some schoolchildren to read. Subsequently, the schoolchildren and adults, by and large, took charge of the library. By now, in three out of eight villages, parents have started demanding specific kinds of books. A few parents in these villages requested the CMWs to teach them to write their names and to learn to read small sentences in the story books. Initially, the CMWs helped these parents in reading and writing and gradually passed this responsibility on to the schoolgoing children. After a month, some paper, pencils and crayons were also provided to these centres.

## A PRELIMINARY ASSESSMENT OF MLE PLUS

Our observations and monitoring of children's progress under the MLE+ show definite signs of positive effects on children's classroom attendance and participation, greater involvement in learning as well as planned activities under MLE+, and community interest in the teaching–learning processes. Teachers also reported better classroom achievement and participation of children. We undertook some formal assessment of classroom achievement in different subject areas at the end of the first year of the MLE as well as MLE+ programmes. All the children in the eight MLE+ schools and children from eight other adjacent MLE schools and eight non-MLE government schools in the vicinity were selected for a comparative assessment of classroom achievement. The Classroom Achievement measures were developed in a workshop with the help of CMWs, some teachers and language coordinators. These measures were directly related to the thematic content of the curricular materials used in the MLE classrooms. The measures used were modelled after the assessment tools used for all the State Government schools of Orissa. The measures used for our assessment were in children's MT and required both oral and written responses from them to specific items. The results of the evaluation undertaken at the end of year I for the Saora MLE+, MLE and Non-MLE schools on Language, Environmental Science (EVS), Mathematics and Drawing subjects are given in Table 18.1. Detailed analysis of the data and also the findings in respect of the Kond programmes are still in process. Further assessment of metacognitive processes underlying language and mathematics are planned. The items for all the assessment tools were developed in a workshop in Kui, Saora and Oriya languages.

The data clearly show that the Saora children from the MLE+ schools performed better than the Saora children from MLE and non-MLE Oriya-medium schools. However, the difference between the Saora students from MLE and non-MLE schools was not very prominent. It is, of course, too early to expect the difference in achievement levels among the children, particularly after only one year of intervention. A continuous evaluation at the middle and the end of the second and third years of the programme for classroom achievement and developments in the cognitive, metacognitive and affective domains will enable us draw preliminary conclusions with a certain amount of confidence. The present data may at best be seen as initial signs of some positive role of the cultural psychological pedagogy in MLE+ schools.

Table 18.1. Achievement scores of grade 1 children in 4 MLE+ schools, 4 MLE schools and 1 Oriya-medium school.

| Subjects | | MLE+ School N=74 | MLE School N=47 | Oriya-Medium School N=55 |
|---|---|---|---|---|
| Language Subject | *Total Marks: 100*<br>Oral: 70<br>Written: 30 | 55.36<br>36.32<br>17.04 | 36.59<br>21.04<br>14.55 | 37.40<br>23.40<br>14.00 |
| Mathematics | *Total Marks: 100*<br>Oral: 40<br>Written: 60 | 58.29<br>25.00<br>33.29 | 38.95<br>19.89<br>19.06 | 40.62<br>18.02<br>22.60 |
| Environmental Science | *Total Marks: 50*<br>Oral: 30<br>Written: 20 | 32.55<br>18.45<br>14.10 | 27.31<br>14.78<br>12.53 | 23.60<br>12.60<br>11.00 |
| Drawing | *Total Marks: 25* | 15.87 | 12.82 | 15.00 |

## MLE Plus: Some Reflections

Our attempt to problematise 'Plus' through a careful planning of activities and our retrospective reconstruction of the processes that were put in place in the first year of the programme such as carrying out an ethnographic survey, training of CMWs, development of classroom activities in children's mother tongues, and developing community reading programmes all reveal that 'Plus' does not mean merely something extra to the existing MLE programme. It is rather a perspective, a metaphor that entails the philosophical underpinnings of critical pedagogy as advocated by Freire (2001), Apple (2004), Giroux (1997) and others and the principles of Cultural Historical Activity Theory (CHAT) as advocated by Vygotsky (Cole and Engeström 2007). This raises a question as to whether MLE and MLE Plus programmes are based on the same or two different perspectives. On the surface, they seem to be based on the same perspective, both aiming at using children's everyday context and materials for classroom teaching and building community awareness for education in their mother tongues. But MLE, being a fairly structured programme, seems to be still adhering to a minimalist agenda. What is required is intense engagement with pedagogic processes, a different quality of community participation, and the establishment of regular give-and-take between school and community resources and knowledge systems with an objective of putting in place a critical pedagogy that helps students question and challenge domination and the beliefs and practices that dominate (Freire 2005). A social and educational vision of justice and equality need to inform all aspects of MLE practices. The MLE Plus programme seeks to strengthen this aspect of MLE through qualitative changes in classroom and community practices and by further reinforcing the cultural bases of school learning. The involvement of our CMWs with the community, such as tracking each individual child, holding regular meetings with the community members, teachers and the tribal leaders, involving tribal leaders at all levels of school education and community initiatives, running synergistic community reading programmes, developing classroom activities on a regular basis from the everyday materials and experiences of tribal children using robust pedagogic principles of cultural psychology, and, finally, using these activities with children in the presence of adults, yielded a unique example of scaffolding. The learning and development of critical consciousness and collective identity is expected to build on the sustained dialectical tension between home and school knowledge systems. This is possible only when there is a more regular give-and-take between the children's own culture and the classroom, without romanticising or privileging[12] any one form of discourse. Such practices can make school learning more meaningful and engaging for tribal children. This will definitely not estrange the tribal children from their land, language and culture as often happens in existing classroom practices.

## Notes

1 This Project is supported by a grant (INA-2006-102) from the Bernard van Leer Foundation, the Netherlands. Both authors are Directors of this project. A team of project staff (one State Project Manger and eight Community MLE Workers who are native speakers of the language) is appointed in the field (Phulbani and Gajapati districts, Orissa, India) in order to carry out the activities decided in periodically organised workshops through a larger consultative process. Two native speakers of both tribal languages, Kond and Saora, with some experience of school education, are appointed as language co-coordinators.

2 Here, discourse means knowledge. Therefore, everyday discourse means everyday knowledge.

3 We have chosen to use Cultural Historical Activity Theory (CHAT) as a general theoretical framework as it captures the paradigmatic essences of Vygotsky, Luria and Leont'ev (for the latest developments, see Engeström 2001 and Cole and Engeström 2007). We use those aspects of CHAT that recognise the role of action, labour and activity settings in the co-construction of mind. The CHAT framework is particularly instrumental because any reform would require a good historical analysis of socio-political conditions that result in certain kinds of arrangement of human life. It privileges children's everyday knowledge without undermining the power of formal literacy and academic practices. More than anything else, it has a clear theory of pedagogy based on a theory of action.

4 The term 'homogenous' does not mean that children are essentially monolingual. It only refers to the fact that most of these children have the same mother tongue albeit with

some regional variation and they may have varying degrees of exposure to the second, third and other languages. Such exposures, however, are still quite limited for the purposes of their direct classroom use.

5 Singh, Deo Ranjan and Mahendra Kumar Mishra 2008. 'Orissa MLE'. Paper presented at the 'International Conference on Multilingual Education: Challenges, Perspectives and Opportunity', New Delhi, 5–8 February, 2008.

6 Some of the routine practices of the state-level programme in India, particularly those in Andhra Pradesh and Orissa, are used as uniform and structured aspects of the MLE procedures, including the Theme web and Calendar approach mentioned earlier. These seem to have percolated into various MLE plans in India through the involvement of SIL (Summer Institute of Linguistics, a US missionary organisation—see Pérez 2009, Phillipson 2009, Skutnabb-Kangas 2009, all this volume) early in the development of the MLE programmes.

7 Culture is often looked at by developmental and educational psychologists as something that is represented in the human mind. Such a definition is mentalistic as it doesn't capture the actual dialectical relationship between different sub-systems or activities that shape the human mind. It rather glosses over the tensions and conflicts that characterise the cultural activities, institutions and artifacts that mediate human learning. Cultural Historical Activity Theory does not subscribe to the mentalistic view of culture as it recommends use of children's language and everyday activities in classrooms so that they learn the concepts in an inter-subjectively shared environment where emotion and identity are part of the learning environment.

8 The idea here is to develop a sense of continuity between oral and written practices by collecting folktales, stories and songs from individual community members and transcribing them into written texts with authorship and photographs. These and other reading resource materials go into community resource centres as well as school libraries. The International Reading Association has implemented similar programmes in African countries.

9 Panda, Minati 2006. 'Ontological qualities of mathematical experiences: Comparison of two cultures'. Paper presented in IACCP 2006, Spetses, Greece.

10 Renshaw, Raymond and Peter Brown 2000. 'Four models of the processing integrating everyday and scientific discourse: Replacement, interweaving, contextual privileging and pastiche'. Paper presented as part of the symposium 'The discourse of science classrooms and popular science texts: Multiplicity in meanings, devices and rhetorical models', at the 3 Conference for Sociocultural Research, Campinas, Sao Paulo Brazil, 16–20 July, 2000.

11 Initiation-Response-Evaluation (I-R-E) refers to a method where the teacher asks students to answer questions, repeats students' responses and prods students to clarify their positions. The interweaving format allows the children to move back and forth between loose everyday talk and scientific discourse. The replacement format differs from the traditional I-R-E script in that it delays teacher evaluations of students' responses in favour of recontextualising what the students 'think' within the discourse practices of a mathematical community (Brown and Renshaw 2000). The discourse format is not about transmitting mathematical knowledge to students, but about motivating students to think of themselves as capable of engaging in the co-construction and interpretation of meaning, about propelling students in different directions through the subject

matter. As such, the replacement format contextualises the learning of mathematical knowledge within a classroom discourse that foregrounds mathematical practices such as 'representing', 'comparing', and 'justifying' and evaluates student products in terms of mathematical norms (e.g. 'efficiency' and 'clarity') that relate to those practices. In this way, students are equipped with the tools necessary to communicate their ways of doing mathematics to a wider classroom audience where the concrete and experiential may be rephrased, re-represented and replaced by the more abstract and general concepts of mathematics.

12 We do not undermine the power of academic mathematics and science discourses for changing the quality of human life, the ability of communities to decide what is good for them as well as for the wider society, and to facilitate their social and politically informed participation in micro- and macro-cultural resource allocation and decision-making. But the politics of knowledge and issues of epistemology need to be understood so that 'validated' scientific knowledge does not function as a basis of oppression. Education, when it works as critical transformative praxis, may expose new modes of colonialism. It can, therefore, be used to empower the marginalised tribal and indigenous communities.

# 19

# MLE Concepts, Goals, Needs and Expense: English for all or Achieving Justice?

*Tove Skutnabb-Kangas, Robert Phillipson, Minati Panda, Ajit K. Mohanty*

This volume has critiqued some practices and theories in multilingual education and presented studies of successful innovation and empowerment. The concluding chapter states that Education For All is a mantra, not reality. It stresses the need for stringency in the concepts or labels used in the area of multilingual education. It draws together some of the significant insights from earlier chapters and other research evidence, including critical Indigenous pedagogy, and relates educational policy to broader social processes. One of them is the role of English worldwide, especially as a medium of education, the issue of popular demand for English, the language that is seen as a panacea. We also provide one possible model for analysing the extent to which multilingual education facilitates structural incorporation without cultural assimilation. Some basic issues around the right to education and Linguistic Human Rights are touched upon. Finally the chapter considers MLE in relation to meeting basic needs and combating poverty, including issues of cost.

## Education for All: A Long Way from Mantra to Reality

Many millions of people in China and India have succeeded in hoisting themselves out of poverty while hundreds of millions remain there. However the globalising economies have failed to deliver successfully the 'Education For All' that political leaders in theory are committed to. The current global economy has in no way bridged the substantial gap between global haves and have-nots. One third of the world's population still live below subsistence levels—the 'wretched of the earth', in Franz Fanon's words in a pioneer study of colonialism—and how a more just world order might be established (1963).

Some of the main causes of educational failure in multilingual societies were correctly diagnosed a century ago in British India (see Curzon as quoted in Skutnabb-Kangas

2009, this volume). UNESCO's 1953 book *The use of the vernacular languages in education* included firm recommendations, written by experts, on how multilingual education can best be organised. Similar informed consultations went into drafting UNESCO's Education position paper in 2003, *Education in a multilingual world.* Alas, a review of achievements in Africa concludes that '[W]e are not making any progress at all' (Alexander 2006: 9); 'most conference resolutions were no more than a recycling exercise' (Bamgbose 2001, quoted in Alexander 2006: 10); 'these propositions had been enunciated in one conference after another since the early 1980s' ( 2006: 11); 'since the adoption of the OAU [Organisation for African Unity] Charter in 1963, every major conference of African cultural experts and political leaders had solemnly intoned the commitment of the political leadership of the continent to the development and powerful use of the African languages without any serious attempt at implementing the relevant resolutions' (2006: 11). This has led to 'the palpable failure of virtually all post-colonial educational systems on the continent' (2006: 16).

Is this book, then, yet another academic 'recycling exercise' of the kind that some African scholars deplore? Not so. It is not merely a set of authorised language policy statements that may or may not be implemented. It brings together critical scholarly evidence of theories and activities in a range of contexts worldwide that are of general, even universal relevance. The critique of much of what has been done, both theories and practices, is also self-criticism; the book represents theoretical innovation but also description of theoretically founded and positive new practices.

## MLE AND OTHER CONCEPTS: USE, MISUSE, MISLABELLING

One step in developing MLE further in a more glocalised direction (enriching more general 'global' theories through local contexts) must be to compare how various central concepts are used in different parts of the world and in different disciplines. When stressing the need to clarify concepts in the area of bilingual education, Skutnabb-Kangas and McCarty wrote (2008: 3):

> The concepts we use are almost never neutral. In contested arenas such as bilingual education, words and concepts frame and construct the phenomena under discussion, making some persons and groups visible, others invisible; some the unmarked norm, others marked and negative. Choice of language can minoritise or distort some individuals, groups, phenomena, and relations while majoritising and glorifying others. Concepts also can be defined in ways that hide, expose, rationalize, or question power relations.
>
> Because concepts and terms develop historically, the same concept may have several definitions. For example, 'language immersion' has historically been associated with French–Canadian immersion for middle-class Anglophones (Cummins and Swain 1986; Lambert and Tucker 1986). The term was misleadingly appropriated by U.S. policymakers to describe submersion programmes (called "structured immersion"), despite protest from the concept's originator (Lambert 1984: 26-27). Recently the

> term has taken on new meaning in Indigenous-language immersion programmes to revitalise endangered Indigenous languages (Bear Nicholas 2005; Hinton and Hale 2001; Hinton et al. 2002). The ideological, historical, epistemic, and empirical bases for these varied uses of "immersion" are distinct, as are program practices.

Skutnabb-Kangas and McCarty also give other reasons for the need to 'unpack and define key concepts' (3–4):

> A further reason for interrogating concepts is the presence of multiple paradigms. For example, literacy can be defined as the ability to read and write. Yet this definition masks two different paradigms informing literacy research and practice. *Autonomous* views characterize literacy as abstract, neutral, and independent from the social context and language users (Ong 1982). *Ideological* views characterize literacy as 'socially and historically situated, fluid, multiple, and power-linked' (McCarty 2005: xvii–xviii; Street 1984, 2001). Educationally, an autonomous view emphasizes discrete language skills, often taught through direct instruction and scripted phonics programs. An ideological view binds reading and writing to oracy, emphasizing the development of different literacies (and multiliteracies) for different purposes through meaningful social interaction and critical examination of authentic texts.

It is noteworthy that 'literacy' is officially defined in Zambia as the ability 'to read and write in English' (Williams 2006: 17). In Malawi it is defined as the ability 'to read and write' (25).

Theoretical concepts and categories are temporally embedded to begin with; they continue to evolve through the flow of knowledge, practices, and analytical processes. Those in the field of MLE are no exceptions. The models and concepts in the field of bilingualism/multilingualism and BE/MLE (such as 'balanced'/additive/subtractive bilingualism) which proved to be extremely powerful explanatory tools are now becoming inadequate for dealing with linguistic heterogeneity and complexity around the globe. Even the common categorical labels such as monolingualism, bilingualism, multilingualism are being increasingly problematised. Pittman (2008) summarises some of the literature on trilingualism where many researchers experience a need for new theories to explain multilingualism because they see it as fundamentally different from bilingualism. Some of the chapters in this volume point to the fluidity of linguistic boundaries, questioning the concept of 'a language' and the psycholinguistic reality of notions like monolingualism (e.g. Agnihotri 2009, this volume).

As the field of BE/MLE research gets enriched by fresh inputs from multilingual societies, in Asia and Africa in particular, it becomes quite clear that monolingualism as a set of codified rules abstracted from the diversity of how a language is actually used is probably rare in oral forms of communication. Heugh (2009, this volume ) describes the 'multilayered and partially connected language chains' (Fardon and Furniss 1994: 4) used among the communities for communication as the *de facto lingua franca* in the African situation. García (2009a, this volume) describes dynamic classroom multilingual discourse as 'translanguaging' with potential implications for pedagogical practices in what is ostensibly monolingual education.

However, while applications of such ideas to the oral practices of children, people and communities in multilingual settings may be less problematic, written text in schools still remains mostly monolingual all over the world regardless of societal multilingualism. Thus, the notion of dynamic multilingualism gets blurred as one moves from oral to written classroom practices. Since the written form must necessarily be a major focus in the classroom, the notion of dynamic multilingualism remains problematic as a pedagogical concept. As long as 'imposed normativity is a feature of most institutions, and the education system is generally a case in point …a system of ideological reproduction' (Blommaert 2008: 428), children who translanguage in writing in official situations lose their voice because '[i]nstitutions have the tendency to "freeze" the conditions for voice: unless you speak or write *in this particular way*, you will not be heard or read' (2008: 428; emphasis in the original).

Even within *one* language, schools need to make children aware of when they engage in what Blommaert (2008: 432) calls 'cross-register transfer' (for instance, using a low-status expression in formal speech, or vice versa). In multilingual situations, children need to be aware of which parts of their multilingual resources to use in which situations. This metalinguistic awareness may develop in more complex ways when a greater number of languages is added. This also increases the potential for adding more benefits that high-level metalinguistic awareness can enhance (e.g. Mohanty 1995), provided teachers know how to support this awareness. As the discussion of the development of scientific concepts below also makes clear, translanguaging can not in any way substitute for good mother-tongue-based MLE where the teachers know and use the children's first language(s).

Furthermore, language labels are themselves monolingual not just as linguistic categories but also as psychological categories, which means that many people and communities like to think of their language as 'a language' and, in the case of multilinguals, their languages as several such forms of 'a language'. Thus, any attempt to de-emphasise that reality may be problematic, particularly when such labels are also very significant identity tags, as in the case of dominated linguistic minorities all over the world.

Thus it is necessary to remind ourselves that when dealing with the real world of languages, the theoretical concepts and categories are prone to be constantly challenged in the light of more and more complex linguistic contexts, especially in urban areas. The field of bilingualism itself evolved with the arrival of 'new' concepts like multilingualism, multilinguality, and plurilingualism. When moving to bilingual and, especially, multilingual education, as contrasted with monolingual education, one also notices a comparable fuzziness and tentativeness of the concepts. This is very true in the endorsement of multilingualism and plurilingualism by the European Union. Concepts/categories in BE/MLE have very different implications for classroom practices. García (2009a, this volume) claims that prestigious programmes of bilingual education (immersion/maintenance) tend to compartmentalise the languages as very distinct and autonomous entities that cannot meet the requirements of heteroglossic multilingual societies. BE/MLE must go beyond just using multiple languages in education. Benson (2009, this volume) sees many early models and categories of BE/MLE as misleading when they are extended to contexts where they do not fit and shows how strongly entrenched notions like immersion are used and abused. In view of the problems encountered, Benson offers the practical suggestion to flexibly adapt context-sensitive learning principles rather than blindly adhering to 'Models'.

It is also important to see our concepts in broader and literally more 'global' historical perspective. For instance democracy is often thought of in purely Western terms, as though patented in ancient Greece, and the idea that democracy is a reality in all Western countries is simply untrue. Contact between China, India and Arabia flourished for two millennia, with translations between Chinese, Arabic and Sanskrit in many scholarly fields (science, mathematics, literature, linguistics, architecture, medicine and music), as explained by Amartya Sen, a winner of the Nobel Prize for Economics, with a distinguished career at Cambridge and Harvard, and passionately committed to his mother tongue, Bengali:

> In so far as public reasoning is central to democracy…, parts of the global roots of democracy can indeed be traced back to the tradition of public discussion that received much encouragement in both India and China (and also in Japan, Korea and elsewhere), from the dialogic commitment to Buddhist organization… The first printed book in the world with a date (corresponding to 868 CE), which was the Chinese translation of a Sanskrit treatise, the so-called "Diamond Sutra" (Kumārajīva had translated it in 402 CE), carried the remarkable motivational explanation: "for universal free distribution" (Sen 2005: 164, 182-3).

The pre-eminence of Western science, in our unstable, inequitable, militarised world, is recent, and legitimated as though 'knowledge societies' are a late capitalist invention:

> Different cultures are thus interpreted in ways that reinforce the political conviction that Western civilization is somehow the main, perhaps the only, source of rationalistic and liberal ideas—among them analytical scrutiny, open debate, political tolerance and agreement to differ…. science and evidence, liberty and tolerance, and of course rights and justice. … Once we recognize that many ideas that are taken to be quintessentially Western have also flourished in other civilizations, we also see that these ideas are not as culture-specific as is sometimes claimed (Sen, 2005: 285, 287).

With the relativity of concepts in mind, we now move to some of the broader prerequisites for working towards the kind of MLE Plus education advocated in this volume. We start with a discussion about the role of English worldwide, English as the big bad wolf/tiger.

## English as the big bad wolf

The prevalent use of European languages worldwide, and especially English, in high-prestige domains has major implications, for democracy, a well-informed public sphere and population, and social cohesion. The prominence given to English is problematical wherever local languages are not *also* used, especially in education. This applies in Europeanised settler countries worldwide (like Canada and Peru, Bear Nicholas 2009, Perez 2009, both this volume). It also holds for former colonies, which as independent countries have generally maintained English as the language of power and privilege. It increasingly also holds in continental Europe, where English is used not only in international links but also within countries in several key domains (Phillipson 2009a, this volume). Many factors contribute to the glamorous pull of English, not least the ubiquitous presence of Hollywood, the massively influential global advertising industry, and the space accorded to English on school time-tables.

It is true that people wish to learn English, and that governments can see pragmatic and economic reasons for facilitating this in education. However, we would claim that whenever English is not the mother tongue, its learning should be promoted through linguistically and culturally appropriate education, meaning MLE for minority groups, and as a foreign language elsewhere. In both cases this represents the addition of English to one's repertoire of language competence. High levels of competence in English can be achieved without sacrificing competence in other languages. In fact this is precisely what is achieved in some continental European countries, especially the Nordic countries and the Netherlands, where the learning of English as a foreign language succeeds without English being a medium of instruction at any level of basic education. It is therefore false to assume that education systems ought to introduce English ever earlier as the medium of instruction or even as a foreign language.

The age variable is merely one among several relevant factors. European scholars from five countries have summarised the criteria that need to be met for any early foreign language learning to succeed: adequate funding and infrastructure, parental involvement, continuity through the various levels of schooling, adequate time, teacher training, sensitivity to learners with different degrees of success, appropriate pedagogy for each age group (summarised in Phillipson 2003: 98). The recommendations stress that all these conditions need to be addressed before innovation is attempted.

Introducing English as a medium of instruction ever earlier in primary education worldwide

- may well be subtractive in multilingual settings, leading to the marginalisation, neglect and dispossession of national languages;
- is an elite project that has overt agendas (the myth of 'development', the demands of globalisation, World Bank strategies) and covert agendas (economic interests, dependency on Western norms and expertise);
- contributes to historical amnesia in postcolonial education, obliterating awareness of the evolution and use of local languages, for instance African languages (Heugh

2009, this volume, who refers to this as revisionism) or Indian languages when children attend exclusively English-medium schools;

- reflects misunderstanding of the nature of learning in several languages, and often misuse of Western bilingual education principles, terms and models;
- an excessive focus on English leads to a false focus and structure in higher education, as in many former colonies, and to an absence of good teacher training for marginalised languages (cf. Bear Nicholas 2009, this volume);
- misleads parents into believing that formal education means education in English, a pernicious backwash effect (Benson 2009, Heugh 2009, both this volume).

There is therefore a major challenge to ensure that parents are better informed about multilingual learning, and what will lead to the best educational results. The faith that an early start in English means good education and ensures success in life is a pernicious myth.

Warnings against an excessive use of English are not new. Rabindranath Tagore, winner of the Nobel Prize for Literature in 1913, and equally proficient in English and Bengali, stressed the importance of good MLE. It is a refrain in the writings of Gandhi and Nehru, who articulated the case for Indian independence and a viable modern state. In Africa the case for MLE has been made most strongly by creative writers like Ngũgĩ and by sociolinguists and educators (references in Benson 2009, and Heugh 2009, both this volume). It is a leitmotiv in the work of scholars who see the maintenance of the dominance of English as serving Western imperialist interests (Phillipson 1992, Skutnabb-Kangas 2000). The European Union is in principle committed to strengthening multilingualism at all levels of European education systems, but the reality is that English is being strengthened at the expense of other languages by the policies that the EU endorses in higher education (Phillipson 2006), by the working practices of the EU institutions, and education systems in member states that are not geared to creating viable MLE. There is in virtually all education systems worldwide an absence of explicit language policies for ensuring multilingualism.

Seeking to constrain English should not be understood as meaning that people have anything 'against' the language English, which, of course, provides access to an infinite range of information, positions of influence, and material well-being. What needs to be resisted and counteracted is policies that privilege English at the expense of other languages. English opens doors, yes, but it closes others. English is an open sesame for some people and some purposes, but it serves to condemn others to poverty and oblivion. A lot of the advocacy in favour of English is one-sided misrepresentation. This is clearly visible in Gordon Brown's plan, announced on the occasion of his first visit as Prime Minister of the UK to China and India in February 2008, to make British English (and not American English or any other form of English) the global language of 'choice', with the para-statal British Council charged with spearheading this operation, a logical continuation of their activities since the 1950s. A key constituent of the new British policy is a plan for the British to train literally millions of English language teachers in India and China. Implementing Brown's plan (which appears to have been announced without prior consultation with the Chinese or the Indians!) has, as the British press noted, billion pound implications for Britain because of the importance for the British economy of the English language industry (reference works, textbooks, university degrees for 'international' students, teacher training expertise, private language schools, educational know-how et al., Phillipson 1992, <http://www.britishcouncil.org>). The rhetoric of 'choice' is pure spin in a world in which 'choice' is as free as the 'free' market. English is the leading language of the unfree neoliberal market, and the new imperialism (Harvey 2005). Linguistic neoimperialism, and whether English functions as a *lingua franca* or *lingua frankensteinia,* are explored in Phillipson 2006, 2008a, 2008b, and 2009b.

### Solid analysis but little change

A diagnosis similar to the African scepticism of Alexander (2006) and others can be made for many Asian contexts. The failures and challenges in India are laid bare in several contributions to this volume. The complexity of language education issues is explored insightfully in Lin and Martin's *Decolonisation, Globalisation: Language-in-education Policy and Practice* (2005, reviewed in Phillipson 2007b) and in Tsui and Tollefson's *Language Policy, Culture, and Identity in Asian Contexts* (2007), with exemplification from many countries. The integration of language with cultural and economic globalisation is revealingly explored in Rassool's *Global Issues in Language, Education and Development* (2007). The case study of Pakistan in the book (Rassool and Mansoor 2007: 218-241) confirms Tariq Rahman's analyses (1998) and shows that the use of English as the sole medium of higher education (for only 2.63% of the population) ensures the cultural alienation of the elite from the rest of the population. 'The global cultural economy is interdependent and, despite the dominant position occupied by English, in practice, it has an organically interactive multilingual base. A narrow monolingual nationalism [a reference to Urdu], an under-resourced educational system as well as unequal access to English as international *lingua franca*, therefore, is counter-productive to national growth.' (ibid., 240).

Thiru Kandiah of Sri Lanka sees countries in the postcolonial world as trapped in a major contradiction. On the one hand, postcolonial countries need the 'indispensable global medium' for pragmatic purposes, even for survival in the global economy: it is a *panacea* for the privileged. On the other there is the fact that the medium —English—is not culturally or ideologically neutral, far from it, so that its users run the 'apparently unavoidable risk of co-option, of acquiescing in the negation of their own understandings of reality and in the accompanying denial or even subversion of their own interests' (Kandiah 2001: 112): a *pandemic* (Phillipson 2009). Kandiah (ibid.) sees the need in relation to English for 'interrogating its formulations of reality, intervening in its modes of understanding, holding off its normalising tendencies, challenging its hegemonic designs and divesting it of the co-optive power which would render it a reproducing discourse'. His concern related exclusively to English, but his worries about hegemonic designs and co-option apply to any dominant language. What he advocates is authentic local projections of reality, and emancipatory action, as in the projects in India and Nepal presented in this volume.

Angel Lin from Hong Kong (2005) makes the methodological point that a 'Periphery' scholar should not merely take over 'Centre' epistemologies, and argues that our research approaches risk being self-referential—purely 'academic'—and lack self-reflection. She demonstrates the value of critical discourse analysis in unmasking the legitimation of an inequitable social structure: proficiency in English remains an elusive goal for the many in postcolonial contexts, but the current education system is functional for the local elite and for global commerce. Lin's worry about choice of appropriate methodology in education holds for all scholars, whether from Centre or Periphery (Heugh 2009, Skutnabb-Kangas 2009, both this volume). Her analysis of the limitations of much 'research' echoes the denunciation of unreflective positivism and academic exhibitionism by one of the key founders of social science research, Max Weber, a century ago (see Kim 2007: 130-131).

We need to relate these major cultural and epistemological considerations to societal goals, those of dominant and dominated groups. How is the place of dominated groups in society seen by both, and how has education been used to achieve these societal goals?

### *Agreement versus disagreement about future goals for Indigenous and tribal peoples and minorities*

Schermerhorn (1970: 80-) has a useful typology of the collective goals of minorities[1] and the extent to which a majority (or dominant group) in a country[2] agrees or disagrees with them. In describing these goals, he distinguishes between two aspects of assimilation, the economic-structural (the alternatives being structural incorporation or autonomy) and the cultural (assimilation or pluralism). Social structure refers to 'the set of crystallized social relationships which [the society's] members have with each other which place them in groups, large or small, permanent or temporary, formally organized or unorganized, and which relate them to the major institutional activities of the society, such as economic and occupational life, marriage and the family, education, government, and recreation' (Schermerhorn 1970: 80). The majority (dominant group) and the minority (subordinated group) can agree or disagree, partially or totally, with the collective goals for the subordinated group. If both groups want the same for the subordinated group in terms of both structure and culture, for instance structural incorporation (SI+) and cultural assimilation (CA+), meaning INCORPORATION at the structural level and ASSIMILATION at the cultural level, there is total agreement. If on the other hand the dominant group wants these two goals (SI+, CA+) for the subordinated group while the group itself does *not* want structural incorporation but wants structural AUTONOMY (SI-), and does *not* want cultural assimilation but cultural PLURALISM (CA-), there is a total disgreement. Partial agreement and disagreement are also possible. There are thus 16 possible outcomes (see Skutnabb-Kangas and Toukomaa 1976: 3–4). Several of them are highly unlikely while some are very realistic. Before relating this typology to situations described in this volume, we present some examples.

US 'melting pot' ideology expects all citizens to adopt the American way of life and ideals, in order to become 'good Americans'. On the other hand, the democratic ideal demands that everyone should be given equal educational and economic opportunities. The official ideology of the majority thus represents cultural assimilation but structural incorporation. This mythical American Dream has always been about granting everybody a chance of structural incorporation into an economically and politically just democratic society (see below). But the price to be paid has also, despite some early tolerance of official multilingualism, been extremely clear: total cultural assimilation. Theodore Roosevelt (the US president 1901–1909) wrote:

> We must have but one flag. We must also have but one language. … We *cannot tolerate any attempt to oppose or supplant the language and culture that has come down to us* from the builders of this Republic…We call upon all loyal and unadulterated Americans to man the trenches against the enemy within our gates' (Roosevelt 1968; emphasis added).

Roosevelt also wrote in 1919, in a letter to the next president:

> In the first place, we should insist that if the immigrant who comes here in good faith *becomes an American and assimilates himself* to us, he shall *be treated on an exact equality with everyone else*, for it is an outrage to discriminate against any such man because of creed, or birthplace, or origin. But this is predicated upon the person's becoming in every facet an American, and nothing but an American ...There can be no divided allegiance here. Any man who says he is an American, but something else also, isn't an American at all. We have room for but one flag, the American flag ... We have room for but one language here, and that is the English language ... and we have room for but one sole loyalty and that is a loyalty to the American people (quoted in Skutnabb-Kangas and Fernandes 2008: 55–56; emphasis added).

Some Indigenous/tribal peoples and minority groups in the USA may want to assimilate culturally, to give up their distinctive cultural features, including their languages and religions, but in general most do not want cultural assimilation. On the other hand, most do want access to goods and services and the institutional benefits of the 'mainstream' society. This would be a case of agreement on structural incorporation but disagreement on the need for cultural assimilation. In particular, if stress is laid on economic and occupational life, political participation and opportunities for a good education for the children, most Indigenous/tribal peoples and minorities globally want structural incorporation, but as the 25-year negotiations preceding the United Nations Declaration on the Rights of Indigenous Peoples 2007 show, most do NOT want linguistic and cultural assimilation. If the dominant group agrees to this, it would be a case of consensus on the goals. This is unusual in today's world. An example would be Swedish-speakers in Finland, with one of the best minority protections in the world and full agreement, with both the (Finnish-speaking) majority and the minority agreeing on the goals: full incorporation politically, economically, and socially and on the labour market, but no cultural and linguistic assimilation:

> In Finland the constitution guarantees the Swedish-speaking minority [5.8% of the population] the right to satisfy its linguistic and cultural needs on the same principles as Finnish-speakers. Both the majority and the minority agree about this, and the principle finds expression in, for instance, the large number of cultural institutions in the minority's own language. For example, Finland-Swedish children can be taught through the medium of their own language right through from Kindergarten to university degree level (Skutnabb-Kangas and Toukomaa 1976: 4).[3]

This total agreement might be an ideal situation for most Indigenous/tribal peoples and minorities. It thus involves two aspects. In cultural pluralism/integration the minority (or, as often is the case, subordinated group), can choose what and how much of its own languages and cultural traits it wants to maintain and develop in the integration process where it also learns and uses as much of the dominant group's language(s) and culture(s) as it chooses, and merges and develops further the resultant evolving hybridities. In full structural incorporation there is agreement that the minority/subordinated group has the same political rights to participate as the dominant group, the same educational opportunities (not only on paper but also in terms of outcomes—and this is where MLE is required), the same chances economically, e.g. on the labour market, and where there is social justice. This might also be the ideal situation in a more just world for all peoples, also in countries which in a numerical sense consist of linguistic 'minorities' only, with no group representing over 50% of the population. Of course, political and economic hierarchies make some of the peoples minorised, regardless of the numbers they represent. Some of the hierarchies are language-based and/or have linguistic consequences.

## Trends, Processes and Variation in Reaching Consensus about Multilingual Just Societies—Possible Futures

In reality, a long, dynamic, historical process, with continuing power struggles, usually precedes a consensus model like the Finnish one. The trends in different subordinated and dominant group situations vary considerably and may include a wide range of stages. Skutnabb-Kangas and Toukomaa suggested[4] (1976: 6) that a 'typical' course of development might well be as follows (Table 19.1):

**Table 19.1.** Possible stages in a development towards agreement between dominant and subordinated groups. on the goals for the subordinated group

| | |
|---|---|
| Stage 1<br>CA SI<br>+ -<br>+ - | Suppressed minority, which the majority consider subordinate. Incorporation not allowed, and the minority culture, including language, despised. The minority has itself adopted the majority's negative picture of it. Consensus situation. |
| Stage 2<br>CA SI<br>+ -<br>- - | The minority starts to awaken and mobilise and to value its own culture and language, but still does not believe it is entitled to the same educational, social, economic and political benefits as the majority. Majority attitude unchanged. Partial conflict situation. |
| Stage 3<br>CA SI<br>+ -<br>- + | The minority begins to demand not only cultural rights but also the same educational, social, economic and political rights as the majority. Majority attitude unchanged. Total conflict situation. |
| Stage 4<br>CA SI<br>- -<br>+ - | The majority gives in to minority demands to hold on to its own culture, but does not grant the minority the same educational, social, economic and political rights as the majority. Minority attitude unchanged, the same as in Stage 3. Partial conflict situation. |
| Stage 5<br>CA SI<br>+ -<br>+ - | The majority and minority agree about cultural pluralism and the right to the same educational, social, economic and political rights as the majority [i.e. structural incorporation]. Consensus situation. |

Now we can relate the typology and the stages to situations described in this volume. All statistics from the USA tell us that Indigenous peoples, African Americans and Spanish-speaking (immigrant) minority groups (e.g. García 2009b) suffer from the results of discrimination socially and economically (see Dunbar and Skutnabb-Kangas 2008 on these results). Indicators of the results of social injustice, including low levels of formal education among these groups, show that the promises of structural incorporation have not materialised for many groups. At the same time, the linguistic and cultural assimilation demands are still as harsh as in Roosevelt's formulations. Most Indigenous peoples in North America have lost their languages (see McCarty 2009, Bear Nicholas 2009, Taylor 2009, all this volume) and recent immigrants are more or less monolingual in English by the third generation. Many groups have paid the price (i.e. tried to assimilate) but have not, at the group level, got what was promised, even if many individuals and even some groups, especially from South Asia, have 'succeeded' economically. There is revealing research by Eddie Williams (1998, 2006) that shows how education fails African children when there is an excessive concentration on English. This reinforces the analyses of Benson and Heugh (2009, this volume).

Williams studied basic education in Malawi (education in an African language, with English as a subject, for the first four years, then English-medium, with an African language as a subject) and Zambia (English-medium from day one; no African languages studied). He documents that the Malawi children in grade 5 do as well in tests of the English language, after one year of English-medium studies, as the Zambian children after 5 years of English-medium. None of them have the competence in English needed for using it as the teaching–learning language, but the Malawi children have a better chance of reaching the required competence. In addition, they are biliterate, and have learned some of the content in their own languages whereas the Zambian children cannot read or write any language well and have therefore missed most of the content teaching. Williams (2006) also reminds us that the medium of education is NOT a panacea—systemic political, economic and societal changes need to accompany changes of teaching language. In addition, teaching methods, teacher training and the entire organisation of schools has to be changed. These results echo results from immigrant minority education in many parts of the world.

Debate about whether the economic success that some groups may have achieved at the cost of being forced to assimilate has been worth it and whether there are alternatives, have not been widespread in the USA or Canada, or, for that matter, Africa, and has not led to large-scale minority organising around linguistic and cultural demands. This may still happen when people realise what the price that they have paid or are in the process of paying might mean.

Some groups/peoples in other countries have mobilised differently, starting with linguistic and cultural demands, as in Table 19.1 above. It is possible that some of them have achieved or are in the process of achieving more rights also in terms of structural incorporation than those who initially strove towards incorporation only, at the cost of language and culture (see. e.g. Aikio-Puoskari 2009, this volume, on the Saami—see also the comparison of the relative success of strategies used by, respectively, the Deaf and the Saami in Skutnabb-Kangas and Aikio-Puoskari 2003).

In many – but by no means all - Asian countries cultural and linguistic pluralism have been much more widely accepted and, in some of them (such as India and Nepal, see Agnihotri 2009, Jhingran 2009, Panda and Mohanty 2009, Hough et al. 2009, Yonjan-Tamang et al. 2009, all this volume, Awasthi 2006) codified in constitutions and other legal texts. Here we can also see that Indigenous/tribal peoples and even many national linguistic minorities are excluded from social justice in the sense of structural incorporation. The structural inequalities are often discussed in addition to linguistic, ethnic and cultural characteristics or even only in terms of class/caste hierarchies which are often language-based or coincide with language-related characteristics, as the following example shows.

For many tribals in India, the formative foundations of social identity are their language, culture and ethnicity, which are often seen as one and the same thing. In a few languages like Saora, the same word is used for land, language and ethnicity. The conceptual distinction between these concepts was less sharp and sometimes non-existent among small tribal communities. Looking back at the history of small and large tribal protests and movements in India, one finds that more often than not, the tribals began their protest essentially for land. They did not want to lose their language, but language was definitely not an issue, since they did not collectively perceive it as a resource or a marker of identity or, at least, did not consider it at risk. Their collective protests were sporadically organised in time and space, and in small groups. Only when these led to big movements, as in the case of Bodos and Santalis, were these three bases of identity conceptually distinguished by the leaders. But for the common people they were one and the same. Non-use of tribal languages in formal/official spaces like school was not construed by the speakers of that language as a process that may lead to loss of their own language and, therefore, their culture and some day their ethnicity, except where collective processes were strong. Therefore the demand for mother tongue based MLE is still weak among tribal parents. In a few states like Andhra Pradesh and Orissa, MLE was implemented in a few pilot schools because of decisions taken at the state bureaucratic level and not because the parents of the tribal children demanded it. However, one can say that many tribal parents have started noticing the benefits of MLE for their children in Orissa and Andhra and therefore have started lending emotional and moral support to these initiatives. They also started seeing language as a resource, a cultural capital. However, an offshoot of the kind of silence mentioned above was strengthening a popular view of the bureaucrats, researchers and educationists that the tribals do not want their children to be taught in their mother tongues in the early years of schooling. This is without doubt a wilful interpretation that is wrong, misleading and dangerous. It is damaging because it delays any kind of collective awareness among tribals of language, education and ethnicity through falsely signifying a mutually exclusive status for each of these three domains of (tribal) life.

Thus in many contexts worldwide Indigenous/tribal peoples and minorities live in societies which are organised so as to exclude them both from structural incorporation that might lead to more just societies socially, economically and politically, and from the right not to be discriminated against on the basis of their languages and cultures and to maintain and develop these, in addition to having access to additional languages and cultures, including the dominant ones. If we take this situation as reflecting the intentions of the dominant groups, regardless of the extent to which the intention is overtly expressed (or even when the opposite is expressed in declarations and laws), what requires analysis is to what extent Indigenous/tribal peoples and minorities agree with these goals. One might safely assume that none of them agree with the goal of *not* having the right and opportunity to achieve full structural incorporation. The three main questions relating to this topic that the authors in our volume grapple with in various ways have to do with the following:

1. Do Indigenous/tribal peoples want linguistic and cultural assimilation or not?
2. What is the role of MLE in reaching *both* goals (structural incorporation and linguistic and cultural pluralism) and how can this be achieved in various contexts?
3. To what extent do those who 'want' linguistic and cultural assimilation think that this is a necessary price to pay for structural incorporation? Do they believe that they have to choose between the two goals? Are they made to believe that it is a zero-sum game? To what extent do they know what the long-term consequences of their choices are, and is there in reality any choice?

One wonders what the future prospects are for the coming generations of Indigenous/tribal peoples, and of both national and immigrated minorities. How are elite parents in the United Arab Emirates and elsewhere in middle eastern oil states going to react when their children, brought up by Philippine nannies and attending English-medium schools, end up with 'neither good Arabic nor good English' (a worry expressed to one of us by a senior educationalist at an English-medium university)? What are those 'second generation' South Asians in the USA going to do who wish to pass on their language and culture to their children but who know too little of their language? Are Internetworks going to support the language use of those youngsters who do not have any speakers of their language in the neighbourhood? Will some of the Indigenous/tribal peoples in Africa, Asia and even Latin America follow the path of Indigenous peoples in other parts of the world who have been deprived of their languages and are now recreating (Amery 2000) or revitalising them (e.g. Huss and Lindgren, in press; Aikio-Puoskari 2009, Bear Nicholas 2009, McCarty 2009, Perez 2009, all this volume) at the same time as they are fighting both assimilation and economic and political exclusion? Or will they be able to maintain and develop their languages and cultures as resources while (successfully?) striving for economic and political self-determination? Is Europe, already the world's linguistically poorest continent (under 3% of the world's languages), succeeding in killing off all immigrant minority languages by the third generation, or will some of the rhetoric about the worth of multilingualism be extended to these languages too? And what is the role of MLE in all of this? We start with what critical MLE should do and move then to human rights, basic needs, and cost.

## Critical Indigenous pedagogy: From everyday concepts to scientific discourse, continuing to build on Indigenous/tribal knowledge

There are absolutely no two opinions on the need to ground MLE in children's everyday knowledge, experiences and perspectives. Without these it is simply futile to talk about MLE practices. Indigenous peoples' knowledge cannot be separated from their epistemological and metaphysical roots, since cultural concepts and meanings are negotiated within epistemological boundaries and metaphysical realities. However, just bringing in a couple or a sample of cultural practices and language uncritically to the classroom may not make the pedagogical practices relevant, innovative and transformative for the young children, though the whole process may superficially appear to be culturally rooted. Experience in India shows that more often than not, we either romanticised the centrality of the children's culture in teaching them or we made our claims and philosophical moorings rhetorical, and therefore only paid lip service to culture when we designed MLE for indigenous and tribal children (Panda 2004; 2006).

What we need is a pedagogical perspective for MLE which goes well beyond Indigenous pedagogy and the pedagogy of mainstream schools in today's world. Hough, Magar and Yonjan-Tamang, and Panda and Mohanty (2009, both this volume) provide a compelling case for this. They extend the case for critical pedagogy of Vygotsky, Freire and Bourdieu to MLE. Hough et al. call this *critical indigenous pedagogy* and draw our attention to a need for not only rooting MLE pedagogy in Indigenous epistemologies and values, but also to allow space for a dialectical tension between one's own Indigenous knowledge systems and Western knowledge systems. Panda and Mohanty present the perspective of CHAT (cultural historical activity theory) that locates Western knowledge (so-called rational discourse in science, mathematics and knowledge of art, literature, history etc.) as yet another cultural artefact added to the sum of artefacts that define the discursive context of the young learners from these language-disadvantaged communities. A pedagogical perspective that allows constant dialogues between these knowledge systems, privileging children's everyday knowledge only in the initial years of formal schooling, serves to awaken a critical consciousness among the learners. Subsequently, a dialectical interplay between different knowledge systems without privileging any one would help the learners rise to a level of critical consciousness in Vygotskyan terms. This would help them to participate optimally in democratic processes and to position themselves vis-à-vis more macro-level discourses, such as the neoliberal economy, patenting, privatisation, and globalisation, since these determine the quality of the political, economic and social lives even of people living in tiny remote villages (Skutnabb-Kangas 2000, Chapter 3).

MLE experts also need to reflect on strategies for building on children's everyday concepts and facilitating their progressive engagement with scientific discourse. They gradually develop the capacity to engage in meta-discursive practices in all areas of school learning such as mathematics, history, science, literature, and human ecology, firstly in their mother tongue and subsequently in the second and other languages. This is, in fact, a precursor to development of CALP (Cummins 1989, 2000, 2009, this volume). And this is possible when children begin with everyday concepts embedded in the mother tongues and rooted in cultural activities like agriculture, food, dance, music, literature, art, religion, knowledge of science, environment and history, and gradually move to scientific concepts and scientific discourse. This, however, does not mean that one form of discourse gets completely replaced by another form of discourse; rather it is more appropriate to state that one form of discourse (i.e. everyday discourse of Indigenous peoples) gets recontextualised into another form of discourse.[5] Panda and Mohanty (2009, this volume) demonstrate that this challenge is met by using the children's cultural knowledge and concepts to develop innovative classroom activities that create multiple contact points between everyday and scientific discourse. Sound, innovative and culturally rooted pedagogic practices based on theories of critical pedagogy and carried out in the children's mother tongue for at least eight years of schooling can enable children to participate in meta-discursive practices, as the Indian and Nepali evidence shows. We strongly feel that this is what the transfer from BICS to CALP is all about. Such transfer empowers all the more when MLE practices are firmly rooted, also in Linguistic Human Rights.

## MLE AND LINGUISTIC HUMAN RIGHTS

Good empowering MLE respects children's educational Linguistic Human Rights (LHRs), including the Indigenous and minority children's right to mainly mother tongue medium education for the first many years (of course with competent teaching of a dominant language as a second language). Today there is no such right in *binding* international human rights conventions (see Varennes 1996). LHRs (including the right not be discriminated against on grounds of language) are in their turn a precondition for enjoying many other human rights, in addition to facilitating access to these other human rights. The international human rights (HRs) system should also be used to protect diversities in a globalised, 'free market' world. Instead of granting market forces free range, HRs, especially economic and social rights, are to act as correctives to the free market, according to human rights lawyer Katarina Tomaševski (1996: 104).

The first international HRs treaty abolished slavery. Prohibiting slavery implied that *people* were not supposed to be treated as market commodities—something that is increasingly happening again today, even if the 1989 International Labour Organisation (ILO) Convention stipulates that *labour* should not be treated as a commodity (see Skutnabb-Kangas and Phillipson 1994 (eds), Appendix: 395). Tomaševski states that the 'purpose of international HRs law is...to overrule the law of supply and demand and remove price-tags from people and from necessities for their survival' (1996: 104). These necessities for survival, minimal prerequisites for social justice, include not only basic food and housing (which come under economic and social rights), but also basics for the sustenance of a dignified life. These have been formulated as basic civil, political and cultural rights, and they include LHRs. These genuinely universal *non-market-values-based* parts of the universal common heritage of humanity include these latter human rights (see Mireille Delmas-Marty's 2003 article 'Justice for sale. International law favours market values', where she shows that the legal protection of market values is incommensurably stronger than the protection of non-market values).

At the moment, many states are denying the HR of access to free and compulsory education by putting price-tags on it, meaning treating *education* as a commodity. More than half of the world's states have introduced school fees for basic primary education in the last decade or two, often prompted by the World Bank and International Monetary Fund's structural adjustment demands.[6] This fact has been strongly criticised by the United Nations former Special Rapporteur on the right to education, Katarina Tomaševski (2000).[7]

Even in other ways, these necessary rights are not being respected nor implemented by governments today. As we see in most papers in this volume, education through the medium of the mother tongue for Indigenous and tribal peoples and minorities is not today a human right, even in countries where it may be legally mandated or at least permitted. When Indigenous and tribal languages are being 'reduced to writing', ostensibly for mother tongue medium education purposes, by missionary organisations like the Summer Institute of Linguistics (SIL), their often covert goals are evangelical as well as linguistic (and ultimately political and economic ones). The version of the Bible, the Living Bible, which is used worldwide for evangelical purposes is considered to be a paraphrase rather than a literal translation. Words with warlike connotations are changed 'in order to pacify those tribes that would otherwise oppose their new masters', a guiding principle for the work of the SIL and the Wycliffe Bible Translators, which have been connected with funding from the CIA and Rockefeller Foundation (see http://www.watch.pair.com/cnp2.html, http://www.wayoflife.org/articles/living.htm). Thus good MLE, for social justice, and good MLE for dominant-language children, to benefit and enrich both them and the whole society, are a long way off.

## Can good MLE help in solving problems in meeting basic needs?

For hungry people, empowerment through LHRs and MLE can sometimes sound like empty words. We have heard many people say: most Indigenous peoples and minorities are struggling to meet even their basic physical needs (for food, housing, health services, jobs, land); languages and cultures are a luxury that they can start thinking of only after their basic physical needs have been met. These are false alternatives: it is not a zero-sum game. We claim that MLE is one of the necessary but not sufficient prerequisites for solving some of the basic needs problems outlined below.

When assessing basic needs, Ngozi Okonjo-Iweala, Managing Director at the World Bank states (2008: 14) that some 550 million people in sub-Saharan Africa (almost 75% of the population) and some 700 million (50%) in South Asia cannot turn on a lamp or have a fridge for the food they might have, because they have no access to electricity. Nearly 2.5 billion people worldwide use traditional biomass fuels for cooking and heating. Simply getting electricity and heating services to them and other deprived people would require an annual investment of $165 billion, and an additional $40 billion for the energy to be green (Okonjo-Iveala 2008: 14). By comparison, the military expenditure of the USA in 2007 was $547 billion, 45% of the world's military expenditure, according to SIPRI, the Stockholm International Peace Research Institute (http://www.sipri.org/contents/milap/milex/mex_data_index.html, accessed 23 August 2008; see Fernandes 2008 for some of the military activities).

The first of the eight United Nations Millennium Development Goals of halving extreme poverty by the year 2015 (see http://www.un.org/millenniumgoals/, accessed 20 July 2008) is to reduce by half the proportion of people living on less than a dollar a day, to achieve full and productive employment and decent work for all, including women and young people, and to reduce by half the proportion of people who suffer from hunger. It is clear by now that this first goal will not be met.

'As has been confirmed by research worldwide since the last century… investment in education spurs economic growth' (Ogutu 2008: 552). If economic growth in the multilingual countries worst hit by poverty is one of the answers, then this education has to support multilingual children through MLE. This is now becoming accepted wisdom even within UNESCO—all their Fact Sheets (called Languages matter!) to celebrate the International Year of Languages take, for the first time, this for granted. After UNESCO's big question[8] that we have discussed above ('how can MLE be done?'), the next question is the cost. Can states afford MLE?

## MLE IS TOO EXPENSIVE?

A further argument that we often hear is: MLE is too expensive. But multilingualism for all does represent both linguistic and cultural capital and added value. The dispossession (in the sense of Harvey 2005) of the mother tongues which is an inevitable consequence of non-MLE programmes for Indigenous/tribal and minority children leaves them without what is generally the only capital that their parents would be able to pass on to them (Skutnabb-Kangas 2000: 404-408). False economic arguments about cost serve as an excuse for of lack of support for many languages. The United Nation's 2004 *Human Development Report* links cultural liberty to language rights and human development (http://hdr.undp.org/en/reports/global/hdr2004) and argues that there is

> no more powerful means of 'encouraging' individuals to assimilate to a dominant culture than having the economic, social and political returns stacked against their mother tongue. Such assimilation is not freely chosen if the choice is between one's mother tongue and one's future.

As Kathleen Heugh (2009, this volume, and references in it) shows, even in one of the world's economically poorest countries, Ethiopia, MLE is possible, and the results show how worthwhile it is. Papua New Guinea, a country with a very small population (under 5 million), with the largest number of languages in the world, (over 700) is a relatively poor country economically. Still their elementary education (admittedly of an early-exit transitional model, so far) is being conducted in over 400 languages (Klaus 2003).

What would, then, be reasonable costs for maintaining Indigenous/tribal languages, respecting children's LHRs, and thus for MLE, and should it be the state that pays them? Grin offers through his discussion of 'market failure' (2003) excellent arguments for resisting market dominance for public or common assets/goods like cultural products:

> Even mainstream economics acknowledges that there are some cases where the market is not enough. These cases are called "market failure". When there is "market failure", the unregulated interplay of supply and demand results in an inappropriate level of production of some commodity (Grin 2003: 35).

In Grin's view, many public goods, including minority language protection, 'are typically under-supplied by market forces' (ibid.). The level becomes inappropriately low. Therefore it is the duty of the state(s) to take extra measures to increase it.

Grin (e.g. 2003: 24–27) differentiates between *moral considerations arguments* and *welfare considerations arguments* in answering the question why anybody, including society as a whole, should bother about maintaining IM languages, and pay for maintaining them. Most of the legal discourse, including the LHRs considerations, refers to moral norms about the right to live in one's own language, even if the extent of the ensuing rights is debated (2003: 24–25). In contrast,

> the emphasis of the welfare-based argument is not on whether something is morally "good" or "bad", but on whether resources are appropriately allocated. The test of an "appropriate'" allocation of resources is whether society is better off as a result of a policy (ibid., 25).

In a moral discourse, in most cases the question of what kind of rights, if any, should be granted to speakers of Indigenous and minority languages, and at what cost, seems to depend on how 'nice' states are. This is a shaky foundation for human rights, as Fernand de Varennes rightly observes (1999: 117):

> Moral or political principles, even if they are sometimes described as "human rights", are not necessarily part of international law. They are things that governments "should" do, if they are "nice", not something they "must" do. Being nice is not a very convincing argument and is less persuasive than rights and freedoms that have the weight of the law behind them.

In addition to new codified LHRs (which might be coming through UNESCO's latest plans?), we need implementation of the existing good laws and intentions —and the political will for that is mostly lacking. Neville Alexander's analysis of reasons for it (2006: 16) states:

> The problem of generating the essential political will to translate these insights into implementable policy…needs to be addressed in realistic terms. Language planners have to realize that costing of policy interventions is an essential aspect of the planning

> process itself and that no political leadership will be content to consider favourably a plan that amounts to no more than a wish list, even if it is based on the most accurate quantitative and qualitative research evidence.

What Alexander advocates necessitates the type of multidisciplinary approach that Grin represents.

In a welfare-oriented discourse one can calculate in much more hard core terms (often but not necessarily always involving cash) who the winners and losers are. Here 'the question is whether the winners, who stand to gain from a policy, can compensate the losers and still be better off' [than without the policy] (Grin 2003: 25). This is an empirical question, not a moral question. If what decides the fate of research-based suggestions for the education of Indigenous peoples and minorities is decided by market-value-based laws, both formalised and non-formalised, then the human rights, including linguistic human rights, of these people, do not stand a chance—unless the rights are formulated in terms of cost-benefit analyses that show the economic market value of both granting these rights and of mother-tongue medium education. If even human rights law is a 'marketable commodity', we as researchers have to discuss whether and how it is possible to market 'our commodity' more effectively and efficiently, while maintaining our integrity.

When assessing the empirical question of why one should maintain minority languages, Grin uses both 'positive' and 'defensive' or 'negative' arguments, but both within a welfare-considerations based paradigm. He asks both what the costs and benefits are if minority languages ARE maintained and promoted, and what the costs (and benefits) are if they are neither maintained nor promoted.

Some of Grin's promising conclusions are as follows:

- 'diversity seems to be positively, rather than negatively, correlated with welfare'
- 'available evidence indicates that the monetary costs of maintaining diversity are remarkably modest'
- devoting resources to the protection and promotion of minority cultures [and this includes languages] may help to stave off political crises whose costs would be considerably higher than that of the policies considered' [the peace-and-security argument].
- 'therefore, there are strong grounds to suppose that protecting and promoting regional and minority languages is a sound idea from a welfare standpoint, not even taking into consideration any moral argument.

We agree. The question whether states can afford MLE should rather be: can states afford *not* to implement MLE?

## Notes

1 If we use 'minorities' alone, it includes Indigenous and tribal peoples whereas the opposite is not true. In a legal sense, Indigenous and tribal peoples are NOT minorities. Indigenous and tribal peoples should minimally have all the rights that minorities have. In addition, they have other rights as Indigenous and tribal peoples—see the UN Declaration on the Rights of Indigenous Peoples (2007) at http://www.un.org/esa/socdev/unpfii/en/drip.html

2 We are fully aware that there are no numerical linguistic majorities in many countries; we use 'the dominant group' and will qualify this later.

3 In terms of Finnish and Swedish, the two official languages, a municipality is officially bilingual if the minority (Finnish- or Swedish-speaking) comes up to 8% of the population. If the municipality has been bilingual and the number of the minority population decreases, as long as the population is at least 3000 people, or, alternatively, does not go down to under 6%, the municipality remains officially bilingual. For language groups in Finland, see http://www.tilastokeskus.fi/tk/tp/tasku/suomilukuina_en.html; for details of the latest Language Act (number 423, from 2003), see http://www.finlex.fi/en/laki/kaannokset/2003/en20030423, for some background for the Act, see http://www.om.fi/uploads/i0qyauwgw18ziqq.pdf, for the Sámi Language Act (number 424), see http://www.finlex.fi/en/laki/kaannokset/2003/en20031086 and the references in Aikio-Puoskari 2009, this volume. For a general presentation, see Latomaa and Nuolijärvi 2002.

4 The table is very slightly modified from the original.

5 Here scientific discourse does not mean 'modern science knowledge' alone; rather it refers to the manner in which networks of concepts exist, interact and make possible furthering of knowledge and discourse beyond the physical limits of everyday knowledge and practices in the cognitive academic language.

6 Laws based on market values are being spread by more or less global organisations such as the WTO (World Trade Organisation) and, it seems to us, even more dangerously, WIPO (World Intellectual Property Organisation). This happens mainly through the 1994 agreement on TRAPS (trade-related aspects of intellectual property rights) which should be concerned with both market values and non-market values such as languages or Traditional Indigenous Knowledge. These laws are being developed extremely rapidly, with harsh sanctions for violations. Since even primary education is now being treated as a commodity, it can come in under TRAPS. A future nightmare scenario might see states taken to court for offering free education—this could be seen as a trade barrier by private schools.

7 See www.tomasevski.net/ and http://www.katarinatomasevski.com/.

8 See, e.g. UNESCO's *Concept Paper Protecting indigenous and endangered languages and the role of languages in promoting EFA [Education For All] in the context of sustainable development*, 24 June 2008. An early version of this is on the web at http://unesdoc.unesco.org/images/0016/001614/161495e.pdf.

# About the authors

**Rama Kant Agnihotri** is a Professor of Linguistics at the University of Delhi. He got his D. Phil. from the University of York (UK) in 1979. He has lectured at several Universities in India, Yemen, South Africa, Canada, UK, Germany, and the USA. Along with A.L. Khanna he edits the Research in Applied Linguistics Series (RAL) of Sage, with six titles published so far. His books include *Crisis of Identity: A Sociolinguistic Study of Sikh Children in Leeds* (Bahri, Delhi, 1987), *Second Language Acquisition: Socio-cultural and Linguistic Aspects of English in India* (Sage, Delhi, 1994, ed. with A.L. Khanna), *Hindi Morphology: A Word-based Description* (Motilal Banarsidass, Delhi, 1997 with Rajendra Singh), *Problematizing English in India* (Sage, Delhi, 1997, with A.L. Khanna), *Adult ESOL Learners in Great Britain* (Multilingual Matters, UK, 1998 with A.L. Khanna, M.K. Verma and S.K. Sinha), *Social Psychological Perspectives on Second Language Learning* (Sage, Delhi, 1998, with A.L. Khanna and I. Sachdev), *Noam Chomsky: The Architecture of Language* (Oxford, Delhi, 2001 ed. with N. Mukherjee and B. N. Patnaik) and *Hindi: An Essential Grammar* (Routledge, London, 2007). He was the Chairperson of the NCERT's (National Council of Educational Research and Training) National Focus Group on the teaching of Indian Languages. agniirk@yahoo.com.

**Ulla Aikio-Puoskari**, University of Oulu, Giellagas Institute and University of Lapland, Arctic Graduate School, Finland. Ulla Aikio-Puoskari has an M.A. in Social Sciences and is a Ph.D. student of the University of Oulu, Giellagas Institute, with Sámi Culture as the major subject. Since 1997 she has held a permanent position as the Educational Secretary and Director of the Office on Education and Instructional Materials for the Sámi Parliament in Finland. She has also worked as a fixed-period researcher (during 1998-2007) for the University of Lapland, the University of Oulu, Giellagas Institute and for Sámi University College, Sámi Institute. In 2001 she published a study on the Linguistic Human Rights of the Sámi in Nordic schools (in Finnish, in the series Juridica Lapponica, nr. 25, University of Lapland) and a study on the Language Rights of the Indigenous Sámi in Finland (with Merja Pentikäinen, in English in series Juridica Lapponica, nr. 26). In 2006 she published a comparative study on The Education of the Sámi in the Comprehensive Schooling of Norway, Finland and Sweden from the viewpoint of the pre-requisites of Indigenous Education (three separate publications, one in North Sámi, one in Finnish and one in Swedish). She has also published numerous articles on the status and position of Sámi Education in Nordic Countries, on Linguistic Human Rights and Sámi Language in school. ulla.aikio@samediggi.fi.

**Andrea Bear Nicholas**, Maliseet (Tobique First Nation) has held the Endowed Chair in Native Studies, at St. Thomas University, in Fredericton, New Brunswick, Canada since 1993. Professor Bear Nicholas teaches courses in native education, colonialism, aboriginal women, Mi'kmaq, Maliseet and Passamaquoddy history, and has published on the subjects of aboriginal women, treaty rights, First Nations history, education, oral traditions, and language survival. With her husband Darryl Nicholas, she has edited a huge collection of Maliseet oral traditions for publication, and is currently researching and compiling a series of community histories in the Maliseet language. She regularly serves as an expert witness in aboriginal and treaty rights cases, and with Dorothy Lazore, one of the founders of the Mohawk Immersion Program, she has developed a unique, certificate program in Native language Immersion teacher-training at St. Thomas University. abear@stu.ca.

**Carolyn J. (Carol) Benson** became interested in educational language issues while working as a Peace Corps teacher trainer in Sierra Leone in the early 1980s. Her subsequent employment and post-graduate study focused on bilingual education, teacher training, anthropology and languages. Benson holds a Ph.D. in Social Sciences and Comparative Education from the University of California, Los Angeles (1994). She is currently based at the Centre for Teaching and Learning at Stockholm University, Sweden, where she designs and facilitates courses in university pedagogy. Benson consults frequently in mother-tongue-based education in multilingual countries, and has experience in the Americas (Argentina, Bolivia, Dominican Republic, Guatemala, Mexico and USA), Europe (Sweden and Spain), Asia (Laos and Vietnam), and Africa (Angola, Cape Verde, Ethiopia, Guinea-Bissau, Guinea-Conakry, Mozambique, Niger, Nigeria, Sierra Leone and South Africa). Benson's research interests include examining the unique talents of students and teachers from bi- or multilingual contexts, determining effective implementation strategies for mother-tongue-based schooling, and exploring how use of the mother tongue may facilitate girls' education. carol.benson@upc.su.se.

**Jim Cummins** is a Canada Research Chair in the Department of Curriculum, Teaching and Learning of the Ontario Institute for Studies in Education at the University of Toronto, Canada. His research focuses on literacy development in multilingual school contexts as well as on the potential roles of technology in promoting language and literacy development. In recent years, he has been working actively with teachers to identify ways of increasing the literacy engagement of learners in multilingual school contexts. His publications include *Minority Education: From Shame to Struggle* (Multilingual Matters, 2008, co-edited with Tove Skutnabb-Kangas); *Language, Power, and Pedagogy: Bilingual Children in the Crossfire* (Multilingual Matters, 2000); *Negotiating Identities: Education for Empowerment in a Diverse Society*. (California Association for Bilingual Education, 2001); *The International Handbook of English Language Teaching* (Springer, 2007, co-edited with Chris Davison); and *Literacy, Technology, and Diversity: Teaching for Success in Changing Times* (Boston: Allyn & Bacon, 2007) (with Kristin Brown and Dennis Sayers). A full list of his publications can be found at: http://www.oise.utoronto.ca/MLC/cumminspub.htm. jcummins@oise.utoronto.ca.

**Ofelia García** is a Professor in the doctoral program in Urban Education at the Graduate Center of the City University of New York, USA. She has been Professor of Bilingual Education at Columbia University's Teachers College, and at The City College of New York; and has been Dean of the School of Education in the Brooklyn Campus of Long Island University. Among her publications are *Imagining Multilingual Schools* (with Tove Skutnabb-Kangas and Maria Torres-Guzmán), *A Reader in Bilingual Education (*with Colin Baker), *Language Loyalty, Continuity and Change: Joshua Fishman's Contributions to International Sociolinguistics* (with Rakhmiel Peltz and Harold Schiffman), and *The Multilingual Apple: Languages in New York City (*with Joshua A. Fishman). She is a Fellow of the Stellenbosch Institute for Advanced Study (STIAS) in South Africa, and has been a Fulbright Scholar, and a Spencer Fellow of the U.S. National Academy of Education. ogarcia@gc.cuny.edu.

**Kathleen Heugh** works in the field of language education policy and planning, teacher education in bilingual and multilingual contexts, literacy and language assessment and programme evaluation. She has served on several government appointed language boards, committees and task groups in South Africa. As a chief research specialist at the Human Sciences Research Council she was involved in several large-scale research projects in sub-Saharan Africa for the UNESCO Institute for Lifelong Learning, the Association for the Development of Education in Africa, the Ministry of Education in Ethiopia and Irish Aid. Currently, Kathleen serves on the editorial board of several publications and is an associate member of SUS.DIV, the Council of Europe's project on sustainable diversity. She is also the co-ordinator of English Language Courses for international students at the University of South Australia and is conducting research on the role of the mother tongue and other languages in the learning of English for educational purposes. kathleen.heugh@unisa.edu.au.

**David A. Hough** is a Professor of Communication at Shonan Institute of Technology in Fujisawa, Japan. For more than thirty years he has been active in the protection and promotion of indigenous, minority and endangered languages and cultures, language planning and policy, linguistic human rights, and the application of critical indigenous pedagogy in multilingual and multicultural education. He has advised ministries and departments of education, institutions of higher learning, local educational bodies and indigenous peoples' organisations in Canada, Nauru, Palau, Micronesia, Russia, Vietnam, Malaysia, India and Nepal. He served in 2007–2008 as Chief Technical Advisor to the Nepal Ministry Education and Sports for the country's Multilingual Education Programme. Funded by the Ministry of Foreign Affairs of Finland, the programme aims at setting up sustainable models where all non-Nepal speaking children can receive education in their mother tongue by the year 2015. In 2001, Dr Hough was awarded a three-year grant by the Ministry of Education, Sports, Science and Technology of Japan to develop multilingual instructional materials for Kosrae in the Federated States of Micronesia. In addition he has written or edited more than 50 language related textbooks, dictionaries and learning materials, and has published widely in the field. DavidA.Hough@gmail.com.

**Dhir Jhingran** is presently Asia Regional Director, Room to Read, an international NGO that works for improving school infrastructure and quality of education for underprivileged children in developing countries. He has worked extensively in the area of elementary education in the past fifteen years in several capacities—as Project Director of Education for All programmes, National Programme Manager of a UN Education Project, in policy level positions in the state and national ministries of education, and as an independent researcher. His work in education has focused on education of children belonging to vulnerable and marginalised groups, community involvement in school processes, quality of education and language policies and teaching practices. He has authored a book—*Language Disadvantage: the Learning Challenge in Primary Education,* based on an empirical research in four states of India. He has strongly advocated for and supported pilot programmes for multilingual education in several states of India as an educational administrator and policy maker. He writes regularly in journals on education and has co-authored a book (with Dr Jyotsna Jha) —*Elementary Education for the Poorest and Other Deprived Groups: The Real Challenge of Universalisation.* djhingran@gmail.com.

**Teresa L. McCarty** is the Alice Wiley Snell Professor of Education Policy Studies and Professor of Applied Linguistics at Arizona State University. She has worked with American Indian education programmes at the local, state, and national levels, including codirecting the American Indian Language Development Institute, an international programme for Indigenous teacher preparation, materials development, and language policy advocacy. Her research and teaching focus on Indigenous/ minority education, language planning and policy, critical literacy studies, and ethnographic methods in education. She has published widely on these topics, including guest editing theme issues of the *Bilingual Research Journal, Practicing Anthropology, Journal of American Indian Education,* and *International Journal of the Sociology of Language*. The former editor of *Anthropology and Education Quarterly,* she currently directs a large-scale study of the impacts of Native language loss and retention on American Indian students' school achievement. Her recent books include *Language, Literacy, and Power in Schooling* (Erlbaum, 2005), *A Place To Be Navajo* (Erlbaum, 2002), *One Voice, Many Voices – Recreating Indigenous Language Communities* (with O. Zepeda, Center for Indian Education, 2006), and *"To Remain an Indian": Lessons in Democracy from a Century of Native American Education* (with K. T. Lomawaima, Teachers College Press, 2006). Teresa.McCarty@asu.edu.

**Mahendra Kumar Mishra** is State Project Coordinator, Scheduled Castes/Scheduled Tribes and Minority Education, Orissa Primary Education Programme Authority (OPEPA), Government of Orissa, India. Dr Mishra has been engaged in the education of tribal children since 1996 in OPEPA. He has successfully implemented the activities of the community-based tribal education programme in District Primary Education Programme and laid a foundation for Multilingual Education Programme under EFA in Orissa. As a practitioner of tribal education Dr Mishra has vast field experience on indigenous knowledge of Orissa tribes. His long-term research with the tribal peoples has enabled him to understand the traditional methods of learning which he incorporates in the curriculum for tribal children. At present Dr Mishra is coordinating the Multilingual Education Programme in ten ethnic minority languages of Orissa. He has substantially contributed to the development of curriculum, instructional materials and teacher training in Multilingual Education, using local knowledge. Dr Mishra is a well-known folklorist for his commendable work on Oral Epics of Kalahandi (2007) and Saura Folklore (2005). He is the recipient of a state Literary Academy Award for his book *Folklore of Kalahandi*. mkmfolk@gmail.com.

**Ajit K. Mohanty** is a Professor of Psychology (and former Chairperson) at the Zakir Husain Centre for Educational Studies, Jawaharlal Nehru University, New Delhi. He has published in the areas of psycholinguistics, multilingualism and multilingual education focusing on education, poverty and disadvantage among linguistic minorities. He has been a Professor since 1983, and Chairperson at the Centre of Advanced Study in Psychology, Utkal University and President of the National Academy of Psychology, India (1997). He was a Fulbright Senior Scholar (University of Wisconsin, Madison), Killam Scholar (University of Alberta), Senior Fellow (Central Institute of Indian Languages), Visiting Scholar (Universities of Geneva and Chicago) and Fulbright Visiting Professor (Columbia University). His books include *Bilingualism in a Multilingual Society, Psychology of Poverty and Disadvantage* (co-editor: G. Misra) and *Perspectives on Indigenous Psychology* (co-editor: G. Misra). He has written the chapters on Language Acquisition and Bilingualism (co-author: Christian Perregaux) in the *Handbook of Cross-Cultural Psychology* (2nd edition) and on Multilingual Education in India in the *Encyclopedia of Language and Education* (eds J.Cummins & N.H. Hornberger). He is on the Editorial Boards of the *International Journal of Multilingualism, Language Policy* and *Psychological Studies*. Ajit Mohanty teaches an M.Phil. level course on Multilingualism and Education in India at JNU. ajitmohanty@gmail.com

**Iina Kaisa Nurmela** started her career working with second language teaching and newly arrived immigrant children in Finland, writing a lot of her own teaching and learning materials in Finnish as a second language due to the lack of existing ones. She is currently working in Nepal to support the development of mother-tongue-based multilingual education in the Multilingual Education Programme, Nepal, a very wonderfully challenging and inspiring setting. Iina has a M.Ed. in International Education from the University of Oulu, Finland. iina.nurmela@gmail.com.

**Minati Panda** is an Associate Professor of Social Psychology of Education at Jawaharlal Nehru University, New Delhi. She is a cultural psychologist with special interests in culture, cognition and mathematics. Her research and publications are mostly in the areas of mathematical discourse and learning, curricular and pedagogic issues and social exclusion. She has been working on mathematical notions and their socio-cultural embedding among the *Saoras* and other tribes in India. She has studied extensively over the past decade the everyday discourse and school mathematics discourse in tribal areas of Orissa and has tried to theorise the common epistemological ground of these two discursive practices in formal classrooms. Her book 'Meaning Making in Ethnomathematics' is under publication. She has been a Fulbright Senior Fellow in the Laboratory of Comparative Human Cognition, University of California, San Diego and a Witkin-Okonji awardee of the International Association of Cross-Cultural Psychology. Prior to joining JNU, Dr Panda was a Consultant for Tribal Education in the District Primary Education Programme and Faculty in Tribal Education in National Council of Educational Research and Training (NCERT). She is also the Co-Director of the MLE Plus Project. minatip@gmail.com.

**Susanne Jacobsen Pérez** worked for several years in an NGO in Peru where she trained Indigenous teachers in Intercultural Bilingual Education. Lately she has worked in Denmark in the Copenhagen Resource Centre for bilingualism and interculturality which trains teachers and does research on immigrants in the Danish education system. Her research and teaching focus on the relationship between formal education and cultural and linguistic minority groups. Susanne has an M.A. in Education and Intercultural Studies from the University of Roskilde, Denmark. susanneperez@gmail.com.

**Robert Phillipson** is a graduate of Cambridge and Leeds Universities, UK, and has a doctorate from the Faculty of Education of the University of Amsterdam. He worked for the British Council in Spain, Algeria, Yugoslavia and London before settling in Denmark. He is a Professor Emeritus at Copenhagen Business School, Denmark. His main publications include *Learner Language and Language Learning* (with Claus Færch and Kirsten Haastrup, Multilingual Matters, 1984), *Linguistic Imperialism* (Oxford University Press, 1992, also published in China and India), *Linguistic Human Rights: Overcoming Linguistic Discrimination*, edited with Tove Skutnabb-Kangas (Mouton de Gruyter, 1994); *Language: A Right and A Resource*, edited with Miklós Kontra, Tove Skutnabb-Kangas and Tibor Várady (Central European University Press, 1999); *Rights to Language: Equity, Power and Education* (as editor, Lawrence Erlbaum, 2000); *English-only Europe? Challenging Language policy* (Routledge, 2003). *Linguistic imperialism continued* (Orient Blackswan, 2009) is a collection of articles and book reviews written over a decade. He has lectured worldwide, and had attachments to universities in Australia, Hungary, India, and the UK. For details of publications, see http://www.cbs.dk/staff/phillipson. rp.isv@cbs.dk.

**G.V. Ramesh** is the MLE Linguist at the State Project Office, Sarva Shiksha Abhiyan, Andhra Pradesh, Hyderabad, India. Mr. Ramesh is a gold medalist in M.A Linguistics from Osmania University, Hyderabad. He has been working for the cause of education of tribal children in the programme of mother-tongue-based multilingual education in eight tribal languages since 2003. He is a Ph.D. student at the Department of Linguistics, Potti Sreeramulu Telugu University, Hyderabad, working on the teaching of tribal languages in primary schools in Andhra Pradesh. Mr. Ramesh is participating in and coordinating the development of textbooks and other teaching-learning materials for mother-tongue-based MLE, development of dictionaries, tribal children's literature, and teacher training modules. He is actively involved in academic monitoring of schools in tribal areas and participates in teacher training programmes as a resource person. He is involved in undertaking an evaluation study of mother-tongue-based MLE textbooks in Andhra Pradesh. rameshgumidyala@gmail.com.

**N. Upender Reddy** started his career as a teacher educator in the Government College of Teacher Education and State Council of Education, Research and Training (SCERT) and worked in various capacities in basic education projects: Andhra Pradesh Primary Education Project as Research and Evaluation Coordinator, District Primary Education Programme as Planning and Evaluation Coordinator. He is now State Pedagogy Coordinator, Sarva Shiksha Abhiyan, Andhra Pradesh, Hyderabad, India. His doctorate (Osmania University, Education) was on school effectiveness and the impact of various basic education projects in Andhra Pradesh. Dr Reddy has coordinated the development of teacher training modules in primary and upper primary stages in various curricular areas. He has coauthored a Source Book in Pupil Assessment Procedures, developed from NCERT, an Elementary Education Source Book from Telugu Academy and textbooks of Physical Science at Secondary Level, for the Government of Andhra Pradesh. Dr Reddy is presently working extensively in the field of mother-tongue-based multilingual education, undertaking evaluation and impact studies and with development of textbooks, teaching-learning materials, children's literature and dictionaries in eight tribal languages, in coordination with DIETs and colleagues from ITDAs, University Departments of Education and Linguistics. nupender@gmail.com.

**Tove Skutnabb-Kangas** is actively involved with minorities' struggle for language rights since five decades. Her main research interests are in linguistic human rights, linguistic genocide, linguicism, MLE, linguistic imperialism and the subtractive spread of English, and the relationship between linguistic and cultural diversity and biodiversity. She has written/ edited around fifty books and monographs and around 400 book chapters and scientific articles in 32 languages. Among her books in English are *Bilingualism or Not—the Education of Minorities* (1984); *Minority Education: from Shame to Struggle*, ed. with Jim Cummins (1988); *Linguistic Human Rights. Overcoming Linguistic Discrimination*, ed. with Robert Phillipson (1994); *Language: A Right and a Resource. Approaching Linguistic Human Rights* ed. with Miklós Kontra, Robert Phillipson and Tibor Várady (1999); *Linguistic Genocide in Education—or Worldwide Diversity and Human Rights?* (2000); *Sharing a World of Difference. The Earth's Linguistic, Cultural, and Biological Diversity* (with Luisa Maffi and David Harmon, 2003) and *Imagining Multilingual Schools: Language in Education and Glocalization*, ed. with Ofelia García and María Torres-Guzmán (2006). Tove has been involved in the Indian and Nepali projects described in this book since their planning phases. She lives on a small organic farm in Denmark with her husband Robert Phillipson. See http://akira.ruc.dk/~tovesk/. skutnabbkangas@gmail.com.

**Shelley K. Taylor** is an Associate Professor in the Faculty of Education at the University of Western Ontario, Canada, and a member of the graduate faculty in French Studies. She teaches graduate courses in bilingualism, minority language issues, first and second language acquisition, second language teaching and learning, and research methods. She is Chair of TESOL's 'Bilingual Education Interest Section' for the 2008-2009 term. She has conducted ethnographic research in bilingual education classrooms with multilingual learners in Canada and Denmark, documenting the need for multilingual education. Her work adopts a macro/ micro perspective, specifically focussing on the theoretical and pedagogical implications of (unexpected) minority populations enrolling in bilingual education programmes, and factors that arise in their language loss/renewal/maintenance and development. Shelley has published her work in refereed journals such as the *Canadian Modern Language Review*, and *Copenhagen Studies in Bilingualism,* and has publications in press with *The International Journal of Bilingual Education & Bilingualism, TESOL Quarterly*, and a chapter co-written with Tove Skutnabb-Kangas in the *Handbook for Social Justice in Education* (2009). She currently holds a major research grant to investigate the implementation of the common European framework in French as a second language programs in a Canadian province. tayshelley@gmail.com.

**Ram Bahadur Thapa Magar** is a member of the 2008 Constituent Assembly of Nepal, which is to draft a new constitution for the country. He also works as a lawyer, legal advisor and public notary. For more than fifteen years he has been actively involved in the foundation and running of several Indigenous associations and federations, most notably the Nepal Federation of Indigenous Nationalities. He is the editor of two Indigenous magazines and has written three textbooks in the Magar language as well as over 40 articles about language, culture, human rights and contemporary issues. He has three MAs, in Nepali literature, in Sociology, and in Political Science, and an Intermediate of Law from Tribhuvan University, Nepal. rthapamagar@gmail.com.

**Amrit Yonjan-Tamang** is the National Technical Advisor to the Multilingual Education Program in Nepal. For more than twenty years he has been actively involved in promoting linguistic diversity and linguistic human rights in Nepal. He is a member of several Indigenous language development committees and has worked as a linguistic consultant in the areas of inclusion of indigenous nationalities, development of educational materials in the Tamang language and in community mobilisation of highly marginalised groups. In addition to having published a dozen articles in various journals, he has written more than 18 books on the Tamang language and other languages of Nepal. He is the editor of four Indigenous magazines and one radio programme. He has an M.A. in Linguistics from Tribhuvan University, Nepal. amrityonjan@yahoo.com.

# References


Abadzi, Helen 2006. *Efficient Learning for the Poor. Insights from the Fontier of Cognitive Neuroscience. Directions in Development*. Washington: World Bank.

Abdulaziz, Mohamed H. 2003. 'The history of language policy in Africa with reference to language choice in education.' In Ouane, Adama (ed.). *Towards a multilingual culture of education*. Hamburg: UNESCO Institute for Education, 181–199.

Adams, Howard 1995. *A Tortured People: The Politics of Colonization.* Penticton, BC: Theytus Books.

Agnihotri, Rama Kant 1988. 'Errors as learning strategies'. *Indian Journal of Applied Linguistics* 14:1, 1–14.

Agnihotri, Rama Kant 1995. 'Multilingualism as a classroom resource'. In Heugh, Kathleen, Amanda Siegrühn and Peter Plüddemann (eds). *Multilingual Education for South Africa*. Johannesburg: Heinemann, 3–7.

Agnihotri, Rama Kant 1997. 'Multilingualism, colonialism and translation'. In Ramakrishna, Shantha (ed.). *Translation and Multilingualism: Post–colonial Contexts*. Delhi: Pencraft International, 34–46.

Agnihotri, Rama Kant 1998. 'Mixed codes and their acceptability'. In Agnihotri, Rama Kant, Amrit Lal Khanna, and Itesh Sachdev (eds). *Social Psychological Perspectives on Second Language Learning*. New Delhi: Sage Publications, 191–215.

Agnihotri, Rama Kant 2000. 'Teacher's space in the classroom'. In Mathew, Rama, R. Lalitha Eapen, and Jacob Tharu (eds). *The Language Curriculum: Dynamics of Change*. Vol I. Hyderabad: Orient Longman, 157–161.

Agnihotri, Rama Kant 2001. 'English in Indian Education'. In Daswani, Chander J. (ed.) *Language Education in Multilingual India*. New Delhi: UNESCO, 186–209.

Agnihotri, Rama Kant 2002a. 'A pre–partition partition: The case of Hindi and Urdu'. In Settar, S. and Indira Baptista Gupta (eds). *Pangs of Partition*, Vol II. New Delhi: Indian Council of Historical Research and Manohar, 29–46.

Agnihotri, Rama Kant 2002b. 'Sociolinguistic theory and practice: The Indian counterpoint'. In Singh, Rajendra (ed.) *The Yearbook of South Asian Languages and Linguistics*. New Delhi: Sage, 11–26.

Agnihotri, Rama Kant 2002c. *Half the Battle and a Quarter*. CIIL Foundation Day Lectures. Mysore: Central Institute of Indian Languages.

Agnihotri, Rama Kant 2005. 'Teaching English in a multilingual classroom'. *Fortell* 6, 2–3

Agnihotri, Rama Kant 2007a. 'Identity and multilinguality: The case of India'. In Tsui, Amy B. M. and James W. Tollefson (eds). *Language Policy, Culture, and Identity in Asian contexts*. Mahwah, NJ: Lawrence Erlbaum, 185–204.

Agnihotri, Rama Kant 2007b. 'Pedagogical paradigm rooted in multilinguality.' *International Multilingual Research Journal* 1:2, 79–88.

Agnihotri, Rama Kant 2009. 'Multilinguality and a new world order'. In Mohanty, Ajit, Minati Panda, Robert Phillipson and Tove Skutnabb–Kangas (eds). *Multilingual Education for Social Justice: Globalising the Local*. New Delhi: Orient Blackswan, 268–277.

Agnihotri, Rama Kant and Amrit Lal Khanna 1997. *Problematizing English in India*. New Delhi: Sage Publications.

Agnihotri, Rama Kant, Amrit Lal Khanna and Aditi Mukherjee 1984. 'The use of articles: errors and pedagogical implications'. *International Review of Applied Linguistics* 22:2, 115–28.

Agnihotri, Rama Kant, Janaki Rajan and Amrit Lal Khanna 2008. *Indradhanush Elementary Textbook Series: From Creation to Reception*. Delhi: State Council of Educational Research and Training.

Aikio–Puoskari, Ulla 2005. *The Education of the Sámi in the Comprehensive Schooling of Three Nordic Countries: Norway, Finland and Sweden*. In series Varsi, Magne Ove (ed.). *Gáldu čála—Journal of Indigenous Peoples Rights*, No. 1/2005. Guovdageaidnu/ Kautokeino: Resource Centre for the Rights of Indigenous Peoples. http://www.galdu.org.

Aikio–Puoskari, Ulla 2006. *Raporta sámeoahpahusas Davviriikkaid vuođđoskuvllain* [A Report on the Sámi Education in the Nordic Compulsory Schools. A Nordic Comparison from the perspective of the basic prerequisites of education]. Three separate publications (original manuscripts in North Sámi and in Finnish, translated into Swedish). Anár/ Inari: Sámi parlamentáralaš Ráđđi/Sámediggi.

Aikio–Puoskari, Ulla 2007. 'Saamelaisopetus osana suomalaista peruskoulua—kielenvaihdoksen vai revitalisaation edistäjä?' [The Sámi Education as a part of the Finnish Comprehensive School—towards a Language Shift or Revitalization?]. In Aikio, Ante and Jussi Ylikoski (eds). *Sámit, sánit, sátnehámit. Riepmočála Pekka Sammallahtii miessemánu 21. beaivve 2007.* Helsinki: Suomalais–Ugrilaisen Seuran Toimituksia = Mémoires de la Société Finno–Ougrienne, 253, 73–84.

Aikio–Puoskari, Ulla 2009. 'The ethnic revival, language and education of the Sámi, an Indigenous People, in three Nordic Countries (Finland, Norway and Sweden)'. In Mohanty, Ajit, Minati Panda, Robert Phillipson and Tove Skutnabb–Kangas (eds). *Multilingual Education for Social Justice: Globalising the Local*. New Delhi: Orient Blackswan, 216–237.

Aikio–Puoskari, Ulla and Tove Skutnabb–Kangas, Tove 2007. 'When few under 50 speak the language as a first language: linguistic (human) rights and linguistic challenges for endangered Saami languages'. In *Revitalizing the Periphery*. Raporta/Report 1/2007. Guovdageaidnu: Sámi Instituhtta, 9–63. [ISBN 978–82–7367–013–7].

Akinnaso, F. Niyi 1993. 'Policy and experiment in mother tongue literacy in Nigeria'. *International Review of Education* 39:4, 255–285.

Albó, Xavier and Amalia Anaya 2003. *Niños Alegres, Libres, Espresivos. La Audacia de la Educación Intercultural Bilingüe en Bolivia.* Cuadernos de Investigación 58. La Paz: CIPCA/UNICEF.

Alexander, Neville 1999. 'An African Renaissance Without African Languages'. *Social Dynamics*, 25:1, 1–12.

Alexander, Neville 2000. *English Unassailable but Unattainable: The Dilemma of Language Policy in South African Education.* PRAESA Occasional Papers No. 3. Cape Town: University of Cape Town. http://web.uct.ac.za/depts/praesa/OccPap3.pdf. (accessed 4 August 2008).

Alexander, Neville 2006. 'Introduction'. In *Intergovernmental Conference on Language Policies in Africa. Harare, Zimbabwe, 17–21 March 1997. Final Report.* Paris: UNESCO, Intangible Heritage Section, 9–16.

Alexander, Neville 2007. 'Some thoughts on the language issue'. *Newsletter of the Language in Education in Africa Project (LEAP)* No. 14. Cape Town: Project for the Study of Alternative Education in South Africa (PRAESA).

Alfred, Taiaiake 1999. *Peace, Power and Righteousness: an Indigenous Manifesto.* Oxford: Don Mills.

Alidou, Hassana 2004. 'Medium of instruction in post–colonial Africa'. In Tollefson, James and Amy B. M. Tsui (eds). *Medium of Instruction Policies: Which Agenda? Whose Agenda?* Mahwah, NJ: Lawrence Erlbaum, 195–214.

Alidou, Hassana, Aliou Boly, Birgit Brock–Utne, Yaya Satina Diallo, Kathleen Heugh and H. Ekkehard Wolff 2006. *Optimizing Learning and Education in Africa—The Language Factor. A Stock–taking Research on Mother Tongue and Bilingual Education in Sub–Saharan Africa.* Paris: Association for the Development of Education in Africa (ADEA). http://www.adeanet.org/biennial–2006/doc/document/B3_1_MTBLE_en.pdf.

Allen, Dawn 2007. 'Just Who Do You Think I Am? The Name–calling and Name–claiming of Newcomer Youth'. In Lyster, Roy and Sharon Lapkin (eds). Theme Issue: Multilingualism in Canadian Schools. *Canadian Journal of Applied Linguistics* 10:2, 165–176.

Amery, Rob 2000. *Warrabarna Kaurna! Reclaiming an Australian Language.* Series Multilingualism and Linguistic Diversity. Lisse: Swets & Zeitlinger.

Anderson, Benedict 1983. *Imagined communities. Reflections on the origin and spread of nationalism.* London: Verso.

Andersson, Theodore and Mildred Boyer 1978. *Bilingual Schooling in the United States.* Austin, Texas: National Educational Laboratory Publishers, 2nd edition.

Annamalai, E. 2004. 'Medium of power: The question of English in education in India'. In Tollefson, James W. and Amy B. M. Tsui (eds) *Medium of Instruction Policies. Which agenda? Whose agenda?* Mahwah, NJ: Lawrence Erlbaum, 177–194.

Anzaldúa, Gloria 1987. *How to Tame a Wild Tongue, from Borderlands/La Frontera: The New Mestiza.* San Francisco: Aunt Lute.

Armstrong, Jeannette 1996. '"Sharing One Skin": Okanagan Community'. In Mander, Jerry and Edward Goldsmith (eds). *The Case Against the Global Economy and For a Turn toward the Local*. San Francisco: Sierra Club, 460–470.

Arthur, Jo 1996. 'Code switching and collusion: Classroom interaction in Botswana primary schools'. *Linguistics and Education,* 8:1, 17–33.

Arviso, Marie and Wayne Holm 2001. ' Tséhootsooídi Ólta'gi Diné Bizaad Bihoo'aah: A Navajo Immersion Program at Fort Defiance, Arizona'. In Hinton, Leanne and Ken Hale (eds). *The Green Book of Language Revitalization in Practice*. San Diego, CA: Academic Press, 203–226.

Ascher, Marcia 1998. *Ethnomathematics: A Multicultural View of Mathematical Ideas*. Boca Raton: Chapman & Hall.

Asociaciòn Pukllasunchis 2006. *Llaqtanchispa yachayninchis. La sabiduría en las comunidades*. Iniciativas desde la escuela. Cusco, Perú: Asociaciòn Pukllasunchis.

August, Diane and Timothy Shanahan (eds) 2006. *Developing Literacy in Second–language Learners*. Mahwah, NJ: Lawrence Erlbaum.

Austin, Granville 2000 [1966]. *The Indian Constitution: Cornerstone of a Nation*. New Delhi: Oxford University Press.

Awasthi, Lava Deo 2004. *Exploring Monolingual School Practices in Multilingual Nepal*. Ph.D. thesis. Copenhagen: Danmarks Pædagogiske Universitet/ Danish University of Education.

Bacon, Francis 1620. *Novum Organum: True Directions Concerning the Interpretation of Nature*. Whitefish, MT: Kessinger Publishing.

Baetens Beardsmore, Hugo and Nathalie Lebrun 1991. 'Trilingual education in the Grand Duchy of Luxembourg'. In García, Ofelia (ed.). *Bilingual Education. Focusschrift in honor of Joshua A. Fishman on the occasion of his 65th birthday.* Volume 1. Strasbourg: John Benjamins, 107–122.

Baker, Colin 2001. 'Review of Tove Skutnabb–Kangas *Linguistic genocide in education – or worldwide diversity and human rights? Journal of Sociolinguistics* 5:2, 279–283.

Baker, Colin 2001. *Foundations of Bilingual Education and Bilingualism.* 3rd edition. Clevedon, UK: Multilingual Matters.

Baker, Colin 2006. *Foundations of Bilingual Education and Bilingualism*, 4th edition. Clevedon, UK: Multilingual Matters.

Baker, Colin and Sylvia Prys Jones 1998. *Encyclopedia of Bilingualism and Bilingual Education*. Clevedon, UK: Multilingual Matters.

Bakhtin, Michel 1981. *Dialogic Imagination: Four essays*. Austin: University of Texas Press.

Bamgbose, Ayo 2000. *Language and exclusion: The consequences of language policies in Africa*. Münster, Hamburg and London: Lit Verlag.

Bankston, C. L. and M. Zhou 1995. 'Effects of minority–language literacy on the academic achievement of Vietnamese youths in New Orleans'. *Sociology of Education* 68, 1–17.

Bartlett, Tom 2005. 'Amerindian development in Guyana: legal documents as background to discourse practice'. *Discourse & Society* 16:3, 341–364.

Battestini, Simon 1997. *Ecriture et Texte: Contribution Africaine*. Québec and Ottawa: Les Presses de l'Université Laval; Paris: Présence Africaine.

Battiste, Marie 1987. 'Mi'kmaq Linguistic Integrity: A Case Study of Mi'kmawey School'. In Barman, Jean, Yvonne Hebert and Don McCaskill (eds). *Indian Education in Canada: The Challenge*. Vancouver: University of British Columbia Press, 107–125.

Bear Nicholas, Andrea 1996. 'Integrated Education and the State of the Maliseet Language: Revitalisation or Linguicide? In Cichocki, Wladyslav, Anthony Lister, Maurice Holder and Anthony House (eds). *Papers from the 20th Annual Meeting of the Atlantic Provinces Linguistic Association*. Fredericton: Graphic Services, University of New Brunswick, Legal Deposit National Library of Canada, ISSN 0831–3520.

Bear Nicholas, Andrea 2001. 'Canada's Colonial Mission: The Great White Bird'. In Binda, K. P. and Sharilyn Calliou (eds). *Aboriginal Education in Canada: A Study in Decolonisation*. Mississaugua: Canadian Educators' Press, 9–34.

Bear Nicholas, Andrea 2003. Linguicide and Historicide in Canada. Paper given at Presence of the Past: The Third National Conference on Teaching, Learning and Communicating the History of Canada. Retrieved 13 July 2008 at http://www.praxismedia.ca/transcripts/transcript_AndreaBearNicholas.pdf

Bear Nicholas, Andrea 2007. 'The Struggle of Indigenous Peoples in Canada for Linguistic Rights and Mother tongue Schooling'. Paper given at a Seminar on Language Revitalisation, Language Rights and Indigenous Peoples, sponsored by the Galdu *Resource Centre for the Rights of Indigenous Peoples*. Elgå, Norway, February 6, 2007.

Bear Nicholas, Andrea 2009. 'Reversing Language Shift through a Native Language Immersion Teacher Training Program in Canada'. In Mohanty, Ajit, Minati Panda, Robert Phillipson and Tove Skutnabb–Kangas (eds). *Multilingual Education for Social Justice: Globalising the Local*. New Delhi: Orient Blackswan, 200–215.

Benally, AnCita and Denis Viri 2005. '*Diné Bizaad* (Navajo Language) at a Crossroads: Extinction or Renewal?' *Bilingual Research Journal*. 29:1, 85–108.

Benson, Carol 2003. 'Possibilities for educational language choice in multilingual Guinea–Bissau'. In Huss, Leena, Antoinette Camilleri and Kendall King (eds). *Transcending monolingualism: Family, school and society*. Lisse, Netherlands: Swets & Zeitlinger, 67–87.

Benson, Carol 2004a. 'Bilingual programmes as educational development: Access, quality, empowerment and equity'. Series A: General and Theoretical Paper No. 592. Essen: LAUD Linguistic Agency/University of Duisburg–Essen.

Benson, Carol 2004b. 'Do we expect too much from bilingual teachers? Bilingual teaching in developing countries'. In Brutt–Griffler, Janina and Manka Varghese (eds). *Bilingualism and language pedagogy*. Clevedon, UK: Multilingual Matters, 112–129.

Benson, Carol 2004c. *The Importance of Mother Tongue–based Schooling for Educational Quality*. Background paper for the EFA Global Monitoring Report 2005. Paris: UNESCO.

Benson, Carol 2008. 'Language "choice" in education'. In Peterson, Karin Anna and Marianne Høyen (eds), *Att sætte spor på en vandring fra Aquinas til Bourdieu—æresbog til Staf Callewaert* [Following the footsteps of a journey from Aquinas to Bourdieu—Festschrift for Staf Callewaert]. Copenhagen: Forlaget Hexis, 487–514.

Benson, Carol 2009. 'Designing effective schooling in multilingual contexts: going beyond bilingual "models"'. In Mohanty, Ajit, Minati Panda, Robert Phillipson and Tove Skutnabb-Kangas (eds). *Multilingual Education for Social Justice: Globalising the Local*. New Delhi: Orient Blackswan, 59–76.

Bernstein, Basil 1996. *Pedagogy, Symbolic Control and Identity: Theory, Research, Critique*. Lanham, MD: Rowman & Littlefield.

Bialystock, Ellen 2001. *Bilingualism in Development: Language, Literacy and Cognition*. Cambridge: Cambridge University Press.

Bloch, Carole 2006. 'Theory and Strategy of Early Literacy in Contemporary Africa with Special Reference to South Africa'. Summary paper of Ph.D. Thesis. http://www.uni–oldenburg.de/zsn/download/CaroleBloch.pdf.

Blommaert, Jan 1997. 'Ideology and Language in Tanzania: A Brief Survey'. In Herbert, Robert K. (ed.). *African Linguists at the Crossroads. Papers from the Kwaluseni 1st World Congress of African Linguistics, Swaziland, 18–22. VII. 1994*. Köln: Rüdiger Köppe, 501–510.

Blommaert, Jan 2005. 'Situating language rights: English and Swahili in Tanzania revisited'. *Journal of Sociolinguistics* 9/3, 390–417.

Blommaert, Jan 2008. 'Bernstein and poetics revisited: voice, globalization and education'. *Discourse & Society* 19:4, 425–451.

Bloom, Jennifer 2008. *Pedagogical Code-Switching: A case study of three bilingual content teachers' language practices*. Unpublished Ed.D. dissertation, Teachers College, Columbia University.

Bloor, Thomas and Wondwosen Tamrat 1996. 'Issues in Ethiopian Language Policy and Education'. *Journal of Multilingual and Multicultural Development* 17:5, 321–338.

Bogale, Berhanu and Mekonnen Alemu Gebre Yohannes 2007. 'History and Context of Language Education Policy in Ethiopia'. In Heugh, Kathleen, Carol Benson, Berhanu Bogale, Mekonnen Alemu Gebre Yohannes. *Final Report. Study on Medium of Instruction in Primary Schools in Ethiopia*. Commissioned by the Ministry of Education, September 2006. Addis Ababa: Ministry of Education of Ethiopia, 44–55.

Bonner, Donna 2001. 'Garifuna Children's Language Shame: Ethnic Stereotypes, National Affiliation, and Transnational Immigration as Factors in Language Choice in Southern Belize'. *Language in Society* 30:2, 81–96.

Bourdieu, Pierre 1991. *Language and Symbolic Power*. Cambridge: Cambridge University Press.

Bowers, C.A. 2002. *Detrás de la apariencia. Hacia la descolonización de la educación*. Lima, Perú: PRATEC.

Bransford, John D., Ann L. Brown and Rodney R. Cocking 2000. *How People Learn: Brain, Mind, Experience, and School*. Washington, DC: National Academy Press.

Brock–Utne, Birgit 2005. 'The Continued Battle over Kiswahili as the Language of Instruction in Tanzania'. In Brock-Utne, Birgit and Rodney K. Hopson (eds). *Languages of Instruction for African Emancipation: Focus on Postcolonial Contexts and Considerations*. Cape Town: CASAS, and Dar es Salaam: Mkuki na Nyota, 57–87.

Bruck, Margaret 1978. 'The Suitability of Early French Immersion Programs for the Language Disabled Child'. *Canadian Journal of Education* 3, 51–72.

Brutt–Griffler, Janina 2003. *World English: A Study of its Development*. Clevedon, UK: Multilingual Matters.

Canada 1969. Statement of the Government of Canada on Indian Policy. Ottawa: DIAND.

Canada, Parliament, House of Commons. Standing Committee on Aboriginal Affairs 1990. *You took my talk: aboriginal literacy and empowerment: fourth report of the Standing Committee on Aboriginal Affairs*. [Ken Hughes, chairperson]. Ottawa: Queen's Printer for Canada.

Canagarajah, Suresh 1999. *Resisting Linguistic Imperialism in English Teaching*. Oxford: Oxford University Press.

Canagarajah, Suresh 2005. 'Dilemmas in planning English/vernacular relations in post-colonial communities'. *Journal of Sociolinguistics* 9/3, 418–447.

Cardinal, Harold 1970. *The Unjust Society*. Edmonton: Hurtig Publishing Co.

Cazden, Courtney and Catherine E. Snow 1990. (Issue eds). *English plus: Issues in bilingual education*. The Annals of the American Academy of Political and Social Science 508.

CBS 2004. *The Population and Socio-Economics Atlas of Nepal*. Kathmandu: Survey Department and Central Bureau of Statistics.

Chamaar, Kanchediar 2007. 'A resolutely uncivilised colonial bumps into postcolonialism'. *Studies in Language and Capitalism* 2:1, 145–154.

Chambers, J. K. 2003. *Sociolinguistic Theory: Linguistic Variation and its Social Significance*. Oxford: Blackwell.

Chatry–Komarek, Marie 2003. *Literacy at Stake. Teaching Reading and Writing in African Schools*. Windhoek: Gamsberg/Macmillan.

Cluver, August 1996. 'Language Development in South Africa'. A Report written for the LANGTAG Report: *Towards a National Language Plan for South Africa*. Pretoria: Department of Arts, Culture, Science and Technology.

Cole, Michael and Yrjö Engeström 2007. 'Cultural-historical Approaches to Designing for Development'. In Valsiner, Jean and Alberto Rosa (eds). *The Cambridge Handbook of Sociocultural Psychology*. New York: Cambridge University Press, 484–507.

Collier, Virginia P. 1989. How long? A synthesis of research on academic achievement in a second language. *TESOL Quarterly* 23, 509–531.

Collier, Virginia P. and Wayne P. Thomas 1999. 'Making U.S. schools effective for English language learners, Part 2'. *TESOL Matters* 9:5, 1, 6.

Comisión de la Verdad y Reconciliación 2003. *Informe Final. Tomo I. Capítulo 1: Los periodos de la violencia*. http://www.cverdad.org.pe.

Cope, Bill and Mary Kalantzis 2000. *Multiliteracies. Literacy learning and design of social futures*. London: Routledge.

Cordero, Graciela, Luis Angel Contreras, Patricia Ames, Don Dippo, Marcela Durán, Steve Alsop, Tove Fynbo, María Luisa Sánchez, Teresa Gonzales and José García 2005. 'Innovación en la educación rural: Reporte de una experiencia de formación de profesores en servicio en el norte de Perú.' *Revista electrónica Iberoamericana sobre*

*Calidad, Eficacia y Cambio en Educación*. 3:1, 832–845. http://www.ice.deusto.es/rinace/reice/vol3n1_e/corderoetal.pdf.

Council of Europe 2000. *Common European Framework of Reference for Languages: Learning, Teaching, Assessment*. Language Policy Division, Strasbourg. *http://www.coe.int/t/dg4/linguistic/CADRE_EN.asp*

Crawford, James W. (ed.) 1992. *Language Loyalties: A Source Book on the Official English Controversy*. Chicago, IL: University of Chicago Press.

Crawhall, Nigel 1992 (ed.). *Democratically Speaking*. Cape Town: National Language Project.

Crosby, Alfred W. 1994. *Ecological Imperialism. The Biological Expansion of Europe, 900–1900*. Cambridge: Cambridge University Press.

Crystal, David 2000. *Language Death*. Cambridge: Cambridge University Press.

Cummins, Jim 1981. 'The role of primary language development in promoting educational success for language minority students'. In California State Department of Education (ed.). *Schooling and Language Minority Students: A Theoretical Framework*. Los Angeles: Evaluation, Dissemination and Assessment Center, California State University, 3–49.

Cummins, Jim 1984. *Bilingualism and Special Education: Issues in Assessment and Pedagogy*. Clevedon, UK: Multilingual Matters.

Cummins, Jim 1989. *Empowering Minority Students*. Sacramento: California Association for Bilingual Education.

Cummins, Jim 1999. 'Alternative paradigms in bilingual education research: Does theory have a place?' *Educational Researcher* 28:7, 26–32, 41.

Cummins, Jim 2000. *Language, Power and Pedagogy: Bilingual Children in the Crossfire*. Clevedon, UK: Multilingual Matters.

Cummins, Jim 2001. *Negotiating Identities: Education for Empowerment in a Diverse Society*. (2nd edition). Los Angeles, CA: California Association for Bilingual Education.

Cummins, Jim 2007. 'Rethinking Monolingual Instructional Strategies in Multilingual Classrooms'. In Lyster, Roy and Sharon Lapkin (eds). Theme Issue: Multilingualism in Canadian Schools. *Canadian Journal of Applied Linguistics*. 10:2, 221–240.

Cummins, Jim 2009. 'Fundamental psychological and sociological principles underlying educational success for linguistic minority students'. In Mohanty, Ajit, Minati Panda, Robert Phillipson and Tove Skutnabb-Kangas (eds). *Multilingual Education for Social Justice: Globalising the Local*. New Delhi: Orient Blackswan, 21–34.

Cummins, Jim, Kristin Brown and Dennis Sayers 2007. *Literacy, Technology, and Diversity: Teaching for Success in Changing Times*. Boston: Allyn & Bacon.

Cummins, Jim and Marcel Danesi 1990. *Heritage Languages: The Development and Denial of Canada's Linguistic Resources*. Toronto: Garamond Press/ Our Schools, Our Selves Education Foundation.

Cummins, Jim and Merrill Swain 1986. *Bilingualism in Education: Aspects of Theory, Research and Practice*. London: Longman.

Dagenais, Diane, Françoise Armand, Nathalie Walsh and Erica Maraillet 2007. 'L'Èveil aux Langues et la Co-construction de Connaissances sur la Diversité Linguistique'. In Lyster, Roy and Sharon Lapkin (eds). Theme Issue: Multilingualism in Canadian Schools. *Canadian Journal of Applied Linguistics* 10:2, 197–220.

Darwin, John 1999. 'Decolonization and the end of empire'. In Winks, Robin W. (ed.). *Historiography*, Vol. 5, *The Oxford history of the British Empire*. Oxford: Oxford University Press, 541–557.

Das, Chittaranjan 2007. *Letters from a Forest School.* New Delhi: National Book Trust India.

Das, Chittaranjan 2008. *Kristen Kold: A Revolutionary in Education.* Delhi: Shipra Publications.

Dasgupta, Probal 1993. *The Otherness of English: India's Auntie Tongue Syndrome,* Delhi: Oxford University Press.

Dauenhauer, Nora Marks and Richard Dauenhauer 1998. 'Technical, Emotional, and Ideological Issues in Reversing Language Shift: Examples from Southeast Alaska'. In Grenoble, Lenore A. and Lindsay J. Whaley (eds). *Endangered Languages: Current Issues and Future Prospects*. Cambridge: Cambridge University Press, 57–98.

Davis, Kanerahtahere Michelle A. 2008. 'Implementation of Language and Cultural Objectives at Kawenni:io/Gaweni:yo School'. Unpublished M.Ed. dissertation, Brock University, St. Catherines, Ontario.

de Swaan, Abram 2004. 'Endangered languages, sociolinguistics, and linguistic sentimentalism'. *European Review* 12:4, 567–580.

de Varennes, Fernand 1996. *Language, Minorities and Human Rights*. The Hague, Boston, London: Martinus Nijhoff.

de Varennes, Fernand 1999. 'The Existing Rights of Minorities in International Law'. In Kontra, Miklós, Robert Phillipson, Tove Skutnabb-Kangas and Tibor Várady (eds). *Language: A Right and a Resource. Approaching Linguistic Human Rights.* Budapest: Central European University Press, 117–146.

de Varennes, Fernand 2004. 'The right to education and minority language'. Eumap.org, at http://www.eumap.org/journal/features/2004/minority_education/edminlang/.

Del Valle, José 2000. 'Monoglossic policies for a heteroglossic culture: Misinterpreted multilingualism in modern Galicia'. *Language and Communication* 20, 105–132.

Delmas–Marty, Mireille 2003. 'Justice for sale. International law favours market values'. *Le Monde Diplomatique*, English version, August 2003.

Deloria, Vine Jr 1988. *Custer Died for Your Sins: An Indian Minifesto*. Norman: University of Oklahoma Press.

Deloria, Vine Jr 2001. 'Transitional Education'. In Deloria, Vine Jr and Daniel R. Wildcat (eds). *Power and Place: Indian Educatoin in America*. Golden, Colorado: American Indian Graduate Centre and Fulcrum Resources, 79–86.

Deloria, Vine Jr 2002. *Evolution, Creationism and Other Modern Myths: A Critical Inquiry.* Golden, Colorado: Fulcrum Publishing.

Deloria, Vine Jr 2003. *God is Red: A Native View of Religion.* Golden, Colorado: Fulcrum Publishing.

Deloria, Vine Jr and Wildcat, Daniel R. 2001. *Power and Place: Indian Education in America*. Golden, Colorado: American Indian Graduate Centre.

Department of Education 1997. *Language-in-Education Policy*. Pretoria: Department of Education.

Department of Education 2002. *Revised National Curriculum Statement Grades R–9 (Schools) Policy. Languages English—First Additional Language*. Pretoria: Department of Education.

Department of Education 2005. *Grade 6 Systemic Evaluation. National Report, South Africa*. Pretoria: Department of Education.

Det kongelige kirke–, utdannings–, og forskningsdepartement [Ministry of Church Affairs, Education and Research] 1997. *O97, Læreplanverket for den 10-årige grunnskolen* [The Curriculum for ten–years comprehensive schooling, Norway]. Oslo.

Dewey, John 1897. 'My pedagogic creed'. *School Journal* 54, 77–80.

Doughty, Catherine and Michael Long (eds). 2003. *The Handbook of Second Language Acquisition*. Maldin, Oxford, Melbourne and Berlin: Blackwell.

Dressler, Cheryl and Michael Kamil. 2006. 'First- and second-language literacy'. In August, Diane and Timothy Shanahan (eds). *Developing Literacy in Second-language Learners. Report of the National Literacy Panel on Language-Minority Children and Youth*. Mahwah, NJ: Lawrence Erlbaum, 197–238.

Dreze, Jean and Amartya Sen 2002. *India: Development and Participation*. New Delhi: Oxford University Press.

Dunbar, Robert and Skutnabb–Kangas, Tove 2008. *Forms of Education of Indigenous Children as Crimes Against Humanity?* Expert paper written for the United Nations Permanent Forum on Indigenous Issues (PFII) New York: PFII. [In PFII system: "Presented by Lars-Anders Baer, in collaboration with Robert Dunbar, Tove Skutnabb-Kangas and Ole Henrik Magga"]. http://www.un.org/esa/socdev/unpfii/documents/E_C19_2008_7.pdf

Duran Eduardo and Bonnie Duran 1995. *Native American Postcolonial Psychology*. Albany: State University of New York Press.

Dutcher, Nadine 2004. *Expanding Educational Opportunity in Linguistically Diverse Societies*. (2nd edition). Washington DC: Center for Applied Linguistics. http://www.cal.org/resources/pubs/fordreport_040501.pdf. (accessed 4 August 2008).

Dutcher, Nadine in collaboration with G. Richard Tucker 1994. 'The use of first and second languages in education. A review of international experience'. *Pacific Island Discussion Paper Series* No. 1. Washington DC: World Bank.

Eastman, Carol M. 1984. 'Language, Ethnic Identity and Change'. In Edwards, John (ed.). *Linguistic Minorities. Policies and Pluralism*. London: Academic Press, 259–276.

Edwards, John 1985. *Language, Society and Identity*. Oxford: Blackwell.

Edwards, John 1994. 'Ethnolinguistic pluralism and its discontents: A Canadian study, and some general observations'. *International Journal of the Sociology of Language* 110, 5–85.

Edwards, Viv 1998. *The Power of Babel: Teaching and Learning in Multilingual Classroom*. Stoke-on-Trent: Trentham Books.

Edwards, Viv 2004. *Multilingualism in the English-speaking World.* Clevedon, UK: Multilingual Matters.

Edwards, Viv and Lynda Pritchard Newcombe 2006. 'Back to Basics: Marketing the Benefits of Bilingualism to Parents.' In García, Ofelia, Tove Skutnabb-Kangas and María Torres-Guzmán (eds). *Imagining Multilingual Schools: Languages in Education and Glocalization.* Clevedon, UK: Multilingual Matters Ltd., 137–149.

Edwards, Viv and Sue Walker 1995. *Building Bridges: Multilingual Resources for Children.* Clevedon UK: Multilingual Matters.

Eidheim, Harald 1997. 'Ethno-Political Development among the Sámi after World War II: The Invention of Selfhood'. In Gaski, Harald (ed.). *Sámi Culture in a New Era. The Norwegian Sámi Experience.* Kárášjohka/ Karasjok: Davvi Girji OS, 29–61.

Elijah, Mary Joy 2002. *First Nations Jurisdiction Over Education. Literature Review —Language & Culture.* Prepared for The Minister's National Working Group on Education, Canada. Draft, October 30, 2002.

Engeström, Yrjö 2001. 'Expansive Learning at Work: Towards an Activity Theoretical Reconceptualisation'. *Journal of Education and Work* 14: 1, 133–156.

Erickson, Frederick 1996. 'Transformation and school success: The politics and culture of educational achievement'. In Jacob, Evelyn and Cathie Jordan (eds). *Minority Education: Anthropological perspectives.* Norwood, NJ: Ablex, 27–52.

Eriksen, Knut and Einar Niemi 1981. *Den Finske Fare. Sikkerhetsproblemer og minoritetspolitikk i Nord 1860–1940.* Oslo: Universitetsforlaget.

*Ethnologue* 2005. SIL (Summer Institute of Linguistics) International Website. http://www.ethnologue.com.

Evans, Stephen 2002. 'Macaulay's Minute revisited: Colonial language policy in nineteenth–century India'. *Journal of Multilingual and Multicultural Development* 23(4), 260–281.

Fairclough, Norman (ed.) 1992. *Critical Language Awareness.* London: Longman.

Fanon, Frantz 1963. *The Wretched of the Earth.* New York: Grove Press.

Fardon, Richard and Graham Furniss 1994. 'Introduction: frontiers and boundaries—African languages as political environment.' In Fardon, Richard and Graham Furniss (eds.). *African Languages, Development and the State.* London and New York: Routledge, 1–29.

Fernandes, Desmond 2008. *The Kurdish and Armenian Genocides: From censorship and denial to recognition?* Foreword by Robert Phillipson. Epilogue by Khatchatur I. Pilikian. Stockholm: Apec Press. [www.apec.nu; ISBN 91–89675–72–X].

Fettes, Mark 1998. 'Life on the Edge: Canada's Aboriginal Languages under Official Bilingualism.' In Ricento, Thomas and Barbara Burnaby (eds). *Language and Politics in the United States and Canada: Myths and Realities.* Mahwah, NJ: Lawrence Erlbaum Associates, 117–149.

Fishman, Joshua A. 1977. 'The social science perspective'. In *Bilingual Education: Current Perspectives.* Social Science. Arlington: Center for Applied Linguistics, 1–49.

Fishman, Joshua A. 1991. *Reversing Language Shift: Theoretical and Empirical Foundations of Assistance to Threatened Languages.* Clevedon, UK: Multilingual Matters.

Fishman, Joshua A. 2006. 'Language Policy and Language Shift'. In Ricento, Thomas (ed.). *An Introduction to Language Policy. Theory and Method.* Oxford: Blackwell, 311–328.

Fixico, Donald L. 2003. *The American Indian Mind in a Linear World.* New York: Routledge.

Foucault, Michel 1991. 'Governmentality'. In Burchell, Graham, Colin Gordon and Peter Miller (eds). *The Foucault Effect: Studies in Governmentality*. Chicago: University of Chicago Press, 87–104.

Francis, David, Nonie Lesaux and Diane August 2006. 'Language of instruction'. In August, Diane and Timothy Shanahan (eds). *Developing Literacy in Second-language Learners. Report of the National Literacy Panel on Language-Minority Children and Youth*. Mahwah, NJ: Lawrence Erlbaum, 365–413.

Francis, Lee 2003. We, The People: Young American Indians Reclaiming Their Identity. In Moore, MariJo (ed.). *Genocide of the Mind: New Native American Writing*. New York: Fawcett Books, 77–83.

Francis, Norbert and Jon Reyhner 2002. *Language and Literacy Teaching for Indigenous Education. A Bilingual Approach*. Clevedon, UK: Multilingual Matters.

Freire, Paulo 1985. *The Politics of Education: Culture, Power and Liberation.* New York: Bergen and Garvey.

Freire, Paulo 2001. *Pedagogy of freedom: Ethics, Democracy, and Civic Courage.* Critical Perspective Series. Lanham, MD: Rowman & Littlefield.

Freire, Paulo 2005 [1974]. *Education for critical consciousness*. New York: Continuum.

Fuller, Norma 2003. 'Introducciòn'. In Fuller, Norma (ed.) 2003. *Interculturalidad y política. Desafíos y posibilidades*. Lima, Perú: Red para el desarrollo de las ciencias sociales en el Perú. Lima, 9–29.

Fuller, Norma (ed.) 2003. *Interculturalidad y política. Desafíos y posibilidades*. Lima, Perú: Red para el desarrollo de las ciencias sociales en el Perú.

Gaffney, Karine S. 1999. 'Is Immersion Education Appropriate for All Students?' *ACIE Newsletter* 2:2, 1–8.

Gajo, Laurent 2007. 'Linguistic knowledge and subject knowledge: How does bilingualism contribute to subject development?' *International Journal of Bilingual Education and Bilingualism* 10:5, 563–581.

Gandhi, Gopalkrishna (ed.) 2008. *The Oxford India Gandhi: Essential Writings.* Delhi: Oxford University Press.

García, Ofelia 1993. 'Understanding the societal role of the teacher in transitional bilingual education classrooms: Lessons from sociology of language'. In Zondag, Koen (ed.). *Bilingual Education in Friesland: Facts and Prospects*. Leeuwarden: Gemeenschappelijk Centrum voor Onderwijsbegeleiding, 25–37.

García, Ofelia 2006. 'Lost in transculturation: The case of bilingual education in New York City'. In Pütz, Martin, Joshua A. Fishman and Neff-van Aertselaer, JoAnne (eds). *Along the Routes to Power: Exploration of the empowerment through language*. Berlin: Mouton de Gruyter, 157–178.

García, Ofelia 2009a. 'Education, multilingualism and translanguaging in the 21st century.' In Mohanty, Ajit, Minati Panda, Robert Phillipson and Tove Skutnabb-Kangas (eds). *Multilingual Education for Social Justice: Globalising the Local*. New Delhi: Orient Blackswan, 128–145.

García, Ofelia 2009b. *Bilingual Education in the 21st century: A Global Perspective.* London and New York: Wiley/ Blackwell.

García, Ofelia, Tove Skutnabb-Kangas and María E. Torres-Guzmán (eds) 2006. *Imagining Multilingual Schools: Language in Education and Glocalization*. Clevedon, UK: Multilingual Matters.

Gebre Yohannes, Mekonnen Alemu 2005. 'Socio-cultural and educational implications of using mother tongues as languages of instruction in Ethiopia'. M.A. Thesis. Oslo: University of Oslo.

Gee, James Paul 1990. *Social Linguistics and Literacies: Ideologies in Discourses.* New York: Falmer Press.

*General Law of Education. No. 28044*, July 2003. Lima, Perú. http://www.minedu.gob.pe/normatividad/leyes/ley_general_de_educacion2003.doc.

Genesee, Fred 1976. 'The Suitability of Immersion Programs for All Students'. *Canadian Modern Language Review* 32:5, 494–515.

Genesee, Fred 1987. *Learning Through Two Languages*. Rowley MA: Newbury House.

Genesee, Fred 2006. 'The Suitability of French Immersion for Students Who Are At Risk: Students with Special Needs and Lower Academic Ability'. Ottawa: Canadian Parents for French.

Genesee, Fred and Patricia Gándara 1999. 'Bilingual Education Programs: A Cross-National Perspective'. *Journal of Social Issues* 55, 665–685.

Genesee, Fred, Kathryn Lindholm-Leary, William M. Saunders, and Donna Christian (eds). 2006. *Educating English Language Learners: A Synthesis of Research Evidence.* New York: Cambridge University Press.

Geva, Esther 2000. 'Issues in the assessment of reading disabilities in L2 children—beliefs and research evidence'. *Dyslexia* 6, 13–28.

Giddens, Anthony 1991. *Modernity and Self-Identity. Self and Society in the Late Modern Age.* Cambridge UK: Polity Press.

Giroux, Henry A. 1997. *Pedagogy and the Politics of Hopes: Theory, Culture and Schooling*: A Critical Reader Boulder, CO: Westview Press.

Goddard, Ives 1996. 'Introduction'. In Goddard, Ives (volume ed.) and William C. Sturtevant (general ed.). *Handbook of North American Indians Vol. 17: Languages*. Washington, DC: Smithsonian Institution, 1–16.

Gonagaslaš girko-, oahpahus- ja dutkandepartementa [Ministry of Church Affairs, Education and Research] 1997. *O97S,10-jagi vuođđoskuvlla sámi oahppoplánat* [The Sámi Curriculum for ten-years comprehensive schooling, Norway]. Oslo.

Gonzalez, Andrew 1998. 'The language planning situation in the Philippines'. *Journal of Multilingual and Multicultural Development* 19, 487–525.

González, Gustavo and Lento F. Maez 1980. 'To switch or not to switch: The role of code-switching in the elementary bilingual classroom'. In Padilla, Raymond V. (ed.). *Theory in Bilingual Education: Ethnoperspectives in bilingual education research* (Vol. II). Ypsilanti, MI: US Department of Foreign Languages and Bilingual Studies, Bilingual Programs, 125–135.

Gopal, Sarvepalli (ed.) 1980. *Jawaharlal Nehru. An anthology.* Delhi: Oxford University Press.

Gorman, Thomas 1974. 'The development of language policy in Kenya with particular reference to the educational system'. In Whiteley, Wilfred (ed.). *Language in Kenya.* Nairobi: Oxford University Press.

Government of India. 1950. *The Constitution of India*. Delhi: Govt of India.

Gramsci, Antonio 1971. *Selections from the Prison Notebooks*. Translated and edited by Hoare, Quintin and Geoffrey N. Nowell-Smith. New York: International Publishers.

Grenoble, Lenore A. and Lindsay J. Whaley 2006. *Saving Languages: An Introduction to Language Revitalisation.* Cambridge: Cambridge University Press.

Grimes, Barbara (ed.) 1992. *Ethnologue: Languages of the World* (12th edition). Dallas, TX: Summer Institute of Linguistics.

Grimes, Barbara F. 2000. *Ethnologue—Languages of the World* (14th edition, 2 volumes). Dallas, TX: SIL International. http://www.ethnologue.com/

Grin, François 2003. 'Diversity as a Paradigm, Analytical Device, and Policy Goal'. In Kymlicka, Will and Alan Patten (eds). *Language Rights and Political Theory*. Oxford: Oxford University Press, 169–188.

Grin, François 2008. The Economics of Language Education. In May, Stephen and Nancy H. Hornberger (eds). *Language Policy and Political Issues in Education.* Volume 1. *Encyclopedia of Language and Education*, 2nd edition. New York: Springer, 83–94

Guthrie, John T. 2004. 'Teaching for literacy engagement'. *Journal of Literacy Research* 36, 1–30.

Gutiérrez, Kris, Patricia Baquedano-López and Hector H. Alvarez. 2001. 'Literacy as hybridity: Moving beyond bilingualism in urban classrooms'. In Reyes, Maria de la Luz and John Halcón (eds). *The Best for our Children: Critical Perspectives on Literacy for Latino Students.* New York: Teachers College Press, 122–141.

Hakuta, Kenji 1986. *Mirror of Language: The Debate on Bilingualism*. New York: Basic Books.

Hakuta, Kenji, Yuko Goto Butler and Daria Witt 2000. *How Long Does it Take English Learners to Attain Proficiency?* Santa Barbara: University of California Linguistic Minority Research Institute.

Hamelink, Cees J. 1994. *Trends in world communication: on disempowerment and self-empowerment*. Penang: Southbound, and Third World Network.

Hare, David 2005. *Obedience, struggle and revolt. Lectures on theatre*. London: faber and faber.

Harmon, David 2002. *In Light of Our Differences: How Diversity in Nature and Culture Makes Us Human*. Washington, D.C.: The Smithsonian Institute Press.

Harvey, David 2005 [2003]. *The New Imperialism*. Oxford: Oxford University Press.

Hawthorne, Harry Bertram (ed.) 1966. *A Survey of the Contemporary Indians of Canada.* 2 vols. Ottawa: Department of Indian and Northern Affairs.

Hemara, Wharehuia 2000. *Maori Pedagogies: A View from the Literature.* Wellington: New Zealand Council for Educational Research.

Herman, Edward S. and Noam Chomsky 1988. *Manufacturing Consent: The Political Economy of the Mass Media.* New York: Pantheon Books.

Heugh, Kathleen 2000a. Giving good weight to multilingualism in South Africa. In Phillipson, Robert (ed.) *Rights to language. Equity, power and education. Celebrating the 60th Birthday of Tove Skutnabb-Kangas.* Mahwah, NJ: Lawrence Erlbaum Associates, 234–238.

Heugh, Kathleen 2000b. *The Case against Bilingual and Multilingual Education in South Africa.* PRAESA Occasional Papers No. 6. Cape Town: University of Cape Town.

Heugh, Kathleen 2002. 'The case against bilingual and multilingual education in South Africa: Laying bare the myths'. *Perspectives in Education* 20:1, 171–196.

Heugh, Kathleen 2003. *Language Policy and Democracy in South Africa.* Ph.D. dissertation. Centre for Research on Bilingualism, Stockholm University. Stockholm: Elanders Gotab.

Heugh, Kathleen 2006a. 'Introduction II—Theory and practice—Language education models in Africa: Research, design, decision-making, outcomes and costs'. In Alidou, Hassana, Aliou Boly, Birgit Brock-Utne, Yaya Satina Diallo, Kathleen Heugh and H. Ekkehard Wolff, *Optimizing Learning and Education in Africa—the Language Factor. A Stock-taking Research on Mother Tongue and Bilingual Education in Sub-Saharan Africa.* Association for the Development of Education in Africa (ADEA), 31–62. http://www.adeanet.org/biennial-2006/doc/document/B3_1_MTBLE_en.pdf. (accessed 4 August 2008).

Heugh, Kathleen 2006b. 'Theory and Practice—Language Education Models in Africa: research, design, decision-making, and outcomes'. In Alidou, Hassana, Aliou Boly, Birgit Brock–Utne, Yaya Satina Diallo, Kathleen Heugh, and H. Ekkehard Wolff. *Optimizing Learning and Education in Africa-the Language Factor. A Stock-taking Research on Mother Tongue and Bilingual Education in Sub-Saharan Africa.* Paris: Association for the Development of Education in Africa (ADEA).

Heugh, Kathleen 2007a. 'Implications of the stocktaking study of mother-tongue and bilingual education in sub-Saharan Africa: who calls which shots?' In Cuvelier, Pol, Theodorus du Plessis, Michael Meeuwis and Lut Teck (eds). *Multilingualism and Exclusion. Policy, Practice and Prospects.* Studies in Language Policy in South Africa. Pretoria: Van Schaik Publishers, 40–61.

Heugh, Kathleen 2007b. 'Language and Literacy Issues in South Africa'. In Rassool, Naz. *Global Issues in Language, Education and Development. Perspectives from Postcolonial Countries.* Series Linguistic Diversity and Language Rights. Clevedon, UK: Multilingual Matters, 187–217.

Heugh, Kathleen 2008. 'Language Policy and Education in South Africa'. In Stephen May and Nancy H. Hornberger (eds). *Language Policy and Political Issues in Education.* Volume 1, *Encyclopedia of Language and Education*, 2nd edition. New York: Springer, 355–368.

Heugh, Kathleen 2009. 'Literacy and bi/multilingual education in Africa: recovering collective memory and knowledge.' In Mohanty, Ajit, Minati Panda, Robert Phillipson and Tove Skutnabb-Kangas (eds). *Multilingual Education for Social Justice: Globalising the Local*. New Delhi: Orient Blackswan, 95–113.

Heugh, Kathleen, Carol Benson, Berhanu Bogale and Mekonnen Alemu Gebre Yohannes 2007. *Final Report. Study on Medium of Instruction in Primary Schools in Ethiopia.* Commissioned by the Ministry of Education, September 2006. Addis Ababa: Ministry of Education of Ethiopia.

Heugh, Kathleen, Gerda Diedericks, Cas H. Prinsloo, Dorethea Herbst and Lolita Winnaar 2007. *Assessment of the Language and Mathematics Skills of Grade 8 Learners in the Western Cape in 2006*. Pretoria: Human Sciences Research Council.

Hinton, Leanne 2001. 'Language Planning'. In Hinton, Leanne and Ken Hale (eds). *The Green Book of Language Revitalisation in Practice.* San Diego: Academic Press, 51–59.

Hinton, Leanne (with Matt Vera and Nancy Steel and the Advocates for Indigenous California Language Survival) 2002. *How to Keep Your Language Alive. A Commonsense Approach to One-on-One Language Learning*. Berkeley, CA: Heyday Books.

Hinton, Leanne and Ken Hale (eds) 2001. *The Green Book of Language Revitalization in Practice*. San Diego, CA: Academic Press.

Hirvonen, Vuokko 2004. *Sámi Culture and the School: Reflections by Sámi Teachers and the Realization of the Sámi School. An Evaluation Study of Reform 97*. Research Council of Norway, Saami University College. English translation by Kaija Anttonen. Kárášjohka/ Karasjok, Norway: ČálliidLágádus.

Hobsbawm, Eric and Terence Ranger (eds) 1983. *The Invention of Tradition*. Cambridge: Cambridge University Press.

Holm, Agnes and Wayne Holm 1990. 'Rock Point, A Navajo Way To Go To School: A Valediction'. *Annals of the American Academy of Philosophy and Social Science* 508, 170–184.

Holm, Agnes and Wayne Holm 1995. 'Navajo Language Education: Retrospect and Prospects'. *Bilingual Research Journal* 19:1, 141–167.

Holm, Wayne 2006. 'The "Goodness" of Bilingual Education for Native American Children'. In McCarty, Teresa L., and Ofelia Zepeda (eds). *One Voice, Many Voices —Recreating Indigenous Language Communities*. Tempe: Arizona State University Center for Indian Education, 1–46.

Hornberger Nancy 1991. 'Extending enrichment bilingual education: Revisiting typologies and redirecting policy'. In García, Ofelia (ed.) *Bilingual Education*. Focusschrift in honor of Joshua A. Fishman on the occasion of his 65th birthday. Vol. 1. Amsterdam: John Benjamins, 215–234.

Hornberger, Nancy 2003. 'Continua of biliteracy'. In Hornberger, Nancy (ed.). *Continua of Biliteracy. An Ecological Framework for Educational Policy, Research, and Practice in Multilingual Settings*. Clevedon, UK: Multilingual Matters, 3–34.

Horton, Myles and Freire, Paulo 1990. *We Make the Road by Walking*. Philadelphia: Temple University Press.

Hough, David A. 2003. 'Micronesia and Japan: Building Communities of Intercultural Praxis'. In *Proceedings: UNESCO Conference on Intercultural Education*. CD ISBN 951–39–1531–X.

Hough, David A. 2005. 'Linguistic Documentation or Critical Pedagogy in Indigenous Language Teacher Education'. Unpublished conference paper, *Language Teacher Education 2005,* Minneapolis, USA.

Hough, David, Ram Bahadur Thapa Magar and Amrit Yonjan-Tamang 2009. 'Privileging Indigenous Knowledges: Empowering MLE in Nepal'. In Mohanty, Ajit, Minati Panda, Robert Phillipson and Tove Skutnabb-Kangas (eds). *Multilingual Education for Social Justice: Globalising the Local*. New Delhi: Orient Blackswan, 146–161.

Hovens, Mart 2002. 'Bilingual education in West Africa: Does it work?' *International Journal of Bilingual Education and Bilingualism* 5:5, 249–266.

Hughes, Arthur 2003. *Testing for Language Learners*, 2nd edition. Cambridge: Cambridge University Press.

Huss, Leena 1999. *Reversing Language Shift in the Far North. Linguistic Revitalization in Northern Scandinavia and Finland.* Studia Uralica Upsaliensia 31. Uppsala: Acta Universitatis Upsaliensis.

Huss, Leena and Anna-Riitta Lindgren 2005. 'Språklig emancipation i Finland och Sverige —projektbeskrivning'. In Huss, Leena and Anna-Riitta Lindgren (eds). *Rätten till eget språk. Oikeus omaan kieleen*. Uppsala: Centrum för multietnisk forskning, Uppsala universitet, 9–24.

Huss, Leena and Anna–Riitta Lindgren, in press. 'Language and Ethnicity in Scandinavia'. In Fishman, Joshua A. and Ofelia García (eds). *Handbook of Language and Ethnic Identity*. 2nd edition. New York & Oxford: Oxford University Press.

ICSU 2002. *Science, Traditional Knowledge and Sustainable Development.* Series on Science for Sustainable Development No. 4. Compiled and edited primarily by Nakashima, Douglas and Derek Elias. UNESCO. ISSN 1683–3686.

Illich, Ivan 1981. 'Taught mother language and vernacular tongue'. In Pattanayak, Debi Prasanna 1981. *Multilingualism and Mother Tongue Education*. Delhi: Oxford University Press, 1–39.

*ILO Convention No. 169 concerning Indigenous and Tribal Peoples in Independent Countries*. http://www.unhchr.ch/html/menu3/b/62.htm, accessed 27 August 2008.

Itkonen, Tuomo 1970. *Pippinä ja pappina.* Porvoo: WSOY.

Jacobson, Rodolfo 1981. 'The implementation of a bilingual instructional model: The new concurrent approach'. In Gonzalez, Pedro (ed.). *Proceedings of the Eighth Annual International Bilingual Bicultural Education Conference at Seattle*. Rosslyn, VA: National Clearinghouse for Bilingual Education.

Jacobson, Rodolfo and Faltis, Christian (eds) 1990. *Language Distribution Issues in Bilingual Schooling*. Clevedon, UK: Multilingual Matters.

Jameison, Kathleen 1978. *Indian Women and the Law in Canada: Citizens Minus*. Ottawa: Advisory Council on the Status of Women, and Indian Rights for Indian Women.

JEP 2005. *Rapid Appraisal on Livelihood Analysis and Need Assessment of Highly Marginalized Janajatis.* Lalitpur: Nayabato, Dhobighat.

Jerome, Christian 2007. 'Community Needs Assessment for the Preservation of Migmewei Tlisuti, ms.,' Gesgapegiag, QC.

Jhingran, Dhir 2005. *Language Disadvantage: The Learning Challenge in Primary Education*. Delhi: APH Publishers.

Jhingran, Dhir 2009. 'Hundreds of home languages in the country and many in most classrooms—coping with diversity in primary education in India'. In Mohanty, Ajit, Minati Panda, Robert Phillipson and Tove Skutnabb-Kangas (eds). *Multilingual Education for Social Justice: Globalising the Local*. New Delhi: Orient Blackswan, 250–267.

Johns, Alana, and Irene Mazurkewich 2001. 'The Role of the University in the Training of Native Language Teachers: Labrador'. In Hinton, Leanne and Ken Hale (eds). *The Green Book of Language Revitalisation in Practice.* San Diego: Academic Press, 355–366.

Johnson, Florian Tom and Jennifer Legatz 2006. 'Tséhootsooí Diné Bi'ólta". *Journal of American Indian Education* 45:2, 26–33.

Jones, Steve 2000 [1994]. *The Language of the Genes*. Toronto: Harper Collins Canada.

Kaini, Prabha Devi 2007. 'Preface'. In Koirala, Bidya Nath, Anju Khadka and Rajan Khadka (eds). *Democratic Indigenous Practices of Nepal.* Kathmandu: Nepal Centre for Creative Research, 3.

Kandiah, Thiru 2001. 'Whose meanings? Probing the dialectics of English as a global language'. In Robbie Goh et al (eds). *Ariels—Departures and Returns: a Festschrift for Edwin Thumboo*. Singapore: Oxford University Press.

Kant, Immanuel 2004. *Kant Political Writings*, ed. Hans Reiss. Cambridge: Cambridge University Press.

Kenner, Charmian 2004. *Becoming Literate: Young Children Learning Different Writing Systems*. Stoke-on-Trent: Trentham Books.

Khubchandani, Lachman M. 1983. *Plural Languages, Plural Cultures: Communication, Identity, Sociopolitical Change in Contemporary India*. Honolulu: East-West Center Book. University of Hawaii Press.

Khubchandani, Lachman M. 2001. 'Language demography and language education'. In Daswani, Chander J. (ed.). *Language Education in Multilingual India.* New Delhi: UNESCO, 3–47.

Khubchandani, Lachman M. 1988 (ed.). *Language in a Plural Society*. Delhi: Motilal Banarasidass and Indian Institute of Advanced Studies, Shimla.

Ki-Zerbo, Joseph (ed.) 2003. *General History of Africa* Vol. 1 (Abridged). *Methodology and African Prehistory.* Cape Town: National Education Association (NEA) and UNESCO.

Kim, Sung Ho 2007. *Max Weber's Politics of Civil Society*. Cambridge: Cambridge University Press.

King, Cecil 1995. 'Cross Cultural Teacher Education: A First Nations' Perspective.' *Journal of Professional Studies* 3:1, 3–11.

King, Christopher R. 1994. *One Language, Two Scripts: The Hindi Movement in Nineteenth Century North India*. Bombay: Oxford University Press.

King, Kendall and Carol Benson 2004. 'Spanish and indigenous language education in the Andes'. In Tollefson, J. and Amy B. M. Tsui (eds). *Medium of Instruction Policies: Whose agenda? Which agenda?* Mahwah NJ: Lawrence Erlbaum, 241–261.

King, Kendall and Alison Mackey 2007. *The Bilingual Edge: Why, When, and How to Teach Your Child a Second Language.* New York: Collins.

Kirkness, Verna 2002. 'The Preservation and Use of our Languages'. In Burnaby, Barbara and Jon Reyhner (eds). *Indigenous Languages Across the Community*. Flagstaff, Arizona: Northern Arizona University, 17–23.

Klaus, David 2003. 'The use of indigenous languages in early basic education in Papua New Guinea: a model for elsewhere?'. *Language and Education* 17:2, 105–111.

Knockwood, Isabelle 1992. *Out of the Depths: The Experiences of Mi'kmaw Children at the Indian Residential School of Shubenacadie, Nova Scotia*. Black Point, Nova Scotia, Canada: Roseway Publishing.

Komarek, Kurt 2003. *Universal Primary Education in Multilingual Societies. Supporting its Implementation in Sub-Saharan Africa and Beyond. 25 Years of Experience in German Technical Cooperation*. Mauritius: BMZ-GTZ/ADEA.

Kosonen, Kimmo 2004. 'Language in education policy and practice in Vietnam'. Consultancy report, September 2004. Hanoi: UNICEF.

Kosonen, Kimmo 2005. 'Overview on the use of local languages in education in South-East Asia'. In *First Language First: Community-Based Literacy Programmes for Minority Language Contexts in Asia*. Bangkok: UNESCO, 3–8.

Krashen, Stephen D. 1982. *Principles and Practice in Second Language Acquisition*. Oxford: Pergamon Press.

Krashen, Stephen D. 1985. *The Input Hypothesis: Issues and Implications*. London: Longman.

Krashen, Stephen D. 1985. *The Input Hypothesis*. Oxford: Pergamon Press.

Krashen, Stephen D. 2002. 'Developing academic language: Early L1 reading and later L2 reading'. *International Journal of the Sociology of Language* 155/156, 143–151.

Krashen, Stephen D. 2004. *The Power of Reading*. (2nd edition). Portsmouth, NH: Heinemann and Westport, CT: Libraries Unlimited.

Krashen, Stephen D. and Clara Lee Brown 2005. 'The ameliorating effects of high socioeconomic status: A secondary analysis'. *Bilingual Research Journal* 29:1, 185–196.

Krashen, Stephen D. and Clara Lee Brown 2007. 'What is academic language proficiency'. *Singapore Tertiary English Teachers Society Language and Communication Review* 6:1, 1–4.

Krauss, Michael 1992. 'The world's languages in crisis'. *Language* 68:1, 4–10.

Krauss, Michael 1995. Paper at a conference of the American Association for the Advancement of Science, reported in *The Philadelphia Inquirer* 19.2.1995, p. A15.

Krauss, Michael 1998. 'The condition of Native North American languages: The need for realistic assessment and action'. *International Journal of the Sociology of Language* 132, 9–31.

Krauss, Michael, Luisa Maffi and Akira Yamamoto, Akira 2004. 'The World's Languages in Crisis: Questions, Challenges, and a Call for Action'. In Sakiyama, Osamu, Fubito Endo, Honoré Watanabe and Fumiko Sasama (eds). *Lectures on Endangered Languages 4*. Suita, Osaka: The Project "Endangered Languages of the Pacific Rim", 23–27.

Kress, Gunther 2003. *Literacy in the New Media Age*. London and New York: Routledge.

Kymlicka, Will 2003. 'Estados multiculturales y ciudadanos interculturales.' In *Realidad multilingüe y desafío intercultural*. Lima, Perú: PUCP–GTZ–MINEDU, 47–69.

L 1987:56 (Norway). *Láhka Sámedikki ja eará sámi vuoigatvuođaid hárrái (sámeláhka)/ Lov om Sametinget og andre samiske rettsforhold (sameloven).*

L 1990:78 (Norway). *Lov om endringer i Lov 12. juni 1987 nr. 56 om Sametinget og andre samiske rettsforhold (sameloven).* The amendment concerning the Sámi language in Chapter 3.

L 1998:61 (Norway). *Lov om grunnskolen og den vidaregåande opplæringa (opplæringslova)* [The Education Act].

Ladson-Billings, Gloria 1995. 'Toward a theory of culturally relevant pedagogy'. *American Educational Research Journal 32*, 465–491.

Laitin, David D. and Rob Reich 2003. 'A Liberal Democratic Approach to Language Justice'. In Kymlicka, Will and Alan Patten (eds). *Language Rights and Political Theory*. Oxford: Oxford University Press, 80–104.

Lamarre, Patricia and Diane Dagenais 2004. 'Language Practices of Trilingual Youth in Two Canadian Cities'. In Hoffman, Charlotte and Jehannes Ytsma (eds). *Trilingualism in Family, School and Community*. Clevedon, UK: Multilingual Matters, 53–74.

Lambert, Wallace E. 1975. 'Culture and language as factors in learning and education'. In Wolfgang, Aaron (ed.). *Education of Immigrant Students*. Toronto: Ontario Institute for Studies in Education, 55–83.

Lambert, Wallace E. 1984. 'An overview of issues in immersion education'. In *Studies on Immersion Education. A Collection for United States Educators*. Sacramento: California State Department of Education, 8–30.

Lambert, Wallace. E. and G. Richard Tucker 1972. *Bilingual Education of Children: The St. Lambert Experiment*. Rowley, MA: Newbury House.

Latomaa, Sirkku and Pirkko Nuolijärvi 2002. *The Language Situation in Finland. Current Issues in Language Planning* 3:2.

Lauhamaa, Pigga 2008. *Saamelaisopetussuunnitelman merkitys. Tutkimus saamelaisopetuksen organisoinnista.* Rovaniemi: University of Lapland, Faculty of Education.

Lave, Jean and Wenger, Etienne 1991. *Situated Learning: Legitimate peripheral participation*. Cambridge: Cambridge University Press.

Le Page, R. B. 1968. 'Problems of Description in Multilingual Communities'. *Transactions of the Philological Society*, 189–212.

Le Page, R. B. and Andrée Tabouret-Keller 1985. *Acts of Identity*. Cambridge: Cambridge University Press.

Leavitt, Robert M. 1979. 'Language and the Community: The Passamaquoddy Bilingual Program'. In William W. Cowan (ed.). *Papers of the Tenth Algonquian Conference*. Ottawa: Carleton University, 60–65.

Lee, Tiffany S. 2007. ' "If They Want Navajo To Be Learned, Then They Should Require It in All Schools": Navajo Teenagers' Experiences, Choices, and Demands Regarding Navajo Language'. *Wicazo Sa Review*. Spring 2007, 7–33.

Lehtola, Veli-Pekka 2002. *The Sámi People. Traditions in Transition.* Aanaar/Inari: Kustannus-Puntsi Publisher.

Leitch, David 2005. 'Canada's Native Languages: Wrongs from the Past, Rights for the Future.' Presentation at a Symposium on Immersion Education for First Nations. Fredericton, St. Thomas University, October 2005.

Letshabo, Kathleen 2002. *Technical Evaluation of Breakthrough to Literacy in Uganda.* Kampala, Uganda: UNICEF. Accessed 12 July 2008 at: http://www.unicef.org/evaldatabase/files/2002_Uganda_Literacy_rec_358398.pdf.

Lewis, Glyn E. 1977. 'Bilingualism and bilingual education—The ancient world to the Renaissance'. In Spolsky, Bernard and Robert Cooper (eds). *Frontiers of Bilingual Education.* Rowley, MA: Newbury House, 22–93.

Lin, Angel M. Y. 1996. 'Bilingualism or linguistic segregation? Symbolic domination, resistance and codeswitching in Hong Kong schools'. *Linguistics and Education* 8:1, 49–84.

Lin, Angel M. Y. 2005. 'Critical, transdisciplinary perspectives on Language-in-Education policy and practice in postcolonial contexts: the case of Hong Kong'. In Lin, Angel M. Y. and Peter W. Martin (eds). *Decolonisation, Globalisation: Language-in-education policy and practice.* Clevedon, UK: Multilingual Matters, 38–54.

Lin, Angel M. Y. and Peter W. Martin (eds) 2005. *Decolonisation, Globalisation: Language-in-Education Policy and Practice.* Clevedon, UK: Multilingual Matters.

Lindgren, Anna-Riitta 1999. ´Pohjoiskalotin vähemmistökielet. Assimilaatiosta emansipaatioon´. In Tuominen, Marja, Seija Tuulentie, Veli-Pekka Lehtola and Mervi Autti (eds). *Pohjoiset identiteetit ja mentaliteetit I, Outamaalta tunturiin.* Rovaniemi/Inari: Lapin yliopisto/Kustannus-Puntsi, 159–174.

Lindgren, Anna-Riitta 2005. 'Oikeus omaan kieleen´. In Huss, Leena and Anna-Riitta Lindgren (eds). *Rätten till eget språk. Oikeus omaan kieleen.* Uppsala: Centrum för multietnisk forskning, Uppsala universitet, 47–66.

Lindholm, Kathryn J. 1990. 'Bilingual immersion education: Criteria for Program Development.' In Padilla, Amado M., Halford H. Fairchild and Concepcion M. Valadez (eds). *Bilingual Education: Issues and Strategies.* Newbury Park: Sage, 91–105.

Lindholm-Leary, Kathryn J. 2001. *Dual Language Education.* Clevedon, UK: Multilingual Matters.

Lindholm, Kathryn J. and Zierlein Aclan 1991. 'Bilingual Proficiency as a Bridge to Academic Achievement: Results from Bilingual/Immersion Programs.' *Journal of Education,* 173(2): 99–113.

Lindholm–Leary, Kathryn J. and Borsato, Graciela 2006. 'Academic achievement'. In Genesee, Fred, Kathryn Lindholm-Leary, William Saunders, and Donna Christian (eds). *Educating English Language Learners.* New York: Cambridge University Press, 176–222.

Littlebear, Richard E. 1996. 'Preface'. In Cantoni, Gina (ed.). *Stabilizing Indigenous Languages.* Flagstaff: Northern Arizona University Center for Excellence in Education, xiii–xv.

Lomawaima, K. Tsianina and Teresa L. McCarty 2006. *'To Remain an Indian': Lessons in Democracy from a Century of Native American Education*. New York: Teachers College Press.

López, Luis Enrique 2008. 'Top-down and bottom-up: counterpoised visions of bilingual intercultural education in Latin America'. In Hornberger, Nancy H. (ed.). *Can schools save indigenous languages? Policy and practice on four continents*. New York: Palgrave Macmillan, 42–65.

López, Luis Enrique and Wolfgang Küper 2000. 'Intercultural Bilingual Education in Latin America: Balance and Perspectives.' Accessed on July 9, 2008 at http://www2.gtz.de/dokumente/bib/00-1510.pdf.

López, Luis Enrique and Carlos Rojas (eds) 2006. *La EIB en América Latina bajo examen*. La Paz, Bolivia: Plural Editores.

Lotherington, Heather 2007. 'Rewriting Traditional Tales as Multilingual Narratives at Elementary School: Problems and Progress'. In Lyster, Roy and Sharon Lapkin (eds). Theme Issue: Multilingualism in Canadian Schools. *Canadian Journal of Applied Linguistics* 10:2, 241–256.

Ludescher, Monika 1998. 'Estado e Indigenas en el Peru: Un análisis del marco legal y su aplicación.' In Küppe, Rene and Richard Pötz (eds.) 1998. *Law & Anthropology. International Yearbook for Legal Anthropology* 10, 122–264.

Luykx, Aurolyn 2000. Gender equity and inteculturalidad: The dilemma in Bolivian education. *The Journal of Latin American Anthropology* 5:2, 150–178.

Macdonald, Carol 1990. *Crossing the Threshold into Standard Three. Main Report of the Threshold Project*. Pretoria: Human Sciences Research Council.

Macdonald, Carol 2002. 'Are the children still swimming up the waterfall? A look at literacy development in the new curriculum'. *Language Matters* 33, 111–141.

Mackey, William 1970. 'A typology of bilingual education'. *Foreign Language Annals* 3, 596–608.

Mackey, William 1978. 'The importation of bilingual education models'. In Alatis, J. (ed.) *Georgetown University Round Table on Languages and Linguistics*. Washington, DC: Georgetown University Press, 1–18.

Maffi, Luisa (ed.) 2001. *On Biocultural Diversity. Linking Language, Knowledge and the Environment*. Washington, D.C.: The Smithsonian Institute Press.

Magga, Ole Henrik 1990. 'The Saami Language in Norway'. In Collis, Dirmid R. F. *Arctic Languages. An Awakening*. Paris: UNESCO, 419–436.

Magga, Ole Henrik, Ida Nicolaisen, Mililani Trask, Robert Dunbar and Tove Skutnabb–Kangas 2005. *Indigenous Children's Education and Indigenous Languages. Expert paper written for the United Nations Permanent Forum on Indigenous Issues*. New York: United Nations.

Máhttodepartementa, Sámediggi and Oahpahusdirektoráhtta/ Kunskapsdepartement, Sametinget and Utdanningsdirektorat 2006. *Máhttolokten—Sámi oahppoplánabuvttus/ Læreplanverket—Kunnskapsløftet Samisk* [The Sámi Curriculum for comprehensive schooling, Norway].

Makoni, Sinfree 2003. 'From misinvention to disinvention of language: multilingualism and the South African Constitution'. In Makoni, Sinfree, Geneva Smitherman, Arnetha Ball and Arthur K. Spears (eds). *Black Linguistics. Language, society, and Politics in Africa and the Americas*. London and New York: Routledge, 132–151.

Makoni, Sinfree and Alastair Pennycook 2005. 'Disinventing and (Re)Constituting Languages'. *Critical Inquiry In Language Studies* 2:3, 137–156.

Makoni, Sinfree and Alastair Pennycook 2007. 'Disinventing and Reconstituting Languages'. In Makoni, Sinfree and Alastair Pennycook (eds). *Disinventing and Reconstituting Languages*. Clevedon, UK: Multilingual Matters, 1–41.

Makoni, Sinfree and Pennycook, Alistair (eds). 2007. *Disinventing and Reconstituting Languages*. Clevedon, UK: Multilingual Matters.

Malone, Susan 2005. *First Language First: Community-Based Literacy Programmes for Minority Language Contexts in Asia*. Bangkok: UNESCO. http://unesdoc.unesco.org/images/0014/001402/140280e.pdf. (accessed 4 August 2008).

Manrique Gálvez, Nelson 2003. 'La mayoría invisible: los indios y la cuestión nacional.' In Karp, Eliane and Linda Lema Tucker (eds). *El tema indigena en debate: aportes para la reforma constitucional.* Lima, Perú: Despacho de la Primera Dama de la nación.

Martin–Jones, Marilyn and Saxena, Mukul 1996. 'Turn taking, power asymmetries, and the positioning of bilingual participants in classroom discourse'. *Linguistics and Education* 8:1, 105–123.

Martinet, André 1962. *A Functional View of Language*. Oxford: Clarendon Press.

Marx, Karl and Friedrich Engels [1848]. *The Communist Manifesto*. In Mendel, Arthur P. (ed.) 1961. *Essential Works of Marxism.* New York: Bantam, 13–44.

Mateene, Kahombo 1999. 'OAU's strategy for linguistic unity and multilingual education'. *Social Dynamics* 25:1, 164–178.

May, Stephen 2001. *Language and Minority Rights*. Harlow: Pearson Education.

May, Stephen 2005. 'Language rights: Moving the debate forward'. *Journal of Sociolinguistics* 9:3, 319–347.

McCarty, Teresa L. 1998. 'Schooling, Resistance, and American Indian Languages'. *International Journal of the Sociology of Language* 132, 27–41.

McCarty, Teresa L. 2002. *A Place To Be Navajo-Rough Rock and the Struggle for Self–Determination in Indigenous Schooling*. Mahwah, NJ: Lawrence Erlbaum.

McCarty, Teresa L. 2008. 'Schools as strategic tools for Indigenous language revitalization: Lessons from Native America'. In Hornberger, Nancy H. (ed.). *Can Schools Save Indigenous Languages? Policy and Practice on Four Continents*. New York: Palgrave Macmillan, 161–182.

McCarty, Teresa L. 2009. 'Empowering Indigenous Languages—What can be learned from Native American experiences?' In Mohanty, Ajit, Minati Panda, Robert Phillipson and Tove Skutnabb-Kangas (eds). *Multilingual Education for Social Justice: Globalising the Local*. New Delhi: Orient Blackswan, 114–127.

McCarty, Teresa L., Mary Eunice Romero-Little and Ofelia Zepeda 2006a. 'Native American Youth Discourses on Language Shift and Retention: Ideological Cross-Currents and Their Implications for Language Planning'. *International Journal of Bilingual Education and Bilingualism* 9:5, 659–677.

McCarty, Teresa L., Mary Eunice Romero-Little and Ofelia Zepeda 2006b. 'Reimagining Multilingual America: Lessons from Native American Youth'. In García, Ofelia, Tove Skutnabb-Kangas and María Torres-Guzmán (eds). *Imagining Multilingual Schools: Languages in Education and Glocalization*. Clevedon, UK: Multilingual Matters, 91–110.

McCarty, Teresa L. and Lucille J. Watahomigie 2004. 'Language and Literacy in American Indian and Alaska Native Communities'. In Pérez, Bertha (ed.). *Sociocultural Contexts of Language and Literacy* (2nd edition). Mahwah, NJ: Lawrence Erlbaum, 79–110.

McCarty, Teresa L. and Ofelia Zepeda (eds), with Victor Begay, Stephanie Charging Eagle, Sarah C. Moore, Larisa Warhol and Tracy M.K. Williams 2006. *One Voice, Many Voices —Recreating Indigenous Language Communities*. Tempe: Arizona State University Center for Indian Education.

McCarty, Teresa (ed.) 2005. *Language, Literacy, and Power in Schooling*. Mahwah, NJ: Lawrence Erlbaum.

McRae, Kenneth D. 1997. *Conflict and Compromise in Multilingual Societies—Finland*. Waterloo, Ontario: Wilfried Laurier University Press.

Mehan, Hugh 1979. *Learning Lessons: Social Organization in the Classroom*. Cambridge, MA: Harvard University Press.

Menk, Antje–Katrin 2000. 'Equality of Opportunity and Assimilation. Or: We German Left-wing Do-gooders and Minority Language Rights'. In Phillipson, Robert (ed.). *Rights to Language: Equity, Power and Education*. Mahwah, NJ: Lawrence Erlbaum, 122–126.

Merrit, Marilyn, Ailie Cleghorn, Jared O. Abagi and Grace Bunyi 1992. 'Socializing multilingualism: Determinants of codeswitching in Kenyan primary classrooms'. *Journal of Multilingual and Multicultural Development* 13:1–2, 103–121.

Mihesuah, Devon A. 2004. *Indigenizing the Academy: Transforming Scholarship and Empowering Communities*. Lincoln: University of Nebraska Press.

Milloy, John S. 1999. *'A National Crime': The Canadian Government and the Residential School System, 1879 to 1986*. Winnipeg, Manitoba: The University of Manitoba Press.

Minde, Henry 2005a. *Assimilation of the Sámi—Implementation and Consequences*. In Varsi, Magne Ove (ed.). *Gáldu čála—Journal of Indigenous Peoples Rights*, No. 3/2005. Guovdageaidnu/Kautokeino: Resource Centre for the Rights of Indigenous Peoples. http://www.galdu.org.

Minde, Henry 2005b. 'The Alta case: from local to the global and back again'. In Cant, Garth, Anake Goodall and Justine Inns (eds). *Discourses and Silences. Indigenous Peoples, Risks and Resistance*. Canterbury, New Zealand: Department of Geography, University of Canterbury, 13–34.

Ministry of Education of Ethiopia 1994. *Education and Training Policy of Ethiopia*. Addis Ababa: Ministry of Education of Ethiopia.

Ministry of Education, Ontario 2003. '*New Funding for ESL and Literacy Programs*'. Retrieved December 18th, 2007 at: http://www.edu.gov.on.ca/eng/funding/0304/eslfund/esl0304.html.

Ministry of Education, Ontario 2007a. 'Aboriginal Education Strategy'. Retrieved June 13th, 2008 at: http://www.edu.gov.on.ca/eng/aboriginal/supporting.html

Ministry of Education, Ontario 2007b. 'Ontario First Nation, Métis, and Inuit Education Policy Framework'. Toronto: Aboriginal Education Office, MEO. Retrieved June 13th, 2008 at: www.edu.gov.on.ca/eng/aboriginal/fnmi**Framework**.pdf

Ministry of Human Resource Development (Department of Secondary and Higher Education) 2004. *Selected Educational Statistics, 2002–2003*. New Delhi: Government of India.

Mishra, Mahendra Kumar 2006. *Cluster Approach to Tribal Education in Orissa*. Bhubaneswar: Orissa Department of Education.

Mishra, Mahendra Kumar 2008. 'Mother Tongue Based Multilingual Education in Orissa: From Theory to Practice'. Paper presented at the International Conference on Language Development, Language Revitalization and Multilingual Education in Ethnolingustic Communities, Bangkok (July 1–3).

Mohanty, Ajit K. 1989. 'Psychological consequences of mother tongue maintenance and the language of literacy for linguistic minorities in India'. *Psychology and Developing Societies* 2:1, 31–51.

Mohanty, Ajit K. 1994. *Bilingualism in a Multilingual Society. Psycho-Social and Pedagogical Implications*. Mysore: Central Institute of Indian Languages.

Mohanty, Ajit K. 2000. 'Perpetuating inequality: The disadvantage of language, minority mother tongues and related issues'. In Mohanty, Ajit K. and Girishwar Misra (eds). *Psychology of Poverty and Disadvantage*. New Delhi: Concept, 104–117.

Mohanty, Ajit K. 2003a. 'Multilingualism and multiculturalism: The context of psycholinguistic research in India'. In Vindhya, U. (ed.) *Psychology in India: Intersecting Crossroads*. New Delhi: Concept, 35–53.

Mohanty, Ajit K. 2003b. 'Psychology of Language Acquisition and Bilingualism in India: The Cultural Input'. In Berry, John W., Ramesh C. Mishra and Rama C. Tripathi (eds). *Psychology in Human and Social Development: Lessons from Diverse Cultures*. New Delhi: Sage, 86–99.

Mohanty, Ajit K. 2006. 'Multilingualism of the Unequals and Predicaments of Education in India: Mother tongue or Other Tongue? ' In García, Ofelia, Tove Skutnabb-Kangas and María E. Torres-Guzmán (eds). *Imagining Multilingual Schools: Language in Education and Glocalization*. Series: Linguistic Diversity and Language Rights. Clevedon, UK: Multilingual Matters, 262–283.

Mohanty, Ajit K. 2008a. 'Multilingual Education in India'. In Cummins, Jim and Nancy H. Hornberger (eds). Vol. 5, *Bilingual Education. Encyclopedia of Language and Education* (2nd edition). New York: Springer, 165–174.

Mohanty, Ajit K. 2008b. 'Perpetuating Inequality: Language Disadvantage and Capability Deprivation of Tribal Mother Tongue Speakers in India'. In Harbert, Wayne (ed.). *Language and Poverty*. Clevedon, UK: Multilingual Matters, 102–124.

Mohanty, Ajit K. 2009. 'Multilingual education—a bridge too far?' In Mohanty, Ajit, Minati Panda, Robert Phillipson and Tove Skutnabb-Kangas (eds). *Multilingual Education for Social Justice: Globalising the Local*. New Delhi: Orient Blackswan, 5–17.

Mohanty, Ajit K., Mahendra Kumar Mishra, N. Upender Reddy and Ramesh Gumidyala 2009. 'Overcoming the language barrier for tribal children: MLE in Andhra Pradesh and Orissa, India'. In Mohanty, Ajit, Minati Panda, Robert Phillipson and Tove Skutnabb-

Kangas (eds). *Multilingual Education for Social Justice: Globalising the Local.* New Delhi: Orient Blackswan, 278–291.

Mohanty, Ajit K. and Panda, Minati 2007. *From mother tongue to other tongue: facilitation transition in multilingual education of tribal children in India.* New Delhi: Project Proposal submitted to Bernard van Leer Foundation.

Mohanty, Ajit K., Minati Panda, Robert Phillipson and Tove Skutnabb-Kangas 2009. 'Foreword'. In Mohanty, Ajit, Minati Panda, Robert Phillipson and Tove Skutnabb-Kangas (eds). *Multilingual Education for Social Justice: Globalising the Local.* New Delhi: Orient Blackswan, 3–4.

Mohanty, Ajit K., Smaranika Panda and Babban Mishra 1999. 'Language socialization in a multilingual society'. In Saraswathi, T. S. (ed.). *Culture, Socialization and Human Development.* New Delhi: Sage, 125–144.

Mohanty, Ajit K. and Christiane Perregaux 1997. 'Language Acquisition and Bilingualism'. In Berry, John W., Piere R. Dasen and T. S. Saraswathi (eds). *Handbook of Cross-Cultural Psychology: Vol. 2, Basic processes and human development.* Boston: Allyn & Bacon, 217–253.

Mohanty, Ajit K., Minati Panda, Robert Phillipson and Tove Skutnabb-Kangas (eds) 2009. *Multilingual Education for Social Justice: Globalising the Local.* New Delhi: Orient Blackswan.

Monbiot, George 2000. *Captive state: the corporate takeover of Britain.* London: Macmillan.

Morton, H.V. 1943. *Atlantic Meeting.* London: Methuen.

Mothibeli, Agnes 2005. *Cross–Country achievement results from the SACMEQ 11 Project —2000 to 2002. A quantitative analysis of education systems in Southern and Eastern Africa.* Edusource Data News No. 49. October. Johannesburg: The Education Foundation Trust.

Mufwene, Salikoko S. 2008. *Language Evolution. Contact, Competition and Change.* London and New York: Continuum.

Mühlhäusler, Peter 1996. *Linguistic ecology. Language change and linguistic imperialism in the Pacific region.* London: Routledge.

Muyeeba, Kyangubabi C–M. 2004. 'Challenges of Making and Implementing Policy in the Multilingual State of Zambia'. *Proceedings of the Third International Conference of the Association for the Development of African Languages in Education, Science and Technology (ADALEST) and the Fifth Malawian National Language Symposium,* University of Malawi and GTZ, Malawi, 167–176. http://www.adalest.com/.

Naik, Chitra 2004. 'India's language policy in an uncertain century'. In Dias, Patrick (ed.). *Multiple languages, literacies and technologies. Mapping out concepts, analysing practices and defining positions.* New Delhi: Books for Change, 246–263.

National Clearinghouse on English Language Acquisition (NCELA) 2002. *How Many Indigenous American Languages Are Spoken in the United States? By How Many Speakers?* Retrieved July 16, 2007 from http://www.ncela.gwu.edu/expert/faq/20natlang.html

National Council of Educational Research and Training (NCERT) 1999. *Sixth All India Educational Survey: Main Report.* New Delhi: NCERT.

National Council of Educational Research and Training (NCERT) 2006. *Position Paper on the Teaching of Indian Languages*. New Delhi: NCERT.

National Council of Educational Research and Training (NCERT) 2005. *National Curriculum Framework 2005*. New Delhi: NCERT.

National Indian Brotherhood 1972. *Indian Control of Indian Education. Policy Paper presented to the Minister of Indian Affairs and Northern Development by the National Indian Brotherhood*. Ottawa.

National Language Project 1994. 'The multilingual classroom: A video'. Salt River, Cape Town: National Language Project.

Nayak, Aradhana 2007. *Classroom Achievement of Students in Mother Tongue Medium and English Medium Schools: A Comparative Study*. Unpublished M.Phil. Dissertation. Delhi: Zakir Husain Centre for Educational Studies, Jawaharlal Nehru University.

NCERT – see National Council of Educational Research and Training Educational Research and Training.

NEFIN 2004. *Training Manual*. Kathmandu: NEFIN (Nepal Federation of Indigenous Nationalities).

Nettle, Daniel and Romaine, Suzanne 2000. *Vanishing Voices: The Extinction of the World's Languages*. Oxford: Oxford University Press.

Neu, Dean and Richard Therrien 2003. *Accounting for Genocide: Canada's Bureaucratic Assault on Aboriginal People*. Blackpoint, N.S. and Winnipeg: Fernwood Publishing and Zed Books.

New London Group 1996. 'A pedagogy of multiliteracies: Designing social futures' *Harvard Educational Review* 66:1, 60–92.

Niranjana, Tejaswini 1993. *Siting Translation: History, Post-Structuralism and the Colonial Context*. Berkeley: University of California Press.

Norris, Mary Jane 2002. *Aboriginal languages in Canada: Emerging trends and perspectives on second language acquisition. Canadian Social Trends*. Ottawa: Statistics Canada—Catalogue No. 11–008.

Norton, Bonnie 2000. *Identity and Language Learning: Gender, Ethnicity and Educational Change*. London: Longman/Pearson Education.

NOU/ Norges offentlige utredninger [Norwegian Committee Reports] 1985:14. *Samisk kultur og utdanning* [The Sámi Culture and Education].

Nyati-Ramahobo, Lydia 2000. 'Language Situation in Botswana'. *Current Issues in Language Planning* 1:2, 243–300.

Nyseth, Torill and Paul Pedersen 2005. 'Globalisation from below: the revitalisation of a Coastal Sámi community in northern Norway as part of the global discourse in Indigenous Identity'. In Cant, Garth, Anake Goodall and Justine Inns (eds). *Discourses and Silences. Indigenous Peoples, Risks and Resistance*. Canterbury, New Zealand: Department of Geography, University of Canterbury, 71–85.

Obanya, Pai 1999. *The Dilemma of Education in Africa*. Dakar: UNESCO Regional Office.

Ogbu, John U. 1978. *Minority Education and Caste*. New York: Academic Press.

Ogbu, John U. 1992. 'Understanding cultural diversity and learning'. *Educational Researcher* 21, 5–14.

Ogutu, James N. 2008. 'Book review of Williams, Eddie. Bridges and Barriers—Language in African Education and Development'. *Discourse & Society* 19: 4, 549–554.

Okonjo-Iveala, Ngozi 2008. The greening of the World Bank. *Developments* 42, 14–15. [http://www.developments.org.uk].

Olthuis, Marja-Liisa 2003. 'Uhanalaisen kielen elvytys: esimerkkinä Inarinsaame'. *Virittäjä* 4/2003. Helsinki: Kotikielen seura, 568–579.

Olthuis, Marja-Liisa 2008. 'Inarinsaamen huoltoa ja elvytystä'. *Kielikello* 1/2008. Helsinki: Kotimaisten kielten tutkimuskeskus, 4–8.

Ong, Walter J. 1982. *Orality and Literacy: The Technologizing of the Word*. London: Methuen.

Organisation for Economic Cooperation and Development (OECD) 2004. *Messages from PISA 2000*. Paris: OECD.

OSCE 1996. *The Hague Recommendations Regarding the Education Rights of National Minorities & Explanatory Note*, October 1996, for the use of the OSCE High Commissioner on National Minorities, Max van der Stoel. The Hague: OSCE (Organisation for Security and Cooperation in Europe). http://www.osce.org/documents/html/pdftohtml/2700_en.pdf.html.

Ouane, Adama 2003. 'Introduction: the view from inside the linguistic jail'. In Ouane, Adama (ed.). *Towards a multilingual culture of education*. Hamburg: UNESCO Institute for Education, 1–22.

Oviedo, Gonzalo and Maffi, Luisa 2000. *Indigenous and Traditional Peoples of the World and Ecoregion Conservation. An Integrated Approach to Conserving the World's Biological and Cultural Diversity*. Gland, Switzerland: WWF International and Terralingua.

Åhren, Mattias, Martin Scheinin and John B. Henriksen 2007. *The Nordic Saami Convention: International Human Rights, Self-Determination and other Central Provisions*. In Magne Ove Varsi (ed.). *Gáldu čála—Journal of Indigenous Peoples Rights*, No. 3/2007. Guovdageaidnu/ Kautokeino: Resource Centre for the Rights of Indigenous Peoples.

Paine, Robert 1992 [1985]. 'Ethnodrama and the "Fourth World": The Saami Action Group in Norway, 1979–1981'. In Dyck, Noel (ed.). *Indigenous Peoples and the Nation-State: 'Fourth World' Politics in Canada, Australia and Norway*. Social and Economic Papers No. 14. Institute of Social and Economic Research, Memorial University of Newfoundland, Canada, 190–235.

Pajuelo, Ramón and Pablo Sandoval (eds) 2004. *Globalización y diversidad. Una mirada desde América Latina*. Lima, Perú: Instituto de Estudios Peruanos.

Pakir, Anne 1991. 'The status of English and the question of "standard" in Singapore: A Sociolinguistic Perspective.' In Tickoo, Makhan L. (ed.). *Language and Standards: Issues, Attitudes, Case Studies*. Singapore: SEAMEO Regional Language Centre, 109–130.

Panda, Minati 2004. 'Culture and Mathematics: A Case Study of Saoras'. In Chanana, Karuna (ed.). *Transformative Links between Higher Education and Basic Education: Mapping the Field*. New Delhi: Sage, 119–132.

Panda, Minati 2006. 'Mathematics and Tribal Education'. *Economic and Political Weekly*. XLI:2, 14–26.

Panda, Minati 2007. 'Saora Culture, As-if Discourse and Mathematics Learning'. In Gang Zheng, Kwok Leung and John Adair (eds). *Perspectives and Progress in Contemporary Cross-Cultural Psychology*. Beijing: China Light Industry Press, 359–369.

Panda, Minati 2008. 'Epistemic give-and-take between home and school mathematics discourse'. Paper presented at the symposium 'Application of Cultural Psychological Research', at the International Congress of Psychology, 20–25 July, 2008, Berlin.

Panda, Minati and Michael Cole 2007. '*As-if* Discourse, Intersubjectivity and Mathematics Learning in Schools: Swapping between two Discourses'. 2nd Socio-cultural Theory in Educational Research and Practice Conference, 10–11 September 2007, University of Manchester, UK. http://www.education.manchester.ac.uk/research/centres/lta/LTAResearch/SocioculturalTheoryInterestGroupScTiG.

Panda, Minati and Ajit Mohanty 2009. 'Language matters, so does culture: beyond the rhetoric of culture in multilingual education'. In Mohanty, Ajit, Minati Panda, Robert Phillipson and Tove Skutnabb-Kangas (eds). *Multilingual Education for Social Justice: Globalising the Local*. New Delhi: Orient Blackswan 295–312.

Pandit, Prabodh Bechardas 1969. 'Comments on J. J. Gumperz's paper: How can we describe and measure the behavior of bilingual groups?' In Kelly, L. G. (ed.). *Description and Measurement of Bilingualism*. Toronto: University of Toronto Press, 255–256.

Pandit, Prabodh Bechardas 1972. *India as a Sociolinguistic Area*. Poona: University of Poona.

Pandit, Prabodh Bechardas 1988. 'Towards a grammar of variation'. In Khubchandani, Lachman M. (ed.). *Language in a Plural Society*. Delhi: Motilal Banarasidass and Indian Institute of Advanced Studies, Shimla, 40–49.

Parasher, S. V. 1991. *Indian English: Functions and Forms*. New Delhi: Bahri Publications.

Parekh, Bhikhu 2001. *Gandhi: A very short introduction*. Oxford: Oxford University Press.

Parenti, Michael, at www.informationclearinghouse.info/article11635.htm, accessed on 15 January 2008.

Pasanen, Annika 2005. 'Kielipesätoiminta osana karjalan ja inarinsaamen kielen revitalisaatiota'. In Kokkonen, Paula (ed.). *Sukukansaohjelman arki. Suomalais-ugrilainen perintö ja arkipäivä*. Helsinki: Castreniaumin toimitteita 64, 67–81.

Pattanayak, Debi Prasanna 1973. *Distribution of Languages in India in States and Union Territories*. Mysore: Central Institute of Indian Languages.

Pattanayak, Debi Prasanna 1981. *Multilingualism and Mother Tongue Education*. Delhi: Oxford University Press.

Pattanayak, Debi Prasanna 1988. 'Monolingual myopia and the petals of the Indian lotus'. In Skutnabb-Kangas, Tove and Jim Cummins (eds). *Minority Education: From Shame to Struggle*. Clevedon, UK: Multilingual Matters, 379–389.

Pattanayak, Debi Prasanna 1997. *Language Curriculum for Teacher Educators*. New Delhi: National Council of Teacher Education.

Pattanayak, Debi Prasanna 2003. 'Language issues in literacy and basic education: The case of India'. In Ouane, Adama (ed.). *Towards a Multilingual Culture of Education.* Hamburg: UNESCO Institute for Education, 129–138. http://www.unesco.org/education/uie/publications/uiestud41.shtml

Patten, Alan and Will Kymlicka 2003. 'Introduction: Language Rights and Political Theory: Context, Issues, and Approaches'. In Kymlicka, Will and Alan Patten (eds). *Language Rights and Political Theory*. Oxford: Oxford University Press, 1–51.

Paulston, Christina Bratt 1994. *Linguistic Minorities in Multilingual Settings. Implications for language policies*. Amsterdam & Philadelphia: John Benjamins.

Pennycook, Alistair 1994. *The Cultural Politics of English as an International Language*. London: Longman.

Pérez, Susanne Jacobsen 2009. 'The contribution of postcolonial theory to intercultural bilingual education in Peru: an indigenous teacher training programme'. In Mohanty, Ajit, Minati Panda, Robert Phillipson and Tove Skutnabb-Kangas (eds). *Multilingual Education for Social Justice: Globalising the Local*. New Delhi: Orient Blackswan, 183–199.

Petrovic, John E. 2005. 'The conservative restoration and neoliberal defenses of bilingual education'. *Language Policy* 4:4, 395–416.

Phillipson, Robert 1992. *Linguistic Imperialism*. Oxford: Oxford University Press.

Phillipson, Robert 2003. *English-only Europe? Challenging Language Policy*. London: Routledge.

Phillipson, Robert 2004. 'Review article, English in globalization: three approaches (books by de Swaan, Block and Cameron, and Brutt-Griffler)'. *Journal of Language, Identity, and Education* 3:1, 73–84.

Phillipson, Robert 2006. 'English, a cuckoo in the European higher education nest of languages?' *European Journal of English Studies* 10:1, 13–32.

Phillipson, Robert 2007a. 'English in Europe: threat or promise?' In Nic Craith, Máiréad (ed.). *Language, power and identity politics*. Basingstoke: Palgrave Macmillan, 65–82.

Phillipson, Robert 2007b. 'Review of Angel M. Y. Lin and Peter W. Martin (eds). *Decolonisation, globalisation: Language-in-education policy and practice'*. *Studies in Second Language Acquisition* 29:1, 139–141.

Phillipson, Robert 2008a. 'The linguistic imperialism of neoliberal empire'. *Critical Inquiry in Language Studies* 5: 1, 1–43.

Phillipson, Robert 2008b. 'Lingua franca or lingua frankensteinia? English in European integration and globalisation'. *World Englishes* 27:2, Forum with seven respondents, 250–284.

Phillipson, Robert 2008c. 'Language policy and education in the European Union'. In May, Stephen and Nancy H. Hornberger (eds). *Language policy and political issues in education*. Volume 1, *Encyclopedia of Language and Education*, 2nd edition. New York: Springer, 255–265.

Phillipson, Robert 2009a. 'The tension between linguistic diversity and dominant English.' In Mohanty, Ajit, Minati Panda, Robert Phillipson and Tove Skutnabb-Kangas (eds). *Multilingual Education for Social Justice: Globalising the Local*. New Delhi: Orient Blackswan, 79–94.

Phillipson, Robert 2009b. *Linguistic Imperialism Continued.* New Delhi: Orient Blackswan.

Pieterse, Jan N. 2004. *Globalization or Empire.* New York and London: Routledge.

Pittman, Iulia 2008. 'Bilingual and Trilingual Codeswitching Between Hungarian, Romanian and English in the Speech of Two Transylvanians Living in North America'. *International Journal of Multilingualism* 5:2, 122–139.

Planning Commission 2004. *Report of the Task Group on Development of Scheduled Castes and Scheduled Tribes on Selected Agenda Items of the National Common Minimum Programme.* New Delhi: Government of India.

Poole, Steven 2007. *Unspeak. Words are Weapons*. London: Abacus (first published in 2006 by Little, Brown in London).

Portes, Alejandro and R. G. Rumbaut 2001. *Legacies: The Story of the Immigrant Second Generation.* Berkeley: University of California Press.

Prince, John Dyneley 1921. *Passamaquoddy Texts.* New York: G. E. Stechert.

ProDoc 2006. *Project Document for Finnish Technical Assistance to the Implementation of the 'Bilingual Education Programme for all non-Nepali Speaking Students of Primary Schools of Nepal'. Final Document (May 2006).* Helsinki: Ministry for Foreign Affairs of Finland.

Quijano, Anibal 2004. 'Colonialidad del poder, eurocentrismo y América Latina'. In Pajuelo, Ramón and Pablo Sandoval (eds) 2004. *Globalización y diversidad. Una mirada desde América Latina.* Lima, Perú: Instituto de Estudios Peruanos, 228–281.

Rahman, Tariq 1998. *Language and Politics in Pakistan.* Karachi: Oxford University Press.

Ram, Tulsi 1983. *Trading in Language: The Story of English in India*. Delhi: GDK Publications.

Ramirez, J. David, Sandra D. Yuen and Dena R. Ramey 1991. *Executive Summary: Final report: Longitudinal study of structured English immersion strategy, early-exit and late-exit transitional bilingual education programs for language-minority children, Submitted to the U. S. Department of Education*. San Mateo, CA: Aguirre International.

Rand, Silas Tertius 1888. *Dictionary of the Language of the Micmac Indians who reside in Nova Scotia, New Brunswick, Prince Edward Island and Newfoundland.* Halifax: Nova Scotia Printing Company.

Rasmus, Minna 2008. *'Sápmelašvuohta lea dego skeaŋka', 'Saamelaisuus on kuin lahja'. Saamelaislasten hyvinvointi ja heidän oikeuksiensa toteutuminen Suomen saamelaisalueella.* Lapsiasiavaltuutetun toimiston selvityksiä 1: 2008. Jyväskylä: Lapsiasiavaltuutettu/Mánáidáittardeaddji.

Rassool, Naz 1999. *Literacy for Sustainable Development in the Age of Information.* Clevedon: Multilingual Matters.

Rassool, Naz 2007. *Global Issues in Language, Education and Development: Perspectives from Postcolonial Countries*. Clevedon: Multilingual Matters.

Ratner, Carl 2001. 'Activity Theory and Cultural Psychology'. In Moore, Carmela C. and Holly F. Mathews (eds). *The Psychology of Cultural Experience*. Cambridge: Cambridge University Press, 68–80.

Reddy, Vijay 2006. *Mathematics and Science Achievement at South African Schools in TIMSS 2003*. Pretoria: Human Sciences Research Council.

Reeves, Cheryl, Kathleen Heugh, Cas H. Prinsloo, Carol Macdonald, Tshilidzi Netshitangani, Hassana Alidou, Gerda Diedericks and Dorethea Herbst 2008. *Evaluation of Literacy Teaching in the Primary Schools of the Limpopo Province*. For the Limpopo Department of Education and Irish Aid. Pretoria: Human Sciences Research Council in association with the Department of Language Education at the University of Limpopo.

Republic of South Africa 1996. *The Constitution of the Republic of South Africa 1996*. Cape Town: The Constitutional Assembly and the National Parliament, Republic of South Africa.

[The] Research Centre for Forest and Landscape 2008. [Skov og Landskab], Copenhagen University, report 4th January 2008, accessed 9 January 2008 at http://www.sl.life.ku.dk/Nyheder/PM_Pragtbille_tit040108.aspx?forside=true.

Reyhner, Jon, Gina Cantoni, Robert N. St. Clair and Evangeline Parsons Yazzie (eds) 1999. *Revitalizing Indigenous Languages*. Flagstaff: Northern Arizona University Center for Excellence in Education.

Ricento, Thomas and Barbara Burnaby (eds). 1998. *Language Politics in the U.S. and Canada: Myths and Realities*. Mahwah, NJ: Lawrence Erlbaum.

Richards, Merle and Barbara Burnaby 2008. 'Restoring Aboriginal Languages: Immersion and Intensive Language Program Models in Canada'. In Fortune, Tara Williams and Diane Tedick (eds). *Pathways to Multilingualism: Evolving Perspectives on Immersion Education*. Clevedon, UK: Multilingual Matters, 221–241.

Ritzer, George 1996. *The McDonaldization of Society. An Investigation into the Changing Character of Contemporary Social Life*. Revised edition. Thousand Oaks, CA/London/New Delhi: Pine Forge Press.

Romaine, Suzanne 1994. *Language in Society: An Introduction to Sociolinguistics*. Oxford: Oxford University Press.

Romero–Little, Mary Eunice, Teresa L. McCarty, Larisa Warhol and Ofelia Zepeda 2007. 'Language Policies in Practice: Preliminary Findings from a Large-Scale Study of Native American Language Shift'. *TESOL Quarterly* 41:3, 607–618.

Roosevelt, Theodore 1968 [1917]. 'The Children of the Crucible'. In *Annals of America*, vol. 14, 916–1928. Chicago: Encyclopedia Britannica, 129–31.

Rosier, Paul and Merilyn Farella 1976. 'Bilingual Education at Rock Point—Some Early Results'. *TESOL Quarterly* 10:4, 379–388.

Rothkopf, David 1997. 'In praise of cultural imperialism'. *Foreign policy*, 38–53.

Rubagumya, Casmir 1994. *Teaching and Researching Language in African Classrooms*. Clevedon, UK: Multilingual Matters.

Rubagumya, Casmir 2003. 'English medium primary schools in Tanzania: A new "linguistic market" in education?' In Brock-Utne, Birgit, Zubeida Desai and Martha Qorro (eds). *Language of Instruction in Tanzania and South Africa (LOITASA)*. Dar-es-Salaam: E and D Limited, 149–169.

Rubagumya, Casmir 2004. 'English in Africa and the emergence of Afro-Saxons: globalization or marginalization'. In Baynham, Mike, Alice Deignan and Goodith White (eds). *Applied linguistics at the interface*. London: Equinox, 133–144.

Saami information: www.samediggi.fi; www.samediggi.no; www.sametinget.se; www.samiskhs.no; www.sameskolstyrelsen.se; www.skolenettet.no; www.saamicouncil.net; www.galdu.org; www.samer.se; www.siida.fi.

Said, Edward W. 1994. *Representations of the Intellectual*. London: Vintage.

Saikia, Jayashree and Ajit K. Mohanty 2004. *The role of mother tongue medium instruction in promoting educational achievement: A study of grade four Bodo children in Assam (India)*. Manuscript.

Sample, Ian 2008. 'Evolution is making it harder to stand still'. *The Guardian Weekly*, January 4–10.2008, 32–33.

Sapir, Edward 1921. *Language: An Introduction to the Study of Speech*. New York: Harcourt, Brace and Co.

Sara, Mikkel Nils 2003. ´Árbevirolaš sámi dieđut ja máhtut sámi vuođđoskuvllas´. In Hirvonen, Vuokko (ed.). *Sámi skuvla plánain ja praktihkas. Mo dustet O97S hástalusaid? Reforpma 97 evalueren*. Kárášjohka/Karasjok and Vaasa: Research Council of Norway, Saami University College/Sámi allaskuvla and ČálliidLágádus, 121–138.

Sarangi, Srikant 2001. 'A comparative perspective on social theoretical accounts of the language-action relationship'. In Coupland, Nikolas, Srikant Sarangi and Chris Candlin (eds). *Sociolinguistics and Social Theory*. Harlow, England: Longman, 29–60.

Schermerhorn, R. A. 1970. *Comparative Ethnic Relations. A Framework for Theory and Research*. New York: Random House.

Schmied, Joseph 1991. *English in Africa: An Introduction*. London and New York: Longman.

Schumacher, E. F. 1977. *A Guide for the Perplexed*. London: Jonathan Cape.

Sema, Toinali 2008. *Classroom Achievement in Sema, Nagamese and English Medium Primary Schools in Nagaland.* Unpublished M.Phil. Dissertation. Delhi: Zakir Husain Centre for Educational Studies, Jawaharlal Nehru University.

Sen, Amartya 1982. *Poverty and Famines: An essay on entitlement and deprivation*. Oxford: Clarendon Press.

Sen, Amartya 1985. *Commodities and Capabilities*. Amsterdam: North-Holland.

Sen, Amartya 2005. *The Argumentative Indian. Writings on Indian Culture, History and Identity*. London: Penguin.

Serra, Cecilia 2007. 'Assessing CLIL at primary school: a longitudinal study'. *International Journal of Bilingual Education and Bilingualism* 10 (5), 582–602.

Seurujärvi-Kari, Irja 2005. 'Saamelaisliikkeen kehitys ja tulevaisuus—saamelaisen identiteetin vahvistuminen'. In Kokkonen, Paula (ed.). *Sukukansaohjelman arki. Suomalais-ugrilainen perintö ja arkipäivä.* Helsinki: Castreniaumin toimitteita 64, 197–222.

SFS, Svensk författningssamling [The Swedish Official Gazette] 1985: 1100. *Skollag* [The Education Act].

SFS, Svensk författningssamling [The Swedish Official Gazette] 1994: 1194. Grundskoleförordningen [The Statute on Comprehensive Schooling].

SFS, Svensk författningssamling [The Swedish Official Gazette] 1995:205. *Sameskolförordningen* [The Statute on Sámi Schools].

SFS, Svensk författningssamling [The Swedish Official Gazette] 2008:97. *Grundskoleförordningen* [The Statute on Comprehensive Schooling]. Äidinkielen opetusta koskevien säännösten uudistaminen.

SFS, Svensk författningssamling [The Swedish Official Gazette] 2008:317. *Skollag* [The Education Act]. Peruskoulun yleisiä säännöksiä (allmänna föreskrifter) koskevien säännösten uudistaminen.

Shimahara, Nobuo K. 1991. 'Social mobility and education: Burakumin in Japan'. In Gibson, Margaret A. and John U. Ogbu (eds). *Minority Status and Schooling: A Comparative Study of Immigrant and Involuntary Minorities*. New York: Garland Publishing Inc., 327–353.

Shiva, Vandana 1997. *Biopiracy: The Plunder of Nature and Knowledge.* Cambridge: South End Press.

Shiva, Vandana 2005. *Earth Democracy: Justice, Sustainability, and Peace.* Cambridge: South End Press.

Shohamy, Elana 2006. *Language Policy: Hidden Agendas and New Approaches*. London and New York: Routledge.

Sibayan, Bonifacio 1978. 'Bilingual education in the Philippines: Strategy and structure'. In Alatis, Jim (ed.). *Georgetown University Round Table on Languages and Linguistics.* Washington, D.C.: Georgetown University Press, 302–329.

Siegel, Jeff 1997. 'Using a pidgin language in formal education: Help or hindrance?' *Applied Linguistics* 18, 86–100.

Simon, R. I. 1992. *Teaching against the Grain: Texts for a Pedagogy of Possibility*. New York: Bergin and Garvey.

Sims, Christine P. 2005 'Tribal Languages and the Challenges of Revitalization'. *Anthropology and Education Quarterly*. 36: 1, 104–106.

Singh, Avtar, V. K. Jain, S. K. S. Gautam and Santosh Kumar 2004. *Learning achievement of students at the end of Class V.* New Delhi: NCERT.

Singh, Kumar S. 2002. *People of India.* New Delhi: Oxford University Press.

Singh, Rajendra 2001. 'Chasing butterflies in a multilingual garden: Grounding even linguistic form in multilinguality'. The R. N. Srivastava Memorial Lecture, Jan 12, 2001. University of Delhi, India.

SKOLFS. Skolverkets författningssamling 1994:1. *Förordning om läroplan för det obligatoriska skolväsendet, förskoleklassen och fritidshemmet, Lpo 94* [The 1994 curriculum for compulsory schooling, pre-school education and free-time activities].

Skutnabb-Kangas, Tove 1981. *Tvåspråkighet.* Lund: Liber.

Skutnabb-Kangas, Tove 1984. *Bilingualism or Not: The Education of Minorities.* Clevedon, UK: Multilingual Matters.

Skutnabb-Kangas, Tove 1988. 'Multilingualism and the education of minority children'. In Skutnabb–Kangas, Tove and Jim Cummins (eds). *Minority Education: from Shame to Struggle*. Clevedon, UK: Multilingual Matters, 9–44.

Skutnabb-Kangas, Tove 1995. 'Review of *Bilingualism in a Multilingual Society: Psychosocial and Pedagogical Implications*, Ajit K. Mohanty'. *TESOL Quarterly*, 29:4, 775–780.

Skutnabb–Kangas, Tove 1999. 'Linguistic Diversity, Human Rights and the Free Market'. In Kontra, Miklós, Robert Phillipson, Tove Skutnabb-Kangas and Tibor Várady (eds). *Language: A Right and a Resource—Approaching Linguistic Human Rights*. Budapest: Central European University, 187–222.

Skutnabb–Kangas, Tove 2000. *Linguistic genocide in education—or worldwide diversity and Human Rights?* Mahwah, NJ: Lawrence Erlbaum. [Republished in a slightly revised form in 2008, New Delhi: Orient Blackswan].

Skutnabb–Kangas, Tove 2003. 'Linguistic Diversity and Biodiversity: The Threat from Killer Languages'. In Mair, Christian (ed.). *The Politics of English as a World Language. New Horizons in Postcolonial Cultural Studies*. Amsterdam & New York: Rodopi, 31–52.

Skutnabb-Kangas, Tove 2004. 'Multiple languages (and literacies) as an expression of diversities'. In Dias, Patrick (ed.). *Multiple Languages, Literacies and Technologies. Mapping out concepts, analyzing practices and defining positions. Series Multilingualism, Subalternity and Hegemony of English, Volume 1*. Frankfurt am Main and New Delhi: Multilingualism Network/Books for Change, 39–85. See http://www.multilingualism.net/.

Skutnabb-Kangas, Tove 2007 [1984]. *Bilingualism or Not—The Education of Minorities*. New Delhi: Orient Longman.

Skutnabb-Kangas, Tove 2007. 'Language Planning and Language Rights'. In Hellinger, Marlis and Anne Pauwels (eds). *Diversity and Change*. Vol. 9. *Handbooks of Language and Communication*. Berlin and New York: Mouton de Gruyter, 365–397.

Skutnabb-Kangas, Tove 2008a. 'Language Rights and Bilingual Education'. In Cummins, Jim and Nancy H. Hornberger (eds). *Bilingual Education*. Vol. 1. *Encyclopedia of Language and Education*. 2nd edition. New York: Springer, 117–131.

Skutnabb-Kangas, Tove 2008b. 'Human Rights and Language Policy in Education'. In May, Stephen and Nancy H. Hornberger (eds). *Language Policy and Political Issues in Education*. Vol. 1. *Encyclopedia of Language and Education*. 2nd edition. New York: Springer, 107–119.

Skutnabb-Kangas, Tove 2008c. Bilingual education and Sign language as the mother tongue of Deaf children. In Kellett Bidoli, Cynthia J. and Elana Ochse (eds). *English in International Deaf Communication*. Bern: Peter Lang, 75–94.

Skutnabb-Kangas, Tove 2009. 'MLE for global justice: issues, approaches, opportunities'. In Mohanty, Ajit, Minati Panda, Robert Phillipson and Tove Skutnabb-Kangas (eds). *Multilingual Education for Social Justice: Globalising the Local*. New Delhi: Orient Blackswan, 35–59.

Skutnabb-Kangas, Tove and Ulla Aikio-Puoskari 2004. 'Exclusion or inclusion-linguistic human rights for a linguistic minority, the Deaf Sign language users, and an indigenous people, the Saami'. In Philip Lee (ed.). *Many voices, one vision: The right to communicate in practice*. Penang: Southbound, 59–88.

Skutnabb-Kangas, Tove and Desmond Fernandes 2008. 'Kurds in Turkey and in (Iraqi) Kurdistan: A Comparison of Kurdish Educational Language Policy in Two Situations of Occupation'. *Genocide Studies and Prevention* 3:1, 43–73.

Skutnabb-Kangas, Tove, Luisa Maffi and Dave Harmon 2003. *Sharing A World of Difference. The Earth's Linguistic, Cultural, and Biological Diversity*. Paris: UNESCO Publishing.

UNESCO, Terralingua, and World Wide Fund for Nature. (ISBN UNESCO 92–3–103917–2). Download at www.terralingua.org/.

Skutnabb-Kangas, Tove and Teresa L. McCarty 2008. 'Clarification, Ideological/ Epistemological Underpinnings and Implications of Some Concepts in Bilingual Education'. In Cummins, Jim and Nancy H. Hornberger (eds). *Bilingual Education.* Vol. 5. *Encyclopedia of Language and Education.* 2nd edition. New York: Springer, 3–17.

Skutnabb–Kangas, Tove and Robert Phillipson 1989. *Wanted! Linguistic Human Rights.* ROLIG-papir 44. Roskilde: Roskilde University Centre. [also available on microfiche from ERIC Clearinghouse on Languages and Linguistics, Center for Applied Linguistics, Washington, D.C.].

Skutnabb–Kangas, Tove and Robert Phillipson 1994. 'Linguistic human rights, past and present'. In Skutnabb-Kangas, Tove and Robert Phillipson (eds), in collaboration with Mart Rannut. *Linguistic Human Rights. Overcoming Linguistic Discrimination.* Contributions to the Sociology of Language 67. Berlin and New York: Mouton de Gruyter, 71–110.

Skutnabb–Kangas, Tove and Robert Phillipson 2008a. 'A Human Rights Perspective on Language Ecology'. In Creese, Angela, Peter Martin and Nancy H. Hornberger (eds). *Ecology of Language.* Vol. 9. *Encyclopedia of Language and Education*, 2nd edition. New York: Springer, 3–14.

Skutnabb-Kangas, Tove and Robert Phillipson 2008b. 'Language Ecology'. (Revision). In Östman, Jan-Ola and Jef Verschueren (eds). *Handbook of Pragmatics.* Amsterdam: Benjamins.

Skutnabb-Kangas, Tove and Shelley K. Taylor 2009. 'The Educational Rights of Kurdish Children in Turkey, Denmark and Kurdistan (Iraq)'. In Ayers, William, Therese Quinn and David Stovall (eds.) *Handbook for Social Justice in Education.* In Henry, Annette (ed.) Section 3 *Race and Ethnicity and Social Justice in Education.* New York: Taylor and Francis. 171–190.

Skutnabb-Kangas, Tove, Robert Phillipson, Minati Panda and Ajit Mohanty 2009. 'MLE concepts, goals, needs and expense: English for all or achieving justice?' In Mohanty, Ajit, Minati Panda, Robert Phillipson and Tove Skutnabb-Kangas (eds). *Multilingual Education for Social Justice: Globalising the Local.* New Delhi: Orient Blackswan, 313–334.

Skutnabb-Kangas, Tove and Pertti Toukomaa 1976. *Teaching migrant children's mother tongue and learning the language of the host country in the context of the sociocultural situation of the migrant family*, Report written for UNESCO. Tampere: University of Tampere, Dept of Sociology and Social Psychology, Research Reports, No. 15.

Skutnabb-Kangas, Tove and Jim Cummins (eds). 1988. *Minority Education: From Shame to Struggle.* Clevedons, UK: Multilingual Matters.

Skutnabb-Kangas, Tove and Kathleen Heugh (eds) forthcoming. *Successful Multilingual Education.* New Delhi: Orient Blackswan.

Skutnabb-Kangas, Tove and Robert Phillipson (eds) 1994, in collaboration with Mart Rannut. *Linguistic Human Rights. Overcoming Linguistic Discrimination.* Contributions to the Sociology of Language 67. Berlin and New York: Mouton de Gruyter.

Smith, Linda Tuhiwai 1999. *Decolonizing Methodologies: Research and Indigenous Peoples.* London: Zed Press.

Smith, Linda Tuhiwai 2007. 'Welcoming Remarks'. International Conference on Language, Education and Diversity, University of Waikato, Hamilton, New Zealand (November).

Smolicz, J. J. 1979. *Culture and Education in a Plural Society*. Canberra: Curriculum Development Centre.

Snow, Catherine E., Margie S. Burns and Peg Griffin (eds). 1998. *Preventing Reading Difficulties in Young Children*. Washington, DC: National Academy Press.

Spicer, Jonathan 2008. 'Toronto Takes on London, New York in Diversity Game'. *Global National* (online). Retrieved January 20, 2008 at: http://www.canada.com/globaltv/national/story.html?id=6625411d–f2c1–4371–a651–88f974932d2b&k=63496.

Spolsky, Bernard 2004. *Language policy*. Cambridge: Cambridge University Press.

Spolsky, Bernard and Elana Shohamy 1999. 'Language in Israeli society and education'. *International Journal of the Sociology of Language* 137, 93–114.

Spring, Joel 1996. *The cultural transformation of a Native American family and its tribe 1763–1995*. Mahwah, NJ: Lawrence Erlbaum.

Spurling, Hilary 2008. 'Book review of Steel, Carolyn: *Hungry City: How Food Shapes Our Lives*'. *The Guardian Weekly* 11.07.2008: 36–37.

SSK, Suomen säädöskokoelma [The Finnish Official Gazette] 1995/974. *Láhka sámedikkis/Laki saamelaiskäräjistä* [Act on the Sámi Parliament].

SSK, Suomen säädöskokoelma [The Finnish Official Gazette] 1998/1186. *Laki opetus– ja kulttuuritoimen rahoituksesta annetun lain (1998/635) muuttamisesta.* [Amendment of the act on financing of education and cultural activities].

SSK, Suomen säädöskokoelma [The Finnish Official Gazette] 1998/628. *Perusopetuslaki* [The Basic Education Act].

SSK, Suomen säädöskokoelma [The Finnish Official Gazette] 1998/635. *Laki opetus-ja kulttuuritoimen rahoituksesta* [Act on the financing of education and cultural activities].

SSK, Suomen säädöskokoelma [The Finnish Official Gazette] 2007/392. *Opetusministeriön asetus vieraskielisten sekä saamenkielisten ja romanikielisten oppilaiden täydentävään opetukseen perusopetuksessa ja lukiokoulutuksessa myönnettävän valtionavustuksen perusteista* [Statute of the Ministry of Education about the grounds for granting state subsidies for the complementary compulsory and upper secondary schooling of immigrants and pupils who speak Sámi, Roma or foreign languages as their native language].

Statistics Canada 2001. '2001 census of Canada'. Retrieved at: http://www12.statcan.ca/english/census01/home/Index.cfm.

Statistics Canada 2007. 'Selected Ethnic Origin for XX, 2001'. Retrieved 30 September 2007 at: http://en.wikipedia.org/wiki/XX,_Ontario#_note–12.

Statistics Canada 2008. 'Immigrants in the Hinterlands'. *Perspectives on Labour and Income, 9*, 1 (online document). Retrieved at: http://www.statcan.ca/english/freepub/75–001–XIE/2008101/article/10505–en.htm.

Stortinget/ Stuorradiggi [The Parliament of Norway] 1993. *Om norsk samepolitikk/ Norgga sámepolitihka birra.* Stortingets melding/ Stuorradikki dieđáhus nr 52, 1992–1993 [Parliamentary Notice].

Street, Brian 1984. *Literacy in Theory and Practice.* New York: Cambridge University Press.

Street, Brian 2001. 'The New Literacy Studies'. In Cushman, Ellen, Eugene R. Kintgen, Barry M. Kroll and Mike Rose (eds). *Literacy: A Critical Sourcebook.* Boston: Bedford/ St. Martin's.

Stroud, Christopher 2003. 'Postmodernist perspectives on local languages: African mother tongue education in times of globalisation'. *International Journal of Bilingual Education and Bilingualism* 6:1, 17–36.

Stroud, Christopher 2007. 'Bilingualism: colonialism, postcolonialism and high modernity'. In Heller, Monica (ed.) *Bilingualism: A Social Approach.* New York: Palgrave Press, 205–229.

Suleri, Sarah 1992. *The Rhetoric of English in India.* Chicago: The University of Chicago Press.

Svonni, Mikael 1997. ′Att lära sig samiska – ett minoritetsspråk. Vilken roll har skolan?′ In Westergren, Eva and Hans Åhl (eds). *Mer än ett språk. En antologi om två- och trespråkigheten i Norra Sverige.* Falun: Norstedts, 130–152.

Swain, Merrill and Robert Keith Johnson 1997. 'Immersion Education: A Category within Bilingual Education'. In Johnson, Robert Keith and Merrill Swain (eds). *Immersion Education: International Perspectives.* Cambridge: Cambridge University Press, 1–16.

Swain, Merrill and Sharon Lapkin 1991. 'Additive Bilingualism and French Immersion Education: The Roles of Language Proficiency and Literacy'. In Reynolds, Allan G. (ed.). *Bilingualism, Multiculturalism, and Second Language Learning: The McGill Conference in Honour of Wallace E. Lambert.* Hillsdale, NJ: Lawrence Erlbaum, 203–216.

Swain, Merrill and Sharon Lapkin 2005. 'The Evolving Socio-Political Context of Immersion Education in Canada: Some Implications for Program Development'. *International Journal of Applied Linguistics* 15, 169–186.

Swales, John 1996. 'English as "Tyrannosaurus Rex" '. *World Englishes* 16:3, 373–382.

Tagore, Rabindranath 1992 [1917]. *My Reminiscences.* New Delhi: Rupa.

Task Force on Aboriginal Languages and Cultures 2005. *Towards a New Beginning: A Foundational Report for a Strategy to Revitalise First Nations, Inuit and Metis Languages and Cultures.* Ottawa: Aboriginal Languages Directorate, Department of Canadian Heritage.

Taylor, Shelley K. 1992. 'Victor: A Case Study of a Cantonese Child in Early French Immersion'. *Canadian Modern Language Review* 48:4, 736–759.

Taylor, Shelley K. 2000. 'Common Practice and Linguistic Human Rights: A- Versus. B–Team Coercion or the Co-construction of "Utopia"?' In Phillipson, Robert (ed.). *Rights to Language: Equity, Power and Education.* Mahwah, NJ: Lawrence Erlbaum, 179–186.

Taylor, Shelley K. 2006. 'ESL in Bilingual Education with a *Twist*: Immigrant Children in Canadian French Immersion'. *Bilingual Basics* 8: 1. http://www.tesol.org/s_tesol/sec_issue.asp?nid=3077&iid=6379&sid=1#135.

Taylor, Shelley K. and Tove Skutnabb-Kangas 2009. 'The Educational Rights of Kurdish Children in Turkey, Denmark and Kurdistan (Iraq)'. In Ayers, William, Therese Quinn and David Stovall (eds.) *Handbook for Social Justice in Education*. In Henry, Annette (ed.) Section 3 *Race and Ethnicity and Social Justice in Education*. New York: Taylor and Francis. 171–190.

Taylor, Shelley K. 2009. 'The caste system approach to multilingualism in Canada: Linguistic and cultural minority children in French immersion'. In Mohanty, Ajit, Minati Panda, Robert Phillipson and Tove Skutnabb-Kangas (eds). *Multilingual Education for Social Justice: Globalising the Local*. New Delhi: Orient Blackswan, 162–180.

Taylor, Shelley K. and Hongfang Yu, in preparation. 'ESL/FSL, Bilingual and Special Education All Rolled into One: Towards Equitable Programming for Exceptional Students in Early French Immersion Without Dismantling the Program'. To be submitted to the *Canadian Modern Language Review*.

Teeter, Karl V. 1967. 'Preliminary Report on Malecite-Passamaquoddy'. In *Contributions to Anthropology: Linguistics: I (Algonquian)*. Ottawa: National Museum of Canada, Bulletin No. 214, Anthropological Series No. 78, 157–162.

Thomas, Jacob (Chief), with Terry Boyle 2001 [1994]. *Teachings from the Longhouse*. Toronto: Stoddart.

Thomas, Wayne P. and Virginia P. Collier 2002. *A National Study of School Effectiveness for Language Minority Students' Long-Term Academic Achievement*. George Mason University, CREDE (Center for Research on Education, Diversity & Excellence). http://www.crede.ucsc.edu/research/llaa/1.1_final.html. Also: Santa Cruz CA: Center for Research on Education, Diversity and Excellence. http://www.usc.edu/dept/education/CMMR/CollierThomasComplete.pdf. (accessed 4 August 2008).

Timbuktu Education Foundation 2002. Discovery of Timbuktu Manuscripts. http://www.timbuktufoundation.org/manuscripts.html

Todal, Jon 2002. '"...*jos fal gáhttet gollegielat*". *Vitalisering av samisk språk i Noreg på 1990-talet*. Avhandling til dr.art.-graden. Tromsø: Det humanistiske fakultet, Universitet i Tromsø.

Todal, Jon 2003. '"Det lappiske Tungemaal til at forstaa"- Nubbingiella gielalaš eaIáskahttima gaskaoapmin'. In Hirvonen, Vuokko (ed.). *Sámi skuvla plánain ja praktihkas. Mo dustet O97S hástalusaid? Reforpma 97 evalueren*. Kárášjohka/Karasjok and Vaasa: Research Council of Norway, Saami University College/ Sámi allaskuvla and ČálliidLágádus, 107–120.

Todal, Jon 2006. 'The Southern Saami Language in Svahken Sijte'. *International Journal of the Sociology of Language* 180, 147–158.

Todal, Jon 2007. *Samisk Språk i Svahken Sijte. Sørsamisk vitalisering gjennom barnehage og skule*. Dieđut 1/2007. Guovdageaidnu/Kautokeino: Sámi Instituhtta.

Tollefson, James W. and Amy B. M. Tsui (eds) 2004. *Medium of Instruction Policies: Which Agenda? Whose Agenda?* Mahwah, NJ.: Lawrence Erlbaum.

Tomaševski, Katarina—see www.tomasevski.net/.

Tomaševski, Katarina 1996. 'International prospects for the future of the welfare state'. In *Reconceptualizing the welfare state*. Copenhagen: The Danish Centre for Human Rights, 100–117.

Tomaševski, Katarina 2004. *Economic, social and and cultural rights. The right to education. Report submitted by the Special Rapporteur Katarina Tomaševski*. Economic and Social Council, UN Commission on Human Rights, Sixtieth session Item 10 on the provisional agenda. E/CN.4/2004/45. 26 December 2003.

Tomaševski, Katarina 2005. 'Has the Right to Education a Future Within the United Nations? A Behind-the-Scenes Account by the Special Rapporteur on the Right to Education 1998–2004'. *Human Rights Law Review* 5:2, 205–237.

Tomaševski, Katarina 2006. *Human rights obligations in education. The 4-A Scheme*. Nijmegen: Wold Legal Publishers.

Traoré, Samba 2001a. 'Convergent Teaching in Mali'. *Prospects: Quarterly Review of Comparative Education* 31:3, 353–371.

Traoré, Samba 2001b. *La Pédagogie Convergente: Son Expérimentation au Mali et son Impact sur le Système Educatif.* Genève: UNESCO Bureau International d'Education.

Trapnell, Lucy 1985. 'Veinticinco años de educación bilingüe en la Amazonía peruana.' In Gasche, Jürg and José M. Arroyo (eds). *Balances Amazónicos. Enfoques Antropológicos*. Perú: CAAP, 121–145.

Trapnell, Lucy 2005. 'Alcances y retos de la educación intercultural en el nivel de inicial.' Paper given at the *IV Congreso Nacional de Investigación en Antropología, 'La Antropología ante el Perú de hoy'*.

Trapnell, Lucy and Eloy Neira 2006. 'La EIB en el Perú'. In López, Luis Enrique and Carlos Rojas (eds). *La EIB en América Latina bajo examen*. La Paz, Bolivia: Plural Editores, 253–355.

Tripathi, P. D 1990. 'English in Zambia: the nature and prospects of one of Africa's "new Englishes" '. *English Today* 6:3, 34–8.

Trivedi, Harish 1993. *Colonial Transactions: English Literature and India*. Calcutta: Papyrus.

Trudell, Barbara and Leila Schroeder 2007. 'Reading methodologies for African languages: Avoiding linguistic and pedagogical imperialism'. *Language, Culture and Curriculum* 20:3, 165–180.

Tsui, Amy B. M. and James W. Tollefson (eds). *Language policy, culture, and identity in Asian contexts*. Mahwah, NJ: Lawrence Erlbaum.

Tubino, Fidel 2003. 'Entre el multiculturalismo y la interculturalidad: mas allá de la discriminación positiva.' In Fuller, Norma (ed.) 2003. *Interculturalidad y política. Desafíos y posibilidades*. Lima, Perú: Red para el desarrollo de las ciencias sociales en el Perú, 51–67.

Tucker, G. Richard 1986. 'Implications of Canadian research for promoting a language competent American society'. In Fishman, Joshua (ed.) *The Fergusonian Impact. Sociolinguistics and the Sociology of Language,* Vol. 2. Berlin: Mouton de Gruyter, 361–369.

Tucker, G. Richard 2003. 'A global perspective on bilingualism and bilingual education'. In Bratt Paulston, Christina and G. Richard Tucker (eds). *Sociolinguistics. The Essential Readings*. Oxford: Blackwell, 464–471.

Turi, Johan 1910. *Muittalus samid* birra = En bog om lappernes liv [A Story about Sámi life]. 2nd edition. Kjøbenhavn: Emilie Demant. [In English: Turi, Johan 1931. *Turi's book of Lappland*. London: Jonathan Cape].

UNESCO 1953. *The use of the vernacular languages in education*. Monographs on fundamental education VIII, Paris: UNESCO.

UNESCO 2000. *Education for All. Status and Trends 2000. Assessing learning achievement, International Consultative Forum on Education for All*. Paris: UNESCO. http://unesdoc.unesco.org/images/0011/001198/119823e.pdf.

UNESCO 2003a. *Language Vitality and Endangerment*. UNESCO Intangible Cultural Heritage Unit's Ad Hoc Expert Group on Endangered Languages. Approved 31 March 2003 by the Participants of the International Expert Meeting on UNESCO Programme Safeguarding of Endangered Languages, UNESCO, Paris-Fontenoy, 10–12 March 2003. http://www.endangeredlanguagefund.org/pdf/ELFN_May_2003.pdf.

UNESCO 2003b. *Recommendations for Action Plan*. International Expert Meeting on UNESCO Programme Safeguarding of Endangered Languages, UNESCO, Paris-Fontenoy, 10–12 March 2003. http://www.unesco.org/culture/en/endangeredlanguages.

UNESCO 2003c. *Education in a multilingual world*. UNESCO Education Position Paper. Paris: UNESCO. http://unesdoc.unesco.org/images/0012/001297/129728e.pdf.

United Nations Declaration on the Rights of Indigenous Peoples 2007; document A/61/L.67: http://www.un.org/esa/socdev/unpfii/en/drip.html.

United Nations Educational, Scientific and Cultural Organization (UNESCO) 2007. *Promoting Literacy in Multilingual Settings*. Bangkok: UNESCO Bangkok.

Urton, Gary 2003. *La vida social de los números. Una ontología de los números y la filosofía de la aritmética quechuas*. Centro de Estudios Regionales Andinos Bartolomé de las Casas. Cusco, Perú.

US Census Bureau 2000. *Native American Language Speakers, 2000. Summary File 3 and 2000 County and County Equivalent Areas Cartographic Boundary File*. Washington, DC: US Census Bureau.

US Census Bureau 2001. *The Native Hawaiian and Other Pacific Islander Population: 2002. Census 2000 Brief*. Washington, DC: US Department of Commerce, Economics and Statistics Administration, US Census Bureau.

US Census Bureau 2002. *The American Indian and Alaska Native Population: 2000. Census 2000 Brief*. Washington, DC: US Department of Commerce, Economics and Statistics Administration, US Census Bureau.

US Census Bureau 2006. *We the People: American Indians and Alaska Natives in the United States. Census 2000 Special Report*. Washington, DC: US Department of Commerce, Economics and Statistics Administration, US Census Bureau.

Valpy, Michael 2007. 'Arabic Study Immersed in Controversy: Public School Language Program Doesn't Count as "Immersion", Ontario Ministry Says'. *CTVglobemedia Publishing* (online). Retrieved May 18, 2007 at: http://www.theglobeandmail.com/servlet/story/LAC.20070518.IMMERSE18/TPStory/TPNational/Ontario/.

Van der Walt, Crista, D. R. Mabule and J. J. De Beer 2001. 'Letting the L1 in by the back door: Codeswitching and translation in science, mathematics and biology classes'. *SAALT Journal,* 35: 2–3, 170–184.

Verhoeven, Ludo 2000. 'Components in early second language reading and spelling'. *Scientific Studies of Reading* 4(4), 313–330.

Vidya Bhavan Society, forthcoming. *Elementary School English Language Textbooks in a Multilingual Perspective*. Udaipur: Vidya Bhavan Society.

Viswanathan, Gauri 1989. *Masks of Conquest: Literary Study and British Rule in India*. New York: Columbia University Press.

Vygotsky, Lev Semenovich 1978. *Mind and Society*. Cambridge, MA: Harvard University Press.

Wade, Tracey 2007. 'Eskasoni Elementary/Middle School'. In Fulford, George (ed.). *Sharing Our Success: More Case Studies in Aboriginal Schooling*. Kelowna: Society for the Advancement of Excellence in Education, 125–150.

Walsh, Catherine 2003. '(De) Construir la interculturalidad. Consideraciones criticas desde la política, la colonialidad y los movimientos indígenas y negros en el Ecuador.' In Fuller, Norma (ed.) 2003. *Interculturalidad y política. Desafíos y posibilidades***.** Lima, Perú: Red para el desarrollo de las ciencias sociales en el Perú. Lima, 115–142.

Walsh, Catherine 2004. 'Geopolíticas del conocimiento, Interculturalidad y Descolonialización'. *Boletín ICCI ARY Rimay*, Año 6, No. 60. http://icci.nativeweb.org/boletin/60/walsh.html#N_1_.

Walter, Steve 2008. 'The language of instruction issue: Framing an empirical perspective'. In Spolsky, Bernard and Francis Hult (eds). *Handbook of Educational Linguistics*. Oxford: Blackwell, 129–146.

Warrior, Robert Allen 1995. *Tribal Secrets: Recovering American Indian Intellectual Traditions*. Minneapolis: University of Minnesota Press.

Watahomigie, Lucille J. and Teresa L. McCarty 1996. 'Literacy for What? Hualapai Literacy and Language Maintenance'. In Hornberger, Nancy H. (ed.). *Indigenous Literacies in the Americas: Language Planning from the Bottom Up*. Berlin: Mouton de Gruyter, 95–113.

Weber, Sandra and Claudette Tardif 1990. 'The Young Child's View of Starting French Immersion'. In Fleming, Berkeley and Margaret Whitla (eds). *So You Want Your Child to Learn French!* (2nd edition). Ottawa, Canada: Canadian Parents for French, 54–66.

Wesche, Marjorie Bingham 2000. 'A Canadian Perspective: Second Language Teaching and Learning in the University.' In Rosenthal, Judith W. (ed.). *Handbook of Undergraduate Second Language Education.* Mahwah, NJ: Lawrence Erlbaum Associates, 187–208.

Wierzbicka, Anna 2006. *English: Meaning and Culture*. Oxford: Oxford University Press.

Wikipedia 2008. 'XX, Ontario'. Retrieved at: http://en.wikipedia.org/wiki/XX,_Ontario. [XX stands for the place name for a school; anonymity prevents the name from being written here].

Williams, Eddie 1998. *Investigating bilingual literacy: Evidence from Malawi and Zambia*. Education Research No. 24. London: Department For International Development.

Williams, Eddie 2001. 'Testimony from testees: the case against current language policies in sub-Saharan Africa'. In Elder, Catherine, Kathryn Hill, Noriko Iwashita, Tom Lumley, Timothy McNamara and Kieran O'Loughlin (eds). *Language Testing: Experimenting with uncertainty*. Cambridge: Cambridge University Press, 200–210.

Williams, Eddie 2006. *Bridges and Barriers-Language in African Education and Development*. Manchester, UK & Kinderhook, NY: St. Jerome Publishing.

Wolfson, Monica 2007. 'Arabic Pilot Project Will Be Curtailed: Deal Brokered to Save Language Program'. *The Windsor Star* (online). Retrieved May 19, 2007 at: http://www.canada.com/windsorstar/news/story.html?id=976a1e64–3cb0–4c89–8fec–fb7f20e0a4f7&k=45221.

Wong Fillmore, Lily 1991. When Learning a Second Language Means Losing the First. *Early Childhood Research Quarterly* 6, 323–346.

Wong, Mary S. and A. Suresh Canagarajah (eds) forthcoming. *Christian Educators and Critical Practitioners in Dialogue: Ethical Dilemmas in English Language Teaching*. London & New York: Routledge, Taylor and Francis.

World Resources Institute, World Conservation Union, and United Nations Environment Programme 1992. *Global Biodiversity Strategy: Policy-makers' Guide*. Baltimore: WRI Publications.

XX Public schools 2007. 'XX Public Schools'. Retrieved at http://www.XXschools.ca/aboriginal/default.aspx?id=581. [XX stands for the place name for a school in Canada; anonymity prevents the name from being written here].

Yonjan–Tamang, Amrit 2006. *Languages of Nepal: Present Situation and Language Planning in Nepal* (in Nepali). Kathmandu: Indigenous Linguistic Society of Nepal (Adivasi Bhasabigyan Samaj).

Yonjan-Tamang, Amrit, David Hough and Iina Nurmela 2009. 'All Nepalese children have the right to education in their mother tongue'-but how? The Nepal MLE Programme'. In Mohanty, Ajit, Minati Panda, Robert Phillipson and Tove Skutnabb-Kangas (eds). *Multilingual Education for Social Justice: Globalising the Local*. New Delhi: Orient Blackswan, 241–249.

# Index

**A**

academic achievement and power relations 28, 30, 34
academic development of minority students 24–31
academic language proficiency 25
  cognitive–academic language proficiency (CALP) 295
activating prior knowledge 32–3
Adams, H. 159
additive bilingualism
  benefits of 24, 27
  education policy in Africa 96–7, 107, 109
  and subtractive bilingualism 62, 130, 131, 132, 133
  *vs* 'early–exit transitional bilingual' model 108–9
affirmation of identity 33–4
Africa
  assessment, monitoring and evaluation 107–12
  colonialism 63, 89, 96, 97, 98–9
  dominance of English 319
  early transition to international language of wider communication (ILWC) 40
  early–exit models 64
  failure of MLE 314
  Molteno Project 109
  post–colonial preoccupation with international languages 99–103
  pre–colonial practices 98–9
  revisionism in language education policy 95–8, 107
  *see also specific countries*
Afrikaans language 101, 106, 107
Alaska Native people *see* native Americans
Alexander, N. 67, 71–2, 314, 332–3
Alfred, T. 159–60
Andhra Pradesh, India 286–90, 297, 326
Angola 75
'Apolitical Intellectuals' (poem) 56
Arabic script (Ajami) 98
archivists' perspective 51–2
Armstrong, D. 82
assimilation
  cultural, and structural incorporation 321–2, 323–7
  of First Nations, Canada 201–3
  of Sámi, Nordic countries 222
  *see also* integration
Association for the Development of Education (ADEA)–UNESCO Insitute of Education (UIE) Report 96–7, 97–8, 110, 112
August, D. and Shanahan, T. 26–7
Austin, G. 274

**B**

backwash effects of testing 68
Bacon, F. 274
Baker, C. 37, 60, 61, 68
Bamgbose, A. 69, 71, 99, 100, 102, 314
Bartlett, T. 54
basic interpersonal communication skills (BICS) 295
Bear Nicholas, A. 201, 205, 207
belief systems and practices, Nepal 158, 247
Benson, C. 64, 66, 70
bilingual education
- and bilingualism 132–4
- concepts in 314–15
- definition of 21
- general outcomes of programs 22–3
- Intercultural Bilingual Education (IBE), Latin America 183, 184–8, 190–1, 198
- language planning 35–6
- literacy instruction in multilingual contexts 31–4
- opposition to 22
- psycholinguistic principles 23–7
- sociological principles 28–31

bilingual education models (North–South relationship) 61–6
- challenges in applying 66–8
- contexts and clarification of language and learning principles 68–72
- effective schooling strategies 72–5
- future strategies and research directions 75–6
- limitations of 60–1

bilingualism
- models 130–2
- questioning assumptions about 129–32
- *see also* bilingual education; translanguaging

Blommaert, J. 45, 316
Bolivia 65, 66
Botswana 100
bridge metaphor of multilingual education (MLE) 8–9, 16–17
Brutt–Griffler, J. 89
Buddhist parables 158
Burakumin minority, Japan 29

**C**

Cambodia 67
Canada
- bilingual programs 21, 65, 205
- bilingualism 129–30, 204
- diversity 162,163
- First Nations/indigenous languages and population 200–6
  - assimilation of 201–3
  - financial barriers to survival of 204–5, 213–14
  - mother tongue medium (MTM) 204, 205, 213
- *see also* French immersion programme, Ontario, Canada; teacher training, Canada, native language immersion programme
- Four Directions Council 150
- Hebrew–English dual language book 33–4
- immersion programmes 133, 134
- 'Indian Control of Indian Education' (ICIE) 202–3
- language legislation issues 204, 212
- Statistics Canada 162, 171, 176

Castillo, O.R. 56
'catch–up' trajectory of minority students 25
Chamaar, K. 80–1
Chichewa language, Malawi 100, 101
China 81,319–20
Chomsky, N. 269, 270

Christian missionaries 330
Africa 98–9,100–1
and English language teaching 81–2
Churchill, Winston 83
code–switching 133,135,139
cognitive–academic language proficiency (CALP) 295
collaborative creation of power 30–1, 34
colonialism
Africa 63, 89, 96, 97, 98–9
Canada 202
decolonisation and postcolonial states 88–9
Latin America 63, 198
'common underlying proficiency' 26, 63
community MLE workers (CMW), India 306–8, 310
community–school relationship, Peru 196–7
competence
in mother tongue (L1) 69, 70–2
in second language (L2) 67–8, 70
content and language integrated learning (CLIL) programs 87, 135
conversational fluency dimension of language proficiency 24
cost issues 204–5, 213–14, 331–3
Crawford, J.W. 120
critical indigenous pedagogy 328
Nepal 152,153–9
cultural assimilation *see* assimilation
cultural diversity *see* diversity, linguistic and cultural; interculturality
Cultural Historical Activity Theory (CHAT) 296, 300, 309
cultural neutrality of English 86
Cummins, J. 26, 30, 63, 68, 70, 72, 108, 109, 164, 165, 168
Curzon, Viceroy of India 42, 262

**D**

Darwin, J. 88
Das, C. 146,160
Dasgupta, P. 90
de Swaan, A. 47
de Varennes, F. 149, 332
decentralisation
Ethiopia 112–13
Nepal 242
Peru 197–8
decolonisation and postcolonial states 88–9
Deloria, V. Jr. 52, 151
democracy 317
democratic and linguistic deficits, EU 84–5
dialects
India 254, 257, 259
and language 271–2
discrete language skills dimension of language proficiency 24–5
discrimination, layers of 166–7, 177–8
diversity, linguistic and cultural
Canada 162,163
and dying languages 38–9
India 250–2
inter–connectedness of 39–40
support continuum 43–7
*see also* multilinguality
documentation, Nepal 152
dominance of English 79–83, 85–93, 317–20
dominant–language medium education 67
negative effects 40, 42, 52
*vs* MLE 39–43
*see also* bilingual education
Dressler, C. and Kamil, M. 26
Dreze, J. and Sen, A. 284

dual language books 33–4
dual medium programmes *62*, 66
Dunbar, R. and Skutnabb–Kangas, T. 42–3
dying languages
  archivists' perspective 51–2
  implications for diversity 38–9
  and linguistic genocide 40,42, 86–7, 148, 149–50, 200, 204, 268, 272, 281
  and marginalised people 6
dynamic bilingualism 131–2
dynamic multilingualism 316

**E**

early French immersion (EFI) *see* French immersion programme, Ontario, Canada
early–exit transitional programmes 41, 63–4
  *vs* 'additive bilingualism' 108–9
Eastman, C. 46
economic issues 204–5, 213–14, 331–3
Education for All 242, 255, 263, 264–5, 295–6
  mantra and reality 313–14
elitism
  English as key language 85–6, 87, 89, 92
  *vs* equality 66–7
empowerment 30–1,34,150,300–1
English
  in Africa 100–9
  *passim*, 319
  in Canada 202, 203–4
  dominance of 79–83, 85–93, 317–20
  as early medium of instruction 318–19
  and globalisation 275–6, 320–1
  in India 42, 80–1, 92, 261–3, 266, 287,
  319–20
  and 'killer languages' 7
  and multilinguality 268
  Navaho immersion students, US 121–3
epistemic interculturality 194, 195
Erickson, F. 129
Eritrea 71, 95
errors
  in advisory documents, Ethiopia 109
  and multilinguality 273
Ethiopia 65, 67, 68, 71, 96, 331
  Amharic language 100, 101, 103–4
  decentralised education policy 112–13
  errors in advisory documents 109
  recent policy developments 103–5
  schooling strategy example 72–5
ethnic identity 46, 196
ethnomathematics/number systems 157–8, 280, 302–6
Europe (EU)
  Bologna process (higher education and research) 87–8
  content and language integrated learning (CLIL) programs 87, 135
  dominance of English 85–93, 319
  language policy 83–5, 87, 132
European Commission *Framework Strategy for Multilingualism* 87
Evans, S. 42, 262
exclusion/marginalisation of tribal languages/mother tongues 6, 7, 100–1, 280–1, 285
extending language 34

**F**

Fardon, R. and Furniss, G. 96, 315
feasts 159
festivals 159, 288
Fillmore, W. 167, 170
Finland 228–30, 323
  Ministry of Foreign Affairs (MoFA) 146, 241
First Nations languages and populations

*see* Canada; French immersion programme, Ontario, Canada; teacher training, Canada, native language immersion programme
Fishman, J. 47–8
fluidity 269–70
foreign language as medium of education 272
Foucault, M. 129
Francis, L. 159
French immersion programme, Ontario, Canada 163
caste–like approach 164–7
ethical questions 169–70
First Nations students and languages 164, 165–6, 170–1, 172, 173, 176–7, 178, 179
investigations 171–3
kindergartens 168
layers of discrimination 177–8
minority non–Aboriginal languages, ranking of 165
minority/immigrant students 170, 171, 178, 179
'multilingual classrooms' 164
Northern Ontario 172–3, 175–7, 178
related research 170–1
results 173–8
Southern Ontario 171–2, 173–5, 178
summary and discussion 179–80
theoretical considerations 167–8
Fuller, N. 187

**G**

games 288, 301, 302, 303, 305–6
Gandhi, G. 80, 83, 86, 90
Garcia, O. 124–5, 126, 128, 133, 136, 140
et al. 164
Gee, J.P. 32
Genesee, F. 65, 167, 169, 179
genocide, linguistic 40, 42, 86–7, 148, 149–50, 200, 204, 268, 272, 281
Ghana 67
Giroux, H. 153
global justice 36–7
approaches 43–52
issues 38–43
opportunities 53–6
globalisation 36–7, 160, 275–6, 320–1
governmentality 129
grammatical rules 273
and Universal Grammar 270, 271
Gramsci, A. 129
Grin, F. 332, 333
Guinea–Conakry 67, 101
Guthrie, J.T. 31–2
Gutiérrez, K. et al. 128

**H**

Hare, D. 86
hegemonic practices 129
herbal medicine and traditional healing practices, Nepal 154–5, 247
heteroglossia, India 134
Heugh, K. 64, 70, 71, 89, 110
et al. 65, 68, 71, 111
Hindi 260–1, 274–5, 287
historical perspectives
African writing systems 98
bilingual education 132–3, 184–8
effects of submersion programmes 41–2
indigenous languages and ethnic groups, Nepal 146–9
Holm, A.D. and Holm, W. 120, 121, 122
home language
as second language 121–3
as teaching medium 119–21
*see also* bilingual education; mother tongue medium (MTM)

homogenisation effect of globalisation 37
Horton, M. 160
Hough, D. 47
Hovens, M. 71
hybridity 45, 46, 128

# I

identity
  ethnic 46, 196
  negotiation 29
  oppositional 28, 29
  regional 260–1
  texts 33–4
immersion programmes *62*, 65
  Canada 133, 134
  Navajo 122, 123
  revitalization 134–5
  *see also* French immersion programme, Ontario, Canada; teacher training, Canada, native language immersion programme
immigrants/migrants 28–9, 170, 171, 178, 179, 254
India
  Census (2001) 251, 253
  Central Institute of Indian Languages (CIIL) 270, 276, 285–6
  English in 42, 80–1, 92, 261–3, 266, 287, 319–20
  heteroglossia 134
  Hindi as link language 260–1
  independence negotiations 86
  language diversity in 250–2
  multilinguality in 268–9
  multiple multilingual education 137–8
  National Curriculum Framework (NCF) 261, 286
  'new' pedagogical approaches 255–6
  possible future strategies 265–7
  pre–school education 266–7
  primary education
    children's language skills 258–9
    classroom situations 252–3
    dialects 254, 257, 259
    English in 261–2
    impact of monolingual teaching practices 256–9
    language in education policies and practice 259–61
    language teaching methodology 257–8
    language used by teachers 256–7
    mediums of instruction and learning disadvantage 253–5, 259–60
    migrants 254
    non–medium of instruction speakers 254–5
    possible future strategies 265–7
    programmes and language related initiatives 262–5
    'quality of education' and learning issue 255–6
    scheduled tribes (ST) 254, 256, 258–9
  regional identity 260–1
  teacher training 265
  Three Language Formula 260–1
  tribal bilingual education 35
  tribal languages/mother tongue
    exclusion of 280, 281, 285
    as language subject 264
    as medium of instruction 281–2, 284
    and multilingual education 285–6
      programmes *see* Andhra Pradesh, India; Orissa, India
    pilots 264–5
    primers 263
    rhymes, riddles and folktales 263
    and state language teaching materials 263

teacher training 264
tribal protests 326
tribes, scheduled (ST) 254, 256, 258–9, 281–2
education, capability deprivation and poverty 284–5
language barrier and education 283–4
literacy, school enrolment, push out rate and educational achievement 282–3
Urdu 260, 274
Indian Constitution 259, 261, 273, 274
indigenous consciousness 159
indigenous knowledge (IK) holders, Nepal 151–2, 154, 245
indigenous knowledge systems 150–1, 153–9, 274–5
and academic knowledge 193–4, 195–6, 197
and everyday practices 301–2, 327–9
indigenous/tribal and minority (IM) people and languages 8–9, 14–17
economic issues 204–5, 213–14, 331–3
exclusion/marginalisation 6, 7, 100–1, 280–1, 285
future goals 321–3
stigma 138–9, 278–9
structural incorporation and cultural assimilation 321–2, 323–7
*see also* dying languages; global justice; *specific countries, indigenous groups and languages*
integration
and language policy, EU 83–5
*see also* assimilation
intellectuals, role of 55–6
inter–connectedness of diversities 39–40
Intercultural Bilingual Education (IBE), Latin America 183, 184–8, 190–1, 198
interculturality
concept of 186–8, 198
epistemic 194, 195
interdependence hypothesis of bilingual education 26–7, 72
International Council for Science (ICSU) 151
'interweaving' and 'replacement' 305,306
involuntary and voluntary minorities 28–9

**J**

Japan, Burakumin minority 29
Jones, S. 37

**K**

Kaini, P.D. 146
Kepa, M. 153, 154
'killer languages' 7
kindergarten education 168, 189, 190
King, K. and Mackey, A. 169, 170
Kiswahili language, Tanzania 99–100, 101
Kold, K. 160
Kond/Kui, India 27, 280, 284–5, 301–2, 303, 306, 307, 308
Krauss, M. 114, 118, 123, 201

**L**

Ladson–Billings, G. 28
language, concept of 269–70
language death *see* dying languages
language disadvantage
primary education, India 253–5, 259–60
vicious circle of 279–81
Language Faculty 269, 270
language proficiency and academic development 24–6
language shift 52, 121–3
late–exit transitional programmes 41,

63–4
Latin America
colonialism 63, 198
Intercultural Bilingual Education (IBE) 183, 184–8, 190–1, 198
*see also* teacher training, Peru, programme for indigenous bilinguals
Lauhamaa, P. 231
Lee, T. 125
life rituals, Nepal 159
Lindholm–Leary, K.J. and Borsato, G. 23
linguistic and cultural diversity support continuum 43–7
linguistic deficit
democratic and 84–5
myth of 279
linguistic genocide 40, 42, 86–7, 148, 149–50, 200, 204, 268, 272, 281
linguistic human rights (LHRs) 53–4, 147–8, 329–30, 332
Canada 204
South Africa 47
linguistic shame 125
literacy
instruction in multilingual contexts 31–4
in non–dominant language 70
transfer of competence 72
*see also* reading; written language
Lomawaima, K.T. and McCarty, T.L. 114–15
López, L.E. 126
and Küper, W. 183, 184–5
Luxembourg 138

**M**

McCarty, T.L. 120, 123
et al. 125
and Skutnabb–Kangas, T. 167
maintenance programmes *62*, 64–5, 68, 133
majority language *see* bilingual education; dominance of English; dominant–language medium education; French immersion programme, Ontario, Canada
Makoni, S. and Pennycook, A. 45
Malawi 67, 97, 99, 107, 315, 325
Chichewa language 100, 101
Maliseet language and population, Canada 206–9, 210, 213
Mäori language 35, 126
marginalisation/exclusion of tribal languages/mother tongues 6, 7, 100–1, 280–1, 285
Martinet, A. 275
Marx, K. and Engels, F. 36
mathematics/number systems 157–8, 280, 302–6
May, S. 45, 46
metalinguistic abilities/awareness 27, 71–2, 75, 139–40, 316
migrants/immigrants 28–9, 170, 171, 178, 179, 254
Mi'kmaq language and population, Canada 170–1, 206, 207, 208–11, 212
minority language *see* bilingual education; indigenous/tribal and minority (IM) languages; linguistic human rights (LHRs); mother tongue medium (MTM)
Mishra, M.K. 160
MLE Plus for tribal children *see under* Orissa, India
Mohanty, A.K. 6, 7, 27, 80, 134, 137, 279, 283, 284, 285, 286, 297
et al. 6, 280
and Panda, M. 149, 166
monolingualism
colonial period, Africa 96
impact of primary level teaching practices, India 256–9
*vs* Kui–Oriya bilingualism, India 27, 284–5

moral *vs* welfare arguments for MLE 332–3
Morton, H.V. 83
mother tongue medium (MTM) 8, 22
  Africa 96–109 *passim*
  Canada 204, 205, 213
  India 281–2, 284
  Nepal 241–9
  Nordic countries 222–3, 224, 228, 229
Mozambique 67, 101, 107
Mufwene, S. 37
Mühlhäusler, P. 137
multilingual education programs 135
multilinguality 268–9
  contribution of linguistics 269–70
  and 'errors' 273
  and globalisation 275–6
  grammatical rules 273
  language and dialect 271–2
  scientific perspective 274–5
  sociolinguistics perspective 269–71, 276–7
  speech and script 272–3
multiple multilingual education 136, 137–8, 143–4

**N**

Namibia 97, 101, 103, 107
National Council of Education Research and Training (NCERT), India 137, 271, 281, 283, 286
national education policy 68
National Foundation for the Development of Indigenous Languages (NFDIN), Nepal 148
native Americans
  classes and decline of languages 114
  demo–linguistic profile 116–19
  legal and political status 114–15
  Navajo 116, 119–23
  repositioning of indigenous languages 126
  youth perspective 123–5
Nehru, J. 80
neo–liberal/neo–conservative perspective 45–7, 54
Nepal
  bottom–up approach 149–53
  critical indigenous pedagogy 152, 153–9
  decentralisation 242
  documentation 152
  future directions 159–60
  herbal medicine and traditional healing practices 154–5, 247
  history, numerical systems, weights and measures 156–8
  indigenous knowledge (IK) holders 151–2, 154
  language/speech communities selection 243, 244
  life rituals, feasts, festivals, songs and poems 159
  mother tongue medium (MTM) project 241–9
  non–Nepali speakers 241–2, 243
  religion, belief systems and practices 158, 247
  schools selection 243–4
  sociohistorical sketch of indigenous languages and ethnic groups 146–9
  teacher training 151
  traditional and modern skills and knowledge 155–6
  transition 248–9
Nepal Federation of Indigenous Nationalities (NEFIN) 148, 248
New Zealand, Mäori language 35, 126
Niger 71
Nigeria 71, 102, 103
Nordic countries *see* Sámi

North–South relationship *see* bilingual education models
Norway 226–7, 231
number systems/mathematics 157–8, 280, 302–6
Nyseth, T. and Pedersen, P. 218

**O**

OECD Programme for International Student Assessment 31
Ogbu, J.U. 28–9
'oppositional identity' 28, 29
oral histories 156–7
oral knowledge 150, 156, 158
oral languages 38
oral multilingual competence 69
oral teaching materials 152
oral and written multilinguality 272–3
Orissa, India 5–6, 7
  Kond/Kui language 27, 280, 284–5, 301–2, 303, 306, 307, 308
  MLE Plus for tribal children 300–1, 309–10
    community MLE workers (CMW) 306–8, 310
    ethnographic survey of everyday practices and knowledge systems 301–2
    everyday to scientific discourse 302–6
    preliminary assessment of 308–9
    *Read Together* programme 301,307–8
  MLE programme for tribal children 286–90, 297–300, 309–10, 326
    cultural–philosophical underpinnings 298–9
    package 299–300
  number systems 280, 302–6
  Oriya language 27, 284–5, 287, 288, 289, 304, 308, *309*
  Saora language 280, 296, 299–308 *passim*
OSCE High Commissioner on National Minorities 43

**P**

Pakistan 34, 92
Panda, M. 280, 295, 302, 328
  and Cole, M. 302, 305
  Mohanty, A.K. and 149, 166
Papua New Guinea 67, 137, 331–2
parental perspectives 47, 102, 204–5
Parenti, M. 36
Pattanayak, D.P. 7, 134, 286
Peru *see* teacher training, Peru, programme for indigenous bilinguals
Philippines 137–8
Phillipson, R. 82, 83, 84, 85, 88, 89, 90, 115, 319
picture dictionary, Nepal 245
plurilingualism 132
poems 159
Portes, A. and Rumbaut, R.G. 29
post-modern perspective 45, 54
postcolonial states
  preoccupation with international languages in Africa 99–103
  role of English 88–9
  *see also specific countries*
posters, Nepal 245, 246
poverty and basic needs 330–1
power relations
  and academic achievement 28, 30, 34
  and empowerment 30–1, 34, 150, 300–1
  native Americans 120
  researchers and subjects 50–1
primary education
  Peru 189
  *see also under* India

primary and secondary discourses 32
psycholinguistic principles, minority students' academic development 23–7
psychological damage, foreign language as medium of education as cause of 272
'push–outs' 5–6

## Q

Quechua language and population *see* teacher training, Peru, programme for indigenous bilinguals

## R

radio programmes, Peru 197
rational choice theory 46
reactive ethnicity 29
reading 157, 299
  *Read Together* programme 301, 307–8
recursive bilingualism 131, 132
regional identity, India 260–1
religion, Nepal 158, 247
'replacement' and 'interweaving' 305, 306
researchers
  and educators' roles 53, 54–6
  perspectives on indigenous and minority (IM) languages 45–51
  and subjects, power relations 50–1
revitalization immersion programmes 134–5
Romaine, S. 137
Roosevelt, Theodore 322
rote memorisation 70, 156–7, 256, 258, 299
Rothkopf, D. 82
Rubagumya, C. 89, 92

## S

Said, E. 55
Sámi 216–19, 230–2, 233–6
  assimilation policies 222
  comprehensive schools 226, 228, 229
  education 218
    integrated 224
  Finland 228–30, 323
  legislation 223, 226, 228
  mother tongue medium (MTM) 222–3, 224, 228, 229
  Northern multilingualism and roots of Sámi education 219–21
  Norway 226–7, 231
  Sámi language and culture in education 222–30
  Sámi schools 223–4
  Sweden 223–5
Sample, I. 37
Sanskrit 274
Saora language, India 280, 296, 299–308 *passim*
Sarangi, S. 270
scaffolding 32–3, 310
Schermerhorn, R.A. 321
'school networks', Peru 188–9
schoolbooks 33–4, 111–12, 193
science
  mathematics/number systems 157–8, 280, 302–6
  *vs* traditional knowledge systems 150–1, 153–9, 274–5
second generation immigrants 29
second language competence 67–8, 70
secondary education
  Nordic countries 226, 228, 229
  Peru 189–90
secondary and primary discourses 32
selective acculturation 29
Sen, A. 284, 317
shamanistic practices, Nepal 158
Shimahara, N.K. 29
Shiva, V. 146, 150

Skutnabb–Kangas, T. 51, 60, 63, 66, 72, 84, 86, 147–8, 150, 167, 169, 200, 203, 204, 272, 281, 319, 331
  Dunbar, R. and 42–3
  and Fernandes, D. 322
  and McCarty, T.L. 205, 314–15
  McCarty, T.L. and 167
  and Phillipson, R. 86
  and Toukomaa, P. 324–5
Smith, L.T. 159
Snow, C.E. et al. 32
social justice principle 140
social practice principle 140
sociological principles, minority students' academic development 28–31
songs 159, 288
South Africa 97, 101, 102, 103
  assessment, monitoring and evaluation 107–9, 110–11, 112
  Bantu 71
  bilingual education models 65, 66, 67
  language rights legislation 47
  recent policy developments 106–7
Spanish
  and Basque bilingual education 26
  and English translanguaging, US 141–3
  native American trilingual communities 123–4
  *see also* teacher training, Peru, programme for indigenous bilinguals
Spicer, J. 162, 163
spoken language *see entries beginning* oral
Spring, J. 81
Spurling, H. 37
stigma of minority language use 138–9, 278–9
stories 157, 159, 245, 263, 288
strong bilingualism *see* additive bilingualism
structural incorporation and cultural assimilation 321–2, 323–7
submersion programmes 7, 41–2, *62*, 63, 66–7
subtractive bilingualism
  and additive bilingualism *62*, 130, 131, 132, 133
  negative effects 52
Summer Insitute of Linguistics (SIL) 51, 82, 185, 330
Swain, M.
  and Johnson, R.K. 65, 167
  and Lapkin, S. 33, 167
Swales, J. 86–7
Sweden 223–5

**T**

Tamang–speaking schools project *see* Nepal
Tanzania 89, 92, 97
  Kiswahili language 99–100, 101
Taylor, S.K. 168, 169, 170, 171
teacher training
  Canada, native language immersion programme
    challenges and possible solutions 211–15
    genesis of 206–9
    impact of 209–11
    Maliseet 206–9, 210, 213
    Mi'kmaq 206, 207, 208–11, 212
  India 264, 265
  Nepal 151
  Peru, programme for indigenous bilinguals 188–92
    bilingual education model (IBE) 183, 184–8, 190–1, 198
    decentralisation 197–8
    Education Law (2003) 186–7
    FORMABIAP programme 185–6
    'hispanification' processes 184–5
    indigenous and academic

knowledge 193–4, 195–6, 197
Quechua language and population 184, 185, 188
Quechua as medium of instruction 190, 192–3
Quechua–speaking teachers 190
school characteristics 189–90
school–community relationship 196–7
Spanish as second language 191–2
Spanish to Quechua translation 193
Spanish–speaking teachers 190
teacher characteristics 190
teachers and schools 188–9
terminological slippage 108–9
Terralingua 39
Thailand 67
theme web approach 288, 297–8, 299–300, 306
Thomas, W.P. and Collier, V.P. 61, 63, 66, 70, 110
Timbuktu manuscripts 98, 99
Tollefson, J.W. and Tsui, A.B.M. 272
Tomaševski, K. 329
traditional knowledge systems *see* indigenous knowledge systems
transfer of knowledge and skills across languages 26–7, 71–2
'transition' *vs* 'transfer' 108–9
transitional programmes *62*, 63–4, 133
translanguaging 124–5, 128, 315
and bilingual education 134–6
potential of 138–40
in US 141–3
tribal languages *see* indigenous/tribal and minority (IM) people and languages; *specific countries, indigenous groups and languages*
Truman, Harry S. 82
Tucker, G.R. 65, 71, 72
Turi, J. 220
two–way/dual medium programmes 62, 66

U

underachievement 23
UNESCO 8, 14–15, 331
*Education in a multilingual world* 314
*Promoting literacy in multilingual settings* 164
*Report on the Use of Vernacular Languages in Education* 99, 314
Trends in International Mathematics and Science Study (TIMSS) 107
*see also* Education for All
United Nations (UN)
*Declaration on the Rights of Indigenous Peoples* 55, 148–9, 200, 248–9
Environment Programme 39–40
*Human Development Report* (2004) 331
Human Rights Council's Minority Forum 14–15
*International Convention on the Punishment and Prevention of the Crime of Genocide* 40, 42
International Year of Languages (2008) 15, 331
Millennium Development Goals 331
Permanent Forum on Indigenous Issues (UNPFII) 42–3
United States (US)
African–American students 28
Board of Indian Commissioners (1880) 41
British relations 86, 88
Census Bureau 116–18
Christian missionaries 81
early bilingual education programs 133
empire and English language dominance 79–80, 82–3, 92, 93

English as *lingua americana* 86
EU–US summit meetings 84
indigenous/tribal and minority (IM) groups 322–3
*see also* native Americans
'melting pot' ideology 322–3
reading 157
social justice issues 324
Universal Grammar 270, 271
Urdu 34, 260, 274

**V**

Vietnam 63
Vollebaek, K. 43
voluntary and involuntary minorities 28–9
Vygotsky, L. 140, 152, 270, 300, 309

**W**

Walsh, C. 194, 195
weak bilingualism *see* subtractive bilingualism
welfare *vs* moral arguments for MLE 332–3
Wierzbicka, A. 90
Williams, E. 100, 315, 324–5
workshop, Nepal 246–8
World Conservation Union 39–40
World Resources Institute 39–40
written language
African 98, 99
and spoken language 272–3
*see also* literacy; reading
Wycliffe Bible Translators 82, 330

**Z**

Zambia 100, 107, 315
Zimbabwe 101